UNDERSTANDING RESEARCH FOR BUSINESS STUDENTS

Sara Miller McCune founded SAGE Publishing in 1965 to support the dissemination of usable knowledge and educate a global community. SAGE publishes more than 1000 journals and over 800 new books each year, spanning a wide range of subject areas. Our growing selection of library products includes archives, data, case studies and video. SAGE remains majority owned by our founder and after her lifetime will become owned by a charitable trust that secures the company's continued independence.

Los Angeles | London | New Delhi | Singapore | Washington DC | Melbourne

UNDERSTANDING RESEARCH FOR BUSINESS STUDENTS

A Complete Student's Guide

Jonathan Wilson

Los Angeles | London | New Delhi
Singapore | Washington DC | Melbourne

Los Angeles | London | New Delhi
Singapore | Washington DC | Melbourne

SAGE Publications Ltd
1 Oliver's Yard
55 City Road
London EC1Y 1SP

SAGE Publications Inc.
2455 Teller Road
Thousand Oaks, California 91320

SAGE Publications India Pvt Ltd
B 1/I 1 Mohan Cooperative Industrial Area
Mathura Road
New Delhi 110 044

SAGE Publications Asia-Pacific Pte Ltd
3 Church Street
#10-04 Samsung Hub
Singapore 049483

Editor: Jai Seaman
Editorial assistant: Hannah Cavender-Deere
Production editor: Victoria Nicholas
Marketing manager: Lucia Sweet
Cover design: Sheila Tong
Typeset by: C&M Digitals (P) Ltd, Chennai, India
Printed in the UK

Library of Congress Control Number: 2021937280

British Library Cataloguing in Publication data

A catalogue record for this book is available from the British Library

ISBN 978-1-4739-5356-7
ISBN 978-1-4739-5357-4 (pbk)

At SAGE we take sustainability seriously. Most of our products are printed in the UK using responsibly sourced papers and boards. When we print overseas we ensure sustainable papers are used as measured by the PREPS grading system. We undertake an annual audit to monitor our sustainability.

This book is dedicated to the memory of my father, Stuart James Wilson

CONTENTS

LIST OF FIGURES

LIST OF TABLES

LIST OF IMAGES

ABOUT THE AUTHOR

Dr Jonathan Wilson works as Associate Professor in Marketing and Business Research at the University of East Anglia (UEA), United Kingdom. He has more than 20 years' experience of teaching marketing and research modules. He has a strong interest in research, marketing and authentic learning. Jonathan is author of the best-selling book *Essentials of Business Research: A Guide to Doing your Research Project* (Sage, 2010). Jonathan has an MPhil in Educational Research from the University of Cambridge and a PhD in International Marketing from the University of Middlesex. For the last five years he has taught 'Understanding Research for Brand Leadership' to students on the MSc Brand Leadership course at Norwich Business School, UEA. In his spare time, Jonathan enjoys cartooning and takes his inspiration from James Thurber, Mel Calman and Saul Steinberg.

PREFACE

The aim of *Understanding Research for Business Students* is to provide students with a clear, comprehensive guide to doing a research project. In this follow up to my first publication – *Essentials of Business Research: A Guide to Doing Your Research Project* – I am grateful to students, colleagues and reviewers for their many comments. This includes support for including material on using social media for research, doing work-based projects and researching your own organization. This book draws heavily on my own teaching methods, in particular, the use of cartoons to illustrate real-world scenarios. These are 'research-related' scenarios, designed to encourage you to think about how you might respond when faced with a certain situation in your research.

My intention with *Essentials of Business Research* was to write a concise, student-focused guide to business research. Pleasingly, the overwhelmingly positive response and success of this book suggests that it has delivered on what I set out to achieve. It has led me to write *Understanding Research for Business Students: A Complete Student's Guide*. So, why another book on business research? The main reasons for this are three-fold. First, an increasing number of business students are undertaking a range of different types of research projects. One example here is the greater attention devoted to group work (Healey et al., 2012). Yet, the majority of business research books continue to largely focus on research methods and/or how to complete a research project. Hence, in Chapter 8, we look at undertaking work-based projects and researching your own organization. Second, we examine specific topics with in-depth content that are often given limited or no attention in other research methods texts. Examples here include the increasing importance of using social media when conducting research (Chapter 11). Third, the book features plenty of student case examples that you can relate to when carrying out your own research.

I have always believed in the importance of explaining research concepts in a language that students can understand. Therefore, the book is written in a straightforward, conversational style with little jargon, making it accessible to a student audience. To support this, a key feature in each chapter is 'The Research Wheel'. This is a simple, visual guide, designed to support your understanding of each of the steps throughout your research.

In my more than 20 years in higher education, I have supervised countless research projects at all levels. Although there is no one single definitive approach to doing a research project, the steps taken in the research process are largely the same. Furthermore, many aspects of doing research are the same no matter what the subject area. For example, all research should start with a research problem, have a clear purpose, involve collecting data, analyzing data and communicating the results.

Consider your research project as a journey. Unlike many other forms of assessment, it is not something that can be completed in a short space of time. A research project is likely to be the culmination of your degree and gives you the opportunity to study a topic of your choosing in significant depth. You will learn a great deal from the process. Writing a research project is challenging, but it can be fun – and very rewarding! To be sure, it is likely to be one of the most rewarding experiences of your degree.

LEARNING FEATURES

- A companion website provides PowerPoint slides, multiple-choice questions and author videos. This is designed to support your learning in addition to material covered in the book.
- 'Research snapshot' boxes within each chapter. The purpose of this feature is to provide you with short 'helpful tips' at different steps in your research; in addition, to highlight typical challenges and how to address them.

- 'Concept Cartoons' provide visual representations of research ideas. The cartoon drawings put forward different views and situations about research and require you to think about potential outcomes. By presenting a number of possible alternative viewpoints, concept cartoons stimulate students to discuss their ideas, in this case about research (Keogh and Naylor, 1999). Furthermore, they provide an opportunity for you to discuss your ideas with fellow students. Each chapter features a concept cartoon putting forward different views about research.
- 'Student Scenarios' provide real student scenarios to help you to understand the potential issues that you may face when conducting your own research.
- Chapter learning objectives provide an outline of what you will learn from reading the chapter.
- End-of-chapter questions for review based on material covered in each chapter.
- A selection of case studies throughout the book in order to support student learning.

THE STRUCTURE OF THE BOOK

The book consists of 18 chapters. Chapter 1 begins by defining 'business research'. Additionally, it considers the approaches to business research and distinguishes between the terms 'research' and 'business research'. Chapter 2 pays attention to the essentials of research direction – research topic, research problem, aims, research questions and research objectives. Chapter 3 covers writing a research project proposal. Emphasis here is on planning your research prior to collecting your data.

Chapter 4 is concerned with searching and critically reviewing the literature. The chapter explains how to identify key literature, structure the literature review and approaches to writing up the literature review. Chapter 5 explores the philosophical underpinnings of research. This chapter will help you to understand key concepts associated with research methodology – research philosophy, approaches and strategies. Chapter 6 examines the different types of research design associated with business research. Chapter 7 pays attention to a range of ethical concerns together with the typical steps required to gain ethical approval from your university or college. In addition, the chapter includes a section on plagiarism and how to avoid it.

Chapter 8 explores doing work-based projects and researching your own organization. A major theme within this chapter is the focus on putting research into practice and the benefits of doing work-based research. Chapter 9 focuses on sampling. The chapter explains the steps in the sampling process and the different types of sampling methods. The chapter ends with examples highlighting the application of different types of sampling techniques. Chapter 10 explores using secondary data, including examples of different types of secondary sources you can consult when doing your research. Chapter 11 deals with social media for research. Social networks such as Twitter can be used for data collection and building research networks. For example, LinkedIn Corp. (www.linkedin.com) is a useful business research tool where subscribers can gather insightful information such as company profile, which could include its size, legal status, headquarters address, website, industry, and maybe even when it was founded (Ojala, 2012). Chapter 12 examines collecting data using focus groups and interviews. In Chapter 13, we focus on observational research, while Chapter 14 explores using questionnaires as a means of data collection.

The next three chapters in the book focus on data analysis. Chapter 15 introduces the analytical tools students can use when undertaking qualitative data analysis. There is also emphasis on how to interpret research findings. The chapter ends with a section on how to present data. Chapter 16 presents the statistical methods students can use when carrying out quantitative analysis. This chapter covers both descriptive and inferential statistics. There is also emphasis on how to interpret research findings. In Chapter 17, students have access to a user-friendly study guide to using the IBM SPSS Statistics software package. The guide will take you through the process of entering, analyzing and interpreting data. Finally, Chapter 18 examines the nature of research conclusions. The chapter devotes considerable attention to the writing up stage of the research project. This includes identifying research limitations and making recommendations. In addition, it presents the options available to you when it comes to disseminating your research findings. The chapter considers various ways to use media options as a means to disseminate your work.

REFERENCES

Healey, M., Lannin, L., Derounian, J., Stibbe, A., Bray, S., Deane, J., Hill, S., Keane, J. and Simmons, C. (2012) *Rethinking Final Year Projects and Dissertations*. York: The Higher Education Academy.

Keogh, B. and Naylor, S. (1999) 'Concept cartoons, teaching and learning in science: An evaluation', *International Journal of Science Education*, *21* (4): 431–446.

Ojala, M. (2012) 'Minding your own business: Social media invades business research', *The Dollar Sign*, July/Aug.

ACKNOWLEDGEMENTS

I am immensely grateful for the support from my family, colleagues and friends during the writing of this book – in particular, my wife, Julie and daughter Jemma. Thank you for your love and support. I am particularly indebted to Jai Seaman and Hannah Cavender-Deere for their patience and encouragement throughout the writing process. Also, thanks go to the anonymous reviewers who provided helpful and comprehensive feedback on many of the chapters. I would also like to acknowledge the constructive feedback from many of my students and colleagues at the University of East Anglia, especially Dr Lucill Curtis and Dr Shahin Assadinia. Finally, my thanks to my former PhD supervisor Professor Ross Brennan for contributing greatly to my educational journey.

ONLINE RESOURCES

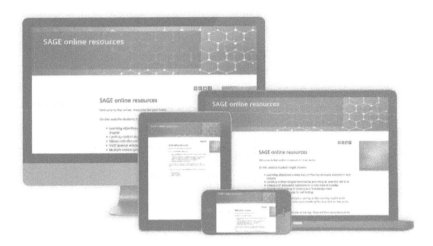

Understanding Research for Business Students is supported by a wealth of online resources for both students and lecturers to aid study and support teaching, which are available at https://study.sagepub.com/jonathanwilsonURBS

FOR STUDENTS

Watch and learn! Author videos for each chapter bring key research concepts to life and provide a clear summary of each step of the research process.

FOR LECTURERS

A **Testbank** containing questions related to the book's key concepts, which can be downloaded and used in class, as homework or for exams.

PowerPoint slides for each chapter featuring interactive tasks and questions, which can be downloaded and customized for use in your own presentations.

Introductory videos explain how you can use the book and the Research Wheel in your teaching.

1

INTRODUCTION TO BUSINESS RESEARCH

Learning objectives

By the end of this chapter, you should be able to:

- understand the nature of research

- explain what is meant by business research

- understand the benefits of studying business research

- appreciate the approaches to business research

- critique the difference between basic research and applied research

- understand 'The Research Wheel'.

INTRODUCTION

The aim of this book is to provide students with a clear, comprehensive guide on how to successfully complete a research project. In particular, it features all of the necessary information you will need at every stage in the research process. This includes choosing a research topic, formulating objectives, conducting a literature review, collecting and analyzing data, writing up and disseminating your research. The book is written with two types of student audience in mind. First, undergraduate students studying on a research methods module prior to doing a research project. Second, both undergraduate and postgraduate students carrying out a research project. In short, the book can be used as a valuable reference point at any stage in your research.

By purchasing this book, there is a likelihood that you are at the beginning of your *research project*. Starting to do a research project is often the most daunting for students. There are many different terms and methods associated with research and it can be challenging deciding which steps to take. Most importantly, though, through reading this book, you will find clear explanations throughout and also recognize that there is no one best way of conducting research. The decisions you take are dependent on a number of factors, such as time, work by earlier researchers, resource constraints and guidance from your research supervisor. Moreover, it is essential to note that decision-making is often shaped by your research direction. This is something we examine in Chapter 2.

This first chapter begins by exploring the nature of research. We examine a fundamental question for business student researchers – *What is research?* It then moves on to examine the benefits of studying business research. Following this, the chapter explores the key differences between academic research and organizational research and looks at whether there is a meaningful distinction between applied research and basic research. Next, we investigate the main stages involved in the research process. This is where you are first introduced to *The Research Wheel*, which is a visual tool specifically intended to guide students throughout their research process. Here, I aim to simplify the research process by dividing it into four distinct layers – *Ethics, Planning, Action* and *Presentation*. There are plenty of things to think about when doing your business research, not least *Where do I start*? Thus, the main purpose of this chapter is to provide you with clear guidance on how to grow and develop your research.

WHAT IS RESEARCH?

> If you are a researcher, you are trying to figure out what the question is as well as what the answer is.
>
> Edward Witten (2005)

The above quote by the American theoretical physicist Edward Witten succinctly captures the role of the researcher. Often, research is viewed from the point of view of answering questions. Certainly, this is a fundamental part of doing research. However, in order to answer the research question(s), it is essential to learn how to formulate your research question(s). We explore this in Chapter 2.

If we consider the etymology of the word 'research' it comes from two syllabi: the prefix 'Re' which means once more or again, while the verb 'search' means examine carefully. Thus, in simple terms, we can view research as 'examining an issue again carefully' through asking questions in order to generate answers to these questions. The 'again' aspect is because research never really stops. For example, an organization might carry out regular market research to better understand consumer attitudes towards data security. Ultimately, the research findings are likely to lead to a further set of questions and follow up research. This is because as a researcher, we are constantly questioning results and asking further questions.

So far, we have established that key aspects of research include questions and answers, together with examining an issue again carefully. However, a starting point for students doing a research project is coming up with a research idea. Think of forming a research idea as similar to embarking on an expedition. This involves organizing your journey, underpinned by systematic planning and a clear purpose. In the process of travelling on the expedition, a range of methods are used in order to successfully complete the journey – arranging a guide, purchasing supplies, booking travel, etc. The culmination in this process is that you successfully reach your intended destination. Your own research 'journey' can be viewed in a similar way. In particular, your research requires systematic planning and a clear research direction (purpose), all of which we explore in subsequent chapters.

The word 'Research' in itself is a broad term. There are many types of research. Media outlets frequently publish articles on the findings from political research. Examples of political research might include voter intentions in the next election or people's views on a particular government policy. Marketers often make strategic decisions on the basis of market research, and advertisers make claims on the popularity of a product or service based on survey findings. In medical research, researchers may report the latest breakthrough in cancer research. Another example is research conducted into sustainability and social responsibility. For instance, a local authority may carry out research to determine the level of recycling within a community, or possibly to find out people's views on how to implement a proposed recycling scheme.

If an organization does not have the resources to conduct research in-house, then they can commission a specialist research organization such as Ipsos Mori to conduct research on their behalf. Of course, research is not only undertaken by commercial organizations. For example, a charity may carry out research with the purpose of increasing charitable donations.

For organizations, business research is important because it can deliver solutions to research problems associated with an organization's marketplace. Gray (2014: 2) notes: 'It also means that those involved in commissioning or sponsoring organizational research is better placed to understand and manage the work of researchers and to objectively evaluate and interpret the outcomes of research'.

So, how can we define research? Given that it is used in a variety of contexts, there is not one definitive definition of what constitutes research. However, there are three themes that are common to most definitions. These themes generally accept that research:

- is a process of enquiry and investigation
- is systematic and methodical
- increases knowledge.

Let us examine each of the above points more closely. First, a *'process of enquiry and investigation'* means that research is driven by having a set of predetermined research questions, and then addressing these questions through the gathering, analysis and interpretation of information. In addition, research can help to solve practical problems. For example, for a small retailer experiencing a loss in sales, research can help to determine the reasons why and address the research problem (loss in sales). Second, *'systematic and methodical'* suggests that research should be carried out in a well-organized and disciplined manner, following a series of steps or stages. Lastly, research *'increases knowledge'*. Through conducting research, researchers are able to develop a better understanding about a particular subject. Moreover, they should be able to demonstrate their knowledge if questioned about their area of research. In the case of business research, an increase in knowledge might relate to a better understanding of customer-buying behaviour, an awareness of opportunities associated with entering a new market or possibly recognition of employee opinions on a range of subjects.

It is worth noting at this point that ethical considerations are an extremely important part of doing research. Perhaps surprisingly, reference to 'ethics' is often overlooked when defining research, but nonetheless, it is something that you will need to contemplate in the context of your own research. Hence, an entire chapter is devoted to ethical issues (Chapter 7).

Although we have examined the nature of research, it is also important to be clear as to what does not count as research in an educational context. Myers (2009: 7) gives examples of these activities. These are as follows:

- the preparation of teaching materials
- the provision of advice or opinion, e.g. consultancy work
- feasibility studies
- routine professional practice.

HOW IS BUSINESS RESEARCH DIFFERENT TO OTHER TYPES OF RESEARCH?

In the last section, we established that *Research* is a frequently used term that applies to so many different contexts. In simple terms, research seems to be associated with discovery and finding answers. The part of the researcher can be likened to 'detective work' in that it is about finding answers to often complex questions. Interestingly, when you rearrange the letters of 'research' you get 'searcher'. You will also find that 'searching' plays a significant part in your research. For example, searching for a research topic, sources of information and research participants.

Before we consider a definition for business research, it is significant to mention that the same generic terms we examined in the last section also apply in the context of business research. Once again, these are that research: *is a process of enquiry and investigation, is systematic and methodological* and *research increases knowledge*. The first part of the definition – *process of enquiry and investigation* – means that business research is concerned with answering research questions. Second, *systematic and methodical* means that you will approach your research in a well-organized and disciplined manner. How can you ensure this takes place when conducting your own research? This is where research planning is important.

Prior to starting your research project, it might be necessary for you to produce a *research proposal*. The purpose of the proposal is for you to plan your research project in terms of time frame, resources and steps in the process.

Often a research proposal is included as a form of assessment within a research methods module. The intention here is to prepare you for your research project. In short, think of a research proposal as 'what you intend to do' prior to actually carrying out your research. The analogy I often tell students is that a research proposal is something like an architect's plan for building a new house. To build the house, it is essential that the builders have a clear understanding of the plan before building work begins. This plan would include the resources required, such as materials, size of the workforce and anticipated completion time. Similarly, as a researcher, you need to have a clear plan and understand the resources required before commencing your research. For a researcher, this is likely to include a clear timetable, access to data and financial resources. Given that a research proposal is about planning, this features early in the book (in Chapter 3).

Finally, *research increases knowledge* can be viewed from both a theoretical and practical perspective. Clearly, through conducting your own research, you are developing your theoretical knowledge about research methods and your chosen subject. Moreover, you are also learning key practical skills associated with doing business research. For example, although not exhaustive, this might include interviewing skills, presentation skills, how to record data and learning quantitative techniques. Additionally, you should be able to demonstrate your knowledge if questioned about your chosen research subject.

There is no one definition of business research. The term *business research* can be viewed as an 'umbrella term' which means that it encompasses research in a range of business contexts. Adams et al. (2014: 3) point out that business research tends to be undertaken in order to achieve one or more of the following objectives.

- to gain a competitive advantage
- to test new products and services
- to solve a management or organizational problem
- to provide information, which may help to avoid future business problems
- to forecast future sales
- to better understand shifts in consumer attitudes and tastes
- to enhance profitability
- to reduce operational costs
- to enable the management to prioritize options for the future.

The above points are typical strategic objectives. Organizations might carry out business research in order to achieve these objectives. Business research in this context might involve conducting research within an organization or outsourcing to a third party, such as a research agency. Thus, business research can be viewed as a study designed to collect and analyze data in order to find solutions to practical problems. If you are undertaking an individual research project or dissertation, then your project is likely to be an academic piece of work. This means that business research in this perspective will ostensibly be more theoretical and perhaps purely based on secondary sources, as opposed to collecting both primary and secondary data.

Business research has also been viewed in the context of its features. Easterby-Smith et al. (2012) argue that business (and management) research is idiosyncratic in the following ways:

- Both employees and managers have a high level of education. Many have undergraduate and post-graduate degrees and are often as well educated as those conducting research about them.
- The nature of business and management means that it draws on knowledge developed in different disciplines, e.g. psychology, sociology, economics and statistics.
- There is an expectation that research has some practical consequence and will lead to action.

Broadly speaking, we define business research as a 'step-by-step process that involves the collecting, recording, analyzing and interpreting data for aid in solving managerial problems' (Wilson, 2014: 3). Simply put, it refers to research undertaken to address a business-related research problem. Of course, managerial problems can be associated with any business function. For example, an organization may wish to conduct research to determine why it is losing market share or perhaps a large multinational intends to carry out research to find out why there is low staff morale. You can describe your research as business research as you are conducting research on a business-related subject and/or in a particular business. Any definition of business research has to take into account the 'business element' associated with research. All research involves the collecting, presenting, analyzing and interpreting of information. In the context of business research, this information is used to address business problems and define business opportunities.

One of the main challenges students often find when doing research is actually deciding on a *research topic*. In some cases, I have known students to have so many possible topics that their difficulty is deciding which topic to choose. Conversely, others find it challenging to identify one particular research topic. Either way, having difficulty choosing a topic is perfectly normal. It is something the vast majority of student researchers encounter at the start of their research.

A factor that can help you to decide on a research topic is identifying a research problem. In essence, a research problem is the rationale for doing the research and addresses something known in research as the 'So what?' question or in other words 'What is the point of the research?'. Thomas (2013) argues that a researcher always has to be able to answer the question 'Why should anyone care?'. The author proposes framing the answer to the 'Who cares?' question by using the mnemonic 'BIS' that captures the relationship between what it is that needs to be explained and the explanation that will hopefully be forthcoming from your research. The BIS should be the core of your introduction:

- Background (the general area which gives rise to the issue)
- Issue (or problem, or question)
- Solution (you promise to throw some light on the issue through your research).

A research problem can be defined as 'A clear statement of an area of concern in academic literature and/or practice that points to the need for significant attention and investigation'.

BOX 1.1: RESEARCH SNAPSHOT

All research should start with a clearly defined research problem. Examples of research problems associated with business practice might include: Why have we seen a downturn in market share? What are the reasons behind a poor customer service rating? Why do consumers no longer view the brand positively?

Only when you have identified your research problem can you start to consider your research questions. Bryman (2007: 5–6) notes the importance attached to the research question as it 'provides a point of orientation for an investigation' and 'helps to link the researcher's literature review to the kinds of data that will be collected'. Your research questions shape the direction of your research by breaking down the nature of the research problem and research topic. Having a focused set of research questions will ultimately influence how you approach your methodology and literature review. For example, if your questions focus on the nature of tax systems, then your literature review will feature studies on this particular topic. We examine a more in-depth analysis of both research topic and research questions later in Chapter 2.

Lastly, all research has a number of generic characteristics. These include research topic, research problem and research questions. All research is about asking questions, explaining problems and reflecting on what emerges in order to make meaning from the data and telling the research story. In terms of the latter, I often tell my students I am interested to learn about their experiences when doing their research projects. This means writing specific details of their research and avoiding a generic discussion. For example, if conducting an interview with someone, mention the where, when, why and how the interview took place.

WHY DO I NEED TO STUDY RESEARCH METHODS?

If you are doing a research project, there is a strong likelihood that you will have undertaken/or be about to start a research methods module. For some students, it might seem that there is little point in studying business research methods and doing a business research project. Yet typically a research methods module is a common feature in business degree programmes. The reason for this is that completing a research project is often the culmination of several years of studying and gives students an opportunity to explore a topic of interest in depth. Moreover, you need to consider the following:

- Awareness of different data collection methods and analytical tools will help you to understand how to address organizational research questions.
- Many of the research methods you study on your course are used in business research across different sectors and by different types of companies. For example, all types of companies conduct business research.
- Studying research methods will make you aware of what constitutes good and bad research. In other words, you can take an informed critical approach as to how you should conduct research.
- By studying research methods, you will understand the different steps in the research process. If required to undertake research at any stage in your career, you will be able to recognize what is required at each step in the research process and understand the relationship between research questions and research methods.
- Studying research methods provides you with an insight into the practices you need to follow when implementing each stage of your research. Thus, the factors required in order to carry out a successful piece of research.

Doing a research project provides you with a wide range of transferable skills. These are outlined in Figure 1.1.

In recent years, the nature of research has witnessed significant developments. Technological innovations such as the rise of multimedia, social media and the Internet of Things (IoT) have driven growth in data. Large data sets or *Big Data* have resulted in leading companies collecting and analyzing data to conduct controlled experiments to make better management decisions (McKinsey Global Institute, 2011). In essence, big data is a large volume of data that has the potential to be mined to extract information that can inform decision-making.

An understanding of research is of benefit if you decide to go on to take a further course of study. Although you might be studying a higher degree or a very different subject, many of the core skills associated with research are generic across subjects. Finally, you may have a number of questions at the start of your research journey. Table 1.1 features some of the more commonly asked questions students often raise when starting a research project.

Figure 1.1   Why research skills are important

Table 1.1   Starting a research project – common questions and answers

Question	Answer
What is research?	Research can be defined as a 'step-by-step process that involves the collecting, recording, analyzing and interpreting of information'.
Why do I need to learn about business research?	An essential part of business-related study programs is the research project. Learning about business research helps you to successfully complete your project as well as provide transferable skills that can be used in a wide variety of business and management positions.
How do I conduct research?	This book fully explains everything you need to know about how to conduct research. A key factor here is the type of research project. By the end of the book, you should be in a position to answer this question!
Where do I conduct research?	If you are an international student you may decide to conduct research in your own country, particularly if focusing on cross-cultural research, while those students who work part-time may conduct some aspects of their research in the workplace.
When do I conduct research?	In general, undertaking your research project commences towards the end of your final year of study. However, check with your university or college.

Source: Adapted from Wilson (2014)

The common questions and answers in Table 1.1 are by no means exhaustive, but intended as a guide to possible questions when starting your research. Try to get into the habit of asking questions throughout your research, in particular to your research supervisor and/or research methods tutor. Taking these steps should help you to become a more accomplished researcher.

APPROACHES TO BUSINESS RESEARCH

In this book, we will use the term 'research project' and 'dissertation' interchangeably to refer to an academic project. An *academic project* has a number of distinguishable features. First, it is carried out as part of a degree or academic course of study. Second, because it is an academic piece of work, there needs to be theoretical content. Third, it needs to meet the guidelines set out by the institution overseeing the research project. Conversely, business research conducted within or on behalf of an organization is designed to establish an opportunity or find a solution to a practical business problem.

In the case of academic research, secondary sources used by the researcher place greater emphasis on academic business journals. These journals contain the latest articles by academics who specialize in business-related research. In addition, they tend to concentrate on specific subject areas. Conversely, business research undertaken by organizations will typically focus on sources of a more practical nature. Examples here include internal sources – customer records, sales records and business reports – together with external sources – business press, government reports and trade magazines. You are likely to consult sources of both a practical and theoretical nature as part of your own research project.

The application of research is sometimes categorized into *basic* and *applied* research. The purpose of *basic* (or *pure*) *research* is to gather information and build on existing knowledge. This process usually involves conducting comprehensive research to gain a deep understanding of a particular theory or phenomenon and to gain an understanding of fundamental principles. For example, a student who studies research philosophy to learn about different research philosophies is doing basic research. In essence, basic research is intended to increase the knowledge base leading to further research. Basic research does not have an immediate commercial objective. By way of example, let us say a university research team is conducting research on the possible health implications of sleep deprivation. The team are interested in their research findings and to further their understanding of the research area. In this sense, the research is very much concerned with the 'How' and 'Why' questions, as opposed to fulfilling a commercial objective. In addition, basic research may not necessarily find a solution to a problem or lead to an invention. In the sleep deprivation example, research is driven by the curiosity of the research team, and/or interest in addressing a scientific question, namely *How does sleep deprivation affect the health of research participants?* In short, basic research lays down the foundation for the applied science that follows.

Applied research is undertaken to solve practical problems and to reduce uncertainty in management decision-making. Examples here might include an organization investigating ways to improve the efficiency of its production system or a marketer who conducts research to find out consumer opinion on a new brand of cola. Different types of organizations conduct research. These include public and private sector, agencies and firms across a variety of industries. Students doing a work-based project often conduct applied research to solve practical problems associated with a particular organization.

Bickman and Rog (2009) make the point that basic research and applied research differ in purposes, context and methods. However, it is important to note, that in many ways the contrast between basic research and applied research is something of a false dichotomy. Applied research can be used to inform theory and vice-versa. Moreover, it is often the case that applied research builds on existing basic research. For example, a marketer who conducts research to find out consumer opinion on a new brand of cola may use research published on consumer behaviour. It is possible to look at research from two different perspectives. First, the purpose of applied research is to improve understanding of a practical business or managerial-related problem. Results from applied research are viewed as providing solutions to the specific problem associated with the organization. Findings are of a practical relevance to an organization and its management. Quite simply, although basic research and applied research are often presented as being opposites, in reality they complement each other. Basic research is typically more of an academic nature and designed to expand knowledge of theories and processes. The outcomes of basic research can have wider societal implications.

Often, the blurring between basic and applied research is evident due to the collaboration between different research stakeholders, especially universities and business.

THE RESEARCH PROCESS

In this part of the chapter, we turn our attention to the *research process*. Your research will entail the completion of several key steps before finishing your project. Examples include defining your research topic, choosing your methodological approach and conducting an extensive literature search on your research subject. Typically, research methods books often refer to these steps or stages as the research process. More specifically, the research process can be viewed as *a systematic and organized series of stages taking you from the start of the process, through to completion.*

Research projects vary in design and approach, but the generic steps in the research project stay largely the same, irrespective of the research topic. Walliman (2011: 30) suggests that four important questions underpin the framework of any research project:

- What are you going to do? The subject of your research.
- Why are you going to do it? The reason for this research being necessary or interesting.
- How are you going to do it? The research methods that you will use to carry out the project.
- When are you going to do it? The programme of work.

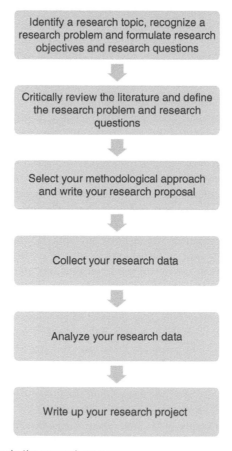

Figure 1.2   An example of stages in the research process

Another feature of the research process is that it is frequently perceived as a linear process consisting of a series of stages (see Figure 1.2). These organized steps generally entail the following: identify a broad research topic, narrow down your topic and recognize a research problem, formulate your research objectives and research questions, conduct a literature review, select your research design, collect data, analyze and present your research findings.

BOX 1.2: RESEARCH SNAPSHOT

The generic research process can be confusing for students. For instance, when deciding on your research topic you will devote considerable time to reading around the literature. Although this is commonly shown as the second or third step in the generic research process, reading the literature is usually undertaken to help to identify your research topic. In short, your literature review is a task that should be ongoing up to approximately three weeks before you are due to submit your project.

The steps shown in Figure 1.2 are all key elements you will undertake in your research process. However, in reality you are unlikely to complete each step in sequence. This is because conducting research requires the researcher to revisit steps in the research process. For example, at the data analysis stage it might arise that your research results do not adequately address the original research questions. Hence, you will then make new plans to revisit the research questions and/ or undertake further data collection. So, if in reality research is not linear, how can we view the research process? An alternative view is that the actual process of doing research can be viewed as an iterative process. This means that you will repeat or revisit steps in your research in order to achieve the desired outcome.

THE RESEARCH WHEEL

Figure 1.3 The Research Wheel is an essential tool intended to guide you throughout your research process. The Research Wheel is an iterative model composed of four layers – *Ethics, Planning, Action* and *Presentation*. In short, these can be referred to as the acronym EPAP. Each layer represents the type of activities you will undertake during the research process – Ethics, Planning, Action and Presentation – while the arrows illustrate the iterative nature of the model. Ethical issues arise at all stages in the research process. Hence, 'Ethics' is shown as the outer ring.

Each layer consists of 'steps' that make up the research process. Completing the steps of one layer means you are in a position to move on to the next layer. For example, completing all of the steps in the 'Planning' layer, indicates you can move on to the 'Action' layer. However, do remember that research is an iterative process, so the likelihood is that you will have to revisit steps in the process. By way of an example, after 'Ethics', the first step in the 'Planning' layer is 'Research direction'. Moving in a clockwise direction, each step represents an aspect of the research process and chapter in the book.

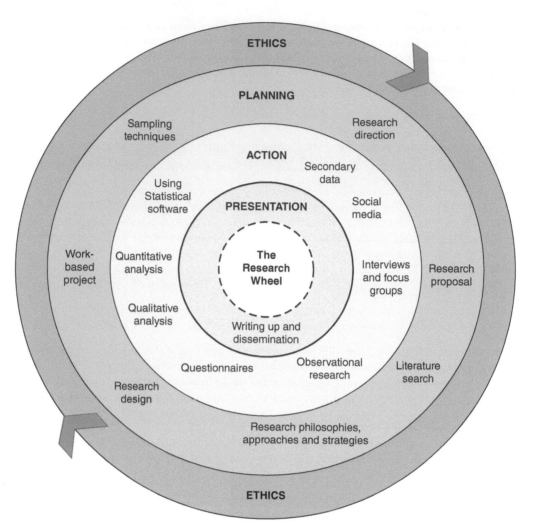

Figure 1.3   The Research Wheel

It is important to note that not all research projects are presented using the same generic structure as highlighted in The Research Wheel. However, all business research projects do have common features, such as formulating research questions, deciding on a methodological approach and presenting research findings.

My intention with The Research Wheel is not to produce a definitive guide, but an essential visual 'checklist' to guide you throughout your research process.

In this section, we will briefly outline the four layers that make up The Research Wheel.

- **Layer 1: Ethics** is a set of principles governing the way in which research is conducted. Researchers face ethical challenges in all stages of the research process. Hence, this is the reason why the outer circles show 'ethics' as ethical issues need to be addressed at all stages of the research process, from designing your research to writing up.

- **Layer 2: Planning** how you develop your research idea and learn about the essential aspects of doing your research. A starting point here is developing your research idea, followed by searching the literature on your research topic and formulating research objectives and research questions. In simple terms, exploring is all about 'finding your feet' and is the starting point in your research process. This stage typically comprises writing a research proposal setting out how you intend to conduct your research.
- **Layer 3: Action** is actively implementing your research proposal and involves key actions associated with addressing your research problem. These include collecting and analyzing your data. If you are doing quantitative research, the latter may also entail using statistical software such as IBM SPSS Statistics.
- **Layer 4: Presentation** is focusing on writing up your chapters and disseminating your work. How you present your research project is likely to be based on written format, although your course may also require a verbal presentation. If the former, presentation will focus on the main generic chapters – Introduction, literature review, methodology, results and analysis and conclusion.

Combined, the four layers of Ethics, Planning, Action and Presentation (EPAP) form your research project. No research project is complete without successfully addressing all four layers in the research process.

Why a wheel model? The arrows in the model are designed to illustrate the iterative process of doing research. For example, although your research will start with developing ideas and refining your research topic (Planning), it is a step you may revisit during the course of your research. Why? Well, although uncommon, I have known students to choose a new research topic part way through their research. One reason for this might be difficulty accessing data, or simply a growing lack of interest in their chosen area of research. Similarly, certain steps in the research process are very much an iterative process. Perhaps the best example of this is searching the literature. This doesn't stop and is an ongoing process. Again, in this sense, the research process can be described as an 'iterative process' that requires revising steps until you have reached a desired result. This is what distinguishes The Research Wheel from other research models typically found in research methods textbooks. My intention is to illustrate the actual 'real-world' process of doing research.

WHAT ARE THE CHALLENGES I AM LIKELY TO FACE DURING MY RESEARCH?

Which is the most difficult step when going through your research process? For many students, the first step tends to be the most challenging. More specifically, choosing a research topic, defining a research problem and formulating research questions and/or hypotheses. There are several considerations and challenges, not least having to complete work within a typically narrow time frame. You can take the following steps in order to overcome these:

- Make sure you understand your university or college project guidelines. This includes structure, word count, time period and ethics approval.

- Meet regularly with your project supervisor(s) and project team. If you are doing a work-based project, then your project team is likely to include an academic supervisor or adviser and a manager from your employer or partner organization.
- Get organized! Keeping a research diary is an ideal way to keep on top of key tasks.

UNDERSTAND YOUR INSTITUTION'S PROJECT GUIDELINES

Your university or college will produce a clear set of project guidelines. These guidelines will contain all the essential information you need when conducting your research and submitting your work. Unsurprisingly, there are differences between institutions when it comes to submission requirements. Considerations here include word count, referencing, format, number of copies due for submission and submission date. My advice here is to make sure you fully understand your institution's project guidelines well in advance of the set submission date. Often, marks are allocated for presentation. This includes structure, referencing and format.

MEET REGULARLY WITH YOUR SUPERVISOR(S) AND PROJECT TEAM

Irrespective of the type of research project you are undertaking, it is important to meet regularly with your supervisory team. Frequent progress meetings will help you to keep on track and complete your project by the research deadline. From my experience, students who fully engage with their research and meet regularly with their supervisor tend to achieve success in their research project.

Remember that your project supervisor may not necessarily be an expert in your chosen topic, but should be fully aware of the research requirements. In addition, your supervisor is there to provide guidance throughout your research journey. However, do not wait for your supervisor to contact you to arrange a meeting. The onus is on the student to work independently and to arrange a supervisor meeting as and when required.

KEEP A RESEARCH DIARY

One of the benefits of keeping a research diary is that it allows you to reflect on your research journey. By being a reflective researcher, you will learn from experience and may make adjustments to work already completed. In addition, by reflecting on earlier stages in your research, this might influence how you approach future actions. What you enter in your diary is of course personal choice. Nadin and Cassell (2006) point out that a research diary is a valuable tool that prompts insights and informs research decisions. The first author refers to the use of a research diary during her PhD. The research diary was in the form of an A5 lined notebook. Each new page included the date, brief biographic information about the firm (i.e. name of the employer, age of the firm, nature of the business and number of employees). Reflections on the interview experience were then recorded. The following are examples of what you might like to include in your research diary:

- brainstorming ideas, research notes and possibly sketch notes
- notes from interviews, discussions with your research supervisor
- follow up questions you want to explore with research participants
- reading material you intend accessing via the library database
- your own personal views on your research topic and/or research direction
- what you have achieved on a day-to-day basis
- a timetable of tasks, including start and completion dates
- reports of research interviews, surveys or observations.

Image 1.1   Keeping a research diary

Source: iStock (photo ID: 582291544)

Quinlan (2011) points out that a research diary is important as it allows the researcher to record their thoughts, ideas, inspirations, references and resources. The format of your diary is up to you. It does not matter if it is electronic or traditional format; choose something that is both practical and manageable. Make sure to keep your diary to hand and try to write clear entries on a daily basis. On some days you will find that you have plenty to write about, but on other days less so. What is important is that regular entries allow you to reflect on your progress at the end of each week. In addition, they help to continuously develop your research. According to Engin (2011) the researcher diary can be seen as an integral part of the development of the researcher and the construction of research knowledge. Hence, a research diary not only helps you to develop as a researcher, but documents the nature of your research and research progress.

Image 1.2   Concept Cartoon 'Research process'

Image 1.2 is the first of our Concept Cartoons. Once again, Concept Cartoons provide visual representations of research ideas. The cartoon drawings put forward different views and situations and are designed to stimulate thinking. In this case, the characters are expressing their views on the research process. What do you think? Do you agree with one of the characters or have a different viewpoint? Remember that Concept Cartoons can also be used to provoke discussion with fellow students.

Date	Task	Objective	Outcome	Personal reflections and next steps
25 June 2019	Conduct a semi-structured interview with the Marketing Manager of Saxon Marketing. The interview is to take place at Saxon Marketing's Head Office in Liverpool.	To ask questions that address the research problem. Questions to focus on marketing performance. In particular, ways in which the organization measures marketing performance and future developments in this area.	The interview took 30 minutes. Pleasingly, the respondent answered all of my questions and agreed to being recorded throughout the interview. The respondent expressed an interest in receiving a summary of the research findings.	This was the third of a total of 25 interviews. Although still at the early stage of data collection, all of the respondents so far have fully participated in the research and agreed to being recorded. The next steps are to continue with data collection and allocate time to transcribing the data.
27 June 2019	Transcribing the data for research participants one and two.	To complete transcribing the data within one day.	Completed transcribing the data. The material is saved on my PC and ready for analysis.	Start analyzing the data and continuing with data collection (interviews).
28 June	Searching the literature	Continue with literature search, specifically on the theme 'marketing performance'.	A number of relevant articles found. Saved on my PC in folder 'key articles'.	There is plenty of literature on this subject. Next steps include identifying key authors and seminal studies in this area.

Figure 1.4 An extract from a research diary

Your research supervisor and/or members of your project team will have other commitments. This can make it difficult to arrange suitable meeting times. However, organizing times well in advance is one way to overcome this problem. At the early stages of your research, plan mutually convenient meeting times with your supervisor. These should be organized at regular intervals, but especially at key stages during your research. For example, prior to collecting your data or carrying out data analysis. Feedback from your research supervisor throughout your research journey is essential to make sure that you are on track to successfully complete your research within the time frame. In addition, organizing meeting times well in advance can help to avoid last minute panic!

A NOTE ON RESEARCH PROCESS, METHODS, METHODOLOGY AND PROJECTS

By now, you should be familiar with the terms research process and research methods. Once again, research methods is a broad term that relates to a range of data collection and analytical techniques adopted during your research. Methodology is viewed as more than simply the methods you intend to use to collect and analyze your data. In essence, methodology is the approach and strategy that outlines the way in which research is to be conducted. The methodology is the overarching approach to the research (Cottrell, 2014). The methodological approach for your study encompasses *research philosophy, research strategy, research approach, research strategy, research design, methods* and *analytical techniques.* The main strategies to business research are qualitative and quantitative. Furthermore, research methods are often associated with two approaches – inductive and deductive. These are all important considerations when conducting your research and something we will address in later chapters.

CHAPTER SUMMARY

- This book is intended for all students in business schools studying business or a business-related subject who have an interest in research methods and business projects.

- Business research can be defined as a 'step-by-step process that involves the collecting, recording, analyzing and interpreting of information'.

- If pursuing a career in business, it is important to have an understanding and the ability to conduct business research as it can apply to all functions of an organization.

- Conducting business research is important because it can deliver solutions to research problems associated with an organization's marketplace.

- A traditional business research project can be defined as 'an academic independent dissertation or project whereby the student chooses a topic aligned to that of their chosen degree'.

- When it comes to the application of research, this can be categorized into basic and applied research.

- The Research Wheel diagram includes four layers – Ethics, Planning, Action and Presentation (EPAP). This is designed to help you to understand the steps in the research process and to successfully complete your research project.

QUESTIONS FOR REVIEW

1. What are the steps you can take to avoid losing your way during the research process?
2. Outline what is meant by the term 'business research'.
3. Provide examples of what you might include in a research diary.
4. Briefly outline each of the layers in The Research Wheel.
5. Discuss the transferable skills gained from conducting your own research project.
6. Outline the benefits of studying business research.
7. What are some of the challenges you may encounter when doing your research?

8. How might you apply the acronym EPAP in the context of conducting your research?

9. Outline what is meant by the term 'basic research'.

10. Outline what is meant by the term 'applied research'.

STUDENT SCENARIO: VANESSA STARTS HER RESEARCH JOURNEY

Vanessa had recently started a final year module in research methods as part of her undergraduate Accounting and Finance degree. Prior to starting the module, she had little in the way of knowledge or experience of doing business research. Yet she perceived research methods as 'boring' and 'a waste of time' given that it was a compulsory module and not linked to her preferred subject area – Accounting. In short, she did not recognize the need to study research methods. Why was reading about research methods worthwhile? Which research methods books did she need to read? What journal articles might an undergraduate read that relate to research methods? Vanessa wanted to know more about how the module linked to the final dissertation. This latter point was clearly explained to Vanessa and other students on the module by the module tutor, in particular by showing the purpose of the research proposal as a plan prior to starting a research project. By the end of the module, Vanessa had learned that an understanding of research methods was essential as it informs other parts of a research project.

All students studying research methods were required to complete a dissertation or a work-based project on an accounting- or finance-related topic. This was the culmination of Vanessa's degree and yet she had not given a great deal of thought to the process involved.

Vanessa arranged a meeting with her supervisor. She asked to read past dissertations and work-based projects by previous students. Vanessa was concerned about the challenges of conducting her own research. The module guide set out the topics covered during the research methods module, but did not illustrate the process of going from a research proposal to completing a research project. She received helpful guidance from her supervisor on the relationship between research methods and the dissertation. Vanessa's supervisor explained that 'methods' are part of methodology and this is typically one chapter within a dissertation.

Thinking about the research journey

Vanessa knew she wanted to undertake a traditional dissertation and already had an area of research in mind. Although early in the research methods module, she was keen to start planning a draft timetable, including setting out the steps she would need to take in order to successfully complete her research. However, given that this was Vanessa's first research project, she was unclear as to how to produce a research timetable and the steps to include. A follow up meeting with her supervisor helped her to identify the key steps in her research journey and to plan her time, taking into account other commitments.

Journal articles

Vanessa was keen to make an early start on her research. This involved reading the literature on research methods and completing a research project. She understood that having a firm grasp of different research methods would ultimately help her when it came to starting her research project. As well as reading key textbooks, Vanesa supplemented this with reading journal articles on the application of different types of research.

Research supervisor

When it was time to start working on her research project, Vanessa had a solid understanding of different approaches to doing research. She found reading journal articles on the application of qualitative and quantitative research methods particularly useful when deciding how to collect and analyze her data. During her research methods module Vanessa had met with her supervisor several times to discuss the module and her thoughts on her proposed research project. Now that she had started her research, Vanessa was keen to continue receiving support and advice on her research journey. She had been allocated a supervisor who took a particular interest in her chosen area of research. As part of her research timetable, Vanessa made sure to organize a series of meetings with her supervisor at mutually convenient dates/times. She felt that taking an organized approach and planning steps in her research well in advance would increase the likelihood of successfully completing her project on time.

Student group discussion

Outline the role of the research supervisor and the research student in the research process.

Hint: Not only reflect on your own experience, but use this as an opportunity to discuss roles with your fellow students and research supervisor.

FURTHER READING

Hart, C. (2005) *Doing Your Masters Dissertation*. London: Sage.

Part of the Sage Study Skills Series. This book gives an essential overview of how to do a Masters dissertation.

Harvard Business School (2016) *Why isn't Business Research More Relevant to Business Practitioners?* Available at: http://hbswk.hbs.edu/item/why-isn-t-business-research-more-relevant-to-business-practitioners (accessed 19 September 2017).

An interesting article that looks at why business research is not more relevant to practitioners. The article also highlights the difference between basic research and applied research.

Levin, P. (2012) *Excellent Dissertations!* Maidenhead: McGraw-Hill Education (UK).

A concise book of 123 pages that divides the process of writing a dissertation into four parts.

REFERENCES

Adams, J., Raeside, R. and Khan, H.T. (2014) *Research Methods for Business and Social Science Students* (2nd edn). New Delhi: Sage.

Bickman, L. and Rog, D.J. (2009) *The SAGE Handbook of Applied Research Methods* (2nd edn). Los Angeles, CA: Sage.

Bryman, A. (2007) 'The research question in social research: What is its role?', *International Journal in Social Research Methodology*, 10 (1): 5–20.

Cottrell, S. (2014) *Dissertations and Project Reports: A Step By Step Guide*. Basingstoke: Palgrave.

Easterby-Smith, M., Thorpe, R. and Jackson, P.R. (2012) *Management Research* (4th edn). London: Sage.

Engin, M. (2011) 'Research diary: A tool for scaffolding', *International Journal of Qualitative Methods*, 10 (3): 296–306.

Gray, D.E. (2014) *Doing Research in the Real World* (3rd edn). London: Sage.

McKinsey Global Institute (2011) *Big Data: The Next Frontier for Innovation, Competition and Productivity*. Available at: www.mckinsey.com/business-functions/business-technology/our-insights/big-data-the-next-frontier-for-innovation (accessed 28 May 2016).

Myers, M.D. (2009) *Qualitative Research in Business & Management*. London: Sage.

Nadin, S. and Cassell, C. (2006) 'The use of a research diary as a tool for reflexive reflections from management research', *Qualitative Research in Accounting & Management*, 3 (3): 208–217.

Quinlan, C. (2011) *Business Research Methods*. Andover, Hampshire: Cengage Learning EMEA.

Thomas, G. (2013) *How to do Your Research Project* (2nd edn). London: Sage.

Walliman, N. (2011) *Research Methods: The Basics*. New York: Routledge.

Wilson, J.S. (2014) *Essentials of Business Research: A Guide to Doing Your Research Project*. London: Sage.

Witten, E. (2005) *Physics' Sharpest Mind Since Einstein*. Available at: http://edition.cnn.com/2005/TECH/science/06/27/witten.physics/index.html (accessed 23 October 2019).

2

GETTING STARTED: CHOOSING YOUR RESEARCH DIRECTION

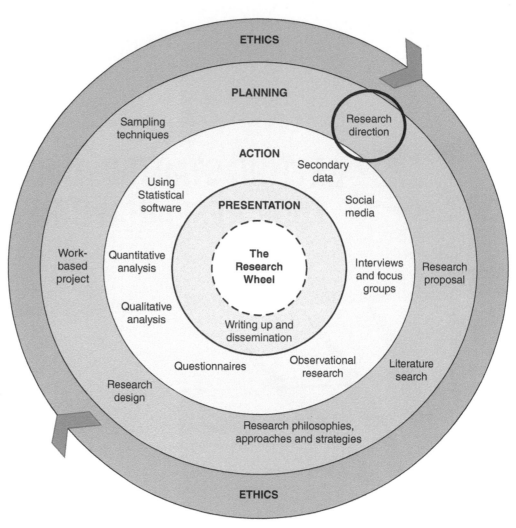

Figure 2.1   The Research Wheel

Learning objectives

By the end of this chapter, you should be able to:

- explain the importance of having a clear research direction

- understand how to choose your research topic

- evaluate how to move from a broad to narrow topic

- understand how to work with a topic that has been assigned to you

- identify and define a research problem

- recognize how to formulate research questions

- understand the relationship between theory, research questions and objectives.

INTRODUCTION

The aim of this chapter is to give you a broad overview of how to shape the direction of your research. This involves making important decisions concerning issues such as research topic, research problem and research questions that will have implications on subsequent stages in your research. Choosing your research topic, defining your research problem and formulating research objectives and research questions are part of the research process and are tasks associated with developing your initial research idea.

An essential part of any research project is understanding the rationale behind the study. As noted in Chapter 1, researchers often refer to this as addressing the 'so what' question. More specifically, what is the purpose of the research and why is it important? As a student researcher, you also need to reflect on how your own research considers the 'so what' question. One way to make sure that you achieve this is by having a clear understanding of the direction of your research. The process starts with the selection of a broad *research topic*. We begin the chapter by devoting significant attention to this subject. In essence, choosing a topic and identifying a research problem is the starting point on your research journey. Subsequently, we examine the next steps in establishing your research direction: understanding and evaluating how to work with a research topic, the research problem and developing an aim, research objectives and research questions. Although these fundamentals of your research may take considerable time to establish, they form the basis of your entire research project.

Figure 2.1 shows the key focus of this chapter – the 'Research direction' (circled). This step is in the 'Planning' layer. Choosing your research direction is the first step in the research process. Before we move onto the 'Action' layer, there is a significant amount of planning that needs to take place. Think of 'Research direction' as an umbrella term that includes research topic, research problem and developing an aim, research objectives and research questions. Your research problem is the issue or opportunity that provides clear reasons for undertaking your research. It is essential that you have a clear understanding of your research problem as this is necessary when it comes to stating the aim of your research, formulating research objectives and research questions. Student researchers often find identifying a suitable research problem particularly challenging. It is your research questions that are the tools that allow you to address the research problem. The chapter culminates with a discussion on making a distinction between research ideas, research objectives and research questions.

KEY STAGES IN YOUR RESEARCH DIRECTION

Figure 2.2 shows the key stages you will go through in developing your research direction. The first stage is to identify a research topic. There are a number of factors to contemplate here, not least making sure to select a topic that is not too broad and relates to your course of study. Having selected your research topic, the next step is to determine a research problem that warrants investigation. You will then need to refine your research problem by providing a clear and concise purpose statement, research objectives and research questions. It is worth remembering that in all likelihood establishing your research direction does not always necessarily follow the sequential stages set out in Figure 2.2. For example, you may decide to change your research topic several weeks into your research. This will involve revisiting earlier stages in establishing your research direction.

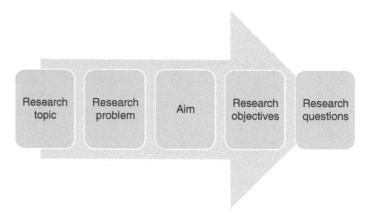

Figure 2.2   The key stages in developing a clear research direction

Figure 2.2 makes a clear distinction between research topic, research problem, aim, research objectives and questions. Why follow these steps at the beginning of your research journey? In developing your research direction, you are moving from the 'general' to 'more specific'. For instance, most students begin their research with a vague idea of a possible research topic. Over time, this needs to become more refined, ultimately leading to a focused set of research questions. Having a well-structured set of research questions is essential if you are to successfully tackle the research problem within the constraints associated with your research project. Examples of typical constraints for student researchers include time frame and word limit. In the next part of the chapter, we will examine each of these stages in Figure 2.2 separately.

HOW DO I GENERATE RESEARCH IDEAS?

'The only way you fundamentally generate ideas is by thinking creatively'

Tony Buzan

There are several approaches you can use for generating ideas for your research. The key to developing ideas is to reflect on your research options and discuss these with your fellow students, research supervisor and research stakeholders. Some of the approaches you can use to generate research ideas are summarized below.

- **Reflect on your work experience.** Ideas can come from your past or existing place of work. Practical work experience can be ideal for informing the direction of your research. For example, through your practical work experience you may have identified a practical problem that warrants research.

- **Examining your own strengths and interests.** It is important that you consider your own strengths and weaknesses when selecting your research topic. One indicator is your performance in assessment undertaken across all modules in your business course.

- **Looking at past projects.** The likelihood is that your university or college library or Course leader will keep past copies of student projects. As noted earlier, looking through past dissertations can help to identify ways to narrow down your research topic. Additionally, there are other benefits of looking at past projects. First, you can see if certain topics are more popular with students than others. You might decide to contribute to a popular area of research among previous students because you believe that there is a contribution to be made. Conversely, you may opt to choose a topic that has yet to be addressed by students. Either way, seeing the topics that your fellow students have chosen is certainly an interesting exercise. Second, looking through past projects gives you an understanding as to your institution's submission requirements. You will also be able to look through projects of varying quality, again, providing a useful guide when it comes to writing up your own research.

- **Scanning the media.** Reading the news, especially the business press and social media can help to generate ideas. Scanning the pages of leading business trade magazines and the business press such as the *Financial Times* might help you to decide to focus on one particular company or industry. Of course, when scanning the media, make sure to refer to media outlets commonly used for business research. This includes media associated with professional bodies, e.g. The Chartered Institute of Marketing (CIM) and the Association of Chartered Certified Accountants (ACCA) and the business pages of the *Times, Telegraph* and the *Guardian*.

- **Searching the literature.** The final choice for your research topic is likely to have been influenced by what is written on the subject. Searching the literature not only helps you to identify a potential topic, but also determines a possible contribution to the literature.

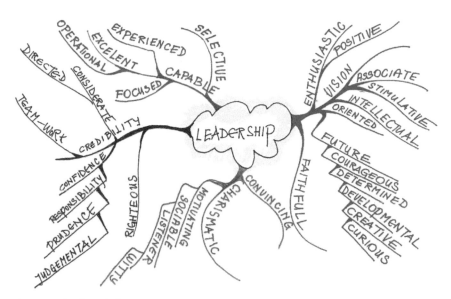

Image 2.1   An example of a mind map

Source: iStock (photo ID: 479993760)

- **Mind Map.** Developed by Tony Buzan more than 50 years ago, a mind map is a diagram representing ideas and concepts. The graphical representation features a central idea surrounded by connected branches of associated topics. Using this approach is also an ideal way to generate ideas and look for relationships between broad themes and sub-themes. Mind maps are a useful way to share your project ideas with your friends, colleagues and research supervisor. Moreover, this visual form of note taking can capture your research thoughts and set your research boundaries.
- **Keeping a notebook of ideas.** In Chapter 1 we examined the usefulness of having a research diary. Similarly, a notebook of ideas can be a useful aid when deciding on your research topic. Keep a notebook on you at all times because you never know when you will develop a research idea.
- **Exploring personal preferences using past projects.** Rather than simply looking at past projects, take a creative approach by selecting projects that fulfil specific criteria. For example, a certain topic, methodological approach or theoretical framework.
- **Relevance trees.** A relevance tree is a structured way of setting out your research ideas. It is similar to a mind map, but more ordered in presentation. The relevance tree is represented by a hierarchical structure that subdivides a broad topic into smaller sub-topics.
- **Brainstorming.** This involves writing down and examining your ideas, generating a list of ideas and/or focusing on a broad issue. A useful activity is arranging a brainstorming session with your fellow research students. Sharing your research ideas and encouraging feedback from other students can often help to narrow your research topic.

    In relation to the final above point, Adrian Furnham (2000: 22) suggests the following conditions in order for a brainstorming session to be correctly carried out:

  - Group size should be about five to seven people. If there are too few people, not enough suggestions are generated. If too many people participate, the session becomes uncontrolled and uncontrollable.
  - No criticism is allowed. All suggestions should be welcome.
  - Freewheeling is encouraged. The more outlandish the idea the better.
  - Quantity and variety are very important. The more ideas put forth, the more likely is a breakthrough idea. The aim is to generate a long list of ideas.
  - Combinations and improvements are encouraged. Building on the ideas of others, including combining them, is very productive.
  - Notes must be taken during the sessions. Either manually or with an electronic recording device. The alternatives generated during the first part of the session should later be edited for duplication and categorizations.

Image 2.2   An example of a brainstorming session

Source: iStock (photo ID: 665394574)

CHOOSING YOUR RESEARCH TOPIC

For many student researchers, choosing a research topic is viewed as the most challenging part of conducting research. When it comes to selecting a topic, students can be categorized into three areas. First, those who have decided their research and are clear on the research direction. Second, those who are undecided and have no idea as to a possible area of research. Finally, students who have multiple research options thereby making it difficult to opt for one particular research topic. Of course, deciding on your research topic early in the process can help to devote sufficient time towards completing each step in your research. However, do not be too concerned if you have a number of potential topics and are yet to decide which is the most appropriate for you. Exploring different topics through searching the literature and asking colleagues, friends and academics is a normal part of doing business research. If you have no idea as to a possible research topic, it is essential that you discuss your frustrations with your research supervisor, rather than losing valuable research time.

Your choice of topic can be key to the success of your research project. We can view a business research topic *as an area of business interest that you decide to explore when undertaking your research project*. Business-related topics are associated with various potential research problems. In some business courses, students are given a particular topic or title which they have to go away and write about. Work-based projects provide an opportunity for students to research a topic based on their employer. The process here is markedly different to undertaking a traditional dissertation, not least because it involves a number of research stakeholders. We explore doing a work-based research project in Chapter 8.

At this early stage in your research, it is also vital that you think about the practicability of your research. For example, have you chosen a topic that you are able to research within the time frame? The most important consideration when selecting your research topic is that it must closely relate to your course of study. Students on business courses typically have the flexibility to choose a topic associated with any area of business. This might include marketing, finance, strategy, human resources or operations. If you are studying one area of business, such as accounting, then clearly your topic must be 'accounting related'. You may also be able to do interdisciplinary research that engages different subject areas.

The significance attached to choosing a topic of personal interest is supported by research conducted by I'Anson and Smith (2004). The authors carried out research into issues of topic selection among tourism students. Although they found that students' motivations for choosing a research topic varied considerably, three main drivers were: personal interest in the subject, a link to career aspirations, and a perceived ease of access to data or the literature.

Blaxter et al. (2010) suggest an interesting measure of whether or not you have chosen the 'right' research topic. They propose if you are in any doubt about whether you have the necessary motivation to carry through the piece of research you have in mind, ask yourself:

'Will it get me out of bed on a wet Monday morning?'

Or, if you are an early morning person:

'Will I want to work on it on Friday evening?'

The need to consider carefully your choice of research topic has been briefly discussed. In this section, we will now take a more detailed look at the factors that may influence your choice of research topic.

RESOURCES

If you are studying business at a university or college you are likely to have a variety of high-quality sources available. For instance, many students make use of sources such as books, academic journals and databases. However, with certain research topics you may experience difficulties finding relevant material. As an example, cross-cultural research focusing on certain developing countries or research on a new technology are potentially subjects where you might find limited sources. Typically, if an institution's library does not have access to a particular book or journal, they may request material via an inter-library loan. Although researching a subject with limited sources can be challenging, it is also liable to provide an opportunity. This is because there is a strong likelihood that you can argue that your research is clearly positioned within the current body of literature. Yet, it is important that you avoid topics that are simply too narrow, with very limited suitable resources. A research project needs to contain a review of the literature and feature academic sources. Clearly, with a dearth of suitable resources on your chosen topic, this will have implications when you come to conduct your literature review. In addition, at this stage it is important to consider the practicability of the research in terms of access to data.

Financial resources are also a consideration. You might be in the fortunate position of having an organization sponsor your research. If not, it is important to think about the likely costs associated with conducting your research. This may include travelling to meet research participants or purchasing data. Remember that your institution will be able to provide many of the resources needed to carry out your research. In terms of travel costs, often there is no need to spend money travelling to meet research participants. Data collection methods such as interviews can easily be conducted via telephone or Skype.

SUPPORT

The potential support you receive when conducting your research can also influence your choice of research topic. To some extent, this depends on the type of project. For example, if you are doing a traditional dissertation, the majority of the support available to you will come from your project supervisor. Conversely, students undertaking a work-based project may receive additional support from a research team and/or organization.

CAREER ASPIRATIONS

What drives your choice of research topic might be based on the perceived benefit to your future career aspirations. Many of my students have selected their topic with this in mind. It is worth mentioning that your research project can be a useful 'selling tool' at interview. By way of example, if you were applying for a job as a data analyst, then your prospective employer would be keen to learn about your research skills, especially data collection and analysis. The research project is an ideal vehicle for demonstrating the transferable skills you have learned while doing your research. Moreover, if it is based on a subject associated with your intended area of employment, this can only be of benefit to you. To gain an understanding of potentially 'hot topics' in your chosen field, seek advice from your research supervisor. Also, your institution's careers office may be able to offer guidance.

PERSONAL INTEREST

In my view, this is the most fundamental consideration when choosing a research topic. You are likely to spend several months working on your research project so it makes sense to choose a topic of interest to you. Select a topic you are passionate about as this helps with motivation. Sometimes you might find it difficult to focus on your research. The scale of the problem will be much greater if you are working on a topic that provides little interest. Research can be an isolating and challenging task at times so make sure that selection of a research topic is 'your' decision. Your research supervisor and/or organization will certainly be pleased to offer advice, but the final decision rests with you, the student.

You may have developed a personal interest in a subject area through studying a particular module on your course. If this is the case, arrange a meeting with your module tutor to discuss your initial research ideas. In addition, your interest could come from practical experience. For example, if you work part-time as an Accounts Assistant for a local accountancy firm and have career aspirations in this area, then this subject can form the basis of your chosen research topic.

POSITIONING

This term refers to the position of your work in the current pool of literature on your research topic. You may have come across the importance attached to 'making a contribution to knowledge' or 'making a contribution to the literature'. The former is certainly a prerequisite for undertaking doctoral research. However, for an undergraduate or postgraduate dissertation, it is often enough to simply recognize how your work is positioned in the context of earlier studies. Certainly, a research project can make a noteworthy contribution to the literature. In addition, if undertaking a work-based project, there is also a practical contribution to the employer/organization. Prior to selecting your topic, it is important that you are familiar with the current body of literature on your potential area of research. A critical review of what has been written on your topic can help to identify the position of your research in the current body of literature.

ETHICAL ISSUES

Another factor that may influence your choice of research topic are ethical issues. Although ethical concerns are something researchers generally address later in the research journey, certain topics will warrant greater ethical scrutiny than others. For example, research involving young children will need to go through a more comprehensive, and very likely, time-consuming ethics approval process. Not surprisingly, this may dissuade some students from selecting a particular topic. If you are passionate about your research topic, do not let this put you off. Create a clear research timetable that makes allowances for ethics approval. Moreover, arrange a meeting with your research supervisor to discuss your institution's ethics approval process. Your supervisor will be familiar with the steps required and may be able to give an indication on length of time needed to gain ethics approval (if required). Ethical issues will be considered more closely in Chapter 7.

CONTACTS

The contacts or personal networks you are able to access may also provide invaluable advice when it comes to selecting your research topic. For example, at my own institution each student on one of the Master's degree programmes is assigned a personal mentor. They often make use of their mentor's contacts as part of their research. Using the wealth of experience and knowledge from practitioners is certainly of benefit when it comes to determining your choice of research topic.

Where you are able to have a say in your choice of research topic, it is always a good idea to discuss these with your potential supervisor. We noted the significance of the research supervisor in Chapter 1. The relationship between a student and their supervisor is likely to have a key influence on the overall success of the project. Deronnian (2011) stresses the importance of the staff–student relationship at all stages of the dissertation process and proposes a possible student–supervisor contract for dissertation preparation (see Figure 2.3).

You may not feel the need to have something formal in place as proposed by Deronnian (2011). However, Figure 2.3 is useful in the sense that it shows expectations from both the student and supervisor perspective. Certainly, you must agree with your supervisor how regularly to communicate and which methods are the most appropriate.

To be discussed and reviewed together at the first dissertation supervisory meeting.

The student and supervisor agree:

- That the dissertation is a substantial, demanding and independently undertaken piece of work
- That mutual trust and respect underpin a successful supervisory relationship
- To engage in a dialogue about the focus of the dissertation, its progress, structure and presentation
- To communicate regularly and by mutual agreement, whether face-to-face, by email, telephone or internet

The student agrees to:

- Read the module guide and become familiar with the requirements and timetables
- Undertake reading, research and writing in line with an agreed timetable
- Take responsibility for arranging and maintaining regular contact with the supervisor
- Submit work for comment by the supervisor in line with an agreed timetable

The supervisor agrees to:

- Offer timely and constructive feedback
- Provide guidance to help keep the student on track
- Identify and clarify uncertainties, such as understanding the marking criteria, at the earliest moment
- Listen to suggestions, discuss issues arising from reading and research, and assist in solving problems that may arise

---

Figure 2.3   Managing the dissertation: A guide for students and their supervisors

Source: Adapted from Deronnian (2011)

If you are in a position where your choice of topic means gaining a supervisor who is an expert in your research area, then ultimately this may influence your decision. However, avoid making a decision on research topic purely on the basis of support. All institutions provide dissertation support. This extends beyond supervisory provision to other areas such as employability. In essence, although support is important, it is not as significant as choosing a topic of interest.

TIME CONSTRAINTS

All student researchers have a set deadline in which to complete their research project. Your project is likely to take anywhere between 6–12 months to complete. Of course, the length of time allocated to doing your project depends on your institution and the course of study. Furthermore, not all projects are undertaken in the final year of study. Where this is the case, projects taken earlier in a course are usually based on a shorter time frame to complete.

To make sure that you are able to submit your project on time it is essential to consider how much time to devote to each research task. Data collection and analysis can often be extremely time-consuming. The time period required to collect and analyze your data will increase if you intend using more than one research method. Students sometimes set out to do multiple research methods without giving much thought to the time involved. Conversely, students who do note the additional time, often underestimate how much time data collection and analysis are likely to take. This is where a clear research timetable is vital. Any timetable should feature the key tasks, start dates and anticipated completion dates. Examples of key tasks include data collection, analysis and when to write up your work. If you have any doubts as to how much time to assign to each task, once again, discuss with your research supervisor.

In summary, we have looked at a number of considerations associated with choosing a research topic. Planning your own research, you might consider some of these factors more important than others, though a priority has to be a topic that will maintain your level of interest.

Let us say that you choose a topic of interest. How do you know that you have chosen a quality topic? What makes a quality topic? The following are characteristics of a quality topic:

* The research is developed from and supported by a sound theoretical base.
* The research is of interest to both the sponsor and the researcher.
* The research problem is well defined and the research questions and objectives that flow from it are specific and possible to address through a rigorous research design.
* Resource requirements are well understood early in the research journey.
* The research is expected to make a contribution to knowledge independently of the orientation of the findings.
* The research can be achieved within the time frame.

Source: Adapted from Hair et al. (2015)

First, as you are undertaking an academic piece of work, your research must by underpinned by a theoretical base. Certainly, you may choose to apply a particular theoretical framework when conducting your research. However, theory may also be an outcome of your research. If this is the case, then your research can be described as an *inductive approach*, while applying theory is viewed as a *deductive approach*. We examine these terms more closely in Chapter 5. Second, if you are undertaking a work-based project, then it might be that the research topic is not only of interest to you, but also the organization(s) taking part in your research. In the previous section, we examined the importance attached to having an interest in the research topic from the point of view of the researcher. Equally, a sponsor such as your employer or partner organization may also have an interest in the topic. Third, having a well-defined research problem and specific set of research questions and objectives increases the likelihood of research success. Fourth, resource requirements such as time, research literature and financial considerations are well-planned for early in your research journey. Fifth, your research should make a contribution to knowledge. This is especially important if undertaking doctoral research. A work-based project will be concerned with making a contribution to practice. Finally, as already noted, the research must be achieved within the time frame.

A TOPIC HAS BEEN ASSIGNED TO YOU

When undertaking commissioned research, you will be presented with your research topic. The *research brief* is the means by which the client presents background to the research topic, the research problem and an indication of research questions. In essence, the research brief is an overview of the client's views on the problem or opportunity and is typically presented in written form. In response to the research brief, the researcher prepares a proposal setting out their opinions on the problem and an outline of their proposed methodology. The research brief is a key part of the process associated with commissioned research.

In some cases, student researchers are required to choose their area of research from a list of potential topics. Consequently, you may find that none of the topics appeal to your research interests. In this situation, you can always ask your course leader or mentor if it is possible to select a topic more in line with your preferred area of research. If this is not workable, the next step is to arrange an initial meeting with your supervisor to discuss topic choices in greater detail. You may find that following an in-depth discussion with your supervisor on various topics, you are better positioned to make an informed judgment on which you would prefer to choose for your research project. There is of course a benefit to having a supervisor who specializes in your chosen area of research. Familiarity with your topic means that they can recommend helpful sources of literature. Moreover, your supervisor will be aware of the challenges you are likely to encounter on your research journey. Examples here may include generating a suitably sized sample or accessing certain secondary sources.

REASONS FOR NOT CHOOSING A RESEARCH TOPIC

Throughout this section, we have examined reasons for choosing, and what makes a quality research topic. However, it is also worth noting some of the reasons students provide for not selecting a research topic. Although by no means exhaustive, examples of these reasons are highlighted below:

- because this is an easy topic
- because there is so much written on this topic
- because my organization selected my topic
- because another student has already chosen this topic.

There is no 'easy' research topic. However, you can take steps to reduce the challenges associated with conducting your research. These include considerations such as choosing a topic of interest and discussing your research ideas with your supervisor. Second, a large body of literature might be an opportunity, rather than a reason not to select a research topic. For instance, although there could be so much written on your subject area, the literature might relate to a broad topic, e.g. finance, with little attention paid to a specific area of finance. In other words, there is a position in the literature which your research can address. Next, if your employer or partner organization(s) insist on you selecting a particular topic, then you may not have the flexibility to decide your own area of research. Although if you have clear justification for making your own topic choice, it is always a good idea to discuss this with your research stakeholders. Lastly, sometimes a student might not select a topic because they believe that a fellow classmate has already chosen their intended area of research. In reality, this is unlikely to be the case. For example, if you have decided to conduct an in-depth research study on Google, and other student(s) have also selected Google as their case study, it is highly improbable that they will select the same focused subject area. In this instance, a narrow topic focusing on Google might address a wide range of subjects, such as cybersecurity, advertising, technological development or search engine optimization (SEO).

HOW DO I NARROW MY RESEARCH TOPIC?

The majority of students tend to have some idea of what they would like to study for their topic choice. Formulation of a research problem begins with selection of a broad research topic. For example, corporate social responsibility is too broad and needs to be narrowed down to something more specific and realistically achievable. After you have narrowed down your topic you can begin to determine a possible research problem. Figure 2.4 shows an example of moving from a broad topic to a narrow, manageable topic. In this case, the broad topic is social media. What follows is an area associated with social media, namely social media marketing (SMM). Next, we can narrow SMM further by focusing on 'The effects of social media marketing on consumer behaviour'. The topic is now much narrower, but potentially still a little broad for our final chosen area of research. Thus, we can go further by selecting 'the effects of SMM on consumer behaviour in the luxury goods market'.

Figure 2.4 provides an insightful illustration of moving from a broad topic to narrow topic. However, it is worthy to note that there is not one particular method for narrowing a research topic. You can consider a number of different options. These include choosing a particular sector, organization, country, culture and/or unit of analysis. Importantly, the options here are by no means exhaustive, but are commonly used by students to narrow their research topic. By way of an example, a study focusing on 'Employee reward systems in the Italian fashion industry' features some of these ways, that is, employee (unit of analysis), Italy (country), fashion industry (sector).

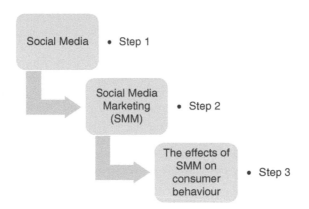

Figure 2.4 Example of moving from broad topic to narrow topic

You need to adopt a narrow focus in order to explore your topic in sufficient depth. However, do not choose too narrow a topic as you will find it difficult to locate relevant literature.

Image 2.3 Concept Cartoon 'Research topic'

Image 2.3 is a Concept Cartoon that shows characters expressing their views on research topic. Think about the different views and use them to provoke a discussion with fellow students. What do you think? Do you share a viewpoint with one particular character?

Looking through past copies of student dissertations is a useful way to understand what makes a narrow research topic. Identifying ways other students have narrowed their area of research may also generate ideas for your own research. Finally, Jasimuddin et al. (2005: 69) make a number of recommendations to researchers about to start searching for a research topic. The list is intended for academic researchers, but equally applies to students.

- Start at the broadest possible level, perhaps using search engines, e.g. Google, Yahoo, etc.
- Set out general ideas about a research problem after interacting with academics who are research active in the area of interest.
- Collect relevant literature from leading journals, focusing either on relevant concepts or on its leading authors.
- Visit conference websites in your research area to access conference papers relevant to your research.
- Analyze existing literature thoroughly and in such a way that themes or trends emerge.
- Subsequently, narrow down the research topic to a workable size.
- Construct a map that synthesizes previous work in the area of study to show the themes identified in the research material and to show the narrowing down of the research focus.
- Re-check and update available materials periodically, with the help of the internet.
- Share knowledge with fellow student researchers through social interactions.

IDENTIFYING AND DEFINING YOUR RESEARCH PROBLEM

The second stage in your research direction is identifying and defining a research problem. Jacobs (2013) also makes the point that nearly all research handbooks advise that stating the problem is among the first steps in the research process. Walliman (2018: 33) argues that for a problem to be researchable, it must be:

- stated clearly and concisely
- significant, for example not a trivial subject or simply repetition of previous work
- delineated, in order to limit its scope to practical investigation
- possible to obtain the information required to explore the problem
- possible to draw conclusions related to the problem, as the point of research is to find some answers.

Let us look at each of the above features in turn. The first feature notes that research is not just about formulating a research problem, but that a research problem needs to be cogent and researchable. Second, a research problem should be based on an interesting subject and not repeat an earlier piece of research. The third feature stresses that the research problem must be explained in order to limit its scope of practical investigation. Fourth, it is important to be able to obtain the information required in order to explore the research problem. Finally, the researcher must be able to generate answers to the problem.

Business research can be viewed as a *problem-solving activity*. The nature of the problem depends on whether the researcher is undertaking applied or basic research. For example, a practitioner is interested in finding out about practical problems and opportunities, while an academic researcher engaged in basic research might be interested in identifying gaps in the theoretical literature. The term 'problem' can be rather misleading as research may also be conducted in order to explore an opportunity, such as the possible benefits for an organization entering a new geographical market. The formulation of your research problem is in effect the starting point of your research journey. A clear definition and statement of the research problem forms the basis for developing your research questions. Moreover, it should also provide the motivation and clarity for you to complete your research project. Why is the research problem important? In essence, it establishes the importance of the topic, creates interest for the readers and explains how the research will add to the current body of literature.

Students typically spend a significant amount of time reading around the subject, sharing the ideas with their supervisor or discussing the issue with various research stakeholders. However, it is certainly worth spending time on formulating your research problem as this will influence your choice of research questions, which in turn will influence later stages in your research journey. What makes the problem different to other areas of your research? Your research problem should be a business-related issue or problem that forms the basis for your research project. A research topic is the subject matter being addressed in your research. In the first instance, students typically begin with a broad topic, before narrowing their topic to a more manageable area of research interest.

Selecting a research problem requires a distinction to be made between a symptom and a problem. A *symptom* indicates the presence of a problem or opportunity. For example, the problem may be defined as 'poor employee retention' when the problem is actually an ineffective reward system or a poor working environment. A question most student researchers ask is 'How do I identify a research problem?'. If you are undertaking a traditional dissertation then you are likely to have the flexibility to locate your own research problem. The research problem can come from a gap in the literature, and conflict in research in the literature, topics that have been neglected in the literature and 'real-life' problems found in the workplace (Creswell, 2014). The sources for business research problems may arise from the following: (1) Your own business experience, (2) Literature review, (3) Theories, (4) Research issues identified by project stakeholders. Let us examine each of these in turn.

YOUR OWN WORK EXPERIENCE

Business practice relies on research to solve problems and identify opportunities. If you currently work for an employer or have work experience, this can prove to be a useful source of research problems. For example, while working in a customer service centre, you may consider how the role of a customer service executive can improve the efficiency of customer service provision. A preliminary review of customer feedback, after sales support and response times might raise significant questions that form the basis of a research problem.

LITERATURE REVIEW

The existing literature can help immensely when it comes to identifying a potential research problem. Searching the literature is a starting point for many students. It is important to know where to find earlier studies on your area of research interest. Do not worry if you have yet to determine your topic, a review of the literature is also an ideal way to identify a possible research subject. As a student researcher, you need to engage with the literature at the early stage of your research to develop your knowledge on your chosen research subject. Research problems of a theoretical nature are found in academic journals. If on the other hand you are commissioned to undertake a consultancy project, also consider internal company information as a possible source for formulating your research problem.

THEORIES

A research problem can exist in a theoretical context. Fred N. Kerlinger (1986: 9) defines theory as 'a set of interrelated constructs (concepts), definitions, and propositions that present a systematic view of phenomena specifying relations among variables, with the purpose of explaining and predicting the phenomena'. For example, a theory may have been applied in earlier studies in a Western cultural context, but yet to be applied in Asian culture. Here, we can interpret the potential problem as evaluating the application of the theory across Asian countries in order to determine the effectiveness in non-Western societies. Students undertaking traditional dissertations usually need to show evidence of theoretical application. In this instance, a theory might be applied to provide a solution to a practical problem.

RESEARCH ISSUES IDENTIFIED BY PROJECT STAKEHOLDERS

If you are conducting research involving a number of project stakeholders, this is also an opportunity to aid formulating your research problem. In particular, your research supervisor will be able to give valuable advice on coming up with a clear and focused problem statement. Examples of how to write a problem statement are presented in Chapter 3. This advice also extends to other research stakeholders. Examples may include your employer, partner organization or fellow business students. Once again, formulating a research problem is one of the most significant steps in your research journey. Thus, do not be afraid to seek guidance from all those who have an interest in your research.

Rather than simply stating your research problem, you should go further by justifying the importance of the problem. Here, justification can be based on what other researchers have found in earlier studies. Second, you can also support your identified research problems by referring to your own past or current business experience. For example, if your problem is associated with a lack of technical skills in the workplace, you may have experienced this issue and therefore are able to refer to this in your study. Finally, justification might be based on the experiences of colleagues in the workplace.

How do I go about locating the research problem? Read the abstract and/or opening paragraphs of existing studies on your chosen area of research. Look for indicators in the article associated with the 'research problem'. For example, terminology such as, What is the issue or research problem? What are the reasons that have led to the need for research? What are the concerns being addressed by the author(s)? Is there an explicit sentence along the lines of 'The research problem being addressed in this research is....'?

Prior to determining whether a problem should be researched you need to answer the following questions:

- Can the problem be researched?
- Do you have access to the resource, time, support and required research skills necessary to address the research problem?
- Does researching the problem contribute to the current body of literature on the subject? Similarly, does it contribute to practice? Will your study inform practice? Will your research extend past research or examine the topic in greater depth?

When identifying your research problem and research direction, you must consider who will read your research project. Your audience is likely to shape the nature of your research problem and subsequent research questions. Typically, traditional dissertations are read by the project supervisor, a second marker and possibly an external examiner. However, work-based projects may have a number of readers. This might include a mentor, company management and other stakeholders in the research. At the early stages in your research journey, it is good practice to communicate regularly with your research stakeholders as to your intended research direction. This is especially the case with a work-based project as the organization may want to be made aware of progress throughout your research.

DEVELOPING YOUR RESEARCH DIRECTION

The first step in developing your research direction is forming a purpose statement. A purpose statement usually consists of one or two sentences on the research intentions. It is sometimes referred to as the 'statement of the problem' and often begins with the wording 'The purpose of this study is to…'. When writing your purpose statement what is important is that it reflects the direction of your research. You may find that you rewrite your purpose statement later in your research. This is because the direction of your research might change during the course of your research journey.

What are the elements of a purpose statement? We can categorize a purpose statement on the basis of quantitative and qualitative research. First, a *quantitative purpose statement* typically identifies variables and their relationships. The terminology used in quantitative purpose statements includes 'relationship', 'variable' and 'compare'. If you are using a particular theory, state the theory that you plan to test. A *qualitative purpose statement* uses words such as 'explore', 'investigate' and 'understand'. When writing your purpose statement, try to be concise and make explicit reference to the purpose of the study.

BOX 2.1: RESEARCH SNAPSHOT

All research should include a clear purpose statement. This sets out the direction of your research and needs to be made explicit within your research project. Write a concise purpose statement and use simple language for your audience to understand. Once again, remember your audience. Non-subject specialists may not be familiar with technical terms, so try to avoid using technical jargon.

DEVELOPING YOUR RESEARCH AIMS, OBJECTIVES AND QUESTIONS

The term 'research aim' typically refers to *the main goal of a research project*. A *research aim* tends to be in the form of a short, lucid sentence. For example:

To investigate factors relating to customer loyalty.

Clearly, the above aim is rather broad and difficult to achieve without greater focus and clarity. Thus, the research aim usually features at the beginning of a research project to indicate the direction of research. In order to develop a more focused approach we need to develop a set of research objectives and research questions.

Although some researchers refer to research objectives and research questions interchangeably, there is a clear distinction between the two terms. *Research objectives* tend to be broader and more statement like, for example, 'To understand the importance of brand identity among UK consumers'. Turning this objective into a research question becomes 'How important is brand identity to UK consumers?'. Thus, research questions are narrower and more focused. Clearly, we can also turn the research objective into a What? Why? Where? or Which? question.

Your research questions are possibly the most important part of your research project as they set to help the direction of your research and 'pull together' subsequent steps in the research process. The importance of research questions is stressed by many researchers. For example, Alvesson and Alvesson (2013) point out that constructing and formulating research questions are one of the most, if not the most, critical aspect of all research.

Research objectives address the purpose of the research. When framing your research objectives and research questions, be sure to illustrate them lucidly. Each research objective should have a corresponding research question. How many research objectives do I need to generate? The answer to this question is that the number should be sufficient to address your research problem. Of course, keep in mind that all of your research objectives need to be achieved prior to your project deadline.

Developing research objectives is no easy task. One of the tools you can use when formulating your research objectives is the acronym SMART (Specific, Measurable, Achievable, Relevant and Timed). The SMART acronym was first devised by Doran in 1981 to improve strategic decision-making. However, the acronym can also be used as a useful guide when formulating research objectives. First, 'Specific' means that your objectives are not too broad and can be broken down into explicit steps. Developing a set of specific objectives is critical to the success of your project. Second, 'Measurable' refers to an objective that features quantifiable increments. For example, rather than simply stating 'To determine the increase in production', by introducing a quantifiable measure we can rework the objective as follows: 'To determine the percentage increase in production over a 5-year period'. Third, 'Achievable' refers to the ability to complete your research, especially within the allocated time frame. Of course, your research requires a high level of commitment and purpose, but it should not result in something that demands your attention 24 hours a day! It may also be influenced by other factors, including access to data, support from your research stakeholders and your research skills. Fourth, 'Relevant' relates to the appropriateness of your research topic. If you are undertaking a traditional dissertation then there is scope to consider a wide range of topics associated with your degree programme. It is important not to go 'off-topic' as this may not meet with your institution's regulations. Students completing a practice-based project, such as a consultancy report, are likely to have less flexibility when it comes to choosing a topic as this is usually done in collaboration with an organization. Finally, 'Timed' is something that can help to motivate you on your research journey by setting yourself clear writing goals. The ability to manage your time and set clear targets is essential to meeting your research deadline. This might involve writing a set number of words each week. Table 2.1 provides examples of research objectives and research questions. In terms of the former, SMART has been taken into consideration when formulating the research objectives.

Table 2.1   Examples of research objectives and research questions

Research objectives	Research questions
To evaluate retail distribution channels and channel members in the UK in order to determine their potential	How to select UK retail distribution channels?
To examine consumer perceptions of the online brand in order to identify improvement opportunities	What are consumer perceptions of the online brand?
To establish factors resulting in a decline in sales so that strategies can be put in place in order to tackle the problem	What are the factors that have led to a decline in sales?
To analyze factors influencing employee turnover in order to identify options for policy changes	What are the factors that influence employee turnover?

Table 2.1 shows examples of research objectives and corresponding research questions. Some researchers suggest subdividing a broad research question into sub-questions. Although this is fine in principle, the benefit of objectives is that they transform research questions into clearly set out aims using action words, such as 'to analyze', 'to interpret', 'to examine' and 'to evaluate'.

In the earlier section, we examined how to formulate research objectives, but how do you know if you have chosen appropriate research questions? Similar to SMART, the 'Goldilocks test' can be considered as a useful means to choosing appropriate research questions. Clough and Nutbrown (2007) developed the Goldilocks test. The authors refer to topics as 'too big', 'too small', 'too hot' and 'just right'. A 'too big' scenario means that the research will be too broad and require too many resources during the research. Conversely, 'too small' results in the research being too narrow and insignificant, while a research question categorized as 'too hot' may result in the researcher having to deal with challenging ethical issues. Finally, Clough and Nutbrown suggested that a researcher should choose a question that is 'just right', thus increasing the likelihood of answering the research question.

An important consideration when developing your research questions is the distinction between quantitative and qualitative. Examples of quantitative research questions may compare two or more groups or possibly relate two or more variables. For example, 'What is the relationship between newspaper sales and advertising spend?' is a question seeking to determine the correlation between two variables (newspaper sales and advertising spend). Begin your quantitative questions with words such as 'How', 'What' and 'Why' to specify the independent, dependent and mediating or control variables. When determining qualitative questions, understand how these types of questions differ from quantitative questions. In the first instance, the terminology lends itself to more open questions and exploratory research. Examples will especially include 'How' and 'Why' questions associated with an in-depth understanding of a particular subject.

How many research questions are appropriate? Similar to research objectives, there is no definitive rule here. To an extent, the number of questions depends on both the nature of your research topic and your ability to address each question comprehensively within your research constraints. Moreover, the word limit is also a factor. If you attempt to tackle too many research questions within your word constraints, then the likelihood is that each question will not be addressed in sufficient depth. If working closely with a research stakeholder, such as an employer, then they may also have a viewpoint as to the type and number of research questions. As your research progresses you will develop and adapt your research questions. The reasons for this are that your literature review and data collection influence your judgment as to your research direction. Once again, this is the iterative process of doing research, as illustrated by The Research Wheel.

Sometimes students do not correctly formulate their questions and they end up more statement like. This makes it difficult when it comes to developing methodology and research direction as the questions drive this process. Below is an example of a student statement. Although interesting and relevant to their research direction, the failure to turn the statement below into research questions would have implications later in the research.

> Digital Marketing among small businesses is developing, but some marketers implement Digital Marketing strategy in a short-term way or more tactical. In terms of the marketing strategies, there appears to be more emphasis on 'digital' strategies in other area of business.

Lastly, research questions may also include a set of *hypotheses*. You will find that in some, typically quantitative studies, the hypotheses might be used instead of research questions. A hypothesis is an unproven proposition or possible solution to a problem. For example, a Finance Director may hypothesize that an increase in the staff training budget will lead to improved organizational financial performance. In essence, a hypothesis is concerned with the relationship between variables, and, through testing, may or may not support the theory. A hypothesis can be stated as a null hypothesis. This states that there is no relationship between an independent variable and the dependent variable. Independent variables are those seen as a 'cause', while a 'dependent' variable is seen as the 'effect' (outcome). We examine hypothesis testing in Chapters 16 and 17.

MAKING A DISTINCTION BETWEEN RESEARCH IDEA, OBJECTIVE AND QUESTION

Table 2.2   The distinction between research idea, research objective and research question

Research idea	Research objective	Research question
Staff training using online videos	To analyze the extent that online training is used among companies	How effective is online training compared to traditional training methods?
Advertising using social media	To examine the importance of social media advertising to marketers	Why are an increasing number of marketers advertising on social media?
The use of marketing semiotics in brand labelling	To establish consumer perceptions in relation to brand labels	How do consumers perceive different aspects of marketing semiotics?

Table 2.2 'pulls together' what we have covered in relation to research idea, research objective and research question. You can see how an initial idea can be transformed into a research objective and a research question, thereby increasing the likelihood of addressing the research problem. Figure 2.5 provides an example of application of each of the key stages in research direction.

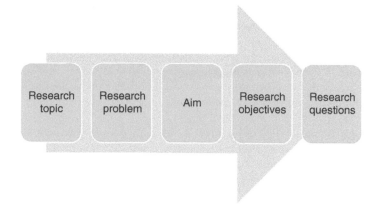

Research topic:	The Globalization of Chinese brands
Research problem:	Why is there a general lack of awareness in the UK of leading Chinese brands?
Aim:	To investigate the extent that Chinese brands have achieved 'global brand status'
Research objectives:	To determine the level of brand awareness of Chinese brands in the UK
	To establish UK consumers' perceptions of Chinese brands
	To evaluate the extent that country-of-origin (COO) effects influence UK consumers' perceptions of Chinese brands
Research questions:	What is the level of brand awareness of Chinese brands in the UK?
	How do UK consumers perceive Chinese brands?
	What are the effects of COO on UK consumers' perceptions of Chinese brands?

Figure 2.5   An example of the relationship between the key stages in research direction

ARTICULATING YOUR RESEARCH DIRECTION USING SPEED RESEARCHING

Once you have developed your research idea, research objectives and research questions, a useful classroom activity you can do is 'speed researching'. This helps to articulate your research direction and also provides an opportunity to share your research. It is an activity I use with my own research students as it gives them an insight into the research being undertaken by each member of the class. 'Speed researching' is like speed dating for researchers! It can be defined as '*A method of sharing and understanding research ideas by briefly talking to fellow researchers on a one-to-one basis within a set time frame*'. Each researcher is allotted a short period of time, e.g. 2–3 minutes, to summarize their research – research topic, research aims, research problem, research objectives and research questions. As preparation, practise articulating the key elements of your research in a coherent and succinct way within the time frame a few days before the event. Speed researching is a two-way process that involves speaking and listening to your partner to make sure that you understand the nature of their research, so you can offer your own views and advice.

CHAPTER SUMMARY

- The key stages in developing a clear research direction include research topic, determining the research problem, developing a purpose statement, identifying research objectives and questions.

- A business research topic is an area of business interest that you decide to explore when undertaking your research project.

- Key considerations when choosing your research topic include personal interest and career aspirations.

- Business research is viewed as a problem-solving activity.

- The research brief is the means by which the client presents background to the research topic, the research problem and an indication of research questions.

- A detailed statement of the problem features research topic, the research problem, audience, purpose statement, background and justification, research objectives and research questions.

QUESTIONS FOR REVIEW

1. What is the difference between a research question and a research objective?

2. Discuss the factors that are likely to influence your choice of research topic.

3. Explain the steps you are likely to take if you are assigned a research topic.

4. Outline the key stages in the research direction.

5. Discuss ways of narrowing down a research topic.

6. What are the features a research problem needs to have in order to be researchable?

7. What are the key reasons for not choosing a research topic?

8. How might you generate and refine your research ideas?

STUDENT SCENARIO: LI HONG FORMULATES HER RESEARCH OBJECTIVES AND QUESTIONS

Li Hong decided to study a degree in Management in order to improve her all-round business knowledge. Her research topic focused on the cultural differences between Western–Chinese joint venture partners. Although a challenging research topic, Li Hong was able to justify her research to her supervisor as she was fortunate to have managerial contacts working in UK–Chinese joint ventures.

Research objectives and research questions

Li Hong developed the direction of her research by reviewing the extensive literature on Western–Chinese joint ventures. She established that the main focus of existing studies tended to be on cultural issues within the joint venture, as opposed to between parent companies. By determining this, she was able to justify the reasons for conducting her research. Moreover, Li Hong used her contacts working in Western–Chinese joint ventures to help formulate her research questions. This involved asking research participants what they consider to be the main cultural themes and issues associated with joint ventures. Using business networks in this way is an ideal approach for determining possible 'hot topics' that can help the researcher to focus on how to frame their research questions. Li Hong produced the following set of research objectives and research questions.

Research objectives

- To establish the importance of cultural understanding between Western and Chinese joint venture partners.
- To determine the relationship between cultural understanding and joint venture performance.
- To understand the level of investment made by Western and Chinese joint venture partners in cultural training.

Research questions

- How important is cultural understanding between Western and Chinese joint venture partners?
- What is the relationship between cultural understanding and joint venture performance?
- How much do Western and Chinese joint venture partners invest in cultural training?

Work experience

Following a discussion with her supervisor and given her work experience in International Accounting, Li Hong decided to change the direction of her research relatively early in her research journey. Originally, she had encountered difficulties accessing potential research participants with her first choice of research topic. Li Hong solved this issue by deciding to select a topic relating to her work experience. Her rationale was to use her knowledge in accounting to focus on the cultural issues, specifically within the accounting departments of Western–Chinese joint ventures. Li Hong learned that although choosing a topic of interest is important, it is also essential to think a few 'steps ahead' when doing research, particularly when it comes to accessing potential research participants.

Questions

1. Give two examples of additional research objectives and research questions Li Hong may wish to include in her research.
2. Apply the Research direction model (Figure 2.5) to Li Hong's research.

Hint: Remember that research objectives are broader than research questions and that there should be a clear link between the two. You do not need to be a subject specialist for this task, focus is on the type of objectives and questions.

FURTHER READING

Lei, S.A. (2009) 'Strategies for finding and selecting an ideal thesis or dissertation topic: A review of literature', *College Student Journal*, 43 (4): 1324–1332.

This short article provides a discussion on how to choose a dissertation topic and includes a useful table of sources for finding an ideal dissertation research topic.

Piotrowski, C. (2015) 'Social media: Major topics in dissertation research', *Education*, 135 (3): 299–302.

This article focuses on social media research. The author includes a table ranking the most researched areas on the topic of social media in dissertations.

Rogers, S. and Earnshaw, Y. (2015) 'Avoiding the dissertation minefield', *TechTrends*, 59 (2): 13–14.

This short article provides brief narratives from the perspective of two recent graduates and offers some suggestions for choosing a topic.

REFERENCES

Alvesson, J. and Alvesson, M. (2013) *Constructing Research Questions: Doing Interesting Research*. London: Sage.

Blaxter, L., Tight, M. and Hughes, C. (2010) *How to Research*. Maidenhead: McGraw-Hill Education.

Clough, P. and Nutbrown, C. (2007) *A Student's Guide to Methodology* (2nd edn). Thousand Oaks, CA: Sage.

Creswell, J.W. (2014) *Research Design: Qualitative, Quantitative and Mixed Methods Approaches* (4th edn). London: Sage.

Deronnian, J. (2011) 'Shall we dance: The importance of staff–student relationships to undergraduate dissertation preparation', *Active Learning in Higher Education*, 12 (2): 91–100.

Doran, G.T. (1981) 'There's a SMART way to write management's goals and objectives', *Management Review*, 70 (11): 35–36.

Furnham, A. (2000) 'The brainstorming myth', *Business Strategy Review*, 11: 21–28.

Hair, J.F. Jr., Wolfinbarger, M., Money, A.H., Samouel, P. and Page, M.J. (2015) *Essentials of Business Research Methods* (2nd edn). London: Routledge.

I'Anson, R.A. and Smith, K.A. (2004) 'Undergraduate research projects and dissertations: Issues of topic selection, access and data collections amongst tourism management students', *Journal of Hospitality, Leisure, Sport and Tourism Education*, 3 (1): 19–32.

Jacobs, R.L. (2013) 'Developing a dissertation research problem: A guide for doctoral students in human resource development and adult education', *New Horizons in Adult Education and Human Resource Development*, 25 (3): 103–117.

Jasimuddin, S.M., Connell, C. and Klein, J.H. (2005) 'The challenges of navigating a topic to a prospective researcher: The case of knowledge management research', *Management Research News*, 28 (1).

Kerlinger, F.N. (1986) *Foundations of Behavioural Research* (3rd edn). New York: Holt, Rinehart & Winston.

Walliman, N. (2018) *Research Methods: The Basics* (2nd edn). New York: Routledge.

3

WRITING YOUR RESEARCH PROPOSAL

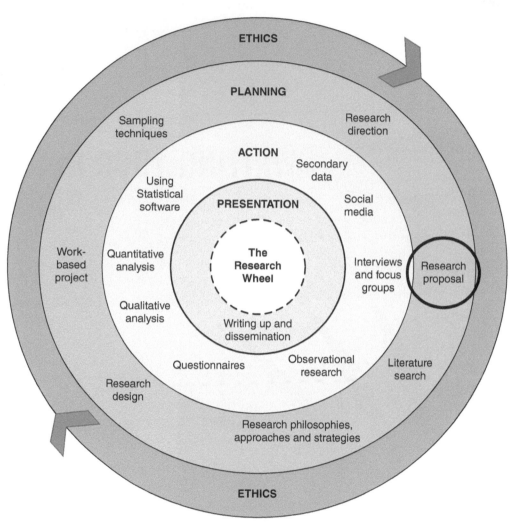

Figure 3.1   The Research Wheel

Learning objectives

By the end of this chapter, you should be able to:

- explain the purpose of a research proposal
- structure a research proposal
- recognize how a research proposal relates to the overall research process
- write your own research proposal
- describe the characteristics of a winning research proposal.

INTRODUCTION

The main way that researchers usually formalize the planning process is to produce something called a 'research proposal' or 'research project proposal' (from this point onwards referred to as research proposal). The structure and length of your research proposal will depend on the requirements set out in your course or institution. Typically, a proposal is an essential document. Students are often required to write a research proposal before doing a dissertation or as part of a research bidding process.

The purpose of this chapter is to examine the process of writing a research proposal. If you are studying for a postgraduate qualification, then the likelihood is that your proposal is an assessed piece of work and used to allocate a research supervisor. In some institutions, the supervisor is then allocated based on choice of research topic.

We start the chapter by defining what is meant by the term 'research proposal' and identify the key points students need to be aware of before starting to write their proposal. Second, the chapter looks at what you need to think about before writing your proposal. This is followed by how to structure your research proposal. At this point, it is important to stress that there is no one definitive approach and that you will need to check the requirements of your institution.

Next, we discuss the typical word length of a proposal and how this impacts your writing. The number of words available will no doubt relate to the type of proposal. In some institutions, a research proposal is purely an outline of the research project. Following this, the chapter moves on to discuss the challenges and approaches associated with writing a winning research proposal.

The chapter then proceeds to show the relationship between the research proposal and the overall research process. The subsequent sections in the chapter cover what a research proposal looks like. I always provide my students with examples of past research proposals. Why? Well, I believe it is important for students to see what a proposal looks like as this helps them to meet assessment expectations.

Lastly, we look at the role of the research supervisor and how they can support you throughout the research proposal process.

As you can see from Figure 3.1, Research proposal (circled), is part of the 'Planning' layer in The Research Wheel. As Gray (2014) notes, a research proposal is constructed through a detailed process of planning and design. Again, remember that the research process is an iterative process that can be challenging and may require you to revisit earlier steps in your research.

WHAT IS A RESEARCH PROPOSAL?

A research project should start with a clearly written plan setting out the proposed actions. The better the plan, the better the project is likely to be and the greater the likelihood that you will successfully complete your research.

A research proposal is a formalized plan that sets out how you intend to conduct your research and is a prerequisite for research investigation. It describes the background of your research, what is known about your chosen research topic, the purpose of your research and the research direction. In addition, it also explains your proposed research methodology, a preliminary review of the literature, the scope of the research, limitations and a research timetable. The latter is an essential part of any proposal as it shows the key tasks in the research and anticipated completion dates.

There is no one universal definition of a research proposal, although there is a general consensus that it is a form of 'planning document'. For example, DeCuir-Gunby and Schutz (2017) refer to the research proposal as a tentative plan for the implementation of your study that contains three major areas (introduction, literature review and research methods) and two minor areas (references and appendices).

You can also think of the research proposal as a 'sales pitch' (O'Leary, 2018). Why? The main reason is that the proposal often has to be 'sold' to the marker, reader and potential research supervisor. You may also need to convince research stakeholders that you are capable of carrying out your research. In this sense, think of the proposal as not only 'selling' the importance of your research, but also your capability as a researcher. I have marked many student research proposals that clearly explain the nature of the research, but they do not always 'sell' why the research is important. Furthermore, a well-written proposal with a focused research topic is likely to make it easier when it comes to allocating a subject specialist research supervisor. Clearly, how supervisors are allocated is not the same across courses and institutions, so a subject specialist is not always available or essential. However, both 'planning' and 'selling' are certainly terms worth considering when it comes to writing your proposal.

A research proposal is also a guide for you as it outlines how you propose to undertake your research. Once again, it contains key elements or building blocks of the research plan, that is, the background to the introduction, preliminary literature review, methodology, summary/outcomes and research timetable. We will examine these elements later in this chapter.

Writing a research proposal is an integral part of the research process. A research proposal contains information you will have decided to use from the planning stage in the research process. This may include key authors, material on your research topic and of course the proposed methodological approach. Sometimes students view a research proposal as a mini or pilot research project. It is not a project, it is a 'proposal'. Remember that your proposal is what you are proposing in terms of 'how' you plan to carry out your research. The subsequent stage in your research is 'Action' (see The Research Wheel) where the 'How' turns into practice. Consequently, any results obtained should feature in the conclusion chapter of your research project and not in the proposal.

In essence, we can say that the main purpose of a research proposal is three-fold. First, producing a research proposal is often a requirement for those students considering doing a research degree. The proposal is a useful indication for an institution to see how much the applicant is familiar with their proposed area of research. It also helps with the process of assigning a potential research supervisor. Second, a research proposal is commonly used as a form of assessment on research methods modules. And finally, a research proposal helps to appoint a supervisor. Depending on the research topic, a supervisor is allocated to support and guide the student throughout their research. In this sense, the proposal is a very effective starting point to discuss the research with your supervisor.

Although these are all key reasons for writing a research proposal, one feature that they all have in common is that they are related to 'procedure', whether it is a part of a course/or applying for a course. Writing a research proposal is also essential when viewed from the point of view of transferable skills.

These are something you will no doubt develop by engaging in the process of writing your proposal. Outcomes include:

- developing your research skills in thinking about and designing a research project
- improving your overall practical research and writing skills
- learning how to conduct a preliminary and later a comprehensive review of the literature
- the ability to critically review and examine different types of data collection and analytical techniques.

One way to think of the research proposal is as an opportunity to master certain research skills prior to actually conducting your research. A key skill is the ability to reflect on the steps you undertake when writing your proposal. By way of an example, critically reviewing the literature and writing as you go along will undoubtedly lead to improvements as to how you write and your ability to review the literature. The process of writing a research proposal is important because it requires deep and reasoned thinking about an area of enquiry and a systematic analysis of the requirements of the research. In other words, the proposal sets out what is required in order to make the research happen (Herrington et al., 2007).

According to Cottrell (2014: 113), the rationale for writing a research proposal is that it helps you to:

- work through, and clarify your thinking about your concept
- synthesize your early ideas and reading
- prepare the groundwork well
- identify potential problems at an early stage, while there is still plenty of time to manage the implications of these
- demonstrate the feasibility of the research from all angles
- make a case for gaining formal approval.

Let us examine each of the above points in turn. First, working through and clarifying your thinking about your concept. This means when actually writing your research proposal, think of it as a process of how each stage relates to the others. For example, when thinking about each step in your proposal, consider the relationships. How does your methodology relate to your research questions? Why have you chosen a certain methodological approach in order to address your research problem? In short, the exercise of producing a proposal is one that promotes thinking.

Second, by synthesizing your ideas and reading you are 'pulling together' the key themes related to your research. By way of example, doing a mind map is an excellent way to synthesize ideas as it provides a visual representation of how different elements 'fit' into your proposal.

Third, think of preparing the groundwork as part of the planning process before you actually conduct your research. Remember the building the house metaphor – that is, you would not build a house without a plan. Your proposal is your plan and your project is the finished product (your house).

Fourth, problems may occur at any stage in the research process, but if they happen at the planning (proposal) stage, then there is a greater likelihood that you will be able to address them. For example, it is not uncommon for a student to change their research topic during writing their research proposal. Why? Well, one of the reasons is that an intended research participant, whether it is an individual or organization, may decide to withdraw from your research project. If you are using a large number of research participants, this may not be an issue. However, if the nature of your research design is based on a single case study design, then the withdrawal of the case will ultimately have a major impact on your research.

On a positive note, it is better for a participant to withdraw at this stage in your research, as opposed to deciding to withdraw when you have started to analyze your data.

Fifth, feasibility of the research at all angles considers the likelihood that you are able to actually complete your research. The advantage of doing a proposal means that you can view the feasibility of your intended research from every step, from formulating your research problem and research questions, through to writing up your research. One key aspect of feasibility is time frame. In other words, is it feasible for you to complete your intended research within the time frame?

Finally, making a case for formal approval depends on the institution. In some cases, a student may not be able to start carrying out their research before producing a suitable research proposal. Suitability might be based on the fact it is a formal assessed piece of work. A proposal can also be assessed formatively. In several cases, my own institution included, the research proposal is a piece of summative assessment that helps to allocate the research supervisor.

Cassuto (2011) suggests one way to view a research proposal is from the inside and out. First, the inside:

- A proposal puts forth your argument. It points toward how it will be proved, giving well-chosen examples.
- A proposal describes how your argument will fit together. What examples will you use, in what order, and why? How is the argument structured?
- A proposal outlines methodology. How will you make your argument? What theoretical, historical, contextual and interpretative tools will you use? Will you employ any particular approach?
- Your proposal should fit your dissertation topic.

From the outside:

- You need to show the place of your dissertation in the critical field. Which critics will you be building on and which ones will you be revising?
- You should include a thorough bibliography in your proposal so that readers may look at what works you plan to consult.

We can also add to the 'outside' that the research proposal should fulfil the requirements of your institution in relation to structure, overall presentation and word count. This 'inside' and 'outside' perspective is just another useful way of viewing a research proposal.

Some universities provide specific guidelines on what a research proposal is and how it should be structured. Others are more flexible in terms of structure and content. Remember that there is no universal definition or structure for a research proposal. Therefore, you need to check with your institution so that you can meet assessment expectations.

CONSIDERATIONS BEFORE WRITING YOUR RESEARCH PROPOSAL

The following section looks at what you will need to consider before writing your research proposal. You might be keen to start writing your proposal straightaway, but first, think about your overall content and structure. One way to address this task is to reflect on a number of guiding questions, as follows:

1. What is your research topic (moving from broad to focused)? What is the nature of your research problem? Why is your chosen research topic important?
2. What is the nature of your research direction? Here, think about formulating your research objectives and research questions.

3. What does the existing literature have to say about your research topic/research questions?
4. What is your methodological approach going to be? How do you propose to collect and analyze your data?
5. Why are you going to use certain data collection methods and analytical techniques to address your research questions?
6. What resources will you need in order to successfully complete your research?
7. What is your research timetable for each stage in the research project? How much time do you intend allocating for each stage?
8. What are the limitations you are likely to encounter when doing your research? How do you intend to access research participants? How will you address the ethical issues in your research?

Take time to read through each of the questions and make brief notes as you go along. By answering each question, you are addressing each of the key points that will need to be discussed in your proposal. In short, the practice of reflecting on your research journey is essential to turning thoughts into writing. Figure 3.2 gives you an illustration of the main preliminary steps before writing your research proposal.

Figure 3.2 The main preliminary steps before writing your research proposal

HOW DO I STRUCTURE A RESEARCH PROPOSAL?

The structure of your research proposal depends on your course or university requirements. In some cases, you may find that you have the option to choose a particular structure. Either way, there are essential elements that you will find in every research proposal. In this section, we look at these elements and how they are applied in practice.

When writing your proposal, it should be well-structured to enable easy reading. You need to produce a document that is clearly written and simple to understand. Consider the reader's perspective. Is the reader able to follow the steps and proposed tasks in your research? The tasks set out in a structured proposal test students' ability to communicate the nature of their research and reasons for their research topic.

Emmanuel and Gray (2003: 309) suggest that the proposal follows the conventional pattern of addressing:

- the research question
- a review of the literature which helps to define both the research question and the terms used in that question
- the methodological assumptions employed in prior research and which will be applied here
- the research methods to be used (together with a simple justification)
- the potential findings and where their contribution to the literature might lie
- limitations
- conclusions.

Although Emmanuel and Gray (2003) provide clear guidance on key elements a proposal should address, they do not summarize the sections in which these elements fall. The first of these sections is the introduction. Locke et al. (2013) argue that a careful introduction is the precursor of three tasks (purpose statement, rationale and background). The authors note that the most common error in introducing research is failing to get to the point. Therefore, when writing your proposal, try to be explicit as to the purpose of your research. A purpose statement sets the direction of your proposal and makes it clear to the reader what you intend to understand or improve by conducting your research.

I would also add that a research proposal should include a clear research direction. This is typically illustrated in the form of a research timetable or Gantt chart setting out when key tasks are due to commence during the research process and completion dates.

What follows is a detailed overview of how to structure a research proposal. I reiterate that you are likely to find your own institution may have a different structure. However, in essence, the general structure is likely to be largely the same. Moreover, what is important is that you know what each element means and how to apply them to your research proposal.

TITLE

A title is the first element your reader will see. Creating a title page as a separate cover page is considered a preliminary feature, as it is included at the beginning of your proposal. A title page contains key information for your institution and the marker(s) of your research project. Notably, for the marker, the most important piece of information is the working title of your project. A *working title* is a temporary title of a project used during the development or planning stage in research. The likelihood is that you will change your title numerous times during your research. This is perfectly normal. Why? Well, aspects of your research such as the methodology or objectives may change during your research. A new working title shows this change. Remember that your title should reflect the research topic, be easy to understand and be free from any grammatical or typographical errors.

The key purpose of a title is to provide the reader with an insight into the nature of the research project. Your title can only contain so much information, so try to avoid using too many words. A maximum of 12 words is a useful guideline. Moreover, try to keep your title clear, concise and avoid unnecessary words. In the past, I have seen some students try to put as much information as they can in their title. A concise, sharp title works best. Often, what you consider to be important information, such as the names of case studies, can be explained early in the introductory section of your proposal.

You can start with a 'working' title, and then after the proposal is written, evaluate it again (Wentz, 2014). The following is an example of a title in development (relating to corporate social responsibility):

- Corporate Social Responsibility
- Corporate Social Responsibility in retailing
- Corporate Social Responsibility in UK retailing
- Corporate Social Responsibility in UK retailing from 2010–2020
- Corporate Social Responsibility in UK retailing from 2010–2020: A case study approach

As you can see from the Corporate Social Responsibility example, each title becomes more specific and focused. The final title is clear, concise and refers to the methodological approach.

Sometimes students ask me 'How do I choose my working title?' or 'What makes a good title?'. For the latter, we have looked at the importance of producing a clear title that reflects the content. However, deciding on a working title can be challenging. Reading examples of titles from leading academic journal articles can certainly help. You might also consider breaking up your title by using a colon. There seems to be a growing trend among researchers to use a colon. Adopting this approach can help to avoid a lengthy 'wordy' title. By way of an example:

Training Small Business Managers: A Reflective Approach

Again, remember that your research proposal is a plan and that the title is likely to change several times before you arrive at your final preferred title. You will find it helpful if you can share your title ideas with your research supervisor and/or fellow students.

ABSTRACT

Your abstract is a brief summary of approximately 300 words. It should summarize all of the key steps in the proposal. This includes the rationale for your study, research objectives and research questions, methodology, time frame and expected results. Note that not all research proposals require an abstract. If this is a requirement for your course, I suggest reading abstracts from academic journals. Often, these will include headings and are based on a very structured approach.

CONTENTS PAGE

A research proposal typically contains a contents page with section headings and page numbers. Once you have produced a draft of your proposal, check to make sure that the headings and page numbers in your contents page correspond to those in the main proposal. Signposting is an important part of academic writing. Therefore, headings and their respective page numbers should be correct.

INTRODUCTION

An introduction is a key element of the research proposal. It should include the background to your study and inform the reader regarding the research aims, objectives and research questions. Start with writing the background and the research problem. Make sure to clarify the statement of the problem or main focus of your research. A problem statement should define the problem and identify the issues to be investigated in the study. We looked at how to define a research problem in Chapter 2. There is no one universal way to write the problem statement. However, by way of example, the two illustrations below show you the commonly used approach to framing a research problem:

1. The purpose of this study will be to investigate consumers' perceptions towards the customer service at ABC plc and evaluate which stores have a better reputation than others.
2. This study will compare the organizational performance for company A and B and identify which variables of performance differ significantly between the two firms.

Ideally, the research problem statement should be clear and expressed in no more than two sentences. Having a clearly defined research problem is one of the most important features in your research proposal as it helps to set a clear research direction. Thus, you may find it beneficial to share your research problem with your supervisor or fellow students to make sure they understand the nature of the research problem or issue. An introduction should also include brief reference to existing studies that are relevant to your own work.

Research objectives and research questions should arrive early in your proposal and usually fall in the introduction. Remember that research objectives should be SMART related and that research questions should relate to each objective. A useful way for presenting your research objectives and research questions is in the form of a table. Similar to your research problem, these are key features in your research and should be made explicit within the proposal. Using a table is an explicit way of presenting objectives and questions.

Be sure to define any key terms the first time you use them. For example, in the background section of your introduction you are presenting the nature of your research topic. Here, you can define key terms using reliable sources, such as those from academic journals. Avoid using unreliable web-based sources such as Wikipedia. Remember that in-text citations should follow your institution's referencing system. In summary, your introduction should address the following questions:

● What is the research about?
● Why is the chosen area of research important?
● What is the research problem, aim, objectives, hypotheses, questions? In short, what is the overall research direction?
● Who are the key authors in your area of research and what is some of the most important work carried out?
● How might your research contribute to the existing literature on the subject?

The introduction to your research proposal is the most important section for two reasons. First, it 'sets the scene'. This means it provides the reader with an insight into the nature of your research topic and the background to the research. Second, the introduction provides the 'research direction'. This includes the purpose of the research and a purpose statement.

PRELIMINARY LITERATURE REVIEW

Your research proposal should include a preliminary review of the key literature. As this is a proposal, you will not be expected to undertake an extensive review of the literature. However, it is important that you are able to recognize the key authors in your subject area and adopt a critical approach to reviewing the literature. Do not produce a descriptive review of the literature that adopts a 'list like' approach. For example, 'Smith, 2008 said …', 'Wong, 2009 noted …', 'Sanchez et al. (2018) commented …'. The best way to avoid this list approach is to read through literature review articles from academic journals to gain an understanding of writing style. It also helps if you regularly read through your work and ask yourself 'Have I been critical here?'.

Start your literature review section with a brief introduction setting out the purpose of the literature review. Your review should demonstrate your knowledge of the key literature and make a critical link with the research questions being investigated. It is also essential to have a summary or conclusion at the end of your review to explain how your research fits into the current body of literature and the 'link' with your study. What do I mean by 'link'? Let us say that you have conducted a preliminary literature review on how cultural differences among employees impact organizational performance. One of the themes in your review might be 'corporate culture' and analyze how the term 'corporate culture' is defined. In your summary, you would explain which definition(s) you will be using for your research. In this example, always try to support your reasons for choosing a particular definition or perhaps a theoretical framework.

The purpose of the preliminary literature review can be summarized as follows:

1.　Recognizes and gives credit to the key authors(s) in your research area.
2.　Makes sure that you are not 'reinventing the wheel'.
3.　Demonstrates your ability to critically analyze relevant literature.
4.　Demonstrates your ability to understand the key theoretical issues relating to your research topic.
5.　Shows your ability to synthesize the existing literature.
6.　Demonstrates to the reader your ability to make a significant contribution to the current body of literature on your chosen area of research.

Conversely, common problems associated with writing a preliminary literature review can be summarized as follows:

* The literature review lacks structure.
* There is a lack of focus and addressing the themes set out in the research questions.
* The review is repetitive in terms of content.
* There is a limited number of citations within the review.
* There is a failure to cite influential authors and papers.
* There is a failure to cite the most relevant papers.

Talk to your supervisor or tutor about how to structure your literature review. It also helps to read through examples written by former students.

METHODOLOGY

The purpose of a methodology section is to fully explain the methodological approach adopted in your study. Your methodology should clarify your chosen research design, data collection methods and what type of data you will collect, such as qualitative and/or quantitative, sampling method(s) and ethical issues. Moreover, it is important to clarify how you intend to analyze your data. The reader will be interested in learning about the specifics of your proposed research. Therefore, avoid using generic-type statements, such as: '25 interviews will be conducted and analyzed'. Tell me more – Where will they be conducted? Why 25 interviews? What type of interviews will you use? (see Chapter 12).

You should be aware of the relationship between the different elements in your research methodology. I often tell my students that there needs to be a common thread that runs through your research philosophy, research strategy, research approach, data collection and data analysis. It is important to think about this relationship as you will need to justify your choice of methodological approach in your proposal. We look at research philosophies, approaches and strategies in Chapter 5.

Typically, most students will also need to highlight issues surrounding reliability and validity in their proposal. The extent that these are discussed depends on the requirements from your institution. However, all students should refer to the nature of the limitations of their research. A *limitation* is a weakness associated with your research. Limitations include time constraints and access to resources. It

REFERENCES

Most academic institutions use the Harvard Referencing System. Although do check with your university or college to see which system they adopt. My advice when writing your research proposal would be to use a wide range of sources. Do not just rely on web-based sources. Often, a key part of the marking criteria is what I refer to as 'strong evidence of research'. In other words, this means asking the following questions: Has the student used a wide range of sources when writing their proposal? Have they identified the key authors in their chosen area of research?

APPENDICES

Your number of appendices is likely to be minimal for a research proposal. What goes in the appendices? Well, examples may include tables, a theoretical framework or your research timetable. As for the latter, I would advise placing this in the main body of your proposal as it will form a central part of your research journey. If unsure, do check with your tutor or research supervisor.

HOW LONG DOES MY RESEARCH PROPOSAL NEED TO BE?

The length of your research proposal will depend on the guidelines set out by your supervisor, tutor, course or institution. Proposal guidelines are usually detailed, not only discussing word length, but also providing essential information on structure and contents. If you find the task of writing several thousand words daunting, break down your proposal into sections. Allocating a set number of words to each section may help you to focus. Use the marking criteria and the weightings for each section as a guide to how much to write. In some cases, I have seen students devote too many words to writing the introduction, and then fail to address subsequent sections in appropriate depth. Of course, your emphasis should be on quality as opposed to quantity, but if you are given a 4,000-word limit for example, try to write up to the word limit. This means that you are then more likely to address each section in sufficient depth. Figure 3.4 illustrates the main elements of a research proposal covered in this section.

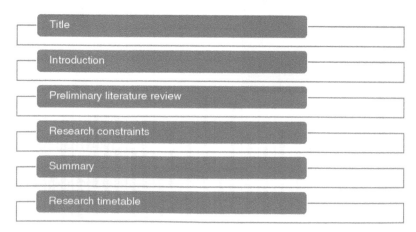

Figure 3.4   The main elements of a research proposal

WHAT ARE THE CHALLENGES OF WRITING A RESEARCH PROPOSAL?

There are a number of challenges you may face when writing your research proposal. The first of these is deciding on your research topic, problem, research objectives and questions. In a study into the experiences of a large cohort of international students as they develop Master's dissertation proposals, Pringle et al. (2019) found that more than half (55.6%) of students noted that topic selection was the most challenging part of formulating the research proposal. The best way to overcome this challenge is by sharing your research ideas with your fellow students and tutor/supervisor.

Starting to write can be a challenge for students. This is normal. Preparation and planning your research can help, together with setting a target number of words to write each day. You can approach your writing in the following ways:

- Develop a writing schedule. Ideally, try to write at the same time each day. Create a comfortable writing environment.
- Think of the proposal as a document to draft and redraft.
- Use a notebook, electronic device or diary so you can write thoughts about your research.
- Although your proposal starts with an introduction, this does not mean it has to be the first section you write. Often, it is easier to begin writing later sections in your proposal, such as the preliminary literature review. Why? Well, your findings from your review are likely to lead to redrafting of other sections in the proposal.
- Remember that your research proposal is not a rigid document, but the foundation of your research. You can amend your proposal at any stage in the research process. However, if you begin to make major changes following submission, this will ultimately lead to additional work.
- Ask your fellow students to form a writing group. This is advice I regularly give to my own research students. Producing a research proposal is possibly the most challenging part of the research process. Quite simply, starting a research journey can be the hardest step, not least because it can take time to arrive at a chosen topic and research objectives. By engaging in a research discussion group, you can share your ideas with fellow students. You will also find that you may share the same or similar features in your research, such as research topic and/or methodology.

HOW DO I WRITE A WINNING BUSINESS RESEARCH PROPOSAL?

As we have seen, there are notable differences when comparing a proposal to other forms of assessment. The likelihood is that this is the first time you have attempted to write one. Therefore, it is important to know what makes a winning research proposal. Understandably, this is a question I am often asked by students. Therefore, later in the chapter I provide an illustration of a research proposal, together with examples of best practice.

Whether you are writing your research proposal as a piece of assessed or non-assessed piece of work, do consider whether you are able to carry out and write up your research project within the set time frame. In my own research methods module, students submit a research proposal as a piece of summative assessment at the end of the module. Subsequently, each proposal is then read, marked and used to assign a research supervisor. Where possible, a supervisor is assigned on the basis of a student's research topic. Thus, there is no point in submitting a proposal and being allocated a supervisor if you have doubts about your chosen topic and don't believe you can write your project within the time frame.

Students have differing views on writing a winning research proposal. For example, some might believe certain sections are more important than others. Similarly, others may view focusing on structure as the most essential part of the proposal. These are all important. However, when considering what makes a winning proposal, in essence, there are four broad areas, as follows:

- Read and edit your proposal a number of times before submission. It is also useful to ask a fellow student and your tutor/supervisor to read your work before submission, although the latter is dependent on the course and university guidelines. Make sure that your proposal is well written and avoid making typographical and grammatical errors. A well-presented proposal creates an impression to the reader that you have taken care and attention when completing the task.
- Make sure to follow your university/course guidance. Conventions do differ between institutions, particularly in terms of structure and word count. Therefore, check with your tutor/supervisor before submitting your work.
- Produce a proposal that is interesting to the reader and has one 'common thread' that runs through it. For example, make sure that your research questions relate to your research topic. Your methodological approach should be designed to address your research problem and the literature review contains citations of key authors and papers that relate to your research topic.
- Make sure that your purpose and research direction are clear and that there is evidence of signposting to 'guide' the reader throughout. Tables and sections should not arrive unannounced, so make good use of headings and sub-headings.

Again, a useful way to help produce a winning research proposal is to ask your fellow students and supervisor to read your work. Do ask for honest and critical feedback. Another useful method you can use in striving to write a winning research proposal is the '5 Cs' rule. Prior to submitting your research proposal, you can check to see if it follows these rules, as follows:

- Clear Is what you are writing easy for the reader to understand? Does it make sense in terms of content and structure or is it rather vague?
- Coherent Does your proposal contain a coherent argument as to why you are conducting the research? In other words, does it address the 'so what' question?
- Critical Does your proposal critically review the literature and the use of the methods used to collect and analyze your data? Or is it simply a description of the different options?
- Compelling Is the proposal an interesting read? Are you able to convince the reader that you are able to conduct the research within the time frame and using the resources available to you?
- Current Does your proposal contain recent sources? Is the topic of current interest?

In this part of the chapter, we have seen some of the steps you can take to help write a winning research proposal. What follows are what I would describe as 'useful tips' that can also go some way to helping you to produce a winning proposal. These are all tips that I share with my own students.

EVALUATING YOUR RESEARCH PROPOSAL

Prior to submitting your research proposal, do reflect on what you have written. Do you have a clear research timetable? Can you complete your research prior to the submission deadline? Is your proposal easy to read? My tip – evaluation before submission.

Again, one of the main reasons why students produce a weak research proposal is because they do not think about the 'common thread' that runs through their research. Moreover, there is sometimes a failure to evaluate whether research objectives are achievable and how key terms are to be measured. By taking time to reflect on your final written proposal and evaluate the content prior to submission, you are more likely to avoid any difficulties when putting your proposal into practice.

CARRY OUT A PILOT STUDY

This is perhaps not so much a tip, but good research practice. A pilot study is a small-scale study typically used to test your proposed research methods. For example, if you intend administering an online survey to a sample of 500 senior managers, a pilot study may involve testing the survey using a small sample of only 25 participants. The outcomes of the pilot could result in you making changes or adapting elements to the survey. Similarly, findings may also result in a complete rethink of how you collect your data. The benefit of a pilot study is that any potential problems can often be easily addressed before carrying out the actual research.

SEEK GUIDANCE FROM YOUR TUTOR AND/OR RESEARCH SUPERVISOR

Research can be a lonely business, especially when working on your research proposal. Your initial enthusiasm for your research topic and planning your research may turn into frustration, a lack of motivation or a feeling of hitting a brick wall. Therefore, it is important to talk to your tutor and/or research supervisor at various points when working on your research proposal. If supervisor allocation does not take place until after you have submitted your proposal, then I suggest asking to meet with a tutor who teaches in your planned area of research. This will certainly help you to gain a better understanding of your chosen research topic and avoid the likelihood of having to make changes to your research proposal.

KNOW WHAT A 'GOOD' AND 'BAD' EXAMPLE OF A RESEARCH PROPOSAL LOOKS LIKE

One of the activities I always do with my research students is to show them what a 'good' and a 'bad' research proposal looks like. A good example can help students to develop ideas about their own research and also gain a better understanding as to how to structure a research proposal. In contrast, a bad example is a useful guide as to what to avoid when developing their own proposals.

Each research proposal I share with students is anonymized and does not include the exact mark, but each one is distinguishable on the basis of a 'high pass' and a 'low pass'. I have also asked students to mark past research proposals so they take on the role of the marker and are able to determine what constitutes a good piece of work. This tip is perhaps more appropriate for your tutor! If you have an opportunity, do ask your tutor if you can look through examples of past proposals. Student feedback I have received using this method has always been positive. One of the best ways you can produce a research proposal is to know what both a good one and a bad one looks like.

For some students, producing a research proposal is an essential requirement in order to be accepted onto a research degree. A poorly written proposal may result in not being accepted onto a degree programme. Robson (2011: 395) cites ten ways to get your research proposal turned down. Although you might not be doing a research degree, the 'ten ways' are still useful irrespective of the type of course. In short, these are things to avoid when writing your research proposal!

1. Don't follow the directions or guidelines given for your kind of proposal. Omit information that is asked for. Ignore word limits.
2. Ensure that the title has little relationship to the stated objectives and that neither title nor objectives link to the proposed methods or techniques.
3. Produce ill-defined objectives.
4. Have a vague statement of the research problem.
5. Leave the research design and methodology implicit.
6. Do not treat your research as some kind of consultancy or poorly conceptualized data that does not bear resemblance to a research project.

7. Be unrealistic in what can be achieved within the time frame and based on the resources available.
8. Be very brief, repetitive and relying on quantity as opposed to quality.
9. Make it clear what your research findings are going to be before conducting your research.
10. Don't worry about a theoretical underpinning or a conceptual framework for your research.

Let us consider the above ten points. First, you would think that following the guidelines set out by your tutor and/or university would be straightforward enough. However, I often see proposals that have not fully followed these guidelines. An example here relates to structure. When writing your proposal, make sure that you follow the structure provided, noting main headings, sub-headings, word limits, and above all, the marking criteria. Typically, the marking criteria will show you how marks are allocated and the breakdown for each section in the proposal. Use this as an indicator when writing each stage of your proposal. By way of example, a 4,000-word proposal means that you will only have a relatively limited number of words to discuss the background of your study.

Second, this relates to the importance of 'linking' and producing a common thread through your proposal. This is something we came across earlier in the chapter, but is worth reiterating. The title of your research proposal relates to the content, this in turn relates to the objectives, the preliminary literature review contains themes that relate to the research questions and so on.

Third, having a clear set of research objectives is essential going forward. Why? Quite simply because your objectives will have implications later in your research. Remember that objectives should be SMART related.

Fourth, an ill-defined research problem is likely to have implications later in your research. In essence, the nature of the research problem is about why you are conducting the research and why it is important.

Fifth, often, a research design, or more broadly, a research methodology, is implicit within a proposal. In other words, there is a lack of detail and perhaps general comments about methodological approach. To some extent, this is perhaps to be expected. It is unlikely that you will have decided upon all aspects of your methodology. However, for those elements you are certain about, try not to be too implicit or general. By way of an example, if you intend administering an online survey to 500 participants, write about the rationale behind the data collection method and sample size. Furthermore, be clear on the sampling method, when and how you intend to produce and administer your survey. Remember that doing research is a personal journey. Thus, avoid generic comments that could almost apply to any research project.

Seventh, underestimating the time it takes to conduct research is often a feature in student research proposals. You might be involved with activities and other commitments outside study. This needs to be considered when producing your research timetable. You may intend using multiple methods and analyzing your data using a variety of techniques. Clearly, using multiple methods can be hugely time-consuming. In addition, it may not be necessary in order to address your research problem. How do I know how much time to allocate to each step in the research process? My advice here would be to consult with your research supervisor.

Eighth, writing a proposal as part of an assignment is likely to have a word limit. Avoid repeating what you have written and simply aiming to write up to the word limit. Aim for your proposal to be quality over quantity. An example here is citations. Use citations to support your argument. This also demonstrates strong evidence of research.

Ninth, remember that your proposal is what you intend to do when actually carrying out your research. It is not the place to start discussing what your findings are going to be before you conduct your research.

Tenth, unless you are doing a practice-based proposal, your proposal should include evidence of theoretical underpinning or a conceptual framework.

In summary, the above ten points are what to avoid when writing your research proposal. If you have an opportunity, try to look through past dissertation proposals and examine each one to see if these points are avoided.

CAN I CHANGE MY TOPIC AFTER SUBMITTING MY RESEARCH PROPOSAL?

Earlier in this chapter we looked at the importance of trying to avoid submitting a research proposal you have reservations about. Although it might be possible to change your research topic after submitting your research proposal, this does have implications. In principle, it is possible to choose a completely new research topic, but if you do so, you will find that takes a considerable amount of time to produce a new proposal. Where I have known students to do this, they usually end up choosing a new topic that is similar to their original choice. For example, perhaps continuing to analyze corporate social responsibility, but deciding to choose a new brand or case in which to study. On rare occasions, I have known students to choose a completely new topic after submitting their research proposal. This means having to basically start their research journey from the beginning. If you do change to a completely different topic after submitting your proposal, my advice is to write a new proposal, as it is essential to have a plan in place before conducting your research.

Remember the whole purpose of a research proposal is in essence a plan or guide to how you are going to carry out your research. Conducting your research without a plan can only increase the likelihood that you will be unable to compete your research to a satisfactory conclusion.

If you do decide to change your topic after submitting your proposal, my advice would be to speak to your supervisor about this. He or she can address any concerns you might have and offer support and guidance on the next steps in your research.

Finally, I suggest producing a research project checklist before submitting your proposal (see Box 3.1). This will ensure that you have covered all of the required material in your proposal. Moreover, it can also help you to avoid changing your topic at a later date.

As you write your checklist, refer to the marking criteria and assessment guidance. Combined, doing this exercise will no doubt increase the quality of your proposal and help you to ensure success when establishing your research plan.

BOX 3.1: RESEARCH SNAPSHOT

Although by no means exhaustive, in this research snapshot I have provided an example of a research project proposal checklist.

1. Have you chosen a suitable research topic?
2. Have you identified a research problem and noted the importance of your research?
3. Do you have a clear research direction, including research objectives and research questions?
4. Do you have the resources required to complete the research?
5. Does your working title reflect the content of your proposal?
6. Have you written a lucid background that 'sets the scene'?
7. Have you written a critical preliminary review of the literature?
8. Does your literature review include a link to how your research fits with the existing literature?
9. Have you explained and justified your chosen methodological approach?
10. Have you produced a realistic research timetable?
11. Have you proofread your work prior to submission?
12. Does your proposal draw on a wide range of sources and are all sources referenced correctly?

HOW DOES MY RESEARCH PROPOSAL RELATE TO THE RESEARCH PROCESS?

As we have established, your research proposal is at the 'Planning' layer in The Research Wheel model. In the context of your overall research process, it is the plan that is designed to help you prior to the 'Action' stage in your research. Typically, students who produce a well-written research proposal tend to do well in their research project. Moreover, usually students have given a lot of thought to the future steps in their research. Examples here include how they intend to analyze their data and present their research findings.

'Can I use material from my proposal in my research project?'. The short answer is yes. However, remember that your research project is putting your research into action and should 'build' on what you have written in your proposal. For example, you can use citations from your proposal in your research project, but the marker of your work will expect to see how you have developed your preliminary literature review. In short, your literature review chapter should not contain lengthy paragraphs that are simply copied from your proposal.

WHAT DOES A RESEARCH PROPOSAL LOOK LIKE?

So far in this chapter, we have explored different aspects of a research proposal. Yet, what does a research proposal actually look like?

Students are often keen to find out what an actual research proposal looks like. This is understandable, as seeing an exemplar can help to understand how to structure a research proposal and know a tutor's expectations. Early in your course, ask the tutor if you can look through past research proposals. Irrespective of the topic, you are likely to find this a useful exercise.

In the next part of the chapter, we examine the main characteristics of a research proposal. The example is based on research looking at dissertation performance and titled: *Selected determinants of dissertation performance: Student perceptions and actual outcomes*. The topic is not important. My intention here is to show you what a research proposal looks like. As you read through the proposal, note the structure, research direction (in this example the author has used a series of hypotheses), writing style and referencing.

AN EXAMPLE OF A RESEARCH PROPOSAL

'SELECTED DETERMINANTS OF DISSERTATION PERFORMANCE: STUDENT PERCEPTIONS AND ACTUAL OUTCOMES'

Introduction

Most undergraduate courses in the social sciences include a dissertation as part of the assessment. The extent a student is successful at completing their dissertation is often an indicator as to their likely degree classification. Therefore, given the importance of the dissertation to both student and university, research to examine factors that can affect performance could be used as a guide to develop teaching methods designed to enhance student performance (Lane et al., 2003).

There are several notable studies on academic attainment (Koh and Koh, 1999; Lane et al., 2003; Sheard, 2009; Richardson et al., 2020). However, these tend to focus on final degree classification, a select number of variables or adopt a cross-sectional research design rather than addressing dissertation performance. Thus, a gap exists in the literature with respect to selected determinants of dissertation performance. The purpose of this study is to investigate the impact of six variables – Research Methods attainment, cultural distance, age, gender, prior educational attainment and mode of study on dissertation performance. The sample consists of undergraduates that have successfully completed an undergraduate business degree programme at a post-1992 UK university. In the UK, Higher Education Institutions (HEIs) are often categorized as 'pre' or 'post' 1992 (Harrison and Whalley, 2008: 403). The institution included in this study falls into the latter category. In order to ensure confidentiality, the university featured in this research will be referred to by a fictitious name – 'Viking University'. The university is located in the South of England and is a former polytechnic. The motivational factors that lie behind this research are as follows:

1. The study of dissertation performance has received scant attention in the literature. Yet, the dissertation is typically the most extensive piece of work that undergraduates are required to complete. A student's performance in the dissertation can quite easily mean the difference between a first and a 2:1, or possibly a 2:1 and a 2:2. It can sometimes be difficult to identify those students that require additional dissertation support. Thus, a study on the determinants of dissertation performance provides much needed empirical research that can help channel resources at those students that require it most.
2. A Research Methods course is typically a prerequisite of the dissertation. In theory, those students that perform well in their Research Methods course should be well placed to successfully complete their dissertation. However, it appears that there is no existing research that explores this relationship. This study intends to fill this gap in the literature by exploring the relationship between Research Methods attainment and dissertation performance.
3. Like many UK universities, Viking University is attracting an increasing number of international students. A changing student profile may require additional student support in the area of Research Methods and dissertation provision. Examining student dissertation performance over a five-year period (2014–2018), is likely to provide an interesting insight to how a changing student profile may have impacted performance figures. Therefore, research is required in this area.

It might be argued that one limitation of the study is that it is based on data from one post-1992 university, though this is an explanatory study that is designed as the 'first stage' of a potentially more in-depth piece of research. The intention in the future is to employ a similar methodology involving a wide range of UK academic institutions. However, the findings from this study are still likely to prove of interest to academics involved in teaching Research Methods and supervising undergraduate students.

The research proposal is structured as follows: Firstly, a short literature review is provided. The next section sets out the six hypotheses that are to be tested. This is followed by an overview of the methodology. Finally, the proposal concludes with sections in ethical considerations and brief reference to proposed timetable.

Relevant literature

Dissertation

The terminology used for 'dissertation' varies. For example, it can be referred to as an 'extended essay', 'independent learning project', 'capstone project', 'senior paper' or 'final-year project' (Smith et al., 2009). For the purpose of this study, in order to ensure clarity, only the term 'dissertation' will be used. Therefore, given the 'type' of dissertation used at Viking University, *dissertation* is defined as 'a 10,000-word piece of academic work written on a business-related topic'.

(Continued)

Dissertation performance

A student's final mark in the dissertation can be a major contributory factor towards their final degree. In simple terms, *performance* is defined as the 'final mark' or level of attainment the student has achieved for their dissertation. In this study, the only dependent variable used is dissertation performance. It is operationalized by classifying dissertation marks into traditional degree classifications, thereby grouping levels of performance. Dissertation marks will be categorized as follows:

- Marks of 70% and above = First class
- Marks between 60 and 69% = Upper second
- Marks between 50 and 59% = Lower second
- Marks between 40 and 49% = Third class
- Marks between 30 and 39% = Bar fail
- Marks below 30% = Fail

Research Methods attainment

For the purpose of this study, *Research Methods attainment* is defined as 'the final mark or level of attainment achieved by a student for the Research Methods module'. Research Methods courses are a common feature in social science curricula. Several studies discuss the complexity of teaching Research Methods (Halfpenny, 1981; Winn, 1995; Edwards and Thatcher, 2004; Lewthwaite and Nind, 2016). Some students also have difficulty with the subject. Edwards and Thatcher (2004) found that it was increasingly apparent that students were experiencing difficulties in understanding Research Methods and that the mode of delivery was not facilitating effective student learning. Papanastasiou and Zembylas (2008) note that 'teaching research methods to undergraduate students is not an easy task' (2008: 165). A problem lecturers face is illustrated by a quote from an article into Research Methods teaching by Morris (2006: 123):

> Our students hate anything to do with numbers and avoid them at all costs, and, since we get so few students interested in quantitative analysis, we concentrate on qualitative techniques.

Winn (1995) proposes that the concerns of students must be taken into account in Research Methods teaching. Ransford and Butler (1982) note that 'Research Methods can be viewed as consisting of professors laboring through lectures as abstract concepts and the tedious details of research techniques, while students often view it as one of those "dreaded requirements"' (1982: 291), although, clearly, this is now a rather dated article. Similar concerns about tutors neglecting quantitative methods and the difficulty in understanding how to deliver the subject to research students have been expressed by Scott Jones and Goldring (2015). In their study into curriculum redesign order to improve the student learning experience, Benson and Blackman (2003) identified that one problem with the delivery of Research Methods is that the way the module can inform other areas of the course (including the dissertation) is not always apparent to students. However, given the pedagogical dilemmas and perceptions of some students towards Research Methods, it is still expected that those students that perform well during the module are more likely to have high levels of dissertation performance. More specifically, this suggests that there is likely to be a correlation between Research Methods attainment and dissertation performance. Therefore, the first hypothesis asserts that:

> H1: Research Methods attainment has a significant effect on dissertation performance.

Similar to dissertation performance, Research Methods attainment will be operationalized by classifying students' marks for the module into traditional degree classifications thereby grouping levels of performance. Marks will be categorized as follows:

- Marks of 70% and above = First class
- Marks between 60 and 69% = Upper second
- Marks between 50 and 59% = Lower second
- Marks between 40 and 49% = Third class
- Marks between 30 and 39% = Bar fail
- Marks below 30% = Fail

Cultural distance

A huge literature exists on culture. Kroeber and Klockhohn (1952), after examining several hundred definitions of culture, came to the conclusion that the term describes the ways that people structure and share information. Hofstede's (1980) seminal work on culture researched the nature and extent of cultural differences. He conceptualizes 'culture' as the 'collective programming of the mind'. Culture can be measured in a number of different ways. One construct that is widely discussed in the literature is *cultural distance*. This measures the distance to which national cultures are different from and similar to the culture of the host (Shenkar, 2001). Although cultural distance has been applied in a number of different contexts in the field of business management, it is unexplored in education. This is perhaps surprising. Arguably, an added challenge for both students and academics can occur when dealing with a class made up of students from a wide variety of cultural backgrounds. For example, in some countries, students may not have come across Research Methods, or are not familiar with academic practice in the UK. A recent illustration of this is a comment made by one of the author's Dutch Master's students:

> Prior to studying in the UK, I was not familiar with the Harvard Referencing System and had never heard of a literature review.

Also, the concept of a dissertation or self-study may be alien to some students. Once again, this creates an additional problem for the lecturer. How to teach Research Methods to international students has taken on greater significance in recent years given the huge number of international students now studying in the UK. The cultural distance that is likely to exist between lecturer and a class consisting of students from a variety of cultural backgrounds generates a number of issues. In the context of Research Methods, key issues are developing appropriate pedagogies, understanding cultural differences and above all making sure that students are able to tackle the dissertation with confidence.

For this study *Cultural distance* will be operationalized by using Hofstede's (1980) cultural dimension 'Long-Term Orientation (LTO) versus Short-Term Orientation (STO)'. The rationale behind using Hofstede's fifth cultural dimension is that it was found using a student-based survey. Hofstede's other cultural dimensions were generated from IBM business employees. Hofstede's fifth cultural dimension was found in a study among students in 23 countries around the world, using a questionnaire designed by Chinese scholars; it can be said to deal with Virtue regardless of Truth. Values associated with LTO are thrift and perseverance; values associated with STO are respect for tradition, fulfilling social obligations, and protecting one's 'face'. Both the positively and the negatively rated values of this dimension are

(Continued)

found in the teachings of Confucius, the most influential Chinese philosopher who lived around 500 BC; however, the dimension also applies to countries without a Confucian heritage.

This study proposes that cultural distance has implications in relation to students' dissertation performance. This leads us to the following hypothesis:

H2: The higher the cultural distance between students' national culture and host culture (UK), the greater the effect on dissertation performance.

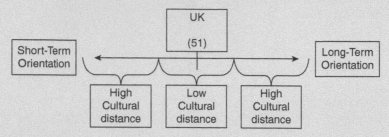

Figure 3.5   The relationship between cultural distance and the measure long-term versus short-term orientation

Age

Age can be used as a factor or independent variable to explain a particular social grouping, social process, or piece of individual or collective behaviour (Finch, 1986). There is no evidence of a consensus among researchers as to the extent that age influences academic achievement. For example, Sheard (2009) found that mature students outperformed younger students in terms of academic attainment. A mature student is an individual who is aged 21 or over when they start their undergraduate degree. Thus, the hypothesis is:

H3: Age has a significant effect on dissertation performance.

Gender

Investigation into attainment differences between males and females are necessary to promote gender equality and to develop supportive mechanisms that concentrate time, resources and attention on those students in greatest danger of being left behind in the educational pipeline (Newman-Ford et al., 2008: 15). Gender has been described as a key variable and one of the most common 'face sheet' variables in social investigations (Morgan, 1986). Gender has been researched from a number of different perspectives and as yet there exists no agreement among researchers as to the extent gender impacts educational attainment. However, research by the Higher Education Statistics Agency in 2008/09 illustrates that female students outperformed male students in relation to the percentage obtaining first and upper second-class degrees, gaining 66% and 60% respectively. Thus, the hypothesis is:

H4: Gender has a significant effect on dissertation performance.

Gender is of course a dichotomous variable. For the purpose of this study, males will be represented by 1, while females a 0.

Prior educational attainment

Recent studies into educational attainment in the UK Higher Education sector tend to focus on degree classification, namely: First, Upper Second, Lower Second, Third and Pass. However, in this particular study *prior educational attainment* is measured by the number of UCAS points achieved by each student. This will involve using categories, which are: 200 points or less, 201–280 points, 281–340 points, 341–420 points, more than 420 points. Yet, prior educational attainment at A level is not necessarily an indicator of degree performance. However, in the case of the dissertation, previous research found core subject scores to be significant. This leads to the formulation of the following hypothesis:

H5: Prior educational attainment has a significant effect on dissertation performance.

Mode of study

This particular variable can be defined as 'the time commitment and work load expected of a student'. There are two modes of study on all Viking University degree programmes – full-time and part-time. Mode of study is a dichotomous variable that will be assigned the following values (full-time = 1) and (part-time = 0). A number of factors have led to an increase in part-time study. However, figures from the Higher Education Statistics Agency indicate that in 2008/09 only 51% of female and 47% of male part-time students in the UK achieved a first or upper second-class degree (Higher Education Statistics Agency, 2010). Perhaps unsurprisingly, these figures compare less favourably with full-time students. This leads to the formulation of the following hypothesis:

H6: Mode of study has a significant effect on dissertation performance.

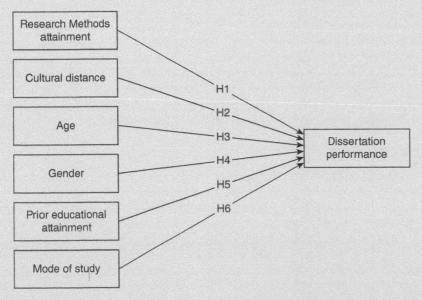

Figure 3.6   The research model that will be tested empirically in this study

(Continued)

Methodology

Research philosophy

The study will adopt a positivist approach as there will be an emphasis on a highly structured methodology and quantifiable observations that lend themselves to statistical analysis (Saunders et al., 1997).

Research approach

The research will adopt a deductive approach of forming a set of hypotheses and then testing these hypotheses through the collection of quantitative data. Typically, a feature of the deductive approach is that the researcher is independent or 'detached' from what is being observed. This is certainly the case in this study as data collection includes using secondary sources and a questionnaire survey.

Research strategy

This study employs a number of research strategies in order to answer the set of hypotheses. First, the empirical material in this research project represents a single case study, explaining the effects of selected determinants of student performance at Viking University. A case study is commonly used to study complex phenomena in their real-life contexts (Yin, 1989). The main intention of the research is to examine the determinants of dissertation performance, thereby examining individual students. However, it must be remembered that these students are all existing or alumni of the post-1992 university featured in this research. Hence, the findings of the research will ultimately affect the university. Second, the research can be defined as an 'explanatory study' as the aim is to explain the relationships between variables.

Time horizons

In terms of 'time horizons' the research does not follow the 'typical' dichotomy of either a cross-sectional or longitudinal study, but adopts elements of both. First, a cross-sectional study in the form of a questionnaire survey will be administered to provide a snapshot of students' perceptions towards determinants of dissertation performance. This will be followed by a longitudinal study intended to analyze secondary data over a five-year period (2014–2018). The intention of adopting both elements is to compare the findings of current student perceptions with actual outcomes.

Data collection methods

This study employs triangulation by using two data collection methods. First, a questionnaire survey will be administered to existing undergraduate Level 3 Business students. All students are currently on a Research Methods course and are at the early stages of undertaking their dissertation. A range of questioning techniques will be used in order to determine students' opinions on the impact of six variables – Research Methods attainment, cultural background, age, gender, prior educational attainment and mode of study on dissertation performance. Next, Viking University student database 'SITS: Vision' will be used to examine the effect of the aforementioned six variables on dissertation performance. Although likely to be a laborious and time-consuming task, the intention is to use student data for all undergraduate business students that graduated during the period 2014–2018.

The reason triangulation will be used is two-fold. First, a questionnaire survey will provide an interesting 'snapshot' of current students' perceptions on dissertation performance. Second, they will act as an effective way of triangulating data collected from the SITS: Vision database. Hopefully, this will of course make for interesting comparative analysis. In addition, the benefit of using a triangulation approach to data collection is that it is likely to reduce the risk of chance associations and of systematic biases (Strauss, 1987). Studies that use only one method are more vulnerable to errors linked to that particular method (e.g. loaded interview questions, biased or untrue responses) than are studies that use multiple methods in which different types of data provide cross-data validity checks.

Once again, the hypotheses to be tested are as follows:

H1: Research Methods attainment has a significant effect on dissertation performance.

H2: The higher the cultural distance between students' national culture and host culture (UK), the greater the effect on dissertation performance.

H3: Age has a significant effect on dissertation performance.

H4: Gender has a significant effect on dissertation performance.

H5: Prior educational attainment has a significant effect on dissertation performance.

H6: Mode of study has a significant effect on dissertation performance.

Finally, the body of research in educational attainment tends to focus on outcomes of performance. Although there is no denying the importance of understanding the significance of selected determinants through analyzing outcomes, there is also a need for research that considers students' perceptions to provide a more complete representation of dissertation performance.

Sampling

Convenience sampling will be used when administering the questionnaire survey to existing Level 3 Undergraduate Business students, the primary reason being that the author has access to this particular group of students. Moreover, the same sampling method will be applied in respect of the sampling frame of former students at Viking University. The sample comprises those students that successfully completed an undergraduate Business-related degree at Viking University between the years 2014–2018. 'Business-related' in this sense means a degree in Business or a key function of business, e.g. Marketing, Human Resources or Finance.

Secondary data

Although an eclectic mix of secondary sources will be used in this study, the main data will be drawn from peer-reviewed academic journals such as *The Journal of Applied Research in Higher Education, British Educational Research Journal* and *The International Journal of Research and Method in Education*. In addition, student data will be drawn from 'SITS: Vision'. This is the student administration software currently used at Viking University. The dependent variable (dissertation performance) is valued as follows: 5 = a mark of 70%, 4 = a mark of 60–69%, 3 = a mark of 50–59%, 2 = a mark of 40–49% and 1 = a mark of <40%. The independent variables are as follows:

- Research Methods attainment
- Cultural background
- Age
- Gender
- Prior educational attainment
- Study mode

(Continued)

Quantitative data analysis

All data will be entered into the statistical software package SPSS. Quantitative analysis will be conducted using a variety of methods. These include descriptive statistics (e.g. means, standard deviations and frequency distribution). Pearson's product-moment correlation coefficient will be employed to ascertain any statistically significant correlations between the six variables and dissertation performance. Independent sample t-tests (t) will be used to analyze differences in dissertation performance between male and females. Finally, multiple regression analysis will be employed to determine the possible relationships between the independent variables and dissertation performance.

Ethical considerations

It must be noted that the author has already sought ethical approval with the Director of Research (DOR) at Viking University. The DOR has verbally confirmed that she is happy to endorse the research and to work with the author to complete the required ethical approval form.

Timescale

It is anticipated that the dissertation will be completed prior to the 18 July 2021 deadline. The researcher is in a fortunate position of having access to students and academics, therefore, no foreseen limitations are expected. From the timetable it is clearly evident that the literature review is an ongoing process. This is essential in order to include the most contemporary articles on the chosen subject.

References

Benson, A. and Blackman, D. (2003) 'Can research methods ever be interesting?', *Active Learning in Higher Education*, 4 (1): 39–55.

Edwards, D.F. and Thatcher, J. (2004) 'A student-centered tutor-led approach to teaching research methods', *Journal of Further & Higher Education*, 28 (2): 195–206.

Finch, J. (1986) 'Age', in Burgess, R. (Ed.), *Key Variables in Social Investigation*. London: Routledge.

Halfpenny, P. (1981) 'Teaching ethnographic data analysis on postgraduate courses in sociology', *Sociology*, 15 (4): 564–570.

Harrison, M.E. and Whalley, B. (2008) 'Undertaking a dissertation from start to finish: The process and product', *Journal of Geography in Higher Education*, 32 (3): 401–418.

Higher Education Statistics Agency (2010) Class of degree achieved by students obtaining first degree qualifications at HEIs in the UK by gender & mode of study 2008/09. www.hesa.ac.uk/dox/pressOffice/sfr142/SFR142_Table6.pdf

Hofstede, G. (1980) *Culture's Consequences: International Differences in Work Related Values*. Beverley Hills, CA: Sage.

Koh Yin Moy and Koh Chye Hian (1999) 'The determinants of performance in an accountancy degree programme', *Accounting Education*, 8 (1): 13–29.

Kroeber, A. and Kluckhohn, F. (1952) 'Culture: A critical review of concepts and definitions', *Peabody Museum Papers*, 487 (1), Harvard University.

Lane, A.M., Devonport, T.J., Milton, K.E., and Williams, L.C. (2003) 'Self-efficacy and dissertation performance among sports students', *Journal of Hospitality, Leisure, Sports and Tourism Education*, 2 (2): 59–66.

Lewthwaite, S. and Nind, M. (2016) 'Teaching research methods in the social sciences: Expert perspectives on pedagogy and practice', *British Journal of Educational Studies*, 64 (4): 413–430.

Morgan, D.H.J. (1986) 'Gender', in Burgess, R. (Ed.), *Key Variables in Social Investigation*. London: Routledge.

Morris, A. (2006) 'Provision of research methods teaching in UK LIS departments', *New Library World*, 107 (314): 116–126.

Newman-Ford, L., Lloyd, S. and Thomas, S. (2008) 'An investigation into the effects of gender, prior academic achievement, place of residence, age and attendance on first-year undergraduate attainment', *Journal of Applied Research in Higher Education*, 1: 13–28.

Papanastasiou, E.C. and Zembylas, M. (2008) 'Anxiety in undergraduate research methods courses: Its nature and implications', *International Journal of Research and Method in Education*, 31 (2): 155–167.

Ransford, H.E. and Butler, G. (1982) 'Teaching research methods in the social sciences', *Teaching Sociology*, 9 (3): 291–392.

Richardson, J.T., Mittelmeier, J. and Rienties, B. (2020) 'The role of gender, social class and ethnicity in participation and academic attainment in UK higher education: An update', *Oxford Review of Education*, 46 (3): 346–362.

Saunders, M., Lewis, P. and Thornhill, A. (1997) *Research Methods for Business Students* (2nd edn). Harlow: FT/Prentice Hall.

Scott Jones, J. and Goldring, J.E. (2015) '"I'm not a quants person": Key strategies in building competence and confidence in staff who teach quantitative research methods', *International Journal of Social Research Methodology*, 18: 479–494.

Sheard, M. (2009) 'Hardiness commitment, gender, and age differentiate university academic performance', *British Journal of Educational Psychology*, 79 (1): 189–204.

Shenkar, O. (2001) 'Cultural distance revisited: Towards a more rigorous conceptualization and measurement of cultural differences', *Journal of International Business Studies*, 32 (4): 519–535.

Smith, K., Todd, M., and Waldman, J. (2009) *Doing your Undergraduate Social Science Dissertation*. Abingdon, Oxon: Routledge.

Strauss, A.L. (1987) *Qualitative Analysis for Social Scientists*. Cambridge: Cambridge University Press.

Winn, S. (1995) 'Learning by doing: Teaching research methods through student participation in a commissioned research project', *Studies in Higher Education*, 20 (2): 203–214.

Yin, R.K. (1989) *Case Study Research: Design And Methods*. London: Sage.

The example research proposal does not include a detailed timetable. This is best illustrated in the form of a Gantt chart, setting out the key tasks, anticipated start dates and completion dates. See Figure 3.3 earlier in the chapter.

Again, before following the structure of the example proposal, do check with your tutor that you are able to follow the same approach. There is no definitive structure. However, most institutions have similar requirements in terms of content and structure.

In the Concept Cartoon shown in Image 3.1, the characters are having a discussion about the research proposal. Again, as with previous examples, think about the different views and use them to provoke a discussion with fellow students. What do you think? Do you share a viewpoint with one particular character?

Image 3.1   Concept Cartoon 'Research proposal'

YOUR RESEARCH PROJECT SUPERVISOR AND THE RESEARCH PROPOSAL

We conclude this chapter with a look at the importance of your research supervisor both during and after completing your research proposal. In many cases, the supervisor is allocated after submitting a research proposal. If this is the case, then the first meeting you have with your supervisor will be on the contents of your proposal. Use this initial meeting to explain the rationale for doing your research direction and the next steps.

On the other hand, if your supervisor is allocated during the research process, then use this as an opportunity. By consulting your supervisor as you develop your process, you are more likely to produce a proposal that provides you with a solid foundation prior to conducting your research.

Rowley and Slack (2004: 10) emphasize the importance of the research supervisor throughout the research process, by focusing on the supervisor's roles, these include:

- Provider of subject expertise, and ready access to the literature of the subject.
- Provider of access to research contexts (e.g. organizations).
- Mentor, to support reflection on the process.
- Director or project management to take the student through the steps in the process in a logical order, and to a time scale.
- Advisor on research methodologies, both in relation to their selection and appropriateness, and in relation to specific design issues.
- Signpost or teacher assisting with access to the literature.
- Editor, supporting structuring and writing of the dissertation.

The likelihood is that your research supervisor is also the marker of your research project and will provide assessment feedback. For an example of a completed research proposal marking form see Figure 3.7.

VIKING UNIVERSITY
VIKING BUSINESS SCHOOL
RESEARCH PROJECT PROPOSAL – MARKING FORM

STUDENT REGISTRATION NUMBER: 1234567

GRADE AWARDED BY 1ST MARKER: 70%

Assessment criteria (weightings in brackets)	First Marker's comments (mark awarded in brackets)
Learning outcomes and scholarship displayed **(10%)**	The learning outcomes are largely addressed. Your assignment contains the main elements one would expect to see in a research proposal. Parts of the methodology are lacking a little detail, but in short, you demonstrate a good understanding of the research process. (8)
Presentation **(10%)**	A table of contents and page numbers would have made a useful addition. A few grammatical and typographical errors. Nice use of main headings and sub-headings. Diagrams are clearly labelled and presented. Your research timetable could have been presented in landscape format. (7)
Proposed methodology **(20%)**	The Honeycomb of Research Methodology provides a nice overview of your chosen methodological approach. You then proceed to discuss each element in the context of your research. Pleasingly, each step is discussed in a lucid way and it is evident that you have thought about the relationship between each step in the research process. I would have liked to have seen a little more detail in terms of data collection, e.g. specific examples of secondary sources, such as the *Journal of Product and Brand Management*. Also, sampling frame, sampling method(s) and sample size could have been fully explored. In places, you could have drawn on a wider range of research methods sources. In short, a decent section. (14)
Argumentation and understanding **(10%)**	A clear introduction to brand thinking. Although some of your points could have been supported using relevant sources, you later demonstrate a solid understanding of the subject and illustrate your research direction using the step diagram (Figure 1). A lucid set of research objectives and research questions. You may also consider adding a 'Why' question. Possibly, 'Why might a company choose to adopt brand thinking?' (7)
Criticality and analysis **(10%)**	Your preliminary literature review starts by discussing the nature of brand and draws on research from key authors. I would have liked to have seen a bit more in the way of sources here. In addition, be careful with some sources as they are now rather dated. Good to see that you recognise the time frame when referring to Millman's work. A more critical approach could have been adopted when discussing Liedtka et. al (2017). Finally, for future reference, when writing your literature review chapter, remember to include a summary that makes a clear link between what you have reviewed and your own study. (7)
Planned sources and use of evidence **(15%)**	A solid range of sources and evidence of sources used to support your arguments in the main text. In some sections of the methodology, I would have liked to have seen a wider range cited in the main text. (10)
Academic referencing **(5%)**	The Harvard Referencing System is largely applied. Remember to include the page number(s) in citing a direct quote in the main text. (4)
Quality of written communication **(10%)**	In general, a well written piece of work that demonstrates one 'common thread' running through your entire proposal. In other words, you have thought about the relationship between each section and your research direction. (7)
Overall Planning for Proposed Investigation **(10%)** -To include a timetable of proposed research	A neatly presented research timetable. I also suggest including supervisor meetings and ethics (ethics approval) on your timetable. In terms of the former, meetings can be scheduled at key stages in the research process. (6)

First Marker: Dr Florida Jones   **Signature:** *F. Jones*   **Date:** 18 May 2019

Figure 3.7   An example of a marking form for a research proposal assignment

Clearly, the nature of the marking criteria used depends on your marker/institution. The same can be said for assessment feedback. However, as we have established in this chapter, the research proposal does contain key elements that you would expect to see in research proposal marking criteria.

BOX 3.2: RESEARCH SNAPSHOT

A useful exercise prior to writing your research proposal is to visualize your research journey. The Research Wheel provides a helpful guide here in terms of the key steps, but also think about any potential obstacles you may encounter on your journey. Think about where you are now in your research journey to the point when you submit your research proposal. For this task, instructions are as follows:

- Use A3 paper and coloured marker pens.
- Illustrate a picture of yourself or a vehicle to show the means of transportation throughout the task of producing your research proposal (Start here).
- Draw the finish line or the point at which you submit your research proposal.
- Sketch the obstacles and milestones along the way.
- Draw a sign showing the future dates to show the next steps in your journey. These are dates that illustrate the key tasks when doing your research. You can discuss these dates with your research supervisor.

Image 3.2   Visualize your research journey

Source: iStock (photo ID: 1140983360)

This chapter has discussed how to prepare your research proposal. It is an important part of the 'Planning' layer in The Research Wheel model, so much so, that if produced well, the likelihood is that you will go on to write an excellent research project.

CHAPTER SUMMARY

- A research proposal is a formalized plan that sets out how you intend to conduct your research and is a prerequisite for research investigation.

- You can start with a 'working' title, and then after the proposal is written, evaluate it again.

- Topic selection is one of the most challenging parts of formulating the research proposal. The best way to overcome this challenge is by sharing your research ideas with your fellow students and tutor/supervisor.

- A useful exercise when writing a research proposal is to consider the '5 Cs' rule: Clear, Coherent, Critical, Compelling and Current.

- Producing a research project checklist before submitting your proposal will ensure that you have covered all of the required material in the proposal.

- Think about the importance of your research supervisor throughout the research process, in particular, the roles that the supervisor undertakes.

QUESTIONS FOR REVIEW

1. Why is it important to write a research proposal before starting a research project?

2. Explain the structure of a research proposal.

3. Outline the characteristics of a 'good' research proposal.

4. What are some of the challenges student researchers may face when writing a research proposal?

5. Imagine you are a research supervisor. What advice would you give your research student who is about to start working on their research proposal?

STUDENT SCENARIO: HOW PEGGY OVERCAME THE CHALLENGES OF WRITING HER RESEARCH PROPOSAL

This example is based on an actual student's experience of writing their research proposal. I have included it here as many students find this part of the research process difficult.

Peggy (not the student's real name), a final year Postgraduate Business Management student, has decided to conduct research analyzing staff retention in the UK advertising industry. As a former practitioner, she has spent several years working for an advertising agency. This is of interest as she is able to draw on her own experience of working in the sector and her business networks.

This experience meant that she had no problem in choosing her research topic. Moreover, Peggy quickly developed a clear set of research objectives and research questions. In essence, the main focus of her research is on the strategies UK advertising agencies need to adopt in order to improve staff retention. Although clear on her research direction, Peggy had never written a research proposal. She had little idea about what to write.

How Peggy progressed from research direction to writing up her research proposal

Although Peggy was ready to start writing her research proposal, she felt anxious about how to actually start writing and structure her proposal. She decided to address her concerns in three ways. First, to speak to her tutor. Peggy had received the marking criteria and guidance on what to include in her proposal, but was still unsure as to how to meet her tutor's expectations.

Peggy explained to her tutor that actually doing the writing was proving difficult. In response, her tutor provided Peggy with an exemplar of a research proposal from last year's cohort. The fact that this exemplar was on a different topic did not matter. Peggy was pleased to receive guidance on how to write each section and to see how to structure a proposal. She viewed meeting with her tutor as the first step in finding out how to approach her writing.

The next step Peggy took was to form a research group with her fellow students. In the beginning, the intention was to set up an informal get together for students with similar concerns about how to write the proposal. Peggy set up the group using the messenger app WhatsApp. She used these meetings as a platform to exchange ideas on how to approach writing and planning research. One of the main advantages of sharing her research concerns was that she found other students had similar experiences. As a result, Peggy soon realized that having difficulty writing was perfectly normal. This made her feel less anxious about writing her proposal.

Finally, Peggy decided to use her social media networks to ask questions about her writing. As an active Twitter user, Peggy had started to follow students and academics engaged in research at other institutions, although until now she had largely followed as opposed to engaged with other Twitter users. However, she saw Twitter as an opportunity to ask questions to the academic community about her proposal. The purpose of posing questions on Twitter to the academic community was to gain viewpoints from people who had gone, or were going through, the proposal process at other institutions. One of the main hashtags Peggy used was #AcademicChatter. This particular hashtag is widely used by students and academics alike. That is, it provides both perspectives. Peggy posed questions on how to approach the research proposal, for example: 'How do other students structure a research proposal?' and 'How do you write a research proposal?'. The last question generated several answers, some of which were really useful and helped Peggy to think about how she might apply the advice given to her own writing.

Outcomes

Although Peggy had a clear view of her research direction, at the start of her research she was concerned about how to actually write her research proposal. In this case, she took three significant steps in order to address her concerns. As a result, she was able to produce an excellent proposal that provided her with a solid foundation prior to undertaking her research project.

The key point here is that Peggy used a variety of ways to go about writing her research proposal. Starting to write is often the most difficult task in research. As well as speaking to her tutor, note that Peggy also used other means to find out more about writing. This included her fellow students. Finally, engaging in an academic community via Twitter was also a useful way to learn from researchers outside of her institution.

Questions

1. Peggy received guidance from her tutor on how to approach the research proposal. Explain how the 5Cs rule might have also helped Peggy when submitting her research proposal.
2. What advice would you give to Peggy if she decided to change her research topic following submission of her research proposal?

FURTHER READING

Denscombe, M. (2019) *Research Proposals: A Practical Guide* (Open up study skills) (2nd edn). Maidenhead, UK: Open University Press.

A book dedicated to research proposals. Contains some helpful information on 'What is a good research proposal?'.

Emmanuel, C. and Gray, R. (2003) 'Preparing a research proposal for a student research dissertation: A pedagogic note', *Accounting Education*, 12 (3): 303–312.

This article provides a useful example of a fictitious research proposal (pp. 305–308).

Heath, A.W. (1997) 'The proposal in qualitative research', *The Qualitative Report*, 3 (1): 1–4.

This short article provides an outline of how to structure a proposal in qualitative research.

Punch, K.F. (2016) *Developing Effective Research Proposals* (3rd edn). London: Sage.

A concise book on developing effective research proposals. The book includes a chapter on examples of research proposals.

REFERENCES

Cassuto, L. (2011) 'Demystifying the dissertation proposal', *Chronicle of Higher Education*, 58 (4).

Cottrell, S. (2014) *Dissertations and Project Reports: A Step By Step Guide*. Basingstoke: Palgrave.

DeCuir-Gunby, J.T. and Schutz, P.A. (2017) *Developing a Mixed Methods Proposal: A Practical Guide for Beginning Researchers*. Sage: London.

Emmanuel, C. and Gray, R. (2003) 'Preparing a research proposal for a student research dissertation: A pedagogic note', *Accounting Education*, 12 (3): 303–312.

Gray, D.E. (2014) *Doing Research in the Real World* (3rd edn). London: Sage.

Herrington, J., McKenney, S., Reeves, T. and Oliver, R. (2007) *Design-based Research and Doctoral Students: Guidelines for Preparing a Dissertation Proposal*. Available at: https://ro.ecu.edu.au/ecuworks/1612 (accessed 10 November 2020).

Locke, L.F., Spirduso, W.W. and Silverman, S.J. (2013) *Proposals that Work: A Guide for Planning Dissertations and Grant Proposals*. London: Sage.

O'Leary, Z. (2018) *Research Proposal: Little Quick Fix*. London: Sage.

Pringle Barnes, G. and Cheng, M. (2019) 'Working independently on the dissertation proposal: Experiences of international Master's students', *Journal of Further and Higher Education*, 43 (8): 1120–1132.

Robson, C. (2011) *Real World Research*. Chichester: John Wiley & Sons.

Rowley, J. and Slack, F. (2004) 'Conducting a literature review', *Management Research News*, 27 (6): 31–39.

Wentz, E.A. (2014) *How to Design, Write, and Present a Successful Dissertation Proposal*. Sage: London.

4

SEARCHING AND CRITICALLY REVIEWING THE LITERATURE

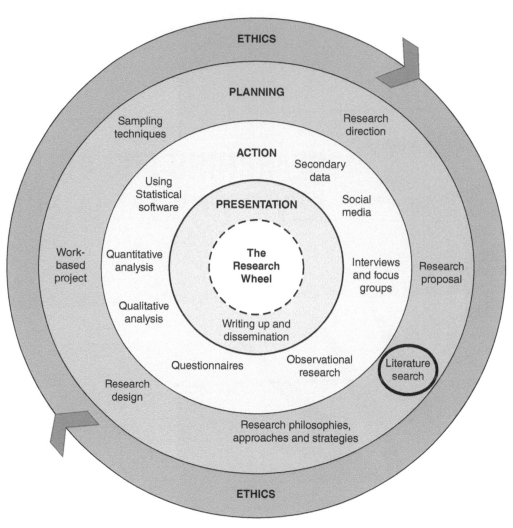

Figure 4.1   The Research Wheel

Learning objectives

By the end of this chapter, you should be able to:

* understand the nature of a literature review

* appreciate why researchers undertake a literature review

* identify different ways of structuring a literature review

* explain how to search the literature

* appreciate when to conduct a literature review

* understand how to adopt a critical approach

* evaluate ways of organizing your literature.

INTRODUCTION

In this chapter, we examine the process and importance associated with conducting a literature review. A *literature review* is a summary of your chosen subject that supports the identification of specific research questions (Rowley and Slack, 2004).

As you can see by Figure 4.1, we have now come to the stage of conducting your literature review in the research process. This step in the research process is important as a methodical review of the current literature is required to understand what has been written on your chosen topic. Furthermore, undertaking a comprehensive literature review is an iterative process as it is ongoing and likely to influence how you approach your research methodology, the next step in your research.

In reality, searching the literature is likely to be the first step you undertake as a student researcher. This is because it can help you to explore a possible research topic that forms the basis of your research project. Only through reading what has been written on your subject area are you able to identify a gap within the literature that your research will seek to address.

You will see from Figure 4.1 that 'Literature search' (circled) is part of the 'Planning' layer in The Research Wheel. This is because you need to search the literature in order to develop your knowledge of your chosen research topic. In addition, searching and evaluating the literature is required so you can refine your research ideas, before moving to the next layer – 'Action'. Conducting a literature review is a challenging task and something that is likely to take up a considerable amount of time. The purpose of this chapter is to provide you with the guidance needed to successfully complete your own literature review. You will have conducted a review of the literature as part of an assignment. However, there is a clear distinction when conducting a literature review for a research project. We begin by exploring what is meant by the term 'literature review' and where this 'fits' within your overall research project. Next, we examine the reasons why researchers undertake a literature review. It is interesting to note that a literature review can be a project in itself. For example, through your literature search you will no doubt find academic journal articles that are based on a review of a particular body of literature. One reason academics write this type of article is to give the reader a comprehensive overview of what has been written on a particular subject.

There is no one approach to structuring a literature review. So, the subsequent section explains the main options available to student researchers. Following on from this, we consider ways to search the literature and when to conduct a literature review. When searching for relevant sources, key questions are likely to include: What are the typical sources you are likely to use? How do you know which sources are relevant to your study? Then, we will look at how to adopt a critical approach when reviewing the literature. A literature review must not be a wholly descriptive piece of work, but show evidence of critical analysis. Finally, we end the chapter with a section on organizing your literature and key success factors when doing a review.

WHAT IS A LITERATURE REVIEW?

An essential part of a research project is the literature review. The format a literature review takes can either be one chapter, two chapters or feature as part of an introduction. We can define a literature review as a *'search and evaluation of what has been written on a particular subject'*. The literature review helps you to identify your chosen research topic. Still further, it helps you to recognize gaps in the literature that warrant greater attention. If you are doing a traditional dissertation then the likelihood is that a literature review forms a key part of your research project. In most instances, a literature review forms one or two chapters within a dissertation. Hart (1998: 13) offers a more detailed definition of literature review:

> The selection of available documents on the topic, which contain information, ideas, data and evidence written from a particular standpoint to fulfil certain aims or express certain views on the nature of the topic and how it is to be investigated, and the effective evaluation of these documents in relation to the research being proposed.

Hart's (1998) definition views a literature review as a *process*. This process starts from the time that you first read an article or book on your research subject. However, process is only one aspect of conducting a literature review. Ridley (2008) recognizes the process as one part, but also notes a second part, namely that of the finished *product*. In essence, this is the chapter or chapters which feature in the final draft of your dissertation or thesis. A literature chapter is a critical review of the current body of literature on your chosen area of research. You need to think of your own literature review as a critical piece of writing on relevant literature. Moreover, it situates the focus of your research within the context of the current body of literature. How you approach and structure your literature review is something that we examine later in this chapter.

Although you will have conducted a literature search as part of writing an assignment or small-scale project, this might be the first time that you embark on a more extensive literature review. One notable difference is that with a dissertation there is greater emphasis on academic journal articles. There is an expectation that the student researcher does not rely solely on books, but places significant attention on academic sources, particularly journals. However, academic journals are by no means the only source to consider when doing a literature review. As a researcher, you will find information applicable to your study across a wide range of literature sources. Some of the sources we examine later in this chapter. An important feature of any literature review is that it is focused and addresses the key themes associated with your original research questions. Again, there must be one common thread that runs through your dissertation.

An important consideration when writing your review is your audience. After reading your review, readers should think of you as an expert on your chosen topic and certainly familiar with the key authors in your field. Your review is likely to be a distinct chapter within your dissertation that falls between the introduction (Chapter 1) and before your methodology (Chapter 3). A high-quality review is complete and is not confined to one research methodology, one set of journals or one geographic region (Webster and Watson, 2002).

WHY DO I NEED TO CONDUCT A LITERATURE REVIEW?

The literature review is where you demonstrate you are both aware of and can interpret what is already known about your chosen topic. In addition, it is where eventually you will be able to point out the disagreements and gaps in existing knowledge. Furthermore, it reveals to the reader your ability to critically evaluate the literature on your chosen research topic. In simple terms, a literature review is 'reviewing' what has been written on a particular subject. The process helps you to further your knowledge on your subject and allows you to determine how your research might be positioned in the current body of literature. However, this is not the only basis for undertaking a literature review. Rowley and Slack (2004: 32) suggest a literature review is important for the following reasons:

- supporting the identification of a research topic, question or hypothesis
- identifying the literature to which the research will make a contribution, and contextualizing the research within that literature
- building an understanding of theoretical concepts and terminology
- facilitating the building of a bibliography or list of the sources that have been consulted
- suggesting research methods that might be useful
- analyzing and interpreting results.

Let us look at each of the above points in more detail. First, conducting a review helps to identify and generate ideas on a possible research topic, questions or hypotheses. Many students often start with an idea of a possible research topic. However, a review of the literature often leads to a more refined research topic, subsequently leading to the development of research questions. In some cases, a review of the literature may lead you to decide to change your original research idea. This may occur if you come across an article based on an unfamiliar topic or appreciate the significance attached to a particular topic. For example, through conducting a literature review on destination branding, you may come across an article that focuses largely on the environmental aspects associated with this topic. Given the importance placed on environmental sustainability, this could lead you to change the direction of your research.

Second, reviewing the literature will allow you to identify and understand how your research will contribute to what has already been written on your chosen subject. If undertaking an undergraduate dissertation or research project, there is less emphasis on contribution than undertaking a doctoral degree. A word that perhaps better explains the rationale for identifying the literature is 'positioning'. In other words, how will your research be positioned in the context of what has been written on your chosen subject? In order to determine this, you need to analyze what has been written on your research topic in a meaningful way.

Third, from a theoretical perspective, conducting a review will develop your knowledge and understanding of the theoretical concepts associated with your topic. Student researchers may be overwhelmed by the different theories and terminologies associated with their research topic. However, familiarizing yourself with theories and terminologies will help you to determine which theory(s) you intend to use as part of your own research.

Fourth, conducting a literature review allows you to develop a list of sources. These sources will feature in your bibliography or reference list towards the end of your research project. They not only act as a useful guide for the reader to look up a particular source cited in your project, but also demonstrate evidence of research. For example, a literature review chapter with a wide range and extensive number of sources shows the researcher has devoted considerable time to the process.

Fifth, as briefly highlighted in the introduction, reviewing the literature can help you to select your methodological approach, especially your research methods. This is because at some point you need to decide which method(s) you will need to use in your research. You might like to adopt research methods that are commonly used, alternatively, you may consider other method(s) that have been given little attention.

Lastly, a literature review is important for analyzing and interpreting results from earlier studies. This is likely to include both qualitative and quantitative data. Existing results may influence how you approach your data collection and choice of analytical techniques.

Consider a project without a literature review. How will the reader know that you are familiar with earlier research? In addition, how do you know that no one else has done anything similar? Your readers will want to know what has already been written on your subject.

THE LITERATURE REVIEW PROCESS

This section examines the steps you need to take when doing your literature review. Conducting the literature review is an organized way to research your chosen topic (Machi and McEvoy, 2016). In the literature review process, each subsequent step builds on the previous one, building a solid understanding of the literature. Thus, the term 'literature view' is a process, as well as a chapter(s) that features within a research project. Conducting a literature review is a systematic process. Figure 4.2 illustrates the typical steps in this process.

Only by performing a comprehensive review process are you able to demonstrate to the readers of your work your knowledge of the current theory, key terminology and leading authors in your subject area. Of course, this will be demonstrated through the content and writing style of your literature review chapter(s). The process of conducting a literature review helps you to develop an important skill set at each stage of the research journey. This includes searching and selecting the literature, analysis and evaluation skills, and finally, synthesis and writing skills. Synthesis involves making connections and identifying relationships between the parts identified in your analysis. Thus, synthesis requires you to have a detailed knowledge of your subject area. Typically, researchers compare and contrast points made by different authors.

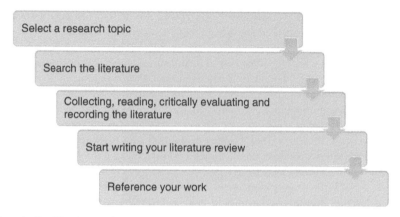

Select a research topic

Search the literature

Collecting, reading, critically evaluating and recording the literature

Start writing your literature review

Reference your work

Figure 4.2   Steps in the literature review process

SELECT A RESEARCH TOPIC

The first step in the literature review process is associated with research topic, research objectives and questions. Establishing your research topic is the starting point to defining the parameters or boundaries prior to searching the literature. Furthermore, formulating your objectives and questions, followed by undertaking a key word search of sub-topics, variables and key concepts will allow you to refine your research. Thus, this makes the process of searching the literature more manageable. In some cases, determining those keywords associated with your research topic may not be straightforward. For example, the term 'place branding' might also be referred to as 'destination branding'.

SEARCH THE LITERATURE

The second stage in the literature process is searching the literature. This is covered in more depth later in the chapter. In relation to the process, the initial searches are a way to get started on finding out more about your chosen research topic. Be sure to search a wide range of sources, in particular key academic journals relating to your research subject. Conducting a search using Google can be a useful starting point, although Google Scholar should be used when searching for academic journals.

Image 4.1   The literature review process – searching the literature

Source: iStock (photo ID: 512051356)

COLLECTING, READING, CRITICALLY EVALUATING AND RECORDING THE LITERATURE

This stage in the literature review process incorporates four tasks. These tasks are generally viewed as interdependent. For example, collecting the literature via various sources requires that you read the book, article or possibly another source. If reading a journal article then the abstract will provide you with a complete overview of the contents of the article. At this point, you can then decide as to whether or not the contents of the article are relevant to your own research. If so, the next task is to read the article, adopting a critical approach as you do so. Adopting a critical stance when reading an article and later writing your literature review chapter(s) is essential and something we examine later in the chapter. Finally, keep a list of all of the sources you intend using in your research as you go along. This will make it easier when it comes to producing your reference list prior to submitting your work. Notetaking can be in electronic format; alternatively, use a traditional notebook to record each source and a brief overview of the nature of the material.

START WRITING YOUR LITERATURE REVIEW

You should start writing your literature early in your research journey. This might be confusing as many research methods books illustrate the literature review as something carried out after deciding on a research topic and formulating research questions. In reality, you need to conduct a literature search in order to identify a suitable topic that makes a contribution to the literature. When should I complete my literature review? As previously highlighted, the literature review is an ongoing process. If I look through a student's timetable setting out each task undertaken during their research, one of the first things I look for is the amount of time allocated to literature review. Quite simply, your review is something that you should be doing right up to your project submission date. It is most certainly not a task that only warrants a few weeks or one narrow block of time during your research journey. Why? Well, in the first instance, material on some topics is likely to develop rapidly over time. This is particularly important if you are doing a longitudinal study, or in other words research over an extended period of time. You need to be able to show that you are aware of how your subject changes over time. In short, there are three points in your research where a review of the literature is required (see Figure 4.3). First, an *early review* is often required to determine the context and reasons for conducting the research, together with clarifying research questions. However, in the case of a work-based project, carrying out a cursory review of the literature may not always be possible until you discuss the nature of your research with the organization(s) involved in your study. Second, an *ongoing review* is essential to make sure that you keep in touch with the current and relevant literature in your subject area. Finally, the *findings review* is intended to analyze the research findings of earlier studies and determine whether these concur or contradict with the findings from your own research project.

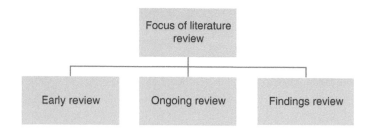

- An early review to determine the context and reasons for your study and to clarify your research questions

- Make sure that you keep in touch with the current and relevant literature in your subject area

- As you begin to analyze and interpret your findings, consider how your findings relate to that of earlier studies

Figure 4.3   Doing a literature review at key points in your research

As you begin to make significant progress selecting sources relevant to your research, you can then start writing your literature chapter(s). Your approach depends on how you intend structuring your review, the options of which we explore later in the chapter. It often makes sense to write your review as you go along. The reason for this is that it maintains your familiarity with the subject and allows the review to develop over time. In contrast, writing the chapter after you believe you have completed the literature review process is more time-consuming and potentially difficult to manage.

REFERENCE YOUR WORK

The final stage in the literature review process is referencing your work. As mentioned, it is useful to reference your work as you go along. This will help avoid trying to locate sources you may have read several weeks beforehand. Quite simply, it is a more effective and manageable way to conduct research. It is not uncommon for large-scale research projects to contain more than 80–100 references.

As noted in earlier chapters, with any research process diagram the stages involved are unlikely to be a series of linear steps. Figure 4.2 is intended to show you the key stages, which should be undertaken in a systematic way. However, in essence you will find that you need to revisit earlier stages. This is certainly the case in terms of 'searching the literature' as your literature search is not something undertaken during one 'block of time' but should be an ongoing process.

Rowley and Slack (2004) provide a slight variation on Figure 4.2 by suggesting the following five steps in the creation of a literature review: scanning documents, making notes, structuring the literature review, writing the literature review and building the bibliography.

1. Scanning documents allows you to become familiar with the range of documents on your chosen topic. Moreover, this may lead to insights into key themes and allow you to group documents on the basis of key themes. When scanning documents there is no need to read an entire document. In the case of journal articles, you will find that the article abstract provides a concise overview of the entire article.

2. Making notes helps you to refine key themes. Remember that it is important to keep an accurate record of your sources as you will need to cite these when writing up your research project. An ideal way to make notes is electronically, for example, using Microsoft Word. Key themes can be colour coded.

3. Structuring the literature review is concerned with identifying the key themes in the review and starting to organize concepts and documents in accordance with the key themes.

4. You can make a start on writing your literature review once you have a broad structure in mind. Your literature review should start with a brief introduction that sets out the purpose of your review. For example, 'the purpose of this chapter is to review the literature on ...'. Having an introduction is important in the context of something called 'sign-posting'. This is how you signal to the reader the path you are taking throughout your project. For instance, reference is likely to be made to the content you are about to cover, the order in which it will come and the focus it will take. Examples of signposting phrases include:

    *   The purpose of this chapter is to ...
    *   This section critically examines ...
    *   In summary, ...
    *   The layout of this section is as follows ...
    *   The aim of this research project is to ...

The headings in your structure can be used to analyze documents based on those headings (themes). When writing your review, be sure to follow the referencing system required by your college or university. Direct quotations can be used for impact, although use these sparingly. Remember to adopt a critical approach, use your own words and cite correctly.

5. Finally, building your bibliography is an ongoing process and something that you will develop throughout your research journey. A bibliography is a list of all of the sources that you have referred to in your literature review. The most important thing to remember is that you correctly cite any sources you refer to in your review chapter(s).

Source: Adapted from Rowley and Slack (2004)

Finally, although there is no one definitive approach to the literature review process, typically, the process involves a number of generic steps as discussed above. These include searching, evaluating, recording, writing and producing a list of references.

HOW DO I STRUCTURE MY LITERATURE REVIEW?

To some extent, how you structure your literature review is likely to be dependent on both your chosen topic and type of research project. This will become clear as we discuss the options for structuring your review. There are a number of ways to structure a literature review, although student researchers normally adopt one of the following approaches – thematic, chronological, theory/methodology or systematic. We will now examine each approach, including how you can determine which option is the most appropriate for your own research.

THEMATIC APPROACH

A popular method of structuring a literature review among business and management students is the thematic approach. In most cases, student researchers select this method as it is a relatively simple and explicit approach to reviewing the literature on their chosen research topic. In essence, a thematic approach to structuring a literature review is based on using themes as main headings and sub-headings. As an example, if your project includes the following research question: 'How do reward systems impact employee performance among UK small businesses?' The key themes are circled below:

How do (reward systems) impact (employee performance) among UK small businesses?

If the focus of the research is purely on UK small businesses, then this might also feature as a key theme as part of the literature review chapter. The advantage of structuring your review using a thematic approach is that it is clear to your audience. Pay special attention to covering all of the themes associated with your research questions. In other words, there must be a lucid relationship between your research questions and the material covered in your literature review. Remember that the purpose of your research questions is to set boundaries when it comes to doing your literature search and writing your literature review chapter(s).

As another example, if your study focuses on cultural differences in the workplace then the main body of your review will feature headings and sub-headings associated with culture. These may include: national culture, cultural dimensions, corporate culture and cultural conflict. The main benefits of using a thematic approach are two-fold. First, it makes it easy for the reader to follow the structure of your review. In addition, you can comment in the introduction of your literature review chapter that the headings and sub-headings follow those in your research questions, thereby clarifying that the important aspects of your research questions are addressed within the review. Second, the thematic approach also has benefits as you are likely to have organized your sources on the basis of key themes when searching the literature. Figure 4.4 illustrates the headings and sub-headings used in a literature review for a marketing-related project, based on a thematic structure.

Project title: A study investigating buyer–seller relationships in the UK construction industry

Chapter 2:   Literature review

2.1   Introduction
2.2   Business-to-Business marketing

    2.2.1   The nature of Business-to-Business marketing
    2.2.2   Business-to-Business marketing – the interaction approach
    2.2.3   Business-to-Business marketing – the network approach
    2.2.4   Theoretical development in Business-to-Business marketing

2.3   Relationship constructs in Business-to-Business marketing

    2.3.1   Trust and commitment
    2.3.2   Satisfaction
    2.3.3   Other relationship constructs

2.4   The UK construction industry

    2.4.1   An overview of the industry
    2.4.2   Key competitors in the marketplace
    2.4.3   Relationships between construction companies

2.5   Summary

Figure 4.4   Example of a literature review structure (thematic approach)

You will see from Figure 4.4 that the structure includes the key themes featured in the title of the research project – *A study investigating buyer–seller relationships in the UK construction industry*. The structure begins with an introduction, the main body of the review features themes divided into sub-themes and finishes with a summary. A well-structured review such as this is easier to write and provides a clear overview of the content to readers.

CHRONOLOGICAL APPROACH

If you choose to structure your review using a chronological approach then your structure is according to changes over time or advances in your subject area. For instance, a study examining the development of learning technologies may lend itself to a chronological approach. The first period to examine might be post-2000, with future development based on increments of every five years. When using a chronological approach, try to justify the reasons for selecting a particular starting date. Consider that even though a chronology is linear, it is important to trace the associations through your timeline (Thomson, 2016). The advantage of this approach is that it works well for subjects where there are key events and milestones over a given period of time. For example, a chronological approach can be applied to an organization's development since inception, to show how an industry has changed over time or referring to a country's economic development. One disadvantage of using the chronological approach is knowing at which point in time to start from. This is why it is important to justify a starting date as the reader will certainly want to know your reasons for selecting a particular starting time.

THEORETICAL/METHODOLOGICAL APPROACH

By using a theoretical approach, your literature review is structured based on selected theories. This approach works particularly well if your project is of a mainly theoretical nature and/or there are several theories relevant to your area of study. As an example, if a student decided to choose a topic focusing on internationalization process theory, several theories are associated with this topic. Examples likely to feature as main headings include Network theory, Born Global and Dunning's eclectic model. A theoretical review is appropriate, if, for example, the dissertation aims to advance a new theory. Moreover, a theoretical review can help establish a lack of theories or reveal that the current theories are insufficient (Randolph, 2009). For large-scale projects, sometimes students may use more than one approach to structuring the literature. In this case, the literature review is often divided into two chapters. One chapter focuses on the theories, thereby adopting a theoretical approach, while the second chapter is of a more practical nature and takes on a thematic structure. However, undergraduate dissertations usually include one literature review chapter, given the word constraints.

Using a methodological approach is another option for business students. This involves reviewing earlier studies on the basis of methodological approaches. In some cases, this might involve structure using different methods – qualitative, quantitative and mixed methods (studies that use the application of both qualitative and quantitative research). The methodological approach works well if you have several studies using different methodologies, but there also needs to be an aspect of commonality in order to have a sufficient number feature under each heading. Conversely, a literature review based on research studies using largely the same or a narrow range of methodologies is perhaps more suited to an alternative approach.

SYSTEMATIC APPROACH

Bettany-Saltikov (2012: 5) defines a systematic literature review as 'A summary of the research literature that is focused on a single question'. Jesson and Lacey (2006: 145) provide a more detailed definition by defining a systematic approach as 'a comprehensive (and if possible complete) review of published articles selected to address a specific question that uses a systematic method of identifying relevant studies in order to minimize biases and errors'. Waddington et al. (2012) view the process of conducting a systematic review as systematically searching defined databases over a specific period of time, with transparent criteria for the inclusion or exclusion of studies, as well as the analysis and reporting of research findings.

In essence, a systematic review is a more rigorous approach to doing a literature review than other approaches. As per Jesson and Lacey's (2006: 145) definition, the review must include all published literature on the research topic or, in other words, be an exhaustive search of all available literature. The 'systematic' reference relates to a well-organized approach to reviewing earlier studies on your subject area. This is supported using an explicit statement as to the criteria used when conducting the literature review. In other words, when doing a systematic review, you must clearly explain each step you went through in your literature review process.

There are a number of key points to consider when conducting a systematic literature review. These include:

- When selecting sources avoid publication bias by selecting journals that promote one particular approach. For example, only publishing articles based on a certain type of research strategy.
- Conduct an extensive review by making an attempt to cover all published material on your research topic.
- Be clear on the methods used when undertaking your review, together with the criteria. In other words, how did you decide to include and exclude material from your literature review?

Although there is no one definitive approach to conducting a systematic literature review, it requires the researcher to have an in-depth understanding of the literature. Researchers often make good use of tables to summarize key findings in a systematic review, although this is something that you can do in any literature review to break up the text. For example, using a table to show key definitions from leading authors or citations. Table 4.1 is an example from Kumar (2015) where the author uses a table to show key studies relating to 'Green Marketing'.

Table 4.1   Example of a table showing how to summarize key earlier studies in a literature review (includes number of citations)

Rank	Citation per year since publication	Article title
1	56.7	Kotler, P. (2011) 'Reinventing marketing to manage the environmental imperative', *Journal of Marketing*, 75 (4): 132–135.
2	53.7	Cronin, Jr. J.J., Jeffery, S.S., Gleim, M.R., Ramirez, E. and Martinez, J.D. (2011) 'Green Marketing strategies: An examination of stakeholders and the opportunities they present', *Journal of the Academy of Marketing Science*, 39 (1): 158–174.
3	43.4	Menon, A. and Menon, A. (1997) 'Enviropreneurial marketing strategy: The emergence of corporate environmentalism as market strategy', *Journal of Marketing*, 61 (1): 51–67.
4	39	Banerjee, S.B., Iyer, E.S. and Kashyap, R.K. (2003) 'Corporate environmentalism: Antecedents and influence of industry type', *Journal of Marketing*, 67 (2): 106–122.
5	39	Peattie, K. and Crane, A. (2005) 'Green marketing: Legend, myth, farce or prophesy?', *Qualitative Market Research: An International Journal*, 8 (4): 357–370.

Source: Kumar (2015)

Assessment as to the quality of a research article is likely to focus on the methodology employed, e.g. sampling method, population and validity of data. Reading systematic literature review articles will give you an understanding of the different methods used by researchers. Look for the steps undertaken by the researcher and assess the quality of the systematic review process using the criteria above.

BOX 4.1: RESEARCH SNAPSHOT

The following article is a good example of how to do a systematic literature review:

- Anees-ur-Rehman, M., Wong, H.Y. and Hossain, M. (2016) 'The progression of brand orientation literature in twenty years: A systematic literature review', *Journal of Brand Management*, 23: 612–630.

Read the above article and identify the following (in pairs/groups):

- Historical context
- Why is the research important?
- Research gap and objectives?
- Methodological approach
- Key findings
- Limitations

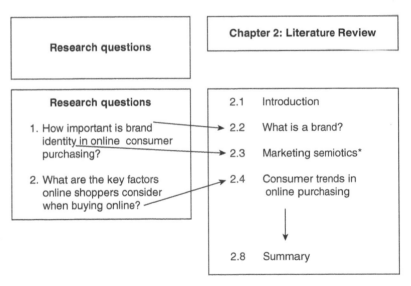

*Semiotics is the study of signs and symbols

Figure 4.5   Making sure that there is a clear link between research questions and literature review

You can see that Figure 4.5 shows you an example of how to 'link' your research questions to your literature review. The arrows point from the themes in the research questions to those in the literature review chapter. The themes or topics covered in your review must relate to your research questions. A literature review should not include any information that is not relevant to your research questions.

CHOOSING THE APPROACH TO YOUR LITERATURE REVIEW

The approach you choose to structure your literature review to a large extent depends on your research topic and research questions. For example, if your questions refer to a specific time frame, e.g. 'What was XYZ PLC's organizational performance between the periods 2000 to 2018?', it is ideally suited to a chronological approach. Similarly, clearly themed-based questions are most likely best addressed by adopting a thematic approach to structuring the literature review. Another factor that sometimes influences choice of approach is the method commonly used by researchers of similar studies. This may allow for ease of analysis when comparing sources and the critical approach adopted by researchers of earlier work.

BOX 4.2: RESEARCH SNAPSHOT

Reading literature review articles in your broad subject area, e.g. Human Resource Management, will give you a valuable insight into how to structure your own literature review. In addition, getting into the habit of reading literature reviews also helps you to develop your writing skills and familiarize yourself with the literature on your broad research topic. A literature review should have a clear introduction, main body and a summary. The last part of the review summarizes the main points and makes a clear link between the existing body of literature and how this relates to your own study.

SEARCHING AND EVALUATING THE LITERATURE

Why search the literature? Searching the literature is an essential part to any research project. As a student researcher you need to understand what has been written on your subject. You need to know how researchers have approached your research topic. This also includes searching the methodological literature on possible methodologies you may decide to adopt for your research. Hart (2011: 3) suggests five reasons for searching the literature:

1. It will help you to identify work already done or in progress that is relevant to your own work.
2. It will prevent you from duplicating what has been done already.
3. It will help you to avoid some of the pitfalls and errors of previous research.
4. It will help you to design the methodology for your project by identifying the key issues and data collection techniques best suited to your topic.
5. It will enable you to find gaps in existing research, thereby giving you a unique topic.

Figure 4.6 shows you the wide range of sources available to you when searching the literature. There are many options here. Try not to restrict your search to a narrow number of sources. Your supervisor will want to see strong evidence of research – this means consulting literature that goes beyond a small number of textbooks.

In the early stages of your research, certainly when choosing a research topic, using a search engine such as Google (www.google.com) will help you to experiment with searching themes and keywords. However, sources without the author's name should not be used. The inclusion of a name is a good 'quality control' mechanism. Without it, anyone could have written the material. Once you have made progress on developing your topic, you can begin to identify more specific sources of literature.

The significant contributions in your area of research are likely to be in leading academic journals. Both books and journal articles include lists of references to other sources. When searching

Figure 4.6   Key sources from where literature can be searched

the literature on your topic, it is essential that you know where to look. A starting point for many students is Google Scholar. This is perhaps unsurprising as Google Scholar allows for ease of access, includes authors' names and is likely to make reference to articles relevant to your study. However, access to the majority of articles will be restricted unless you access via your institution's electronic library. Your university or college library website should be the starting point for your literature search.

Given that you are likely to have a wide range of written material on your subject, what steps can you take to evaluate the literature? This is a key question as a literature review is not an exhaustive list of everything written on your topic. There are a number of considerations when evaluating journal articles for use in your literature review, including:

- *Relevance.* Are the contents of the article relevant to your research topic?
- *Reputation.* Is the article published by a reputable publisher in a peer-reviewed academic journal?
- *Author.* Is the author recognized as a specialist in your area of research?
- *Content.* Is the article up-to-date and does it contain new and/or interesting material on your research topic?
- *Referencing.* Does the article contain a wide range of references and an in-depth review of the literature?
- *Presentation.* Is the article clearly presented and structured in such a way that it is easy to follow?
- *Up-to-date.* Does the article feature contemporary sources?

Books and websites also provide useful sources. However, like journal articles, you should also evaluate and determine whether to include them in your review. Of course, web-based sources are easy to access via popular search engines such as Google or Yahoo! However, the difficulty with web-based sources is knowing the extent to which they are reliable and relevant to your own study. Certainly, reliability can be problematic to determine. For example, a website's domain name might suggest a reliable source, although how can you be certain? It is worth noting the following points when making a judgment as to the reliability of a particular website. First, does the domain name sound like an authoritative and reliable source? Make sure that you avoid sources that are widely recognized as being unreliable, e.g. Wikipedia. Next, who is the intended audience? How frequently is the material on the website updated? Are there links to other websites of authority? Who writes the articles on the website? Are they considered an authority in their field? Are there any reviews on the website and are they up-to-date?

Lastly, a useful indicator as to whether a website is reliable is the extent that the website is cited by other researchers. For example, the Organization for Cooperation and Economic Development (OECD) is a globally recognized organization that 'provides a forum in which governments can work together to share experiences and seek solutions to common problems', is viewed as a reliable and trusted source and material from its website is commonly cited in articles.

SEARCHING FOR BUSINESS-RELATED INFORMATION

If you are undertaking a work-based project, the likelihood is that you will have access to business-related information. This includes company specific sources relating to your employer or research organization. For example, company reports, customer records and data sources can provide valuable information and could be essential when it comes to addressing your research problem. A key consideration here is the ethical issues that will need to be addressed. Accessing any kind of company information will require ethical approval from your employer/organization.

LITERATURE SEARCH TOOLS

Your library will give you access to a wide range of search tools. Library catalogues are ideal for locating hard copies and e-books on your research topic. In addition, your library is likely to subscribe to the leading journals, thus giving access to articles written by key authors on your subject. Online databases are particularly useful if you require information on organizations and market data. Important statistical data can be found on websites such as Statista and databases such as Mintel. For examples of selected databases see Table 4.2.

Online databases typically give access to a wide spectrum of sources. Other examples include conference papers, newspapers, reports and past copies of student dissertations. Finally, search engines provide ease of access to sources, but access to academic journals is usually restricted. So, be sure to use your library if trying to access journals! Examples of key selected journals in business and management are highlighted in Table 4.3. Using a search engine allows keyword searches using a basic or advanced search.

Table 4.2   Selected databases in Business and Management

Name of database	Brief description
Business Source Complete	Business Source Complete is the industry's most used business research database, providing full-text for more than 2,300 journals.
Emerald E-Journals Collection	A full-text of 100 management and accounting journals and e-books published by Emerald.
FAME	A fully searchable database containing information on public and private companies in the UK and Ireland.

Name of database	Brief description
Google Scholar	Google Scholar searches academic publishers, professional societies and pre-print archives.
JISC Journal archives	Enables you to search over 3.745 million journal articles.
MarketLine Advantage	Provides information on 10,000 companies, 2,000 industries and 50 countries. Includes company and industry reports, case studies, business news and financial deals.
Mintel	Provides access to consumer and market research used by professionals.

Table 4.3   Examples of selected academic journals

Area of business	Journal titles
Accounting	*Accounting Review*
	Accounting, Organizations and Society
	Journal of Accounting and Economics
	Journal of Accounting Research
Finance	*Journal of Finance*
	Financial Economics
	Financial Studies
	Corporate Finance
Entrepreneurship	*Entrepreneurship, Theory and Practice*
	Journal of Business Venturing
	Strategic Entrepreneurship Journal
	Entrepreneurship and Regional Development
Human Resource Management	*British Journal of Industrial Relations*
	Human Resource Management (USA)
	Human Resource Management Journal (UK)
	Industrial Relations: A Journey of Economy and Society
International Business	*Journal of International Business Studies*
	Journal of World Business
	African Affairs
	Asia Pacific Journal of Management
Marketing	*Journal of Consumer Psychology*
	Journal of Consumer Research
	Journal of Marketing
	Marketing Research
Operations and Technology	*Journal of Operations Management*
	International Journal of Operations and Production Management
	Production and Operations Management
Strategy	*Strategic Management Journal*
	Global Strategy Journal
	Long Range Planning
	Strategic Organization

If you are doing a keyword search on a database such as EBSCO or Emerald, using Boolean operators such as 'and', 'or' and 'not' will allow you to combine research terms and limit the scope of your research. For example, in Boolean searching, an 'and' operator between two terms, e.g. 'Brand AND Loyalty' means you are searching for articles containing both of the terms, not just one of them, while using the Boolean operator 'Or' between two terms, e.g. 'Brand OR Loyalty' means that you are searching for articles containing either of the words (see Figure 4.7). The Venn diagram shows search results for 'Brand', 'Loyalty' and 'Brand Management'.

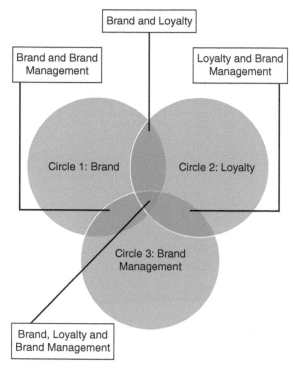

Figure 4.7   Boolean operatives used to specify and limit a literature search

Source: Adapted from Burns and Burns (2008: 55)

Based on using the search engine Google Scholar, the first column in Table 4.4 shows the keyword search items associated with the research question 'How much do UK millennials spend online each month?'. Clearly, the words 'millennials' and 'online' are far too broad and generate thousands of articles. The 'Advanced search' column shows the same search terms; however, this time an 'Advanced search' has been selected, followed by 'In the title of the article' under the heading 'Where my words occur'. If you know more specific information about an article, e.g. the author's name or title of the article, you can use the advanced search function.

Table 4.4   How much do UK millennials spend online each month?

Search item	Hits	Hits (Advanced search)
Millennials	69,400	3,790
Online	7,680,000	287,000
'Millennials Online'	15	74
'Spend online'	4,380	107
'Millennials spend online'	2	0

Image 4.2   Concept Cartoon 'Conducting a literature review'

Image 4.2 is a Concept Cartoon that shows characters expressing their views on literature review. Again, think about the different views of the characters and, if possible, use them to provoke a discussion with fellow students. In short, what do you think?

Your research supervisor and/or members of your project team are likely to provide useful guidance on literature and sources of information. If your supervisor is a specialist in your selected research topic, they will know the leading authors in your chosen field. This includes seminal articles that are essential to your literature review. Discussing literature and company information with your research stakeholders early in your research journey can help to save you time spent searching the literature. As the literature review is an ongoing process, it is important to discuss your progress at each meeting with your research supervisor.

What if I can't find any relevant sources? Again, your supervisor can help to determine why you are having difficulties, although in essence, the reasons are probably due to one of the following causes:

- you are looking for the wrong type of source
- you are looking in the wrong place
- you have problems with the parameters or keywords for your research
- you really have found an uncharted research area.

Source: Wilson (2014: 67)

ADOPTING A CRITICAL APPROACH

It is essential that you take a critical approach when reviewing the literature and writing up your literature review. A literature review is not simply a long list of what others have said about your subject.

Do not start each paragraph with a reference to avoid making your review 'list like'. What follows are two examples of extracts from a literature review. The first example is very 'list like', while the second example shows you how to adopt a critical approach.

Wong (2012) notes that country-of-origin (COO) is a key factor in influencing consumer decision-making among millennial shoppers. Henderson and Banks (2016) also suggest price is an important factor in the buying process. This view is shared by Wilkins (2018).

Note how Example 1 reads as being rather 'list like' and fails to provide any real detail in relation to the content of each study. Moreover, there is no evidence of critical analysis. Once again, consider your audience when writing your review. What are the questions your readers are likely to want to know when reading your review? Have you addressed their questions in your writing? For instance, not only does the example above demonstrate a very descriptive piece of writing, but it also fails to critically analyze important elements of each study.

Conversely, Example 2 shows a written paragraph providing evidence of critical analysis:

There are several different definitions of customer loyalty (see Wong, 2012; Sanchez, 2014; Hartley, 2016; Boyle and Khan, 2018). However, only Wong has examined customer loyalty in the context of retail consumers in Malaysia, although it is worth noting that this study was conducted using a relatively small sample size consisting of only one hundred respondents. Thus, clearly there is a need for further research in this area. This view is supported given the growth in size of Malaysia's middle class (see Turner, 2015).

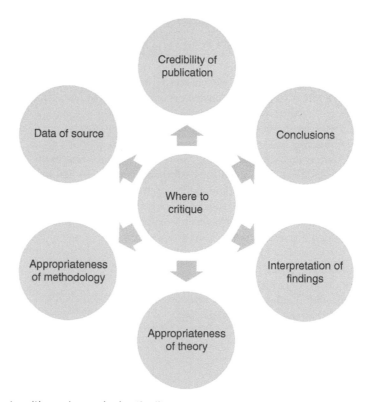

Figure 4.8   Where to critique when reviewing the literature

Comparing both examples in this section, you can clearly see the difference between the two approaches to writing a literature review. In essence, be sure to keep this critical approach in mind when writing your own literature review. A literature review is not a repetition of what every book and journal article has written on a particular subject. It should not contain extracts based on unconnected themes without comments. Avoid a list of quotations and make sure to introduce your voice. The reader will want to know your views on the subject. In addition, a key part of the literature review should be how your research relates to or links to the current body of literature.

Adopting a critical approach when reviewing the literature does not mean 'criticizing' other works, but evaluating the literature. Make notes that are analytical. Consider:

- Who is saying it?
- When did the study take place?
- Why are they saying it?
- What is the nature of their argument and is it supported?
- What have other researchers said about this work?
- How does it relate to your research problem and research topic?
- What is the particular methodological approach in which the topic was studied?

Figure 4.8 shows areas where to critique when conducting your literature review. Let us examine each of these in turn.

CREDIBILITY OF PUBLICATION

Sites such as Wikipedia and Google are often used by students as a means of research topic. This is fine as the original sources can be looked up through Wikipedia. Arguably, if you question the credibility of a publication then the source should not feature in your literature review. On the other hand, including the odd reference from potentially unreliable sources is an indicator to readers that you have conducted a comprehensive review across multiple sources. Examples of publications where credibility might be called into question includes articles in selected newspapers. Remember that a newspaper article is written by a journalist and does not go through the same rigorous peer review process employed by leading academic journals, like many who write for Wikipedia and work that appears on Google.

CONCLUSIONS

Reviewing the conclusions set out by author(s) of earlier studies provides another opportunity to take a critical approach. For instance, to what extent do you fully agree with the author(s) conclusions? Do you agree with their interpretation of the research findings? As an example, this is the kind of terminology you might use to be critical here – 'Although Baker and Allen (2014) conclude that employees prefer in-house training, it is important to note that their study is based on a relatively small sample size.'

INTERPRETATION OF FINDINGS

When criticizing how the author(s) interpret their research data, a distinction can be made between qualitative and quantitative data. For example, qualitative data tends to be based on exploratory research and involves the author(s) interpreting data based on a subjective approach. The nature of qualitative research and the subjective viewpoint adopted by the researcher means that it is subject to criticism. An example here is how the researcher(s) interprets a verbatim quotation from a respondent. You may not agree with their interpretation, so, state why you do not agree. The nature of quantitative research is that it is more objective and usually concerns the interpretation of numerical data. Here, the likelihood is that you agree with the numerical results, but not how the researchers have interpreted the reasons for the result. For example, you may agree with the median number of hours spent per week using social media, yet not the reasons behind the number of hours.

A researcher's interpretation of the findings may concur or disagree with that of earlier studies. Whether you agree or disagree with aspects of a researcher's interpretation of the findings, be sure to give your reasons why and support your argument.

APPROPRIATENESS OF THEORY

When reviewing the theoretical application applied by a researcher, consider the following question: Have the researcher(s) included a rationale for using their chosen theory? If not, then this is one area where you can be critical. Moreover, do you view the author(s) choice of theory appropriate for their research? There are two areas that come to mind when it comes to criticizing appropriateness of theory. The first relates to the original date of publication of the theory. Some theories are viewed as being seminal or, in other words, ground-breaking and are therefore still used in contemporary studies. Yet, this does not mean we cannot be critical of applying the theory in a modern context. For instance, in my subject area of marketing, many marketers and marketing researchers still commonly refer to and apply the marketing mix (4Ps). Otherwise known as McCarthy's (1960) marketing mix, the framework has been around since the early 1960s. Second, you can also be critical of a theory that has been applied in a different cultural context. Many theories in business and management tend to be Western and applied in a Western context. However, can these theories be applied in a non-Western, for example, Asian context?

APPROPRIATENESS OF METHODOLOGY

In this instance, you may consider that the methodological approach undertaken by the researcher(s) is not appropriate for the research topic. Of particular note here is the research methods employed in the study. For example, let us say that a researcher was interested in finding out about bullying in the workplace of a particular organization. If the researchers collected data using structured interviews, you might argue that this does not adequately capture the views of research participants. Why? Because the sensitivity of the topic may mean that respondents are uncomfortable sharing their experience face-to-face. You might argue that an anonymous questionnaire survey provides an appropriate means of data collection.

DATE OF SOURCE

An article's date of publication is important as it can impact whether you agree or disagree with the author(s) argument. For example, a study on the nature of the UK economy may make claims as to the success of the country's economic performance, yet the article could have been published more than ten years ago. Be careful when criticizing a researcher's argument from a dated source. Remember that the basis of their argument may have changed over time.

ORGANIZING YOUR LITERATURE AND KEY SUCCESS FACTORS

Early in your research journey you will start to collect a wide range of sources. Furthermore, the majority of these sources will be in electronic format. This certainly helps when organizing your literature.

Although there is no one definitive approach, it makes sense to organize your literature on the same basis as you intend structuring your literature review. For example, if your review is likely to follow a thematic structure, then this is how you organize the literature.

It is important to get into the habit of organizing your literature early as this will have implications later in your research. Save your articles on file under relevant names using Microsoft Word. Ridley (2008) suggests three types of record keeping systems which are particularly helpful when it comes to organizing your approach to the literature review:

- keep a record of all of your keyword searches
- keep a record of all of the bibliographical details you will need for your list of references at the end of your dissertation or project
- keep a personal library: a filing system of hard copies and/or notes of key texts.

KEY SUCCESS FACTORS

This section is devoted to what I refer to as 'key success factors' when writing your literature review. In other words, these are likely to be key areas of your review that the reader and/or marker will look for when reading through your work. The key success factors can be summarized as follows:

- Start your literature search early in your research journey.
- Conduct a comprehensive literature search to identify your research topic.
- Adopt a clear approach to structuring your literature review.
- Be sure to undertake a critical approach when reviewing the literature.
- Do not rely too heavily on a small selection of sources.
- Avoid using dated sources.
- Make sure that your review has an introduction, main body and summary.
- Be sure to state how your study 'fits' within the current body of literature.
- Meet regularly with your supervisor to discuss your literature review.
- Be sure to follow your institution's guide to referencing.

BOX 4.3: RESEARCH SNAPSHOT

When approaching a literature review, being organized is a key factor to success. Start off writing at a general level before moving to the specific. Use headings and sub-headings to easily guide the reader through your research. How you 'sign-off' your review is particularly important. The summary/conclusion is not the place to introduce new material and must give an overview of the review and note any gaps in knowledge. If you are using certain aspects from the review, e.g. a definition, make this clear in your summary.

In the earlier section we looked at what makes a good literature review in terms of the key success factors. Conversely, Biggam (2008: 52) noted that a bad literature review exhibits too many of the following:

- irrelevant rambling
- ideas are presented in no particular order (so difficult to follow thread of student discussion)
- too descriptive (with no/little attempt to give an opinion, much less support it with reasoned argument)
- ends abruptly, devoid of any clarification of main findings
- limited sources used (mainly websites), coupled with inconsistent referencing styles.

REFERENCING AND AVOIDING PLAGIARISM

The final key success factor when writing your literature review is 'be sure to follow your institution's guide to referencing'. The purpose of referencing is to demonstrate to the reader that you have conducted a comprehensive and appropriate literature search. When writing your research project, it is important to reference your work correctly to acknowledge the work of other authors. Your university or college will have academic requirements governing the process of referencing your work. Plagiarism is such an important subject that we discuss the subject in greater length in Chapter 7. Although there are several styles that can be used for referencing, The Harvard Referencing System is one of the most commonly used conventions within academia. Accurately referencing your work is essential in order to avoid plagiarism. Your university or college will certainly provide plenty of essential information on how to reference and avoid plagiarism.

You should reference all sources of literature you use when writing your work. Referencing does not only apply when citing a direct quotation within your project, but also referring to another person's work and/or ideas. The term 'references' is sometimes used interchangeably with the term 'bibliography'. However, there is a distinct difference. A *bibliography* typically refers to sources which you have consulted for your project, but not cited. These items can be listed at the end of your research project under the heading of 'bibliography'. Every item you cite in your work will be listed at the end of your project under a heading of 'References'. A *citation* means referencing another person's work in the main text of your project.

The commonly used examples of citations using the Harvard style are highlighted below:

Citing one author

If the source has one author, the author's name can be placed at the beginning or the end of a sentence.

Wade (2019) has studied the impact of semiotics on consumer behaviour.

A recent piece of research investigated the impact of semiotics on consumer behaviour (Wade, 2019).

Citing two or three authors

If the source has two or three authors, include all names in your citation.

The latest research findings show that educational attainment in this area is improving (Stapleford & Drew, 2018).

Earlier studies show that investment in this type of reward system is likely to increase employee retention (Moss, Peterson & Granger, 2019).

Citing four or more authors

If the source has four or more authors, then convention using the Harvard style is to use the abbreviation 'et al.', which is an abbreviation for the Latin 'et alia' which means 'and others'. It is important to note that this may vary as some institutions use 'et al.' with three or more authors.

Trust and commitment are important factors in UK-Chinese joint venture relationships (Holland et al., 2019).

Citing a direct quotation

If citing a direct quotation, use single quotation marks and state the page number.

David, Marks and Sanchez (2018) suggest that the customer dissatisfaction is now widely 'communicated across a range of social media platforms' (p. 9).

Compiling a reference list

When compiling a list of all of the sources cited in your project, list all of the sources under one heading of 'References'. There is typically no need to include separate headings for each type of source, e.g. 'Journals' or 'Books'. The format of your reference list is as follows:

- References are listed in alphabetical order by author.
- Your list of references includes all sources cited or directly quoted from within your work.
- Books, journals, electronic, web-based sources, etc. are written in a certain format.
- When citing more than one piece of work from the same author, you must list the work in date order within your reference list, beginning with the most recently published work first.

Compiling your reference list as you progress will make sure that you avoid failing to include any sources.

CHAPTER SUMMARY

- A literature review is a summary of your chosen subject that supports the identification of specific research questions.

- A review of the literature is essential in order for you to develop an understanding of your research topic.

- Your literature review demonstrates your knowledge of the current theory, key terminology and leading authors in your subject area.

- The approaches to structuring a literature review include themes, chronology, methodology/theory and systematic.

- Adopt a critical approach when writing your literature review.

- Use a recording system when organizing your approach to the literature review.

- Make sure to correctly reference your work throughout your literature review.

- Meet regularly with your supervisor to discuss your progress when conducting your literature review.

QUESTIONS FOR REVIEW

1. How would you define a literature review?

2. Why is searching the literature an essential part of your research project?

3. What are the steps you can take to successfully complete your literature review?

4. Explain the advantages of structuring a review using a thematic approach.

5. Discuss why it is important to adopt a critical approach when writing your literature review.

6. Why might a literature review be divided into two chapters?

7. Outline key sources you are likely to refer to when searching the literature.

8. What are the key success factors when writing your literature review?

STUDENT SCENARIO: ANITA DEVELOPS HER LITERATURE REVIEW

Anita is a final year undergraduate business management student. She has produced a draft of her literature review and received feedback from her research supervisor. Anita's literature review is on the 'Organizational performance of Nigerian small and medium sized enterprises from 1980 to 2020'. Although only a draft, Anita is pleased with the comments received from her supervisor. The review includes a clear introduction setting out the purpose of the review chapter. In addition, within the main body of the chapter, Anita addressed each of the themes associated with her research topic using a series of headings. Anita's usage of headings throughout her literature review is a good example of signposting as it 'guides' the reader through her review.

Structure

Although Anita's literature review featured a well-structured main body, there were two areas where her supervisor made constructive recommendations as to how she should develop her review. The first of these referred to adopting a more critical approach and using a wider range of sources. Anita had clearly used relevant sources within the review, however, there needed to be evidence of 'denser referencing'. In other words, drawing on a greater number and wider range of sources. In terms of the latter, the majority of her references were from web-based sources with only limited inclusion of articles from leading academic journals.

Her supervisor also suggested that she break up her lengthy review chapter by including two tables. The first of these was to focus on the definitions of the key terms associated with her research project. In this table, Anita's supervisor also suggested that she include the author(s), title of the study and year of publication to provide a brief overview of the source of each of the definitions. In the second table, her supervisor suggested examples of methodologies employed by researchers conducting similar research studies. Anita learned that by including a table showing methodologies employed by researchers of similar studies, she was providing a useful 'snapshot' for the reader of her review and how her research might be positioned in the current body of literature from a methodological perspective.

Summary

The summary section of Anita's literature review failed to make a clear link with her own study. Her supervisor noted the importance of being explicit as to which of the definitions of 'trust' Anita intended using for her own research. Also, her supervisor commented that he would like to see reference to how Anita's research will contribute to the existing body of literature on her subject area.

Revised draft

Anita began amending her literature review, taking into account the feedback provided by her research supervisor. Part of this process involved revisiting the literature and adopting a systematic approach to her literature review.

Questions

1. Discuss different ways Anita can structure her literature review.
2. Advise Anita on how to critique a literature review.

Hint: Remember that the research topic may influence how to structure a literature review.

FURTHER READING

Cronin, P., Ryan, F. and Coughlan, M. (2008) 'Undertaking a literature review: A step-by-step approach', *British Journal of Nursing*, 17: 38–43.

This article defines literature review, includes types of literature reviews and explains steps in the literature review process.

Fink, A.G. (2011) *Conducting Research Literature Reviews: From the Internet to Paper* (5th edn). Thousand Oaks, CA: Sage.

A comprehensive book on conducting research literature reviews. The book includes sections on the 'How?' and the 'Why?' when it comes to reviewing the literature.

Knopf, J.W. (2006) 'Doing a literature review', *Political Science & Politics*, 39 (1): 127–132.

In order to create a literature review of existing knowledge, the author includes a useful set of questions to ask and answer.

Price, R.H. (2017) 'The four-part literature review process: Breaking it down for students', *College Teaching*, 65 (2): 88–91.

This short article provides helpful tips for students writing a literature review, including 1) Developing a topic; 2) Searching the literature; 3) Narrowing the scope; and 4) Synthesizing prior research.

Synder, H. (2019) 'Literature review as a research methodology: An overview and guidelines', *Journal of Business Research*, 104: 333–339.

A comprehensive paper that discusses literature review as a methodology for conducting research and offers an overview of different types of reviews, as well as some guidelines on how to both conduct and evaluate a literature review paper.

REFERENCES

Bettany-Saltikov, J. (2012) *How to do a Systematic Literature Review in Nursing*. Glasgow: McGraw-Hill Education.

Biggam, J. (2008) *Succeeding with your Master's Dissertation: A Practical Step-by-step Handbook*. Maidenhead: Open University Press.

Burns, R.B. and Burns, R.A. (2008) *Business Research Methods and Statistics Using SPSS*. London: Sage.

Hart, C. (1998) *Doing a Literature Review*. Thousand Oaks, CA: Sage.

Hart, C. (2011) *Doing a Literature Search: A Comprehensive Guide for the Social Sciences*. London: Sage.

Jesson, J. and Lacey, F. (2006) 'How to do (or not to do) a critical literature review', *Pharmacy Education*, 6 (2): 139–148.

Kumar, P. (2015) 'State of Green Marketing research over 25 years (1990–2014)', *Marketing Intelligence & Planning*, 34 (1): 137–158.

Machi, L.A. and McEvoy, B.T. (2016) *The Literature Review: Six Steps to Sampling Success* (3rd edn). Thousand Oaks, CA: Corwin Press.

McCarthy, E.J. (1960) *Basic Marketing: A Managerial Approach*. Homewood, IL: Richard D. Irwin.

Randolph, J. (2009) 'A guide to writing the dissertation literature review', *Practical Assessment, Research & Evaluation*, 14 (13).

Ridley, D. (2008) *The Literature Review – A Step-by-step Guide for Students* (Sage Study Skills Series) (2nd edn). London: Sage.

Rowley, J. and Slack, F. (2004) 'Conducting a literature review', *Management Research News*, 27 (6): 31–39.

Thomson, P. (2016) *Five Ways to Structure a Literature Review*. Available at: https://patthomson.net/2016/08/29/five-ways-to-structure-a-literature-review/ (accessed 2 February 2019).

Waddington, H., White, H., Snilstveit, B., Hombrados, J.G., Vojtkova, M., Davies, P., Bhavsar, A., Eyers, J., Koehlmoos, T.P., Petticrew, M. and Valentine, J.C. (2012) 'How to do a good systematic review of effects in international development: A tool kit', *Journal of Development Effectiveness*, 4 (3): 359–387.

Webster, J. and Watson, R.T. (2002) 'Analyzing the past to prepare for the future: Writing a literature review', *MIS Quarterly*, 26 (2).

Wilson, J.S. (2014) *Essentials of Business Research: A Guide to Doing your Research Project* (2nd edn). London: Sage.

5

RESEARCH PHILOSOPHIES, APPROACHES AND STRATEGIES

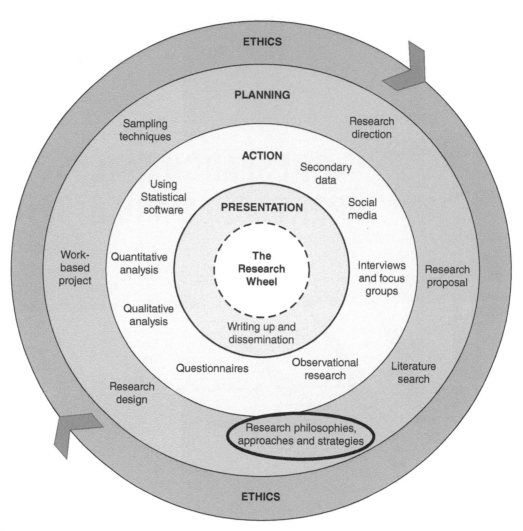

Figure 5.1   The Research Wheel

INTRODUCTION

Research philosophies, approaches and strategies are the first elements that make up *research methodology*. Other elements include research design, data collection and data analysis techniques. We examine these elements later in the book. The research methodology can be viewed as the 'central approach and strategy used to conduct the research' (Wilson, 2014).

At this stage in your research, you should have identified a clear research direction and started to become familiar with the key literature written on your research topic. Figure 5.1 shows where on The Research Wheel, 'Research philosophies, approaches and strategies' takes place in the research process (circled). Here, we are still very much at the 'Planning' layer. This is because decision-making needs to take place, for example, in terms of choice of research approach and strategy, before actively collecting and analyzing your data (the 'Action' layer in The Research Wheel).

The chapter starts by discussing the nature of research methodology and moves on to examine different types of research philosophies. Next, we examine approaches to doing your research, namely inductive and deductive. Usually, students have little, if any, prior understanding of research approaches. This is a key part of research methodology as your research approach will impact how you consider the role of theory in your research. This is followed by a section on research strategies. Finally, we look at the principles associated with validity and reliability.

RESEARCH METHODOLOGY

As briefly highlighted in the introduction, the methodology is the overarching approach to the research. Denzin and Lincoln (2005) view methodology as 'how to carry out the research relative to the question and context'. In this chapter, we look at the first three of the key elements that make up research methodology, namely research philosophy, approaches and strategies.

One way to think of methodology is the combining of all of the six elements highlighted in Figure 5.2. You will notice that Figure 5.2 also includes three other elements associated with research methodology – research design, data collection and data analysis. We examine these elements later in the book. Collectively, these six elements make up research methodology.

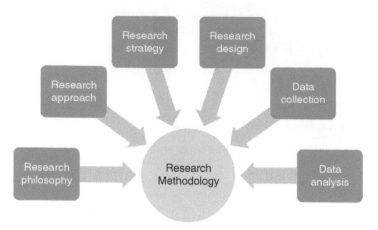

Figure 5.2   The elements that make up research methodology

When deciding on your research methodology you are considering the 'big issues' associated with your research. These include key factors such as the following:

- Your role as a researcher and how your views and the way you approach your research may impact your research outcomes.
- The role of theory in your research. Will you be applying one particular theory(s) or is your project of a more practical nature?
- The preferred methods that allow you to address your research questions.
- The ethical issues that are relevant to your study.
- The extent to which your research methodology compares to that of earlier studies. Adopting a similar methodological approach might permit for interesting comparative analysis. Conversely, there might be an argument to adopt a completely different methodology.

In short, the methodological choices you make are dependent on your role as a researcher, but also the nature of your research objectives.

Rather confusingly, you will find that there is a general lack of consistency in the literature on research terminology. Terms such as 'approach' and 'strategy' and 'methods' may vary in relation to how they are defined and applied by researchers. Further evidence of the number of elements associated with 'methodology' is Hudson and Ozanne's (1988: 508) definition that refers to methodology as 'how one answers research questions and not only data gathering techniques, but also research design, setting, subjects, analysis, reporting and so on'. However, although there is no one consistent definition for many research terms, typically you are still able to understand how each of these terms are defined and their overall context. Two terms that are often confused are 'methods' and 'methodology'. Remember that methodology is not the same as methods. The former is concerned with your overarching approach and strategy to the research, while 'method' refers to the 'different ways in which data can be collected and analyzed' (Wilson, 2014).

WHAT IS RESEARCH PHILOSOPHY?

Research philosophy is the first element and starting point in your research methodology. Often, student researchers will be keen to select a particular method of data collection and start collecting data.

However, when considering your own choice of data collection methods, it is necessary to understand the relationship between methods and research philosophy. In simple terms, research philosophy relates to the development of knowledge and the nature of that knowledge. Quite simply, it requires that you consider the way in which you view the world and your role as a researcher. Your views will influence the approach to your research, particularly in terms of data collection methods and analytical techniques. By way of example, one researcher may view financial metrics, such as profit and turnover, as ideal measures of organizational performance. Conversely, another researcher doing a similar study may argue that employee satisfaction and managerial opinions are essential measures of organizational performance. Clearly, both researchers are conducting research with the intention of measuring organizational performance. However, they have opposing views as to how organizational performance should be measured. You will see that later in the chapter the different approaches such as these are often down to how individuals view their role as a researcher.

When evaluating the philosophical stance that you are likely to take when conducting your research, there are three areas that need to be considered – *epistemology, ontology* and *axiology*. We examine each of these philosophies in the next section.

UNDERSTANDING RESEARCH PARADIGMS AND THE 'OLOGIES'

A paradigm is a deep-rooted set of perspectives that includes an ontological and an epistemological position and a set of values for operating in the world (Kuhn, 2012). The two dominant paradigms in social sciences are *Positivism* and *Interpretivism*. Positivist researchers argue that in order to understand the social world it is necessary to take an objective viewpoint. Thus, to adopt the methods used by the natural sciences. The researcher is independent of the research project and values are independent of the research. Conversely, interpretative researchers consider that in order to have knowledge of the social world it is important to understand language, meanings and cultures which are typically understood using qualitative research methods.

EPISTEMOLOGY

It is likely that few student researchers actually think about epistemology when carrying out their research. *Epistemology* is concerned with what constitutes acceptable knowledge in a field of study. How do we know what there is to be known? Your ontological position is likely to inform the way you view knowledge. The example earlier in this chapter of the researchers measuring organizational performance illustrates two different epistemological viewpoints. The researcher who considers employee satisfaction and managerial opinion as the most important measures of performance can be described as the 'views' researcher. More specifically, this researcher is concerned with the feelings or the subjective viewpoints from respondents. In contrast, the researcher who views performance on the basis of profit and turnover is taking an 'objective' viewpoint. We can describe the position adopted by the objective researcher as a positivist perspective, while that of the 'views' researcher as an interpretivist position. If you adopt an approach similar to that of a natural scientist, then your epistemological approach is likely to be positivist. In contrast, if you intend undertaking an approach similar to that of a social scientist, then your epistemological approach is likely to be interpretivist.

POSITIVISM

If you decide to take a positivist approach to your research, then you are taking an objective view of reality. For a positivist researcher, reality is a concrete and objective structure that is viewed as external to the researcher. Thus, being external or independent of the research means that you have little, if any, interaction with your research participants. Moreover, the researcher typically seeks to verify hypotheses and collect data using quantitative methods. The purpose of a positive study is often to generalize findings to the wider population. In order to do this the chosen sampling technique and sample size are important. There is a strong sense of reliability (repeatability) in a positivist research project. In other words, if a different researcher were to undertake the same study, then the likelihood is that they would achieve the same results. *Positivism* does not focus on any in-depth understanding and explanation of what is observed. In this respect it does not enable 'How?' and 'Why?' questions to be answered, but often comprises describing phenomena and finding relationships between independent and dependent variables. Emphasis is on searching for regularities and causal relationships between its constituent elements (Burrell and Morgan, 1979: 5). Table 5.1 provides an overview of the philosophical assumptions of positivism.

Table 5.1   Philosophical assumptions of positivism

- *Independence*: the observer must be independent from what is being observed.
- *Value-freedom*: the choice of what to study, and how to study it, can be determined by objective criteria rather than by human beliefs and interests.
- *Causality*: the aim of the social sciences should be to identify causal explanations and fundamental laws that explain regularities in human social behaviour.
- *Hypothesis and deduction*: science proceeds through a process of hypothesizing fundamental laws and then deducing what kinds of observations will demonstrate the truth or not of these hypotheses.
- *Operationalization*: concepts need to be defined in ways that enable facts to be measured quantitatively.
- *Reductionism*: problems as a whole are better understood if they are reduced into the simplest possible elements.
- *Generalization*: in order to move from the specific to the general it is necessary to select random samples of sufficient size, from which inferences may be drawn about the wider population.
- *Cross-sectional analysis*: such regularities can most easily be identified by making comparisons of variations across samples.

Source: Easterby-Smith et al. (2012)

Researchers critical of positivism argue that interesting insights are liable to be lost if taking a positivist approach. For example, if you conducted a study on product quality on behalf of a manufacturer, and you decide to take a positivist view, then your measure of 'quality' may focus on the number of product returns. Of course, product returns are only one measure of quality. Thus, an interpretivist would be interested in gaining insights as to why the products are being returned and how the products came to be sold in the first place. Research of this nature is likely to use qualitative methods such as interviews to gather data that address these questions. Post-positivists argue that reality can never be fully apprehended, only approximated (Guba, 1990: 22). Researchers now recognize the case against positivism, thus post-positivism relies on multiple methods as a way of capturing as much of reality as possible.

INTERPRETIVISM

Having read the earlier section, you might not consider your own philosophical stance as that of a positivist researcher. If this is the case, then you may regard your views as being more closely aligned to that of an interpretivist researcher. *Interpretivism* is a philosophical stance that advocates the importance attached to human actors. It seeks to provide 'culturally derived and culturally situated interpretations of the social-life world' (Crotty, 1998: 67). It supports the view that the researcher must be a part of the social world that is being examined. This means that the researcher is interdependent with their research and likely to regularly interact with research participants. An example here would be a researcher conducting research by living and travelling with a group of explorers. The emphasis here on the part of the researcher might be observation, interaction and collaboration with research participants. Interpretivists view the world as complex and open to interpretation. Taking a subjective viewpoint also means that bias cannot always be avoided.

Critics of interpretivism tend to focus on the subjective nature of this type of research. Typically, interpretivism is associated with qualitative research and small sample sizes. Often, a sample may not be representative of the population and therefore it is not possible to generalize to the wider population. However, this is not necessarily a weakness as typically with research of this nature the purpose is to examine a small number of cases in depth and not to generalize.

Positivist and interpretivist research are often presented as a dichotomy of two approaches to doing research. However, in reality it is not unusual for researchers to draw on aspects of both approaches to conducting research. The paradigm provides the rationale for one particular method over another. In your research project, the extent that you need to focus on research philosophy depends on the type of research project and the expectations of your research supervisor. Certainly, for most postgraduate research projects research philosophy is an essential feature.

PRAGMATISM

Pragmatism rejects the so-called 'paradigm wars' often viewed as reference to either positivism or interpretivism by advocating the role of the researcher. It is a deconstructive paradigm that debunks concepts such as 'truth' and focuses instead on 'what works' on the truth regarding the research questions and overall aim of the research (Tashakkori and Teddlie, 2009). Pragmatism is generally considered as the most popular paradigm for mixed methods social enquiry (Greene, 2007). However, it is important to note that mixed methods research can be undertaken with any paradigm. Although the research philosophy sometimes focuses on the dichotomy between interpretivism and positivism, there is another philosophical viewpoint. If you are of the view that your research is not aligned with interpretivism or positivism, then you are perhaps a pragmatist. Pragmatist researchers focus on the practicalities of doing the research. Moreover, pragmatist researchers centre on the 'what' and the 'how' of the research problem (Creswell, 2003: 11). Pragmatism places the research problem and research questions at the centre of research and use the methods they consider to be the most suitable in generating significant insights into their research. In short, pragmatists do not wish to be 'constrained' by one particular philosophical approach.

ONTOLOGY

Ontology is concerned with the nature of reality. The central question relating to ontology is whether social entities are perceived as objective or subjective. In simple terms, it considers how we perceive the social world. For example, one viewpoint of ontology is that researchers consider the world as external to social actors, or the perceptions and actions of social actors create social phenomena. Your own position in the world and how you perceive it is likely to inform your ontological position. There are two aspects associated with ontology – *Objectivism* and *Subjectivism*. First, objectivism implies that social phenomena are based on external realities that are beyond our reach or influence (Bryman, 2016). Social phenomena and their existence are external to social actors. Researchers taking an objective view set out to discover the objective truth; they should attempt not to include their own values. However, an objective view can still be undertaken when analyzing the subjective nature of research respondents. For example, a researcher may want to conduct research on the beliefs and attitudes consumers hold towards sustainability; however, this must be done from an objective viewpoint. In comparison, subjectivism holds that individuals construct their own meaning about a particular subject. In other words, a researcher would impose their views on a particular subject. These views are dependent on an individual's cultural background, social class, religion and unconscious bias.

BOX 5.1: RESEARCH SNAPSHOT

How you view ontology determines your approach to research methodology. For example, let us say that you intend to carry out research on a leading international banking group. The aim of your research is to measure the organizational performance across the group. If you decide that the world is external to social actors, then you will consider objectivism. Here, emphasis will be on measuring performance based on profit, turnover and market share. Conversely, subjectivism holds that you view the perceptions and actions of social actors to create social phenomena. Thus, likely measures are customer attitudes and perceptions towards the bank. Moreover, quite possibly your own views on the bank's organizational performance.

AXIOLOGY

Axiology is a branch of philosophy concerned with our views about values. In a research context, axiology considers how the values of the researcher relate to all stages of the research process. Each researcher will have their own set of values. When considering ontology, a researcher who holds their view of the world as subjective considers that they are interdependent with their research. They are unlikely to be value free and have a certain bias towards how the research is conducted. For example, a researcher conducting research into food branding may judge brand image as the most important feature of a brand. Yet, another researcher may have strongly held values that sustainability is the most important feature. Clearly, as a researcher strongly held values and feelings may lead to bias and influence overall research results. This interdependence means it is difficult to detach yourself from your research. If discussing your research philosophy as interpretivist and your ontology as one of subjectivism, it is important to note your values in your research. By noting your values and biases you are acknowledging to the reader that there is a potential issue. This is especially important if you are collecting value-laden data. An example here would be conducting research on your own organization. As both an entrepreneur and researcher, it is extremely difficult to detach yourself from your own biases and values towards your own start up.

In contrast, positivists consider the process of research as value free. The main reason for this is that they are independent or external to their research. One area where positivists tend to be detached is in relation to data collection. A typical example of a data collection method associated with positivism is the questionnaire survey. This is usually administered in such a way that the researcher is detached from their research. Examples include online, postal and email.

If adopting a pragmatist approach to your research then axiology is viewed as holding a potential bias and value-free. Based on pragmatism, there is a likelihood that data collection is centred on mixed methods. The combination of research methods means that there might be circumstances relating to biased views and those that are value-free.

Table 5.2 shows the relationship between epistemology, ontology, axiology and research approach. The latter we examine later in the chapter. At this stage, you should be starting to recognize how choice of research philosophy is likely to influence other elements of research methodology.

Table 5.2   Positivism, interpretivism and pragmatism epistemologies

Epistemology	Research approach	Ontology	Axiology
Positivism	Deductive	Objective	Value-free
Interpretivism	Inductive	Subjective	Biased
Pragmatism	Deductive/inductive	Objective and subjective	Value-free/biased

Source: Adapted from Wilson (2014)

WHY DO I NEED TO LEARN ABOUT RESEARCH PHILOSOPHY?

An understanding of research philosophy allows you to reflect on your role as a researcher. There is no one 'best' research philosophy. By now, you should recognize that what determines your research philosophy is two-fold. First, the nature of your research questions. For example, if your research questions are seeking answers to 'How' or 'Why' questions, then this suggests that you are an advocate of an interpretivist philosophical stance. The likelihood is that you are interested in finding answers of a subjective nature, based on the views of research participants. Conversely, if your research seeks to find answers to a set of research hypotheses, then your intention is likely to be on establishing objective answers.

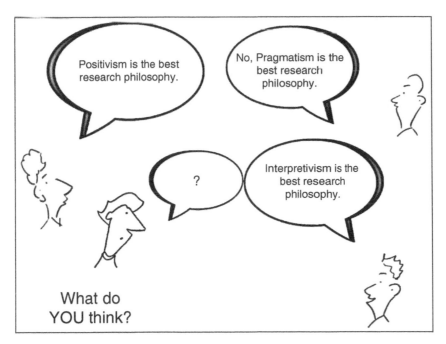

Image 5.1   Concept Cartoon 'Research philosophy'

Image 5.1 is a Concept Cartoon that shows characters expressing their views on research philosophy. One character has the view 'positivism is best', another 'interpretivism is best', the third 'pragmatism is best', finally the fourth character is uncertain. Think about the different views. Working in groups, use them to provoke a discussion with fellow students. Do you share a viewpoint with one particular character?

Students sometimes find the terminology associated with research philosophy difficult to grasp. At the point of formulating your research objectives and research questions, try to consider the methodological approach you are likely to use. In particular, your research philosophy. Remember that types of research questions or hypotheses are likely to be more closely associated with certain types of methodologies. Do not be too concerned that your research has to 'fit' into one particular type of philosophy. If you are taking a pragmatic approach to your research, then justify why you have opted for this philosophical stance. Research philosophy might seem daunting at first. However, it is important to recognize that there are usually arguments for and against each type of philosophy.

APPROACHES TO DOING RESEARCH

The next section of this chapter explains the different approaches to doing research. This is the second element of research methodology. Approach in this case refers to '*the relationship between theory and data*'. Researchers often make a distinction between an inductive and deductive research approach, although the pragmatic approach relies on a version of abductive reasoning. This recognizes that the research approach does not require a decision to be made on the basis of a false dichotomy.

INDUCTIVE APPROACH

Inductive refers to 'a theory-building process, starting with observations of specific instances, and seeking to establish generalization about the phenomenon under investigation' (Hyde, 2000: 83). If you adopt an inductive approach to your research then the role of theory is that of an outcome in your research. For example, let us say that you were interested in conducting a focus group with consumers to determine their views on a government green initiative scheme. As a result of your literature review, you may arrive at a conclusion that you do not wish to apply one particular theory. In essence, your research does not start from one theoretical viewpoint. In this case, the observations made during your research will lead to a proposed theoretical framework. This is the outcome of your research. Many students find an inductive approach challenging as often they are more comfortable with applying theory. However, for certain research topics adopting an inductive approach might be the preferred option. This is especially the case where this is very little written on a research topic.

An inductive approach is associated with the following:

- a qualitative research strategy
- less emphasis on sample size and the need to generalize research findings
- axiology or values are liable to be biased/value laden
- an interpretivist epistemology
- the researcher interacts closely with research participants.

Although the above points refer to a qualitative strategy as being inductive, Patton (1987: 62) notes the following:

> The extent to which a qualitative approach is inductive or deductive varies along a continuum. As evaluation fieldwork begins, the evaluator may be open to whatever emerges from the data – a discovery or inductive approach. Then, as the inquiry reveals patterns and major dimensions of interest, the evaluator will begin to focus on verifying and elucidating what appears to be emerging – a more deductively orientated approach to data collection and analysis.

Qualitative research does not necessarily apply to a purely inductive approach. This is what Patton (1987) means when he refers to 'a continuum'. Once again, you can see that although researchers often view research philosophy as a number of different dichotomies, in reality, this is not always the case.

DEDUCTIVE APPROACH

An inductive study starts with the collection of empirical data. This is a flexible approach to doing research as the research questions and process is likely to change. Analysis leads to an understanding of reality and leads to the generation of theories. By comparison, a *deductive* approach applies theory from the start and is viewed as a 'top down' approach to doing research. Hypotheses are derived from the theory and what has been written on the topic. These are then tested empirically. An example of a deductive approach would be a researcher developing a set of hypotheses derived from Michael E. Porter's (1980) Five Forces model to assess the competitiveness within an industry, and then testing these hypotheses on a particular case(s).

A deductive approach is associated with the following:

- moving from theory to observation
- a positivist epistemology
- the generation of hypotheses from theory
- a quantitative research strategy
- the researcher is independent or 'detached' from what they research
- axiology or values are value-free
- the study of large representative samples in order to make generalizations to the wider population.

The following factors may lead you to adopt a deductive approach to your research:

- There exists a large body of literature on your chosen research subject. You may find that there are a number of theories of interest to you. Thus, there is every reason to apply a theory(s) to your own research.
- An objective of your research is to compare your research findings with that of earlier studies. This will involve applying the same theory and evaluating your research in the context of other studies.
- Quite simply, adopting a deductive approach might be your preferred approach to doing your research. Again, often students are more comfortable with this approach vis-à-vis an inductive approach.

Choosing an inductive or deductive approach is not a precursor for selecting a particular type of data collection method. However, inductive approaches are commonly associated with qualitative research, while deductive approaches are usually more common in quantitative research.

ABDUCTIVE APPROACH

A number of research texts refer to the dichotomy of a deductive or inductive approach; actually, your actual process of doing research never operates in one direction. In the context of your research methodology, including your actual design, collection and analysis of research findings, it is impossible to operate in an exclusively theory or data driven fashion (Plano Clark and Creswell, 2008). The *abductive* approach is associated with a pragmatic approach and involves moving back and forth between induction and deduction. An example here would be a researcher developing a theoretical framework by adopting an inductive approach and then testing the framework through theoretical application.

Again, it is impossible to be completely 'subjective' or completely 'objective', thus pragmatists recognize that there is a single 'real world' and also acknowledge that all individuals have their own interpretations of that world (Plano Clark and Creswell, 2008).

TYPES OF RESEARCH STRATEGY

The third element of research methodology is research strategy. Again, terminology may vary in the literature with 'research strategy' also referred to as 'research approach'. For example, Collis and Hussey (2009: 7) refer to 'approach' but their interpretation is consistent with qualitative and quantitative research in general. A common theme running through discussions of research methods is the contrast (or contest) between qualitative and quantitative research (Hakim, 2012).

QUALITATIVE RESEARCH

Of course, not everything can be quantified. *Qualitative research* involves finding out what people think, how they feel and how they behave. Subjective aspects such as perceptions, consumer experience and ideas can only be described using words. The information provided is subjective and not numerical. Qualitative researchers are interested in knowing how individuals understand and experience their world in terms of a particular time and contact. This is very much based on an interpretivist philosophical stance, which is embedded in the qualitative approach (Merriam and Grenier, 2019).

Qualitative research can provide meaningful and in-depth findings behind quantitative research. By way of illustration, quantitative research may establish that a large restaurant chain is losing on average 5% of its customers every six months. Clearly, this figure doesn't tell us why the restaurant chain is losing customers. In this instance, following up with qualitative research can determine the reasons behind the loss in customers.

If you decide to undertake a qualitative research strategy then you intend answering your research questions by collecting qualitative data and analyzing your data using qualitative methods. A qualitative strategy is associated with an inductive approach. Typical examples of data collection methods include interviews, focus groups and observational research. The latter is sometimes paid less attention to than other research methods. Yet, observational research is a commonly used technique for researchers with an interest in consumer behaviour. It also demonstrates that qualitative research not only applies to the 'written or spoken word' but also how individuals behave. We look at observational research in Chapter 13. Other characteristics of qualitative research include the following:

- purpose of the research is on gaining insights and understanding
- uses subjective data, for example interpreting written or spoken words
- aims to obtain meaning from data
- qualitative data collection techniques include focus groups and in-depth interviews.

Qualitative research is commonly associated with 'What' and 'Why' questions, although 'What' questions can also be used when undertaking quantitative research using comparative questions. We look at examples of these later in this section. The following questions all focus on the same research theme 'car brands' and are designed to generate a set of qualitative answers:

- What is your favourite car brand?
- What word do you associate with your chosen car brand?
- Why do you prefer your chosen car brand over other brands?

It is important to note that the term 'qualitative research' can be misleading. This is because researchers sometimes prefer to analyze qualitative data using quantitative methods. For example, you might expect a researcher studying TV coverage devoted to cookery programmes to be adopting a qualitative research strategy. Certainly, observational research of this nature can be viewed as qualitative. However, the research may also be interested in counting the number of hours allocated to TV cookery programmes each week. In this instance, the researcher is carrying out quantitative analysis of qualitative data. Table 5.3 summarizes the advantages and disadvantages associated with conducting qualitative research.

Table 5.3   The advantages and disadvantages of qualitative research

Advantages	Disadvantages
Allows for the development of new theories	Reliability (replicability) can be difficult
Uses subjective data	Researcher bias
Examines challenging research topics that can be impossible to address using quantitative research	Data analysis is especially time consuming
Explores area of research in depth	Resource intensive
The researcher is not detached from their research	No one approach to critical analysis

QUANTITATIVE RESEARCH

Quantitative research is considered by its concern for objective data collection, focus on research control, and development of systematic and consistent procedures. If you decide to adopt a quantitative research strategy, then your research is based on the collection of quantitative data and analysis involving statistical methods. Some students prefer to avoid quantitative research because they are not familiar with statistical methods. However, quantitative research does not have to go beyond descriptive statistics. What is important is that you use appropriate methods that address your research questions. An example of a quantitative research strategy would be a study on the relationship between sales and advertising spend for a leading drinks brand. Examining the relationship between these two variables may focus on the correlation by undertaking statistical analysis. This type of research is based on a relationship-based research question. There are other types of research questions that are designed to generate quantitative answers. These include comparative and descriptive questions. In terms of comparative research questions, emphasis here is on examining the differences between two or more groups on one or more dependent variables. As an example:

What is the difference in the number of hours spent commuting to work each day between managerial and non-managerial employees?

Here, the dependent variable is the number of hours spent commuting to work, while the two groups are (1) managerial employees, (2) non-managerial employees.

Descriptive research questions are designed to describe the variable you are measuring. This type of question may use such terminology as 'How many', 'How much' or 'How frequently'. Using the same research topic that we used for the comparative research question, reworking this to form a descriptive question may read:

How many hours do managerial and non-managerial employees spend each day commuting to work?

Both the comparative and descriptive questions above will give us an objective answer. The unit used for analysis in this case is number of hours. Of course, the type of units used for later quantitative analysis depend on the type of research questions. From an ontological viewpoint, quantitative research is objective in nature, while in relation to an epistemological perspective, the researcher is independent from their research. This independence is underpinned by the data collection method(s) commonly used, such as a questionnaire survey. Administering a survey means that there is often minimal contact and interaction between the researcher and research participants. We have now examined both qualitative and quantitative research. Researchers sometimes discuss qualitative and quantitative research in the context of a dichotomy between these two strategies. However, there is third option – mixed methods or multi-strategy research. We will explore this in the next section.

Table 5.4   Comparing qualitative and quantitative research

	Qualitative research	Quantitative research
Kind of descriptions	General and detailed descriptions, difference in kind	Numerical descriptions, qualifications, difference in number/degree
Cases	Few cases	Many cases
Examples of methods	Focus groups, in-depth interviews, diaries, observations/ethnography, content analysis	Questionnaire surveys, observations, content analysis
Ontology/perception of reality	No reality exists outside perceptions	The reality is independent of our perceptions
Epistemology/theory of knowledge	Knowledge is subjective, bias cannot be avoided	Aim to collect objective data
Generalization to population at large	Limited potential	Possible (if accurate sampling)

Source: Dahlberg and McCaig (2010)

MIXED METHODS (MULTI-STRATEGY RESEARCH)

Gorard (2001: 5) refers to two extreme viewpoints about numerical data – 'numbers are fab' and 'numbers are rubbish'. He points out that he regularly encounters among students and researchers, in essence, two extreme viewpoints and that without a combination of approaches we are often left with a lack of clarity of deciding between competing conclusions. Combining these approaches, or more specifically integrating qualitative and quantitative research, is often referred to as 'mixed methods'.

Research that involves the integration of quantitative and qualitative research is being increasingly used by researchers (Bryman, 2006). Tashakkori and Teddlie (1998: 17–18) view mixed method studies as those that 'combine the qualitative and quantitative approaches into the research methodology of a single study or multi-phased study'. Students often set out to use mixed methods. In some cases, method is a starting point. However, you need to be aware that choosing mixed methods is not always a necessity and depends on your research questions. Certainly, research strategy should not be viewed as a dichotomy between qualitative and quantitative. Mixed methods research is associated with a pragmatist approach to doing research. Let us say that you intend researching the shopping habits of a group of millennial business professionals. The first phase of your research might involve conducting a focus group with 6–8 people to explore themes associated with shopping. Phase two in your research may entail developing a questionnaire survey on the basis of the research findings from your focus group. This follow up study would be to a much larger representative sample with a view to generalizing your results to the wider population. You will find that in the literature mixed methods are sometimes referred to as 'multi-strategy'. Bryman (2006: 97–98) refers to three approaches or terms associated with the combining of qualitative and quantitative research – 'multi-strategy' (Bryman, 2004), 'multi-methods' (Brannen, 1992) and 'mixed methods' (Creswell, 2003; Tashakkori and Teddlie, 1998).

One of the arguments supporting the adoption of mixed methods research is that qualitative and quantitative methods rest on different paradigm assumptions and cannot be easily combined. Mixed methods also raise a number of challenges for researchers. The first of these is time. As a student researcher, you will have limited time in which to complete your research. This becomes even more of a challenge if doing a work-based project as you may also have work commitments on top of your study. Second, resources can be an issue, especially if travelling to various destinations to conduct interviews. Finally, not all researchers have the required skills to do mixed methods research. Researchers sometimes have a preference and better skill set with either qualitative or quantitative research.

WHICH RESEARCH STRATEGY SHOULD I CHOOSE FOR MY RESEARCH PROJECT?

The answer to this question is three-fold. First, consider the type of research questions you developed in order to address your research problem. If your questions are 'Why' and 'How' questions then your research is likely to be exploratory in nature. In other words, emphasis is on generating interesting insights and depth in your study. These types of questions are usually associated with qualitative research. In contrast, quantitative research is often based on the testing of a set of hypotheses. If your research aims to test a set of hypotheses developed from a particular theory, then your research will typically involve quantitative analysis. This is certainly the case if your intention is to analyze relationships between variables and are concerned with objective measures. Alternatively, you may decide that to fully address your research questions you need to undertake a mixed methods piece of research that 'captures' both the qualitative and quantitative aspects of your research problem. An essential question here is – How do I combine the different methods? For example, you may decide to opt for a two-phase study by moving from qualitative to quantitative. Conversely, another option would be to begin with quantitative research, before starting qualitative data collection. We explore the different approaches to data collection later in the book.

VALIDITY AND RELIABILITY IN QUALITATIVE AND QUANTITATIVE RESEARCH

The issues of validity and reliability are considered in different ways in qualitative and quantitative research. In simple terms, validity is defined as 'is one measuring what one intends to measure?' (Frankfort and Nachmias, 1992: 158). In other words, it refers to the relationship between a construct and its indicators. Researchers may use multiple indicators when measuring a particular construct. By way of example, if a researcher wanted to measure the performance of a sales team, they could use number of sales as an indicator of success. However, this is one objective measure and is certainly not the only measure of the sales teams' success. In simple terms, indicators here can be divided on the basis of objective and subjective measures. This includes profit, customer satisfaction, employee satisfaction and so on. Thus, by using multiple indicators such as these the researcher can create a measure that covers the construct (in this case, 'performance') in its entirety. Another way to think of validity in simple terms, is that the researcher's conclusion is either true or correct (McBurney and White, 2009). One analogy to illustrate the difference between reliability and validity is to consider measuring shoe size to determine footballing ability. A researcher may measure someone's shoe size every day for a week and generate the same results. In this sense, the test is reliable as it provides consistent results. However, it is not valid as shoe size does not have anything to do with footballing ability.

There are several different types of validity. However, Calder et al. (1982: 240) list four types of validity to consider when designing and analyzing a research project – internal validity, construct validity, external validity and statistical conclusion validity. We can add a fifth type to this list, namely content validity, which we examine later in this section. The types of validity include:

- Internal validity – which addresses whether or not an observed covariation should be considered a causal relationship.
- Construct validity – which considers whether or not the operational variables used to observe covariation can be interpreted in terms of theoretical constructs.
- External validity – which examines whether or not an observed causal relationship should be generalized to and across different measures, persons, settings and times.
- Statistical conclusion validity – which refers to whether or not statistical inference or covariation between variables is justified.

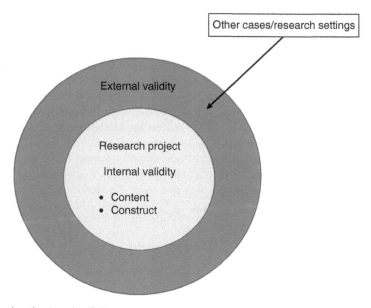

Figure 5.3   Internal and external validity

Figure 5.3 illustrates validity on the basis of *internal* and *external* validity. Internal validity can be broken down into *content* and *construct*. In the next section, we examine the different types of validity more closely.

INTERNAL VALIDITY

Internal validity refers to how well an experiment is done. It examines the extent to which a study provides evidence of a cause-and-effect relationship between the independent and dependent variables. An experimental design has internal validity if you believe that you have solid reason to believe that a cause-and-effect relationship has taken place. For example, let us say you ran an experiment on the effect of music on purchasing behaviour. Group A conducted the experiment listening to classical music, while group B conducted the experiment listening to rock music. Group A were tested on a Sunday, while Group B participants were tested on a Monday. There are two issues with this experiment. The first is that each group were subjected to different types of music. Second, each group was tested on a different day of the week. Thus, it is impossible to assign any changes in the differences in purchasing behaviour to music or day of the week. As a result, this experiment lacks internal validity because we cannot conclude that the music caused the results. This particular problem when undertaking an experiment is referred to as 'confounding'. In this example, time was confounded with music as each variable was not tested separately. There are a number of confounding variables that could affect purchasing behaviour, examples including the shopping environment, retailer, pricing, etc. How do you know which are the confounding variables? It is impossible to make allowances for all confounding variables. Often, it is simply a matter of judgment. By way of an example, researchers interested in carrying out a blind taste test on a new brand of health drink will be aware that eating or drinking shortly before the test may invalidate the results. This is why research participants are advised not to eat or drink anything up to two hours before taking part in the experiment.

You can control for confounding variables. The way to do this is by trying to make sure that all of the research participants in each group are comparable in terms of characteristics. Going back to the new brand of health drink example – if the brand is aimed at a predominantly millennial, female market, then both groups need to share the same characteristics.

It is not always possible to determine a straightforward cause-and-effect relationship. For example, if you establish a positive association between stress in the workplace and alcohol consumption. Does alcohol consumption lead to greater stress in the workplace? Or does stress in the workplace lead to greater alcohol consumption?

There are two main types of internal validity – content and construct validity. The former we examine more closely later in this section. First, *Face validity* is also often viewed as a type of internal validity. This concerns the extent to which an instrument appears (at face value) to measure what it is supposed to measure. As an example, in order to address face validity when conducting a questionnaire survey, you can ask your research supervisor to check the content and type of questions. Alternatively, if doing a survey as part of a work-based project you may ask your immediate line manager to check the structure and type of questions. Asking both your supervisor and mentor or manager can lead to increased validity. Of course, in order for there to be validity there needs to be agreement among the experts or specialists who check the questionnaire.

In qualitative studies internal validity can be addressed in a number of ways. These include:

- using multiple researchers
- expert checking
- conducting a literature review
- keeping an audit trail.

First, using multiple researchers, such as working as part of a research team, means that other people are able to contribute and validate the analysis. Similarly, expert checking may involve your research supervisor and/or manager checking the validity of your results. In particular, your research supervisor will be familiar with research methods and understand the significance of validating your analysis. Conducting a literature review means that your results can be compared with those of earlier studies. It is essential to examine to what extent your results correspond to or contradict with studies of a similar nature. Finally, keeping an audit trail is important when presenting your research findings. An audit trail is a lucid description of the research process from the beginning of your research project to the presentation of your findings.

CONSTRUCT VALIDITY

Construct validity is particularly important in quantitative research. Yin (2003: 34) defined it as 'establishing correct operational measures for the concepts being studied'. Examples of constructs include trust, commitment, attitude and satisfaction. A construct is valid to the extent that it measures what it is supposed to measure. For example, does an IQ test actually measure intelligence or some other variable/s? Using questions that have been pre-tested using a pilot study, and are also based on relevant literature, is one method of aiming for construct validity.

EXTERNAL VALIDITY

External validity is the extent to which the findings from your study can be generalized to other cases or settings. External validity tends to be more important to those researchers who have adopted a positivist approach to their study. A positivist researcher will often strive to claim generalizability of their results. This is where sampling becomes important; the aim is to achieve a representative sample. For those researchers who tend to adopt an interpretivist approach, particularly through case study research design, the intention is often not to generalize. The purpose of the research is to explain a particular case in the context of one particular research setting. This is often to provide new insights that can later be followed up with research that looks at the potential to generalize.

External validity can be difficult to achieve in a study based on qualitative research. This is due to qualitative studies typically being based on case studies and small samples. Clearly, a small sample size is unlikely to be representative of the entire population, thereby making it difficult to argue external validity. However, there are steps that researchers can take in order to address external validity. One of these is to keep a lucid, accurate account of your research so that others can make a judgment as to the extent that the research findings from your research are generalizable.

STATISTICAL CONCLUSION VALIDITY

Statistical conclusion validity refers to the degree to which statistical analyses lead to good conclusions. This type of validity is based on quantitative data. By way of an example, let us say that you conducted research to establish if doubling marketing spend is more effective than keeping the current annual spend. Having analyzed the data, you conclude that there is a positive relationship between doubling the marketing spend and an increase in sales. Conclusion validity will illustrate how reliable that conclusion is.

CONTENT VALIDITY

Content validity is concerned with the extent to which a test covers all of the essential items in order to measure a particular behaviour or trait. Thus, it is key that the content of the test matches what is being taught to individuals. By way of an example, a one-day intensive course on learning to drive is designed to provide all of the information required to pass the driving test. The course is taught by former examiners who are familiar with the driving test and know the types of questions you are likely to find in the test paper. The former examiners will make sure that what is delivered on the one-day course matches the material included in the driving test. The examiners will want to ensure that their learning methods increase the likelihood that you will pass the test. One way that they ensure this is to hold a mock test based on exam conditions, thereby increasing levels of content validity.

WHAT ARE THE THREATS TO VALIDITY?

The following list, adapted from Robson (1993), highlights the main considerations.

Effects of pre-testing

Conducting a pre-test may impact the validity of your results when carrying out your actual study. For example, if you do research on employee satisfaction using a pilot study made up of a small sample of employees, then decide to use the same employees in the main test, you may find that they opt to change or alter their answers.

History

A relevant historical occurrence may impact the validity of your research findings. For example, if a researcher carried out a survey on consumer perceptions of a leading food brand 24 hours before a product recall, this is likely to have a significant influence on research findings.

Instrumentation

This threat refers to how instruments are used in the research. If a restaurant has received an instruction that they are going to receive a visit from a health inspector then they are going to make sure that the restaurant meets the health and safety standards required. However, if the following year the standards and the instrument used to measure health and safety becomes more rigorous, then changes in the restaurant's rating may not be due to health and safety, but to changes in the instrument used to measure ratings.

Mortality

This refers to participants dropping out of a research study. You may find that there is a greater likelihood of this happening if your participants are engaged in demanding jobs, e.g. those in management positions. Mortality rates can be particularly problematic if conducting longitudinal research based on different demographics, particularly baby boomers. Unfortunately, death is also a contributing factor to mortality rate in research studies. In short, if your research is based on a longitudinal design, there is a greater risk of higher drop-out rates.

Maturation

The *maturation effect* is when any biological or psychological process within an individual that occurs with the passage of time has an impact on research findings (Frey, 2018). Let us say that your research focuses on a longitudinal design (over 12 months) into technology skills of different age groups. Results of the experiment might be influenced by participants becoming more knowledgeable about technology. Maturation is considered a threat to validity when it has not been considered in the research.

If you recall, earlier in the chapter we looked at internal validity in the context of qualitative research. The section below goes further by examining more closely some of the ways to improve validity when conducting qualitative research (adapted from Mays and Pope, 2000).

1. *Methodological triangulation.* This compares the results from either two or more different methods of data collection or two or more data sources. An example here would be comparing data from focus groups and an online survey. The researcher looks for patterns of convergence in the data to develop or substantiate an overall interpretation.
2. *Respondent validation.* This includes techniques in which the researcher's account is compared with those of the research participants to establish the level of correspondence between the two sets. Research participants' reactions to the analyses are then incorporated into the research findings. This also generates further original data, which in turn requires interpretation.
3. *Clear exposition of data collection and analysis.* It is important to have a clear account of the process of data collection and analysis. In particular, how early classification evolved into more detailed coding structures.

4. *Reflexivity*. This is defined as sensitivity to the ways in which the researcher and the research process have shaped the collected data, including the role of prior assumptions and experience. Any personal and intellectual biases need to be clearly stated at the beginning of the research in order to enhance the credibility of findings. Potential biases are not something that should be shared late in the research process.

5. *Attention to negative cases*. Qualitative research can be improved by searching for, and discussing elements in the data that contradict, or seem to contradict, the emerging explanation of the phenomenon under study.

6. *Fair dealing*. It is important to ensure that the research design explicitly incorporates a wide range of different perspectives so that the viewpoint of one group never dominates the findings but rather that these results represent the whole truth about a situation.

RELIABILITY

Reliability concerns the extent to which a measurement of a phenomenon provides stable and consistent results (Carmines and Zeller, 1979). It is also concerned with the extent that a study can be replicated. This is difficult when conducting qualitative research as the research is subjective and typically based on a snapshot of time. In quantitative research, particularly if undertaking an experiment, a test is said to be reliable if repeat measurements made by it under constant conditions will give the same result (Moser and Kalton, 1989: 353).

When conducting your research, it is necessary to view the quality of your research both in terms of validity and reliability. For example, if you use a pedometer to count the number of steps you take on your daily commute to work, the device may register a total of 3,400 steps. However, you later realize that a malfunction with the device results in an additional 500 steps being added to the final total. This occurs every day for the entire month. Notably, the number of steps calculated each day is reliable as the pedometer counts the same number of steps each day. However, we cannot say the results are valid as the device adds an additional 500 steps walked on to every journey.

There are three main types of reliability: inter-judgmental reliability, testing and retesting reliability, and parallel forms of reliability.

Inter-judgmental reliability

Inter-judgmental reliability is used to establish the extent to which individuals with the required skills and/or authority agree in their assessment decisions. For example, if conducting research as part of a work-based project you may seek to promote inter-judgmental reliability by consulting with your research supervisor, mentor or other research stakeholders. Inter-judgmental reliability is commonly undertaken in qualitative research, given the subjective nature of the research.

Testing and retesting reliability

Testing and retesting reliability relates to the measurement of the same reliability test on more than one occasion. Research of this nature is conducted over an extended period of time using the same research participants. By way of an example, let us say that you administered an online survey to assess employees' views on the outcomes of an organizational restructure. The survey can then be administered on two separate occasions, three months apart. The feedback from time 1 (T1) and time 2 (T2) can then be correlated to see if there is a relationship between them.

Parallel forms of reliability

Parallel forms of reliability measures reliability that uses two different types of assessment tools. Each tool must contain items that are intended to measure the same things. It must also be carried out on the same group of individuals. The scores from the two versions can then be correlated in order to evaluate the consistency of results across alternative versions. For example, if a researcher intended to test the reliability of strategic knowledge assessment, you may develop a large set of items that all apply to strategic knowledge and then randomly divide the questions up into two sets, which would represent the parallel forms.

WHAT ARE THE THREATS TO RELIABILITY?

There are a number of threats to reliability. Examples include subject error, time error and observer-caused effects. These are examined below:

Subject error

Subject error refers to the nature of the subjects being observed. For example, let us say that you were interested in the purchasing behaviour of food buyers at a local food festival. Your methodology may involve collecting data by observing buyers at the festival. However, if the intended subjects in your research are individual buyers, then you may find that on certain days or at certain times the festival is largely attended by organizational buyers. Thus, potential observation of organizational buyers is an example of subject error – rather than solely observing individual buyers, your observations also include those working for business buyers.

Subject error can also be associated with bias. Continuing with the food festival example, if you decided to conduct interviews with festival attendees on the first day of the event, you may find that the majority of those attending are in some way connected with the organization of the event. Hence, when questioning the people on the quality of the event, there is the potential for subject bias.

Time error

Time error is also a threat to reliability. By way of illustration, let us say that you decided to conduct research into customer loyalty. Your proposed measure for this study is the number of times customers visit the retailer in question during a four-week period. There are two issues here. The first is that the number of visits does not necessarily measure customer loyalty. Second, if people had recently been sent discount vouchers through the post, then this means that the number of visits measured at this time may not be a 'true' reflection of people's shopping habits. An approach to address potential time error is to adopt a longitudinal research design.

Observer-caused effects

Observer-caused effects concerns the researcher undertaking observational research and the effect this might have on research participants. For example, a field researcher's presence may cause the research participants to change their behaviour and communication. If this occurs, then clearly the researcher is not observing the participants in their natural setting. Conducting research based on a work-based project can be problematic for this reason. If part of your research is to observe your fellow employees' behaviour in the workplace, how do your colleagues view your role? If they are aware of your research then there is a likelihood that this will ultimately change their behaviour. Potentially, one solution to this fear of a change in behaviour is to take on the role of a covert observer. In other words, you observe the subjects in the research setting, but do so without their knowledge. However, be aware that carrying out research of a covert nature does have ethical implications, particularly in terms of how you will use the data. For example, will it be broadcast across social media? A more ethical approach is to advise those subjects that you are observing them, and will do so over an extended period of time. This is in the hope that over time they will become familiar with your presence and will be more likely to maintain their 'normal' behaviour.

Observer influence can also relate to possible bias on the part of the researcher. Let us say that you are studying the role of management within your own family business. Your observations may suggest a possible positive bias towards those managers who are family members. In all fairness, this may be something that has arisen subconsciously. Given this, it is worth reflecting on your role as an observer.

We conclude this chapter with a discussion on the interrelationship between the first three elements of research methodology. Again, elements four, five and six, namely research design, data collection and data analysis are explored later in the book. When considering your methodological approach to your research, it is important that you consider this relationship. Your choice of methodology is largely determined by the nature of your research topic and type of research questions. In your research project, the marker will be looking for you to justify your choice of methodology. A key argument you can make is that it is the 'right' methodology in order to address your research questions. In addition, your argument can be supported by earlier research that has adopted the same or a similar methodological approach. For example, you might argue that you have adopted an interpretivist philosophical stance, inductive approach and qualitative strategy as the current body of literature is dominated by positivist, quantitative-based studies. Thus, your research is clearly adding to the extant literature on your chosen area of research.

CHAPTER SUMMARY

- Your research methodology is the overarching approach to the research. The methodology consists of research philosophy, research strategy, research approach, research design, data collection and data analysis.

- Research philosophy relates to the development of knowledge and the nature of that knowledge.

- When evaluating your philosophical stance, be sure to consider epistemology, ontology and axiology.

- Approaches to research include deductive, inductive and abductive. Reflecting on the quality of your research considers both validity and reliability.

- Reliability concerns the extent to which a measurement of a phenomenon provides stable and consistent results.

- When considering qualitative and quantitative research strategies, note that this is not a straightforward dichotomy of two strategies. There is also the option to use mixed methods.

QUESTIONS FOR REVIEW

1. What are the different types of research philosophies?

2. Explain the nature of axiology.

3. Why might a researcher decide to adopt an inductive approach?

4. Outline an example of the first three elements of methodological approach for your own research. Your answer should include research philosophy, research strategy and research approach. Give reasons for your answer.

5. Give examples of different types of validity.

6. How might you improve validity when conducting qualitative research?

7. What are the threats to reliability?

8. Explain what you understand by the term 'mixed methods' or 'multi-strategy'.

STUDENT SCENARIO: MARCEL'S RESEARCH DIARY

Marcel decided to arrange a meeting with his research supervisor as he was unsure as to the methodological approach to adopt for his research project. The nature of Marcel's research was on employee perceptions on post-mergers and acquisitions. He had made significant progress with his literature review, although only identified a small number of authors in his area of research. However, what was clear from his literature review was that there was no one dominant methodological approach adopted by researchers. Marcel was hoping that by reviewing the literature he would be able to develop his ideas on his own choice of research methodology. Given his uncertainty, Marcel decided to arrange a meeting with his research supervisor to discuss how he should approach his methodology.

Marcel's meeting with his research supervisor

At the meeting, Marcel's supervisor asked him to reflect on his role as a researcher. Although Marcel had a clear research timetable, he admitted to largely focusing on each of the tasks, without devoting time to reflecting on his progress. Marcel's supervisor suggested that reflective practice should start with his research topic, followed by research problem and research questions. Marcel's research questions included 'How do employees respond to a merger or acquisition?' together with, 'Why do mergers and acquisitions take place?'. Marcel's supervisor also asked him to think about his role as a researcher from a philosophical viewpoint. In this respect, Marcel considered his epistemological approach to be that of interpretivism. His supervisor then asked him to think about other elements of research methodology, and the relationship with research philosophy and research questions. Marcel soon learned that the two key factors that would influence his choice of methodology were the nature of his research questions and his role as a researcher.

Outcomes

Following the discussion with his research supervisor, Marcel was able to outline his chosen methodological approach. Again, this approach was largely determined on the basis of his research questions – 'How' and 'Why' questions – and his role as a researcher – 'interpretivist'. Thus, Marcel's methodology was to follow an interpretivist philosophical stance, adopt an inductive approach (given the small number of researchers in his area of research) and a qualitative research strategy. Finally, Marcel recognized the importance of not just completing each of his research tasks, but to also reflect on his progress throughout his research. To support this, he started using a research diary to record each of his research tasks, the outcomes and reflections on overall progress.

(Continued)

Questions

1. Identify some of the research tasks Marcel might include in his research diary.
2. What are the advantages of keeping a research diary?

Hint: You may want to think about all stages in the research process when considering the tasks that Marcel might enter into his research diary.

FURTHER READING

Brinkmann, S. (2018) *Philosophies of Qualitative Research*. New York: Oxford University Press.

This book introduces philosophies associated with qualitative research and defines key terms, such as research philosophy and epistemology.

Bryman, A. (2006) 'Integrating quantitative and qualitative research: How is it done?', *Qualitative Research*, 6 (1): 97–113.

An interesting article that is based on a content analysis of 232 studies that combine qualitative and quantitative research.

Flick, U. (2018) *An Introduction to Qualitative Research* (6th edn). London: Sage.

Chapter 1 provides a clear introduction to qualitative research, while Chapter 2 examines combining qualitative and quantitative research.

REFERENCES

Brannen, J. (1992) 'Combining qualitative and quantitative approaches: An overview', in J. Brannen (ed.), *Mixing Methods: Qualitative and Quantitative Research* (pp. 3–37). Aldershot: Avebury.

Bryman, A. (2004) *Social Research Methods*. Oxford: Oxford University Press.

Bryman, A. (2006) 'Integrating qualitative and quantitative research: How is it done?', *Qualitative Research*, 6 (1): 97–113.

Bryman, A. (2016) *Social Research Methods* (5th edn). Oxford: Oxford University Press.

Burrell, G. and Morgan, G. (1979) *Sociological Paradigms and Organizational Analysis*. Aldershot: Gower.

Calder, B.J., Phillips, L.W. and Tybout, A.M. (1982) 'The concept of external validity', *Journal of Consumer Research*, 9: 240–244.

Carmines, E.G. and Zeller, R.A. (1979) *Reliability and Validity Assessment*. Newbury Park, CA: Sage.

Collis, J. and Hussey, R. (2009) *Business Research: A Practical Guide for Undergraduate and Postgraduate Students* (3rd edn). Basingstoke: Palgrave Macmillan.

Creswell, J.W. (2003) *Research Design: Qualitative, Quantitative and Mixed Methods Approaches* (2nd edn). Thousand Oaks, CA: Sage.

Crotty, M. (1998) *The Foundations of Social Research: Meaning and Perspective in the Research Process*. Thousand Oaks, CA: Sage.

Dahlberg, L. and McCaig, C. (eds) (2010) *Practical Research and Evaluation: A Start-to-finish Guide for Practitioners*. London: Sage.

Denzin, N.K. and Lincoln, Y.S. (2005) *Handbook of Qualitative Research* (3rd edn). Thousand Oaks, CA: Sage.

Easterby-Smith, M., Thorpe, R. and Jackson, P.R. (2012) *Management Research* (4th edn). London: Sage.

Frankfort-Nachmias, C. and Nachmias, D. (1992) *Research Methods in the Social Sciences* (4th edn). London: St Martin's Press.

Frey, B. (2018). *The SAGE Encyclopedia of Educational Research, Measurement, and Evaluation* (Vols. 1-4). Thousand Oaks, CA: Sage.

Gorard, S. (2001) *Quantitative Methods in Educational Research: The Role of Numbers Made Easy*. London: Bloomsbury Publishing.

Greene, J.C. (2007) *Mixed Methods in Social Enquiry*. San Francisco, CA: John Wiley & Sons.

Guba, E.G. (1990) *The Alternative Paradigm Dialog*. Newbury Park, CA: Sage.

Hakim, C. (2012) *Research Design: Successful Designs for Social and Economic Research*. New York: Routledge.

Hudson, L.A. and Ozanne, J.L. (1988) 'Alternative ways of seeking knowledge in consumer research', *Journal of Consumer Research*, 14: 508–521.

Hyde, K.F. (2000) 'Recognising deductive processes in qualitative research', *Qualitative Market Research: An International Journal*, 3 (2): 82–89.

Kuhn, T.S. (2012) *The Structure of Scientific Revolutions* (2nd edn). University of Chicago Press.

Mays, N. and Pope, C. (2000) 'Qualitative research in healthcare: Addressing quality in qualitative research', *British Medical Journal*, 320 (1st Jan): 50–52.

McBurney, D.H. and White, T.L. (2009) *Research Methods* (8th edn). Belmont, CA: Cengage Learning.

Merriam, S.B. and Grenier, R.S. (2019) *Qualitative Research in Practice: Examples for Discussion and Analysis* (2nd edn). San Francisco: Jossey-Bass.

Moser, C.A. and Kalton, G. (1989) *Survey Methods in Social Investigation*. Aldershot: Gower.

Patton, M.Q. (1987) *How to Use Qualitative Methods in Evaluation*. Newbury Park, CA: Sage.

Plano Clark, V.L. and Creswell, J.W. (2008) *The Mixed Methods Reader*. Thousand Oaks, CA: Sage.

Porter, M.E. (1980) *Competitive Strategy*. New York: Free Press.

Robson, C. (1993) *Real World Research*. Oxford: Blackwell.

Tashakkori, A. and Teddlie, C. (1998) *Mixed Methodology: Combining Qualitative and Quantitative Approaches* (Applied Social Research Methods Series Volume 46). London: Sage.

Tashakkori, A. and Teddlie, C. (2009) *Foundations of Mixed Methods Research: Integrating Qualitative and Quantitative Approaches in the Social and Behavioural Sciences*. Thousand Oaks, CA: Sage.

Wilson, J.S. (2014) *Essentials of Business Research: A Guide to Doing Your Research Project*. London: Sage.

Yin, R.K. (2003) *Case Study Research: Design and Methods* (3rd edn). Thousand Oaks, CA: Sage.

6

FORMULATING THE RESEARCH DESIGN

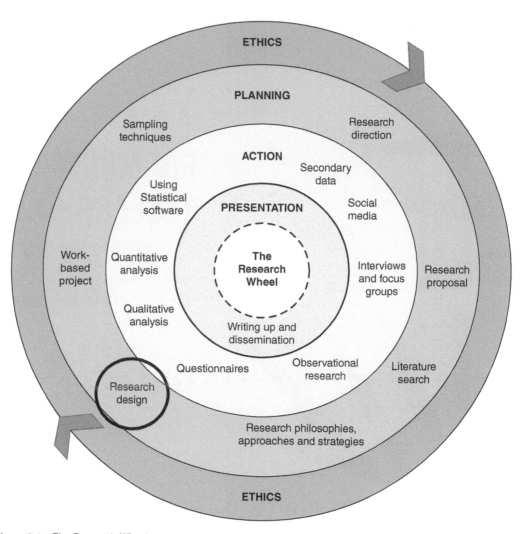

Figure 6.1   The Research Wheel

INTRODUCTION

The purpose of this chapter is to define research design and discuss the different types of research designs for you to consider when conducting your research. Think of your *research design* as a plan or framework that is intended to help you to achieve your research questions. Choosing your research design is an important part of the research process as it is likely to influence later stages in your research, especially how you decide to collect and analyze your data.

As you can see from Figure 6.1, The Research Wheel shows that we have now arrived at the research design element in the research process. This element is part of the 'Planning' layer in The Research Wheel because research design is part of your planned methodological approach. Exploring research design options also means considering the possibility of combining research designs, which we will consider later in the chapter.

Selecting a research design can be a difficult decision as there are an array of choices available to the researcher. Furthermore, each research design is not mutually exclusive so you may find that you decide to combine different designs when doing your research. The intention of this chapter is to help you to make these decisions. The chapter starts by examining what we mean by the term 'research design' and the purpose of research design. Next, we consider what can be referred to as 'types' of research studies.

Following this, we explore types of research design, including case study research. This type of design is a common feature in business and management research and is almost certainly a type of design you are likely to have come across as part of your degree programme. However, have you ever wondered what is meant by the term 'case study research' and how it might be used as part of your research? This is something we examine in detail later in this chapter.

A key consideration when selecting a research design(s) is how much time you intend spending on your research. This is the time-bound or time horizon associated with your study. In essence, there are two options here – cross-sectional and longitudinal. We consider both options and explain how they relate to different types of research design. Next, the chapter explores ways to combine different types of research design and comparative research designs. The chapter concludes by looking at whether there is one 'best' research design, how to select your research design and examples of research design.

WHAT IS RESEARCH DESIGN?

There is no one universally accepted definition of research design. To confuse matters, researchers sometimes use the terms 'research design' and 'methodology' interchangeably. You will also find in the literature that there is a lack of consensus as to what constitutes a research design. In my view, it is not so much the definitions you use, but that you are consistent throughout your project and clearly reference your work.

Let us look at some of the definitions given for the term 'research design'. Punch (2014: 114) defines research design as 'at the most general level it means all the issues involved in planning and executing a research project – from identifying a problem through to reporting and publishing the results'. This definition refers to planning. In this sense, research design is part of the planning process, as we saw in Figure 6.1.

Similarly, the definition by Van Wyk and Taole refers to research design as 'the blueprint which directs you in finding your way towards executing your plan for your research methodology' (2015: 164). In other words, research design is not just about planning, but helps to direct other elements of research methodology. For example, your choice of research design is related to other elements of methodology, namely, research philosophy, research approach, research strategy, data collection and analytical techniques.

Rowley (2002: 19) points out that research design contains the following components:

- the study's questions
- the study's propositions
- the study's units of analysis
- the logic linking the data to the propositions
- the criteria for interpreting findings.

Rowley's (2002) definition is more closely associated with methodology or perhaps the research process as it refers to 'the study's questions' and 'interpreting findings'. However, it is clear from the

Image 6.1   A key characteristic of research design is 'planning'

Source: iStock (photo ID: 1074983828)

many definitions of research design that a key characteristic is 'planning' and how the researcher intends to conduct their research. Hence, we can define research design as '*A detailed framework or plan that helps to guide you through the research process, allowing a greater likelihood of achieving your research objectives*'.

The term 'research design' relates to the choices and decisions you make about your research questions. Research designs are generally related to the following type of research questions (in brackets). The first three terms below are types of studies. We will examine these later in the chapter.

- Exploratory (Why)
- Descriptive (Who, Where, What, When, Which, How)
- Causal or experimental (Cause-and-effect)
- Case study (How, Why)
- Action research (How)
- Cross-sectional (Who, What, Where, How many, How much)
- Longitudinal (Who, What, Where, How many, How much)
- Comparative (How, Why, What)
- Archival (Who, What, Where, How many, How much)

WHAT IS THE PURPOSE OF A RESEARCH DESIGN?

Prior to selecting a research design(s), it is important to understand the function of your research design and the criteria to use when making your selection. For example, Blumberg et al. (2005: 195) make the following points in relation to the purpose of research design:

- the design is always based on the research question
- the design is an activity and time-based plan
- the design guides the selection of sources and types of information
- the design is a framework for specifying the relationships among the study's variables
- the design outlines procedures for every research activity.

The above points made by Blumberg et al. (2005) illustrate the interrelationship between your research questions, selection of sources (literature) and research procedures. The latter can be interpreted as how you intend to collect and analyze your data. As is a common theme in research, elements of the research process are interrelated. In other words, for example, the type of research questions you choose are likely to impact your choice of research design.

TYPES OF RESEARCH STUDIES

It is essential to understand the type of research study you intend conducting from the point of view of your overall purpose or objective. Research projects are undertaken for different purposes or objectives. These can be categorized as exploratory, descriptive or causal (explanatory). Each type of research is very much related to your chosen research direction, in particular, the nature of your research questions. In this section, we examine each of these types of research and give examples of research questions that are typically associated with each one.

Table 6.1   Types of research studies

	Exploratory	Descriptive	Causal (explanatory)
Purpose	Conducting research into a problem where there currently exists very little, if any, literature on the area of research.	Descriptive research seeks to describe existing or past phenomena. For example, describing a population based on important variables.	Causal research studies place a major emphasis on determining cause-and-effect relationships and is involved with learning 'why'.
Research statement	Questions	Questions	Hypotheses
Type of questions	Why	Who, Where, What, When, Which, How	Cause-and-effect
Examples of research objectives	An investigation into the ways of improving employee retention in the UK car manufacturing industry. A study into the role of sustainable packaging as an effective means of attracting new customers. An investigation into the ways to develop more efficient batteries in the Australian electric bicycle market.	To determine the number of students who shop at ABC supermarket. To estimate the proportion of over 50s in Canada who take skiing holidays. To establish the most frequent mode of market entry method among US multinational organizations.	To assess the impacts of foreign direct investment on economic growth in China. To analyze the effects of a new training programme on staff morale. To assess the impact of a customer reward scheme on the levels of customer satisfaction.

EXPLORATORY RESEARCH

Exploratory research is associated with research whereby the researcher conducts research into a problem where there currently exists very little, if any, literature on the area of research. An example here might be a researcher interested in the views of consumers on the use of facial recognition in paying for products. Given this type of technology is relatively new and there currently exists limited literature on this subject, the researcher is interested in gaining insights and a better understanding of the research topic. In essence, an exploratory research study is used if there is little or no data on a particular topic and limited sources.

There are three commonly used ways of conducting exploratory research – searching the literature, interviewing experts in the subject and conducing focus groups interviews. Of these three ways, we examined searching the literature in Chapter 4. The other two ways we explore in Chapter 12. Exploratory research studies typically use data collection methods associated with qualitative research. This includes observational research, in-depth interviews, focus groups and historical analysis.

Sometimes exploratory research is the prerequisite to causal research. The outcomes of the exploratory research may help the researcher to decide on a set of hypotheses that are then tested. These hypotheses may seek to explore cause-and-effect relationships.

Hart and Dewsnap (2001) provided an example of exploratory research in their study of consumer behaviour in the fashion industry. Having recognized that the vast majority of research into consumer decision-making tended to focus on outer clothing apparel, the authors set about carrying out research into inner apparel, the main emphasis being on the purchasing of bras and lingerie. Their rationale for undertaking an exploratory study was that little attention had been paid to their chosen topic within the existing literature.

Another characteristic of exploratory research is that it is unstructured informal research undertaken to gather background information about a research problem. Once again, it is all about discovering insights. Hence, research questions often linked to exploratory research are 'Why' questions. For example, 'Why has Organization X experienced a decrease in market share?'. Exploratory research can also be used to address a research problem that lacks clarity and may involve the collection of secondary data.

DESCRIPTIVE RESEARCH

Descriptive research seeks to describe existing or past phenomena. For example, describing a population based on important variables. The key features of descriptive research are structure, precise rules and procedures (Ghauri and Grønhaug, 2005). Public opinion polls are typically descriptive in nature as they seek to describe the proportion of respondents who hold various views. By way of example, if you want to know what percentage of the population would be interested in switching to renewable energy, then participants are expected to give a descriptive answer.

Descriptive research provides answers to questions such as Who, Where, What and How. For example, understanding the frequency in relation to product usage or number of times a consumer visits a particular retailer or 'What is the average age of mobile phone users?'. Descriptive research can be either qualitative or quantitative, although it is usually associated with a quantitative research strategy as the intention is to collect quantifiable data to be used for statistical analysis. Researchers often use a survey method to collect data, and similar to exploratory research, descriptive studies are often preliminary studies that lead to further research.

An advantage of undertaking descriptive research is that studies typically provide accurate information, e.g. descriptive statistics. They also present useful information for decision-making. However, one criticism of descriptive studies is that they do not determine cause-and-effect relationships. Further, a series of 'what' questions might mean that your study ends up being too descriptive. A dissertation that is too descriptive is likely to lose marks as you should include critical analysis of your research findings. Also, too much focus on description can degenerate to mindless fact gathering (de Vaus, 2001). Highlighted below are examples of descriptive research questions:

- What is the market share for Neptune PLC?
- What is the current level of customer satisfaction across all of our branches?
- What percentage of participants in the study are British?
- What is the main reason for online shopping among consumers?
- How much money do consumers spend on plastic bags each year?
- How often do employees take part in work-related activities each week?
- How many hours do millennials spend each week watching TV?
- What are the important factors that affect the choice of washing powder among consumers?

CAUSAL RESEARCH

Causal research studies place a major emphasis on determining cause-and-effect relationships and is involved with learning 'why'. For example, in marketing, a commonly researched cause-and-effect relationship is the relationship between an increase in price (cause) and sales (effect).

In a research study by Singh (2018), the researcher explored the cause-and-effect relationship between dependent (job performance) and independent variables (stress dimensions). The author distributed 280 questionnaires among medical representatives to explore the relationships between job stress and job performance. Findings confirmed the impact of job stress on job performance. All the job stressors (work load, role conflict, role ambiguity and inadequate monetary rewards) influence the job performance.

Another term for causal research is explanatory research. The purpose of this type of design is to understand and explain presumed causal links between variables. According to Gavin Dick et al. (2008: 695), causality is usually accepted in empirical research as requiring three conditions:

- there is an association between variables that logically might influence one another
- the causal variable must produce its influence before the outcome occurs
- other possible explanations must be eliminated, such as a third variable that influences both variables.

The presence of cause-and-effect relationships can be established only if specific causal evidence exists. Zikmund and Babin (2006: 54) point to three pieces of causal evidence:

- temporal sequence
- concomitant variance
- nonspurious association.

Temporal sequence

Temporal sequence is concerned with the time order of events. This is one key criterion for causality. It is essential that the cause takes place before the effect. For example, if a car dealership experiences a heavy downturn in sales prior to employing a new marketing manager, they will be unable to hold the marketing manager responsible. Similarly, if a new employee training programme causes an improvement in customer satisfaction scores, then the customer training programme must take place before the change in customer satisfaction scores.

Concomitant variance

Concomitant variance occurs when two events 'covary'. This means that when a change in the cause occurs, a change in the outcome is also observed. Causality cannot exist when there is no systematic variation between the variables. For example, if a company never changes its employee away day programme, then the employee away day programme cannot be responsible for a change in staff morale. Clearly, there is no correlation between the two events. However, if two events vary together, one might be causing the other. If a book retailer starts selling online and finds that it leads to a decrease in sales across traditional retail outlets, then the online retail part of the business might be causing the decrease.

Nonspurious association

Nonspurious association means any covariation between a cause and an effect is true and not simply due to some other variable. 'Spurious' means one that is not true. Often, it can be difficult to make a causal inference because two variables as the association might be influenced by a third variable. For example, let us say that when there is an increase in the number of picnic tables booked in a national park, there are more visitor accidents. Should the park authority ban picnics? No, because the concomitant variation observed between picnic table bookings and accidents is spurious. On days when the park is particularly busy, more picnic tables are booked and more visitors have accidents.

In sum, although there are three different types of research studies, you may find that your research questions have an element of all three types of study. For example, your research questions might seek to explore, describe and examine cause-and-effect relationships. However, remember that what determines the type of study is the nature of your research problem. Often, a research problem is associated with one particular study. A research problem may focus on 'why organization A has decided to enter into a partnership with organization B'. In this example, the nature of the problem suggests that the study is likely to be exploratory in nature.

TYPES OF RESEARCH DESIGN

In the previous section, we examined the three types of research studies. Again, the three types of research are not necessarily mutually exclusive. For example, you may combine exploratory research with causal research. Going back to our earlier example of a research problem that is exploratory in nature – 'why organization A has decided to enter into a partnership with organization B' – an exploratory study could be combined with causal research. For example, the outcomes from your exploratory research findings inform the type of hypotheses you develop and test.

The three research studies, or (sometimes rather confusingly) referred to as the 'three basic research designs', are commonly used in academic and marketing research. Once you have chosen the type of study(s), it is time to think about your research design. In this next section, we will examine the main types of research designs, including perhaps the most commonly used of these designs in business and management – case study research design.

CASE STUDY RESEARCH DESIGN

Students studying business and management are likely to be familiar with the term 'case study' or 'case'; however, when I ask my students to define 'case study' many of them express it in organizational terms. This is understandable, as working on case study-related tasks typically involves analyzing a particular organization or organizations, but is a case study just about organizations? Let us look at some of the definitions of case study.

Swanborn (2010) mentions that a case is not just about an organization(s), but also people, groups, individuals, local communities or nation-states, in which the phenomenon to be studied enrol. From this definition, we can see that 'case' goes beyond simply reference to an organization.

In business and management, investigating a real-life context or scenario encompasses several different case options. Stake (1995) does not view the case study as a method, but the object of study. For Stake (1995: 11), case study research is defined as 'the study of the particularity and complexity of a single case, coming to understand its activity within important circumstances'. Interestingly, Stake's (1995) definition suggests that research is limited to a single case, such as one organization. However, is it possible to examine multiple cases, such as multiple organizations?

Creswell et al. define case study research as 'a qualitative approach in which the investigator explores a bounded system (a case) or multiple bounded systems (cases) over time through detailed, in-depth data collection involving multiple sources of information (e.g. observations, interviews, audio visual material, and documents and reports) and reports a case description and case-based themes' (2007: 33). Comparing the two earlier definitions, there is a lack of consensus in terms of number of cases as Creswell et al. (2007) refer to 'multiple cases' and also refer to a 'qualitative approach'.

Perhaps the most widely cited definition of case study research comes from Robert Yin (2014). The author defines case study as 'an empirical enquiry that investigates a contemporary phenomenon in depth and within its real-life context, especially when the boundaries between phenomenon and context may not be clearly evident.' Robert Yin outlines the following five components of a case study research design:

- a study's questions (How/Why?)
- its propositions/purposes
- its unit of analysis
- the logical linking the data to the propositions
- the criteria for interpreting the findings.

In terms of data collection, case studies typically combine data collection methods such as interviews, archives, questionnaires and observations. Evidence may be qualitative, quantitative or both (Eisenhardt, 1989). In Chapters 11 to 14 we look at different types of primary data collection.

What can we conclude from examining the literature on case study research design? Well, it is clear that there is no one definitive definition of 'case study'. However, there are three commonalities that emerge from the definitions. First, a 'case study' is examining a phenomenon or phenomena in a real-life context. Second, when doing case study research, consider the research questions typically associated with case study research design. Finally, understand the unit(s) of analysis and that a case study has a number of characteristics. These include depth rather than breadth, natural settings and multiple sources and data generation methods. Again, when analyzing definitions in your research, try to adopt a critical approach and be clear on which definition(s) you intend using in your study. For example, if adopting Yin's definition of case study research, be clear as to why and be consistent on the use of the definition throughout your research. Also, I always make it clear to my students that they should justify why they have chosen a particular definition. Possible justification might be because a definition is the most widely used, you want to compare your findings with that of earlier studies or it encapsulates the nature of your research.

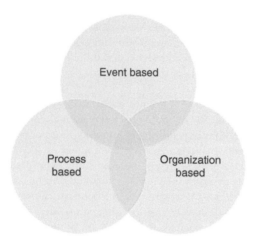

Figure 6.2   Case selection options

In Figure 6.2, you can see that there are three case selection options – process, event and organization. Let us look at each of these in turn. First, an organization can relate to any type of organization. This includes public or private sector, global brand, independent retailer or franchise. Examples of organization case studies include:

- A single organization such as a university, charity, multinational organization – what is happening in terms of a particular strategy.
- A particular community – an issue concerning a community such as a resident's association.

In essence, a researcher choosing an organization as a case study option is interested in investigating an aspect of the organization. This might be how the organization trains its employees, its level of customer service, financial performance or development over time. For example, I might be interested in investigating to what extent Google's organizational culture has changed over the last five years.

Second, an event is another case study option. Although this tends to be less popular amongst students than investigating an organization, it still remains worthy of consideration. Typical events may include a sporting, charity, arts or business event. In terms of the latter, this may comprise a business trade fair or exhibition. For example, in the UK there is an annual Franchise exhibition that attracts leading franchises from around the world. A potential research project might investigate how successful the exhibition is at recruiting new franchisees. Again, the case study in this example is the Franchise exhibition (event).

Finally, a process-based case study is another option for researchers. Examples of a process include marketing, recruitment, planning or internationalization. A process involves a series of steps. So, irrespective of the nature of the process, the purpose of the research project might be to examine each step in the process. Let us look at internationalization as an illustrative example. If you work for a Nigerian-based organization considering entering the German market, then the nature of your research topic may focus on the process of internationalization. In other words, exploring the steps involved when moving from a domestic to an international market.

You will notice that Figure 6.2 illustrates each of these case study options in the form of a Venn diagram. This is because each of the options can be overlapping or interconnected. For example, going back to the franchise example, perhaps you are not only interested in investigating the extent to which the exhibition is successful, but also how it has impacted on a particular organization(s). Similarly, you might be concerned with comparing the corporate planning process of two organizations. In short, each case study option is not mutually exclusive. Doing case study research may involve more than one case study option. Choosing more than one case study option or more than one case is referred to as a 'multiple case study design'. So, a useful starting point for considering case study research is whether you intend doing single or multiple case study research. Table 6.2 shows examples of projects and whether the nature of the research design is either a single or multiple case study.

Table 6.2   Examples of projects involving single or multiple case study research designs

Project	Type of case study design
Investigating consumer perceptions of Ford's latest motor vehicle	Single case study – the case study in this example is Ford (organization).
A comparative case study design – comparing the customer service programme of two leading supermarkets	Multiple case study – in this example there are two cases (two leading supermarkets)
Investigating the process of launching a new product and the impact this will have on organizational culture	Multiple case study – this is a multiple case study using two case study options (process and organization based)
Analyzing the experience of those attendees at the London 2012 Olympics	Single case study – this is an example of a single event-based case study
Investigating the process and impact on an organization when launching a new brand of lawn mower at a horticulture exhibition, together with comparing how this new brand is perceived by attendees against other exhibitors	This case study design appears rather challenging because it is a multiple case study involving all three case study options – event based (horticulture exhibition), organization based (impact on organization) and process based (launching a new brand of lawn mower)

You can see from Table 6.2 that if you decide to select multiple case studies, then this can either be as part of the same case option, for example, choosing three organizations; alternatively, across case options, such as analyzing the process of launching a new product and how this product is received at a trade exhibition. Clearly, opting for a multiple case study research design across different case-based options is going to be more challenging than choosing a single case study, not least because you are likely to spend more time gathering and analyzing data relating to each of the cases. The latter is particularly important and something we examine in Chapter 15.

WHEN SHOULD I USE A CASE STUDY RESEARCH DESIGN?

According to Yin (2014), case study research design works particularly well when the research question starts with 'How' and 'Why'. For example, 'How does Amazon respond to customer complaints in the UK market?' or 'Why do an increasing number of global brands use brand mascots?'. What both of these questions have in common is that they are designed to explore and generate insights relating to a particular research topic. The case study design also works especially well when exploring a number of different actors or goals.

Punch (2014) notes that properly constructed case studies have a valuable contribution to make to social science research in three ways.

- What we can learn from the study of a particular case, in its own right. The case being studied might be unusual, unique or not yet understood, so that building an in-depth understanding of the case is valuable.
- Only the in-depth case study can provide understanding of the important aspects of a new or persistently problematic research area. This is particularly true when complex social behaviour is involved, as is the case in much social science research. Discovering the important features, developing an understanding of them and conceptualizing them for further study, is often best achieved through the case study strategy.
- The case study can make an important contribution in combination with other research approaches.

Coming back to my earlier point about justifying how you define key terms such as 'case study' and 'research design', the same principle applies when selecting your choice of research design. Punch's (2014) points above provide excellent justification for choosing case study research design.

HOW DO I SELECT MY CASES WHEN DOING MY RESEARCH?

I have found that in the early stages of the research process, students will often pay more attention to refining their topic or thinking about research methods, rather than focusing on selecting cases. Although they may be interested in a particular organization or brand, they do not often think of this in terms of a 'case' and rarely in terms of case study research design. If you are considering adopting a case study research design, then do think about the criteria you use to select your case(s).

Remember that when choosing a case study research design, a case can be viewed as an individual, organization, group, process or even an event. From my experience, the most commonly selected case by students is the organization – but this does not have to be your choice. Similar to your research topic, choose a case(s) that you find interesting. For example, it might be a community group that you are a part of, or a one-off event, such as a music festival. Clearly, selecting your case(s) and being explicit as to your case(s) in your research is important as it sets 'boundaries'. In other words, choosing a case(s) helps to narrow your research topic. Furthermore, it also makes it clear to the reader as to what it is you are analyzing (see below for a more detailed discussion on case study analysis). How do you determine your case boundaries? Well, the boundary of the case selection is determined by those boundaries set by the researcher. For example, if choosing a single case design and holistic analysis, then you have explicit case boundaries given your choice of an in-depth case study research design.

IDENTIFY YOUR CASE AND UNIT(S) OF ANALYSIS

Possibly one of the most important considerations when doing case study research is identifying your case. For example, being explicit when selecting your choice of case study design will make things clearer when it comes to analyzing your research. This brings us on to units of analysis. Let us say that you have chosen to do case study research on a single design (organization). When it comes to analyzing the organization, what exactly is your unit(s) of analysis? This is something students often consider quite late in the research process, but in reality, it is essential to be clear on what it is you are analyzing prior to starting your data collection. Figure 6.3 makes a distinction between analysis and case design. We shall look at these in the next part of the chapter.

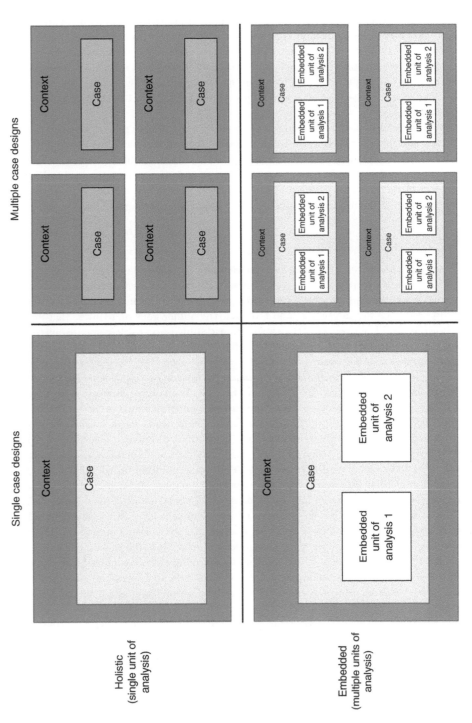

Figure 6.3   Case study research designs and types of analysis

SINGLE CASE STUDY DESIGNS

A case study can be conceptualized along two distinct lines – holistic versus embedded and single case versus multiple cases. First, let us examine the latter two. Single cases can be viewed as single experiments. I have found that students cite a number of reasons for choosing a single case study. For example, the decision to select a particular case might be because the example is unique or an extreme example. An illustration of this might be research examining the collapse of the former UK travel company Thomas Cook. This is a unique case as it is the biggest failure to date of a UK package holiday company (Collinson, 2019):

Single case studies can be used to test a particular theory or as part of a pilot study prior to extending the research to a multiple set of cases. An example here might be conducting research into employee satisfaction in one particular supermarket chain (single case), before furthering the research to look at several supermarket chains (multiple cases, see below). Lastly, selecting a single case is ideal for in-depth studies. If you are in the fortunate position to have access to a particular organization (case), then this creates the potential to examine various aspects of the organization at length.

MULTIPLE CASE DESIGNS

If multiple cases are used in research, then we can view this as multiple experiments. The more cases that feature within a research project to establish or refute a theory, the more robust the research outcomes. Wahyuni (2012) argues that ideally case study research should use a multiple case study design and use multiple methods to analyze the collected data. The author goes on to stress that the rationale behind the choice of multiple case study over a single case study is to enable comparisons between the observed practices by subjects stated in order to obtain a more comprehensive understanding of the practices. However, we can argue against this view by perhaps saying 'The chosen research design is that of a single case, adopting holistic analysis. The rationale for selecting a single case is two-fold. First, the case is unique in its sector, and second, the focus of the study is on an exploratory in-depth analysis'.

How many cases should I include in a multiple case design? It depends on several factors. First, it is not so much the number, but the quality of the cases. There needs to be careful selection so that they either produce similar results (literal replication), or produce contrasting results but for predicable reasons (theoretical replication). Usually, six to ten cases may produce literal replication, whereas more cases might be needed to examine other patterns of theoretical replication (Rowley, 2002: 21–2). Second, time constraints do not allow students to typically go beyond ten cases. Third, it may not be necessary to select a large number of multiple cases in order to achieve your research objectives. Certainly, there will be an expectation on you to justify why you have chosen your selected cases. I often remind students that if a case does not add anything of value to your research, such as being unique or chosen in order to compare findings with that of earlier studies, then do not include it in the research. Finally, having too many cases is likely to make it difficult when it comes to analyzing each of your cases sufficiently within the word limit. The majority of institutions require students to write to a word limit and meet a deadline when undertaking a research project. Clearly, the nature of the word limit and timetable for submitting a research project varies between courses.

By way of example, a multiple case design may examine the legacy of the Olympic Games in each of the host cities post-2000. This is an example of an event-based case study using multiple cases (events). Zeng and Mackay (2019) conducted an interesting study using multiple case design. In their article on internet platforms in China, the authors adopted a case study approach tracing the evolution of two of China's leading tech brands – Alibaba and Tencent. The study also adopts a longitudinal design as it focuses on a period of 15 years from formation to market dominance. Thus, their study uses multiple cases (two case study organizations). The rationale given was that adopting multiple case organizations enabled comparison of organizational information, augment external validation, guard against observer bias and allow for analytical replication logic.

HOW TO CHOOSE AND COMBINE RESEARCH DESIGNS

Holistic analysis

If your case study research adopts a single unit of analysis, then this can be referred to as holistic analysis. Typical units of analysis in case study research include an organization, business function, and an individual, such as a Finance Director. Identifying your unit of analysis early in your study will help to set boundaries when conducting your research. For example, let us say you intend conducting research on a leading confectionary brand. At some point early in your research you need to decide the unit of analysis – is it the entire organization, production department or possibly you are interested in the financial performance of the company and thus, the Finance Director is your chosen unit of analysis.

Embedded analysis

If you decide to choose an embedded case study, then this is a case containing more than one sub-unit of analysis (Yin, 2014). This is referred to as *embedded analysis.* This type of analysis focuses on different sub-units of an entity. For example, in an organization, units of analysis might include employees, management, directors, departments or a combination of these. Thus, when doing case study research, think of 'case study' as an umbrella term, and underneath this are various units of analysis. To illustrate my point, Figure 6.4 shows you the various options when it comes to selecting case study design and units of analysis. This diagram is something I actually encountered when doing my PhD on UK–Chinese joint venture performance. In brief, a joint venture is a separate company (entity) formed by two or more parent companies. Thus, I needed to decide early in my research whether to investigate a single case (joint venture), multiple cases (joint venture and parent companies) and the units of analysis. Consequently, my research emerged as a single case design (joint venture) and the units of analysis were those joint venture managers responsible for the day-to-day running of the joint venture.

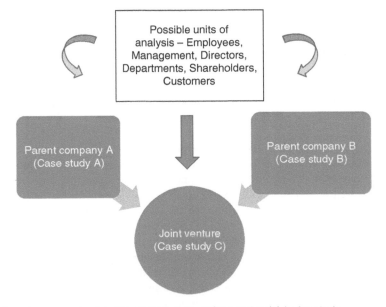

Figure 6.4   Joint venture example showing possible case options and unit(s) of analysis

Lastly, when it comes to analysis in case study research design, the main issue that arises with my students is a lack of clarity as to the unit(s) of analysis. Early in your research, do think about what exactly it is you intend analyzing and how this relates to your research questions. For example, if your unit of analysis is 'employees' within one particular organization (case), then this should be reflected in your research questions; for instance, 'How do employees respond to a change in working environment?'

WHAT ARE IDIOGRAPHIC AND NOMOTHETIC CASE STUDIES?

Two terms you may come across in the research design literature are 'idiographic' and 'nomothetic' case studies. First, the word 'idiographic' originates from the Greek word 'idios', which means 'own' or 'private'. In the context of case study research, an idiographic case means that the researcher focuses in-depth to achieve a unique understanding of an organization, process or event. By way of an example, a study exploring why the UK Tour Operator Thomson went out of business. In this example, the entire research, including observations and measurement, is on one single case (Thomson).

In contrast, the term 'nomothetic' comes from the Greek word 'nomos' meaning 'law'. Here, a case study adopting this approach involves investigating large groups of cases in order to find general laws of behaviour that apply to everyone.

Idiographic and nomothetic case studies have been viewed in philosophical terms (Gerring, 2006). For example, the former often refers to an in-depth study and typically an interpretivist research approach, while nomothetic studies are often concerned with multiple cases and more positivist studies.

ACTION RESEARCH DESIGN

The term action research was first coined by the social psychologist Kurt Lewin in 1946. A researcher undertaking action research will take an active role in the research, as opposed to being an outside observer. The purpose of action research is to produce both an outcome and actions. Action research is usually illustrated in the form of spiralling cycles of action and research (Lewin, 1946). The four elements associated with this cycle are as follows:

1. Planning – a collaborative process that should involve all members of the action research group.
2. Action – at this stage, plans are implemented.
3. Observation – at this stage, actions are observed to see how they perform.
4. Reflection – at this stage, reflection involves evaluating whether or not the actions were appropriate and how they might influence any future planning.

A major feature of action research is the cyclical nature of the process. Thus, 'Reflection' is not the final stage in the process. This stage is followed by the 'Revision' stage and may require changes to the original plan. Revision will then be put into 'Action' and will be observed again, and so on. The cyclical nature of action research promotes continuous improvement and allows for learning and development as research participants in the process work through the stages from planning to reflections and back again (Nyanjom, 2018). As the researcher is part of the 'action' and the 'research', there needs to be a rigorous and transparent process of data collection and analysis.

Greenwood and Levin (2006) point out that action research is social research carried out by a team that encompasses a professional action researcher and the members of an organization, community or network ('stakeholders') who are seeking to improve the participants' situation. Action research promotes broad participation in the research process and supports action leading to a more just, sustainable or satisfying situation for the stakeholders. In simple terms, you can think of action research as professionals pursuing ACTION and RESEARCH at the same time in order to improve their own practice.

In one respect, an advantage of action research is that it is a continuous process. This is particularly suited to some contexts, for example, if an organization has invested in a programme of Continuing Professional Development (CPD) and intends to adopt action research as a means of measuring the success of the programme. Conversely, there are likely to be ethical and resource issues associated with adopting such an approach to research. Employees may not welcome the constant pressures that are likely to come with using action research in connection with CPD. Typically, action research raises the following limitations for students:

- the ability to access key individuals within an organization
- the student is not in a position to instigate organizational change
- the project deadline does not allow a sufficient time frame in which to carry out action research.

EXAMPLE OF ACTION RESEARCH DESIGN

This section includes an illustrative example of a student's research project using an action research design. The purpose is to show you how action research is applied in a real-world context.

Rachel is a Customer Service Manager for a small independent hotel. For her research project, she decided to adopt an action research design as she was able to take an active role in her research and in a fortunate position to put the findings from her research into action.

- Planning – this involved planning how to address the research problem, focusing on 'why there had been a decline in customer satisfaction'. Rachel developed a set of research questions, methodology and consulted with her colleagues about the nature of the research. In short, the purpose centred on improving the customer experience.
- Action – Rachel implemented her plan by asking both customer and employees questions about how customer experience might be improved. Data collection involved face-to-face interviews, followed by a questionnaire survey.
- Observation – following feedback from employees and customers, Rachel implemented changes to how customers were greeted at the hotel, together with other changes centred on guest services.
- Reflection – Rachel reflected on the changes by observing how customers and employees reacted. This also involved asking employees and guests again what they thought of the changes (planning). Not all feedback was positive, so Rachel decided to adapt some of the changes made (action)....

In the above example, you can see the cycles of action adopted by Rachel when doing her research. Of course, there comes a point at some stage with action research where the researcher has to decide when to stop and complete their research. This can be challenging for a student researcher, not least because of the time constraints in which to complete their research project.

Examples of action research objectives:

- To improve the customer service practice going on presently within the organization.
- To make the finance and marketing personnel more cooperative within the workplace.
- To make the organizational environments more conducive for effective communication between functions of business.

EXPERIMENTAL DESIGN

An experimental design posits that experiments are conducted along the lines of the natural sciences, i.e. in a laboratory or in a natural setting, in a systematic way. Experimental studies allow causal relationships to be identified. The aim is to manipulate the independent variable (e.g. an increase in employee commission) in order to observe the effect on the dependent variable (e.g. advertising sales levels for a business magazine). A typical scenario for an experimental design is as follows:

> Research participants are selected and split into two groups. Participants are assigned at random to each group. This means that the two groups will be similar in all aspects relevant to the research whether or not they are exposed to the planned intervention or manipulation. In the first of these groups, the experimental group, some form of planned intervention or manipulation is made, for example a pricing discount. In the control group (the other group), no such manipulation is made. In this example, the dependent variable (purchasing behaviour) is measured before and after the manipulation of the independent variable (the price discount) for both the experimental group and the control group. This means that a before and after comparison can be undertaken. On the basis of this comparison, any difference between the experimental and control groups for the dependent variable (purchasing behaviour) is attributed to the intervention, in this example the 'price discount'.

EXAMPLE OF EXPERIMENTAL DESIGN

The example below shows you how an experimental design applies to an actual study. In this case, the example provides an overview of the entire study. This includes the purpose, methodology and research findings. The study by Sääksjärvi et al. (2015: 7) is from the *Journal of Product & Brand Management*.

- Purpose – This study aims to propose that a brand can be kept both prominent and fresh by using existing logos as well as logo varieties (i.e. slight modifications to the brand's existing logo).
- Design/methodology/approach – In two experimental studies, the authors exposed respondents to either the existing brand logo or to logo varieties, and examined their influence on brand prominence and freshness.
- Findings – The findings suggest that consumers subconsciously process logo varieties to which they are exposed in a similar way as they subconsciously process the existing logo of the brand, making both types of logo exposure effective for building brand prominence and freshness.
- Research limitations/implications – It would also be worthwhile to study the effect of logo varieties using other dependent measures than the ones employed in this study, such as purchase intent and behavioural measures (such as consumption behaviours).
- Practical implications – This research shows that logo varieties can be used alongside the existing brand logo to build prominence and freshness. These findings diverge from the findings typically reported in the branding literature that state that consumers resist changes to logos.
- Originality/value – This research not only demonstrates that exposure to logo varieties and existing logos evokes automatic effects (both types of logos outperform a control group in fostering brand-related outcomes) but also confirms that exposing consumers to the existing logo or logo varieties give fewer differential effects than one may think.

The above example is an adapted version of the abstract from Sääksjärvi et al.'s (2015: 7) article. A structured abstract such as this provides an interesting snapshot of an entire study. It also gives you an insight as to how steps in the research process are related to one another.

TIME HORIZONS

Sometimes a researcher may wish to analyze a case study over a long period of time. In this context, case study research can be viewed as longitudinal. A longitudinal study may involve one particular case or a group of cases. For example, a researcher might be interested in examining how the introduction of an organization's rebranding strategy is viewed by consumers. The researcher would then gather and analyze data at certain points over a prolonged period of time – this is often over a period of several years.

Conversely, if a researcher doing the same study is only concerned with consumers at a particular moment in time, then this is what is referred to as a cross-sectional design. Think of a cross-sectional time horizon as involving the collection of data from a multiple number of cases at one point in time. Again, remember that research designs are not mutually exclusive. Thus, a researcher may decide to investigate a single case study design over a long period of time (longitudinal design). If you are thinking about opting for a case study design when writing your research project, consider the various options and decide which option is likely to allow you to successfully answer your research questions. Further, reflect on the resources you have when doing case study research, especially time.

CROSS-SECTIONAL DESIGNS

A cross-sectional design can be defined as the collection of data from any given sample of the population only once. In essence, it is a 'snapshot' of a phenomenon at a particular moment in time. A cross-sectional design is the most commonly used time horizon design by student researchers. If you decided to conduct a single cross-sectional design, then only one sample from the population is used and data from this sample is obtained only once. Conversely, in a multiple cross-sectional design two or more samples are drawn from the population and data from each sample is collected over time.

Cross-sectional studies typically employ the survey method as a form of data collection. For example, many of my students use an online survey as it is easy to administer and provides a 'snapshot' of a particular phenomenon, such as describing how consumers perceive a particular brand (at a particular point in time). However, in reality, a cross-sectional design may involve different data collection methods. By way of an example, interviews and focus groups also provide insights at a particular moment in time.

The likelihood is that your research will be cross-sectional; this is because most research projects taken by students are time-constrained. If you do have several months in which to complete your research, then a longitudinal study is an option available to you.

One of the key advantages of a cross-sectional design is that it is less resource intensive than a longitudinal design. This is because the research is a snapshot as opposed to evaluating changes over time. Yet, a notable disadvantage is that a snapshot may not be a true representation of a phenomenon (or phenomena) as it may change or develop over time. In the earlier example of how consumers perceive a particular brand, asking consumers 'How do you perceive the brand?' may generate very different results if asking the same question 6 months or 1 year later.

LONGITUDINAL DESIGNS

A longitudinal design is analyzing a sample or samples from the target population over a prolonged period of time. Typically, this period of time is over a number of years. Clearly, the implications of this are that this type of design is not an option for many student researchers. A notable advantage of longitudinal design over cross-sectional design is the ability to monitor changes in variables from the same sample over time. For example, let us say a researcher is interested in examining consumer views on product performance associated with the launch of a new mobile phone brand. Short-term, perceptions may well be positive as the brand offers new features and higher quality when compared to the competition. However, over time, perceptions are likely to change given the nature of the product and rapidly changing market. Hence, a study may focus on changes in perception over a period of five years. The results produced from such a study are likely to be very different to a similar piece of research adopting a cross-sectional design.

Longitudinal studies repeatedly draw sample units of a population over time. Essentially, there are two methods for doing this. First, is to draw different units from the same sampling frame. Second, is to use a panel where the same individuals are asked to respond periodically. An organization can use the services of a panel provider to recruit and manage the panel.

EXAMPLES OF LONGITUDINAL DESIGNS

Although many of my students do not choose a longitudinal design, it is still an option given the time frame in which they complete their research. Unfortunately, for the majority of students doing a research project, choosing a longitudinal design is not an option. However, it is still useful to understand how researchers may use this type of design. In this section, I have included two examples of real-world studies that have used a longitudinal design.

Example A

In this example, Sydney-Hilton and Vila-Lopez (2019) conducted a study to analyze whether the correlations between four marketing strategies and seven financial measures had increased (or not) over time. To achieve their objectives, the authors analyzed secondary information about 500 companies operating in the USA.

The longitudinal design in this example involved the collection of data for eight different periods of time (from year 2009 to year 2016) and for 11 different industries. Research findings showed that two marketing investment decisions out of four (brand value and price) displayed a significant and incremental change over time, while the other marketing investment decisions (brand rank, communication and service) did not increase their importance with time. Second, in two investment decisions (brand value and price), correlations found with financial measures strengthened over time.

In terms of research limitations, the authors note that the study was conducted on large US companies and that studying other sectors within the US can lead to future discoveries, while looking at similar companies in different countries, could provide compare and contrast opportunities. The other limitation is that no qualitative data were collected in the study, leaving the potential for gaps in knowledge.

Why is this longitudinal study of value?

The authors make the point that the value of the study was to adopt a longitudinal perspective to analyze the evolution of marketing investment over time and its interesting results, given that, until now, most of the studies have focused on a specific period. Furthermore, they stress that previous works have scarcely noticed that by better understanding how marketing investments impact regularly used financial variables, stakeholders can better assess the inner workings of a company. Sydney-Hilton and Vila-Lopez (2019) note that bridging this academic gap from a longitudinal perspective will enable marketing workers and accounting workers to act cohesively to cultivate successful companies.

This is a good example of a study using a longitudinal research design based on secondary information. The authors justify usage of a longitudinal design as it clearly contributes to the existing body of literature on the subject area. In essence, this is because the vast majority of studies to date have adopted a cross-sectional design, thus only providing a snapshot of the research findings. Another key advantage of doing longitudinal research is the ability to analyze a change over time.

Example B

In this second example of a longitudinal research design the authors – Murillo and King (2019) – carried out research examining the evolution of brand understanding and its antecedent variables over time, by using a longitudinal panel survey of recently hired employees in a service organization. The authors' methodological approach involved surveying employees working for a restaurant chain in Mexico City. Commencing in June 2016, all new recruits completed the first survey on their first day of joining the company. The purpose of the survey was to determine their view on brand values. Subsequently, second and third surveys were administered some months later to see how employees' views on brand understanding may have changed over time. The authors noted that some employees failed to complete the second or third survey or failed to provide complete data to the security questions, making matching impossible. At the conclusion of data collection, a 105-member panel was built. The authors later conducted statistical analysis on their research findings.

In this illustrative example, longitudinal or panel analysis takes place. This is statistical analysis of pooled data which consists of a cross-section of units (e.g. countries, firms, households, individuals) for which there exist repeated observations over time (Grill, 2017). In this example, the repeated observations were employees working for the Mexican restaurant chain. Again, as with all longitudinal studies, the research is able to examine changes over time. In this case, assessing employees' views on brand understanding from the point of joining the firm over a period of several months makes for an interesting study. Clearly, conducting research involving three surveys is resource intensive, even though in this study the response rate in the first instance was 90%.

ARCHIVAL DESIGN

Archival design relates to public records or documents. It is sometimes referred to as raw data. Archival data are a type of secondary data that exist in the form in which they were originally intended. Examples of archival data include staff records or minutes for a resident association, country reports, business reports and governmental reports.

Archival design is most commonly used by historians and perhaps for this reason tends not to be a favoured choice amongst business and management students. Yet, Moore et al. (2017: 3) argue that while some contents may be 'old' and 'closed' (that is, nothing new is added to them), others are very much 'new' and 'open' and with continual accretion or modification a driving force. Given the capabilities provided by digitization, some previously old and closed data has become very much new and open.

To an extent, the level of emphasis on archival research depends on the nature of the research topic. For example, if you are interested in investigating the development of an organization over time, then you may consider drawing on archival data. The focus of this type of study is on a chronology of organizational development. Reasons for using archival design include the following:

- It might be a favoured research design in your chosen area of research. For example, if your broad topic is human resource management, then if this is a favoured research design it ultimately means that there is likely to be plenty of material available to you.

- You intend to carry out archival analysis as part of an exploratory study, prior to conducting more detailed research.
- You may combine this with a case study design, allowing you to access company documents such as staff records.

COMBINING RESEARCH DESIGNS

By now, you should be aware that research designs are not mutually exclusive. Researchers often combine designs. Typically, the rationale for combining different designs is because the researcher views this as the 'best' way of addressing the research problem. Mika Gabrielsson et al. (2004: 596–597) provide an interesting example of how to combine research designs in their article investigating the influence of financial strategies and finance capabilities on the globalization of born global companies. A born global company can be defined as a company that is global from inception. The authors carried out analysis using longitudinal design based on the organizations' finance records and knowledge accumulation processes when globalizing their operations. Multiple case study research was also selected. This involved interviewing different respondents among 30 companies based in Finland. Finally, the authors supplemented this with archival material such as newspaper articles, press releases and the company material.

BOX 6.1: RESEARCH SNAPSHOT

How you combine research designs should be made explicit when writing your methodology chapter. For example, let us say that you intend to carry out research on a leading international banking group. The aim of your research is to measure the organizational performance across the group. If you decide that the world is external to social actors, then you will consider objectivism. Here, emphasis will be on measuring performance based on profit, turnover and market share. Conversely, subjectivism holds that you view the perceptions and actions of social actors to create social phenomena. Thus, likely measures are customer attitudes and perceptions towards the bank. Moreover, quite possibly, another measure is your own views on the bank's organizational performance.

EXAMPLES OF COMBINING RESEARCH DESIGNS

As mentioned earlier in the chapter, the likelihood is that your research will combine different types of research design. What follows are case examples that illustrate some of the ways researchers combine research designs. The first example is from a journal article. The second example is an actual student example. Again, my intention with these examples is to show you how combining research designs can be done in practice. Of course, there are many different ways of combining research designs. These are purely an illustration.

Example A

A study by Raes et al. (2007) looked at the process of top management teams (TMTs) sensemaking about leadership of middle managers.

The authors used a longitudinal case study design, by analyzing observational data from 23 TMT meetings and transcripts from interviews with TMT members. Results indicate that TMT sensemaking consisted of images of middle managers, the TMT self-image, and reflection on action and action planning. In this example, the authors selected two different types of research design, namely, case study and longitudinal. The latter point is associated with the 'time horizon' aspect of research design.

Question

How would you combine a multiple case study design, longitudinal design and archival design?

The answer to this question is that there is no one definitive answer. Again, you could look at existing studies to examine the relationship between these designs. These studies do not necessarily have to be in your chosen area of research. Start with archival research as this may help to set your research direction. Next, think about the cases you will use in your multiple case study design and the unit or units of analysis. Finally, remember that longitudinal design refers to time horizon. For a start, consider the period of time for your intended research project.

Example B

Henry conducted research into the new employee training scheme to see how it had been received by employees. As a Human Resources Manager in his organization, he decided to conduct action research to see how the scheme had been implemented and to reflect and make changes in response to employee feedback. In keeping with action research, he chose to follow the 'cycle' associated with action research design. Fortunately for Henry, he had a 12-month period in which to conduct his research, so he also selected a longitudinal design as his chosen time horizon. Finally, he supplemented his research with archival material such as the organization's staff newsletter, company records and reports.

In this student example, Henry has decided to select three research designs – action research, longitudinal research and archival research. Thus, you can see how different research designs can be incorporated into one research project.

COMPARATIVE RESEARCH DESIGN

A comparative research design compares two or more groups on one variable. A variable is a characteristic that can be measured. By way of example, comparing the turnover (variable) of Chinese organizations to the turnover (variable) of Indian organizations can be interpreted as a comparative research design. The variable in this case is 'turnover', while the two groups are 'Chinese organizations' and 'Indian organizations'. Note that this is purely an illustrative example. This example also applies to the turnover of organizations from other countries.

A comparative research design can make for an interesting study. For example, one of my former students conducted a comparative analysis of private label and leading brands. The variable in this case was 'consumer perception'. A comparative research design does present a number of challenges. One of the potential problems you may face is ensuring that the variable in your study is interpreted the same way by your chosen groups. This can be particularly problematic when comparing groups across distinctly different cultures. Let us say that your chosen variable is satisfaction and the purpose of your research is to compare levels of satisfaction between cultural groups from China, France, Brazil and Russia. How do you know that the concept of satisfaction is interpreted in the same way across these respective cultures? This is an issue for researchers conducting cross-cultural research – the ability to measure comparisons can be challenging due to cultural differences.

Image 6.2 is another example of a Concept Cartoon. In this scenario, the characters are discussing research design. Think about the different views and, if possible, use them to provoke a discussion with fellow students. Do you share a viewpoint with one particular character?

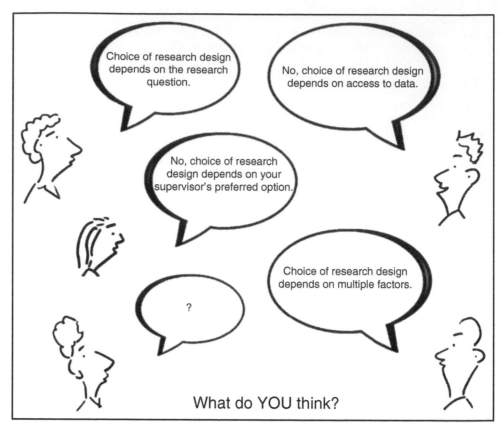

Image 6.2   Concept Cartoon 'Research design'

WHICH IS THE 'BEST' RESEARCH DESIGN FOR MY RESEARCH?

The short answer is that there is no one 'best' research design. Every research design has limitations. Your choice of research design is dependent on a number of factors, in particular other elements you have chosen in your methodological approach and your research direction. I have found that the most popular choice of research design for my students is the case study design. The reason for this is that many students have a passion for a particular brand or brands, currently work for an organization or have a view to work for a potential organization(s).

HOW TO SELECT YOUR RESEARCH DESIGN(S)

Your choice of research design is likely to be largely determined by the nature of your research questions. According to Draper (2004), when deciding the best approach (design) to answer the research question, researchers must take account of their own experience, any support or supervision they will need, any cost and other resource implications, the accessibility of the sample and whether there are any complex ethical considerations. For example, let us say that you decided to choose a single case study design, focusing on a leading security organization. The sensitive and ethical considerations associated with this type of case may lead you to select a different design, such as archival research. In addition, how you select your research design might also be influenced by earlier studies. There are two approaches here. First, adopting the same research design(s) may allow for comparative analysis. In contrast, if you adopt a largely untested research design, you can make the argument that this is a valuable contribution to the literature on your chosen research topic.

One way to think about the relationship between research questions and research design is that there must be a congruence between questions and study design. In other words, a 'common thread' must link these steps, and all steps in the research process. For example, 'How' and 'Why' questions are particularly suited to case study research and exploratory research design as they generate insights and understanding when doing research.

EXAMPLES - WHICH RESEARCH DESIGN(S) DO THESE EXAMPLES REPRESENT?

To give you a better understanding of research design, the mini scenarios below are asking you which research design or study does each example represent. Answers at the end of this section.

1. A washing powder manufacturer is considering launching a new detergent that produces double the number of washes compared to its nearest competitor.
2. A tea producer wishes to examine the effect of tea bag shape on the purchasing behaviour of regular tea drinkers.
3. A group of managing directors from start-up tech organizations have been interviewed qualitatively and will be re-interviewed each year to examine their individual performance and its long-term effects on their well-being.
4. A marketing researcher is conducting a comparative study on two major competitors.
5. A supermarket has used two sample groups to examine the effect of smell on purchasing behaviour. The first group has been exposed to 'fresh bread' smells and the second has not.
6. A research student is interested in conducting research into place branding by analyzing visitor perceptions of London.

Answers:

1. Exploratory.
2. Causal.
3. Longitudinal.
4. Multiple case study.
5. Experimental.
6. Single case design.

HOW RESEARCH DESIGN 'FITS' WITH OVERALL RESEARCH DIRECTION

The example below shows the relationship between research design and other elements of research. This is taken from Rowley (2004).

- **Background:** An exploratory study into the approaches to the delivery of brand messages through a website, using McDonald's as a case study.
- **Research problem:** To what extent does the internet contribute to brand building?
- **Aim of the research:** A case study analysis of the internet presence of McDonald's, and a review of some of the devices that it uses to build the brand through this channel.

Reasons for choice of research design:

- A case study approach has been adopted because understanding of online branding is relatively undeveloped.

- Single case designs are appropriate when the case has something special to reveal.

- Case studies are a valuable way of asking 'How' and 'Why' questions.

- **Future research:** How can online brand building help to raise awareness?

CHAPTER SUMMARY

- A research design is a detailed framework or plan that helps to guide you through the research process, allowing a greater likelihood of achieving your research objectives.

- The three types of research studies are exploratory, descriptive and causal.

- Case study selection options include organization based, process based and event based.

- The four elements associated with the spiralling cycles of Action research are: Planning, Action, Observation and Reflection.

- Case study designs can be either single case or multiple case.

- Time horizon relating to research design can be either cross-sectional or longitudinal.

- Consider different ways of combining research designs as each design is not mutually exclusive.

QUESTIONS FOR REVIEW

1. How would you define research design?

2. What are the different types of case study research design?

3. Explain the time horizons associated with research design.

4. Give an example of combining different types of research design.

5. Outline the nature of an exploratory research study.

6. Explain what you understand by the term 'archival design'.

7. Give an example of how an experimental design might be used in practice.

8. Outline the benefits of using a longitudinal research design.

STUDENT SCENARIO: NINA SELECTS HER RESEARCH DESIGN(S)

For her research project, Nina wanted to measure the levels of corporate social responsibility among leading energy companies. As a supervisor for one of the 'Big Four' energy companies, she was in the fortunate position of having access to secondary data and employees. She also wanted to look at how consumers viewed corporate social responsibility in terms of importance when choosing an energy supplier. Nina was in the process of putting together her research proposal and had made good progress in narrowing down her topic, formulating research objectives and research questions. However, although she had an idea as to her choice of data collection methods, Nina had some doubts as to which of the research design option(s) she should select for her research. Nina thought that the best way to select her research design would be to look at what designs are commonly used in previous research studies.

Choosing a case study research design

Nina was of the view that a case study research design might be a suitable option for her research, given that the focus was on energy companies (cases). In terms of analysis, Nina was unclear as to whether her research would benefit from holistic or embedded analysis. She was aware of the benefits associated with each approach. Furthermore, as Nina was studying on a part-time degree, she had more than 12 months in which to complete her project. This gave her ample time in which to collect her data.

Questions

1. What do you consider to be an appropriate research design(s) for Nina? Try to justify your answer.
2. Discuss the advantages and disadvantages of combining case designs.

Hint: Remember that there is no one 'best' research design. However, it is always good practice to justify your methodological approach.

FURTHER READING

Farquhar, J.D. (2012) *Case Study Research for Business*. London: Sage.

A comprehensive guide to conducting case study research. This book contains everything from how to define case study research, to the ethical issues associated with case study research.

Hakim, C. (2000) *Research Design: Successful Designs for Social and Economic Research* (2nd edn). London: Routledge.

Chapter 5 provides examples of different types of case studies, while Chapter 10 focuses on choices and combinations of research design.

McNiff, J. (2017) *Action Research: All You Need To Know*. London: Sage.

An in-depth book on action research. Answers the how, what and why of action research.

Perry, C. and Gummesson, E. (2004) 'Action research in marketing', *European Journal of Marketing*, 38 (3/4): 310–320.

Presents a broad definition of action research in marketing.

REFERENCES

Blumberg, B., Cooper, D.R. and Schindler, P.S. (2005) *Business Research Methods*. Maidenhead: McGraw-Hill.

Collinson, P. (2019) 'Thomas Cook collapse: Your questions answered', *The Guardian*, 23 September. Available at: www.theguardian.com/business/2019/sep/23/thomas-cook-collapse-your-questions-answered (accessed 25 November 2019).

Creswell, J.W., Hanson, W.E., Plano Clark, V.L. and Morales, A. (2007) 'Qualitative research designs: Selection and implementation', *The Counseling Psychologist*, 35 (2): 236–264.

De Vaus, D.A. (2001) *Research Design in Social Research*. London: Sage.

Dick, G.P., Heras, I. and Casadesús, M. (2008) 'Shedding light on causation between ISO 9001 and improved business performance', *International Journal of Operations & Production Management*, 28 (7): 687–708.

Draper, J. (2004) 'The relationship between research question and research design', in P.A. Crookes and S. Davies (eds), *Research into Practice: Essential Skills for Reading and Applying Research in Nursing and Health Care* (2nd edn) (pp. 69–84). Edinburgh: Bailliere Tindall.

Eisenhardt, K.M. (1989) 'Building theories from case study research', *The Academy of Management Review*, 14 (4): 532–550.

Gabrielsson, M., Sasi, V. and Darling, J. (2004) 'Finance of rapidly growing Finnish SMEs: Born internationals and born globals', *European Business Review*, 16 (6): 590–604.

Gerring, J. (2006) 'Single-outcome studies: A methodological primer', *International Sociology*, 21 (5): 707–734.

Ghauri, P. and Grønhaug, K. (2005) *Research Methods in Business Studies: A Practical Guide* (3rd edn). Harlow: Prentice Hall.

Greenwood, D.J. and Levin, M. (2006) *Introduction to Action Research: Social Research for Social Change*. Thousand Oaks, CA: Sage.

Grill, C. (2017) *Longitudinal Data Analysis, Panel Data Analysis*. Wiley Online Library. doi: 10.1002/9781118901731.iecrm0134

Hart, C. and Dewsnap, B. (2001) 'An exploratory study of the consumer decision process for intimate apparel', *Journal of Fashion Marketing and Management*, 5 (2): 108–119.

Lewin, K. (1946) 'Action research and minority problems', in G.W. Lewin (ed.), *Resolving Social Conflicts*. New York: Harper & Row.

Moore, N., Salter, A., Stanley, L. and Tamboukou, M. (2017) *The Archive Project: Archival Research in the Social Sciences*. Abingdon: Routledge.

Murillo, E. and King, C. (2019) 'Examining the drivers of employee brand understanding: A longitudinal study', *Journal of Product & Brand Management*, 28 (7): 893–907.

Nyanjom, J. (2018) 'Cycles within cycles: Instilling structure into a mentoring self-study action research project', *Educational Action Research*, 26 (4): 626–640.

Punch, K.F. (2014) *Introduction to Social Research: Quantitative & Qualitative Approaches* (3rd edn). London: Sage.

Raes, A.M., Glunk, U., Heijltjes, M.G. and Roe, R.A. (2007) 'Top management team and middle managers: Making sense of leadership', *Small Group Research*, 38 (3): 360–386.

Rowley, J. (2002) 'Using case studies in research', *Management Research News*, 25 (1): 16–27.

Rowley, J. (2004) 'Online branding: The case of McDonald's', *British Food Journal*, 106 (3): 228–237.

Sääksjärvi, M., van den Hende, E., Mugge, R. and van Peursem, N. (2015) 'How exposure to logos and logo varieties fosters brand prominence and freshness', *Journal of Product & Brand Management*, 24 (7): 736–744.

Singh, B. (2018) 'Modeling of effect of job stress on medical representative's job performance', *Research Review International Journal of Multidisciplinary*, 3 (11): 522–526.

Stake, R.E. (1995) *The Art of Case Study Research*. Thousand Oaks, CA: Sage.

Swanborn, P. (2010) *Case Study Research: What, Why and How?* London: Sage.

Sydney-Hilton, E. and Vila-Lopez, N. (2019) 'Are marketing strategies correlated with financial outputs? A longitudinal study', *Journal of Business & Industrial Marketing*, 34 (7): 1533–1546.

Van Wyk, M.M and Taole, M. (2015) *Educational Research: An African Approach*. Cape Town: Oxford University Press.

Wahyuni, D. (2012) 'The research design maze: Understanding paradigms, cases, methods & methodologies', *Journal of Applied Managing Accounting Research*, 10 (1): 69–80.

Yin, R.K. (2014) *Case Study Research: Design and Methods* (5th edn). Thousand Oaks, CA: Sage.

Zeng, J. and Mackay, D. (2019) 'The influence of managerial attention on the deployment of dynamic capability: A case study of internet platform firms in China', *Industrial & Corporate Change*, 28 (19): 1173–1192.

Zikmund, W. and Babin, B. (2006) *Exploring Marketing Research* (9th edn). Mason, OH: Cengage Learning.

7

PLAGIARISM AND ETHICS IN BUSINESS RESEARCH

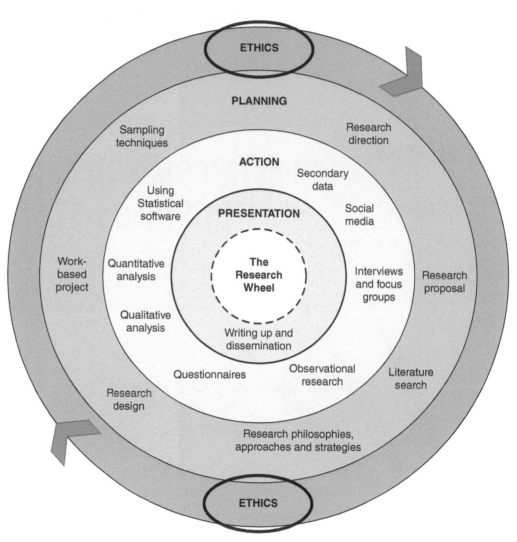

Figure 7.1   The Research Wheel

Learning objectives

By the end of this chapter, you should be able to:

- understand what is meant by the term 'research ethics'

- know why business ethics is important

- appreciate why student researchers need to understand research ethics

- appreciate how research ethics may impact research stakeholders

- know how to address different types of ethics issues

- understand plagiarism and self-plagiarism

- understand the importance of ethics approval

- know the different ways of negotiating access when carrying out your research.

INTRODUCTION

The focus of this chapter is on the ethical issues you will need to consider when doing your research. For some students, research ethics can be something of an afterthought. However, it is essential not to treat research ethics retrospectively as all research must be conducted in an ethical manner and in accordance with your institution's ethical standards. Typically, any research involving human participants requires ethics approval. This approval may come from your supervisor or an ethics committee, depending on the research ethics policy of your university or college. In most cases, gaining ethics approval in business and management subjects is relatively straightforward although there are certain subjects, for example, research involving children, which are more complex. In this chapter, we examine the ethical concerns and processes you will need to consider when doing your research.

The chapter starts by considering what is meant by 'research ethics' and why ethics is important in business. The latter explores business ethics in a real-life context by discussing how organizations address ethical issues. Following on from this, the chapter moves on to look at why it is important for student researchers to learn about research ethics. Subsequently, we consider the ethical responsibilities you have towards your research stakeholders. Remember that your research is not only the relationship between you (the researcher) and research participants. Other stakeholders also have an interest in your research and thus should be viewed in the context of research ethics. Examples of other stakeholders include your research supervisor, employer or organizations(s) you are doing your research on and, finally, your institution.

Next, we examine the different types of ethical issues you will need to consider when doing your research. At this stage, it is important to note that there are several types of ethical issues. Perhaps the most well-known to students are plagiarism and to a lesser extent self-plagiarism. These are terms you are likely to have come across earlier in your course as they are associated with other forms of assessment. Similarly, plagiarism is also something to think about when doing your research project.

Following this, we explore the actual process of gaining ethics approval. In addition, we also look at the role of the research ethics committee and what to do if you encounter difficult ethical issues. Lastly, the chapter concludes with a discussion on some of the ways to negotiate access. This last point can be a challenge even for the most accomplished of researchers.

As you can see from Figure 7.1, research ethics falls in the outer layer of The Research Wheel model. It is essential to consider research ethics in the early stages of your research as ethical issues can arise at all steps in the research process. For example, although plagiarism is something to think about at the start of your research, it is particularly important when you come to writing up your research. Similarly, a research participant's request to withdraw from your study could come at any stage following their acceptance to take part in your study. McKee and Porter (2012) echo this view by commenting that the research process requires ethical revisionings and the need for researchers to be recursive in their thinking and actions; to be open to adjusting not only what they are doing, but why and how they are doing it. Pilkington et al. (2019) point out that ethical issues continue throughout the research process, starting with the drafting of the research question through to the dissemination of the research findings. Hence, the outer layer in The Research Wheel represents 'ethics' as relating to all stages in the research process, while the arrows represent addressing ethical issues as an iterative process.

Many colleges and universities now require that students who undertake a research project concerning human subjects must gain ethics approval for their work. Typically, the process is usually straightforward, although this may not be the case if the research is of a sensitive nature or high risk. Again, as you will see later in the chapter, ethical issues can arise at any stage in the research process.

BOX 7.1: RESEARCH SNAPSHOT

It is always a good idea to start thinking about your ethical considerations when writing your research proposal. Certainly, ethical considerations should form a key part of the 'planning layer' in The Research Wheel model. Why? Well, one reason I have found is that students often fail to allow enough time to gain ethics approval. In many cases, business research ethics is low risk. If this is the case in your research, then it might be possible that your research supervisor is able to approve your research. However, research involving higher risks, for example, sensitive topics such as satisfaction in the workplace, may take several weeks to gain research approval. This is because an ethics application requires approval from a research committee. The length of time it takes to gain ethics authorization depends on your institution, but forward planning can help to avoid any last-minute panic in the research process.

WHAT ARE RESEARCH ETHICS?

Before we examine what is meant by 'research ethics', it is important to stress that the implications of failing to follow ethical guidelines can be serious. Reports of ethical misconduct are becoming increasingly common in the national press. In recent years, there have been a number of high-profile cases where senior politicians have been accused of plagiarism. For example, in 2013 the German education minister Annette Schavan resigned after being stripped of her doctorate because of plagiarism. The decision was made by the University of Dusseldorf to void Schavan's PhD because parts of her doctoral thesis had been copied (*The Guardian*, 2019).

Ethics is derived from the Greek word 'ethos' which means a person's fundamental orientation towards life. There is no universal consensus as to what 'ethics' means. However, there is one common theme that the majority of definitions have, and that is that they consider ethics from a stakeholder perspective. In essence, this means that ethics is not only viewed from the point of the research, but all those actors who have a vested interest in the research. 'Actors' in this sense does not mean all those who take to the stage! What it does mean is all those who are involved with the research to some extent. For example, if you are conducting research comparing the organizational performance of two leading brands, the actors in your research are likely to be you (the researcher), your research supervisor, employees/managers for each of the brands, your university or college and other research participants. A definition of the stakeholder view of ethics is provided by Linda Treviño and Katherine Nelson (2011: 17). They define ethics as 'the principles, norms, and standards of governing an individual or group'.

The Economic Social Research Council (ESRC) has six key principles for ethical research:

- Research should aim to maximize benefit for individuals and society and minimize risk and harm.
- The rights and dignity of individuals and groups should be respected.
- Wherever possible, participation should be voluntary and appropriately informed.
- Research should be conducted with integrity and transparency.
- Lines of responsibility and accountability should be clearly defined.
- Independence of research should be maintained and where conflicts of interest cannot be avoided, they should be made explicit.

In the literature you will see the terms 'ethics' and 'social responsibility' often used synonymously. However, there is a notable difference when comparing these two terms. First, social responsibility relates to the public's expectations of an organization to act in a manner that is socially responsible, while ethics relates to morality rather than society's interests. What is perceived as moral is down to an individual's perception of what is right or wrong. In short, as a researcher, you have a moral responsibility to conduct your research in an accurate and honest way. This includes respecting the views of your research participants, even if you disagree with their views. This last point refers to taking what is called an impartial viewpoint when doing your research. Maintaining a non-biased view can be particularly challenging for researchers carrying out research on a topic where they have strongly held views. However, maintaining a non-biased or impartial view is essential if a researcher is to produce credible results.

Respecting research participants is echoed by Rowley and Slack (2004: 210) who comment that

conducting research ethically is concerned with respecting privacy and confidentiality, and being transparent about the use of research data. Ethical practices hinge on respect and trust and approaches that seek to build, rather than demolish relationships.

If we examine the definition more closely, we can see that a key term used to express the relationship between a researcher and a research participant is 'trust'. Having conducted many interviews over the years, I can tell you that it takes time to develop trust between the researcher and participants, although this is likely to be achieved sooner if you respect the privacy and confidentiality of your participants. In short, acting in a professional manner when doing your research builds credibility, which in turn leads to an increased level of trust.

Lastly, when considering ethical issues in your research, try to do so from a stakeholder perspective, not simply your own views as a researcher. Put yourself in the shoes of a research participant. How would you want your data to be used? Where would you like your data to be stored? Would you like the information you provide to remain confidential? I tell my students to think of research ethics in a holistic way, not just from the point of view of the researcher.

WHY ARE BUSINESS ETHICS IMPORTANT?

It takes 20 years to build a reputation and five minutes to ruin it. If you think about that, you'll do things differently.

Warren Buffett

Before discussing the importance of research ethics in the context of your research project, it is worth considering why ethics is such an important subject in real-world business.

In essence, the same ethical principles apply to both the student researcher and the research practitioner. There are numerous definitions of business ethics. It is often discussed together with corporate social responsibility (CSR). The term 'business ethics' comprises two words 'business' and 'ethics' which cover the areas of moral principles, beliefs, values, culture, governance issues and code of conduct for business (Dimitriades, 2007).

Treviño and Nelson (2011: 21) view ethics from an employee's perspective and wider society:

> As workers, we should care about ethics because most of us prefer to work for ethical organizations. We want to feel good about ourselves and the work we do. As responsible citizens, we must care about the millions of people who lost retirement savings because of the greed of those at AIG, Citigroup, Lehman Brothers, Merrill Lynch, and other financial firms that brought down the global economy in 2008. These people are our parents, spouses, siblings, children, and friends – they're us! We live in a world community, and we're all inextricably connected to each other and to the environment that surrounds us.

Given the importance attached to business ethics, many organizations now have their own code of ethics. Having an explicit ethics policy is especially important for large energy companies such as BP and Exxon Mobil. The following provides an interesting insight into BP's code of conduct in respect of its relationship with its customers:

> Our code applies to all BP employees, officers and members of the Board. Business partners, including operated joint ventures and third parties, can have a direct impact on our reputation through their behaviour. For this reason, we want to work with business partners that share our commitment to safety and ethics and compliance. We expect and encourage all our contractors and their employees to act in a way that is consistent with our Code. We will take appropriate measures where we believe they have not met our expectations or their contractual obligations. (BP, 2019: 4)

There are certain organizations who pride themselves on their approach to research ethics. How an organization approaches ethical issues can be a source of competitive advantage. For example, the coffee brand Kenco ran an advertising campaign in 2014 to promote its ethical values as part of a project which has seen 20 young people at risk of entering a gang and giving them an education and training to become a coffee farmer. The Coffee v Gangs campaign ran across TV, cinema and online and was designed to show the brand's 'ethical coffee' and Kenco has differentiated through ethics for many years (Faull, 2014).

WHY IS IT IMPORTANT FOR ME TO LEARN ABOUT RESEARCH ETHICS?

For some student researchers, research ethics is unlikely to be high up on the agenda of project tasks. Yet, the importance attached to understanding and addressing ethical issues cannot be underestimated. The reasons why it is important for you to learn about research ethics are as follows:

- Your university or college will have a set of ethical standards that need to be followed when doing your research.
- Understanding and implementing ethical guidelines provide essential transferable skills.
- You will be able to view ethics from the point of view of the researcher and the research participant.
- The implications of not following ethical standards can be serious and damaging to your own credibility as a researcher and possibly the integrity of your research stakeholders.

First, when carrying out your research you will need to be aware of a range of ethical issues that may impact different research actors. Second, all organizations need to be aware of business ethics so the knowledge and practical skills you learn can be used in the real world. For example, a piece of research conducted by Purcell (1977) found that those US MBA students who participated in a seminar on business ethics were still positively influenced by the contents of the seminar many years later. Thus, the content had a positive impact on their ethical views.

As a researcher, you have an ethical responsibility to carry out your research honestly and with integrity. In order to do this, you need to have a clear understanding of research ethics. Failure to carry out your research in an ethical manner can have serious implications. This includes failing your research project and potentially expulsion from your course. Not following research ethics is essentially fraud and can come in several forms (Adams et al., 2014: 21):

- being selective in sampling
- not reporting survey response/participation rates
- deliberately biasing the data collection instruments – for example, asking leading questions in surveys
- making up data because you cannot be bothered doing the data collection
- falsifying results to make them fit in with your analysis – this may be a legitimate thing to do but you must make it clear what has been done and why
- biased or inappropriate analysis.

WHAT ARE MY ETHICAL RESPONSIBILITIES TO MY RESEARCH STAKEHOLDERS?

Walliman (2011: 43) notes that there are two aspects to ethical issues in research:

1. The individual values of the researcher relating to honesty, frankness and personal integrity.
2. The researcher's treatment of other people involved in the research, relating to informed consent, confidentiality, anonymity and courtesy.

It is the second point above that we focus on in this section. Earlier in the chapter, I mentioned that as a researcher you should consider the views of all research stakeholders when thinking about ethical issues. In this part of the chapter, I will provide you with a detailed guide to the main ethical responsibilities that you have to each of your research stakeholders (see Figure 7.2). Clearly, not all of the stakeholders listed here may be involved in your research. In essence, my intention here is to give you a checklist of possible stakeholders. It is important that you check with all those involved in your research that you are satisfying your ethical commitments throughout the entire research process.

Figure 7.2 Consider ethical responsibilities in the context of your research stakeholders

YOUR INSTITUTION

As a student researcher, you have an ethical responsibility to your university. Conducting research as a university or college student adds credibility to you as a researcher. It also means that you need to follow your institution's ethics regulations when doing your research. Why? This is because any ethical issues that might arise have the potential to not only damage your reputation as a researcher, but also that of your institution. Hence, it is essential that you seek ethical approval from your university or college in order to avoid any ethical problems.

YOUR EMPLOYER

If you are doing a part-time course or a work-based project, there is a likelihood that your research project will be based on your employer. As such, you have to consider how ethical issues may impact your employer. For example, if conducting interviews with your fellow employees, how do you intend to record the data? How will you address issues centred on confidentiality and anonymity?

One of the main issues I have found with students doing research on their employer is knowing who to ask for permission to conduct the research. For some organizations, this may be straightforward as you can ask the owner of the business. However, for large multi-national organizations, it can be both difficult and time-consuming to determine who to ask in order to gain ethics approval.

Of course, the key advantage you have by doing research on your employer is ease of access. Having to negotiate access is a challenge for all researchers and something we address later in the chapter. Given the sensitive nature and ethical issues surrounding research involving a student's employer, it is always a good idea to talk through these ethical issues with your research supervisor.

YOUR RESEARCH PARTICIPANTS

Prior to colleting primary data, a key question all researchers face is 'How am I going to select my research participants?'. Although students often use their fellow students or friends and family as their research participants, it is essential to recognize the limitations that come with selecting such a sample. Using participants known to the researcher does not mean that ethical concerns can be avoided. On the contrary, all participants taking part in your study still need to be fully briefed on the nature of your research and understand the implications of taking part. This process should involve completion of a consent form. Even though you know your participants, they must still be given the option to withdraw at any stage of your research without recrimination. Irrespective of the research participants, your responsibilities towards all those taking part in your research are foremost to offer the level of protection that participants expect.

The researcher on any project is ultimately responsible for the ethical conduct of research with human participants. This includes being responsible to ensure the welfare of all your research participants. 'Welfare' not only includes physical, but also mental well-being. Protection of your research participants should be based on the same thorough, professional process, irrespective of age, gender or ethnicity. Knowing the background of your research participants can help you to better protect their well-being, though it can sometimes be difficult doing research on particularly sensitive topics as there can be a fine line between protecting their well-being and asking questions that are essential to addressing a research problem.

Recruiting your research participants and informed consent

From my experience, students sometimes find it difficult to recruit research participants. Knowing how to target and the process of inviting people to take part in your research can be challenging.

To an extent, the process does depend on your choice of sampling method. This is something we examine later in the book. At this point, let us look at the whole issue surrounding informed consent. Consent can be defined as 'seeking permission for something to happen or for something to be done'. Another important aspect of consent is 'informed consent'. This is a term some students struggle to understand. In essence, think of informed consent from the researcher's perspective. Quite simply, it means that it is the responsibility of the researcher to accurately explain the nature of the research they are conducting and the role the prospective participant is likely to play in it. Research participants are only able to give informed consent on the basis that they have a full understanding of the nature of the research project.

YOUR RESEARCH PROJECT SUPERVISOR

You also have an ethical responsibility to your research supervisor as they will take an active interest in your research. In many cases, the supervisor is also the first marker of a research project and is able to provide guidance on how to do your research. Therefore, it is essential that you are open and honest with your supervisor throughout the entire research process.

THE RESEARCH COMMUNITY

As a researcher, you are a member of an ethical community and this brings with it ethical responsibilities. You have a responsibility to be honest, objective, transparent and independent in your work to the research community. The research community can be defined as all those researchers who engage in research.

PREVENTING HARM TO THE RESEARCHER

The final key stakeholder in your research is you, the researcher. As well as protecting your research participants it is also essential to make sure that you are not harmed when conducting your research. Again, potential risks are not only physical, but also psychological. In business research, studies on sensitive subjects, such as childhood obesity and well-being in the workplace, may carry a greater likelihood of psychological risk. You need to take into account all safety issues when doing your research so as to reduce the risk to your own welfare. To address safety issues relating to your research, it is always a good idea to consult with your research supervisor. In some cases, your research may require insurance to protect against any unforeseen eventuality. This may include travel insurance or personal liability insurance.

ETHICAL ISSUES AND YOUR RESEARCH

This section examines the ethical issues you will need to consider when doing your research project. As we saw earlier in the chapter when looking at The Research Wheel, research ethics is not something to view at one point in your research, as ethical concerns apply to all stages of the research process. The majority of universities and colleges have their own research ethics code of conduct. However, if your institution does not have a formal code of conduct, it is still important for you to note the ethical issues you will need to consider when doing your research. If you are in any doubt about expectations when it comes to ethics, be sure to consult your research supervisor.

Table 7.1   A summary of ethical issues you need to consider for your research

Ethical issues	Brief summary
Voluntary participation	Voluntary participation refers to a human research subject's exercise of free will in deciding whether to participate in a research activity.
Anonymity and confidentiality	Anonymity – the protection of research participants by making sure that their names are not published with the information they provide.
	Confidentiality – protecting research participants by making sure that sensitive data are not disclosed to any third party.
The Data Protection Act (2018) and UK General Data Protection (GDPR)	The Data Protection Act controls the way data are handled including how personal information is used by organizations, businesses or the government.
Plagiarism and self-plagiarism	Plagiarism is passing off the work of others as your own. Self-plagiarism is including work in your research project that you have already submitted as part of a previous piece of assessment.
Personal conduct	Your own professional conduct when conducting your research must be professional, honest and transparent.
Potential physical and mental harm	As a researcher, the core principle when conducting your research is to cause no harm to your research participants.
Informed consent	The principle of informed consent requires that prospective participants in research are provided with information about the project in which they are being invited to participate.
Recording data	If you are thinking about conducting interviews, using focus groups or carrying out observational research, do reflect on how you record your data. Avoid oversimplifying transcripts.
The right to withdraw from the research	Participants have the right to withdraw at any stage in your study.
Deception	Deception means gaining access to a participant or data in a dishonest way.
Respect	Respect means considering the feelings and rights of your research participants and treating them with courtesy and appreciation throughout your research.
Debriefing	Debriefing usually takes place at the conclusion of a participant's role in the research. It informs participants about the intentions of the research in which they took part.
Collusion	Collusion occurs when two or more individuals cooperate to product a piece of research or a research project that is presented as the work of one student alone.
Conflict of interest	A set of circumstances that creates a risk that an individual's ability to apply judgement or act in one role is, or could be, impaired or influenced by a secondary interest.
Storing data	All electronic data should be password protected and do not share your password with anyone else.
Dissemination	How you intend to do this should be made clear to research participants when seeking informed consent.
Disposing of your research material	Deciding how to dispose of your data or research findings is likely to be your final ethical concern in the research process.

VOLUNTARY PARTICIPATION

Voluntary participation refers to a human research subject's exercise of free will in deciding whether to participate in a research activity. International law, national law and the codes of conduct of scientific communities protect this right (Lavrakas, 2008). A key ethical principle is that coercion should not be used to force individuals to take part in the research. I advise against offering rewards or financial incentives to induce people to take part. People should not feel under any pressure to take part in a research project and should be given all of the necessary information about the research. This includes how their data will be collected, stored and used. The latter point is particularly important in the context of social media. Although a person may consent to taking part in your research, this does not necessarily mean that you have the freedom to disseminate their personal data online. The use of social media platforms such as Twitter and YouTube provide researchers with an excellent opportunity to disseminate their research findings, but consent should be sought first from participants before sharing such information in the public domain.

You may find that it can take time to gain consent from your intended research participants. This can be the case when asking employees to take part in your research as they have to ask permission from their immediate line manager or possibly even another branch/office in the organization.

ANONYMITY AND CONFIDENTIALITY

Some students use these two words interchangeably. However, there is a notable difference. First, it is important to offer all participants both anonymity and confidentiality. If a participant intends to remain anonymous, this means that they will not be identified from the information they provide. A positive aspect of offering anonymity is that this tends to lead to a higher response rate, particularly in questionnaire surveys. In particular, sensitive research topics and/or sensitive questions are likely to have a greater response rate if you can guarantee anonymity. A key question to ask yourself as a researcher is 'Do I really need to know the identity of my research respondents?'. If the answer is no, then it is perhaps best to ensure anonymity. In some cases, though, knowing the identity of participants is essential as it adds to the credibility of the research or possibly it is a requirement of your research questions(s). In these situations, it is essential that the participant gives their consent.

If you intend guaranteeing anonymity, be careful how you disguise the identity of your participants. By way of example, let us say that you are doing research into staff retention among leading aircraft manufacturers. Citing the location of the manufacturer is not sufficient to hide an organization's identity given the small number of manufacturers that operate within this sector.

Confidentiality focuses on the data collected rather than the identity of the participant. It provides protection to research participants by making sure that sensitive information is not disclosed. If confidentiality is a condition for a participant to take part in a research project, what you can do is agree with the participant that their information will not be disclosed in the public domain. This is something that I have suggested to my students in the past. Sometimes, agreeing with a participant that the information they disclose will remain confidential and not shared beyond the student's supervisor, second marker and possibly an external examiner, is enough for them to agree to be involved in the study. At the point of submission, the student includes a note stating these facts and that their dissertation is not to be placed in the library or shared in the public domain.

THE DATA PROTECTION ACT (2018) AND UK GENERAL DATA PROTECTION (GDPR)

The Data Protection Act controls the way data are handled including how personal information is used by organizations, businesses or the government. The Act requires that everyone responsible for using personal data has to follow strict rules called 'data protection principles'. They must make sure the information is:

- used fairly, lawfully and transparently
- used for specified, explicit purposes
- used in a way that is adequate, relevant and limited to only what is necessary
- accurate and, where necessary, kept up to date
- kept for no longer than is necessary
- handled in a way that ensures appropriate security, including protection against unlawful or unauthorized processing, access, loss, destruction or damage.

Source: www.gov.uk/data-protection

The Data Protection Act (2018) sits alongside and supplements the UK GDPR, for example by providing exemptions. The main principle of data protection is to respect the privacy and rights of stakeholders associated with the research. The UK General Data Protection Regulation (GDPR) is a UK law which was implemented on 1 January 2021. It sets out the key principles, rights and obligations for most processing of personal data in the UK, except for law enforcement and intelligence agencies (ICO, 2021). Although the Data Protection Act (2018) is not specifically designed for conducting research, it is important to follow advice and guidance provided in the DPA 2018 and UK GDPR so that you understand and take responsibility for using personal data.

PLAGIARISM AND SELF-PLAGIARISM

Out of all of the ethical considerations associated with writing a research project, plagiarism is possibly one of the most well-known to students. The reasons for this are that it not only applies to writing a research project, but also other types of assessments.

Plagiarism is passing off the work of others as your own. This not only means using words from other writers, but also taking someone else's idea and passing it off as your own idea. In recent years, plagiarism has hit the headlines as a number of high-profile individuals have openly admitted to plagiarizing their work while studying at university. The use of the internet has led to an increase in the publicity surrounding such cases.

The best way to avoid plagiarism is to correctly attribute your sources. Using others people's work, including an idea or concept that is not your own must be correctly referenced within your research project. The majority of universities adopt the Harvard Referencing System, although there are other systems such as the Vancouver style. Thus, it is important to check which method your institution adopts before you begin referencing your work. Correctly attributing your sources is undertaken through:

- correctly citing the source in the main text of your research project, again, using your institution's referencing system
- providing full details of the source in the full list of references at the end of your project
- taking care to note when citing someone else's work whether you are using a direct or verbatim quote or paraphrasing.

Although by no means exhaustive, some of the reasons plagiarism happens are listed below:

- a lack of understanding as to what constitutes plagiarism
- poor time management and planning
- deliberate cheating

- a failure to record notes accurately
- a lack of understanding as to how and when to use references
- a lack of understanding as to how to read critically and include your own 'voice'
- a lack of attention to detail when referencing or checking your work.

Self-plagiarism is including work in your research project that you have already submitted as part of a previous piece of assessment. A simple way to avoid self-plagiarism is to avoid choosing a research topic covered in other modules. Sometimes a student may have concerns that there is a possibility of self-plagiarism if using material from their research proposal in their final research project. In theory, this should not be a concern as the research proposal is purely the research plan, while the project is the finished product.

PERSONAL CONDUCT

Your own conduct when conducting your research must be professional, honest and transparent. Honesty is an essential quality in a researcher in order to produce a level of credibility and trust in your research. This applies to all researchers, irrespective of the level of the researcher and the type of research being conducted. Intentionally misrepresenting data or results is a serious lapse in honesty and could have serious consequences for the researcher and the research participants. For example, misrepresenting a quote on career progression from a research participant could have a damaging effect on their job and future career prospects. This is all the more likely to happen if the participant has waived their right to anonymity.

POTENTIAL PHYSICAL AND MENTAL HARM

As a researcher, the core principle when conducting your research is to cause no harm to your research participants. Ideally, your research participants should feel that they are gaining something from taking part in your research, not in a financial sense, but they believe that taking part is producing something of value. First, taking precautions to avoid your participants suffering physical harm might seem fairly straightforward when doing research in business and management. However, I have known students wanting to conduct research in war zones. Where this is the case, it is essential to make sure that the students go through the ethical approval process.

Avoiding mental harm means not subjecting your participants to mental distress or affecting their mental well-being. Again, you might think that this is not such an issue in business research. Although do bear in mind that there are subjects in business that are of a sensitive nature. Examples include well-being in the workplace, discrimination in the workplace and career progression.

INFORMED CONSENT

We came across informed consent earlier in the chapter. According to Crow et al. (2006: 83),

> The principle of informed consent requires that prospective participants in research are provided with information about the project in which they are being invited to participate that is sufficiently full and accessible for their decision about whether to take part to be considered informed.

Once again, remember that when inviting potential participants to take part in your study that you fully brief them on the nature of your research. This includes making it clear they have the right to withdraw from your study at any time. The 'informed' part of informed consent is explaining the nature of the research, while the 'consent' part seeks to gain approval from the participant that they are willing to take part. It is important to record this willingness to take part in writing. This is done using something called a consent form. Almost certainly your institution will have an example or template you can use for your research. Figure 7.3 shows an example of a participant consent form. The purpose of the consent form is that it provides the participant with a written overview of the nature of the research and confirms their agreement to take part in the research. This agreement is confirmed through signing the form. Make sure to keep copies of all consent forms as these are evidence of agreement and an important point of reference when reviewing people who have agreed to participate in your study.

Viking University

Participant Consent Form

NAME OF PARTICIPANT:

Title of the research project:

Main investigator and contact details:

Members of the research team:

I confirm that I agree to take part in the above research. I have read the Participant Information Sheet which is attached to this form. I understand what my role will be in this research project, and all my questions have been answered to my satisfaction.

I understand that I am free to withdraw from the research at any time, for any reason and without prejudice.

I have been informed that the confidentiality of the information I provide will be safeguarded.

I am free to ask any questions at any time before and during the study.

I have been provided with a copy of this form and the Participant Information Sheet.

Data Protection: I agree to Viking University processing personal data which I have supplied. I agree to the processing of such data for any purposes connected with the Research Project as outlined to me.*

*Note to researchers: please amend or add to this clause as necessary to ensure that it conforms to the relevant data protection legislation in your country.

Name of participant (print)…………....…...................………..Signed………………......……...Date……....………..

YOU WILL BE GIVEN A COPY OF THIS FORM TO KEEP

If you would like to withdraw from the research, please complete the form below and return to the main investigator named above.

Title of project:

I WISH TO WITHDRAW FROM THIS STUDY

Signed: ……………………….............................…..........   Date: ………..……….

Figure 7.3   Example of a participant consent form

RECORDING DATA

If you are thinking about conducting interviews, using focus groups or carrying out observational research, do reflect on how you record your data. Avoid oversimplifying transcripts. Recording data in qualitative research often involves transcribing data and interpreting the results. There are two ethical issues here. First, when transcribing your data, make sure to accurately record the data and avoid leaving out and/or adapting your participant's responses. Second, when interpreting the results, adopt an impartial view and avoid being biased.

THE RIGHT TO WITHDRAW FROM THE RESEARCH

Earlier in the chapter, I explained the nature of the consent form. Every consent form should make reference to a participant's right to withdraw from the research. Your participants have a right to withdraw at any stage in your study. This might seem frustrating, especially if you have a small number of research participants. However, remember that a participant is giving up their time and sharing their personal views, so they may wish to retract this at any stage in the research. Actually, in all my years of doing research, on very few occasions has a participant requested to withdraw from the research. Certainly, being clear on the nature of the research and securing informed consent can help to reduce the possibility of withdrawal of consent. If you do receive a request to withdraw from the research, thank the participant and respect their wishes to withdraw from the study. It is important to confirm that none of the information they provide will be included in the research findings.

DECEPTION

Deception means gaining access to a participant or data in a dishonest way. For example, giving a false identity in order to gain access to a participant is clearly deceptive. Have confidence in your own abilities as a researcher. The fact that you are doing research as part of a degree programme already adds to your credibility as a researcher. It is essential that you do not set out to deceive any of the stakeholders involved in your research.

RESPECT

Respect means that you should consider the feelings and rights of all those participating in your study. Respect can take time to develop, but if you adopt a professional manner from the start of your research, then there is a greater likelihood that participants will show respect towards you and your research.

DEBRIEFING

Debriefing usually takes place at the conclusion of a participant's role in the research. For example, this may involve sharing with participants any additional information they need to further their understanding of the research after the data have been collected. It also informs participants about the intentions of the research in which they took part.

COLLUSION

Collusion occurs when two or more individuals cooperate to produce a piece of research or a research project that is presented as the work of one student alone. Of course, some forms of research are group projects. However, where the project task is intended as an individual piece of work, then you must not collude with other students.

CONFLICT OF INTEREST

The possibility of conflict of interest is unlikely if you are doing research on an external organization. However, it is something that is very much applicable to students undertaking research on their own organization. By way of example, if you are conducting interviews with senior management within your own organization, are you able to remain impartial and provide an honest representation of the findings?

UK Research and Innovation (UKRI, 2019) defines a conflict of interest as,

> a set of circumstances that creates a risk that an individual's ability to apply judgment or act in one role is, or could be, impaired or influenced by a secondary interest. Even a perception of competing interests, impaired judgment or undue influence may be damaging to UKRI's reputation.

The organization states that conflicts might occur if individuals have for example:

- a direct or indirect financial interest
- non-financial or personal interests
- competing loyalties between an organization they owe a primary duty to and/or some other person or entity.

The existence of an actual, perceived or potential conflict of interest does not necessarily imply wrongdoing on anyone's part. However, any private, personal or commercial interests which give rise to such a conflict of interest must be recognized, disclosed appropriately and either eliminated or properly managed. Reporting, recording and managing potential conflicts effectively protects staff and can help to generate public trust and confidence.

STORING DATA

Having taken part in countless research studies, one of the key questions I have for the researcher(s) is, 'Where do you intend to store your data?'. For students, data storage is not always high on the list of ethical concerns, but it should be. All electronic data should be password protected and do not share your password with anyone else. Why? Remember that on your consent form, as far as the participant is concerned you are the sole researcher. All hard copies of data should be stored under lock and key. Make sure to produce backup copies of your data storage – again, this must be security protected.

DISSEMINATION

How and where you disseminate your work is also an ethical concern. Again, how you intend to do this should be made clear to research participants when seeking informed consent. If you decide to disseminate your work in outlets not mentioned in the consent form, you must seek approval from your participants. For example, your original intentions might have been to disseminate extracts of your work on your own personal blog, but on reflection, you have decided to also share aspects of your findings in a journal article.

DISPOSING OF YOUR RESEARCH MATERIAL

Deciding how to dispose of your data or research findings is likely to be your final ethical concern in the research process. For example, think about how you tend to dispose of documents such as interview transcripts and completed surveys. Considerations here include anonymity and confidentiality. My advice would be to dispose of such documents using a paper shredder.

See Images 7.1 and 7.2 – what are the ethical considerations here? First, Image 7.1 is a researcher conducting research on efficiency in manufacturing. Image 7.2 is a researcher conducting research into children's classroom behaviour. Discuss with your fellow students.

Image 7.1   What are the ethical considerations here? (Manufacturing site)
Source: iStock (photo ID: 1278915839)

Image 7.2   What are the ethical considerations here? (Classroom observation)
Source: iStock (photo ID:1194312424)

GAINING ETHICS APPROVAL FOR YOUR RESEARCH

If your research involves human participants, then the likelihood is that you will need to seek ethics approval from either your supervisor or an ethics committee. The latter we examine later in the chapter.

The purpose of an ethics application is to make sure that the student identifies all possible ethical concerns or problems and methods for addressing them. It is unlikely that students will be able to identify all ethical issues without some kind of assistance (Polonsky, 1998). Given this, it is important that any ethics application should include guidance from your supervisor.

YOUR RESEARCH ETHICS CHECKLIST

The UK Research Integrity Office (UKRIO) has produced a useful checklist for researchers (see below). The checklist lists the key points of good practice in research for all types of research projects and is applicable to all subject areas. Several of the points on the checklist relate to the ethical issues discussed in this chapter. Your institution may provide their own checklist; if not, then the following is a comprehensive guide.

Before conducting your research, and bearing in mind that, subject to legal and ethical requirements, roles and contributions may change during the time span of the research:

1. Does the research address pertinent question(s) and is it designed either to add to existing knowledge about the subject in question or to develop methods for research into it?
2. Is your research design appropriate for the question(s) being asked?
3. Will you have access to all necessary skills and resources to conduct the research?
4. Have you conducted a risk assessment to determine:

    a)   whether there are any ethical issues and whether an ethics review is required
    b)   the potential for risks to the organization, the research, or the health, safety and well-being of researchers and research participants
    c)   what legal requirements govern the research?

5. Will your research comply with all legal and ethical requirements and other applicable guidelines, including those from other organizations and/or countries if relevant?
6. Will your research comply with all requirements of legislation and good practice relating to health and safety?
7. Has your research undergone any necessary ethics review (see 4(a) above), especially if it includes animals, human participants, human material or personal data?
8. Will your research comply with any monitoring and audit requirements?
9. Are you in compliance with any contracts and financial guidelines relating to the project?
10. Have you reached an agreement relating to intellectual property, publication and authorship?
11. Have you reached an agreement relating to collaborative working, if applicable?
12. Have you agreed on the roles of researchers and responsibilities for management and supervision?
13. Have all conflicts of interest relating to your research been identified, declared and addressed?
14. Are you aware of the guidance from all applicable organizations on misconduct in research?

When conducting your research:

15. Are you following the agreed research design for the project?
16. Have any changes to the agreed research design been reviewed and approved if applicable?
17. Are you following best practice for the collection, storage and management of data?
18. Are agreed roles and responsibilities for management and supervision being fulfilled?
19. Is your research complying with any monitoring and audit requirements?

When finishing your research:

20. Will your research and its findings be reported accurately, honestly and within a reasonable time frame?
21. Will all contributions to the research be acknowledged?
22. Are agreements relating to intellectual property, publication and authorship being complied with?
23. Will research data be retained in a secure and accessible form and for the required duration?
24. Will your research comply with all legal, ethical and contractual requirements?

Research ethics is an important part of any research project, as evidenced by the lengthy list above! Often, students focus on developing their research topic, questions and methodology before thinking about addressing ethical issues. To some extent, this is understandable. Taking an ethical approach is about being thoughtful and forward planning, addressing ethical issues is more than simply producing a checklist. It is about your attitude, credibility and professionalism as a researcher.

Polonsky (1998: 1230–1233) provides a useful summary of the key issues contained in an ethics application. It is worth thinking about these issues if applying for ethics approval in your own research project.

1. Have students described the objectives, hypothesis, rationale for methodology, etc.?
2. What is the student's relationship with the subject organization and the subject group?
3. Obtain clearance from the organization being studied or the location being used in the research.
4. Subject recruitment issues.
5. Autonomy and information issues.
6. Data analysis issues.
7. Harm issues.
8. Training issues.
9. Information sheets and consent forms.
10. Anonymity and confidentiality issues.
11. Feedback issues.
12. Plagiarism and academic fraud.

WHAT IF I UNCOVER DIFFICULT ETHICAL ISSUES?

If ethical concerns occur early in your research project, this does not necessarily mean that you should change your research topic. Identifying issues early means that you are more likely to be able to overcome them in some way. This is why it is imperative to consider research ethics early in the research process. Clearly, whether you decide to change topic depends on the nature of the ethical issues. For example, I have found that students who have chosen particularly sensitive topics, such as employee satisfaction or retention, are more likely to uncover difficult issues early in their research. In the case of this example, the issues stem from gaining ethical approval from line managers and how to deal with particularly sensitive answers. If you do find yourself in the situation where you uncover serious ethical concerns, then do raise them immediately with your research supervisor.

This chapter has been about understanding the ethical issues which you will need to consider when doing your research. It is important that you discuss the ethical issues associated with your research with your research supervisor. The onus is on the student to gain ethical approval before starting their research. Also, remember that ethical approval cannot be obtained retrospectively, but must be obtained before your research commences.

THE RESEARCH ETHICS COMMITTEE

The process of gaining ethics approval varies from one institution to another. However, if your research involves human participants, then this is likely to involve an ethics approval process. In some cases, low risk studies may be able to be approved by your research supervisor. Typically, this involves the student completing an ethics checklist. A checklist usually consists of approximately 20 closed-ended questions. Questions are based on issues such as whether the research involves children, is of a medical nature and dissemination of research. Low risk studies are often approved by a research supervisor. Typically, high risk research is referred to an ethics committee. If the latter, then this may require providing more detail by completing an ethics application form (see Figure 7.4).

Viking University

Ethics Application Form

SECTION A: Project/Researcher details

Title of Research Project:

Name of Student Researcher:

Student Number:

Name of Project Supervisor:

Is this research sponsored by any external organization by either the provision of access to data or by funding in cash or in kind?

Will the research be carried out on the premises of another organization? (If so, please attach written consent from this organization.)

SECTION B: Project aims and objectives

Please include a brief outline of your research project. Please make clear the rationale and benefits of the project. In addition, please include whether or not your research will make reference to your affiliation to the college.

Does the project involve the direct participation of individuals other than your research supervisor? If no, please go to the last section (SECTION F). If yes, please continue.

SECTION C: Research methodology

Please provide details of when you intend to commence your project and indicate the likely duration. In addition, please provide details of the proposed methodology.

SECTION D: Ethical issues

Risk – does the proposed research place any of the participants at risk of physical, psychological or emotional harm? If yes, please provide details of how you intend to deal with this issue.

Sponsorship – is the project sponsored by an individual or external organization? If so, will the project require the signing of a confidentiality agreement with an external organization? (If so, this needs to be agreed by the college's research office.)

Will the sponsor need to see the data that you have collected or the report of your research findings? If so, please provide details.

Are there any other ethical issues that you wish to highlight to the research ethics committee?

SECTION E: Consent

It is essential that all those who participate in your research do so of their own free will. For consent to be valid, participants must be informed about the nature of the research, and they must be competent to understand the implications of their participation.

Please provide details of how it is intended that informed consent be obtained from the participants. Copies of relevant documentation should be included, especially any explanatory material given to participants and the consent form.

Discuss the procedures you intend to undertake for gaining permission from participants who are unable to give informed consent. If you intend conducting research without informed consent of participants, detailed reasons must be provided.

Finally, give a detailed account of how you will comply with the Data Protection Act 2018.

SECTION F: Signatures

Student:

Supervisor:

Director of Research:

Date:

Figure 7.4   Example of an ethics application form

Studies of a higher risk may need to seek approval from an ethics committee. If submitting an ethics application to an ethics committee, try to do this as early as possible in the research process. The committee may only meet on an infrequent basis and can be viewed as a gatekeeper who have an important role to play in the ethics approval process. Their role is not to hinder your ethics approval process, but to be vigilant and to make sure that all steps have been taken by the researcher to address ethical issues, particularly all possible sources of harm.

If you find your ethics application rejected by the committee, then you might be asked to resubmit your application. If this is the case, prior to resubmission make sure to follow the feedback provided by the committee. At this point, I also advise you to meet with your supervisor to talk through the feedback and the changes required to your application. Clearly, all of this takes time and means a delay to your data collection. Hence, the need to start your ethics application early.

Image 7.3   An application for ethics approval

Source: iStock (photo ID: 147606195)

From my experience, the relationship between a student and their supervisor is particularly important when seeking ethics approval. If submitting your application to an ethics committee, make sure
that your supervisor reads through and comments on your application. This is almost certainly likely to
increase the chances of gaining approval.

Over the years, very few of my students have had to radically change aspects of their research due
to an application being rejected by an ethics committee. In reality, your supervisor should be able to
provide advice on research ethics to help avoid difficulties gaining ethics approval.

Doyle et al. (2010: 50) provide a typical example of an ethics application in their paper on the issues
experienced by a Research Ethics Committee in a Business School in Ireland:

> A manager in a large corporation asks one of his charges to participate in a research project. The
> manager is pursuing a Master's program at the Business School and this research is deemed to
> be a necessary part of his/her Master's dissertation. In this instance we will take it as given that
> such research does fall within the remit of the local ethics committee. There are various distinct
> scenarios to consider and what follows captures some of the issues that have been debated during
> our committee meetings. The research may be focused on a highly technical issue, for instance
> whether or not a new technological innovation is functioning well. This type of research, is, in
> the main, low risk and even though the issue of voluntarily given informed consent remains, the
> prospect of harm is seen as minimal.

The authors add that this type of project could be approved using an ethics checklist as opposed to an
ethics committee.

Robson (2011: 224) makes the following suggestions on how to get your application approved:

1. Plan the ethical aspects of your study from the beginning.
2. Try to start a dialogue with the chair of the committee at an early stage.
3. If allowed, attend one or more meetings of the committee. All committees develop their own inter-
    nal culture, which has a bearing on how they function, the ways they interpret the guidelines, and
    the values and views they express in the committee. Such observation, and the dialogue mentioned
    above, can be invaluable in helping to shape your application, and to sensitize you to issues they
    are likely to find problematic.
4. If the committee regulations allow this, attach a cover letter to your application summarizing your
    study, giving special attention to key issues such as informed consent and data protection.
5. Know the timetable for meetings and the deadlines for submission prior to the meeting. Approval
    may be conditional, possibly requiring further discussion at a later meeting.
6. If possible, attend the meeting at which your application is discussed, and be prepared to answer
    questions or concerns.
7. If you disagree with a decision, seek a personal meeting with the chair to discuss things.
8. If this does not resolve the situation, or if you feel (after discussion with experienced colleagues)
    that the committee has shown bias or otherwise dealt inappropriately with your case, there should
    be a formal appeal process.

ETHICS ACROSS CULTURES

As there is no universal consensus as to how to define 'ethics', you may find it particularly challenging
if doing cross-cultural research, or, in other words, research involving participants from two or more
different countries. The 'ethical relativist' maintains that nothing is 'really' or 'simply' good or bad; it is
only good or bad in relation to the moral code of a given culture or historical era. If you are engaging in
cross-cultural research, the main considerations are three-fold. First, be prepared to follow 'written' and

'unwritten' codes of conduct. For example, when doing my PhD on UK investment in China, I travelled to several major cities to interview joint venture managers. Prior to commencing each interview, I gave each interviewee a gift from my home country to thank them for their time. Although this might be viewed as not particularly 'ethical', such practice is common when conducting business in China. Second, be sure to understand sensitive issues when producing a questionnaire survey. By way of example, in the UK it is typically considered as disrespectful to ask someone how much they are paid. Yet, in some cultures, this is perfectly acceptable. Finally, as a researcher you need to show respect and willingness to adapt to different cultures.

HOW DO I NEGOTIATE ACCESS?

A key aspect of any research project is knowing how to negotiate access. This can be viewed as negotiating access to individuals and also key sites. For example, the former may focus on managers working within an organization, while the latter may mean how to access particular organizations. Negotiating access to respondents can be challenging for even the most experienced researcher.

Wallace and Sheldon (2015) note that gaining access can be challenging as the researcher's research issues or topic may have little interest or relevance for those managing the organizations invited to participate. In short, there is no perceived benefit for the participant.

Below you will find a useful guide on how to negotiate access.

- *Use all available networks.* This includes family, friends and your research supervisor. Access to participants can be enabled by friends or acquaintances of friends or family. Also, your supervisor is likely to know people you can contact who might be willing to take part in your research. This is likely to be the case if your supervisor is an expert in your chosen area of research.
- *Be explicit in relation to the nature of your research project.* Prospective research participants are far more likely to take part in your research if they fully understand the purpose and benefits of your research. Often, research participants are of the view 'What is in it for me?' when considering taking part in a research study. Thus, be sure to clearly explain your research and its importance.
- *Use one or two individuals as part of a snowball sampling strategy.* We examine sampling methods at length in Chapter 9. For now, snowball sampling is a useful technique if you only know one or two individuals you are able to invite to take part in your research. In essence, snowball sampling is about an individual contacting individuals in their networks asking if they would like to take part in the study. Hopefully, the sample size will grow as a result of the networks of one or two key individuals.
- *Address 'What benefits will I get from taking part in the research?'.* In other words, will your participants gain any tangible or intangible reward for taking part in the research? From my experience, I have found that promising your research participants a summary of your research findings, and/ or a condensed version of your research project, can be a major selling point.
- *Communicate your credibility as a researcher.* This point I regularly communicate to my own research students. The fact that you are doing research at a reputable institution already adds credibility to you as a researcher. Further, when contacting potential research participants, try to 'sell' your research and communicate your skills as a researcher. By way of an example, do not simply state 'I am a student doing research on ...'; consider 'I am currently in the final year of my degree at the University of ... doing an important study on ...', 'I view the benefits of my research as ...'.
- *Do not take 'no' straightaway.* When contacting a potential research participant, whether it is via email, post or telephone, the likelihood is that you may receive no answer or possibly a 'no' straightaway. Before accepting a no answer, explain the merits of your research. Occasionally,

'name dropping' can help to encourage potential participants to take part. For example, if you were carrying out research on a national chain of food retailers, mentioning that the largest chain of food retailers is taking part may persuade competitors to participate. However, prior to mentioning other participants, remember to consider issues surrounding confidentiality and anonymity.

- *Build relationships.* In this section I have already highlighted the importance of networks. Developing your own networks with individuals and organizations is not only an important skill as part of your research, but also something that promotes key transferable skills that you will likely find invaluable.

Image 7.4   Concept Cartoon 'Negotiating access'

In this Concept Cartoon example, the discussion is on negotiating access. One character is saying that negotiating access is impossible for student researchers, the second character states that negotiating access is easier with the help of your supervisor, while finally, the third character mentions that the best way to avoid negotiating access is to use fellow students as a research sample. What do you think? Again, you can participate in a group discussion with your fellow students to see if you arrive at the same conclusions.

ETHICS SCENARIOS

This section presents three mini ethics scenarios. Each scenario requires you to explain the ethical issues that need to be considered. In this respect, think of your role as that of the Chair of the Research Ethics Committee, tasked with identifying the ethical issues associated with each research project.

(A) An international student researcher conducting research into place branding in Oxford has received consent from the Ministry of Tourism. The student intends interviewing 20 hotel managers on the impact of the Covid-19 pandemic on tourism in the city.

  •   What are the ethical issues that need to be considered?

(B) A student researcher intends to interview employees at the Japanese Head Office of a leading accountancy organization. The interview questions will focus on job satisfaction in the workplace. She is from Brazil and has some experience of doing interviews.

  •   What are the ethical issues that need to be considered?

(C) A part-time student researcher works for a leading Indian soft drinks brand. She conducts a focus group with work colleagues on their perceptions of brand names and logos in the soft drinks industry.

  •   What are the ethical issues that need to be considered?

GROUP TASK

In groups of 4 or 5, discuss the ethical considerations when recording interviews.

CHAPTER SUMMARY

- Ethics can be defined as 'the principles, norms and standards of conduct governing an individual or group'.

- You have an ethical responsibility to all of your research stakeholders.

- The term 'business ethics' comprises two words – 'business' and 'ethics' – which cover the areas of moral principles, beliefs, values, culture, governance issues and code of conduct for business.

- As a researcher you have an ethical responsibility to carry out your research honestly and with integrity.

- The purpose of an ethics application is to make sure that the student identifies all possible ethical concerns or problems, and methods for addressing them.

- The 'ethical relativist' maintains that nothing is 'really' or 'simply' good or bad; it is only good or bad in relation to the moral code of a given culture or historical era.

- Key documents associated with ethics approval include the ethics checklist, approval application form and participant consent form.

QUESTIONS FOR REVIEW

1. How would you define research ethics and why is it important to have an understanding of ethical issues when doing your research project?

2. What is meant by the term 'informed consent' and at what point in your research are you likely to seek this?

3. Discuss some of the ways to increase the likelihood of securing ethics approval from a Research Ethics Committee (REC).

4. Explain how your research supervisor might be able to support you when addressing your ethical concerns.

5. Conducting cross-cultural research raises different ethical issues. Discuss.

6. Outline the reasons why many leading brands have an ethics code of conduct.

7. Discuss the steps you can take when negotiating access.

8. What are some of the questions you are likely to find in an ethics checklist in relation to 'conducting your research'?

STUDENT SCENARIO: THE ETHICAL ISSUES IMPACTING MAX'S STUDY

Max worked as a Customer Services Manager for a large retail chain, while also studying on a part-time MBA programme. In order to avoid having to go through the challenges of negotiating access, he decided to adopt an action research design and focus on customer service policies within his own organization. He intended conducting interviews with customer service staff across three of the branches located in the Eastern region of the UK. Max had considered the ethical issues associated with his research early in the research process and had also consulted with his research supervisor. As he was conducting research involving human participants, he submitted his ethics approval form to the University's Research Ethics Committee (REC). Following approval from the committee, Max proceeded to collect his primary data.

Ethical issues

Max was confident that he had addressed all of the ethical issues in his research. He had followed the correct process by speaking to his supervisor and submitting an ethics approval form. Although Max's ethics application had been approved by the REC, he still had some reservations about the sensitivity of his research, especially as data collection involved asking sensitive questions to colleagues such as, 'What are your current views on the level of customer service provided by the organization?' and 'How would you develop customer service support over the next 12 months?'. Part of Max's ethics application included a letter from the Managing Director of his employer confirming that Max could proceed with his data collection. In Max's application he covered all ethical issues, including informed consent, anonymity, confidentiality, data storage and dissemination.

Data collection involved interviewing a total of five customer service employees. However, following completion of the interviews, Max received requests from 3 of the participants to withdraw from the study. Although unexpected, Max understood that participants had the right to withdraw from his re-search at any stage in the research process. Unfortunately, this meant that he now only had data from 2 employees. In Max's view, this was not enough to address his research problem and research questions. As a result, he decided to amend his study by also interviewing managers at two supplier firms to de-termine their views on customer service. Thus, he then proceeded to interview these new participants.

Research consequences

Following his interviews with the supplier firms, Max shared his changes with his research supervisor. To his frustration, Max's supervisor explained that as Max had made changes to his research, he should have sought ethics approval from the REC. Participants withdrawing from his research, combined with the interviews of managers at two of his employer's suppliers, were significant changes to his research. Why did he need to seek new ethics approval? In short, because the REC approved his original research, not the revised process.

Retrospective ethics approval

After completing his data collection, Max submitted another ethics application form to the REC. However, although the REC approved his application (on condition that all ethical issues were addressed in accordance with ethical standards), they made it clear that retrospective ethics approval is not possible and is only ever considered in exceptional circumstances.

Questions

1. Identify the ethical issues Max should have considered prior to making changes to his data collection.
2. Why is it important to consider ethical issues early in the research process?

Hint: Think about Max's relationship with his research supervisor and the REC when answering the question.

FURTHER READING

Mertens, D.M. and Ginsberg, P.E. (eds) (2009) *Handbook of Research Ethics*. London: Sage.

Section III provides helpful information on ethics and different types of research methods.

Oliver, P. (2003) *The Student's Guide to Research Ethics*. Maidenhead: Open University Press.

A comprehensive book on research ethics that focuses on ethics before the research commences, during the research and post data collection.

Richardson, J.C. and Godfrey, B.S. (2003) 'Towards ethical practice in the use of archived transcripted interviews', *International Journal of Social Research Methodology*, 6 (4): 347–355.

This article explores how ethical approaches can be developed for the use of transcripted archived interviews.

Wiles, R. (2013) *What are Qualitative Research Ethics?* London: Bloomsbury.

This book provides an introduction to research ethics relevant to researchers conducting qualitative research. It covers all of the main ethical considerations and features a chapter on 'Where next for research ethics?'

REFERENCES

Adams, J., Raeside, R. and Khan, H.T.A. (2014) *Research Methods for Business and Social Science Students* (2nd edn). New Delhi: Sage.

BP (2019) *Ethics Code of Conduct*. Available at: www.bp.com/content/dam/bp/business-sites/en/global/corporate/pdfs/who-we-are/our-code-our-responsibility.pdf (accessed 18 February 2021).

Buffett, W. (2020) *The Three Essential Warren Buffett Quotes to Live By*. Available at: www.forbes.com/sites/jamesberman/2014/04/20/the-three-essential-warren-buffett-quotes-to-live-by/?sh=5a3364f26543 (accessed January 2021).

Crow, G., Wiles, R., Heath, S. and Charles, V. (2006) 'Research ethics and data quality: The implications of informed consent', *International Journal of Social Research Methodology*, 9 (2): 83–95.

Dimitriades, Z.S. (2007) 'Business ethics and corporate social responsibility in the e-economy: A commentary', *Electronic Journal of Business Ethics and Organizational Studies*, 12 (2).

Doyle, E., Mullins, M. and Cunningham, M. (2010) 'Research ethics in a business school context: The establishment of a review committee and the primary issues of concern', *Journal of Academic Ethics*, 8: 43–66.

Faull, J. (2014) 'Kenco coffee gangs campaign', *The Drum*, 13 August. Available at: www.thedrum.com/news/2014/08/13/kenco-s-coffee-v-gangs-campaign-highlights-brand-ethics (accessed 20 December 2019).

Information Commissioner's Office (ICO) (2021) *Some Basic Concepts*. Available at: https://ico.org.uk/for-organisations/guide-to-data-protection/introduction-to-data-protection/some-basic-concepts/ (accessed 15 December 2020).

Lavrakas, P.J. (2008) *Encyclopedia of Survey Research Methods*. Thousand Oaks, CA: Sage.

McKee, H. and Porter, J. (2012) 'The ethics of archival research', *College Composition and Communication*, 64 (1): 59–81.

Pilkington, A., Bowen, P. and Rose, R. (2019) 'Ethical decision making in a mixed methodological study investigating emotional intelligence and perceived stress amongst academics', *International Journal of Academic Management Science Research*, 3 (8): 15–26.

Polonsky, M.J. (1998) 'Incorporating ethics into business students' research projects: A process approach', *Journal of Business Ethics*, 17 (11): 1227–1241.

Purcell, T.V. (1977) 'Do courses in business ethics pay off?', *California Management Review*, 19 (4): 50–58.

Robson, C. (2011) *Real World Research*. Chichester: John Wiley & Sons.

Rowley, J. and Slack, F. (2004) 'Conducting a literature review', *Management Research News*, 27 (6): 31–39.

The Guardian (2019) 'German education minister quits over PhD plagiarism', 9 February. Available at: www.google.co.uk/amp/s/amp.theguardian.com/world/2013/feb/09/german-education-minister-quits-phd-plagiarism (accessed 16 November 2019).

Treviño, L.K. and Nelson, K.A. (2011) *Managing Business Ethics: Straight Talk About How To Do It Right* (5th edn). Hoboken: John Wiley & Sons.

UK Research and Innovation (2019) *Conflicts of Interest*. Available at: www.ukri.org/about-us/governance-and-structure/conflicts-of-interest/ (accessed 15 October 2019).

Wallace, M. and Sheldon, N. (2015) 'Business research ethics: Participant observer perspectives', *Journal of Business Ethics*, 128: 267–277.

Walliman, N. (2011) *Research Methods: The Basics*. New York: Routledge.

8

DOING WORK-BASED PROJECTS AND RESEARCHING YOUR OWN ORGANIZATION

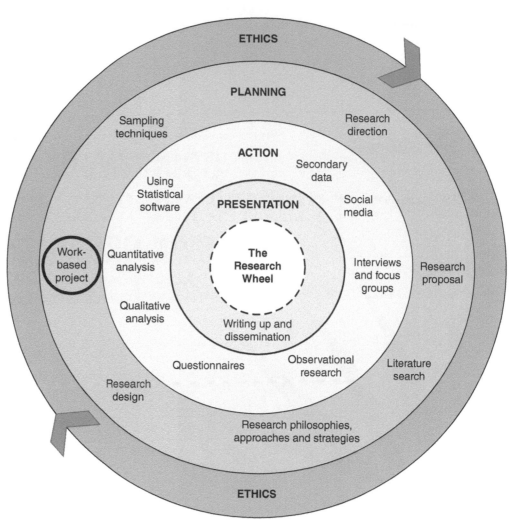

Figure 8.1   The Research Wheel

Learning objectives

By the end of this chapter, you should be able to:

- understand what is mean by 'work-based project'
- appreciate the differences between a work-based project and a dissertation
- carry out the steps involved in undertaking a work-based project
- know how to structure a project proposal
- know how to design, plan and implement a work-based project
- appreciate supervision, support and relationships when doing a work-based project
- understand the benefits and challenges of doing a work-based project
- understand the importance of reflection when doing a work-based project
- explain the ethical considerations when researching your own organization.

INTRODUCTION

The purpose of this chapter is to explore the process of conducting a work-based project and researching your own organization. In simple terms, a *work-based project* can be viewed as a project based on a particular aspect of an employee's organization. However, there is no one universal definition. For example, some institutions view a work-based project as a piece of research conducted at an organization's request, while others view it as something carried out as a more collaborative process between a student, student's employer and an academic institution. We will examine these interpretations and others later in the chapter.

Increasingly, universities and colleges are assessing students using alternative assessment methods to the traditional dissertation. Although doing a dissertation offers a wide range of research skills, it does not always involve research based on a particular organization(s). The increasing emphasis on employability, together with flexible degrees, means that academic institutions are adapting their assessment to meet these changes. One way to address the added focus on employability is the introduction of work-based projects. In this chapter, we will look at all of the factors associated with conducting a work-based project. If you are required to complete a work-based project as part of your course, then you should find this chapter useful.

The chapter begins by explaining what is meant by work-based learning. Undertaking a work-based project is taken in the context of work-based learning, so it is important to discuss the nature of this association. Next, we explore what is meant by the term 'work-based project' and the role of the researcher. If doing a work-based project, your role as a researcher can be viewed from a dual perspective. In other words, you are both an employee and a researcher.

Following this, the chapter discusses the differences between a traditional research project (dissertation) and a work-based project. In this section, you will find useful information on how the two types of project differ, together with similarities. Subsequently, the chapter provides an outline of the steps involved when undertaking a work-based project.

We then analyze what is involved when planning and managing a work-based project. An important consideration here is the relationships you have with your supervisor and the organization.

The chapter then explores the benefits and challenges of doing a work-based project. Finally, the chapter examines the significance attached to reflecting on your research and the ethical issues to consider. Although we explored research ethics in Chapter 7, in this chapter emphasis is given towards doing research on your own firm.

As you can see by Figure 8.1, we have now come to the stage of 'work-based project' in the research process. Clearly, if you are doing a traditional dissertation, then undertaking a work-based project does not apply to you. However, if this is a requirement of your course, then you will note that work-based project is in the 'Planning' layer of The Research Wheel.

Why the 'planning' layer? Well, many students have little, if any, prior knowledge of how to do a work-based project. Hence, a great deal of exploration is required to get to know what is required. Many of the latter stages in the research process (as illustrated in The Research Wheel) are generic, irrespective of the type of research project. There are, of course, differences when carrying out a work-based project. One example here is that it requires more collaboration with research stakeholders, in particular, the organization. This is because there is a greater focus on collaboration with this type of research, in contrast to a traditional dissertation, where the researcher has more autonomy.

WORK-BASED LEARNING

'Work-based project' is typically discussed in the context of *work-based learning*. Lester and Costley (2010) provide a comprehensive overview of work-based learning. They define *work-based learning* as 'any learning that is situated in the workplace or arises directly out of workplace concerns'. They distinguish between work-based learning on the basis of 'planned' and 'unplanned'. The latter is informal and can relate to on-the-job learning in the workplace, while the former might be organized by an individual, their employer or possibly a third party such as an educational institution. The focus of this chapter is primarily on the last of these, where there is some kind of involvement or collaboration from an academic institution.

Lemanski et al. (2011) pointed out that there are many work-based learning courses throughout the UK education system, including in higher education institutions and businesses, and there are many means by which the student is engaged and assessed. For example, assessment may take the form of a group presentation, exam or portfolio of work. Although work-based learning involves all of these types of assessment, this chapter focuses on work-based project. A project is normally the culmination of any work-based learning programme or course. Work-based learning is a process, according to Raelin (2008: 2), which has three critical elements:

1. It views learning as acquired in the midst of action and dedicated to the task at hand.
2. It sees knowledge creators and utilization as collective activities, wherein learning becomes everyone's job.
3. Its users demonstrate a learning-to-learn aptitude, which frees them to question underlying assumptions of practice.

The above points view work-based learning perhaps as more of an on-the-job process, as opposed to learning and assessment. Although learning can be undertaken and assessed in-house, within an employer, it is not clear how 'learning' relates to 'learners', 'employers' and 'assessment'.

Seagrave et al. (1996) suggested three key strands to work-based learning which should be relevant to all learners and employers – learning at work, learning through work and learning for work. These three key strands are something for you to reflect on if engaged in work-based learning as they are relevant to your role as a 'learner'.

LEARNING AT WORK

The first of these strands is learning 'at' work. Emphasis here might be on doing vocation training or in-house training, which is all about learning on the job. This may involve some kind of assessment, but often not a formalized work-based project.

LEARNING THROUGH WORK

The second strand is learning 'through' work and utilizes the higher education perspective of developing critical skills and application of learning which can be fostered through higher education.

LEARNING FOR WORK

Finally, learning 'for' work is associated with the concept of professional development, which can of course be provided by higher education.

What does learning in the workplace mean? In relation to work-based learning that is accredited and formally assessed, Ebbutt (1996) proposed a classification scheme consisting of four basic modes.

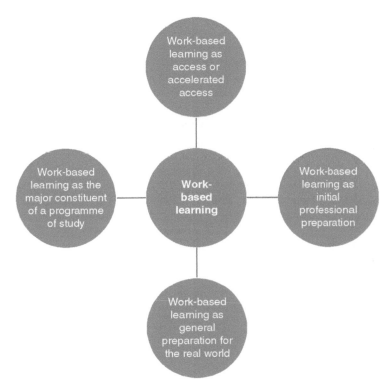

Figure 8.2   A classification of work-based learning

Source: Adapted from Ebbutt (1996)

- Work-based learning as access or accelerated access
  This is where a student draws on their learning experiences at work as a means to secure a place on a degree programme. This is mainly achieved through Accreditation of Prior Learning (APEL). An APEL claim may also entitle the student to credits from the programme.
- Work-based learning as initial professional preparation
  This is where full-time students gain access to a workplace as part of their degree programme. For example, an Undergraduate Business student spending a six-month placement working for a financial institution.

- Work-based learning as general preparation for the real world
  This is where a degree course focuses on a key set of transferable skills as part of 'real-world learning'. Examples may include communication, teamwork, problem-solving and leadership.
- Work-based learning as the major constituent of a programme of study
  This is where students are full-time employees, and study on a part-time programme; most of the research-based fieldwork is carried out in the student's own workplace. The academic institution retains control over assessment, but there may also be consultation between the institution and the student's employer. Students are likely to meet regularly with tutorial staff from the institution to discuss research methods.

The above classification scheme gives a clear overview of different types of work-based learning. In terms of work-based project, we are primarily concerned with the second and fourth of these: *Work-based learning as initial professional preparation* and *Work-based learning as the major constituent of a programme of study*. If you are doing an academic programme with a large 'work-based element' then this is the course that you are likely to be doing. It is these types of programmes that usually require students to complete a work-based project. The strong academic element in work-based learning is evident in the definition by Garnett (2016: 305), who defines work-based learning as '... used to describe higher education programmes of study where the learning which takes place is undertaken primarily at and through work and is for the purposes of work'. By way of an example, a work-based degree may describe a part-time degree programme where a student studies and works part-time. This allows an employee to gain a degree while working. A key advantage of this type of learning is that an employee can learn best practice with the entire organization.

Brennan and Little (2006) proposed the following distinct types of work-based learning. First, a student in higher education doing an extended or several short periods of work placement. Second, the student based in employment studying on either a higher education-based programme with integrated taught content and activities in a work context, or, finally, an employment-based programme with content negotiated between the university, the employer and learner.

For a better understanding of the role of work-based learning, it is always a good idea to read academic articles on the subject as this will give you an insight into how programmes are implemented and the role of the student.

For example, in their study on the partnerships in work-based learning, Maclaren and Marshall (2006) reflect upon their own learning from the setting up and running of a work-based learning module, on the part-time degree programme run by the Institute of Continuing Education at The Queen's University of Belfast. Reflection was based on the questions below, as noted by Guise (1995). These are fundamental questions associated with a work-based learning programme that are applicable to all three-parties – the student, employer and adviser – and certainly something for you to consider if doing a work-based learning module.

- Are the learning outcomes agreed by all parties?
- Are the assessment criteria agreed by all parties?
- What sort of evidence of learning is appropriate?
- Who should do the assessment? The tutor? The work-based supervisor?
- Can work-based learning be graded?
- What specific support do learners need?

ARE THE LEARNING OUTCOMES AGREED BY BOTH PARTIES?

Prior to starting your work-based programme, make sure that all parties are aware of the learning outcomes. The university typically produces the learning outcomes as part of a work-based learning programme and project. However, often this is done with an employer, particularly if a work-based learning programme is delivered in-house.

Some work-based programmes require that all parties sign up to a Learning Agreement or contract. Learning contracts are drawn up between tutor or supervisor and the learner to construct individual learning plans and outcomes of the learner. Contracts can be drawn up to satisfy both the needs of the learner as well as their employer (Lemanski et al., 2011). This demonstrates a commitment by all parties and also provides the employee (student), employer and university with a clear overview of expectations throughout the programme.

For you, as a student, it is important to know the nature of the commitment made by your employer. For example, key questions for you to know might include: How many hours each week will I be permitted to work on my work-based project? Will I have a dedicated mentor? What support will my employer give me to help me to achieve the learning outcomes?

Furthermore, make sure you know the level of authority you have when accessing data. Having limited access to data and difficulty gaining permission to access may of course affect views and ability to achieve the learning outcomes. For your first research meeting with your academic adviser and/or work supervisor, it is essential to take a checklist to go over key points (see Figure 8.3).

Checklist

- Expectations of all parties – the student, adviser and work supervisor.
- Frequency of face-to-face meetings and communication via email and telephone.
- Meeting topics, dates and times of meeting (planned in advance).
- Key deadlines and submission date of final project.
- Research topic and discussion on key steps.
- Planned discussion of research findings.

Figure 8.3   Work-based project initial meeting with supervisor and/or adviser checklist

ARE THE ASSESSMENT CRITERIA AGREED BY ALL PARTIES?

Again, the amount of input you have in contributing to the assessment criteria depends on the type of work-based learning programme. Usually, the assessment criteria are well established when it comes to a work-based programme. To a large extent, the nature of project work is quite generic in several aspects, for example when it comes to formulating objectives, data collection and analysis.

WHAT SORT OF EVIDENCE OF LEARNING IS APPROPRIATE?

A work-based learning programme may include several different assessment methods for evidence of learning, for example you might be required to keep a research diary, produce a portfolio of work or most commonly a work-based project. Also, if the course you are doing is at or in collaboration with an academic institution, then your project will be driven by specified learning outcomes.

WHO SHOULD DO THE ASSESSMENT? THE TUTOR? THE WORK-BASED SUPERVISOR?

The assessment might be set by the university if it is a work-based learning programme delivered to a number of employers. In contrast, some employers, especially those wanting in-house, bespoke programme delivery, are likely to want a greater say on assessment. The setting of the assessment might be done by the university, but allocating marks and feedback might be a more collaborative approach.

CAN WORK-BASED LEARNING BE GRADED?

Grading work-based learning can involve assessment criteria set by your institution or employer. In some cases, assessment and the marking criteria is a collaboration between an employer and university. Certainly, a work-based project can be graded and often follows a similar set of marking criteria to that of a traditional dissertation. As with a traditional dissertation, a work-based project usually starts with a research proposal. This is something we look at later in the chapter.

WHAT SPECIFIC SUPPORT DO LEARNERS NEED?

Gray (2001) notes that work-based learning programmes typically focus on work-based problems and issues which could involve their own personal development, the management of employees, communication, or the management of change. In this sense, learning is an inductive approach, as the learner moves from a research problem to implementation and later evaluation. In essence, this is action research or action research design as we examined in Chapter 6.

Why is it important to understand the different interpretations of work-based learning? The answer to this question is that it makes you think about the nature of your work-based learning degree and assessment. Furthermore, it encourages you to reflect on your role as a learner. If there is a significant work-based element, then the likelihood is that you will be required to do a work-based project. We now consider the nature of a work-based project in the next section.

WHAT IS A WORK-BASED PROJECT?

As we have seen, perhaps rather confusingly, there are many varieties of work-related, workplace or work-based learning (the terms are unfortunately used interchangeably) in higher education (Boud and Costley, 2007). The same extends to projects. For example, in the literature, 'work-based project' can also be referred to as 'work-based learning project'. From this point forward, I will use the term 'work-based project'.

Essentially, a work-based project allows you to develop a workplace activity into a meaningful learning experience, which will benefit the workplace, you as a learner and your university (Workman, 2010). A work-based project might take place at any point during a course, although like a traditional degree programme, a large-scale project is usually the culmination of a course of study.

Doing a work-based project is not only beneficial to a student, but can also be advantageous to the partnering institution. For example, according to Boud and Soloman (2001: 37), work-based learning 'provides the university with the opportunity to establish long-term relationships with corporations and this potentially has an impact on many kinds of education and research, ranging from new forms of course provision to collaborative research projects'. Relationships in general are an important part of the work-based learning process and something we examine in greater depth later in the chapter.

A key aspect of work-based research is that it is within the researcher's own work practice (Costley et al., 2010). In some cases, students have the option to undertake a work-based project as opposed to a dissertation. In essence, a work-based project involves doing a piece of research about your employer or a partner organization. Typically, the focus of the research is on one organization, although this may also be narrow in the sense that emphasis is on a particular department or function of the business.

Normally, a work-based project is relatively small compared to a traditional dissertation. This is reflected in the time frame given to students in which to complete their research. Clearly, this varies between institutions, although usually the time period can be anywhere from 8 to 12 weeks. Hence, in this sense the nature of the research task is likely to be extremely focused and often in response to a request from a student's employer. For example, topics may focus on improving or introducing a new feature within the organization. By way of example, one of my former students produced a marketing communications plan for their employer. This was a small, local organization, with limited knowledge and experience of strategic marketing.

By addressing a particular work-based issue, research in this area has a usefulness and can be applied to an organization. As an insider, a challenge for researchers is conflict of interest, but this can be outweighed by the benefits of doing work-based research, not least, seeing the outcomes of your research implemented by the organization.

The work-based project has been viewed as having its own characteristics which differentiate it from the traditional dissertation. Examples of these characteristics include the dual role of the worker as researcher, the organizational context and culture including the knowledge held within the organization and by its individuals, and the ethical values underpinning working practice (Armsby and Costley, 2000, cited in Workman, 2007).

If you are doing research on your own organization, think of yourself as an 'insider'. Costley et al. (2010) support this view of work-based research from an insider's perspective. So much so, that they refer to a work-based project as 'an insider-led work-based project'. The authors stress that as you are an insider within your own organization, this gives you easy access to people and information.

COMPARING A WORK-BASED PROJECT AND A DISSERTATION

In terms of the research process, there are a number of differences when comparing a work-based project and traditional dissertation. Table 8.1 summarizes the key differences when comparing a work-based project with other projects. The table is from Boud and Costley (2007) and provides an interesting comparison. As well as differences, it is also important to note that there are many similarities. For example, both types of research will require a clear research direction, methodology, data analysis and presentation of research findings.

Table 8.1   Common differences between work-based projects and other student projects

Work-based project	Typical student project
• Student is insider to problem/context	• Student is outsider
• Focus on work and learning for work	• Focus on learning disciplinary knowledge
• Setting defines what is required (in part)	• Greater emphasis on supervisor to define
• Practice drives use of theory	standards
• Primary abilities to be fostered: reflexivity, development	• Theory privileged over practice typically
• Draws on wide range of resources/support within work organization	• Variable abilities to be fostered, often critique and analysis
• Embraces knowledge-in-practice	• Draws on resources/support within educational institution
• Time-limited by real-world constraints	• Knowledge-in-practice limited or non-existent
• Driven by the exigencies of work usually interpreted widely	• Time-limited by timetable and university deadlines
• Paradigm/methodology not necessarily evident	• Driven by specified learning outcomes and interests of student and adviser
• Outcomes – mix of pragmatic/organizational and academic	• Works within defined paradigm/methodology
• Applied in real settings	• Outcomes predominantly academic
• Student knows about existing context and knowledge boundaries	• Not normally applied in real settings
	• 'Supervisor' has knowledge that is passed on to the student

Source: Costley and Boud, 2007

Similarly, Workman and Nottingham (2015) note the following differences between work-based projects and dissertations:

- Dissertations are theory orientated rather than practice.
- Dissertations often are purely desk-based research with no field work.
- Workplace ethical issues are less prevalent in dissertations.
- Personal and reflective learning is not explicitly included in a dissertation.
- It is customary for a dissertation to reflect the conventions of its subject discipline, while work-based projects consider the transdisciplinary aspects of a workplace.
- A dissertation format is usually an extended piece of narrative, unsuitable for a work-based project, which involves a report with critical reflection.

Let us look at some of the above points in relation to what characterizes a work-based project in greater detail.

STUDENT IS INSIDER TO PROBLEM/CONTEXT

As highlighted earlier in the chapter, doing work on your organization means that you are an insider researcher. This means that you have the benefit of access and possibly first-hand experience of the research problem or research context. An advantage is that you may also be able to instigate change and monitor changes within the organization. For example, one of my former students undertook a work-based project on her retail organization. As a Marketing Executive, she was able to implement the changes to marketing strategy as per the recommendations in her project.

Clearly, one of the issues of being an insider researcher is the importance of ethical issues and getting the message across that you are an impartial researcher.

FOCUS ON WORK AND LEARNING FOR WORK

A work-based project is based on a work-related research problem designed to support your learning. The 'learning for work' aspect means that an outcome is that you can put into practice what you have learned from doing the project. By way of an example, I have taught banking and finance students on part-time degree programmes. The course requires students to complete a work-based project on a work-related topic. The topic is agreed between the employer, student and the academic institution.

SETTING DEFINES WHAT IS REQUIRED (IN PART)

Sometimes a requirement of a work-based learning programme is the research topic being set by the employer. For example, the employer may choose a topic on the basis of furthering an employee's learning. Setting a topic may also in part be based on collaboration with the employee (student).

PRACTICE DRIVES USE OF THEORY

Typically, work-based projects are largely practice based. An academic work-based learning programme is likely to still require theoretical application, but there is less emphasis on theory. If you are doing a work-based project as part of a short course, possibly delivered in-house, as your place of employment, the main attention will perhaps be on applied research. If you remember, students doing a work-based project often conduct applied research to solve practical problems associated with a particular organization.

PRIMARY ABILITIES TO BE FOSTERED: REFLEXIVITY, DEVELOPMENT

A key skill when doing a research project of any kind is the ability to critique and be analytical. However, with a work-based project, abilities to be fostered include personal development.

DRAWS ON WIDE RANGE OF RESOURCES/SUPPORT WITHIN WORK ORGANIZATION

Students doing a work-based project are in a fortunate position to have access not only to academic sources, but also access to resources and support from their employer. Support from your organization includes access to secondary sources. Examples here may include customer records, sales records and company reports. Access to secondary data requires agreement from your employer and consideration of ethical issues.

EMBRACES KNOWLEDGE-IN-PRACTICE

This point refers to the emphasis on knowledge development through practice. For example, adopting knowledge in relation to workplace activity. If work-based learning is a major constituent of your programme of study, then much of your knowledge will be developed through working in practice. When it comes to writing your work-based project, you are already starting from a position of knowledge, although the project is an opportunity to develop this through reading what has been published on your chosen area of research.

TIME-LIMITED BY REAL-WORLD CONSTRAINTS

Certain work-based learning programmes are delivered in-house or part-time. If you are doing your work-based project while still working, then you need to balance your research with the demands of work. As with any research project, a clear research timetable is required to make sure that you can devote adequate time to your research. Figure 8.4 shows you an example of a work-based project research timetable. There are many similarities to a traditional dissertation, although students are typically given less time in which to complete their project. Remember that if you are doing a programme of study that is largely a work-based learning programme, then it is important to meet with your work supervisor and/or mentor, as well as your academic adviser on a regular basis. Here, I have used the term 'adviser' as opposed to 'supervisor'. This is because students doing a work-based project usually have two key stakeholders – that of an adviser from the academic institution and a work supervisor from their employer.

DRIVEN BY THE EXIGENCIES OF WORK USUALLY INTERPRETED WIDELY

This point depends on the nature of your work-based learning programme. For example, if you are driven by the exigencies, or, in other words, the demands of work, this will inform how you approach your research project. Your interpretation of the research problem and what you need to achieve as a result of doing your project is communicated via your employer. This type of work-based learning tends to take place where there is no collaboration or partnership with an academic institution. However, in reality, if an academic institution is involved, then to a certain extent your research will be driven by learning outcomes and your adviser and work supervisor.

Timetable for completing a work-based project

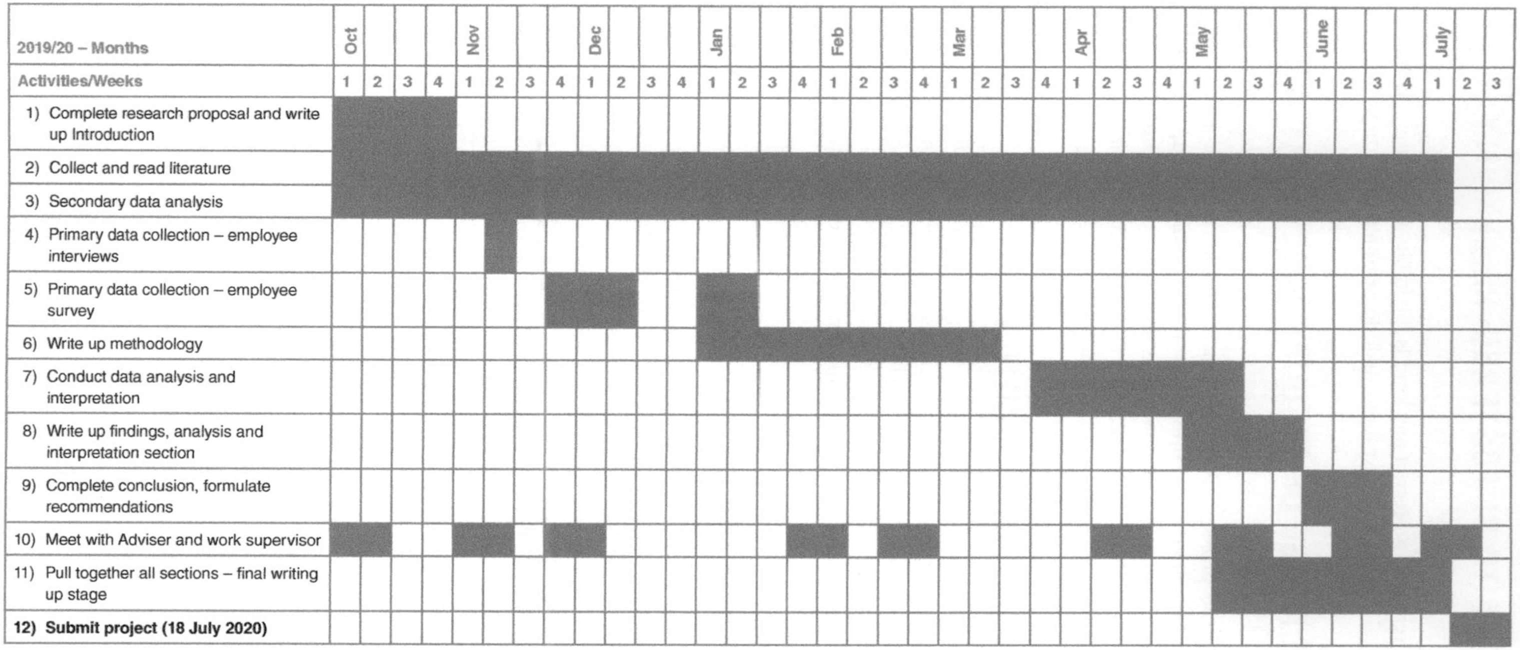

2019/20 – Months	Oct			Nov				Dec				Jan				Feb				Mar				Apr				May				June				July		
Activities/Weeks	1	2	3	1	2	3	4	1	2	3	4	1	2	3	4	1	2	3	4	1	2	3	4	1	2	3	4	1	2	3	4	1	2	3	4	1	2	3
1) Complete research proposal and write up Introduction	■	■	■																																			
2) Collect and read literature				■	■	■	■	■	■	■	■	■	■	■	■	■	■	■	■	■	■	■	■	■	■	■	■	■	■	■	■	■						
3) Secondary data analysis					■	■																																
4) Primary data collection – employee interviews								■	■																													
5) Primary data collection – employee survey												■	■																									
6) Write up methodology																■	■																					
7) Conduct data analysis and interpretation																							■	■	■	■												
8) Write up findings, analysis and interpretation section																												■										
9) Complete conclusion, formulate recommendations																														■	■							
10) Meet with Adviser and work supervisor		■		■				■								■			■							■						■				■		
11) Pull together all sections – final writing up stage																															■	■	■	■	■	■	■	
12) Submit project (18 July 2020)																																						■

Figure 8.4 Example of a work-based project research timetable

PARADIGM/METHODOLOGY NOT NECESSARILY EVIDENT

As a work-based project tends to be largely practice based, there is much less emphasis on research philosophy and methodological approaches. This does not mean to say that you should totally ignore research theory, but focus on research paradigms may not be a requirement by your institution and/or employer. It is still important to be clear when explaining your research process. By way of example, avoid being too generic, e.g. 'I conducted 10 interviews with colleagues, recorded the interviews and transcribed my data'. Remember that this is your 'research journey' so try to write about your personal experience of doing research. For example, What type of interviews did you conduct? Why did you record the interviews? Where did the interviews take place? In short, although this is a work-based project, do not skip on the detail.

OUTCOMES – MIX OF PRAGMATIC/ORGANIZATIONAL AND ACADEMIC

The outcomes of your research are likely to have both practical and theoretical implications. In other words, the findings from your research may benefit and/or contribute to your organization, while the 'academic' outcome may relate to theoretical contribution to your research. Often, a work-based project will involve the application of theory to underpin practice, for example applying a particular theory in the context of your organization.

APPLIED IN REAL SETTINGS

The key difference here is that a work-based project can have application in a real-world setting, whereas a traditional dissertation tends to be more academic and may not be applied to the real world. Similar to the above point, this is not always a straightforward dichotomy. If you are doing a work-based project, you might be fortunate that aspects of your research recommendations can be implemented within your organization. In short, the likelihood of real-world application is much greater with a work-based project.

STUDENT KNOWS ABOUT EXISTING CONTEXT AND KNOWLEDGE BOUNDARIES

In relation to a traditional dissertation, the supervisor is normally a subject specialist and able to pass on knowledge to the student. In contrast, for a work-based project, a student typically has a wealth of practical knowledge about their subject.

WHAT DOES A WORK-BASED PROJECT LOOK LIKE?

Prior to going through the typical structure of a work-based project, it is important to explain a little about the research proposal. Although this is something we examined in Chapter 3, when doing a work-based project, the proposal is for the benefit of the employer and adviser (academic). In a traditional dissertation, the main purpose of the proposal is to help you to set out your research direction, and also to allocate a research supervisor. Typical steps in the proposal are below and see Figure 8.5 for the main items.

TITLE PAGE

To include:

- the title of your dissertation research proposal
- module code
- module title
- student registration number
- date
- contents page (to include section headings and page numbers).

1.0 INTRODUCTION

- should include background to your research topic
- the research problem or issue that is the focus of the study
- the purpose of the study – aims, research objectives and research questions.

2.0 PRELIMINARY LITERATURE REVIEW

- a critical review of the main research published that is relevant to your research problem
- do not adopt a 'list approach' but be critical when reviewing the literature
- establish a link to your own research.

3.0 METHODOLOGY

- explain and justify your proposed research philosophy, approach, strategy and research design
- consider ethical issues
- how do you intend to analyze your data?

4.0 RESEARCH CONSTRAINTS

- clearly state the likely constraints you will encounter when doing your research
- examples include access to data, time and financial resources.

5.0 SUMMARY

- a brief summary of the main points set out in your proposal.

6.0 RESEARCH TIMETABLE

- in the form of a Gantt chart or table setting out the key tasks, start dates and anticipated completion dates.

Figure 8.5 includes a preliminary literature review. This may not be required for some courses involving a work-based project, as emphasis might be more on practice-based content and methodology. How to approach searching and writing up the literature is a key part of a work-based project, so do clarify with your adviser and work supervisor as to expectations.

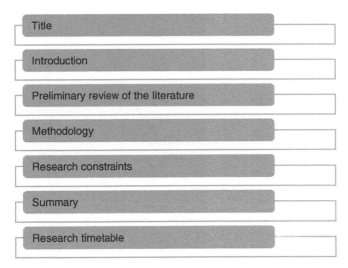

Title

Introduction

Preliminary review of the literature

Methodology

Research constraints

Summary

Research timetable

Figure 8.5   Writing your work-based project research proposal (the main items)

UNIVERSITY OF NEPTUNE

WORK-BASED PROJECT – MARKING GRID

STUDENT REGISTRATION NUMBER:

GRADE AWARDED BY 1ST MARKER:

Assessment criteria (weightings in brackets)	First Marker's comments
Learning outcomes and scholarship displayed (10%)	
Presentation (10%)	
Proposed methodology (15%)	
Argumentation and understanding (10%)	
Criticality and analysis (15%)	
Planned sources and use of evidence (15%)	
Academic referencing (5%)	
Quality of written communication (10%)	
Overall planning for proposed Investigation (10%) – to include a timetable of proposed research	

First Marker: **Signature:**   **Date:**

Figure 8.6   A work-based project proposal marksheet

Figure 8.6 illustrates an example of a work-based project proposal marksheet showing weightings for each section. Although the sections are similar to that of a traditional research proposal, there is one notable difference, that is, the overall planning for the proposed investigation is especially important. This is because you will need to consider your employer's role, together with work and study commitments.

Many universities require students to complete a work-based project using report format. You may have already written reports as part of your work or course. Report writing is a useful skill to have as the ability to write a professional report is an essential requirement in business and management. A typical report structure is as follows:

- *Title page*. To include the title of your work-based project, student number and date of submission.
- *Terms of reference/acknowledgements*. An opportunity to thank all of those who helped you on your research journey, including your adviser and work supervisor.
- *Abstract/synopsis/summary*. Provides a complete overview of your project, typically in no more than 300 words.
- *Contents page*. Shows the main headings, sub-headings, title of figures and tables, and page numbers.
- *Aims/objectives*. To include situation, problem statement, objectives and possibly research questions.
- *Introduction*. Includes background to the research, in particular the organization and how the research is anticipated to change the organization.
- *Methodology*. To include methodological approach, data collection methods and sources of information, nature of data (qualitative, quantitative), research instrument and methods of data collection.
- *Findings/results*. To include presenting, analyzing and interpreting your results.
- *Conclusions/recommendations*. A summary of the key research findings and recommendations, limitations. Evidence all team members have contributed.
- *References/bibliography*. Using your institution's preferred referencing guide, e.g. Harvard Referencing.
- *Appendices*. Typically, these are kept to a minimum, but often include charts and tables.

If you are unsure as to the structure required for your work-based project, again, make sure to check with your adviser and work supervisor. We have now examined the typical structure of a work-based project, let us now move on to look at the steps involved.

WHAT ARE THE STEPS INVOLVED IN UNDERTAKING A WORK-BASED PROJECT?

Your first step in your work-based project should be to consider 'why' you are doing research on your own organization. The initial idea might come from your manager or perhaps you have identified a research problem that warrants research. As with all research, a starting point in the research process should be your research problem. A work-based project is no different. If you are having difficulties in determining your research problem, remember that with a work-based project, it is likely that you will have support and guidance from your employer and access to information on the company.

Sekaran and Bougie (2016: 38) suggest gathering relevant contextual factors can be useful when raising appropriate issues relating to a research problem. The authors point out relevant background information might include:

1. The origin and history of the company.
2. Size in terms of employees, assets, or both.
3. Charter – purpose and ideology.
4. Location – regional, national or other.
5. Resources – human and others.
6. Interdependent relationships with other institutions and the external environment.
7. Financial position during the previous five to ten years, and relevant financial data.
8. Information on structural factors, e.g. roles and positions in the organization.
9. Information on the management philosophy.

In essence, the extent that each of the above are researched depends on the nature of the research problem you are researching within the organization. For example, if your research focuses on 'organizational change' or more specifically, 'how to improve staff morale within the organization', then when writing the background to your study, you are likely to cover most of the above points.

Moving on from your research problem, you then need to think about your overall research direction, especially research questions. Moore (2006: 9) points out the importance of thinking about the following questions before starting your project:

- What are you trying to achieve?
- What are the important issues?
- Who will benefit from, or be affected by the project?
- What things will change as a result of the project?

If you have the option of doing a work-based project, then do consider a number of reasons for undertaking this type of research. The steps involved largely depend on the nature of the project and the relationship between the student, university and organization. The university or college often plays an active role in recruiting organizations to take part in work placement schemes, sometimes involving a work-based project. By way of an example, in the paper on 'Pre-placement work-based projects within a retail sandwich degree' Stephen et al. (1997: 51–52) note that students doing a five-week work placement in retail were allocated placements as a result of their university approaching potential retail participants in the Greater Manchester area.

A range of retailers within Greater Manchester were approached with a view to participating in the work-based project by staff at the University. The retailers' response was very favourable and the majority of the participants were national companies including BHS, Boots, C&A, Debenhams, House of Fraser, IKEA, Marks & Spencer, MFI, Sainsbury's and Tesco, along with a small number of local retailers. All first-year students on the retail marketing degree were successfully placed following selection interview. The overall standard of the final written projects was good and, in many cases, they were supported by formal presentations to the company's Head Office for more senior consideration.

The above illustration shows you that a starting point in the research was first finding potential organizations to take part in work-based learning programmes and this then culminated in the completion of a work-based project.

Fergusson et al. (2019) assert that the steps in conducting a work-based project are more of a cyclical nature. They state that practitioners come into Professional Studies with a sense of the type of work-based project they wish to embark upon in their Masters and doctoral journey, through a micro-reflective cycle of:

1. Having a real-world experience (be it educational or work-related).
2. Reflecting on the experience by reviewing it critically and thereby learning from it.
3. Planning and trying out something new at work on the basis of what she/he has learned.
4. Having a concrete experience, and so on in related loops, the researching practitioner begins to understand the nature of her own experience, skills and aptitudes (and the lifelong learning which has occurred as a consequence of them) and is thereby in a position to develop a defensible, work-based research plan.

Fergusson et al. (2019) go on to argue that this micro-reflective cycle in turn is dovetailed at the macro-reflective scale to:

1. Reflect, learn and engage in work and in Professional Studies.
2. Scope and plan a work-based project and the investigative method required to examine it, resulting in:
3. A research proposal which in turn leads to:
4. Further reflection and engagement and thereby to more learning and understanding about oneself, one's work and one's professional practice domain.

In essence, this reflective process to research is very much in line with action research as we examined in Chapter 6. Remember that action research is all about a researcher undertaking an active role in the research, as opposed to being an outside observer. The purpose of action research is to produce both an outcome and actions. This is something you might be able to do through work-based research, as the result of your project may possibly be put into action within your organization. The outcomes of your research and 'the next steps' is something for you to discuss with your employer.

HOW DO I PLAN AND MANAGE MY WORK-BASED PROJECT?

A key part in the planning and managing of your work-based project is regular communication with your adviser and work supervisor. Your research proposal is the 'plan' and foundation for your work-based project. Although producing a research proposal may not be a requirement of your work-based learning programme, as with all business research, it is advisable, so have some kind of proposal document before doing a work-based project. This is for the simple reason that it provides a plan (in writing) that is not only for your benefit, but also your employer and adviser.

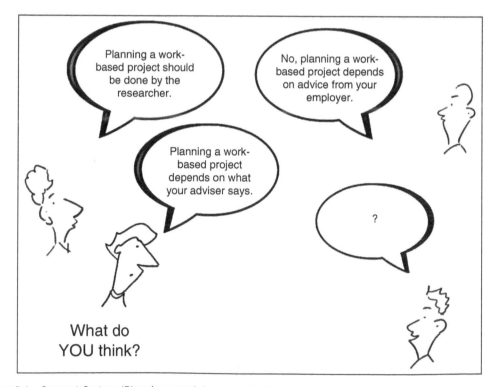

Image 8.1   Concept Cartoon 'Planning a work-based project'

Image 8.1 is a Concept Cartoon that shows characters expressing their views on planning a work-based project. Again, think about the different views of the characters and, if possible, use them to provoke a discussion with fellow students. In short, what do you think?

BOX 8.1: RESEARCH SNAPSHOT

Managing and planning your project should be viewed as a collaborative approach. From my experience, students who tend to do well when completing a work-based project seek to collaborate closely with their adviser and organization. Further, the organization usually has one key point of contact who the student can consult all the way through their research. If your organization does not have one point of contact, see if you can arrange this through your supervisor and the organization.

Figure 8.7 is a useful checklist for you to use if you are at the proposal stage in your research.

Project Proposal Checklist	✓
I have discussed my work-based project with my mentor	
I have identified an area of work that is a possible research topic	
My work-based project is an area related to my work/responsibilities	
The project is related to my longer-term career aspirations	
The project will have a significant impact on my work and colleagues	
My work-based project has been agreed with my line manager	
I have set dates for regular meetings with my mentor	

Figure 8.7   Work-based project proposal checklist

WHY RELATIONSHIPS ARE IMPORTANT WHEN DOING A WORK-BASED PROJECT

In traditional research, the main relationship throughout the research process is that between the student and their supervisor. However, when we consider work-based learning and undertaking a work-based project, there are a number of stakeholder relationships. Little and Brennan (1996) point out that the three key stakeholders in work-based learning are the individual, their employer and the academic institution. They distinguish between the interests associated with each of these three stakeholders as a result of a work-based learning agreement.

- *The student.* Possible gains may include career advancement, personal development and a formal qualification.
- *The employer.* Might be seeking to motivate employees, establish effective staff development opportunities, access a wider knowledge base that may in turn increase the competitiveness of the organization.
- *The academic institution.* Work-based learning might be seen as a way to enhance its teaching and learning and to fulfil its social responsibilities.

The above list is by no means exhaustive and there is likely to be a certain amount of overlap. For example, an interest in enhancing your personal development is likely to be a key goal for all three stakeholders.

Although it can be argued that the relationship with research stakeholders is important for any type of research, they are particularly significant when doing a work-based project. Clearly, the relationship you have with your employer is key as they play a major involvement in your research. In particular, the relationships you have with your employer are likely to be fundamental all the way through your research. For example, gaining access to key individuals, data and reporting your research findings are all dependent on the nature of the relationship you have with your employer.

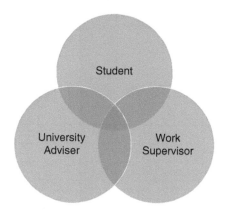

Figure 8.8   The three-way relationship when doing a work-based project

Figure 8.8 shows you the key stakeholders that make up the three-way relationship when doing a work-based project. Let us examine these relationships more closely.

THE RELATIONSHIP BETWEEN STUDENT, ADVISER AND WORK SUPERVISOR

Boud and Costley (2007: 127) compared the relationships between the adviser, work supervisor and student. The key points in this three-way relationship can be summarized as follows:

- The three-way relationship is often mediated between student, adviser and work supervisor.
- Commonly involves parties other than the student, adviser and work supervisor.
- Multi-mode contact.
- Negotiation of topic and process.
- Plan negotiated at start.
- Formalized three-way learning agreement.
- May be assessed by practitioner.
- The project itself can be highly varied, but typically includes a reflective component.
- The learner is an insider and an expert in their subject area.
- The adviser is an expert in frameworks and levels of achievement.
- The adviser is an expert in epistemology of practice.
- The adviser and learner have distinct areas of expertise.

Another term and role in the work-based learning literature is 'mentor'. Similar to that of a work supervisor, a mentor is an important role in any work-based programme. For example, Benefer (2007: 215) provides an interesting example of the role of a mentor in a work-based learning programme. The example here is the University of Staffordshire's Foundation Degree in Applied Technology, delivered in partnership with JCB, the global construction manufacturer:

> At the start of the programme, the mentor sits down with the college tutor, the student employee and JCB training manager to plan three-month placements within various sections in the company. The mentor can also schedule-in assignment dates, and ensure that the assessment tasks are matched to the employee's day-to-day work activities.

THE LEARNING AGREEMENT/CONTRACT

Something that underpins the relationship between the student, employee and adviser is the 'learning contract'. Anderson et al. (1998: 163) referred to a 'learning contract' as typically 'A formal written agreement between a learner and a supervisor which details what is to be learnt, the resources and strategies available to assist in learning it, what will be produced as evidence of the learning having occurred and how that product will be assessed'. A learning contract used for a work-based programme may take a variety of different forms; however, key criteria should include learning objectives, assessment criteria and expectations of the employee. In some cases, universities may use the term 'agreement' rather than 'contract'. More recently, the term 'agreement' has become a substitute for the term 'contract' as it carries a less legalistic overtone.

THE BENEFITS AND CHALLENGES OF RESEARCHING YOUR OWN ORGANIZATION

There are a number of key benefits to be gained from doing research on your own organization. In an article on the impact of work-based research projects at postgraduate level, Costley and Abukari (2015) questioned a sample of alumni, who had graduated from work-based Masters, professional doctorate programme and their corresponding employers. The findings were as follows:

- *Motivation and support.* The authors found that the main motivation for undertaking work-based learning was down to personal enthusiasm and their desire to gain more professional expertise. A challenge in the research was the administrative difficulties encountered with the university by some work-based learners and their employers.
- *Value.* The authors found it difficult to find examples for a business case that work-based learning is or is not cost-effective in terms of benefits to employees or employers.
- *Enhanced personal and professional confidence.* Findings showed that the culmination of a work-based project often brings about enhanced personal and professional confidence, aspirations and expertise.
- *Enhanced personal and professional credibility.* The less tangible benefits of work-based projects are identified and include prestige and credibility.
- *Direct benefit and impact to an organization or professional area.* Candidates undertaking the work-based projects recorded a greater understanding of both their fields of expertise and generic understanding of management, leadership and generally how things work and better communications with other people.

BENEFITS OF WORK-BASED LEARNING

Costley and Abukari's (2015) study provide a useful checklist for you if doing a work-based project. Certainly, it gives you a useful insight into the challenges you may encounter and how to prepare, or ideally, avoid them. However, the above list is by no means comprehensive when it comes to benefits of doing a work-based project. Below you will find other additional benefits.

- A better understanding of your work culture

  Meeting with your employer and possibly different functions of business is going to lead to a better understanding of your work culture. Depending on the nature of your research, it might also give you an insight into corporate culture that extends beyond your department. For example, if you work in one particular function of business, e.g. marketing, then if possible, try to conduct research that goes beyond your department. Why? Consider it an opportunity for you to compare how departments operate at a strategic level within your organization. Furthermore, it also develops your overall knowledge of the business.

- Raising your profile within the company

  Developing relationships with individuals within your organization will help to raise your profile with the company. It is likely that only a few people at your organization are aware of your research, so use the opportunity to share your research findings. This can only help to raise your profile and potentially work in your favour if applying for any further promotions.

  I have known former students doing work-based projects to disseminate their work in all sorts of ways. Examples here include writing a summary of the research findings on their organization's blog, to sharing their research with senior management.

- Furthering your career prospects

  Similar to the previous section, working closely with your employer on what is likely to be a valuable piece of research can only benefit your future career prospects. If anything, a work-based project goes further than a traditional dissertation as skills learned extend to conducting in-house research and learning what is required to be an insider researcher.

- Gaining a better understanding of your research topic

  Having completed a work-based project, you will have gained a better understanding of your research topic. This includes being familiar with the key authors in your chosen area of research and how your research compares to earlier studies. In the case of a work-based project, this understanding also comes from the ability to potentially put what you have learned into practice.

- Developing theoretical knowledge

  For some students doing a work-based project, the majority of their knowledge about their organization and area of employment is most likely to be practice-based. Rogers (2011) points out that managers undertaking work-based learning can not only develop their experience, but also acquire theoretical learning. Furthermore, completing a work-based project provides a tangible return for their employer.

Workman (2007:151) cites the following benefits of being an insider-researcher doing a work-based learning project:

1. Organization:

   - Knowledge of organization and culture, colleagues, clients, information, working norms, networks and language.
   - Project design reflects needs and methodological choice.
   - Contributes to organization's aims.

2. Co-workers/clients/customers:

    - Improve practice, efficiency and cost effectiveness.
    - Involve others – gives clients a voice, positive impact through involvement in project.
    - Access key informants – purposive sample, established working relationships.

3. To insider-researcher personally:

    - Practitioner insights and role duality in the project provides additional benefits such as reflection upon different aspects of their role.
    - Synergy between worker and researcher.
    - Knowledge of organization, problem, depth and breadth extended.
    - Personal knowledge and experience contributed to the organization.
    - Choice of methodology to suit situation.
    - Improve own capabilities and skills.
    - Develop autonomy and can champion project and choose key informants.
    - Choose own support systems, e.g. mentor.

The above benefits are considered from a stakeholder perspective. The second point – 'co-workers, clients and customers' – makes clear that being an insider-researcher means that the results of your research can have benefits for all stakeholders. By way of an example, if you worked for a retailer and your research focused on how to improve customer satisfaction, it is quite likely that your findings could be put into practice. In broad terms, doing a work-based project can have positive benefits that can be put into action, a typical feature of action research.

CHALLENGES OF WORK-BASED LEARNING

Although doing a work-based programme and project has its benefits, there are also notable challenges. Many of the challenges associated with doing a work-based project are similar to those of undertaking a traditional dissertation. For example, Costley and Armsby (2007) note that problems students encounter when managing work-based projects centred on methodology, together with choosing and formulating project aims, managing data collection and evaluating the project findings. Lemanski et al. (2011: 23) viewed challenges associated with work-based learning for all three parties – the university, employer and student – as follows:

1. Work-based learning modules could increase the learner's workload too much both in and outside the workplace.
2. Learners may find that not obtaining the desired levels of support from both higher education and employers may pose a problem; they may not know who to seek advice from.
3. Too little collaboration between higher education establishment and employer; neither establishment sure who is the main contact for assistance with work-based learning modules.
4. Module outlines and learning outcomes may be too diffuse if they are flexible enough for all students.
5. Students may not feel as though they are part of a community of learners.
6. Inadequate focus on individualized learning outcome or study plan.
7. Perceived irrelevance of certain topics over which they may have no control.
8. The balance between job-specific learning and obtaining a broader education which may equip them for employment in another sector.

Of the above list, in my view, the most important of these challenges is point 3 – 'Too little collaboration between higher education establishment and employer; neither establishment sure who is the main contact for assistance with work-based learning modules'. From my experience, I have found that if there is close collaboration between the academic institution and employer, then this helps to alleviate other challenges such as perceived irrelevance of certain topics and learners not obtaining the desired level of support. You, as both a student and employee, have a role to play in the relationship by making sure that the above points are addressed before they become an issue during your research. One way to do this is to communicate with your stakeholders on your research process.

THE IMPORTANCE OF REFLECTION WHEN DOING A WORK-BASED PROJECT

Reflection is an important part of any project, but this is especially the case when doing a work-based project as the outcomes are likely to have implications for both you and your employer. Moon (1999) defines reflection as 'a process of learning and a representation of that learning'.

One way to view reflection is as a cyclical process. Applying Gibbs' (1988) reflective cycle is a useful means of continuously questioning and developing your personal and professional practice. This includes the following steps:

- *Description*. The first stage of the cycle is all about what happened in your research, e.g. in terms of collecting and analyzing data, communicating with your adviser and work supervisor.
- *Reflect*. Here, your thinking should consider the extent it was a good or bad experience, e.g. using evidence from adviser feedback and observations.
- *Making sense*. On what took place, forming your own explanations and discussing with colleagues. As part of your research project, you will interact with a number of stakeholders, in particular, your colleagues in your department. Use this as an opportunity to share your research experiences.
- *Plan*. How would you do a research project next time based on your understanding and experience? At the end of a research project, always reflect on your research and put plans in place for future research projects and disseminating your research findings.

Reflection is an ongoing process and is good practice, both in terms of learning 'on the job' and part of a work-based learning programme. Through reflection you can see how you might do things differently. For example, your main data collection in your work-based project might be interviews with senior management. Following the interviews, reflect on how they went. Did they go as planned? Did respondents' answers help to address the research problem? Do you need to adapt elements of your research, such as follow up with a different data collection method? Making sense of these questions can lead you to plan 'how' you do things differently.

THE ETHICAL CONSIDERATIONS WHEN DOING A WORK-BASED PROJECT

As noted earlier in the chapter, being an insider-researcher brings with it certain benefits, not least, easy access to research participants, though it also raises key ethical considerations. We examined the main ethical considerations in Chapter 7. However, there are particular issues that take on greater importance in the context of an insider-researcher. These can be summarized as follows:

- *A conflict of interest.*

  If doing a work-based project, there is a much greater potential for conflict of interest. This is because your employer is taking a much more vested interest in your research. Furthermore, your employer may have a view to implementing your findings. Consequently, it is essential to go through the correct ethical channels. Once again, consult with your research adviser about how to do this. It may also require you to consult with your main contact or mentor at your organization. For example, students on one of my modules I deliver have a mentor and an adviser when doing their work-based research project. In many cases, students consult with both when seeking ethics approval to gain an academic and a practitioner perspective.

- *Access to privileged information.*

  The extent to which you have access to your employer's privileged and private information, of course, depends on your employer. Clearly, from your perspective as a researcher, it would be beneficial to your research to have unrestricted access to all information you require for your project. However, in reality it is unlikely that you will be fortunate enough to be in this position. You need to take ethical responsibility as a researcher (and employee) to balance your research objectives with that of the rights of your employer and colleagues.

- *Employer responsibilities.*

  An employer must be supportive and transparent about the nature of the research problem, resources and information available and the time allocated for doing the research project. An employer should not attempt to influence or manipulate the result by requesting that certain information be exaggerated or omitted from the report. As a researcher and employer for the organization, you should refuse to carry out such a request. This is where it is key to adhere to both the university and employer ethical standards. No pressure or contractual conditions should be contingent upon a particular outcome. This is where the learning agreement or contract is key as it clarifies in writing what all parties have signed up to.

- Competency and credibility as a researcher.

  Ethical issues should be discussed early in any work-based learning programme. As an employee and researcher, you need to reflect on your ability to carry out the research and attempt to communicate your credibility as a researcher to both your employer and academic institution.

This chapter concludes with examples of work-based projects. Each one is designed to show you the role of the student, organization and the university.

EXAMPLE A

This first example is an illustration from Garnett (2016: 307) that shows you the flexibility associated with work-based learning. In this example, the process culminates with a work-based project.

Chris was referred to the university by his employer to see if it were possible that he could undertake a work-based higher education programme. Chris had no formal qualifications beyond secondary school level but had been investigating accidents and acting as an expert witness for over 20 years. The university assigned an adviser to work with Chris to put together a portfolio identifying and evidencing relevant learning from experience. The outcome of the portfolio assessment proved that Chris was already working at, and in some areas beyond, the level associated with the final stage of an honours degree. The work-based learning programme of study incorporated his accredited prior learning and extended his knowledge and skills at Master's level through a module in practitioner enquiry and a major work-based project.

Source: Garnett (2016: 307)

EXAMPLE B

In this second example, from Benefer (2007: 215–216), a collaboration between Burton College and JCB, students undertake a Foundation degree programme that also requires the completion of a work-based project.

In the JCB model of the Foundation degree in Applied Technology there is a firm partnership between the employer, the college and the university. The qualification has a strong vocational focus that is meeting the skills needs of the employer. It is delivered in a college with a strong reputation for its engagement with employers and which is committed to work-based learning and to meeting the skills needs of local industry. The employer contributes to the design of the programme, particularly in the provision of 'real' projects and assignments to support the assessment of learning. Delivery on site helps to ensure that work-based learning and academic learning are integrated. Company-based mentoring supports and guides student progress. Staff from the college, the university and the company work as a team to ensure the quality of the student's learning experience.

Source: Benefer (2007: 215–216)

These additional examples provide a summary of both an undergraduate and postgraduate work-based project. Each one includes the project title, a brief summary of the research methods used and research findings. When reading each example, consider the similarities and differences to that of a traditional dissertation.

AN EXAMPLE OF AN UNDERGRADUATE WORK-BASED PROJECT

Title: 'Reviewing employee development and training provision in a UK engineering company'.

Summary of the project: The work-based project reviews the current development and training provision, and seeks feedback from employees at different levels of the organization. The project adopted secondary data and primary data collection. Primary research involved interviews with a convenience sample of 10 employees, thus mainly applying a qualitative research strategy. The project was fortunate to have full cooperation from senior management and the research findings were subsequently presented to the work supervisor and senior management. Recommendations focus on training in key areas such as technological expertise and presentations skills.

AN EXAMPLE OF A POSTGRADUATE WORK-BASED PROJECT

Title: 'Analyzing how employees view mergers and acquisitions in a German multinational retailer'.

Summary of the project: The work-based project analyzes how employees respond to a recent merger and acquisition within a German multinational retailer. The research seeks the views of employees at a regional level and from corporate headquarters. The key stakeholders in the research included the student, supervisor and organization mentor. The project adopted secondary data and primary data collection. Primary research involved an online survey with a sample of 300 employees. This was a quantitative study, using a random sampling method to target employees within the firm. Given the sensitivity of the subject, all participants were ensured anonymity. Research findings were subsequently presented to the board of directors. Recommendations focus on cultural training to ensure a smooth transition, post-merger and acquisition.

CHAPTER SUMMARY

- A work-based project can be interpreted in different ways and is sometimes referred to as a 'work-based learning project'.

- A key difference between a work-based project and other projects is that a student is an insider-researcher when doing a work-based project.

- Three subsequent benefits associated with doing a work-based project include those related to the organization, those related to co-workers/clients/customers and those related to the insider-research personally.

- A key ethical consideration when researching your own organization is conflict of interest.

- Doing a work-based project can help to further your career prospects.

- Sharing the results of your work-based project can help to raise your profile in the organization.

- Undertaking a work-based project means that the choice of topic and research process may require negotiation between the student, adviser and work supervisor.

QUESTIONS FOR REVIEW

1. How would you define a 'work-based project'?
2. What are the key differences when comparing a work-based project with a traditional dissertation?
3. What are the ethical considerations when doing research on your own organization?
4. How does being an insider-researcher compare with being an outsider-researcher?
5. How would you define 'work-based learning'?
6. What are the potential benefits to the student of doing a work-based project?
7. What are the potential benefits to the organization of doing a work-based project?
8. What steps are you likely to take when planning your work-based project?

STUDENT SCENARIO: AYOMIDE'S COLLABORATION WITH KEY RESEARCH STAKEHOLDERS

Ayomide was about to start her work-based project. As a part-time Masters student, her course enabled her to complete a short work-based project on an area of 'change' associated with her organization. In Ayomide's case, her university was not heavily involved in setting up the three-way relationship between student, adviser and her work supervisor, as Ayomide was able to instigate this herself. The purpose of Ayomide's project was negotiated primarily with her work supervisor. In essence, it involved analyzing the impact of a recent change to the working environment in the sales department. The main change centred on employees moving from individual offices to an open plan office.

(Continued)

Ayomide had a good relationship with her university adviser, although she had only met with her work supervisor a couple of times before the project. Ayomide was aware that her supervisor had limited experience of collaborating with employees and her institution on work-based projects. Her supervisor suggested that the three of them meet regularly in order to monitor progress. Ayomide had a three-month period in which to complete her research, upon completion, she needed to submit a copy of her project to both her work supervisor and university adviser. As Ayomide had never undertaken such a large scale and important project, she asked her adviser if she could have access to past student work-based projects. Ayomide's adviser was only able to share a small number of exemplars. This is due to the issues surrounding anonymity and confidentiality associated with each project.

Summary

Although Ayomide was excited to be doing research that would have a direct impact on her organization, she was apprehensive about communicating the results. Her supervisor had little experience of working in this type of three-way partnership and had mentioned that she could disseminate her findings across all media, including the organization's in-house monthly magazine. In some respects, Ayomide was pleased that her work supervisor was so supportive, but she was uncertain if her supervisor had the authority to do this.

Questions

1. Identify the steps Ayomide will need to take in order to maintain a successful relationship with her work supervisor and adviser throughout her research process.
2. Create a work-based project proposal checklist Ayomide can use for her research.

Hint: When creating a proposal checklist, take a stakeholder perspective.

FURTHER READING

Doherty, O. and Bennett, B. (2010) 'Work based learning partnerships: A match made in Heaven?', *Advances in Higher Education*.

This article looks at the stakeholder nature of work-based learning. The objective of the article is to identify the critical success factors for a Work Based Learning (WBL) partnership between a Higher Education (HE) provider and an employer and to make recommendations for successful WBL partnerships.

Gibson, D. and Tavlaridis, V. (2017) 'Work-based learning for enterprise education? The case of Liverpool John Moores University "liv" civic engagement projects for students', *Work-based Learning for Enterprise Education*, 8 (1): 5–14.

The focus of this study is on the experience of work-based learning projects done by students at the Liverpool John Moores University and if they developed their entrepreneurial competencies through these projects.

Helyer, D.R. (2010) *The Work-Based Learning Student Handbook*. UK: Palgrave Macmillan.

Chapter 5 provides a detailed overview on the nature of a work-based project. This includes the characteristics, planning and the ethical issues to be considered.

REFERENCES

Anderson, G., Boud, D. and Sampson, J. (1998) 'Qualities of learning contracts' in J. Stephenson and M. Yorke (eds), *Capability and Quality in Higher Education*. London: Kogan.

Armsby, P. and Costley, C. (2000) 'Research driven projects', in D. Portwood and C. Costley (eds), *Work Based Learning and the University: New Perspectives and Practices*, No. 109. London: SEDA Publications.

Benefer, R. (2007) 'Engaging with employers in work-based learning: A foundation degree in applied technology', *Education + Training*, 49 (3): 210–217.

Boud, D. and Costley, C. (2007) 'From project supervision to advising. New conceptions of the practice', *Innovations in Education and Teaching International*, 44 (2): 119–130.

Boud, D. and Soloman, N. (2001) *Work-based Learning: A New Higher Education?* Buckingham: Open University Press.

Brennan, J. and Little, B. (2006) *Towards a Strategy for Workplace Learning: Report of a Study to Assist HEFCE in the Development of a Strategy for Workplace Learning*. London: Centre for Higher Education Research & Information.

Costley, C. and Abukari, A. (2015) 'The impact of work-based research projects at postgraduate level', *Journal of Work-Applied Management*, 7 (1): 3–14.

Costley, C. and Armsby, P. (2007) 'Methodologies for undergraduates doing practitioner investigations at work', *Journal of Workplace Learning*, 19 (3): 131–145.

Costley, C., Elliott, G.C. and Gibbs, P. (2010) *Doing Work-based Research: Approaches to Enquiry for Insider-researchers*. London: Sage.

Ebbutt, D. (1996) 'Universities, work-based learning and issue about knowledge', *Research in Post-compulsory Education*, 1 (3): 357–372.

Fergusson, L., Shallies, B. and Meijer, G. (2019) 'The scientific nature of work-based learning and research: An introduction to first principles', *Higher Education, Skills and Work-Based Learning*, 10 (1): 171–186.

Garnett, J. (2016) 'Work-based learning: A critical challenge to the subject discipline structures and practices of higher education', *Work-based Learning*, 6 (3): 306–314.

Gibbs, G. (1988) *Learning by Doing: A Guide to Teaching and Learning Methods*. Oxford: Further Education Unit, Oxford Polytechnic.

Gray, D. (2001) *A Briefing on Work-Based Learning*, Assessment Series No. 11, Higher Education Academy, York.

Guise, S. (1995) 'Collaboration between higher education and employers: A case study', *Proceedings of the 1995 UACE CVE Conference*, Lancaster University, 30 May–1 June: 23–29.

Lemanski, T., Mewis, R. and Overton, T. (2011) 'An introduction to work-based learning: A physical sciences practice guide', *The Higher Education Academy*, Feb.

Lester, S. and Costley, C. (2010) 'Work-based learning at higher education level: Value, practice and critique', *Studies in Higher Education*, 35 (5): 561–575.

Little, B. and Brennan, J. (1996) *A Review of Work-based Learning in Higher Education*, Department for Education and Employment, Sheffield, Open Research Online. Available at:

https://oro.open.ac.uk/11309/1/A_review_of_work_based_learning_in_higher_education.pdf (accessed 3 November 2019).

Maclaren, P. and Marshall, S. (2006) 'What is the learner? An analysis of the learner perspectives in work-based learning', *Journal of Vocational Education and Training*, 50 (3): 327–336.

Moon, J.A. (1999) *Reflection in Learning and Professional Development*. London: Routledge Falmer.

Moore, N. (2006) *How to do Research: A Practical Guide to Designing and Managing Research Projects* (3rd edn). London: Facet Publishing.

Raelin, J.A. (2008) *Work-based Learning: Bridging Knowledge and Action in the Workplace*. San Francisco: Jossey-Bass.

Rogers, B. (2011) 'The value of work-based projects in management education', *Industrial and Commercial Training*, 43 (6): 335–342.

Seagrave, L., Osbourne, M., Neal, P., Dockrell, R., Hartshorn, C. and Boyd, A. (1996) *Learning in Smaller Companies* (LISC), Final Report, University of Stirling, Educational Policy and Development.

Sekaran, U. and Bougie, R. (2016) *Research Methods for Business: A Skill-building Approach* (7th edn). Chichester: John Wiley & Sons.

Stephen, J., Jones, P. and Huntington, S. (1997) 'Pre-placement work-based projects within a retail sandwich degree', *Industrial and Commercial Training*, 29 (2): 49–52.

Workman, B. (2007) '"Casing the joint": Explorations by the insider-researcher preparing for work-based projects', *Journal of Workplace Learning*, 19 (3): 146–160.

Workman, B. (2010) 'Work-based projects: What they are and how to do them', in R. Helyer (ed.), *The Work-based Learning Student Handbook* (pp. 127–154). Basingstoke: Palgrave Macmillan.

Workman, B. and Nottingham, P. (2015) 'Work-based projects', in R. Helyer (ed.), *The Work-based Learning Student Handbook* (2nd edn) (pp. 253–277). London: Red Globe Press.

9

SAMPLING TECHNIQUES

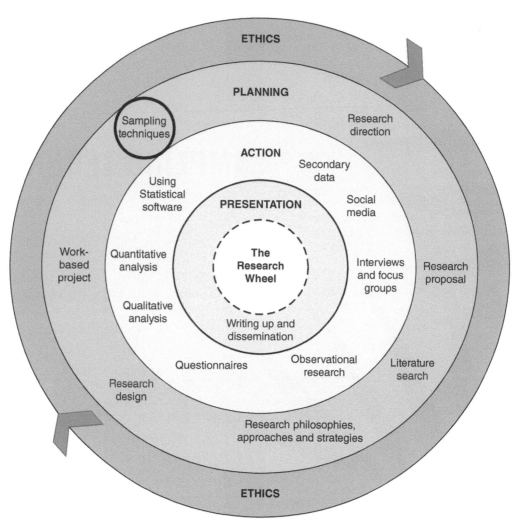

Figure 9.1   The Research Wheel

Learning objectives

By the end of this chapter, you should be able to:

- understand what is meant by sample, sampling frame and population
- understand the steps in the sampling process
- appreciate why researchers use sampling methods
- understand the differences between probability and non-probability sampling
- know how to determine sample size
- recognize issues associated with response and non-response
- appreciate how sampling methods are applied in practice
- understand how to use multiple sampling methods
- know how sampling techniques relate to other elements in the research process.

INTRODUCTION

The purpose of this chapter is to explain the different types of sampling methods, how to determine sample size and to examine the steps in the sampling process.

Two of the most common questions I am asked by students doing a research project are 'How many participants should I include in my sample?' and 'Which sampling method(s) should I use when doing my research?'. These are important questions to consider prior to collecting your primary data. We will address these questions later in the chapter. The chapter begins by discussing what is meant by sample, sampling frame and population; we then examine the steps in the sampling process. In essence, sampling is a systematic process that starts with clearly defining your target population. Understanding key terms such as 'population' and 'sampling' is a fundamental part of the sampling process and something we look at in depth in this part of the chapter.

Following this, we look at why researchers use sampling methods. This is illustrated using case examples of real-world studies to show you why researchers use sampling. The chapter then moves on to discuss the various types of sampling techniques. There are two main types of sampling techniques – probability sampling and non-probability sampling. You will also find in some books these are also referred to as 'random sampling' and 'non-random sampling' respectively. Each of these techniques has different sampling methods that can be used when doing your research.

Next, we examine how to determine sample size. A number of different factors influence choice of sample size. These include nature of the research design, research questions and earlier studies. Following this, we look at issues surrounding response and non-response rate. Generating an adequate number of responses can be challenging for student researchers and something we examine at length.

The next part of the chapter explores sampling methods in practice and combining sampling methods. The emphasis in this section is on showing you how sampling methods can be applied in actual student research.

Subsequently, we look at how sampling methods are applied in practice. You can also learn about how to apply sampling methods by reading past dissertations and journal articles. Irrespective of the topic, it is interesting to see 'how' and 'why' researchers have chosen certain sampling methods. This may help you to consider how to apply methods within your own study. The chapter then moves on to explain and give examples of multiple sampling methods. Lastly, we look at how sampling methods relate to other steps in the research process.

As you can see by Figure 9.1, we have arrived at 'Sampling techniques' in The Research Wheel. This forms part of the 'Planning stage' in your research journey. Why? Well, it is essential to plan how you identify your potential research participants. Rather than simply aiming for a certain number of responses, your chosen sampling method(s) is based on a number of factors. This includes your research questions and methodological approach. For example, adopting a qualitative strategy means the likelihood is that you will have a small sample size. Hence, your chosen sampling method will reflect this.

A key part of doing research is understanding how your choice of sampling method(s) will work in practice. 'Sampling techniques' is the final step in the 'Planning stage' in The Research Wheel. Now that your planning is done, it is time to go through the 'Action' stage in your research. The first step – secondary data – is something we examine in the next chapter.

WHAT IS A SAMPLE?

Prior to examining the steps in the sampling process, it is important for you to understand how to define the key terms associated with sampling. First, a *sample* can be defined as a sub-set of the population, while sampling means selecting a suitable sample for research. The term 'population' refers to a clearly defined group of cases in which the researcher can draw. Sampling can be used to make inferences about a population or to make generalizations in relation to existing theory. Figure 9.2 shows you the relationship between population, sampling frame and sample. The small circles represent individual cases, while the large circle represents the entire population, the inner circle the sampling frame, and the centre circle the sample. In numerical terms, the population might be 500 organizations, a list of some of the cases (sampling frame) might represent 400, while the sample might be 100 (a sub-set of the sampling frame).

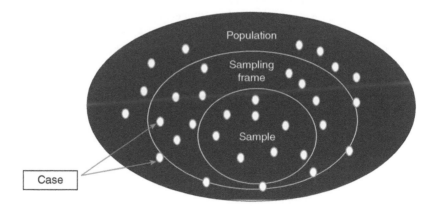

Figure 9.2   Relationship between population, sampling frame and sample

As a helpful guide, this section concludes with a summary of the terminology of key terms associated with sampling:

- **Population:** all members of a specified group.
- **Target population:** the population to which the researcher ideally wants to generalize.
- **Accessible population:** the population to which the researcher has access.
- **Sample:** a sub-set of a population.
- **Sampling frame:** refers to a list of the accessible population in which a researcher is able to draw a sample.
- **Subject:** a specific individual participating in a study (sometimes referred to as 'case').
- **Sampling technique:** the specific method used to select a sample from a population.

WHAT ARE THE STEPS IN THE SAMPLING PROCESS?

Figure 9.3 shows you the steps you should follow in the sampling process. As with many models in business and management, the process is illustrated as a systematic, linear process. However, in reality, this is not always the case as conducting research often produces unplanned circumstances requiring the researcher to adapt accordingly.

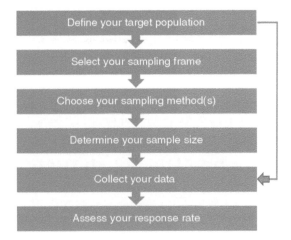

Figure 9.3   Steps in the sampling process

STEP 1: DEFINE YOUR TARGET POPULATION

The first step in the sampling process is to clearly define your target population. The word 'population' is often used in the context of a country's population. However, it also applies to other scenarios. By way of an illustration, in the aircraft manufacturing industry, the population may include all major global aircraft manufacturers. Given the likelihood that the number of organizations in this sector is relatively small, it might be possible to include all subjects in the population as part of your research; thus, there is no need to engage in sampling.

Defining a population is not always straightforward. Factors that determine the ease with which to determine the population include earlier research, your research questions and access to data. Furthermore, a population can often be narrowed by moving from the general (or broad) to the narrow (or more specific). For example, the population of Europe can be sub-divided based on West/East, countries and regions.

STEP 2: SELECT YOUR SAMPLING FRAME

Although students are familiar with the term 'population', they are less likely to be familiar with the term 'sampling frame'. Think of a sampling frame as a list of the actual cases from which your sample is drawn. A sampling frame should be representative of the population; however, in reality it is difficult to know when a sample is unrepresentative and should not be used.

A key part of your sampling frame is to think about how easily a list of people or organizations (it can be either) can be located. For example, if your objective is to survey advertising agencies in your region, you may identify your population as all those organizations within a five-mile radius of your address. Today, finding a list of advertising agencies is likely to be relatively straightforward as obvious sources include Google/Google maps. Yet, there is a chance that not all agencies are listed on Google. Therefore, how do you know that those organizations listed on Google are representative of the population? We address issues surrounding sample representativeness later in the chapter.

Unfortunately, determining a sampling frame is not always easy. If your research is based on an organization(s) or a particular sector, usually this type of information is readily available in business directories. This can be either in hard copy or electronic format. Your institution's library will likely allow access to business directories via databases such as Mintel or Business Monitor. However, if you are unable to access a pre-determined sampling frame, then the only option is to create one. Of course, this is a time-consuming process and something I have done several times when doing my own research in China. The downside is that you are faced with the problem of having to ensure that your sampling frame is representative of the population. In contrast, creating your own sampling frame increases your familiarity with the organization and/or sector in which you are doing research.

By way of an example, one of my former students undertook research on how to measure organizational performance among Brazilian branding agencies. At the time, there did not exist a directory of all the branding agencies in Brazil. She therefore devoted considerable time to creating her own sampling frame. This was achieved by using a combination of sources, such as personal networks in branding, online sources and material from academic studies and government reports. Following the creation of your sampling frame, the next step is to think about your sampling method(s).

STEP 3: CHOOSE YOUR SAMPLING METHOD(S)

Choosing a sampling method(s) is a task all researchers engage with. This includes everything from academic research to research undertaken by a market researcher. Before choosing your sampling method(s), ask yourself if it is possible to include the entire population in your research. Organizations engaging in research will ask the same question. By way of example, a UK soft drinks manufacturer is in the process of launching a new flavour of soft drinks. In essence, there are two ways in which the manufacturer can determine consumers' opinions on the product. First, it could ask every consumer in the UK who might purchase the new flavour of soft drink whether or not they will actually buy it, and how much they would be prepared to pay. Second, it could take a sample of consumers, ask them whether or not they will buy the new product, and then estimate the likely demand from the population as a whole.

Clearly, when considering the above two options, the first is unrealistic given the number of consumers, together with the time and resources necessary to undertake such a major task. For many organizations, the second option is far more feasible as sampling can be used to generate dependable results, rather than focusing efforts on the whole population. There are several reasons associated with not surveying an entire population. These can be summarized as follows:

- time constraints make it impossible to survey the entire population
- the skills to collect all of the data and interpret findings are lacking
- there are not the resources, particularly, not the budget, to survey the entire population
- the size of the population is too large
- surveying the entire population is not required to address your research problem
- it is too difficult to access the entire population
- you wish to compare your research to that of previous studies.

Let us examine each of the above points in turn. First, an obvious factor making it difficult to survey an entire population is that of time constraints. The likelihood is that your population is spread out, rather than in one particular cluster. In some cases, such as the UK biotechnology sector, organizational clusters do exist – in this example, many of the UK's biotechnology firms are located in the city of Cambridge. However, having a population in the form of a cluster is unlikely and even if this is the case, it is still a time-consuming process to contact all cases in the population.

Second, not all researchers possess the skills required to survey the entire population. For example, if your research is cross-cultural in nature and involves collecting data from respondents in different countries, you may not have the necessary language skills in which to do this task. In practical terms, large research agencies wishing to engage in this type of research will have branches across different countries and employees with the necessary skills needed to undertake such a large-scale piece of research.

Third, a student researcher is unlikely to have the resources, including budget, needed to survey the entire population. Of course, time is also a resource (as mentioned earlier); however, financial resources, e.g. travelling and accommodation costs, make it difficult to involve all cases within a population in your research. Certainly, one way to reduce the costs of doing research is to use technologies, such as Skype, email and/or telephone interviews. Although this may help to reduce the resources required to survey an entire population, they all still take time, thus making it impractical to involve all cases in a population in your study.

Fourth, if the size of the population is too large then clearly it is impractical to even begin to consider using the entire population. Realistically, too large may mean a relatively small number of cases. For example, a population may only consist of 50 organizations; however, if they are located in different regions throughout the world, then it is not possible to use all cases in your research.

Fifth, why survey an entire population if this is not required to address your research problem? I have known students to conduct research on one organization, in essence, a sample of one case. Why? Often, the main reason is that the purpose of their research is to examine an organization in depth. This is in contrast to surveying the entire population or a large sample so as to make generalizations to the wider population. By way of an example, I once had a student conduct an in-depth piece of research on her own jewellery-making business. The rationale behind the research was to look at how consumers perceive the business and to determine future strategic direction.

Sixth, quite simply it may well be too difficult to survey the entire population. The main reason for this is one of access. For instance, although you may wish to carry out research exploring the corporate social responsibilities associated with leading technology brands, in reality, it is unlikely that you will be able to contact individuals representing each brand.

Finally, your primary reason for not wanting to survey the entire population might be because you want to use a similar approach to sampling adopted in earlier studies. These studies are likely to be based on the same area of research and in order to compare your findings, you decide to use the same method(s) and/or sample size.

In this part of the chapter, we have discussed several reasons for selecting a sample as opposed to surveying the entire population. Next, the chapter looks at the different sampling methods available to you when doing your research.

PROBABILITY SAMPLING (RANDOM SAMPLING)

In sampling, there are two main categories or techniques – probability sampling, or random sampling, and non-probability sampling, or non-random sampling. For the purposes of this book, I have chosen to use the terms 'probability' and 'non-probability' as these tend to be better understood by students.

Prior to choosing your sampling method(s), a starting point in your research should be which sampling categories you intend to use. Figure 9.4 highlights the different types of sampling methods associated with each technique (probability sampling and non-probability sampling).

If you decide to choose probability sampling, this means that every item in the population has an equal chance of being included in your sample. An example of probability sampling in action would be if you put all 55 lottery numbers into a hat, then without looking, chose six numbers at random. In this example, every one of the 55 lottery numbers has an equal chance of being chosen.

Another way to engage in probability sampling would be to use a sampling frame first and then use a random number generator to select a sample from the sampling frame. Probability sampling has the greatest freedom from bias but may represent the costliest in terms of time and energy for a given level of sampling error (Brown, 1947: 337). Furthermore, probability sampling may not be your chosen method as the purpose of your research is to select unique or special cases, and not to choose cases at random.

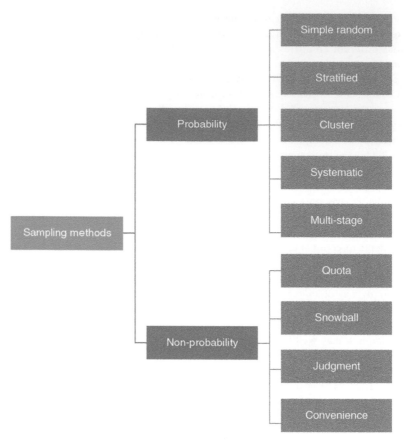

Figure 9.4   Sampling methods

The term 'Probability sampling' can be viewed as an umbrella term. Under this, we have several different types of sampling methods, the first of which we examine in the next section.

Simple random sampling

Figure 9.5   Simple random sampling

Figure 9.5 illustrates *simple random sampling*. By adopting a simple random sampling method, every case in the population has an equal probability of inclusion in your sample. Simple random sampling is a suitable choice if the population is small, homogenous and easy to access.

By way of an example, let us say that you want to carry out an online survey on preferred brand of cereal among members of an online discussion group. If you want to survey 100 members of the group, and the total membership is 500, the probability of the inclusion in the sample is:

P (inclusion) = Online discussion group members = 100 = 0.2 (i.e. 1 in 5)

Total membership   500

The main advantage with simple random sampling is that it is easy to use. Notable disadvantages include a list of all of the units or cases in the whole population is needed, and the costs of obtaining the sample can be high if the units are geographically dispersed. Lastly, another disadvantage is that if simple random sampling is carried out with a small sample size, then the composition of the sample is likely to be different to that of the population.

Stratified sampling

The second of our probability sampling methods is stratified sampling. In *stratified sampling,* the population is divided into two or more groups called strata, and random samples are taken in proportion to the population from each of the strata or sub-groups. Examples of the latter include occupation, nationality, or possibly number of employees in an organization. Stratified means 'in layers', so in order to select a stratified random sample we first need to make the layers.

Lohr (1999: 74) points out that stratified sampling is used for one or more of the following reasons:

* To protect against taking a really bad sample.
* We may want data of known precision from sub-groups of the population.
* A stratified sample may be more convenient to administer and may result in a lower cost for the survey.
* Stratified sampling often gives more precise estimates for population means and totals.

Stratified sampling is typically used when there exists a significant amount of variation within a population. The purpose is to ensure that every stratum is adequately represented. Thus, the number of items selected from each sub-group may be proportionate to the size of the stratum in relation to the population. For this reason, when making inferences in relation to the wider population, stratified sampling usually has a smaller sampling error than simple random sampling. One of the problems associated with stratified sampling is that it can sometimes be difficult to gather sufficiently detailed information on your entire sampling frame, thereby making it problematic when it comes to identifying your strata.

The steps or stages involved in undertaking stratified sampling are as follows:

1. Choose your stratification variables, e.g. gender, occupation.
2. Divide sampling frame into discrete strata.
3. Number each of the cases within each stratum with a unique number.
4. Select sample using simple random or systematic sampling.

By way of illustration, let us look at how stratified sampling works in practice. A shoe manufacturer has recently introduced a new training programme for all of its employees. The organization employs a total of 5,000 people. Using a sampling frame of 2,500 (50%) of the total workforce, the purpose of your research is to see how many of the employees have participated in what is a voluntary training programme on using technologies in the workplace.

You have determined the following strata – occupation and gender (Stage 1). The total workforce is made up of 250 people in senior management positions (150 female and 100 male) and 3,000 and 1,750 female and male employees respectively (Stage 2). Using stratified sampling, your sample would consist of 50 male and 75 female managers, and 1,500 female and 875 male employees. Figure 9.6 shows a simple illustration of proportional stratified sampling based on two strata: 'happy' and 'unhappy' consumer responses. The size of the sample from each stratum is proportional to the relative size of the stratum in the population.

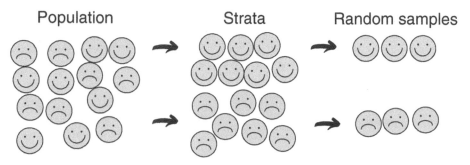

Figure 9.6   Stratified random sampling

Cluster sampling

Cluster sampling is a method used in which the entire population is divided into clusters or groups. Following this, a simple random sample of clusters is selected from the population. This type of sampling method is particularly useful where subjects are fragmented over a large geographical area, as it saves time and money. By way of example, if a researcher wanted to carry out a study into dental care provision among dentists in the UK, rather than target the entire population, the researcher may use cluster sampling. As a starting point, the researcher may start by recognizing regional dental groups as clusters. Subsequently, a sample of these groups can be chosen at random, with all organizations in each group included in the final sample.

Finally, steps to the cluster sampling process are highlighted below. In relation to the earlier dentist example, an advantage of adopting cluster sampling for the researcher is that it saves both time and money in having to travel to every dentist in the UK.

1. Choose cluster grouping for your sampling frame, e.g. type of organization or geographical region.
2. Number each of the clusters.
3. Select your sample using random sampling.

Figure 9.7 shows a graphic of cluster sampling. First, the cluster group is all of the blocks within a large housing development. Next, we number each of the blocks. There are 30 blocks (four are illustrated). We then use probability sampling to choose two blocks from the total of 30 blocks to take part in the research. Households residing in each of these blocks will take part in the research (circled).

Figure 9.7 Cluster sampling

Systematic sampling

In *systematic sampling*, the researcher selects a sample from a randomly generated list that represents the sampling frame. The researcher selects every nth case after a random start is selected. The interval is determined by the size of the sample needed from the list until the desired sample size is reached. For example, if surveying a sample of employees, every fourth employee may be selected from your sample. Thus, the subjects in the population need to be ordered in some way. For example, the names and address of businesses in a business directory, a list of customer records or a sales database based on key accounts.

The advantages of systematic sampling include the fact that the sample is easy to select, it is evenly spread over an entire target population and finally the sampling frame can be identified easily. One of the main disadvantages associated with this sampling method is the sample may be biased if there is an unknown periodicity in the population that coincides with that of the selection. Let us say for example that a confectionary producer of luxury chocolates decides to implement a system of total quality management (TQM). A key feature of their TQM strategy is regular quality control checks of their most expensive selection box. By adopting a systematic sampling method, the process of checking for quality might sound perfectly fine in principle; however, in practice, this could lead to a major problem. For example, what if the packaging machine developed a fault? If this fault leads to the boxes of chocolate failing to correctly seal the packaging at regular intervals, then this is likely to generate widely inaccurate data as to the overall quality of the production output. A way to avoid this problem is to adopt random, rather than systematic checks. Figure 9.8 shows an illustration of systematic sampling.

Figure 9.8 Systematic sampling

Multi-stage sampling

The final probability sampling method we will examine in this chapter is *multi-stage sampling*. This is a sampling method where the sampling is carried out in a number of stages such that the sample size gets reduced at each stage. In short, the process involves moving from a broad to a narrow sample.

Let us say, for example, a Dutch publisher of a monthly fitness magazine were to carry out an online survey – it could take a random sample of gym goers from the entire Dutch population. As we saw earlier in the chapter, surveying the entire population typically raises a number of challenges for a researcher. Thus, a less costly alternative would be to use multi-stage sampling. In practice, this would require the researcher to divide the country (The Netherlands) into different geographical regions. Subsequently, some of these regions are chosen at random, and then sub-divisions are made, possibly based on local government areas. Following this, some of these are again chosen at random and then divided into smaller areas, e.g. towns or cities. The aim of multi-stage sampling is to select samples which are concentrated in a few geographical regions.

For the student researcher, multi-stage sampling is challenging in the sense that it requires time and resources to fully implement this type of sampling method. Typically, this is a method used by research agencies and organizations employing several market researchers engaging in this activity.

Figure 9.9 shows you an illustration of multi-stage sampling. This is once again our housing development example, but there is an extra layer. Probability sampling is once again used to select two blocks at random, then households are selected at random from within each chosen block. So, initially this study has gone from city, to blocks, to households – a series of stages. Hence the term multi-stage sampling.

Figure 9.9   Multi-stage sampling

NON-PROBABILITY SAMPLING (NON-RANDOM SAMPLING)

Students often use non-probability sampling methods as they allow for easy access to research participants. For example, students often invite other students to take part in their research. Asking students to take part in your research can be described as 'non-probability sampling'. In essence, non-probability sampling means that the probability of each subject being selected from your total population is not known. Consequently, it is not possible to make inferences in relation to the wider population.

Non-probability sampling is typically associated with case study research design and qualitative research strategy. Data collection methods usually involve interviews, focus groups or possibly observational research. The sample size tends to be small as the purpose of the research, particularly with case study design, tends to focus on analyzing a small number of cases in depth. As the purpose of the research is not to make statistical inferences in relation to the wider population, the sample need not be representative, or random. Conversely, with probability sampling, research strategy is often quantitative and data collection focusing on questionnaire surveys, whereby the intention is usually to make inferences in relation to the wider population.

Quota sampling

Quota sampling is a non-probability sampling method where a researcher looks for a specific characteristic in their research participants, e.g. nationality. Pre-determined characteristics are selected so that the total sample will have the same distribution of characteristics as the wider population. An issue with this sampling method is that researchers may find it difficult to gather data on the characteristics of those in their intended sample. Going back to the earlier nationality example, this may not be a characteristic that is published in secondary sources.

The main difference between quota sampling and random sampling is that once the general breakdown of the sample is decided, e.g. how many people in each age group to include, the choice of the actual sample units is left to the researcher (Moser, 1952). A problem with quota sampling is that the sampling procedure often results in a lower response rate than would be achieved in a probability sample (Lavrakas, 2008). See Figure 9.10 for an example of quota sampling. In this example, the researcher has segmented the population into 'happy' and unhappy' sub-groups. Then used their judgment to select the cases from each segment based on a proportion of 50:50.

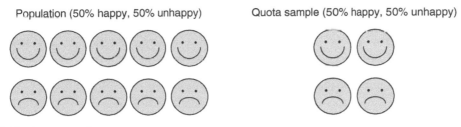

Figure 9.10   Quota sampling

Snowball sampling

Snowball sampling is a sampling method I have used many times when doing research in China. Basically, with snowball sampling, the clue is in the name 'snowball'. The way that this method works is that the researcher contacts a small number of subjects about their research and asks them to use their contacts or networks to make contact with a group. This in turn helps to develop sample size. The *snowball sampling* method is so called because the number of sample cases increases over time, similar to a snowball gathering snow as it rolls down a hill.

This type of method works particularly well in small populations that are difficult to access and have a gatekeeper or 'barriers' making it difficult to develop contacts. Furthermore, Baltar and Brunet (2012) note that snowball sampling is a useful sampling method in exploratory and descriptive research studies where respondents are few in number or a high degree of trust is required to initiate the contact.

By way of example, when researching in China, I found it particularly challenging trying to develop my sample of UK managers working in UK–Chinese International Joint Ventures. I had a small number of contacts, largely through academia and my work with a professional body. Hence, I used these contacts by telling them about the nature of my research and asking them to mention it and put me in contact with potential research participants. I have also used this approach when doing research on UK–Chinese retailers, using a contact working in a senior role at a UK retailer to help develop my sample.

Image 9.1   The snowball sampling method is so called because the number of sample cases increases over time, similar to a snowball gathering snow as it rolls down a hill

Source: iStock (photo ID: 479475029)

A key advantage of snowball sampling is that other individuals can do a lot of the work of developing a sample for you. They can take much of the time-consuming aspects of making contact, following up and building relationships with potential research participants. However, disadvantages do exist. These are three-fold. First, by using your contacts to develop your sample, ultimately you will find that you lose some control in the research process. For example, a senior manager, one of your close contacts, may ask a colleague to act as a research participant. Yet, this colleague may not meet the criteria you set out in your research. What steps should you take? Involve your contact's colleague in the research, thereby going against the criteria set out in your research proposal, or, politely tell your contact that their friend does not meet the research criteria? As you can see, this may lead to a delicate issue and potentially result in damaging the friendship you have with your research contact.

Second, as individuals are likely to contact close friends and/or business associates, then you may find that your research produces similar views and/or results. For example, let us say that you use snowball sampling in order to learn more about the political views of employees working in the US banking sector. If one of your contacts is a member of a political party, and thereby makes contact with other members, clearly this is likely to lead to a biased set of results. Finally, snowball sampling can be problematic if you attempt to use it where you do not have a particularly strong relationship with a contact. For example, Robson (2011: 275) describes snowball sampling as the researcher identifying one or more individuals from the population of interest, interviewing each individual, then after they have been interviewed, use the individual as an informant to identify other members of the population, who are themselves used as informants, and so on. Figure 9.11 shows you how snowball sampling works in practice.

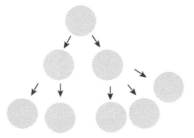

Figure 9.11   Snowball sampling

Judgment sampling

This sampling method is also sometimes referred to as *purposive sampling*. It is a strategy in which particular settings, persons or events are selected deliberately in order to provide important information that cannot be obtained from other choices. The researcher includes subjects in the sample because they are deemed to warrant inclusion. For example, if you intend doing research on online retailers and business ethics, based on your judgment, you might be of the view that it is essential to include Amazon in your research, given the organization's dominance in online retailing.

There are three key reasons why you may opt to include certain subjects, but exclude others:

- a critical case
- a unique case
- a focus on heterogeneous or homogeneous groups.

First, a critical case is one that is essential to your research. As previously mentioned, Amazon might be viewed as a critical case if researching online retailing and business ethics. Second, a unique case is one that demonstrates a feature that is not shared by other cases. If, for example, you were carrying out research on leading automobile manufacturers, let us say that in recent years the 'rising star' of automobile brands is the Chinese firm Geely (owner of Volvo). The fact that Geely is China's leading automobile manufacturer and has not been in business as long as many of the more established manufacturers, then perhaps this makes the firm a unique case. Thus, the inclusion of Geely in your research may generate insightful findings that perhaps can be explored in future research studies.

Lastly, you might consider exploring either heterogeneous or homogeneous groups. Heterogeneous means 'diverse in character or content'; as such, a heterogeneous group might comprise employees in different positions, working across all functions of a business. In contrast, homogeneous can be defined as 'the same or a similar nature'; thus, staying with our employees' example, a homogeneous group may refer to managers employed in the marketing department. The disadvantage associated with this type of sampling method is that cases are subject to some degree of bias. Figure 9.12 illustrates judgment sampling by using a light bulb to represent the researcher 'thinking' which cases to include in their sample.

Figure 9.12 Judgment sampling

Convenience sampling

Robson (2011: 275) makes the point that 'Convenience sampling is sometimes used as a cheap and dirty way of doing a sample survey. You do not know whether or not findings are representative'. This is one way to describe convenience sampling, although it is popular among students as potential participants (often other students) are easily and readily available.

Convenience sampling is commonly used in 'vox pops' or people on the street interviews in journalism. 'Vox pops' comes from the Latin phrase meaning 'voice of the people' and in English means 'the opinion of the majority of the people'. In journalism, vox pop or person on the street refers to short interviews with members of the public.

Market researchers also adopt convenience sampling as a sampling method as it is a simple and straightforward method of selecting individuals that are easy to reach. For example, if a market researcher wanted to conduct a survey on the shopping habits of young people, they may decide to survey employee members of a professional body. Why use convenience sampling? Quite simply, it is probably the easiest of all sampling methods as it provides ease of access to a known population group and a good response rate. A drawback is that a researcher cannot generalize their findings so cannot move beyond describing the sample.

Convenience samples can also be viewed on the extent that they are conventional or homogeneous. If adopting a homogeneous convenience sample, researchers can be more confident that the findings are more generalizable. Using a sampling frame that is more homogeneous ultimately means that the more probable it is that convenience sampling generates a representative sample. Figure 9.13 shows an illustration of convenience sampling. In the illustration, the researcher has chosen cases that are in close proximity to include within their sample. Including neighbours or those living in close proximity is an example of possible convenience for a researcher.

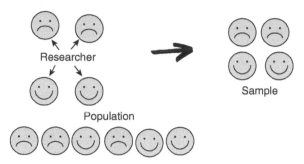

Figure 9.13   Convenience sampling

In this section of the book, I have covered all of the main sampling methods. Of course, there is no such thing as 'the best' sampling method. What determines your choice of sampling method depends on several factors, probably the factor that students consider the most important is time and access to potential participants. That said, there are advantages and disadvantages associated with each sampling method; these are summarized in Table 9.1.

Table 9.1   Advantages and disadvantages associated with selected sampling methods

Sampling method	Advantages	Disadvantages
Simple random sampling	Easily understood, results projectable	Difficult to construct sampling frame, expensive, lower precision, no assurance of representativeness
Convenience sampling	Least expensive, least time-consuming, most convenient, ideal for students	Selection bias, not representative, not recommended for descriptive or causal research
Judgment sampling	Low-cost, convenient, not time-consuming, ideal for exploratory research designs	Does not allow generalization, subjective

Sampling method	Advantages	Disadvantages
Quota sampling	Sample can be controlled for certain characteristics	Selection bias, no assurance of representativeness
Multi-stage sampling	Appropriate with a highly dispersed population, high degree of flexibility	Subjective and can be difficult to implement, more complex than cluster sampling
Snowball sampling	Can reach potentially difficult to reach cases	Time-consuming, lack of control
Systematic sampling	Can increase representativeness, easier to implement than simple random sampling, sampling frame not always necessary	Can decrease representativeness
Stratified sampling	Includes all important sub-populations, precision	Difficult to select relevant stratification variables, not feasible to stratify on many variables, expensive
Cluster sampling	Easy to implement, cost-effective	Imprecise, difficult to compute and interpret results

STEP 4: DETERMINE YOUR SAMPLE SIZE

Probably the most commonly asked question I receive from students about sampling is, 'What is a suitable sample size for my study?'. The short answer to this question is, 'It depends'. This may not seem helpful! However, it is a fair answer given that the answer to this question is complex and depends on a number of factors, including the type of sampling method used, the confidence level, sampling error, precision, standard deviation and analytical methods (Hernon, 1994).

The purpose of this section is to introduce you to the considerations to make when choosing your sample size. At this point, it is also important to reiterate that prior to selecting your ideal sample size, you are able to clearly define your population and, second, you have determined your sampling frame.

Your methodological choice is a key determining factor of sample size. For example, an interpretivist approach, qualitative strategy and data collection involving interviews and focus groups are likely to result in a small sample size, but how small? How many interviewees is enough? Do I need to interview a minimum of five participants? Again, these are all questions I have been asked by students.

Basically, your choice of sample size comes down to the following factors:

- the comparative sample size of earlier studies in your research area
- the confidence you need to have in your data, i.e. the level of certainty that the characteristics of the data collected will represent the characteristics of the total population
- the margin of error that you can tolerate, i.e. the precision you require for any estimate made from your sample
- the types of analysis you are going to undertake, in particular the number of categories into which you wish to subdivide your data, as many statistical techniques have a minimum threshold of data cases for each cell
- the size of the total population from which your sample is being drawn
- using formulas and published tables.

According to Hoinville and Jowell (1985), in some respects the final sample size is almost always a matter of judgment rather than calculation. Roscoe (1975) contends that the most suitable size for social research is to select a sample size larger than 30 and less than 500.

Let us examine each of the above factors in turn:

1. Basing your sample size on that of earlier studies in your area of research can be a valid justification for your chosen sample size. The advantage of this is that it allows for a direct comparison with other studies. For example, let us say that the majority of research into entrepreneurship from the point of view of multimillionaires has adopted a narrative analysis, using interviews of CEOs. In this case, a narrative analysis involves asking CEOs about their career journey. In order to draw direct comparisons with this type of research, you may also decide to interview a small sample of CEOs, using the same data collection method. Conversely, if all or most of the studies in this area adopt the same sampling method(s) and size, then by adopting different methods and size of sample you can argue that your study is making a contribution to the literature. In short, always consider the ability to compare and contrast when doing your research.

2. If you intend to make inferences to the wider population, as a 'rule of thumb' your sample size should consist of at least 30 cases. Ideally, where the sample size is less than 30, then the entire population should be included in the study. This also depends on the nature of the sample, for example, the extent that it is homogeneous or heterogeneous. If the latter, then you can probably use a relatively small sample size. In contrast, the more heterogeneous a population, the larger the sample required to acquire a representative sample.

    The confidence you have in your data is referred to as the *confidence level* and is expressed as a percentage, typically 95% or 99%. It is how confident you are that a parameter falls within a specific range of values. A parameter is a population characteristic such as a proportion (P) or mean. For example, if you adopt a 95% confidence level, then you expect 95 out of 100 samples will have the true population value within the range of precision, e.g. +/- 5%.

3. The level of precision or *sampling error* is the range in which the 'true' population value is estimated to be. This range is typically illustrated using percentages, e.g. +/- 5%. For example, if a student researcher finds that 70% of students use the library on Saturdays with a precision rate of +/- 5%, then the student can conclude that between 65% and 75% of students in the population use the library on Saturdays. Every sample statistic you calculate will have a sampling error, no matter which sampling technique you use. The lower the sampling error required, the larger the probability sample needs to be. The only way to eliminate sampling error is to undertake a census of the entire population.

4. The type of analysis you intend to undertake is also another factor. For example, often with a case study research design the focus is on 'depth' and may involve a sample size of one. Conversely, with large-scale quantitative studies, focus is likely to be on generating a large sample size in order to undertake meaningful statistical analysis.

5. If the population is small, e.g. less than 150, then you may be in a position to carry out a census of the entire population. The advantage of being able to do this is that it eliminates sampling error data on all individuals. However, once again, it can be resource intensive having to target the entire population.

6. Lastly, there exist several different formulas and tables used for determining sample size. The range of methods is beyond the scope of this book. For a more in-depth discussion on sampling methods see Cochran (1977).

Krejcie and Morgan (1970) produced a table for determining required sample size given a finite population. This can be applied to any population of a finite size (see Table 9.2). As you can see, the larger the sample size, the better it represents the population. Thus, if an aim of your research is to make inferences about your results in relation to the wide population, then it is important for you to determine the minimum sample size to reflect the size of the population.

Table 9.2 shows that a minimum sample size of 384 is considered to be representative for a population greater than or equal to 1,000,000. The population range is in fact from 1,000,000 to 10,000,000 (at a 95% confidence level).

Table 9.2 Required sample size, given a finite population

Size of population	Sample size
10	10
15	14
50	44
100	80
120	92
150	108
250	152
500	217
1,000	278
10,000	370
50,000	381
1,000,000	384

Source: Krejcie and Morgan (1970)

In short, there is no one definitive method used for calculating sample size. It is important to think about non-responses when considering sample size (see below), as this will ultimately affect how many subjects you aim to contact in order to achieve your desired sample size. For example, it is typical for non-response rates to be anywhere between 20% and 40%. Hence, if you are aiming to receive a total of 200 completed surveys, your sample will need to make allowances for non-responses.

Thus far, the focus of this chapter has been on selecting sample size in accordance with the steps in the sampling process. However, if you recall, the sampling process is not always linear. This can certainly be the case when we consider sample size. Silverman makes the point that one of the strengths of qualitative research is that it allows flexibility when it comes to sampling; in particular, flexibility may be appropriate in the following cases (Silverman, 2015: 275):

- As new factors emerge you may want to increase your sample in order to say more about them (for instance, a gatekeeper has given you an explanation that you doubt on principle).
- You may want to focus on a small part of your sample in the early stages, using the wider sample for later tests of emerging generalizations.
- Unexpected generalizations in the course of data analysis led you to seek out new deviant cases.

STEP 5: COLLECT YOUR DATA

The next step in your sampling process is collecting your data. The various methods used to collect data are discussed at length later in the book, so I will only make brief reference in this section. Data collection can be categorized on the basis of primary and secondary methods. The former is based on you gathering your own data relating to your research, while secondary data is concerned with using data already published. In terms of sampling, this is really concerned with primary data collection and includes methods such as surveys, focus groups, interviews and observation. Certainly, if doing something like administering an online survey, the next logical step is to assess your response rate. This brings us to the final part in the sampling process.

STEP 6: ASSESS YOUR RESPONSE RATE AND SUITABILITY OF RESPONSES

Response rate can be defined as the number of subjects agreeing to take part in your research; this may relate to the number of interviews or possibly the number of surveys completed and returned to the researcher. A response rate is represented as a percentage or actual number. By way of an example, let us say that you have administered an email survey. The survey was undertaken using convenience sampling and involved emailing 60 of your fellow music club members. After a period of a few days, including chasing non-responses, you finally managed to receive a total of 50 completed surveys. Thus, your response rate can be expressed as:

$$50/60 \times 100 = 83\% \text{ (response rate)}$$

In this short example, an 83% response rate can be considered as excellent and something many researchers would be extremely pleased with!

Personally, I have yet to carry out research where I have received a 100% response rate. Often, research can produce very low response rates, although there are steps that can be taken in order to try and increase the number of responses. According to Dillman et al. (2009), one way to raise the possibility of improved response rates is to use two or more survey modes in a single data collection. The authors tested whether response rates could be improved by offering a second survey mode after multiple attempts to collect data by the first mode. For example, starting with telephone, followed by mail. Their results showed that response rates can be improved by this sequential offering of survey modes. Yet, for student researchers, adopting a sequential offering of survey modes is likely to be challenging. Notably, for reasons cited earlier in the chapter, such as time constraints.

Why do response rates tend to be so low? Well, reasons for this include a poorly targeted survey, a survey containing too many and/or sensitive questions and a poor response mechanism. Consequently, it is essential to give a great deal of thought into how you can generate the best possible response rate before collecting your data. Do consult with your research supervisor to get their views on how this might be possible.

An important part of collecting data is following up and trying to encourage non-respondents to take part. This needs to be done sensitively, as being too persistent is liable to lead to complaints towards you, or worse still, your university.

BOX 9.1: RESEARCH SNAPSHOT

Difficulty in generating responses is something that all researchers face at some point. Discuss with your supervisor ways to increase your response rate. In addition, note typical response rates in your area of research. This can be a useful guide in terms of a benchmark for you to aim for when doing your research.

In reality, the final step in the sampling process does not end with assessing response rate, as it is also important to consider the quality of your responses. Irrespective of the data collection method, there is always the likelihood when doing research that interviewees will not answer questions, or respondents will not accurately answer survey questions. One way to increase the suitability of responses is to carry out a pilot study. Using a pilot will help to determine whether participants understand your questions. If not, the fact you have only carried out a pilot study still leaves scope to make amendments to your survey questions before administering the actual survey.

HOW ARE SAMPLING METHODS APPLIED IN PRACTICE?

As we saw in the last section, understanding the sampling process is an essential part of sampling. By seeing how different methods are applied in practice, you can begin to develop your own ideas about which methods might work best for your research project. What follows are three brief examples of how students have used sampling methods as part of their research projects. Again, the purpose of including these examples is to show you just some of the ways the sampling methods we discussed earlier in the chapter can be applied in practice.

EXAMPLE A

The first example is based on a study carried out by Michael, one of my former students. The purpose of Michael's research was to examine how both managers and consumers viewed a co-branding strategy between two technology companies. *Co-branding* can be defined as a strategic marketing and advertising partnership between two brands wherein the intention of the partnership is to bring success to both brands.

The first step in Michael's research involved interviewing a key contact within one of the brands to gain their opinion on the co-branding alliance. As Michael knew very few people working for both brands, he used one of his leading contacts to help to develop his sample size (snowball sampling).

The second step involved gathering a consumer perspective. Since Michael had easy access to his fellow students, he decided to use them for this part of his research (convenience sampling). The rationale behind Michael seeking perceptions from students and employees working for each of the partnership brands, was that he wanted to compare and contrast his research findings, in particular with that of earlier studies.

The final step in Michael's research brought together a small number of employees from each partnership brand and students. Michael gathered data using focus groups. The purpose was to examine how all participants interacted and to see if any views changed/adapted as a result of the focus group. He invited participants to take part in the focus group that he considered important to his research (judgment sampling). Lastly, Michael decided to use the data from his study in future research. This focus of an online survey would be to use questions, informed from his research project, to examine perceptions in other co-branding relationships. He intended distributing his survey using a stratified random sample of the whole population of Brand Managers, working in a co-branding partnership, within the East of England region.

In this student example, you can see how Michael implemented three sampling methods, namely snowball, convenience and judgment. In addition, in his follow up research he intended to use stratified random sampling.

EXAMPLE B

Vanessa's research focused on the levels of trust and cooperation between buyers and sellers in the UK automotive sector. Vanessa was fortunate that the significant amount of secondary data available on the subject meant it was easy enough for her to identify the population and a sampling frame. The latter came from a reliable publisher who produces key company information on all UK firms working in the automotive sector.

The first step in Vanessa's research involved contacting a sample of 300 organizations working in the sector. In keeping with earlier studies, Vanessa decided to use simple random sampling to generate her sample. Using a random number generator, Vanessa selected 300 organizations to send her postal survey to. The business directory included the names of the marketing director for each of Vanessa's target organizations, so she addressed her survey to each of these individuals.

Two weeks after administering her survey, Vanessa was disappointed to receive only 28 fully completed surveys. This number fell well below the typical response rate achieved in similar studies. Thus, after consulting with her research supervisor, Vanessa decided to change the methodological approach used in her research. Data collection would now centre on interviewing marketing directors for carefully chosen organizations that met a number of set criteria. This included years in business, location of both the buyer and seller, product range and financial turnover. To a large extent, selection of the case to be interviewed was based on Vanessa's judgment (judgment sampling), but also with input from her supervisor and consulting experts as to which case to choose.

In this example, you can see how an unplanned for circumstance (low response rate) may lead to a change in methodological approach and possibly sampling method(s).

EXAMPLE C

In this final example, we look at the application of one sampling method – snowball sampling. For her research project on Chinese branding, Yang Mei decided to seek the views of Brand Managers working for some of China's leading technology brands. Fortunately for Yang Mei, negotiating access to Brand Managers was relatively straightforward in the first instance, as she had spent several years working in the Chinese technology industry before commencing her business degree. However, she still did not have a sufficient number of contacts in which to develop her sample.

Following a meeting with her supervisor, Yang Mei chose to use a snowball sampling method to develop her sample. She was able to justify using this method given the sensitivity of her research topic (employee retention in the Chinese technology industry), access to a small number of contacts/informants and no other studies in her subject area had used a snowball sampling method. This last point meant that Yang Mei argued adopting snowball sampling would make a welcome contribution to the existing literature.

In summary, what these examples show is that there are a number of factors that influence choice of sampling method. Furthermore, your originally planned method(s) might change as you progress through the research process.

CAN I USE MULTIPLE SAMPLING METHODS?

The short answer is yes. From my experience, students often use multiple sampling methods when doing their research project. The reasons for this are four-fold:

- The research is based on mixed methods. If you recall, mixed methods involve the use of qualitative and quantitative research strategies. Typically, qualitative research is based on non-probability sampling, while quantitative studies adopt probability sampling methods.
- The use of multiple sampling methods is a common approach in your chosen area of research. In order to draw direct comparisons with earlier studies, you might want to adopt the same multiple sampling methods. By way of an example, if an earlier study uses convenience sampling based on focus groups in phase 1 of their research, while phase 2 is an online survey, then you may want to justify using the same methods so that you can compare and contrast this step in your research process.
- Changing/adding sampling method(s) in response to participants' views. Occasionally, research brings up interesting findings that warrant further investigation. This might mean introducing a different sampling method as part of a new phase in your research. For example, following exploratory research, you may wish to extend the research by examining the insights at greater length. Thus, research may involve conducting a large-scale survey, possibly using probability sampling methods such as simple random or stratified random.
- A variety of research questions require different sampling methods. For example, for simple research questions or in-depth studies sample size might be quite small. Yet, for complex questions, large samples and a variety of sampling techniques might be necessary.

SAMPLING METHODS AND OTHER STEPS IN THE RESEARCH PROCESS

As we mentioned earlier in the chapter, your choice of sampling methods(s) is very much dependent on the nature of your research questions and elements of your chosen methodological approach. For example, if you have chosen an interpretivist philosophical stance, intend undertaking an exploratory study, case study research design that addresses 'How' and 'Why' questions and adopting a qualitative research strategy, then the likelihood is that you will choose a non-probability sampling method. By way of example, if your research focuses on interviewing female entrepreneurs to understand their 'journey' using narrative analysis, then two possible broad approaches to sampling are convenience and judgment, the latter based on you selecting participants that are perhaps unique or critical to your research.

Image 9.2 is a Concept Cartoon that shows characters expressing their views on sampling. Think about the different views and use them to provoke a discussion with fellow students. What do you think? Do you share a viewpoint with one particular character?

To conclude, in this chapter we have focused on issues relating to sample, sampling frame, population, and finally, sampling process. Furthermore, we looked at the differences between probability and non-probability sampling techniques and the methods associated with each one. Once again, the most commonly asked question I receive about sampling is sample size. Hopefully, by now, you are able to answer this question, while at the same time able to recognize the different options governing sampling methods available to you.

Image 9.2   Concept Cartoon 'Sampling'

CHAPTER SUMMARY

- The sampling method(s) you choose largely depends on whether or not you wish to infer that your findings apply to the wider population.

- A population is a clearly defined group of research subjects that is being sampled.

- Several factors need to be considered when determining sample size. These include the confidence that you have in your data, earlier studies, the margin of error you can tolerate, the types of analysis you are going to undertake, the size of the total population, and using formulas and published tables.

- Sampling techniques can be categorized on the basis of probability (random) or non-probability (non-random) sampling.

- It is possible to change the size of your sample during your research.

- A high response rate is essential if you want to infer your results to the wider population.

- Generating a low response rate is likely to lead to a greater likelihood of sample bias.

QUESTIONS FOR REVIEW

1. How would you define sample, sampling frame and population?

2. Explain each of the steps in the sampling process.

3. Give an example of how you might use a combination of sampling methods in your research.

4. Discuss ways in which you might develop a suitably sized sample.

5. Outline three examples of probability sampling methods, including the advantages and disadvantages for each one.

6. Outline three examples of non-probability sampling methods, including the advantages and disadvantages for each one.

7. What steps can a researcher take in order to increase response rate?

8. What are the three key reasons why you may opt to include certain subjects but exclude others when using judgment sampling?

STUDENT SCENARIO: MOHAMMED'S CHOICE OF SAMPLING METHODS

Mohammed's research topic related to customer satisfaction within his family's restaurant business. He was particularly interested in this topic because he intended to work in the family business upon completing his degree programme.

Mohammed's research involved several interviews with family members employed in the business. He used the case study research design and planned to share his research findings with all of his family members. Mohammed hoped that by sharing details of his research, his fellow family members would be keen to take part in his study. He was sure that negotiating access would be no problem, given that these were his family members.

Mohammed also wanted to ask customers what they thought about the service provided by his family's restaurant, so he planned to contact customers to form a focus group. He viewed obtaining perspectives on customer service from both employees and customers would give him a useful insight into the business. Mohammed has already established that the focus group will take place prior to collecting data from his family members. The rationale behind this is that he wants the feedback from the focus groups to inform the questions to ask his family members.

Choice of sampling methods

As Mohammed's research was based on a qualitative study, he chose to use non-probability sampling methods. First, a judgment sampling method was undertaken to select the employees and customers. Mohammed did not just select customers who were positive about their experience at the restaurant, he was also sure to ask customers who had a negative experience. Customer contact details were gained from comment cards collected over a 12-month period. Mohammed was only able to contact those customers who had left their name and address.

Mohammed believed that his choice of judgment sampling was appropriate for addressing his research questions and choice of research design. However, he did have some reservations about using

(Continued)

judgment sampling when selecting family members to take part in the focus groups. The reason for this was because of possible accusations of bias. Furthermore, by acting as moderator during the focus groups, he would of course have to include this information as part of the informed consent when asking customers to take part in the research. Thus, this may impact participants' willingness to take part in the study.

Prior to collecting his data, Mohammed arranged a meeting with his research supervisor to discuss his approach to sampling. His supervisor explained the steps in the sampling process and how choice of sampling method(s) relates to other elements in the research process. In addition, he suggested that Mohammed consider other sampling options before collecting his data, especially in the context of the methods used in earlier studies.

Questions

1. Identify a minimum of two sampling issues Mohammed may encounter that might cause him to change or add to his choice of sampling methods.
2. What factors might Mohammed consider when determining sample size?

Hint: You may want to focus your discussion on both the potential positive and negative outcomes that lead Mohammed to change or add to his choice of sampling methods.

FURTHER READING

Daniel, J. (2012) *Sampling Essentials: Practical Guidelines for Making Sampling Choices*. London: Sage.

A book that covers the key aspects of sampling, including probability sampling, non-probability sampling and guidelines for preparing to make sampling choices.

Etikan, I. and Bala, K. (2017) 'Sampling and sampling methods', *Biometrics & Biostatistics International Journal*, 5 (6): 00149.

A short article that provides a useful guide to the different types of non-probability and probability sampling methods.

Koerber, A. and McMichael, L. (2008) 'Qualitative sampling methods: A primer for technical communicators', *Journal of Business and Technical Communication*, 22 (4): 454–473.

The authors attempt to clarify some of the current confusion over qualitative sampling terminology, explain what qualitative sampling methods are and why they need to be implemented.

REFERENCES

Baltar, F. and Brunet, I. (2012) 'Social research 2.0: Virtual snowball sampling method using Facebook', *Internet Research*, 22 (1): 57–74.

Brown, G.H. (1947) 'A comparison of sampling methods', *Journal of Marketing*, XI (4): 331–337.

Cochran, W.G. (1977) *Sampling Techniques* (3rd edn). New York: John Wiley & Sons.

Dillman, D.A., Phelps, G., Tortora, R., Swift, K., Kohrell, J., Berck, J. and Messer, B.L. (2009) 'Response rate and measurement differences in mixed-mode surveys using mail, telephone, interactive voice response (IVR) and the Internet', *Social Science Research*, 38 (1): 1–18.

Hernon, P. (1994) 'Determination of sample size and selection of the sample: Concepts, general sources, and software', *College and Research Libraries*, 55 (2): 171–180.

Hoinville, G. and Jowell, R. (1985) *Survey Research Practice*. Aldershot: Gower.

Krejcie, R.V. and Morgan, D.W. (1970) 'Determining sample size for research activities', *Educational and Psychological Measurement*, 30: 607–610.

Lavrakas, P.J. (2008) *Encyclopedia of Survey Research Methods*. Thousand Oaks, CA: Sage Publications.

Lohr, S.L. (1999) *Sampling: Design and Analysis*. Boston, MA: Dewsbury.

Moser, C.A. (1952) 'Quota sampling', *Journal of the Royal Statistical Society*, 115 (3): 411–423.

Robson, C. (2011) *Real World Research*. Chichester: John Wiley & Sons.

Roscoe, J.T. (1975) *Fundamental Research Statistics for the Behavioural Sciences* (2nd edn). New York: Holt, Rinehart and Winston.

Silverman, D. (2015) *Interpreting Qualitative Data*. London: Sage.

10

SECONDARY DATA

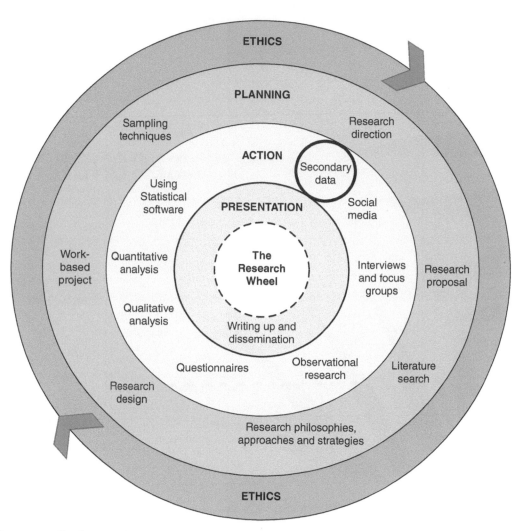

Figure 10.1   The Research Wheel

INTRODUCTION

Using secondary data is a key part of any research project. Some projects are only based on secondary data, while others start with secondary data prior to primary data collection. In this chapter, we examine all aspects associated with secondary data. This includes how to access and evaluate secondary sources.

In simple terms, secondary data are data collected by other researchers for other purposes. Having marked many research projects over the years, one of the most common issues associated with secondary data is that students could have used a wider range of sources. There is likely to be a wealth of secondary sources available on your research topic. Later in the chapter, we examine various sources you can consult when doing your research.

This chapter starts by looking at defining secondary data and how secondary data compares to primary data. The latter encompasses several different types of data collection methods, which we shall explore in subsequent chapters. Following this, the chapter then considers how businesses use secondary data, a classification on the basis of 'internal' and 'external' data and writing a research project based only on secondary data. Moving on, the chapter will then look at different sources of secondary data, before focusing on using secondary data sets and the advantages and disadvantages of secondary data. In terms of the latter, there are plenty of opportunities to do research using existing data sets. The main issue for students is knowing where to access relevant data sets and how this type of research may prove beneficial. Both of these points we address later in the chapter.

Next, the chapter looks at evaluating and presenting secondary data. Your ability to evaluate and decide whether or not to use a secondary source is an important part of being a researcher. This is for two reasons. First, there is a strong likelihood that there exists a significant number of secondary sources on your chosen research topic. Thus, evaluating which sources to use in your research is essential. Second, part of your evaluation is based on assessing the reliability of the source.

We then consider the nature of the relationship between primary and secondary data. Relationship in this context looks at how both primary and secondary data inform your research analysis. The chapter culminates with examples of studies using multiple sources of secondary data.

As you can see by Figure 10.1, we have now reached the 'Action' layer in The Research Wheel model (EPAP). This first step in the Action layer at this stage in the research process involves you conducting a number of activities, not least collecting and analyzing data. Prior to reaching the action layer you should have a clear understanding of your research direction. This will have been achieved through exploring the nature of business research, writing your research proposal and determining your methodological approach (all of which are part of the planning layer). Secondary data is the first step in the Action layer and will ultimately be heavily influenced by what you have found while working on your research proposal.

WHAT ARE SECONDARY DATA AND SECONDARY SOURCES?

While 'primary data' are used to describe information that is collected for a specific purpose, secondary data are best viewed as 'second-hand', because such data are 'old' primary data (Bradley, 2013). In simple terms, *secondary data* are data that already exist. Ellram and Tate (2016) go further by defining secondary data as quantitative or qualitative data that has been collected by someone other than the researcher(s) for a different purpose than its proposed use in research. Rabianski (2003) provides a clear illustrative example of the difference between primary and secondary data:

- The best example of this relationship is the data of the US Bureau of the Census. The Bureau is responsible for counting the population every ten years to establish the districts of representation in the House of Representatives. Over time, this charge 'to count the population' evolved into the analysis that the Bureau currently conducts of the demographic and economic characteristics of the population, characteristics of retail trade, composition of the industrial sector, nature of the housing stock, etc. This wide array of data is all primary data to the Bureau of the Census.
- When census data is used in a market evaluation for an appraisal or a market study, it becomes secondary data. Appraisers and market analysts use many data sets that are gathered as primary data. Any demographic and economic data generated by any government agency (federal, state, and local) for whatever purpose they deem necessary becomes someone else's secondary data.

Secondary data includes everything from annual reports, an organization's promotional documentation, journal articles, published case descriptions, magazines, newspaper reports to online government statistics. We can describe all of these examples as secondary sources. In other words, a *secondary source* contains secondary data.

The likelihood is that your research will begin with secondary analysis. This approach to doing research is typical when doing a research project. The outcome of your secondary analysis may dictate whether or not you decide to undertake primary research. However, do check with your research supervisor and/or course leader as doing primary research might be a condition of your course. If you have the option of basing your entire project only on secondary data, then do consider this. Why? Well, if an extensive range of secondary sources exists on your topic, it might be that you can address your research problem without the need to do primary research. Remember the purpose of your research is to address the research problem and ultimately answer your research questions.

There are other reasons that may influence your decision on whether or not to use secondary data. These include your choice of research design, whether you are undertaking international or cross-cultural research and whether you are unable to conduct primary research.

First, your choice of research design may influence your decision whether or not to conduct a project based exclusively on secondary data. Let us say, for example, that you intend analyzing how CEOs of pharmaceutical companies view the latest trends in measuring organizational performance; this is unlikely to be possible using primary research given the difficulties associated with accessing individuals in high-ranking positions. Other than difficulty accessing primary sources, another argument you can make for only focusing on secondary data is because you wish to compare and analyze existing studies. This type of research is commonly used when researchers carry out an extensive literature review on what has currently been written on a particular topic.

Before setting out to start collecting primary data, ask yourself the question 'Do I really need to undertake primary research?' and perhaps a follow up question 'Am I able to address my research problem and answer my research questions only using secondary data?'. I often find that students who are eager to do research start thinking about different types of research methods associated with primary research. This sometimes extends to using multiple methods, such as conducting interviews, focus groups and observational research. Remember that research should not start with methods. The starting point in your research is the initial idea, followed by the research problem and overall research direction. This includes research objectives and questions.

Some students seem to view using secondary data as 'an easy option'. However, this is certainly not the case. Collecting, presenting, analyzing and interpreting someone else's data can be a challenging prospect for all researchers. This is because using secondary data means that you are unfamiliar with the data collection process. Moreover, using another researcher's data means it has been collected to address a different set of research questions.

Second-hand shoes are used as a metaphor for secondary data. For example, if a pair of second-hand shoes are bought by someone else, there is a likelihood that they will not fit properly. We can think of secondary data in a similar way – that is, it has been collected to address another researcher's research problem, so is unlikely to 'fit' with your research.

In this chapter, we look at 'secondary data'. Other similar terms you will come across are 'secondary sources', 'secondary research', 'desk research' and 'secondary analysis'. Confusingly, you may also come across terms such as 'secondary data research'. Although these terms may look similar, they do have differences. Let us look at some of these examples.

First, when you see reference to 'secondary data' this means data collected by another researcher, while 'secondary research' means conducting research using secondary data. The term 'desk research' means the same as secondary research. Occasionally, you will find researchers use these terms interchangeably. If you see the term 'secondary analysis' this is simply analyzing secondary data. As you are probably aware by now, some of the terminology associated with doing research can be misleading! This is partly due to the fact that there is a lack of consensus among researchers as to what terms mean, and/or how they are defined.

Lastly, I have read many excellent research projects based exclusively on secondary data. These types of projects typically demonstrate two types of characteristics. First, a comprehensive understanding of the research topic, and second, an extensive review of the literature.

HOW DO BUSINESSES USE SECONDARY DATA?

All types of organizations use secondary data. A challenge for all organizations is knowing how to incorporate secondary data into their research. By way of an example, if an automobile manufacturer is in the process of launching a vehicle in a new geographical market, then the organization will carry out its own primary research to understand consumer opinions. Similarly, if the manufacturer wants to find out more about the external environment, then there are plenty of secondary sources they can access.

INTERNAL AND EXTERNAL SECONDARY DATA

Organizations use internal and external data to inform decision-making. This is one way we can classify secondary data. There are numerous ways of classifying secondary data. For example, one approach is to classify secondary data on the basis of 'electronic' or 'written' format (see Wilson, 2014). However, using a binary approach on the basis of 'electronic' or 'written' does not provide a 'true' classification as electronic or digital sources are so ubiquitous and there is often an integration of digital and written sources. Hence, for organizations, we can use two broad classifications – internal and external data (see Figure 10.2).

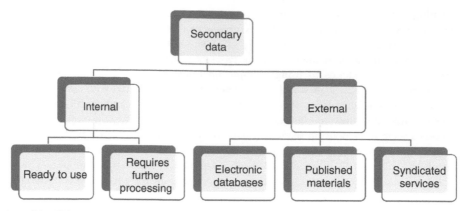

Figure 10.2   Classifying secondary data on the basis of internal and external data

Examples of internal sources used by organizations include sales invoices, customer records, marketing research reports, company newsletters and minutes from board meetings. In some cases, internal data are ready to use, although they may require further processing so that they are in a suitable format for research.

There are plenty of external sources available to organizations. To a point, the types of sources are dependent on the nature of the organization and the sector in which they operate. Examples here include everything from sector reports produced by government organizations to literature produced by leading competitors. A distinction can be made between electronic databases, published material and syndicated services (see Figure 10.2). First, a syndicated service includes studies conducted by market research organizations but not for any specific client. Mintel is an example of an organization that conducts syndicated research. Second, published materials are secondary data which are intentionally used for publication. Examples here include government data and material published on the website of an organization. Finally, electronic databases may include statistical data or possibly text data.

Although classifying secondary data on the basis of internal and external is rather simplistic, it does provide an organization with a useful 'checklist' of what data sources to consider when doing research. Certainly, considering what data are available in-house or within an organization is important as this can help to inform decision-making in relation to whether or not to use the services of an external agency to collect data or conduct primary research.

Of course, an organization's size and availability of resources is also likely to influence its ability to access secondary data when conducting market research. Smaller firms may have limited secondary sources because they have been in business for a short period of time or simply do not have the resources to search and process secondary sources in-house. If this is the case, then they may not have an option but to carry out primary research.

In contrast, large organizations are likely to have access to an extensive number of secondary sources in-house. However, interestingly many large firms still buy in secondary data, or mailing lists, from specialized agencies. By way of an example, let us say that a fruit juice producer wishes to sell their new flavoured drink to Dutch retailers. If no published data are available, then one option is to buy in the data from a specialized agency. Yet, 'buying in' secondary data from a third party does not guarantee that the data will help an organization to address its research questions. Furthermore, it can be associated with a number of problems, as follows:

- The data might be out of date. In other words, it is worth remembering that a key problem with secondary data is that it can soon become dated and therefore almost useless. Certain types of data are more likely to become dated quicker than others. Buying secondary data on the technology sector is particularly problematic given the fast-paced changes associated with the industry.

- The data list may be unreliable. There are likely to be literally thousands of data lists available. How does the organization (buyer) know they are buying a reliable list? An organization needs to know that it is buying data from a reputable source.
- Another issue is that secondary data bought for the purpose of direct marketing activities are unlikely to be exclusive to one organization. This is especially true in business-to-business markets, where several companies compete with a small number of customers.

Although classifying secondary data on the basis of internal and external is relatively straightforward for businesses, what about student researchers? Using the same classification is unrealistic given that the majority of students do not have the luxury of being able to access an organization's internal data. Furthermore, not all students conduct research based on an organization(s). For example, some of my past students have carried out research on an event, such as the London 2012 Olympic Games. In this example, the focus was not on an organization, but those people who attended the games. Hence, there is a notable difference when classifying secondary data from a student's perspective. However, the purpose of sharing the classification here is for you to use it as a guide when searching and evaluating secondary sources.

It is clear that the size and resources available to an organization will impact how it approaches secondary data. Often, small organizations conduct research only using secondary data. The reasons for this are three-fold. First, small organizations do not have the resources to conduct primary research. This extends to not having the skilled employees capable of collecting and analyzing primary data. Second, in some sectors, organizations may decide there is no need to carry out primary research given the large amount of secondary data available. Finally, in some cases, small organizations may not be particularly market-oriented, thus they do not recognize the need to conduct primary research. Generally, where primary research is carried out, this tends to lack strategic planning. Examples here include the use of customer comment cards and informal questions delivered by customer service employees.

In contrast, large organizations have the resources to buy in secondary data, such as statistics on industry competitors, mailing lists and research on sector growth. Organizations can go to specialist agencies who provide data, while data on sectors can be bought from market research companies such as Mintel. By way of illustration, let us say that an herbal tea manufacturer wants to promote their products to German retailers. If no published material exists, then the organization has two options. The first is to conduct primary research, while the second option is to buy the data from a specialized agency. However, using the services of a specialized agency is costly and does not guarantee success.

Buying in secondary data does raise a number of issues. First, the secondary data needs to be accurate and help an organization to address its research objectives. Quite simply, data is only as good as the research questions you ask. Second, secondary data can soon become out of date. Reasons for this include organizations going out of business, moving address or a change in personnel. Using customer records can be a useful form of secondary data as it is free and easy to access; however, it needs to be updated regularly.

Third, data bought for marketing activities are unlikely to be exclusive to one organization. By way of an example, a soft drinks manufacturer buying access to market reports from Mintel needs to recognize that its competitors are also able to purchase the same data. The only way to avoid this situation is to commission an agency to carry out research on your behalf.

In short, secondary data can benefit all types of organizations. The nature of the data depends on the research questions being asked. For businesses, secondary data can be particularly useful when conducting exploratory research, such as looking for insights to aid identifying a research problem. Yet, all organizations need to be aware of the limitations associated with secondary data, namely data might be available to competitors, it can soon become dated, it is sometimes difficult to verify the credibility of a source, and finally, it may not fully address the research problem.

WRITING A RESEARCH PROJECT BASED ONLY ON SECONDARY DATA

In the last section, we looked at secondary data from a business perspective. The likelihood is that when doing your research project, you will not be conducting research on behalf of an organization, unless of course you are doing a work-based project. In essence, your research is your own individual project that allows for flexibility in terms of how you approach secondary data.

In this part of the chapter, we discuss the reasons for conducting research only using secondary data. A question I am often asked by students is 'Can I base my research project on secondary sources?'. Well, the short answer is 'it depends'. First, check with your tutor or research supervisor to see if you have to conduct primary research. I know that on some courses there is an expectation that students will complete their research project having carried out some kind of primary research. If you are unsure as to whether or not this applies to you, do check with your supervisor/tutor early in the research process.

The second reason why a research project might only be based on secondary data is down to the nature of your research topic. In essence, certain research topics are more likely to merit a greater focus on secondary data. By way of illustration, let us say that you intend doing a single case study research design on Facebook and issues surrounding online security. This can be described as something of a 'hot topic' as so much has been written about the subject in recent months. Furthermore, Facebook is a global brand and a popular choice for academic writers and not just journalists. Thus, you are likely to find the brand feature in plenty of journal articles. In this case, you can perhaps argue that there is no need to carry out primary research. This is for the simple reason that plenty has already been written on the subject.

If permitted by your institution, how do you decide whether or not to conduct research using only secondary data? Several factors might influence your decision: whether you are unable to conduct primary research, whether you are undertaking international or cross-cultural research, your choice of research topic and availability of secondary data. Let us look at each of these points in turn. First, as highlighted earlier in this section, the fact that your university or college does not require you to conduct primary research might be reason enough to just focus on secondary data. However, my advice would be to always consider the nature of your research topic before making your decision. In short, do not just base your decision on university regulations.

Second, if your research involves undertaking international or cross-cultural research, this is another reason to just focus on secondary data. In reality, carrying out this type of research within what is likely to be a narrow time frame is going to be challenging for student researchers. In addition, if you are in the advantageous position of being able to converse in the target language(s) then this of course gives you access to a wider range of secondary sources. However, you will still need to be cautious of potential differences in how terms and keywords are interpreted across cultures. Clearly, inability to access international sources may not be a particularly strong argument for just doing secondary research. Today's technologies means that it is more straightforward than ever before to conduct primary research, using Skype, Facetime or simply carrying out interviews over the telephone.

Third, as highlighted earlier in the chapter, your choice of research topic may influence your decision as to whether to conduct primary research. For example, more contemporary topics, such as Artificial Intelligence, might have limited secondary data on the subject. If this is the case, then you may have no option but to conduct primary research.

Lastly, a lack of availability and/or difficulty accessing secondary data are also reasons why conducting primary research might be necessary. Certainly, access to academic journals is unlikely to be problematic as you should be able to access these through your institution. However, attempting to access specialized reports, such as those produced by commercial market research organizations, might not be possible as often there is a significant charge for accessing such material.

I have read many research projects over the years. A large number of them have only been based on secondary data. Although it is essential to consider the rationale for doing a project based on secondary data, there is no reason why this should prevent a student from producing an excellent research project.

SOURCES OF SECONDARY DATA

In this section, we look at sources of secondary data (see Figure 10.3). You can consider this as a form of checklist when considering sources to consult during your research.

Figure 10.3 Sources of secondary data

THE INTERNET

A starting point for many students seeking to search secondary sources is to search in Google (other search engines also apply!). Certainly, turning to the internet can be a useful place to begin searching secondary data on your research topic. In a business context, organizations may view it as a useful vehicle for gathering information from competitors' websites, accessing industry data or assessing potential environmental threats to the business. However, 'offline' or traditional secondary sources should not be ignored. These may include printed business directories, government reports and, of course, internal data.

As a student researcher, my advice would be to try to avoid exclusively relying on the internet or web-based sources. Why? Over-reliance is likely to have a negative impact on the reliability of your research, especially if your chosen sources are unknown and cannot be tested for their reliability. Instead of Google, first turn to your university or college library to search for secondary sources. Databases such as FAME and MarketLine Advantage provide invaluable information on UK and International companies respectively. All of these are likely to be free and easy to access via your institution.

Key websites for student researchers

Clearly, the internet provides all sorts of possibilities when it comes to secondary data. However, there are two important issues worth considering before you start searching various websites. They are credibility of the site and relevance of the information. Always try to find out the credibility of the site by checking the name(s) of the authors. Is the website widely cited by other authors? How regularly is the website updated? In general, remember to use clearly reliable sources, such as those summarized in Table 10.1. In some cases, the databases listed here require registration and/ or payment to access, although it is likely that you will be able to access the likes of FAME via your institution's electronic library.

Table 10.1 Useful databases you may wish to use for your research

Name of database	Web address	Brief summary
FAME	www.bvdinfo.com/en-gb/our-products/data/national/fame	Database containing detailed information on public and private organizations in the UK and Ireland.
Mintel Trends	www.mintel.com/mintel-trends	Provides insights on how today's consumers think, feel and act. Analyses changes in society.
Business Source Complete	www.ebsco.com/products/research-databases/business-source-complete	The industry's most used business research database, access to more than 2,300 journals.
Emerald E-journals Collection	www.emerald.com/insight/	A full-text database of 100 management and accounting e-journals and e-books published by Emerald.
MarketLine Advantage	www.marketline.com/	Information on 10,000 companies in 50 countries.
UK Government database	https://data.gov.uk/	A variety of data sets.
Scopus	www.scopus.com/sources	Scopus is the largest abstract and citation database of peer-reviewed literature: scientific journals, books and conference proceedings.
Google Scholar	https://scholar.google.com/	A searchable database of news, academic journals and essays.
World Bank database	https://data.worldbank.org/	A variety of data sets.
US Government database	www.usa.gov/statistics	A variety of data sets.
Pew Research Center	www.pewresearch.org/download-datasets/	A variety of data sets on different research areas including: internet and tech, social and demographic trends, and science and society.

GOVERNMENT WEBSITES

Many governments have statistical departments that regularly provide a list of publications available for external use. This includes census records and specialist censuses on different sectors, for example, on consumer purchasing, agriculture, telecommunications and education. Table 10.1 provides some examples of useful government websites, together with general business-related sites often used by business and management students.

Image 10.1   Government websites can provide a useful source of secondary data

Source: iStock (photo ID:1300682358)

MULTILATERAL ORGANIZATIONS

Leading multilateral organizations can be a useful source for statistics. In many cases, material is free to access online and/or likely to be available via your institution's electronic library. Examples include The European Union, Organization for Economic Cooperation and Development (OECD), Asia-Pacific Economic Cooperation (APEC), United Nations Educational, Scientific and Cultural Organization (UNESCO).

COMPANIES

For many student researchers, particularly those doing research on a particular organization(s), one of the most important sources of secondary data will be companies themselves. Much of the material on companies is easy to access and freely available. You may find that Annual reports and accounts provide useful information that may help to address your research questions. The Chairperson's statement can be used to analyze the mission and strategic direction of the company. Thus, a company provides both quantitative and qualitative data.

An organization's data can be combined with other secondary data. An example of a study that used primary data from an organization and secondary data is a study by Tasneem and Jain (2017). In an attempt to understand the work done by a public sector and a private sector organization in the field of corporate social responsibility (CSR), the researchers based their study on the primary data of Oriental Insurance Company Ltd (OICL) and secondary data of Reliance Life Insurance Company Ltd (RLIC). The primary data for Oriental Insurance Company Ltd was collected through a semi-structured interview and the secondary data for Reliance Life Insurance Company Ltd was collected through their web portal.

THE PRESS

Newspaper articles can be a useful source of secondary data. Their usefulness is likely to depend on the nature of the article and the publication. For example, if it is clear that the article is based on a 'source' with little evidence of facts, then it is perhaps best to avoid citing information from the article. Similarly, remember that newspapers have a certain political stance.

The 'media' can also include useful information for the student researcher. For example, newspapers occasionally commission opinion polls on everything from political views to consumer purchasing. These provide 'free access' to potentially interesting findings.

DIRECTORIES

Directories provide details of companies that buy or sell in different markets. For example, key publishers that provide business-to-business directories include Dun & Bradstreet and Fitch Solutions.

ACADEMIC JOURNALS

Although research published in newspapers and the 'media' has to be treated with caution, student researchers are likely to be more comfortable with material from academic researchers. Material here is often produced in peer review journals. Increasingly, other researchers are disseminating their work online, via social media and blogging. Many academics now use their own website as a tool to promote and share their work, thus making it freely available in the public domain. Although this creates potentially interesting sources of secondary data, it is still important to check the credentials of the researcher. As we examined earlier in the book, academic journals are an essential source when conducting your literature review and as such are an essential secondary source.

CONFERENCE PAPERS

Leading academic conferences often make conference papers freely available via their website. For example, in marketing, the Industrial Marketing & Purchasing Group (IMP) freely publish their papers on the conference website (www.impgroup.org). To the student researcher, an advantage of consulting academic conference papers is that they are written by academic specialists.

BOOK REVIEWS

Book reviews are available on leading e-retailer websites such as Amazon and Goodreads. These give you a 'snapshot' into the nature of the book and reader perceptions. Of course, given the nature of the review site, it is difficult to determine the credibility of each review.

TEXTBOOKS

Textbooks are essential reading on modules; they are also an essential secondary source when conducting research. The advantages of accessing textbooks are two-fold. First, a textbook is written by an authority on the subject. Second, it has gone through a peer review process, which adds to the reliability of the source. Finally, textbooks are easy to access. However, there are potential limitations. Often, textbooks will not include the latest research on a particular subject. They also tend to cover topics at a general level.

Textbooks can be a useful resource if you are focusing on a particular case study. In addition, they often feature case studies on leading organizations.

LECTURE NOTES

Lecture notes provide an invaluable source of information. If one of the modules taken during your course is the inspiration for your chosen research topic, then you may find secondary sources studied during the module relevant to your research.

USING SECONDARY DATA SETS

A data set (or dataset) is a collection of data. Many data sets are publicly available via open access, while others may require a license. Greenhoot and Dowsett (2012) point out that there are a number of reasons why a researcher may decide to carry out secondary analyses of an existing data set rather than design a new study to collect original data:

- The data have already been collected, thus freeing the researcher to focus their time on other steps in the research process.
- Many shared data sets have very large samples and longitudinal designs which enable researchers to address research questions that they may otherwise lack the time or resources to investigate.
- There is the potential to draw on longitudinal data and examine changes over time. Student researchers do not often have the time available to adopt a longitudinal research design.
- Some public-use data sets are collected using complex sampling procedures, thereby resulting in representative samples and highly generalizable findings.
- Large sample databases may provide unique opportunities to study specialized sub-populations.

THE ADVANTAGES AND DISADVANTAGES OF USING SECONDARY DATA

I have already highlighted some of the advantages associated with using secondary data, including ease of access. However, there are other advantages. In this section, we will first examine some of the other advantages, followed by disadvantages (for a summary, see Table 10.2).

Table 10.2   The advantages and disadvantages of using secondary data

Advantages	Disadvantages
Can be integrated and compared with primary data	Difficult to verify the reliability of the data
Less resource intensive	Secondary data not in a manageable form
Easy to access for fellow students and other researchers	The data not matching the research problem and research questions
Useful for longitudinal research	The measures may not be directly comparable
Large amount of secondary data can facilitate different types of analysis	Collecting primary research leads to the development of more research skills
Unforeseen relationships in the data can be made	Sensitivity of secondary data
Fast and less expensive	You will need to familiarize yourself with the data
May provide information otherwise not accessible	You do not have any control over the quality of the data

ADVANTAGES

Can be integrated and compared with primary data

An advantage when using secondary and primary data in your research, is that it allows for comparison and integrating your data. What do I mean by this? Well, first comparing secondary and primary data makes for interesting reading. Let us say, for example, that you are conducting research on consumers' perceptions of vegan food among 18- to 25-year-olds. Your secondary findings may indicate that there is a growing trend towards buying vegan food and healthy eating in general among this age group. However, your primary findings contradict this national finding by showing that there is no such trend among the participants who took part in your online survey. Similarly, you can integrate these findings when discussing the results of your research. It is always good practice to discuss the extent that your primary research findings concur or contradict with earlier research.

Less resource intensive

Typically, searching and accessing secondary data are less resource intensive when compared to primary research. Remember that conducting primary research means that you have a number of data collection options. Although some are less resource intensive than others, they all take a considerable amount of time and effort. Focusing on secondary data means that you are likely to have easy access to a wide range of sources via your institution's electronic library. In terms of resources, Martins et al. (2018: 3) provide a helpful example as to why secondary data is preferable to primary data when conducting research involving multiple countries:

> A team of researchers want to understand the influence of regional institutions in location choice of cross-border acquisitions. Whereas gathering data first-hand for dozens of countries is certainly possible (however long this may take), it is much easier to find world databases that gather at least a sub-set of the intended data and complement them with smaller national statistics databases.

Easy to access for fellow students and other researchers

Secondary data can facilitate access for your fellow students and other researchers in your area. The advantage of this is that by other researchers citing secondary sources they are making it easier for you to identify key sources in your subject area. Similarly, citing and sharing secondary sources with your fellow students will aid their research. As I have mentioned, establishing your own informal research group is an excellent way to share data.

Useful for longitudinal research

Although students do not always have the option of doing longitudinal research, it is still useful to recognize the benefits associated with using secondary data for this type of study. Typically, much of the data compiled by governments and organizations such as Statista and Pew Research Center is compiled over many years. By way of an example, Statista has data on GDP growth in the UK from 2000 to 2019. As with all secondary data, you still need to consider how it relates to your research problem. Other examples of longitudinal studies that may feature secondary data over time include those looking at changing demographics and consumer buying habits.

Large amount of secondary data can facilitate different types of analysis

In secondary data analysis, the researcher(s) that analyzes the data is not involved in the planning of the experiment or the collection of the data (Church, 2002). An advantage that secondary data gives the researcher is the ability to facilitate different types of analysis. What does this mean? Well, let us say that you were conducting research on entrepreneurship among family businesses in Vietnam. It is fair to say that this is quite a narrow subject. Thus, your secondary data analysis may extend to similar types of businesses in other countries in the region, such as China and Thailand. Given likely resource constraints, accessing data using primary research across these different countries is something you would not be able to do using primary research.

Unforeseen relationships in the data can be made

Using a wide range of secondary sources means that you may discover unforeseen relationships or patterns in the data. By way of an illustration, a study looking at employees' views on flexible working, may discover that views are dependent on seasonal factors and certain external factors, such as changes in fuel costs. This type of association may not have been discovered using primary research, as the researcher is using multiple secondary sources.

Fast and less expensive

A key advantage of using secondary data is that it is typically quick to access and less expensive. In many cases, large data sets are available to the public and do not require registration to access.

May provide information otherwise not accessible

Typically, large data sets are a result of research conducted by a large research organization, such as Pew Research Center or a government organization. As a result, these organizations are almost certainly going to have access to information otherwise not accessible to the student researcher.

DISADVANTAGES
Difficult to verify the reliability of the data

Typically, your ability to determine the reliability of secondary data is down to the source. A major disadvantage of using secondary data is that the secondary researcher did not participate in the data collection process and does not know exactly how it was conducted (Johnston, 2017). If using academic journals, then you can be confident that most journals are reliable. Certainly, articles published in journals that use a peer review process tend to be more reliable, although it is still important to consider reliability based on number of citations and journal ranking. In business, you can check the Chartered Association of Business Schools (CABS) listings to see if a journal is listed. If so, where it features in the table. Long established and well-known publications such as the *Harvard Business Review* offer high levels of reliability.

Limited access to primary data can be addressed by using multiple secondary sources, especially if they are easily accessible. By way of an illustration, Guruswamy and Adugnaw (2016) used multiple secondary sources in their article on the determinants of capital structure of selected insurance companies in Ethiopia. To achieve the objective, researchers used only secondary data obtained from the annual financial statement of selected insurance companies, National Bank of Ethiopia (NBE) and The Ministry of Finance and Economic Cooperation (MoFEC). The authors used an explanatory research design, purposive sampling method and quantitative research strategy. The statistical data provided by these secondary sources made for an interesting quantitative study.

The application of secondary research methods is dependent on the ability to access pre-existing data sets that are appropriate for addressing the research question(s) of the secondary study (Manu et al., 2021).

Secondary data not in a manageable form

One of the key problems associated with secondary data is that it may not be in manageable form. This is often referred to as 'raw data'. Hence, it can take time to process data so that it can be used for your research.

The data not matching the research problem and research questions

Again, remember that there is always a likelihood that secondary data may not match your research problem and research questions. This is because the data was intended to address other researcher(s) set of research questions. Similar issues relating to not addressing the research questions include too much data, the data is collected for a different purpose and there are gaps in the data. In terms of the latter point, an example here might be a study examining well-being in the workplace among UK small companies from 2000 to 2020. However, the researcher is only able to access secondary data that looks at well-being up to and including 2014. Clearly, this is a limitation and should be acknowledged by the researcher, although it is not unusual to only have access to secondary data that is two or more years old. This is because it takes time to reach publication. Furthermore, some organizations only publish data at set time frames, e.g. annually or biannually.

The measures may not be directly comparable

One of the problems associated with secondary data, especially for studies centred on cross-cultural research and between countries, is that the data might not be comparable. By way of an example, let us say that you are interested in measuring social class across different countries. In essence, this may seem a simple task. However, it is important to note that governments may use different metrics to measure social class. In some instances, the level of education might be used, while in other examples a country may use type of occupation.

Collecting primary research leads to the development of more research skills

A reason many courses insist that students must conduct primary research is that it helps to develop key transferable skills. Examples include interviewing techniques, how to produce a questionnaire survey, negotiating access and recording data.

Sensitivity of secondary data

Company data may be seen as commercially sensitive. This makes it difficult to access company archives. There are also access issues and knowing who to contact. For example, although you may have permission to access certain secondary data from within an organization, it is essential to check that the person granting you permission has the authority to do so. It is always worth mentioning to the person 'do I need to seek permission from elsewhere inside the company?', and make sure that you have confirmation in writing.

You will need to familiarize yourself with the data

Quite simply, as you are dealing with data produced by a third party, you are not going to be familiar with the data. For example, having to deal with large amounts of secondary data and/or large data sets can make it challenging when it comes to analyzing the data.

You do not have any control over the quality of the data

An unfortunate downside of using secondary data is that you are not aware of the control measures untaken by the researcher(s). For example, how do you know that the work has not been plagiarised from other sources? How do you know the research participants provided informed consent? In short, the data might not be up to your high standards of conducting research. One would hope that if you are using secondary data from a generally accepted source such as a leading academic journal, that issues surrounding the quality of data have been tackled by the researcher(s).

EVALUATING SECONDARY DATA

In the last section, we looked at the advantages and disadvantages associated with secondary data. Another important consideration is knowing how to evaluate secondary data. It is essential that you evaluate secondary data before using it in your research. A useful starting point is to identify the aim of the original study before moving on to other aspects, such as methodology. For example, is it clear what and how the researcher(s) measured the data? Did they use a consistent approach over time and potentially across different data sets? If you find that you have doubts about the reliability of the data, then you should consider disregarding the data or look to use alternative secondary sources.

There are a number of ways you can evaluate secondary sources. For example, when evaluating web-based sources, Walliman (2005: 55) suggests the following seven different tests you can make to determine the quality of the contents:

- Is it accurate?
- What authority is it based on?
- Is it biased?
- How detailed is the information?
- Is it out of date?
- Have you cross-checked?
- Have you tried pre-evaluated 'subject-gateways'?

Let us look at each of these tests in turn:

First, is it accurate? Does it say what sources the data are based on? To address this, you can compare the data with other sources. If there is a significant difference, ask yourself if there is a reason for this.

Second, what authority is it based on? Find out who authored the pages. This is not always transparent and may require searching the website to find out. You can find out whether the author(s) are viewed as an expert on their subject by checking to see if they are cited in other websites and publications. The web address can be an indicator as to the reliability of the source. Web addresses that end in 'ac' (meaning academic) are likely to be university or college addresses and therefore point to some intellectual credibility.

Third, is it biased? Remember that many commercial organizations and pressure groups use the web to promote their ideas and products, and present information in a one-sided way. It may require a little research, but can you find out if the author has a vested interest in the subject on the website? For example, are they a writer who is employed by the organization?

Fourth, how detailed is the information? Is the information so general that it is of little use or so detailed and specialized that it is difficult to understand? Investigate whether it is only fragmentary and misses out important issues in the subject, and whether the evidence is backed up by relevant data.

Fifth, is it out of date? Pages stay on the web until they are removed. For certain subjects, the date an article is published online can be particularly important. Clearly, if you are conducting research comparing economic growth among developing countries, you would aim to gather the most up-to-date data available. Using data from ten years ago is unlikely to be an accurate reflection of a country's current economic position. Thus, try to find out a date or when it was published. Note some updates may not update all the contents. Check any links provided to see if they work.

Sixth, have you cross-checked? Compare the contents with other sources of information such as books, articles, official statistics and other websites. Does the information tally with or contradict these? If the latter, can you say why?

Finally, have you tried pre-evaluated 'subject gateways'? The information on these sites has been vetted by experts in the relevant subjects so can be relied upon to be of high quality.

In addition to the points above, there are other ways in which you can evaluate secondary data:

- Purpose
  When evaluating as to whether you are going to use secondary data, do consider the purpose of the research. To what extent does the secondary data relate to the purpose of your own research project? It is unlikely the secondary source is going to 'exactly match' your research aims and objectives. Remember that this is a limitation of secondary data. However, there does need to be similarities in order for you to justify its inclusion in your research. Let us look at an example. If a researcher is interested in examining the recruitment practices of leading global financial companies, they might find a study focusing on US banks. Yet, the nature of their research is to examine the recruitment practices of leading Canadian banks. Clearly, the fact that the secondary source is based on research relating to US banks implies that there are potentially differences in business practice and culture. However, this does not necessarily mean that this secondary source should be discounted as there are likely to be similarities to your own research. This is especially true if the researchers have used or propose a theoretical framework. In short, there might be a contribution here as the theory has yet to be applied in a Canadian context.
- Format
  The format of the data, for example electronic or hard copy, dictates the ease with which you can access and interpret the data. Typically, the majority of sources today are likely to be in electronic format. This makes it easier when it comes to organizing secondary data as you can save files in folders based on themes.

In summary, it can be challenging assessing the reliability of secondary sources. Below you will find a summary of questions to ask when making the decision whether or not to include a secondary source in your research:

- What is the purpose of the research?
- Who wrote the article?
- How accurate is the data?
- How old is the information?
- Is the research likely to be biased?
- How closely does the research align with your own study?
- How detailed is the information?
- How closely do the contents compare to other sources of information?
- What are the credentials of the author(s), institution or organization sponsoring the information?
- Where does the information exist?
- Who is the intended audience?
- How easy is it for you to access the data?
- Can the information be downloaded into a spreadsheet or Word document?

BOX 10.1: RESEARCH SNAPSHOT

When analyzing secondary data, this can be viewed as a systematic process involving a series of steps. According to Johnston (2017), this process begins with the development of the research questions, then the identification of the data set, and finally, thorough evaluation of the data set. First, remember that the research questions guide your work and that secondary data should allow you to address your questions. The final step, evaluation, will inform your decision, based on the evaluation criteria we examined earlier in the chapter.

PRESENTING SECONDARY DATA

When presenting your secondary data there are two considerations. First, are your data qualitative or quantitative? Second, consider whether your data are raw data, or cooked data. If the former, then you will need to convert the data into a manageable format that can be used for your research project. By way of an example, the UK Government Department for Business, Energy & Industrial Strategy produces longitudinal research on small business survey reports. The *Small Business Survey 2018: SME Employers'* data contains nearly 150 tables on statistics associated with small business. This is clearly too much data to include in a research project so, therefore, requires managing so that the key information is extracted and presented in a manageable form.

In terms of quantitative secondary data, you do not have to present the data in its original format. For example, a table might be turned into a pie chart or bar chart. How do you know which format works best when presenting secondary data? To a point, this is a matter of choice, but do try to avoid using the same format throughout. I remember once reading a research project that contained nothing but a series of pie charts! Yes, a pie chart can be a suitable way of presenting quantitative data, but using a whole series is not especially interesting for the reader! Furthermore, it demonstrates a lack of creativity and understanding of how to present secondary data.

Presenting secondary data also includes qualitative data. Here, like quantitative data, there exist several ways to present the data. Let us say that you are interested in the views of leading financial journalists on the future economic prospects of the UK. One way to illustrate their views is to illustrate them directly, alternatively you may decide to use something a little more creative, such as a word cloud or present themes in the form of a table.

Lastly, my advice when presenting secondary data is to look at how researchers in your chosen area of research are presenting secondary data. By all means, you can use the same approaches, but also think about how you might adapt or present secondary data using alternative methods.

HOW DOES PRIMARY DATA RELATE TO SECONDARY DATA?

As we explored earlier in the chapter, you may find that your research does not go beyond using secondary data. However, if using both secondary and primary data, it is important to consider the relationship between the data types. First, primary data can be used to support secondary data. For example, let us say that you are researching market entry strategies among Japanese multinational companies. Your primary findings may show that the favoured market entry method is direct exporting. If the secondary data from various sources also shows this, then you can refer to these sources to support your argument.

In contrast, your primary findings may differ to results from other studies. In this case, try to examine why this is the case. Could it be that the secondary data does not wholly match your research questions? Or are the findings from the secondary data part of a study that took place several years ago?

EXAMPLES OF STUDIES USING MULTIPLE SOURCES OF SECONDARY DATA

In this section, we look at two short examples of studies that have used secondary data. One of the best ways to gain an understanding as to how secondary data might be used in your research is to read journal articles that use multiple sources of secondary data. The topic of the article is not particularly important, as the purpose is for you to see how secondary data is used in a research study, as opposed to types of secondary sources. By reading articles focusing on secondary data, the likelihood is that you will learn about potentially new sources of secondary data.

Example A

In their study into the relationships between tourism destination competitiveness determinants and tourism performance, Hanafiah and Zulkifly (2019) adopted secondary data as their primary source of data for their research. Notably, the authors provide clear justification for using secondary data, namely that secondary data sources were viewed as the most favourable for achieving the objectives of their study given the country-oriented macro–micro focus.

The research compares the tourism destination competitiveness and tourism performance across 115 nations. Secondary sources consulted include The Travel and Tourism Competitiveness Index (TTCI), while data on the Gross Domestic Product (GDP), the Balance of Payments (BOP) and fuel prices were derived from an International Monetary Fund (2013) report, and data on Foreign Direct Investment (FDI) were collected from a United Nations Development Programme (UNDP, 2012) report.

It is worth noting that conducting research based on multiple countries is often suitably addressed using secondary data. The reasons for this are two-fold. First, it is easier and less resource intensive to use secondary data, and second, there usually exists a wide range of sources that provide such information, much of which is produced by governments.

Example B

In their study into service satisfaction, Becerril-Arreola et al. (2017) examined the effects of emphases on two aspects of service satisfaction – relational service (interactions with the service provider's staff) and service environment (service provider's facilities) – on the market shares of service and goods components of partnered hybrid offerings. The authors used multiple secondary data sources from the US automobile industry between 2009 and 2015. This included collecting data on car sales, marketing mix, and other control variables from AutoData Corp, Kantar ad$pender, WardsAuto, the JD Power and Associates' IQS, and other sources (e.g. World Bank, the Bureau of Labor Statistics) (2017: 91).

Again, this example shows the wide range of secondary sources used in one study. Here, the researchers draw on secondary data from government, industry, commercial organizations and multilateral organizations.

Image 10.2 is a Concept Cartoon that shows characters expressing their views on secondary sources. Think about the different views and use them to provoke a discussion with fellow students. What do you think? Do you share a viewpoint with one particular character?

Lastly, this chapter has explored how secondary data can be used in your research. In the chapter, we looked at the nature of secondary data, together with the advantages, disadvantages, examples of studies using secondary data and different ways of presenting secondary data.

Image 10.2   Concept Cartoon 'Secondary sources'

CHAPTER SUMMARY

- Secondary data are data that have been collected by other researchers, not specifically for the research questions at hand.

- A key advantage of secondary data is that it can save time and money for the researcher. Other advantages include being useful for longitudinal studies and it can facilitate different types of analysis.

- Secondary data can be classified on the basis of internal and external data.

- Secondary data can be checked for reliability when considering accuracy, authority, potential bias, level of detail, whether it is a dated source, cross-checking the source, pre-evaluating subject gateways, purpose and format.

- Qualitative and quantitative secondary data can be presented in a variety of ways. Avoid using the same method throughout your research project.

- Raw data will require time to present the data in a manageable form. Conversely, cooked data can be presented in its original format.

QUESTIONS FOR REVIEW

1. How might you define secondary data?

2. Explain why a research project might be only based on secondary data.

3. Give three examples of secondary sources associated with a commercial audience.

4. Suggest the possible advantages of using secondary data in your research project.

5. Why might the use of raw data be problematic for a researcher?

6. What are the disadvantages associated with using secondary data?

7. How might a researcher test for the reliability of secondary data?

8. What are the potential problems associated with using only web-based sources?

9. What are the ways you might combine primary and secondary data?

10. Why might you decide to base your entire research on secondary data?

STUDENT SCENARIO: HAKEEM'S CHALLENGES OF ACCESSING AND EVALUATING SECONDARY DATA

Hakeem is a final year business student. Hakeem's research topic focuses on Twitter usage among US teenagers. Given the vast amount of secondary data available, Hakeem decided to use only secondary sources when conducting his study. Hakeem arranged a meeting with his research supervisor as he was unsure as to the secondary sources he should be consulting in his research. Hakeem was hoping that by meeting with his supervisor he would be able to identify possible sources and begin to evaluate whether or not to include data in his research.

Accessing secondary data

At the meeting, Hakeem's supervisor asked him to think about his research questions prior to identifying possible data sets. Hakeem's supervisor made the point that his research questions should guide his research and choice of secondary data should allow him to address his research questions. Furthermore, his supervisor explained that an important part in the secondary data analysis process involved evaluating secondary data. Given the nature of his research topic, Hakeem's supervisor suggested that he access The Pew Research Center data set on 'Teens and Tech Survey 2018'.

Assessing the reliability of secondary data

Following the discussion with his research supervisor, Hakeem registered with The Pew Research Center and began analyzing the 'Teens and Tech Survey 2018' data set. However, although the survey contained data on Twitter, the majority focused on teens' social media usage of other platforms, such as Instagram and Snapchat.

Questions

1. What action should Hakeem now take in his research? Give reasons for your answer.
2. Give examples of questions Hakeem can ask when making the decision whether or not to include a secondary source in his research.

Hint: Remember that research questions should guide your research. Start by thinking about the nature of the research questions, then consider secondary data options.

FURTHER READING

Heaton, J. (2004) *Reworking Qualitative Data: The Possibility of Secondary Analysis*. London: Sage.

A comprehensive guide to all aspects of qualitative secondary analysis. The book includes how to define secondary analysis and distinguish between quantitative and qualitative secondary analysis.

Largan, C. and Morris, T. (2019) *Qualitative Secondary Research: A Step-by-step Guide*. London: Sage.

A helpful guide if doing a secondary research project. This book guides the reader through finding, managing and analyzing qualitative secondary data.

Stewart, D. and Kamins, M. (1993) *Secondary Research Information Sources and Methods* (2nd edn). Thousand Oaks, CA: Sage.

This book includes a useful table listing the general directories and guides to secondary source material.

REFERENCES

Becerril-Arreola, R., Zhou, C., Srinivasan, R. and Seldin, D. (2017) 'Service satisfaction: Market share relationships in partnered hybrid offerings', *Journal of Marketing*, 81 (5): 86–103.

Bradley, N. (2013) *Marketing Research: Tools and Techniques*. Oxford: OUP.

Church, R.M. (2002) 'The effective use of secondary data', *Learning and Motivation*, 33 (1): 32–45.

Ellram, L.M. and Tate, W.L. (2016) 'The use of secondary data in purchasing and supply management (p/sm) research', *Journal of Purchasing and Supply Management*, 22 (4): 250–254.

Greenhoot, A.F. and Dowsett, C.J. (2012) 'Secondary data analysis: An important tool for addressing developmental questions', *Journal of Cognition and Development*, 13 (1): 2–18.

Guruswamy, D. and Adugnaw, M. (2016) 'Determinants of capital structure of selected insurance companies in Ethiopia', *Developing Country Studies (IISTE)*, 6 (10).

Hanafiah, H.M. and Zulkifly, I.M. (2019) 'Tourism destination competitiveness and tourism performance: A secondary data approach', *Competitiveness Review: An International Business Journal*, 29 (5): 592–621.

Johnston, M.P. (2017) 'Secondary data analysis: A method of which the time has come', *Qualitative and Quantitative Methods in Libraries*, 3 (3): 619–626.

Manu, E., Akotia, J., Sarhan, S. and Mahamadu, A. (2021) 'Identifying and sourcing data for secondary research', in E. Manu and J. Akotia (eds), *Secondary Research Methods in the Built Environment*. Oxon: Routledge.

Martins, F., da Cunha, J. and Serra, F. (2018) 'Secondary data in research: Uses and opportunities', *Iberoamerican Journal of Strategic Management (IJSM)*, 17 (4): 01–04.

Rabianski, J.S. (2003) 'Primary and secondary data: Concepts, concerns, errors, and issues', *The Appraisal Journal*, 71 (1): 43.

Tasneem, R. and Jain, S. (2017) 'Corporate social responsibility in India: A case study of public and private sector', *IOSR Journal of Business and Management*, 19 (6): 67–74.

UNDP (2012) African Economic Outlook 2012, Country Note Burundi.

Walliman, N. (2005) *Your Research Project: A Step-by-step Guide for the First-time Researcher*. London: Sage.

Wilson, J.S. (2014) *Essentials of Business Research: A Guide to Doing Your Research Project*. London: Sage.

11

SOCIAL MEDIA FOR RESEARCH

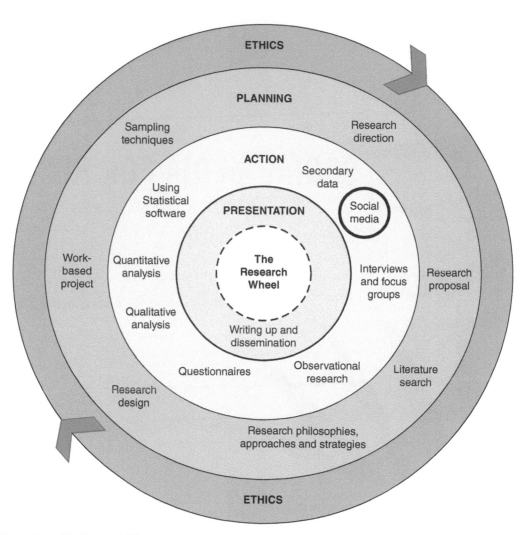

Figure 11.1   The Research Wheel

Learning objectives

By the end of this chapter, you should be able to:

- appreciate what is meant by social media
- understand the classification of social media
- be able to conduct research using social media
- understand the benefits and challenges of using social media for research
- be aware of the analytical techniques associated with social media research
- be aware of the ethical issues associated with social media research.

INTRODUCTION

So far in this book we have largely focused on what can be described as 'traditional' approaches to doing research. For example, in the context of secondary data, emphasis has been on sources such as books, journals and research websites.

Social media is ubiquitous in today's society and offers all sorts of possibilities when doing research, not least access to data and the ability to share your research findings. You may decide to choose a research topic based on social media. Examples here might include focusing on participants' use of single social media channels or analyzing social media trends over time. In contrast, you may prefer to draw on social media as a source of secondary data. It is this last point that is the main focus of this chapter – to consider ways social media can be used as part of your methodology. However, the chapter also takes a broader view, to look at the following:

- using social media as a research topic
- social media as a methodological consideration
- social media and ethical issues.

The chapter begins by defining social media. This leads to a discussion on how to classify social media research. Social media in the context of research is a broad term. Classification is designed to categorize the different aspects of social media, thereby making it easier for you to determine how to incorporate each aspect(s) in your research.

Next, we explore the use of social media as a data collection tool. Here, social media platforms such as Twitter can be used as both a recruitment tool and to collect observational data. Following this, the chapter discusses the benefits and challenges associated with social media research.

Moving on, we examine social media analytics and look at the ethical issues you will need to consider when conducting social media research. In Chapter 7, we explored plagiarism and ethical issues in business research. However, although there are many similarities when comparing ethical issues with traditional research, there are also notable differences. Finally, the chapter culminates with 'Top tips' or key takeaways if you are considering using social media as part of your research.

As you can see in Figure 11.1, 'Social media' is in the 'Action' layer in The Research Wheel model (EPAP). Remember that prior to reaching the Action layer you should have a clear understanding of your research direction – achieved during the planning stage in The Research Wheel model. Your emphasis on social media research will be heavily influenced by what you have found while working on your research proposal.

WHAT IS SOCIAL MEDIA?

Social media allows individual users and organizations to engage with, reach, persuade, and target audiences across multiple platforms (Freberg, 2019). According to The Pew Research Center (2019), the most popular platforms are YouTube and Facebook, while smaller shares of Americans use sites such as Twitter, Pinterest, Instagram and LinkedIn.

Prior to examining social media for research, it is essential to define social media. The term is widely associated with social media platforms such as Twitter, Facebook, Instagram and Pinterest. However, social media has multiple meanings and its definition has become highly contested and it is not always clear what tools, platforms and social phenomena count as social media (McCay-Peet and Quan-Haase, 2017).

Social media is often defined in relation to 'content' or 'content creation'. For example, Kaplan and Haenlein (2010: 61) define social media as 'a group of Internet-based applications that build on the ideological and technological foundations of Web 2.0, and that allow the creation and exchange of user-generated content'. Similarly, according to the *Oxford English Dictionary* (2021), social media is defined as 'Websites and applications that enable users to create and share content or to participate in social networking'. It is the 'sharing' and 'networking' aspects that present opportunities when doing your research. As we shall see later in the chapter, networking can aid data collection, while sharing content can relate to disseminating your research. Wilson (2019: 17) notes the creation of content is user-generated and can be defined as: 'Material such as personal opinions, news, ideas, photos and video published by users of social networks, blogs, online communities and product/service review sites'. The author goes on to explain that online social networks allow individuals to communicate with one another, as well as share a variety of content.

McCay-Peet and Quan-Haase (2017) also recognize that social media is about creating content, but go further to stress that although there is a proliferation of research on social media, it is not particularly easy to define. The authors conducted a review of the literature and make a distinction on the basis of themes:

- what social media enables
- how social media does it
- content of social media.

The authors arrive at a conclusion that social media 'allows individuals, communities, and organizations to interact with one another by providing a service that enables them to communicate and collaborate and to create, modify, and share content' (2017: 6).

The McCay-Peet and Quan-Haase (2017) definition is interesting as it highlights an important consideration when doing research on a social media-related topic – what is your unit of analysis? For example, this could be consumers, communities or organizations. Unit of analysis is something we look at later in the chapter. Wilson (2019: 16) makes a distinction between 'individual' social networks and 'object' social networks. The former includes platforms such as Facebook and LinkedIn, while 'object' includes Flickr, Instagram or Pinterest (where photographs form the object) and YouTube (where videos form the object). Making this distinction between 'objects' and 'individuals' is noteworthy as it may influence how you approach your own research. For example, if the purpose of your research is to analyze the use of advertising messages in the promotion of fashion brands, then your choice of social media platform(s) is likely to be Instagram and/or YouTube.

The European Society for Opinion and Marketing Research (ESOMAR) defines social media as 'internet-based platforms and technologies that permit users' interaction and/or facilitate the creation and exchange of user created content'. Whilst the scope is evolving, currently the most frequently used examples include:

- online forums/discussions, communities, blogs, social networks (e.g. Facebook)
- video/photo sharing (e.g. YouTube)
- multi-person/group communication and/or collaboration platforms (e.g. Twitter)

Source: ESOMAR (2021: 3)

Many definitions have focused on types of social media platforms, the creation and exchange of content and building communities. The latter point is particularly popular among researchers as online communities generate consumer opinions and feedback, which we look at later in the chapter.

CLASSIFYING SOCIAL MEDIA AND DATA COLLECTION

As we have seen in the last section, social media is a broad term. It includes the following: social networks, blogs, discussion forums, wikis and other applications. In this section of the chapter, we will look at how to classify, or in other words, divide social media into groups with similar characteristics. This process can help to make it easier for you to decide which social media platform(s) are best suited to your research. Following this, we look at different examples of the more commonly used social media platforms, together with how they may be used as part of your research.

Certain social media sites, such as Twitter and YouTube, are more commonly used in research than others. Given this, greater attention will be given to these platforms.

According to Kaplan and Haenlein (2010: 62), social media can be classified on the following basis:

1. Collaborative projects (for example, Wikipedia)
2. Blogs and microblogs (for example, Twitter)
3. Social news networking sites (for example, Digg, Reddit)
4. Content communities (for example, YouTube)
5. Social networking sites (for example, Facebook)
6. Virtual worlds: game worlds (for example, World of Warcraft); social worlds (for example, Second Life)

Image 11.1   Social media platforms can provide research opportunities

Source: iStock (photo ID: 1133848951)

As with many classifications, although useful, Kaplan and Haenlein's (2010) six points overlap and are not mutually exclusive. For example, microblogs such as Twitter are now the 'go to' place for up-to-the minute news.

Irrespective of your choice of research topic, social media provides a wide range of ways in which to conduct research. However, it also presents challenges. These include knowing where to look for information and how to select data. In large part, these challenges can be overcome by understanding the options social media presents and having a clear set of research questions. Before we examine closely the different types of social media platforms, it is worth considering how social media might feature as part of a research project. By no means exhaustive, options here for you to consider are listed below.

EVENTS

At the time of writing, the hot topic of discussion on social media is the US elections. Using the hashtag #USElection2020 brings up a whole magnitude of posts on Twitter. Hashtags are ways to connect content to a particular topic. In this respect, they act as a useful tool for researchers when focusing on a certain theme or topic. By way of example, analyzing events on social media might involve analyzing post-event evaluation comments following a major sporting event. These comments can then be compared across two different social media platforms.

USER GROUPS OR COMMUNITIES

A user group is a set of people who share similar interests or goals. As we shall see later in the chapter, Reddit is a useful platform for analyzing user groups and communities. Again, using hashtags is an ideal way to engage with a community online. For example, as an active Twitter user, I engage with the Learning and Teaching in Higher Education (#LTHEChat) community. The community organizes a weekly Twitter Chat on a topic related to teaching and learning in higher education. More on Twitter Chats later in the chapter.

PRACTICES

In this context, practices refer to a type of profession or activity. By way of example, if you were keen to analyze the views of accountants on Twitter, you can use a series of accountancy-related hashtags. Similarly, there is also overlap with groups here as accountancy practice and interactions can also be analyzed using a platform such as Reddit.

AUDIENCES

Finally, a focus of your research might be on the individual and/or organizational level when conducting social media research. Although by no means exhaustive, examples here may include:

- How do brands communicate via social media?
- What impact do influencers have across different social media platforms?
- How do organizations handle crisis management on social media?
- How do organizations use social media as a form of customer service?
- Business performance and social media
- Social media in financial services
- The impact of social media on small businesses

The above examples give you an insight into some of the areas and topics involving social media research. As mentioned, research involving social media is not just about focusing on social media as a research topic, but also considering how to use social media for research in other ways. This latter point we examine in the next section when applying and discussing Kaplan and Haenlein's (2010) classification of social media.

COLLABORATIVE PROJECTS

Collaborative projects enable the joint and simultaneous creation of content by many end users. Within collaborative projects, one differentiates between wikis – that is, websites which allow users to add, remove and change text-based content – and social bookmarking applications which enable the group-based collection and rating of internet links or media content (Kaplan and Haenlein, 2010). Perhaps the best-known example of a collaborative project is Wikipedia.

Wikipedia

Wikipedia (www.wikipedia.org/) needs no introduction. Launched in 2001 by Jimmy Wales and Larry Sanger, there are Wikipedia sites in 300 different languages, with some 46 million articles accessed by 1.4 billion unique devices every single month (Barnett, 2018). Wikipedia is a free online encyclopaedia featuring openly editable content created and sourced by users from around the world. Wikipedia has become the go-to site for students seeking information on any topic. As a volunteer service, the site is powered and maintained by a full-time staff and thousands of contributors who work for free.

Wikipedia can be used as a source for your research; however, it should not be cited within a research project. This is because Wikipedia is typically not viewed as being a reliable source. Instead, you can use the sources at the bottom of the wiki page when searching the literature.

BLOGS AND MICROBLOGS

There are a wide range of social tools available to student researchers. A blog is perhaps one of the most commonly used tools. What is a blog? In simple terms, a blog is a chronological series of posts by an author or authors.

A blog is a type of website, or at least part of a website. The word 'blog' is a shortened version of the term 'weblog'. Blogs contain a range of opinions and feature a variety of topics. Typically, blogs tend to focus on one particular theme, e.g. cooking or fashion, so as they are best placed to aim at a particular target audience. For your research, they can provide a useful source of information. Furthermore, you can create your own blog and use it as a platform to share your research. Most blogs have a comments section, allowing you to post comments on a particular article. WordPress is probably the most popular blogging tool. A valuable way to have a better understanding of blogging and how it can work is to look at some examples. Here is a varied selection:

- *Seth Godin's blog* (https://seths.blog/). The daily thoughts of marketing guru Seth Godin. As a marketer, I subscribe to Seth's blog and have the joy of receiving his daily musings in my email inbox. Unfortunately, one of the drawbacks of Seth's blog is that it does not allow comments.
- *Marketoonist* (https://marketoonist.com/blog). Tom Fishburne is the marketer and cartoonist behind Marketoonist. He regularly blogs about marketing topics. What makes Tom's blog so engaging is that each blog also features one of his humorous cartoons illustrating a particular marketing scenario.
- *Venus Williams* (http://venuswilliams.com/). The global tennis star's blog is not just about tennis, but also includes videos and visuals on travel, fashion and charity.
- *Crunch* (www.crunch.co.uk/knowledge/blog). Crunch is a blog that includes information on business guides and articles written by the experts, featuring a range of topics from UK tax law, being self-employed, managing a limited company.
- *TEDBlog* (https://blog.ted.com/). Here, you can access news about Ted Talks and Ted Conferences.
- *Richard's blog* (www.virgin.com/branson-family/richard-branson-blog). Sir Richard Branson's blog features the latest information on his business ventures and philanthropic projects. As one of the world's most successful entrepreneurs the blog also features information on the Branson family.

In terms of a resource for accessing data, blogs may provide interesting insights for your research. However, one has to proceed with caution in terms of the credibility of the blogger. Is the blogger viewed as an authority on their subject? If the answer is 'yes', then parts of their blog can potentially be used in your research. Using blogs allows the researcher to access data that have been produced by the author, usually for specific reasons that are communicated by the author (Benzon, 2019).

Microblogging are 'Services that focus on short updates that are pushed out to anyone subscribed to receive the updates' (Grahl, 2013: n.p.). Examples include Twitter and Tumblr. The next section provides an overview of the former.

Twitter

Twitter (https://twitter.com/?lang=en-gb) is a leading social media platform, with over 68 million users in the US and 16 million in the UK (Statista, 2020). Twitter is a microblogging system that allows you to send and receive short posts called tweets. Tweets are restricted to a maximum of 280 characters and can include links to websites, hashtags and links to other resources. A key feature of posting tweets is the hashtag (#). This links tweets about a topic, such as (research), (politics) or (education). Although Twitter allows the user to catch up on a topic at any time, Twitter Chats provide an especially useful way to gather data on a particular topic.

In essence, Twitter Chats provide a synchronous environment for users to post their answers to a series of questions posted by a facilitator. Participants in the chat gather at a specified time to discuss a particular topic. Typically, a Twitter Chat usually lasts for one hour and is on one particular topic or theme.

Twitter users can follow other users and organizations. If you follow someone you can see their tweets in your timeline. Some Twitter users prefer to use the platform in a passive way by largely retweeting content, while others choose to engage in dialogue and tweet and retweet information. What can you tweet about? All kinds of information. This includes:

- writing your own tweets about your research
- replying to other people's tweets
- posting a link and a request asking Twitter users to complete an online survey
- links to any blog posts you have written about your research
- news information relevant to your research.

You can learn how to sign up to Twitter at www.wikihow.com/Make-a-Twitter-Account.

Personally, I find Twitter to be the most useful platform to share my own research and to network with the academic community. The main reason for this is that it is simple to use, easily accessible, the majority of students already have their own Twitter account and it is a wonderful tool for social networking. This latter point is particularly important. At the start of your research journey, try to engage with fellow researchers via Twitter. You will find there is a large research community often willing to answer questions and offer support. Depending on the nature of your research, you can experiment with different hashtags to see which is the most widely used. Examples of hashtags associated with research communities includes - #PhD Forum, #PhDChat and #Dissertation. Although you may not be doing a PhD, you will find the first two hashtags include information relevant to all types of research. For example, how to manage your time and organize your research.

In the next section, we look at ways in which Twitter can be used as a data collection tool and examine examples of social media research using the microblogging system.

Twitter as a data collection tool

As a data collection tool, Twitter offers certain advantages over alternative online methods of data collection. O'Connor et al. (2014) suggest an advantage of recruitment via Twitter is that it can attract a heterogeneous sample from many different locations. In addition, selection bias of a sample should be taken into account, although this is the same using other social media platforms across the internet.

Social media platforms such as Twitter can be useful for recruiting research participants. See Table 11.1 for advantages and disadvantages of using social media to recruit research participants.

Table 11.1   Advantages and disadvantages of using social media to recruit research participants

Platform	Mechanisms to recruit	Advantages	Disadvantages
Twitter	• Recruitment Tweet > Retweets • Tag users and organizations who would find research relevant or interesting who have large follower bases • Add a relevant hashtag (i.e., #UKBusiness) • Consider building an online community	• Able to loosely target people in a particular field or area of interest • Ability to 'pay' to 'promote' the tweet (gets in the feeds of users who do not follow you)	• Sampling bias • Not right for all research projects • Very little control over the message once posted • People who do not fit your criteria will see message
Facebook	• Facebook targeted advertisement	• Largest social media platform	• Sampling bias • Not right for all research projects
Instagram	• Ads (owned by Facebook and linked on both platforms)	• Ability to reach a younger age demographic	• Sampling bias • Not right for all research projects

Source: Adapted from Arigo et al. (2018)

My own dissertation students typically turn to easy to access online survey platforms such as SurveyMonkey, Qualtrics and Google Forms when creating their surveys. A survey link is then shared via blogs, websites and social media platforms. Although easy to set up, a difficulty is often generating a suitable number of responses. There may also be a cost involved, especially if you intend developing a large number of questions and generating a large sample. Conversely, Twitter Chats are free to administer and have the potential to reach a large audience if using an established facilitator. Another option for recruiting business research participants is to send a direct tweet to your potential participant. You can find lists of Twitter users in different areas of business via Google. For now, here are some examples of marketers using Twitter:

- *Dr Jonathan Wilson* (https://twitter.com/WilsoJS). Okay, I know this is a little self-promotion! I tend to tweet about teaching, learning, research and marketing.
- *Professor Scott Galloway* (https://twitter.com/profgalloway). Professor Galloway is professor of marketing at the New York University Stern School of Business, and a public speaker, author, podcast host and entrepreneur. He tweets frequently on marketing topics, particularly those relating to technology brands.
- *Mark Ritson* (https://twitter.com/markritson). Former professor of marketing at Melbourne Business School and an international keynote speaker for conferences and organizational events. Mark is a columnist for *Marketing Week* magazine and tweets about all things marketing and brand.
- *Helen Edwards* (https://twitter.com/helenedw?lang=en). Helen is a Brand Consultant, columnist for *Marketing Week* magazine, Teaching Fellow at London Business School and author of *Creating Passion Brands*.

One useful application of Twitter is to recruit research participants using snowball sampling. We looked at snowball sampling in Chapter 9. In essence, the principles of snowball sampling using Twitter are the same as in a traditional context, in that the attributes of those invited to take part in research are not always known to the researcher. This includes personal information such as gender and age (O'Connor et al., 2014).

One of the challenges of Twitter is the almost completely disorganized nature of incoming tweets. Twitter offers an unobtrusive flow of information when compared with Facebook or a blog. However, what is important is matching the right social networking tool with the right purpose (Pennington, 2012).

Twitter research in action

The following case example illustrates one way Twitter can be used as a data collection tool. In this particular example, the researchers are conducting a comparative study between China's Weibo microblogging site and Twitter.

Kim et al. (2021) carried out a study into the differences between China's Weibo and Twitter. The focus of their research is on how users carry out online 'firestorms'. An online firestorm can be defined as the 'sudden discharge of large quantities of messages containing negative word-of-mouth and complaint behaviour' (Pfeffer et al., 2014). The authors undertook exploratory research through the use of quantitative content analysis of top trending words and associated top tweets over a six-month period on the social media platforms.

Their findings suggest that the threshold for considering online reaction to an online firestorm is significantly higher in China than in the US. In addition, Chinese users rarely target government and politics. Conversely, in the US, government and politics are targeted extensively.

SOCIAL NEWS NETWORKING SITES

Social news networking sites are

> services that allow people to post various news items or links to outside articles and then allows its users to 'vote' on the items. The voting is the core social aspect as the items that get the most votes are displayed the most prominently. The community decides which news items get seen by more people. (Grahl, 2013: n.p.)

Digg

Digg (https://digg.com/) is a social network and a news aggregating site. Users submit stories for promotion, and they are subsequently either voted for (digged), which is a positive vote, or against (buried). If you like a story, by giving it the thumbs up you are contributing to the stories that people want to read about. The most popular stories are posted to the front page, which can drive a lot of traffic to the corresponding sites. Users can share stories read on Digg with other social media networks.

How might Digg be used for research? Digg can be particularly useful for generating ideas for your research. The more 'Diggs' the greater the popularity of the topic. Furthermore, the search function allows you to search for information on your chosen research topic.

Reddit

Reddit (https://www.reddit.com/) claims to be 'the front page of the Internet' and is a network of communities based on people's interests. Reddit users vote on the entries posted and use good (upvotes) and junk (downvotes). Each entry gets a submission score computed by calculating the differences between the upvotes and the downvotes (Wasike, 2011).

Conducting a keyword search brings up the 'best results', 'Posts' and 'Communities and users'. It is this last function that can be used for research. By way of an example, let us say that you want to engage and be part of a social network on auditing. You have decided that this will be your broad research topic, but want to find out more about the subject from a practitioner's perspective. A subreddit is like a niche online community. **Each subreddit has a particular focus.** For example, the subreddit /r/ArtsandCrafts features questions, feedback and creative ideas regarding arts and crafts. In terms of a business example, at the time of writing, entering 'Auditing' in the search box, followed by clicking on 'Communities and users' brings up '/r/auditing' 631 members. The auditing community describes itself as:

> Internal auditors, external auditors, financial auditors, regulatory auditors, and information technology auditors are all welcome. Relevant news, business happening, certification questions, career discussions, engagement discussions.

Joining a Reddit community not only means it can be used to recruit possible research participants, but used for ethnographic research. This is a type of qualitative research in which the research participants are observed and interact within an environment that can be online and/or offline. In both contexts, the focus here might be on either participant or non-participant research whereby the aim is to observe the interactions, themes and relationships of participants within a particular community. In the case of Reddit, an example of ethnographic research might be observing the interactions among the Harry Potter subreddit community (/r/harrypotter) of which there are 991,000 members. We examine ethnographic research in Chapter 13.

CONTENT COMMUNITIES

Content communities are platforms that provide an opportunity to share media content between users. An obvious example here is YouTube (videos), Slideshare (PowerPoint presentations) and Pinterest (visuals, pictures). For the researcher, YouTube in particular offers a rich source of data. Given their popularity, they are likely to contain information on your chosen research topic.

YouTube

YouTube (www.youtube.com/) is the world's most popular video sharing site and the most visited site after Google. YouTube channels generate a huge amount of content every week. According to The Pew Research Center, as of January 2019, nearly 44,000 YouTube channels had at least 250,000 subscribers (van Kessel, 2019).

According to Lifewire (2020a), YouTube is a video platform that is driven by two types of users:

- Video creators: People who have channels and upload videos to those channels.
- Video viewers: People who watch videos, interact with videos and subscribe to channels.

To the student researcher, YouTube provides an easy and free access to a plethora of information. Yet, it is sometimes overlooked as a source of data collection or a means of developing research ideas. These research ideas might be generated by simply browsing videos by entering a keyword or phrase in the search box. Later in the chapter, we will examine how YouTube can be used as a means to collecting data.

Slideshare

Founded in 2006, Slideshare (www.slideshare.net/about) is a slide hosting service acquired by LinkedIn in 2012. It is a way to put your PowerPoint slides online. SlideShare's homepage sums up what the site is all about – 'Discover. Share. Learn'. First, 'Discover' allows the user to narrow their search by showing a wide range of the most popular topics. This includes Design, Engineering, Food, Environment and Technology. To search for any particular topic, use the search function. You can also do a general search in the search box. Second, 'Share' allows users to share slides via Facebook, Twitter and LinkedIn. Finally, the focus on 'Learn' comes from the slide content.

Slideshare is a popular tool with academics. The platform is also used by universities and conference organizers to post PowerPoint slides for those unable to attend an event. By way of an example, Image 11.2 shows an illustration of a set of my own PowerPoint slides posted to Slideshare. These are from a conference I attended on educational development.

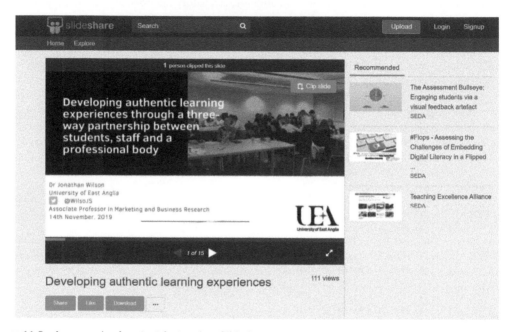

Image 11.2   An example of content featured on Slideshare

The ways you can use Slideshare in your research are three-fold. First, you can simply search for possible research topics at the start of your research journey. Second, many of the presentations on Slideshare include references. These can be helpful if undertaking a literature review. Finally, Slideshare can also be used to share your research ideas and presentations.

Pinterest

Pinterest (https://about.pinterest.com/en-gb) is an online pinboard used for photo sharing. Users can visually share and discover new interests by posting, known as 'pinning' images or videos to their own boards. One way to think of your Pinterest board is that of a traditional cork board. A collection of pins usually centres on a common theme, e.g. interior design. Pinterest is a social network very much focused on visual orientation so ideal if your research is based on some kind of visual analysis.

According to Wilkinson (2013: 3):

Pinterest is not an inherently social medium. People use Pinterest to save images and links that they like whether collections of recipes, pictures of cats with humorous captions, or ideas for crafts. A Pinterest user would be free to use the site simply to store interesting photos and ideas.

Using the platform for pictures or designs is also a key emphasis of the site. This makes it ideal if the nature of your research is on visual research. For example, you might share on Pinterest research on how participants are able to recall and illustrate leading brand logos. Sashittal and Jassawalla (2015) note that Pinterest is unique in many ways. First, it is an online medium devoted almost entirely to visuals. Second, users engage in posting original images but more often 'like' and/or 'repin' the images posted by others to produce curated albums.

SOCIAL NETWORKING SITES

Social networking sites allow users to connect by creating a personal profile. The largest social networking site is Facebook. LinkedIn is also another example. Social networking sites are web-based services 'that allow individuals to (1) construct a public or semi-public profile within a bounded system, (2) articulate a list of other users with whom they share a connection, and (3) view and traverse their list of connections and those made by others within the system' (Boyd and Ellison, 2007: 211).

Facebook

Facebook (www.lifewire.com/what-is-facebook-3486391) is a social networking website where users can post comments, share photographs, and post links to news or other content on the web, chat live, and watch short-form video. According to Lifewire.com (2020b), the key features of Facebook are as follows:

- Facebook allows you to maintain a friends list and choose privacy settings to tailor who can see content on your profile.
- Facebook allows you to upload photos and maintain photo albums that can be shared with your friends.
- Facebook supports interactive online chat and the ability to comment on your friend's profile pages.
- Facebook supports group pages, fan pages and business pages.
- You can video live using Facebook live.

LinkedIn

LinkedIn (https://gb.linkedin.com/) is a social network site for the business community to share, connect and learn. One way to think of LinkedIn is as an online networking event where you go to network with individuals. On LinkedIn, you network with other users by adding them as 'connections'. You converse via private message or by using available contact information. A key feature of LinkedIn is the profile page where you can show your name, photo, location and work experience, similar to a CV or resume. In this respect, LinkedIn is a place where you can create your online profile. In addition, LinkedIn can be used to find and apply for jobs.

An interesting example of how to use LinkedIn in research is a study by Huang et al. (2019). The authors were interested in the role of social media websites, LinkedIn and Twitter in disseminating sustainability knowledge. The social media networks were used as a form of data collection. First, snowball sampling was used to recruit participants through the referrals or connections of one member of a particular group. To begin with, participants were recruited from Twitter followers and LinkedIn connections who shared similar interests in sustainability.

The final sample included participants recruited from one of the author's own Twitter and LinkedIn sites. Next, a structured survey was administered via both Twitter and LinkedIn. For example, participants were asked about their attitudes toward each social media site disseminating sustainability knowledge on three items (1 = strongly disagree, 7 = strongly agree):

- The information about the implementation of sustainable community plans offered on LinkedIn is useful.
- The information about the implementation of sustainable community plans offered on LinkedIn is understandable.
- The information about the implementation of sustainable community plans offered on LinkedIn is sufficient.

The participants were also asked about three motivations for engaging in LinkedIn (1 = strongly disagree, 7 = strongly agree):

- I browse or participate in the LinkedIn community to obtain relevant information about sustainable community plans.
- I browse or participate in the LinkedIn community to learn more about sustainable community plans.
- I browse or participate in the LinkedIn community to seek advice on sustainable community plans.

The authors used different analytical tools, including content analysis, to analyze their data. What is interesting about this study is that social media features in different ways throughout the research. First, it is used as an effective tool for recruiting research participants. Second, for sharing a survey. And finally, also forms the basis of the research topic. Notably, the research is not only focusing on one popular social media platform. This study shows you the opportunities social media presents when thinking about your own research project.

Instagram

Launched in 2010, Instagram has quickly become one of the most widely used social networking platforms in the world (Duggan, 2015). As of June 2018, the social network reported more than 1 billion monthly active users worldwide and the social media network's daily active users stood at 500 million (Clement, 2020).

Instagram (www.instagram.com/) is a social networking app which allows users to share photos and videos. Unlike Facebook, which relies on both text and pictures, Instagram is designed to enable users to share images or videos with their audience. In short, Instagram is all about visual sharing. Its visual nature is what distinguishes it from social media that are relatively more text-focused (Carpenter et al., 2020)

On Instagram, user roles are divided into posters and followers. A poster can be described as the owner of an Instagram account and only posters can publish a new picture or video on their accounts, while a follower is someone who subscribes to a poster's account and then receives pictures and videos (updates) (Russmann and Svensson, 2016).

How might Instagram be used for research? The visual nature of Instagram provides a whole host of opportunities to engage in research based on visual analysis. By way of an example, Salleh et al. (2015) used web-based content analysis on the top ten restaurant-brand Instagram accounts in Malaysia. Of the ten brands, only seven had an Instagram account. Content and comparative analysis focused on the following characteristics:

- type of restaurant
- year began operation
- specialty
- number of outlets
- date adopted Instagram

- page age (number of days)
- total videos
- total photos
- number of followers.

The authors used the Diffusion of Innovations (DOI) model as their theoretical underpinning in the research. The DOI model describes the innovation adoption and implementation processes at both the individual and organizational levels (Rogers, 2003). Organizational adoption studies investigate factors influencing the adoption of innovations, adoption rates and adopter categories while diffusion examines the implementation of technology in an organization. One key conclusion from their findings was that early adoption (joining Instagram early) does not necessarily lead to early implementation, meaning that two of the seven brands posted content on an irregular basis.

Although a relatively straightforward research project, this example of using visual analysis on Instagram shows you how different metrics can be used as part of a comparative study. This type of research also has the potential to be extended to other social media networks.

WeChat

Released in 2011, WeChat (web.wechat.com/?lang=en_US) is an instant messaging app developed by the Chinese technology giant Tencent. Known as 'Weixin' in Chinese, WeChat has similar features to WhatsApp to generate both text and voice messages. WeChat is free to install, use and download, and supports all smartphone platforms (Lien and Cao, 2014). As of December 2018, WeChat is one of the world's most popular social media platforms with over one billion monthly active users (Montag et al., 2018). Although popular in China, WeChat is less commonly used in Western countries.

An example of how WeChat is used in research is a study conducted by Xue et al. (2019). The study explored how a group of online educators in China used WeChat to build an online Community of Practice (CoP). A CoP can be defined as 'groups of people who share a concern, a set of problems, or passion about a topic, and who deepen their knowledge and experiences in this area by interaction on an ongoing basis' (Wenger et al, 2002: 4). The authors adopted a qualitative study and collected data from multiple sources, including online interaction excerpts, teachers' reflections, classroom observation and interviews.

The study aimed to investigate how WeChat may be used by teachers to build online CoPs for professional learning and what transformative effects it may have on teachers' teaching practices. The authors addressed the following research questions:

1. How do the participating teachers utilize WeChat for online CoP building?
2. What are their perceptions on participating in the teacher WeChat group for professional learning?
3. What are the teachers' transformational changes in their teaching practice?

Data collection involved setting up a WeChat group for research participants to join. The first author was also in the chatting group in order to observe the participating teachers' interactions and to ask any questions raised. In this sense, the study can be described as 'participant observation'. This is a type of observational research and something we examine in Chapter 13. Consisting of five teachers, members of the WeChat group were asked to submit reflections on how they use mobile social media in their teaching at the end of each month.

Phase two of the research involved conducting semi-structured interviews with participants in order to understand their perceptions of this form of communication, challenges encountered and suggestions for effective use of teachers' groups for professional learning. Data were analyzed using content analysis.

What is interesting about this study is that it is conducted using two phases. First, social media is used to create a WeChat group and as a platform to share experiences. Second, a more traditional method is used, namely semi-structured interviews, to follow up the responses from the five participants.

VIRTUAL WORLDS

Game worlds

Peachey et al. (2010) divide virtual worlds into two categories: 1. Game worlds including Eve Online, City of Heroes and World of Warcraft, usually roleplaying games that attract hordes of players and foster the creation of shared social norms and behaviours, often through language; 2. Social worlds, including The Palace and Second Life (SL), which may be viewed as an extension of bulletin/discussion boards, chat and social networks, providing a graphical environment in which to communicate.

Social worlds

According to Kaplan and Haenlein (2009) virtual social worlds have three characteristics that differentiate them from other social media applications. First, virtual worlds allow users to interact with others in real time. Second, virtual worlds allow users to create fully customized virtual self-presentations in the form of avatars. Finally, avatars within virtual worlds have the possibility of exploring their

Image 11.3   Concept Cartoon 'Social media platforms for research'

virtual environment in three dimensions. An example of research based on social worlds is a study by Mackenzie et al. (2013: 354) involving Second Life®:

> Using an avatar to research Second Life®, one of the authors examined the sites of twenty real-world businesses, each located in its own geographical location. The avatar, self-identified as a researcher, visited various business sites, used text chat to converse with other avatars, accepted calling cards offered within business sites and took visual snapshots. At the same time, she recorded document field notes of her observations in the real world. Descriptive content analysis was used to assess the businesses' virtual settings, visual displays, the use of customer service avatars, virtual product offerings and promotional objects, the range and types of navigational aids on offer, and the overall aesthetics and atmosphere of the setting. The study was conducted between July and October 2007, at a time when Second Life® had over ten million registered residents.

What is interesting to note about this extract from an article by Mackenzie et al. (2013) is that although the research focused on Second Life®, the recording of field notes is based on the real world.

Image 11.3 is a Concept Cartoon that shows characters expressing their views on types of social media platforms. Think about the different views, and if possible, use them to provoke a discussion with fellow students. What do you think? Do you share a viewpoint with one particular character?

STRATEGIES FOR DATA COLLECTION

The first step in conducting research using social media is to have a research question. Given the volume of data available via social media, an error sometimes made by students is to start with data first.

Sloan and Quan-Haase (2017) advises that the initial question should be:

1. Which social media platforms would be the most relevant for my research question? (Single platform vs. multi-platform approach)

Once decided, the next step is to prepare to collect your data from the selected platform(s), while asking the following questions:

2. What are my main criteria for selecting data from this platform? (Basic approaches for collecting data from social media)
3. How much data do I need? (Big vs. small data)
4. What is (unproportionally) excluded if I collect data this way? (Collection bias)

The above questions are very useful in helping to formalize your research. However, like many aspects of research, think about the process. Applying a process model such as the one in Figure 11.2 will help you to clarify the steps involved.

Figure 11.2   A process model for using social media in your research

Figure 11.2 acts as an important reference point for you in relation to the following key questions:

5.   How will social media be used in my research?
6.   Will social media form the basis of my research topic?

The steps in the social media process shown in Figure 11.2 are:

*   *Purpose*: Here, include objectives relating to social media, for example, 'to recruit research participants online'. Objective 2 might be: 'to distribute a survey online'.
*   *Strategy*: This might include utilizing multiple channels to both recruit research participants and to distribute the survey.
*   *Tools*: An example here relating to my own teaching material might include Twitter, my own blog, post link to the module Blackboard discussion board (online course management system).
*   *Results*: This is likely to include reflecting on the outcomes of using social media in your research, together with understanding the tools and their benefits.

SINGLE PLATFORM VS. MULTI-PLATFORM STUDIES

The majority of social media studies tend to focus on a single social media platform. Focusing on a single platform allows you to conduct a study in-depth and to fully understand user engagement. For example, if you decide to carry out research examining retweets, hashtags and twitter chats, then clearly Twitter is going to be your chosen platform. An alternative approach is to compare aspects of two or more social media platforms. The rationale for doing this might be to see if research findings are unique to one particular platform.

By way of an example, let us say that you want to study online communication in the run-up to an election, but how do you choose your platform? Start by thinking about your research questions and the type of information you need. The next step is to review all of the social media platforms that are available to you. Also, consider access, popularity and the profile of users. Returning to our example of the run-up to an election, you may find that Twitter and YouTube are suitable platforms. Firstly, Twitter is widely used by the public, organizations and politicians as a means to share opinions. Second, the use of hashtags makes it easy for the researcher to follow and gather data. Similarly, YouTube also has a diverse range of content and users. In particular, videos are an important part of sharing information.

BASIC APPROACHES FOR COLLECTING DATA FROM SOCIAL MEDIA

As with traditional research, there are a number of ways data can be collected. Before hastily choosing your data collection method(s), think about how much time you want to devote to data collection. Your chosen time frame will ultimately influence how you approach your data collection, including your sampling method. For example, should data be collected from social media accounts on one particular day of the week? Should social media users be selected at random? If so, what type of sampling method? Criteria you can use for your data collection are as follows:

Based on topics, themes or keywords

An approach commonly used by researchers is to collect social media content based on topics, themes or keywords. For example, a topic might refer to a particular process (such as a brand promoting a new product using social media), to a sport or political event (like the Olympic Games or general election). As examined earlier in the book, topics usually start at a broad level and then become narrower. Again, using the Olympic Games as a broad topic, then you can subsequently narrow this topic down so it is more manageable when conducting research, e.g. by focusing on a particular sport.

Topics are typically labelled using hashtags, especially on Twitter. Popular topics of course tend to be trending and thus make it easier to capture information. Although using hashtags are beneficial for researchers, there are drawbacks. As highlighted earlier in the chapter, hashtags are keywords or phrases preceded by the # symbol that make it easier for users to find and follow information by grouping similar topics. For example, if you are interested in finding out about the latest information on business news, you can search for information using #Business. Clearly, this is likely to provide you with a broad range of information, so we can narrow down our search. For instance, if the focus of your research is UK organizations, then you can use #UKBusiness.

Users may not all use the same terminology when posting tweets and using hashtags. The latter can be particularly frustrating. By way of an example, the US elections has a series of hashtags, including #USelectionresults2020, #USelections, #USelections2020 #Trump and #Biden.

Other problems include some users may not use a hashtag or may not be explicit in their response. Going back to the US elections example, simply analyzing hashtag #elections may not necessarily relate to the US election. An example of the possible confusion when using hashtag #Piers is that this can refer to the UK broadcaster and journalist and also a platform on pillars projecting into the sea! In addition, sometimes users have a tendency to overuse the number of hashtags. This blanket approach can make it difficult if you are researching a topic such as views on climate change; the hashtag climate change may also be combined with other topics, for example, #climatechange, #Humanrights, #AnimalRights. This is an actual example! Although these topics may all be of concern to the user, they are unlikely to contain a clear, succinct message.

When using hashtags, how do you know which hashtags to use? What are the most popular hashtags? The answer is you can use a tool to monitor hashtags in real time (see Table 11.2), such as RiteTag, Trendsmap and Hashtagify.

Table 11.2   Tools researchers can use to monitor hashtags on Twitter in real time

Tool	Description
RiteTag https://ritetag.com/	If you want to analyze which hashtags are the most popular, or best to use for your research, then one of several tools available is RiteTag. Free to use, RiteTag also provides suggestions for related hashtags. This is useful for researchers looking at the most commonly used hashtags relating to their research topic.
Hashtagify https://hashtagify.me/	Hashtagify provides some useful graphics on hashtags, including a word cloud showing related hashtags. The Tweets Wall also provides an interesting overview of users engaging with the hashtag. Also, reference to key influencers.
Trendsmap www.trendsmap.com/	Trendsmap shows the latest Twitter trending hashtags and topics from anywhere in the world. To analyse trends over different time periods requires a certain type of subscription.

HOW MUCH DATA DO I NEED?

A distinction can be made between 'Big data' and 'Small data'. Big data is large volume data that has the potential to be mined to extract information that can inform decision-making. In contrast, small data tends to be limited in volume and based on samples, as opposed to entire populations. The data you capture in social media research depends on: data required in order to address research objectives, the sampling frame, social media platform(s) used in your research, your methodological approach and how the data are classified. Reading earlier studies on social media research will provide a useful insight into how researchers use data.

POSSIBLE DATA COLLECTION BIAS

Selection bias is a consideration when conducting social media research. For example, in some countries certain social media platforms are banned or there is limited access for researchers. An example of this is in China, where both Facebook and Twitter are banned. Most social media providers restrict access to their users' data, thus making it difficult to access personal data. However, do think about where this type of data is important in the context of your research.

Sampling bias is another consideration. For example, collecting tweets only using one particular hashtag, e.g. #USelection, excludes those tweets by users who have not used a hashtag or used an alternative hashtag, such as #USElections2020.

Finally, data collection bias may also relate to bias in the context of social media platforms. If you are only accessing one particular social media site, e.g. LinkedIn, it is likely that the users of the platform are not representative of the general population. Thus, it is rarely possible to make generalizations to the wider population.

According to McCay-Peet and Quan-Haase (2017), social media research can answer the following questions:

1. Methodological questions

   Methodological questions emerge from social media. For example, consider how you might use social media to collect, analyze and visualize your data. Although social media allows easy access to large quantities of data, how do you know which data to include and exclude, how to analyze your data and interpret the results. Of course, these are also questions you may ask when conducting traditional research. However, one of the challenges of social media research is the volume of data available.

2. Ethical questions

   Social media research raises numerous ethical questions. Examples include privacy, dissemination of data and informed consent. We examine these issues more closely later in the chapter. Although social media data is often publicly available, this does not mean that you should not consider all of the ethical issues that you would typically do with traditional research. For example, certain websites may not be comfortable with their data being used for research purposes. Similarly, doing qualitative research using a small sample size may make the ability to protect the identity of an individual (anonymity) difficult to do.

3. Questions of scale

   Questions of scale is a challenge for researchers doing social media research. Social media provides an opportunity to examine large data sets of information or to focus on small-scale studies that focus on the behaviour of a small number of users. Each serves a different purpose. In the context of your own research, questions of scale are likely to be determined by the nature of your research objectives and methodology. In terms of the latter, in particular your chosen data collection method(s) and analytical techniques. We examine these later in the chapter.

THE BENEFITS AND CHALLENGES OF USING SOCIAL MEDIA FOR RESEARCH

Before discussing the benefits and challenges associated with social media for research, it is useful to look at the benefits of using social media in general. According to the Economic and Social Research Council (ESRC, 2020), social media allows you to:

- promote your research and increase its visibility
- communicate directly and quickly with others who have an interest in your research
- develop new relationships and build networks
- reach new audiences, both within and outside academia
- seek and give advice and feedback
- generate ideas
- share information and links (e.g. journal articles and news items)
- keep up-to-date with the latest news developments, and forward it to others instantly
- follow and contribute to discussions on events (e.g. conferences that you can't get to in person)
- express who you are as a person.

Source: https://esrc.ukri.org/research/impact-toolkit/social-media/using-social-media/

There are a number of benefits and challenges associated with using social media for research. First, an advantage of social media is that it is easily accessible. The majority of social media platforms are straightforward to access and easy to use. Other benefits include the following:

1. Andreotta et al. (2019) note that collecting social media data may be more scalable than more traditional approaches. Once the necessary equipment is in place, it can be relatively straightforward to collect your data. Conversely, traditional data collection methods such as interviews and surveys can be time-consuming when it comes to collecting data from participants.
2. Social media data emerges from 'real-world' environments where the researcher is a non-participant and is observing interactions in their natural setting. In addition, social media research also provides an opportunity to observe an environment made up of a large and diverse range of participants. For example, although research shows that Twitter tends to be more popular with users over the age of 35, the platform is still used by people from a diverse range of backgrounds.
3. Perhaps the most notable benefit of using social media for research is that for something like Twitter, the data is free. Conducting traditional research using a survey typically requires paying for survey software, whereas wanting to collect additional data using Twitter is quick and easy.
4. Social media offers a wide reach and plenty of opportunities for you to share your research. For example, you can set yourself up a YouTube channel to diary each step in your research journey. Viewers can then follow your research and comment on each video.
5. Compared to traditional research methods, such as focus groups and interviews, social media research is typically less expensive.

For all the benefits of using social media for research, there are a number of notable challenges.

1. Social media research does not always focus on the researcher as an observer. For example, rather than observing and analyzing a series of tweets, the focus of your research might be to actually engage with Twitter users. These conversations might provide interesting data. However, a problem you might find is knowing the 'boundaries of your research' and the unit(s) of analysis. Conversations with multiple users may make it difficult to decide what information to include within your research. It is the potential viral nature of social media that can make it challenging for researchers.
2. Social media content is huge in comparison to traditional data sets. Postings to a social media site may be diverse in nature and largely unrelated. So, when conducting your research, you might find that postings may not always fully relate to your research topic.

3. Content is dynamic and temporary. In relation to the last point, the time when you carry out social media research may influence your results. By way of an example, if you were conducting research on the topic of the public relations of Amazon, then a perceived negative experience from a customer may cause their post to go viral. Ultimately, this is a 'snapshot' of how the technology brand is viewed on social media.

4. How do you know the information provided on social media is from a credible source? If you are using information from a blog, then the likelihood is that the blogger will provide some kind of personal details, including experience and qualifications. However, their credibility is more difficult to determine if referring to a social media platform with limited information, such as Twitter. In theory, LinkedIn is arguably one of the more reliable social media sites given that the content is based on people's profile and work experience.

5. Not everyone is on social media. This means that certain key cases might be excluded from your research for this simple reason. One way to address this issue is to use more than one type of data collection method. For example, combining different social media platforms with conducting conventional focus groups.

BOX 11.1: RESEARCH SNAPSHOT

Planning how to incorporate social media into your research is something that should be decided early in your research. Although there are notable differences compared to traditional research, the fundamental principles are the same, in particular, that research is a systematic process. A useful exercise is to use a sheet of A1 paper to draw out the steps and to write down how you intend to use social media in your research.

There are two main areas of research where there are notable differences when comparing traditional and social media research. These are data collection and data analysis. In this section, we start by examining the methods associated with collecting data using various social media platforms. Following this, a discussion on the typical methods used to analyze data when conducting social media research.

SOCIAL MEDIA ANALYTICS (SMA)

Social media platforms such as Twitter offer a large resource of data for student researchers. As we have seen in this chapter, social media platforms present a vast amount of data on a daily basis. A challenge you are likely to find in your research is knowing which data to use and how to narrow down your data collection. The process of social media analytics takes three steps (Zeng et al., 2010) – capture, understand and present.

CAPTURE

The capture process involves collecting the data from your chosen social media platform(s). The data are then saved in a database for further processing. Examples of the type of data you may capture for your research includes events, moments or the online profile of users. For example, through the use of hashtags, Freelon et al. (2018) identified the Twitter activity of three separate communities – 'Asian-American Twitter', 'Feminist Twitter' and 'Black Twitter' in tweets from 2015 to 2016.

UNDERSTAND

This stage in the process involves deciding on analytical techniques, the main options include:

Thematic analysis

Thematic analysis involves a rigorous process in order to locate patterns within data through data familiarization, coding and developing a revising theme. Thematic analysis is also used in more traditional research, for example when analyzing data collected from a face-to-face interview. We examine this type of thematic analysis later in Chapter 15.

Content analysis

Content analysis can be systematically used for labelling text, audio and/or video communication from social media, and can provide a numerical output. We look at content analysis later in the book.

Semantic analysis

Semantic analysis can be used for examining the meaning of language and also the relationship between occurrences of words, phrases and clauses. One of the most powerful techniques for semantic analysis is the hashtag, which was popularized by Twitter and is now used by all major social media platforms (apart from Wikipedia) (Wills, 2016).

PRESENT

The final step in SMA is to present your data. There are a number of visualization techniques you can use to show your data. Canva (www.Canva.com) is my favourite free online tool for designing and illustrating graphics. The tool gives you the option to produce your own infographics, poster, presentations and mind maps. You will also find templates helping you to prepare your design. We examine ways of presenting qualitative and quantitative data in Chapters 15 and 16 respectively.

ETHICAL ISSUES IN SOCIAL MEDIA RESEARCH

Research conducted using social media platforms must be subject to the same ethical scrutiny as off-line. Several ethical societies have introduced ethical principles based on digital principles. These include The British Educational Research Association (BERA), The European Society for Opinion and Market Research (ESOMAR), The Chartered Institute of Marketing (CIM) and The Association of Certified and Chartered Accountants (ACCA).

A fundamental aspect of ethical principles is the notion of research involving human subjects. However, if research involves using an avatar, is this still a human subject? What about if someone posts a review to a public site such as Trustpilot? Does this require ethics approval? Is social media research conducted without revealing your identity to the research participants viewed as covert observation? These are just some of the ethical considerations that social media research presents.

INFORMED CONSENT

As you saw earlier in the book, informed consent is based on the principle that a participant is provided with all relevant information on the research so that they make a decision as to whether or not to take part in the research. Although the consent process might not be so unlike the traditional method of mailing surveys to potential research participants, it can be much more straightforward to click a consent box as opposed to completing a survey and consent form and mailing this back to the researcher.

Obtaining informed consent online may involve the researcher posting to communities or individually contacting users and providing them with participant information sheets and consent forms to sign (Sugiura et al., 2017).

There are difficulties in trying to gain consent from participants in online communities. For example, not all participants may actively engage with a community. They may simply make a post and leave. One way to address ethical concerns is for you to read the conditions set out by the forum. These are likely to refer to ethical issues and provide guidance for researchers. Where you find that these do not exist, you can try to contact the moderator of the site, but this cannot be viewed as informed consent for all members of the group.

Determining the best place for consent information within a digital survey shared on social media requires careful consideration. Clearly, a limitation of social media is the number of characters within a post, so consent has to be placed within the survey tool or linked to an institutional webpage (Carey et al., 2020).

USING SOCIAL MEDIA FOR RESEARCH: TOP TIPS FOR STUDENTS

The chapter culminates with eight top tips or takeaways for student researchers considering using social media for research. Many of these tips are equally applicable to traditional research.

Figure 11.3   Using social media for research: Top tips for students

1. Plan your time

    Although planning your time is equally applicable to all types of research, arguably it is more important when using social media for research. Why? Well, the nature of social media means that it is easy to spend too much time scrolling through tweets, for example, without making any kind of research progress.

2. Choosing your platform(s)

    As already highlighted in this chapter, your choice of social media platform is dependent on a number of factors. First, think about the nature of your research problem and research questions. From your research, is there one particular platform that is more likely to allow you to address your research problem? Second, think about the unit of analysis. If, for example, your research is analyzing fashion brands, then you may decide to select a site that is largely all about visuals, e.g. Instagram or Pinterest. Third, choice of platform may also be dependent on how familiar you are with a particular platform and user access.

3. Consider your audience

    Understanding the nature of social media users associated with each platform will help you to decide which sites to use in your research. A key factor here is demographics. Organizations such as Pew Research Center and Statista publish data on the profiles of the 'typical' social media user for each platform. For example, Snapchat is a relatively new platform and is typically associated with a teenage audience. In contrast, LinkedIn is viewed as the go-to site when targeting business professionals.

4. Plan your research

    As highlighted earlier in the chapter, planning your social media research is essential. The most fundamental questions are: Are you using social media for research and/or as a research topic? How does social media 'fit' into your planned methodological approach?

5. Consider visuals

    An advantage of social media is that certain platforms are designed with visuals such as videos or images in mind. Social media data is much more than just text. Many of my own students have made good use of @Canva, the free design platform to create all types of visuals to illustrate their research, including word clouds, graphs, infographics and pictures.

6. Develop your research networks

    Using platforms such as Twitter makes it easier to develop research networks and join a research community. In addition, Twitter Chats also offer ideal opportunities to engage with individuals with similar interests.

7. Consider your research stakeholders

    If your research is based on your employer or you have established links with a particular organization, then it might be possible to use their social media, e.g. blog to recruit research participants and/or share your research. A key research stakeholder is your supervisor who may also have experience of doing research on/using social media.

8. Understand your unit(s) of analysis

    Finally, think about your unit(s) of analysis. When searching social media, what are you interested in analyzing? This could be an event, user group or possibly an organization. Again, are you conducting research on a social media related topic, using social media for research or both?

CHAPTER SUMMARY

- Social media is defined as 'Websites and applications that enable users to create and share content or to participate in social networking'.

- A distinction can be made between social networks on the basis of 'objects' and 'individuals'.

- Social media can also be classified on the basis of collaboration projects, blogs and microblogs, social news networking sites, content communities, social network sites and virtual worlds.

- An example of social media research is ethnographic research (from observing online social behaviour to participating and collecting primary data in various forms, including 'friending' users).

- Social media research can also study events, practices, user groups and audiences.

- Hashtags are keywords or phrases preceded by the # symbol that make it easier for users to find and follow information by grouping similar topics.

- Twitter Chats provide a synchronous environment for users to post their answers to a series of questions posted by a facilitator. Participants in the chat gather at a specified time to discuss a particular topic.

- Social media analytical techniques include thematic, semantic and content.

QUESTIONS FOR REVIEW

1. How would you define social media?

2. Explain how you would categorize social media.

3. Give an example of a social media platform suitable for conducting research into a healthy eating consumer group.

4. Discuss ways in which you might use hashtags to conduct social media research into corporate social responsibility in the fast fashion industry.

5. Outline three ways to analyze data collected via social media.

6. Outline three examples of ethical issues that need to be considered when doing social media research.

7. Explain how you might develop a suitably sized sample using social media.

8. Outline three key differences between social media research and traditional research.

9. Explain what is meant by the term 'blogging' and how you might use your own blog when conducting social media research.

10. Give two examples of possible selection bias when conducting social media research.

STUDENT SCENARIO: TIFFANY'S USE OF TWITTER TO COLLECT DATA

Tiffany is a BSc Business Management student. Tiffany's undergraduate project focuses on the acquisition of traditional bricks and mortar retailers by their online competitors. In essence, Tiffany wanted to determine how the public and consumers viewed such an acquisition. She decided to adopt a qualitative research approach. Social media would be used to provide interesting, exploratory insights as to how people viewed the downfall of many leading traditional high street retailers, and how these would be viewed by the public. Tiffany's research began by refining her research topic and coming up with one overriding research question, '*How do Twitter users view the increasing rise in acquisitions of high street retailers by increasingly dominant online retailers*'.

Choice of hashtags (keywords and themes)

Following a cursory search of recent stories on Twitter about acquisition, Tiffany identified a series of keywords and hashtags to use in her research. Subsequently, she put together a list of hashtags and decided to devote a period of seven days in which to monitor and analyze the data.

Choice of analytical method

Tiffany decided to use a thematic approach to analyzing Twitter users' responses to acquisition of bricks and mortar retailers. Research started by looking at broad themes and then narrowing this down on the basis of positive, negative and 'mixed' response to the acquisitions. Tiffany chose a convenience sampling method, as the purpose of her research was not to generalize to the wider population but to explore selected comments on the acquisition.

Presentation of research findings

Tiffany used a variety of ways to present her research findings. These included the use of word clouds, verbatim comments (screenshots of user tweets) and tables. The use of Twitter screenshots was exported from the social media platform into Word, thus giving an interesting visual first-hand insight into users' responses. Tiffany made sure to not only present her findings, but to also analyze her data and look for patterns and relationships between comments.

Interestingly, a key finding from Tiffany's research was that although many users professed to shop online, they were equally saddened about the closure and acquisition of leading high street brands. Furthermore, users commented on the importance of certain brands, suggesting that brands may be able to make the successful transition from traditional retail outlet to online retailer.

Questions

1. Identify the extent that time frame might impact Tiffany's research findings. Remember that Tiffany decided to choose a seven-day period in which to collect her data.
2. Tiffany chose Twitter as the social media platform in which to conduct her research. Recommend other platforms Tiffany may consider using for future research. Justify your answer.

Hint: For question 2, think about the purpose and target audience when making your recommendations.

FURTHER READING

Nwangwa, K.C.K., Yonlonfoun, E. and Omotere, T. (2014) 'Undergraduates and their use of social media: Assessing influence on research skills', *Universal Journal of Educational Research*, 2 (6): 446–453.

This article investigates the influence of social media usage on research skills of undergraduates at six different universities in Nigeria. In addition, the authors include a useful table on categories of social media.

Woodfield, K. (2017) *The Ethics of Online Research*. Bingley: Emerald Group Publishing.

This book provides a detailed discussion on ethical issues relating to social media research, including users' views of ethics in social media research.

Xue, S., Hu, X., Chi, X. and Zhang, J. (2019) 'Building an online community of practice through WeChat for teacher professional learning', *Professional Development in Education*. doi: 10.1080%2F19415257.2019.1647273

This article explores how a group of higher education teachers in China used the Chinese messaging app WeChat to build an online Community of Practice, which supported their professional learning. A qualitative study was designed. Data were collected from multiple sources including online interaction excerpts, teachers' reflections, classroom observation and interviews.

REFERENCES

Andreotta, M., Nugroho, R., Hurlstone, M.J., Boschetti, F., Farrell, S., Walker, I. and Paris, C. (2019) 'Analyzing social media data: A mixed-methods framework combining computational and qualitative text analysis', *Behavior Research Methods*, 51 (4): 1766–1781.

Arigo, D., Pagoto, S., Carter-Harris, L., Lillie, S.E. and Nebeker, C. (2018) 'Using social media for health research: Methodological and ethical considerations for recruitment and intervention delivery', *Digital Health*. doi: 10.1177%2F2055207618771757

Barnett, D. (2018) 'Can we trust Wikipedia? 1.4 billion people can't be wrong', *The Independent*, 17 February. Available at: www.independent.co.uk/news/long_reads/wikipedia-explained-what-it-trustworthy-how-work-wikimedia-2030-a8213446.html (accessed 31 January 2021).

Benzon, N. (2019) 'Informed consent and secondary data: Reflections on the use of mothers' blogs in social media research', *Area*, 51 (1): 182–189.

Boyd, D. and Ellison, N.B. (2007) 'Social network sites: Definition, history, and scholarship', *Journal of Computer-Mediated Communication*, 13: 210–230.

Carey, L., Jacobson, L., Pritchard, A. and Sadera, W. (2020) 'April. If you tweet it, data will come: Using social media for education research', in *Society for Information Technology & Teacher Education International Conference* (pp. 751–754), Association for the Advancement of Computing in Education (AACE).

Carpenter, J.P., Morrison, S.A., Craft, M. and Lee, M. (2020) 'How and why are educators using Instagram?', *Teaching and Teacher Education*, 96: 103–149.

Clement, J. (2020) 'Instagram: Statistics and facts', *Statista*, 14 May. Available at: www.statista.com/topics/1882/instagram/ (accessed 2 February 2021).

Duggan, M. (2015) 'Mobile messaging and social media 2015', *Pew Research Center*. Available at: www.pewinternet.org/2015/08/19/mobile-messaging-and-social-media-2015/ (accessed 3 January 2021).

Economic and Social Research Council (2020) *Using Social Media: What are the Benefits of Using Social Media?* Available at: https://esrc.ukri.org/research/impact-toolkit/social-media/using-social-media/ (accessed 10 January 2021).

ESOMAR (2021) *Ethics*. Available at: www.esomar.org/uploads/public/knowledge-and-standards/codes-and-guidelines/ESOMAR-Guideline-on-Social-Media-Research.pdf (accessed 2 February 2021).

Freberg, K. (2019) 'Social media and emerging media', *Public Relations Theory: Application and Understanding*: 97–111.

Freelon, D., Lopez, L., Clark, M.D. and Jackson, S.J. (2018) 'How black Twitter and other social media communities interact with mainstream news (Tech. Rep.)', *Knight Foundation*, 20 April. Available at: https://knightfoundation.org/features/ twittermedia (accessed 3 January 2021).

Grahl, T. (2013) *The 6 Types of Social Media*. Available at: http://timgrahl.com/the-6-types-of-social-media/ (accessed 26 November 2020).

Huang, L., Clarke, A., Heldsinger, N. and Tian, W. (2019) 'The communication role of social media in social marketing: A study of the community sustainability knowledge dissemination on LinkedIn and Twitter', *Journal of Marketing Analytics*, 7 (2): 64–75.

Kaplan, A.M. and Haenlein, M. (2009) 'The fairyland of Second Life: Virtual social worlds and how to use them', *Business Horizons*, 52 (6): 563–572.

Kaplan, A.M. and Haenlein, M. (2010) 'Users of the world, unite! The challenges and opportunities of social media', *Business Horizons*, 53 (1): 59–68.

Kim, S., Sung, K.H., Ji, Y., Xing, C. and Qu, J.G. (2021) 'Online firestorms in social media: Comparative research between China Weibo and USA Twitter', *Public Relations Review*, 47 (1): 102010.

Lien, C.H. and Cao, Y. (2014) 'Examining WeChat users' motivations, trust, attitudes, and positive word-of-mouth: Evidence from China', *Computers in Human Behavior*, 41: 104–111.

Lifewire (2020a) 'What is YouTube: A beginner's guide', *Lifewire*. Available at: www.lifewire.com/youtube-101-3481847 (accessed 10 February 2021).

Lifewire (2020b) 'What is Facebook?' *Lifewire*. Available at: www.lifewire.com/what-is-facebook-3486391 (accessed 11 February 2021).

MacKenzie, K., Buckby, S. and Irvine, H. (2013) 'Business research in virtual worlds: Possibilities and practicalities', *Accounting, Auditing & Accountability Journal*, 26 (3): 352–373.

McCay-Peet, L. and Quan-Haase, A. (2017) 'What is social media and what questions can social media research help us answer', in L. Sloan and A. Quan-Haase (eds), *The SAGE Handbook of Social Media Research Methods* (pp. 13–26). Thousand Oaks, CA: SAGE.

Montag, C., Becker, B. and Gan, C. (2018) 'The multipurpose application WeChat: A review on recent research', *Frontiers in Psychology*, 9: 2247.

O'Connor, A., Jackson, L., Goldsmith, L. and Skirton, H. (2014) 'Can I get a retweet please? Health research recruitment and the Twittersphere', *Journal of Advanced Nursing*, 70 (3): 599–609.

Oxford English Dictionary (2021) *Social Media Definition*. Available at: www.lexico.com/definition/social_media.

Peachey, A., Gillen, J., Livingstone, D. and Smith-Robbins, S. (eds) (2010) *Researching Learning in Virtual Worlds*. London: Springer Science & Business Media.

Pennington, D.R. (2012) *Social Media for Academics: A Practical Guide*, Chandos Social Media series. Available at: https://search.ebscohost.com/login.aspx?direct=true&db=cat07845a&AN=uea.812323391&authtype=sso&custid=s8993828&site=eds-live&scope=site (accessed 25 January 2021).

Pew Research (2019) *Which Social Media Platforms are Most Popular?* Available at: www.pewresearch.org/internet/fact-sheet/social-media/#which-social-media-platforms-are-most-popular (accessed 25 January 2021).

Pfeffer, J., Zorbach, T. and Carley, K.M. (2014) 'Understanding online firestorms: Negative word-of-mouth dynamics in social media networks', *Journal of Marketing Communications*, 20 (1–2): 117–128.

Rogers, E.M. (2003) *Diffusion of Innovations* (5th edn). New York: Free Press.

Russmann, U. and Svensson, J. (2016) 'Studying organizations on Instagram', *Information*, 7 (4): 58.

Salleh, S., Hashima, N.H. and Murphy, J. (2015) 'Instagram marketing: A content analysis of top Malaysian restaurant brands', *E-Review of Tourism Research*, 6: 1–5.

Sashittal, H.C. and Jassawalla, A.R. (2015) 'Why do college students use Pinterest? A model and implications for scholars and marketers', *Journal of Interactive Advertising*, 15 (1): 54–66.

Sloan, L. and Quan-Haase, A. (2017) *The SAGE Handbook of Social Media Research Methods*. Thousand Oaks, CA: Sage.

Statista (2020) *Leading Countries Based on Number of Twitter Users as of October 2020 (in Millions)*. Available at: www.statista.com/statistics/242606/number-of-active-twitter-users-in-selected-countries/ (accessed 3 January 2021).

Sugiura, L., Wiles, R. and Pope, C. (2017) 'Ethical challenges in online research: Public/private perceptions', *Research Ethics*, 13 (3–4): 184–199.

van Kessel, P. (2019) *10 Facts about Americans and YouTube*. Available at: www.pewresearch.org/fact-tank/2019/12/04/10-facts-about-americans-and-youtube/ (accessed 25 January 2021).

Wasike, B.S. (2011) 'Framing social news sites: An analysis of the top ranked stories on Reddit and Digg', *Southwestern Mass Communication Journal*, 27 (1): 57–67.

Wenger, E., McDermott, R. and Snyder, W.M. (2002) *Cultivating Communities of Practice. A Guide to Managing Knowledge*. Cambridge, MA: Harvard Business School Press.

Wilkinson, Z. (2013) 'Oh, how pinteresting! An introduction to Pinterest', *Library Hi Tech News*, 30 (1): 1–4.

Wills, T. (2016) 'Social media as a research method', *Communication Research and Practice*, 2 (1): 7–19.

Wilson, A. (2019) *Marketing Research: Delivering Customer Insight* (4th edn). London: Red Globe Press.

Xue, S., Hu, X., Chi, X., and Zhang, J. (2019) 'Building an online community of practice through WeChat for teacher professional learning', *Professional Development in Education*. doi: 10.1080%2F19415257.2019.1647273

Zeng, D., Chen, H., Lusch, R. and Li, S.H. (2010) 'Social media analytics and intelligence', *IEEE Intelligent Systems*, 25 (6): 13–16.

12

INTERVIEWS AND FOCUS GROUPS

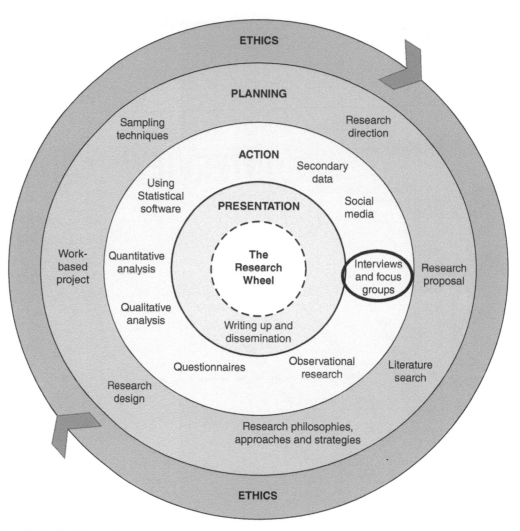

Figure 12.1   The Research Wheel

Learning objectives

By the end of this chapter, you should be able to:

- recognize different types of interviews

- understand the purpose of a research interview

- be aware of how to use various types of interview methods

- understand the questioning techniques used in interviews

- recognize the different types of focus groups

- know how to organize a focus group

- understand the benefits and disadvantages of conducting a focus group.

INTRODUCTION

This chapter introduces you to two important data collection methods – interviews and focus groups. The latter is sometimes referred to as a 'Group interview' or 'Discussion group'. There are differences, which we will examine. Hence, throughout this chapter, we use the term 'Focus group'.

The chapter begins by defining 'interview' and examines the different types used by researchers. The term 'interview' is a broad term. Similarly, the same can be said for focus groups. Therefore, in this section we begin by defining and looking at the various types of interviews you may consider when doing your research. This is then followed by a discussion on the purpose of the research interview and how to recruit interviewees. Knowing how to recruit research participants is often a challenge for students. Consequently, in this part of the chapter, considerable attention is given to how to approach this task.

Following this, the chapter discusses how to conduct an online interview. Although online interviews have much in common with conventional face-to-face interviews, there are notable differences. For example, how will technology change the interview experience?

Next, the chapter moves on to the topics of telephone interviews and elite interviewing, followed by questioning techniques used in interviews. An interview is only as good as its questions. This first part of the chapter concludes with a discussion on recording interviews.

The second part of the chapter explains how to define and organize a focus group, together with the benefits and disadvantages associated with this data collection method. Finally, the chapter culminates in an example of a focus group in practice.

As you can see by Figure 12.1, 'Interviews and focus groups' is in the 'Action' layer in The Research Wheel model (EPAP). Remember that the Action layer at this stage in the research process involves you conducting a number of activities, not least collecting and analyzing data. Hence, in this chapter we continue with the theme of data collection, something we also examined in Chapter 11 (Social media for research). Subsequent to this chapter, we continue with data collection by exploring observational research.

WHAT IS AN INTERVIEW?

The term 'interview' is a broad term that can be used in a variety of contexts. For example, it may be used in the context of a job interview or possibly someone being interviewed as part of a research project. The first thing to note is that interviews are typically associated with a qualitative research strategy. This is because the purpose of an interview is to explore and to gain insights and understanding about a particular topic. It is also possible to think of an interview conducted on an individual basis and involving a group.

According to Watts and Ebbutt (1987: 25), an interview is 'a conversation initiated by an interviewer for the specific purpose of obtaining research relevant information and focused by him/her on content specified by research objectives'.

If we consider this definition of an interview, we can see that the research interview is a tool designed to collect information from an interviewee. Furthermore, what drives the focus of this information are the research objectives. This is an important point. The questions asked by a researcher to an interviewee must be formulated with the sole purpose of allowing the researcher to address the original research objectives and questions.

As mentioned earlier in this section, an interview can be conducted between an interviewer and an interviewee, or as a group. The latter is sometimes referred to as a 'Focus group'. However, there is one key difference between an individual interview and a focus group, that is, a group interview has a moderator whose job it is to gather information and to keep the discussion moving. We will examine the role of the moderator more closely later in the chapter.

An interview is best conducted in an environment that is free from distractions and comfortable for both the interviewer and interviewee. This makes it easier to record the conversation. Unfortunately, sometimes the researcher as the interviewer may not have much say in where or when an interview takes place. This is particularly the case when trying to access senior managers. Interviews can be conducted in various ways, although the most common method is face-to-face. However, before we examine this and other interview methods, let us look at types of interviews.

TYPES OF INTERVIEWS

In a research context, types of interviews refer to how to organize and approach questioning when conducting an interview. There are essentially three different types of interviews – structured, unstructured and semi-structured (Gill et al., 2008). In this section, we will consider each of these three types of interviews. Furthermore, there are examples of how each type of interview can be applied in practice.

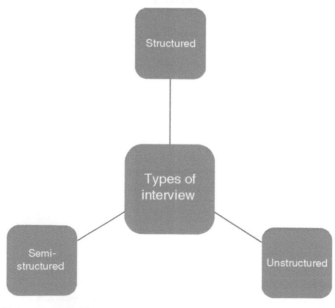

Figure 12.2   Types of interview methods

STRUCTURED INTERVIEWS

First, think of a *structured interview* as the researcher administering a questionnaire by reading out the questions to the research participant. Using a set of pre-determined questions, the researcher will read through each one systematically and record the participant's responses. The structured nature of this type of interview means that there is no scope to be flexible. Hence, no additional questions or themes are asked to the interviewee, irrespective of their answers.

Sometimes referred to as *directed interviews*, a notable advantage of structured interviews is that they present the same experience for all research participants. Moreover, they are relatively quick and straight-forward to administer. Another advantage is that by asking the same set of questions to all research partici-pants, the researcher is able to conduct comparative analysis. For example, asking a participant the following closed-ended question – 'Does your organization work with a local charitable organization?' – means simple analysis can examine the number of respondents who replied 'Yes', 'No' or possibly 'Don't know'.

Disadvantages of structured interviews include a lack of flexibility and they do not allow for new topics or themes to be introduced. For example, if you are interviewing the Finance Director of a large multinational organization, there is a likelihood that the interviewee will share unexpected information. Quite simply, this is because the Director has more experience and knows more about their business than you do. Yet, structured interviews do not give you the option to explore new or unexpected infor-mation that might arise from an interview.

Structured interviews can be used for both qualitative and quantitative research. If you are interested in quantitative research, then your questions are likely to be more closed-ended, while open-ended ques-tions can be used for qualitative research. For example, 'Please explain why your organization partners with a local charitable organization.'

UNSTRUCTURED INTERVIEWS

Unlike structured interviews, *unstructured interviews* – sometimes referred to as *in-depth* or *non-directive interviews* – do not start with any pre-determined questions or ideas. In my own research, I have often used unstructured interviews when aiming to learn about my participants' 'journey' or 'story'. This is referred to as narrative research, a research approach that commonly uses unstructured interviews. Similarly, Fossey et al. (2002: 727) explain that,

> Unstructured interviews are usually conducted in an everyday conversational style, in which par-ticipants take the lead, to a greater extent, in telling their stories, rather than the researcher direct-ing the interview.

To start the interview, an opening question might be 'Can you tell me how you arrived where you are today?'. Unstructured interviews can generate some particularly interesting findings. Research participants have the opportunity to talk about a subject they are likely to be passionate about, while at the same time not being restricted to a set of pre-determined questions. However, unstructured interviews do have their limitations. First, they can be difficult to manage as participants may go 'off topic' and talk too long about a particular subject. Second, they are typically very time-consuming. For this reason, it can be challenging for the researcher to manage their time, especially if trying to organize multiple interviews on any given day. Lastly, unstructured interviews can make it difficult to compare data. By way of an example, let us say that you ask ten managers to discuss 'organizational performance'. Given that there are multiple definitions, along with different ways of viewing this term, the strong likelihood is that you will receive ten very different answers.

What are unstructured interviews mostly used for? As mentioned, they work particularly well when conducting exploratory research, such as finding out about a participant's journey or story. In addition, they are also suited to studies that require interviewees to answer sensitive questions. This is because the interviewee might be uncomfortable answering pre-determined questions. Furthermore, they may also prefer to talk about a particularly sensitive topic in their own words.

SEMI-STRUCTURED INTERVIEWS

The final of the three interview types are *semi-structured interviews*. You can think of semi-structured interviews as a hybrid form of structured and unstructured interviews. In essence, they include a number of pre-determined questions, while at the same time also give the researcher the flexibility of being able to explore themes and ideas that may emerge from the interview.

A key advantage of semi-structured interviews is that they encourage two-way communication. For example, if an interviewee shares an interesting piece of information, the interviewer can use a mix of open and closed-ended questions, making this a more natural way of interacting.

THE PURPOSE OF THE RESEARCH INTERVIEW

According to Gill et al. (2008: 292), the purpose of the research interview is 'to explore the views, experiences, beliefs and/or motivations of individuals on specific matters'. This definition features the word 'explore' which suggests that the research interview is a data collection tool designed for exploratory research. However, as discussed earlier in the chapter, interviews can be used as part of both qualitative and quantitative research.

The purpose of an interview may not necessarily just involve verbal communication. For example, as part of your own research, you may be interested in understanding non-verbal communication. An example here might be exploring the body language of interviewees when asked sensitive questions about bullying in the workplace. Clearly, this type of question raises ethical issues, which is something we explored in Chapter 7.

According to Rowley (2012: 262), interviews are useful when:

- the research objectives focus on understanding experiences, opinions, attitudes, values and processes
- there is insufficient knowledge about the subject to be able to draft a questionnaire
- the potential interviewees might be more receptive to an interview than other data gathering approaches.

FACE-TO-FACE INTERVIEWS

A face-to-face interview is an interview conducted in person between the interviewer and interviewees. Here, you will notice I use the term 'interviewees'. This is because you may decide to undertake a group interview involving several participants. Carrying out a face-to-face interview presents a number of benefits to the researcher. These can be summarized as follows (Wilson, 2014):

- the ability to observe both verbal and non-verbal communication
- greater flexibility in how the interview is managed
- interviews are typically conducted in an interviewee's natural setting
- completion is immediate and straightforward
- the respondent's feedback can be recorded.

First, having the ability to observe both verbal and non-verbal communication means that you may observe interesting insights from your research. Often, a researcher conducting cross-cultural research will note both verbal and non-verbal communication, the reason being that they are interested in examining similarities and differences in cultural traits among research participants. For example, in business research, this may include how to greet a business associate, the importance of gift giving and time-keeping.

Second, face-to-face interviews offer a degree of flexibility not experienced by some other methods. A notable example here is introducing an additional question. Asking a participant a direct question is often more difficult for the person to say no if they are being asked face-to-face.

Third, conducting an interview in an interviewee's natural setting, such as their office, also offers advantages. For example, I have known circumstances where an interviewee has been unable to answer a question, but looked through their files so that they may answer the question.

Fourth, unlike administering an online survey, completion is immediate and usually straightforward to complete. However, the extent an interview is straightforward depends on the pre-planning prior to the interview taking place.

Fifth, your ability to record verbal communication has a number of advantages, not least that it allows the researcher to concentrate on asking questions and the participant's answers. Furthermore, it also has the advantage of freeing the interviewer to guide the interview. We will examine recording interview data more closely later in the chapter.

There are also some notable challenges associated with conducting face-to-face interviews. These are summarized as follows:

- arranging and carrying out the interview can be challenging
- some questions might be perceived as embarrassing or sensitive by interviewees, particularly if conducting cross-cultural research
- the interviewee might express an unwillingness to answer certain questions
- transcribing and analyzing data is time-consuming
- the participant perceives a lack of credibility and experience on the part of the interviewer.

From my own experience, I know that arranging interviews can be challenging. The main difficulty I found when conducting interviews in China was identifying the right person and their role. There were also logistical difficulties, such as travel arrangements and resourcing. Of course, all of this is also time-consuming. However, having an individual agree to be interviewed makes it all worth it. If you are considering conducting interviews, do look ahead to the possible outcomes of your research and how much you are likely to learn by using this type of data collection method.

Once you have decided who you would like to interview, you will need to arrange an appointment. Make sure to allow sufficient time for each interview. In some cases, you may find that an interviewee is only able to devote 30 minutes to the interview, whereas other interviewees are much more flexible with their time. Although frustrating, this is typical when setting up interviews. How does a researcher address this issue? The answer is by taking a willingness to accept that research requires flexibility and that conducting interviews often entails adapting to the needs of the interviewees.

As the interviewer, your role is to control the interview. This requires giving your interviewee time to answer questions, ensure understanding and keep the interview 'on topic' and relevant. Another consideration for researchers is choosing where the interview(s) should take place. The main advantage of doing interviews at your university or office compared to the interviewee's location, is one of familiarity and convenience. Clearly, this may not always be possible as the interviewee may not have the time and/ or is comfortable to travel to your choice of interview location. The simple answer to where an interview should take place is – a place suitable for everyone. This may mean meeting at a café or restaurant, but do bear in mind the environment, ethical issues and whether your interviewee is likely to be comfortable being interviewed in a busy public place.

A challenge an interviewer may face is one associated with questions and questioning techniques. There is also a risk that with face-to-face interviews, too much rapport could lead to the conversation drifting and losing its focus (Farooq and de Villiers, 2017). To address this point, it is important to have some kind of interviewing guidelines, even if you intend conducting unstructured interviews. As the interview progresses through different stages or topics, it can become difficult to remember all of the topics covered. Interview guidelines help to keep you on track. Guidelines contain information such as contact details of the interviewee, interview location, interview questions, timings and key themes.

WHAT IS THE PROCESS OF CONDUCTING A FACE-TO-FACE INTERVIEW?

If you decide to conduct a face-to-face interview, then it is essential to consider the steps involved in the interview process. Gaining access to an individual is often the first step on what can be a lengthy process. What follows (in Figure 12.3) is a breakdown of the series of steps you should plan for when doing the interview. In reality, the process is unlikely to be linear. For example, at the end of the interview, your participant may agree to being interviewed for a second or possibly even a third time. Ultimately, this will mean starting the process again from Step 1. Similarly, if your participant notifies you that they wish to withdraw from the study part way through organizing the interview, then clearly this means the entire interview process will not be fully completed.

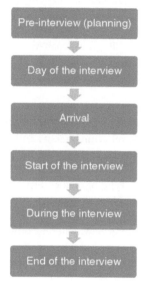

Figure 12.3   Navigating your way through the interview process

Source: Wilson (2014: 155)

Let us examine Figure 12.3 more closely.

Stage 1: Pre-interview planning

First, before even conducting your interview, there needs to be a great deal of planning that takes place. For example, what type of interview do you wish to conduct? What are the type of questions you would like to ask? How do your questions relate to your overall research objectives? Has your participant asked to see a copy of the questions before the interview takes place? On this last point, although advice here differs, my personal view is that it is always best to avoid sending a participant a copy of the interview questions. Why? Well, the reasons for this are two-fold. First, let us say that you email your participant the exact questions before the interview takes place. There is always the likelihood that they may answer the questions via email, then request that the face-to-face interview does not take place as they have answered all of your questions! Of course, you could email the participant and comment that you have further questions to ask. However, this is rather unprofessional and unlikely to be met with a welcome response. Second, by providing the questions in advance, your participant has an opportunity to prepare their answers. In principle, this may seem fine, although prepared answers might be delivered on the basis of research the participant has undertaken. Furthermore, how do you know it is the participant's answers? They may have simply asked a colleague or consulted a more senior member of staff for their opinion.

At the planning stage, you also need to be clear on where the interview will take place, if you are able to record the interview, and time allocated to the meeting. This last point is essential. Only prepare questions that can be answered within the allocated time. If you are unsure as to how many questions to ask, say, within a 60-minute interview, consider doing a dry run with a fellow student or your research supervisor.

Stage 2: Day of the interview

On the day of the interview, make sure that you take with you all of the required information. This includes the name and contact details of the participant, the venue address (map), your questions, stationery and recording device. If you intend to largely rely on a recording device, be sure to take a spare set of batteries or a second device. Of course, most mobile phones also have a recording function, so ensure that your phone is suitably charged. It is important to present yourself in a professional manner. Smart attire or a suit is usually best.

Stage 3: Arrival

Once you have arrived at your interview location, you should have enough time to go over your questions and make sure you know the location of your interviewee. Once you meet your research participant, a nice firm handshake, followed by a little small talk can help to settle your nerves.

Stage 4: Start of the interview

Start your interview by reiterating the nature of your research, the purpose of the interview, the types of question that you will be asking, and how the interview is likely to take place. Remember that it may have been some time since your participant read through the details of your study. Clarifying the type of questions will help to put your interviewee at ease. In addition, at this point, explain the ethical issues such as anonymity and confidentiality. Lastly, if your interviewee has agreed to be recorded, set up your recording device and/or notebook.

Stage 5: During the interview

Once your interview commences, ask your questions in a lucid, professional manner. Make sure to listen attentively and give your interviewee time to answer. Remember that the purpose of the interview is to gather information to help you to answer your research objectives.

With this in mind, make sure to refer to your interview questions and themes. Adopting a simple checklist by adding a 'tick' once an interviewee has answered a particular question or theme can be a useful way to ensure you have covered everything.

Stage 6: End of the interview

At the end of the interview, it is important to explicitly close the interview by telling the interviewee 'Thank you, I do not have any further questions. Do you have any comments to make?'. This last point gives the interviewee an opportunity to perhaps raise a topic or question not included in the interview. In addition, they may have a question about research ethics or possibly future research opportunities. Once you have thanked your interviewee, try to be clear that you will keep in contact via email or other means. Most interviewees are likely to be very interested in your research and would welcome an opportunity to engage in a second interview. They may also be keen to see a summary of your research results.

These steps are intended as an outline to the interview process. Clearly, in the real world, there are likely to be other factors to consider, in particular, the implications of culture and language issues if engaging in cross-cultural research.

Jacob and Furgerson (2012: 7–8) suggest the following considerations when conducting a face-to-face interview:

- start with your script
- collect consent
- use some type of recording device
- arrange to interview your respondent in a quiet place
- block off uninterrupted time for the interview
- have a genuine interest in your interviewee
- use basic counselling skills
- keep it focused
- listen
- end with your script.

Let us look at each one in turn:

1. Start with your script
   Your script is there to make sure that you do not forget to mention any key information. In particular, ethical issues and reiterating the purpose of the research and how and where the results will be disseminated.
2. Collect consent
   Collecting consent should be at the start of your script. Your interview should not take place without the participant having read and signed the informed consent form. Ideally, informed consent should be obtained early in the interview process, and certainly not retrospectively.
3. Use some type of recording device
   Attempting to get your notes right and constantly looking down at your notebook means a loss of eye contact, hence making it difficult to engage with your interviewee. Recording your interview helps to overcome this issue. Some researchers prefer not to take notes and rely on one or possibly two recording devices, should one break or run out of batteries. However, my view is that taking brief notes is positive as it is a means of showing to the interviewee that you are actively listening and engaging in the interview process.
4. Arrange to interview your respondent in a quiet, semi-private place
   A coffee shop, airport waiting lounge or restaurant all have the advantage of being convenient. However, they may have too much background noise to produce a quality recording. If you are unable to understand what is on your recording device later, then this is of no use to your research and hugely frustrating. An ideal location in which to conduct interviews is your university or a public library.
5. Be sure that both you and the interviewee block off plenty of uninterrupted time for the interview.
   Blocking off time means no distractions from email, phone calls and clearing your schedule. My advice here would be to block more time than is probably needed. From the interviewer's perspective, the reason for this is two-fold. First, an interviewee may take longer to answer questions and/ or want to explore a topic in greater depth. In unstructured interviews this is not uncommon, as

interviewees are often talking about a topic they are passionate about, such as their career journey or business. Second, if you have a multiple number of interviews planned during one day, make sure to allow sufficient travel time between interviews.

Do not schedule yourself too tightly by trying to cram in too many questions. Remember that the time agreed with the interviewee in which to conduct the interview should not result in them having to rush off to another meeting. Similarly, you do not want a situation where poor planning means that you are unable to ask all of your interview questions.

6. Have genuine care, concern, and interest for the person you are interviewing

    Show that you are interested and engaged with your interviewee. Listen intently and find out what is interesting about them. Prior to asking a question, I always start with an icebreaker question, such as 'How are you doing today?'. This helps to put your interviewee at ease and quickly demonstrates that you are a credible interviewer.

7. Use basic counselling skills to help your interviewees feel heard

    The authors recommend reading a basic book on counselling techniques so that you may learn how to become a good listener with whom people feel comfortable sharing their stories. When people feel heard and understood they are more likely to share.

8. Keep it focused

    Occasionally an interviewee strays off topic. In some instances, they provide interesting material that you may not have considered when compiling your interview research questions. In other instances, it might be the case that your interviewee has not understood the question or has simply moved away from the topic. As the interviewer, it is down to you to take control and to bring them back on topic.

9. Listen!

    It is important to remember that interviewing is not just about asking questions, but also very much about listening. You can certainly share things about yourself in order to build a relationship with the interviewee. However, by not listening or constantly interrupting, you may miss something key about an individual's life experience. In the case of narrative research, this is especially important. You are likely to know very little about your participant's life story so listening takes on added significance.

10. End with your script

    Just as the beginning of your script contains key information, so does the end of your script. For example, be sure to tell the interviewee the next steps in your research, how the information will be used and where it will be disseminated. You do not need to read your script verbatim; however, use it as a prompt to help you to remember how to end the interview.

RECRUITING YOUR INTERVIEWEES

How you recruit your interviewees depends on your sampling method(s), resources and the demographics of your intended research participants. Students typically use convenience sampling and recruit fellow students. Social media and discussion forums also provide another avenue in which to recruit participants. There are also more traditional methods, such as putting an advertisement in a local paper, email, letter or telephone call.

Rowley (2012: 264) suggests the following when aiming to recruit a research participant via an initial letter, email or telephone call:

- indicate who you are (including the university and course that you are attending) and why you are conducting this research
- capture the interest of the potential interviewee with a brief explanation of your research, and if appropriate send them the interview schedule

- be clear as to the amount of their time that the interview will take
- ask their permission to record the interview
- assure them of confidentiality
- provide any details regarding benefits to them, such as a summary of your research
- give your contact details, and invite them to indicate their availability over the next, say, two weeks, remembering that they may be away from the office when you first try to contact them
- follow up if your initial contact does not provoke a response.

HOW TO CONDUCT AN ONLINE INTERVIEW

Before we look at how to conduct an online interview, it is important to clarify what the term means. Salmons (2011: xviii) defines online interviews as

> interviews conducted with information and communications technologies (ICTs). The primary focus is on interviews conducted with synchronous technologies including text messaging, videoconferencing or video calls, multi-channel meetings, or 3-D immersive environments. Asynchronous technologies such as email, blogs, forums, wikis, social networks, or websites are used to prepare for, conduct, or follow up on the interview.

This definition of online research by Salmons makes a distinction between synchronous and asynchronous technologies. The former means at the same time or real time. Conversely, asynchronous means not at the same time, or not in real time. Thus, we can see that how you factor in the time aspect of your online interviews will ultimately influence your choice of technology. For example, if your research is about a sensitive, rapidly changing topic such as people's political views leading up to an election, then your preference is likely to be for synchronous technology, such as videoconferencing.

In many respects, an online interview is just the same as an in-person interview. However, there are notable differences – in particular, understanding how to use the technology and what I refer to as 'the interview environment'. The technology you use to conduct your interviews is often based on the preference of the interviewee. Using leading video conferencing services such as Zoom or Microsoft Teams are convenient, easily accessible and straightforward to use. However, it is always useful to test the technology before carrying out an interview. Conducting a pilot or practice interview with a fellow student first is ideal preparation before the main interview(s).

At the time of writing, the pandemic has meant that researchers have little option but to conduct interviews online. I know many of my own research students had to change from conventional face-to-face to online interviews. As a result, conducting online interviews is currently viewed as the norm.

If you are conducting online interviews, then do consider your interview environment. This is the room/location where your laptop or PC is located. Privacy concerns can be addressed by using a screen background to protect the privacy of your space.

TELEPHONE INTERVIEWS

Prior to examining how to conduct a telephone interview, it is important to clarify how to define the term 'telephone interview'. Perhaps surprisingly, there is little in the way of definitions of telephone interview. According to Carr and Worth (2001: 512), 'A telephone interview in research terms is a strategy for obtaining data which allows for interpersonal communication without a face-to-face meeting'.

Similar to face-to-face interviews, a telephone interview can be used as part of qualitative and quantitative research. There are several advantages of using the telephone as a mode of data collection. These can be summarized as follows:

- interviews can be easily recorded
- they are a relatively quick and low cost means of data collection
- they provide flexibility for both the researcher and the interviewee
- they do not require the same level of organization as face-to-face interviews
- they can work particularly well with certain research topics, e.g. cross-cultural research
- they can help to overcome research limitations, such as travel constraints.

Vogl (2013) states that there are a number of disadvantages associated with telephone interviews when compared to face-to-face mode including:

- trust is more difficult to establish
- impersonal, anonymous character
- no visual aids
- less cues for understanding
- less depth of responses
- controlling the conversation is more difficult to attain for the interviewer.

ELITE INTERVIEWING

Elite interviewing can be defined as 'Conducting interviews with key decision-makers and/or those in high-ranked positions, e.g. company directors, politicians or leading academics'. According to Harvey (2011: 433), elites can be defined as 'those who occupy senior management and board level positions within organizations'. Why would you want to conduct research focusing on these people? There is no one definitive answer to this question. By way of an example, if your research focuses on how a particular organization grows over time, then you may decide that the person 'best' able to answer this question is the founder of the company. Similarly, you may view that the CEO of an organization is in the best position to comment on organizational performance.

One of the earliest studies on elite interviewing was carried out by Kincaid and Bright (1957). The authors conducted interviews with high-ranking business executives during the 1950s. Although their study was conducted more than 70 years ago, many of the issues that the researchers encountered are equally applicable today. These include:

- enlisting the cooperation of large organizations requires careful planning
- respondents are likely to consider carefully the qualifications of the interviewer
- consider access: interviews with top-level executives should be requested using letters to the chief executive, which include the aims, details of the study and the reasons for requesting an interview with a high-level executive
- a request is likely to be successful if it stresses the practical aspects of the research problem and relates them to the company's own particular research
- an excellent means of getting entrance to a corporation is through persons in a well-established business school who have personal acquaintances among business people
- this research can be slow moving and rather expensive, for example, arranging the interviews, preparation and writing up limit the number of interviews
- careful attention must be given to the respondent's conception of his or her role in the interview.

In addition to these points, it is also important to think about how silence can be used in the interview. For example, according to Empson (2018: 66):

> Silence can be useful also, as elite interviewees often keep talking to fill the space – they are not typically the ones who listen in meetings – but silence only works if you have first established your credibility. Professionals will not respond well to an interviewer who appears too passive or seems to have nothing interesting to say.

On the point of credibility, this can be established by ensuring you know your research topic, have researched the company and individual you are interviewing, and have a clear interview guide or script.

QUESTIONING TECHNIQUES USED IN INTERVIEWS

Conducting an interview is all about gathering information. How you go about gathering this information depends on the type of questions you ask. In broad terms, remember that an interview is likely to consist of mostly open-ended questions if conducting an unstructured interview. In contrast, an interviewer conducting a structured interview is likely to rely on largely closed-ended questions. However, there are examples of other questioning techniques you can use. Here is a brief summary that includes both closed-ended and open-ended questions:

- *Dig deep* to get past what respondents think interviewers want to hear...!
- *Open-ended and non-directive* – allow them to respond in their own way, in own language, with no direction on how to answer...
- *Probing...* Exactly what happened next? Can you tell me more about that? These are useful for gaining clarification and for asking your interviewee to provide you with more information.
- *Closed and precise questions* to confirm the context or facts, for example, How much did you pay for that? How many people benefited from that? 'Polar' questions provide a simple 'Yes' or 'No' answer, for example, 'Are you entering the Japanese market?'
- *Prompting* – repeat the question, rephrase, use non-verbal cues and give them space to answer...

RECORDING INTERVIEWS

It is now common place for researchers to use a recording device, such as a mobile phone or voice recorder to record interviews. Even so, it is still important to seek permission from the participant before starting the interview. This should be done early in the interview process, and certainly not something that is done five minutes before the interview is due to begin! It is always useful to record participants' feedback. This ensures that you can gather their verbatim answers, you do not lose or forget any of the information, and finally, it helps when it comes to analyzing your data. However, recording should not be used as a substitute for taking notes.

There are a couple of counter-arguments against the recording of interviews: the first being the participant may feel uncomfortable being recorded. Second, you may find that even though an interviewee has agreed to be interviewed, clearly from their body language this is not the case. If this situation should arise, my advice would be to suggest to the interviewee that you turn off the recording equipment.

WHAT IS A FOCUS GROUP?

The majority of interviews conducted by researchers in business and management are individual face-to-face. However, if a researcher is interested in participants' views within a group setting, then a focus group can be used.

The Insights Association (2020) defines a focus group as

… a marketing research technique for qualitative data that involves a small group of people (6–10) that share a common set of characteristics and participate in a discussion of predetermined topics led by a moderator. There are opportunities to conduct focus groups with the use of focus group software.

Although this definition refers to 'marketing research', a focus group can be used for many different types of research, such as consumer, academic, medical or business research.

Morgan (1996: 130) defines a *focus group* as 'a research technique that collects data through group interaction on a topic determined by the researcher'. The author explains that this definition has three essential components. First, it clearly states that focus groups are a research method devoted to data collection. Second, it locates the interaction in a group discussion as the source of the data. Third, it acknowledges the researcher's active role in creating the group discussion for data collection purposes.

A distinct feature of a focus group is group dynamics. Conducting the interviews as a group rather than on an individual basis allows for a wide range of interpersonal communication, as the group dynamic encourages participants to interact with each other (Richard et al., 2018). For the researcher, focus groups provide a wide range of information on how participants view a particular topic.

WHY USE FOCUS GROUPS?

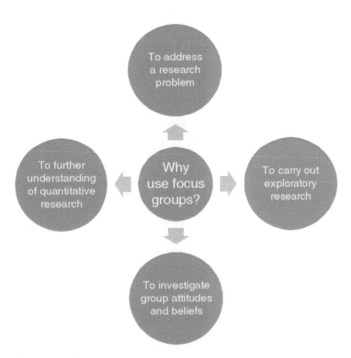

Figure 12.4   Why use focus groups?

Figure 12.4 shows four reasons why a researcher might decide to conduct a focus group. In simple terms, the purpose of a focus group is 'to get collective views on a certain defined topic of interest from a group of people who are known to have had certain experiences' (Myers, 2009: 125).

A focus group is a form of qualitative research in which a group of people are asked about their attitudes, opinions, beliefs towards a particular product, service, concept, advertisement or packaging. On this last point, an example might be a researcher interested in finding out consumers' perceptions towards a cereal product's rebranding campaign. Hence, the nature of the focus group is not only likely to involve questions about the rebrand, such as the name, colours, logo and packaging, but also other methods might be used. Examples here include the new physical branded product and also a video of the brand's latest advertising campaign.

What makes a focus group work? Focus groups work well 'when participants feel comfortable, respected, and free to give their opinions without being judged' (Krueger and Casey, 2015: 4). In order to achieve this, the focus group moderator has an essential role to play. The moderator is sometimes referred to as a facilitator and has the task of keeping the discussion on topic. We will look at other aspects of the role later in this chapter. A focus group is conducted by an experienced moderator among a group of respondents or participants. Typically, the focus group will be conducted in the form of a group discussion, usually among 6 to 10 participants. The qualitative nature of the focus group means that the discussion is unstructured and natural in such a way that participants are free to express their views and concerns (see Figure 12.5).

Figure 12.5   Characteristics of a focus group

During a focus group, questions are asked in an interactive group setting. This setting could be 'formal', for example, within a dedicated room designed specifically for focus group interviews (see Image 12.1). Many larger organizations will use the services of a market research agency as opposed to conducting focus groups in-house. In contrast, an informal setting might be someone's living room. Ultimately, using an informal approach has the advantage of reducing the costs involved. However, the informal setting may distract group participants (see Image 12.2).

Image 12.1   An example of a formal focus group setting

Source: iStock (photo ID: 1146552587)

Image 12.2   An example of an informal focus group setting

Source: iStock (photo ID: 689947888)

The term 'focus group' is often viewed as a 'focused interview'. It is also a broad term that encompasses different approaches or types of focus groups. Nyumba et al. (2018) note that there are seven types of focus groups. These approaches are briefly summarized below:

- *Single focus group.* This is the most commonly used focus group where all participants are together in one group to interact and discuss a topic. An advantage of the single focus group is its simplicity to administer as there is only one group and one moderator.
- *Dual moderator focus groups.* Here, the moderators work together with one moderator asking the questions and the other moderator keeping a check that all questions and themes are asked. For a dual moderator focus group to be successful, careful planning and an understanding of the tasks of each moderator is required.
- *Two-way focus groups.* This type of focus group involves using two groups. The process here is that one group actively discusses the topic and the other group observes the first group and then discusses their conversations. What is interesting about this type of focus group is that through observing the first group, participants views might be influenced as a result of the interactions from the group one participants.
- *Respondent moderator focus group.* Here, the respondents will temporarily act as the moderator. This is likely to change the dynamics of the group. A challenge with this type of group is that respondents are unlikely to have experience of acting as a moderator. Hence, the outcomes of this approach may not deliver the desired results.
- *Duelling moderator focus groups.* In this type of focus group, the two moderators intentionally take on opposing sides on a topic in order to fuel discussion. This type of approach needs to be managed carefully so as to achieve the right balance of arguments between the two moderators.
- *Mini focus groups.* This type of focus group uses a smaller number of participants, typically in the region of only 4 to 5 people. An advantage of a smaller focus group is that each respondent has more time in which to interact and share their views. This increases the possibility of generating more meaningful and in-depth answers. This approach is particularly suited to exploring views on a sensitive topic.
- *Online focus group.* The online focus group is increasing in popularity among researchers. This is largely due to the flexibility and cost saving that comes with conducting focus groups online. Real-time online focus groups can be conducted using specialist software or a web-based video conferencing platform (see Table 12.1 for the advantages and disadvantages of online focus groups).

Image 12.3   An example of an online focus group using video conferencing

Source: iStock (photo ID: 1254705170)

Table 12.1   The advantages and disadvantages of online focus groups

Advantages	Disadvantages
Research participants can be located anywhere in the world making it ideal for cross-cultural research	Recruitment can be challenging, especially as potential participants may not have access to the technology
Convenient for participants	Participants might be easily distracted
Large numbers and multiple focus groups can take place	Identifying the targeted research participants can be challenging
The moderator is unable to see both verbal and non-verbal communication	The technology/connection may breakdown during the focus group
No need to record the information	The moderator may find it difficult to facilitate the meeting
Convenient for participants to access, no travel required	The moderator needs to learn a different skillset
Can be inexpensive compared to face-to-face focus groups	A lack of depth in data compared to face-to-face focus groups
Easy to organize to ensure privacy and anonymity	Two-way focus groups and other types can be more difficult to implement online

TYPES OF ONLINE FOCUS GROUPS

SYNCHRONOUS (REAL-TIME) ONLINE FOCUS GROUPS

Similar to individual face-to-face online interviews, the usual distinctive contexts for online focus group method applications are of two types – asynchronous and synchronous (Morrison et al., 2020). Synchronous focus groups take place in real time at a time agreed by the moderator and research participants. Typically, online focus groups take place between 30 and 60 minutes and consist of 6 to 10 participants. As is the case with conventional focus groups, a moderator facilitates the group discussion and the data collection takes place for the duration of the focus group. An advantage of synchronous focus groups is that because they take place in real time, participants can interact with each other.

Synchronous online focus groups are particularly useful where participants are located across multiple locations, especially in different countries. This type of data collection method is ideal for exploring insights into topics that have an international dimension, such as examining consumers' perceptions of a multinational advertising campaign.

ASYNCHRONOUS ONLINE FOCUS GROUPS

Asynchronous focus groups do not take place in real time and may involve the use of a bulletin or discussion board. Longitudinal tracking is used to analyze participants' engagement in an online community. The time period for running this type of focus group could well be days, months or even years. Users can engage with each other using text, post pictures and other means. The flexibility and different ways of posting messages make asynchronous online focus groups attractive to researchers conducting longitudinal research. An example here might be a luxury fashion brand launches a new brand of swimwear and is interested to see how consumer perceptions change over time.

Conducting online focus groups is based on many of the same principles as conventional focus groups. In particular, it is essential to plan the questions and themes to ask during the focus group. Oringderff (2004: 6–9) provides useful suggestions for researchers considering undertaking an asynchronous online focus group. Although in 2021 the first point is perhaps less of an issue, the other points are still important to consider if doing online focus groups.

1. Bring participants who are comfortable participating in an electronic medium
    One of the potential barriers of conducting online focus groups is finding participants comfortable participating in an electronic medium. Although this is less likely today, technologies do change. So, when choosing which technology to use, make sure to think about accessibility and ease of use.

2. Make procedures clear, and make sure they are followed by the moderator and participants
    Set up a user's guide, including Frequently Asked Questions (FAQs). For example, you may want to make it very clear on the type of content that is not permitted on the site. Another consideration is whether you want to allow the use of pictures and/or videos to be posted. You may also want to make it clear that the discussion board is not a place to promote other sites. Giving clear guidance to users from the outset will help to avoid potential problems during the focus group. In addition, it also demonstrates your credibility as a researcher.

3. Choose a capable and knowledgeable moderator
    This point may not be an option as it depends on whether your institution or course regulations permit a third party to act as moderator. Irrespective of this, my advice would be to try to learn the skills required to be an effective moderator. Why? Well, what you learn are essential skills. You also have the advantage of taking an active role in the entire focus group process. Acting as moderator means you can see first-hand how participants engage with fellow group members. Wilson (2019) suggests that the moderator role is critical and has to bring together a group of strangers, build a rapport between the group, focus their discussions on the research topics, and make sure that they all have an equal opportunity to contribute, while also preventing any participants who would like to dominate the group.

    The role of the moderator includes the following:

    - understand the nature of the research topic and research objectives
    - make the research participants feel at ease
    - build trust and credibility through careful planning and demonstrating control
    - listen and observe interactions between group participants
    - be attentive to non-verbal behaviour
    - encourage participation of each participant
    - maintain control over the conversation
    - be flexible, but try to keep 'on topic'
    - facilitate and encourage interaction between participants.

4. Consider how and where you are going to find participants
    Probability sampling is not really necessary for focus groups, as it is usually a target group that is required, although some form of systematic strategy should be employed and consideration given to screening criteria (Brown, 2018). To recruit your focus group participants, you have a number of options. For example, more conventional methods may include asking your fellow students. For an online focus group, it also makes sense to post a message on discussion forums and social media sites. If you receive an expression of interest, check that the person meets with your selection criteria. For example, this may involve asking interested respondents to provide you with demographic information.

5. Keep the discussion focused
    Although keeping the discussion focused is something to consider when conducting both conventional and online focus groups, there is one important difference. People in an online environment sometimes use a tone that they would not use in a face-to-face situation. This is where the role of the moderator is key to keep the discussion on track.

6. Make time limitations clear
    If your intention is to only run the focus group for a set period of time, be clear on when the deadline is going to be. This is something for you to clarify in the focus group instructions.

HOW TO ORGANIZE A FOCUS GROUP

There are a number of steps involved in organizing a focus group. The steps may differ when comparing a conventional to an online focus group. However, the generic key steps highlighted in Figure 12.6 are the same.

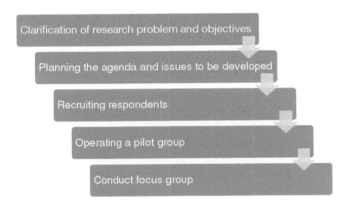

Figure 12.6   The key steps involved in organizing a focus group

1. Clarification of research problem and objectives
   Understanding the nature of your research problem and objectives is important for three reasons. First, it will influence how and who you recruit to take part in your focus group. For example, let us say that your research topic focuses on the perceptions of millennials (anyone born between 1981 and 1996) towards sustainability in the Canadian fashion market. Clearly, when selecting participants for your focus group, you would want them to be representative of this particular age group.

2. Planning the agenda and issues to be developed – discussion and topic guide
   The planning stage requires the researcher to begin to develop an agenda and something called a discussion and topic guide. The latter consists of the themes and questions the researcher or moderator will ask during the focus group. It is important that the topics featured in the guide allow the researcher to address the research problem and research objectives. Developing a discussion guide includes the following (adapted from Wilson, 2019):

   - introduction (objectives of the session, explanation of the task, agenda)
   - discursive phase (topics discussed may include the use of stimulus material)
   - summarizing phase (prompts for summarizing what has been discussed, closing remarks).

   During a focus group, researchers also commonly use stimulus materials. These may include storyboards, products, adverts, product samples.

3. Recruiting respondents
   For student researchers, it can be challenging recruiting members of the public to take part in a focus group. As highlighted earlier in the chapter, recruiting your fellow students to take part is likely to be much more straightforward. Students are easy to contact and may only be too keen to express their views about a particular topic. In this case, recruitment can be undertaken via word-of-mouth communication, posting a message via social media or possibly using your School/University blog.

The disadvantage of using students is that they may not be representative of your target audience. Conversely, recruiting participants through a local newspaper, for example, is likely to generate a much more representative sample of the population.

4.   Operating a pilot group

If possible, it is always useful to conduct a pilot focus group before the actual focus group is conducted. In focus groups, although recruiting participants may not be difficult, you will find that the main challenge is understanding the role of the moderator. There exists a number of issues that might arise. For instance, as a moderator you may run out of time to ask all of your intended questions, fail to manage the group dynamics or quite simply forget to record the group discussion! These are all potential problems that may occur. For these reasons, it is always advisable to conduct at least one pilot focus group first.

5.   Conduct focus group

The next step in the focus group process is actually conducting the focus group. If you have carried out a pilot focus group, then it is important to reflect on what went well and areas for improvement prior to carrying out the main group interview.

6.   Analyzing of transcripts

Figure 12.6 highlights the key steps in organizing a focus group. However, there are two additional steps. These are analysis and presentation of findings. Analysis is the most time-consuming part of the process – transcribing the data. To give you some idea of time, if you have conducted a one-hour focus group, then this is likely to equate to transcribing in the region of 6,000 to 8,000 words. As with any transcription, it is advisable to transcribe your own data. We look at qualitative data analysis later in the book.

7.   Presentation of findings

Presentation of findings may take several different forms. For most students, the presentation of qualitative data might take the form of verbatim comments within the main body of their research project. Furthermore, it may also involve a verbal presentation.

BENEFITS AND DISADVANTAGES OF CONDUCTING A FOCUS GROUP

Using a focus group as a data collection tool does not tend to be as popular with students as other methods such as online surveys or interviews. This is surprising, as a focus group does offer a number of benefits for student researchers. These include:

- A focus group provides a platform for a free and open discussion among participants that can lead to interesting results and new ideas.
- The moderator can keep the discussion 'on topic' by using the discussion guide and closely monitoring the dynamics in the group.
- A focus group is a fluid discussion that allows the moderator to make any changes and/or change the direction of the discussion. The moderator can also control the interaction by inviting quieter members of the group to take part.
- A large-scale research project has the potential to allow other researchers to observe the discussion. Typically, observers are behind a two-way mirror so as not to influence the interaction in the group.
- The moderator also has an opportunity to observe non-verbal communication, such as how participants respond to a particular product or video.

However, there are also a number of disadvantages to consider when conducting a focus group. These include:

- Some participants might be reluctant to actively participate and share their views. This is more likely to occur with sensitive topics, such as political views.
- An inexperienced moderator may find it difficult to control some participants who try to dominate the group. Conducting a pilot focus group or using role plays can help to address this problem. Another option is for an inexperienced moderator to observe or shadow a more experienced moderator.
- The nature of the environment where the focus group takes place may seem unnatural to some participants, thus making it difficult for them to be put at ease and to actively participate in the discussion.
- Focus groups provide an interesting insight into how a group of individuals view a particular topic. However, due to the small sample size and heterogeneity of individuals, the research findings may make it difficult to make suitable projections.

The above section provides a brief overview of the benefits and disadvantages of conducting a focus group, but how do you know when to use a focus group? If the nature of your research is exploratory, qualitative research and aims to understand participants' insights, then the focus group is certainly a data collection method worth considering. Furthermore, conducting this type of exploratory research can be a useful first phase in a research project. For example, the findings generated from your focus group(s) may inform the type of questions you include within an online survey.

Conversely, if the emphasis of your research is more of a quantitative nature, based on a large sample size, then clearly, the focus group is not an ideal data collection method.

AN EXAMPLE OF A FOCUS GROUP IN PRACTICE

This short example is from an actual study by Brown et al. (2020) where the researchers have used a focus group as one of their methods of data collection. My reason for sharing this example is in order to illustrate the relationship between data collection (focus group) and another data collection method.

Background to the study

The aim of the research is to understand American premium chocolate consumer perception of craft chocolate and desirable chocolate product attributes.

Research objectives

1. To gain insight into American premium chocolate consumer perception of craft chocolate.
2. To identify search, experience and credence attributes that are important to American premium chocolate consumers.

Methodology

The authors used a mixed methods approach, using focus groups and project mapping. The rationale for using focus groups is that there is no previous literature or reports describing American premium

(Continued)

chocolate consumer attitudes to craft chocolate or desirable chocolate attributes, thus, a focus group is an appropriate method for exploratory research. The second method used is projective mapping. This is a technique used in which consumers place products on a blank space in terms of their relationship with one another (e.g. flavour, quality) (Risvik et al., 1994).

In this short example, notice how the research objectives refer to words such as 'insight' and 'identify' – these clearly suggest that the research is exploratory in nature, hence demonstrating a relationship between objectives and chosen methodological approach.

BOX 12.1: RESEARCH SNAPSHOT

Like all research methods, focus groups have benefits and drawbacks. However, as we have seen in this chapter, they work particularly well when research aims are exploratory in nature. One of the biggest drawbacks is the amount of time required to plan, organize and analyze data from a focus group discussion. Hence, it is always advisable to start planning your focus group early. Your research supervisor can help you with how to organize a focus group, so be sure to discuss with them early in your research.

Image 12.4   Concept Cartoon 'Type of interviews'

Image 12.4 is a Concept Cartoon that shows characters expressing their views on type of interviews. Think about the different views, and if possible, use them to provoke a group discussion with fellow students. What do you think? Do you share a viewpoint with one particular character?

CHAPTER SUMMARY

- An interview is 'a conversation initiated by an interviewer for the specific purpose of obtaining research relevant information and focused by him/her on content specified by research objectives'.

- The purpose of the research interview is 'to explore the views, experiences, beliefs and/or motivations of individuals on specific matters'.

- There are essentially three different types of interviews – structured, semi-structured and unstructured.

- Think of a structured interview as the researcher administering a questionnaire by reading out the questions to the research participant.

- Unstructured interviews are sometimes referred to as in-depth or non-directive interviews as they do not start with any pre-determined questions or ideas.

- Elite interviewing can be defined as 'Conducting interviews with key decision-makers and/or those in high-ranked positions, e.g. company directors, politicians or leading academics'.

- Developing a discussion guide includes the following: an introduction, a discursive phase and a summarizing phase.

- Examples of questioning techniques used in interviews include dig deep, open-ended, probing, closed and precise questions, and prompting.

- A telephone interview in research terms is a strategy for obtaining data which allows for interpersonal communication without a face-to-face meeting.

QUESTIONS FOR REVIEW

1. What are the advantages of conducting a structured interview compared to other interviewing methods?

2. Outline the type of research topic(s) that are likely to be best suited to an unstructured interview.

3. Why is it important to conduct a pilot focus group before carrying out your actual focus group?

4. Discuss ways in which you might recruit focus group participants.

5. Outline three benefits associated with conducting telephone interviews.

6. Outline three advantages of conducting online interviews.

7. Explain three considerations when conducting a focus group.

8. Outline a way to present your focus group findings.

9. Explain the challenges associated with elite interviewing.

10. What are the advantages and disadvantages of online focus groups?

STUDENT SCENARIO: CONDUCTING YOUR OWN FOCUS GROUP (4–6 PARTICIPANTS)

For this task, you will be conducting a focus group. The task requires 4–6 people. Highlighted below you will find a focus group discussion guide (which reviews consumer behaviour in the fast coffee market). First, select one person to be the moderator to run the group. The moderator should be the only person to have the discussion guide open in front of them and ask the questions. Second, select one person to record the key points of the focus group discussion (that is, to act as a 'scribe').

Pre-focus group preparation – both the moderator and scribe to agree process. Consider how you will record the information.

Discussion guide

- Good morning – today we will be discussing various aspects of the coffee shop industry.
- How many times a week do you visit a coffee shop?
- Why do you choose to visit a coffee shop, rather than drink coffee at home?
- How often do you visit one of the coffee shop chains such as Starbucks or Costa Coffee?
- Why/why not visit more often?
- What new products have Starbucks introduced in recent years?
- Do these new products make you more/less likely to visit Starbucks?
- What recent Starbucks advertising campaign are you aware of?
- What is the main message/s of this advertising?
- Does this advertising make you more/less likely to visit Starbucks?
- What new products or other changes could Starbucks make for you to visit their shops more often?
- Thank you for participating in this focus group.

Questions

1. How smoothly did your focus group run? Were there any problems with running the group?
2. Discuss the key findings of the focus group.
3. How valuable would this information be for coffee shop chains such as Starbucks?
4. What do you see as the limitations of this style of qualitative market research?
5. How might the findings from your focus group be combined with other research methods?
6. How would you improve upon the above group discussion guide?

FURTHER READING

Barbour, R. (2018) *Doing Focus Groups* (2nd edn). London: Sage.

A book dedicated to focus groups. Includes how to analyze focus group data and getting the most out of focus groups.

Guest, G., Namey, E., Taylor, J., Eley, N. and McKenna, K. (2017) 'Comparing focus groups and individual interviews: Findings from a randomized study', *International Journal of Social Research Methodology*, 20 (6): 693–708.

As per the title, an interesting article that compares focus groups and individual interviews as a means of data collection. The study sample consists of 350 African–American men living in Durham, North Carolina.

Smith, T.M. (2014) 'Experiences of therapists and occupational therapy students using video conferencing in conduction of focus groups', *The Qualitative Report*, 19 (19): 1–13. Available at: http://nsuworks.nova.edu/tqr/vol19/iss19/3.

An interesting article on the use of video conferencing to conduct a focus group. Compares traditional focus groups and highlights the advantages and disadvantages of each method.

Stewart, D.W., Shamdasani, P.N. and Rook, D.W. (2007) *Focus Groups: Theory and Practice*. Thousand Oaks, CA: Sage.

This book includes many of the essentials associated with focus groups, including conducting a focus group, the role of the moderator and analyzing focus group data.

REFERENCES

Brown, A.L., Bakke, A.J. and Hopfer, H. (2020) 'Understanding American premium chocolate consumer perception of craft chocolate and desirable product attributes using focus groups and projective mapping', *PloS one*, 15 (11): e0240177.

Brown, J. (2018) 'Interviews, focus groups and Delphi techniques', in P. Brough (ed.), *Advanced Research Methods for Applied Psychology: Design, Analysis and Reporting* (pp. 95–106). London: Routledge.

Carr, E.C. and Worth, A. (2001) 'The use of the telephone interview for research', *NT Research*, 6 (1): 511–524.

Empson, L. (2018) 'Elite interviewing in professional organizations', *Journal of Professions & Organization*, 5 (1): 58–69.

Farooq, M.B. and de Villiers, C. (2017) 'Telephone qualitative research interviews: When to consider them and how to do them', *Meditari Accountancy Research*, 25: 291–316.

Fossey, E., Harvey, C., McDermott, F. and Davidson, L (2002) 'Understanding and evaluating qualitative research', *Australian & New Zealand Journal of Psychiatry*, 36 (6): 717–732.

Gill, P., Stewart, K., Treasure, E. and Chadwick, B. (2008) 'Methods of data collection in qualitative research: Interviews and focus groups', *British Dental Journal*, 204 (6): 291–295.

Harvey, W.S. (2011) 'Strategies for conducting elite interviews', *Qualitative Research*, 11 (4). doi: 10.1177%2F1468794111404329

Insights Association (2020) *Definition of Focus Group*. Available at: www.marketingresearch.org/issues-policies/glossary/focus-group (accessed 10 January 2021).

Jacob, S.A. and Furgerson, S.P. (2012) 'Writing interview protocols and conducting interviews: Tips for students new to the field of qualitative research', *Qualitative Report*, 17: 6.

Kincaid, H.W. and Bright, M. (1957) 'Interviewing the business elite', *American Journal of Sociology*, 63 (3): 304–311.

Krueger, R.A. and Casey, M.A. (2015) 'Overview of focus groups', in R.A. Krueger and M.A. Casey (eds), *Focus Groups: A Practical Guide for Applied Research* (Ch. 1). Thousand Oaks, CA: Sage.

Morgan, D.L. (1996) 'Focus groups', *Annual Review of Sociology*, 22 (1): 129–152.

Morrison, D., Lichtenwald, K. and Tang, R. (2020) 'Extending the online focus group method using web-based conferencing to explore older adults online learning', *International Journal of Research and Method in Education*, 43 (1): 78–92.

Myers, M.D. (2009) *Qualitative Research in Business & Management*. London: Sage.

Nyumba, T.O., Wilson, K., Derrick. C.J. and Mukherjee, N. (2018) 'The use of focus group discussion methodology: Insights from two decades of application in conservation', *Methods in Ecology and Evolution*, 9 (1): 20–32.

Oringderff, J. (2004) '"My way": Piloting an online focus group', *International Journal of Qualitative Methods*, 3 (3): 69–75.

Richard, B., Sivo, S., Orlowski, M., Ford, R., Murphy, J., Boote, D. and Witta, E. (2018) 'Online focus groups: A valuable alternative for hospitality research?', *International Journal of Contemporary Hospitality Management*, 30 (11): 3175–3191.

Risvik, E., McEwan, J.A., Colwill, J.S., Rogers, R. and Lyon, D.H. (1994) 'Projective mapping: A tool for sensory analysis and consumer research', *Food Quality and Preference*, 5 (4): 263–269.

Rowley, J. (2012) 'Conducting research interviews', *Management Research Review*, 35 (3/4): 260–271.

Salmons, J. (2011) *Cases in Online Interview Research*. London: Sage.

Vogl, S. (2013) 'Telephone versus face-to-face interviews: Mode effect on semi-structured interviews with children', *Sociological Methodology*, 43 (1): 133–177.

Watts, M. and Ebbutt, D. (1987) 'More than the sum of the parts: Research methods in group interviewing', *British Educational Research Journal*, 13 (1): 25–34.

Wilson, A. (2019) *Marketing Research: Delivering Customer Insight* (4th edn). London: Red Globe Press.

Wilson, J. (2014) *Essentials of Business Research: A Guide to Doing Your Research Project* (2nd edn). London: Sage.

13

OBSERVATIONAL RESEARCH

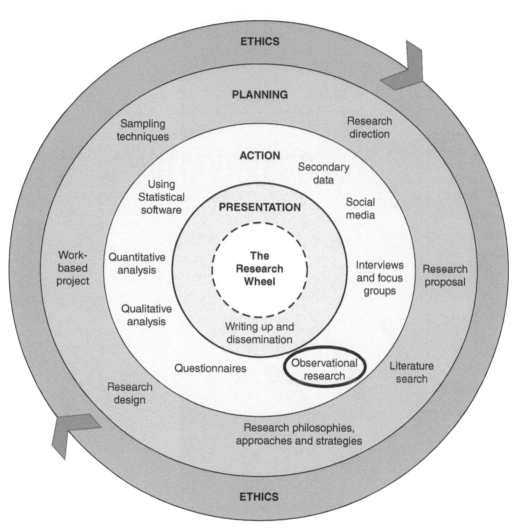

Figure 13.1   The Research Wheel

INTRODUCTION

In this chapter, we continue to examine primary data collection methods by examining observational research. Observation is an important data collection method in business research. However, from my experience, the method tends not to be as popular with students as surveys or interviews. There are perhaps a number of reasons for this, including the perception that observation is difficult to obtain ethics approval and a lack of understanding as to how to conduct observational research.

The chapter begins by defining observational research. It then considers the different types and methods of observational research, followed by the advantages and challenges associated with this research method. Next, we consider the steps involved in the observational research process. Like many aspects of research, this process is systematic and involves a series of steps. Moving on, the chapter will then explore what to observe when conducting observational research and recording your observations. In terms of the latter, examples here include audio equipment, video and using a notebook. We then look at ethnography, netnography and observation. The terms ethnography and participant observation are often referred to interchangeably. However, there is a difference, which we examine later in the chapter.

The next part of the chapter looks at what makes an effective observer and how to use observation in your research. Finally, the chapter concludes with examples of research studies that combine observational research with another data collection method, namely interviews.

As you can see by Figure 13.1, 'Observational research' is in the 'Action' layer in The Research Wheel model (EPAP). Remember that the Action layer involves you conducting a number of activities, not least collecting and analyzing data. Prior to reaching the action layer you should have a clear understanding of your research direction. This will have been achieved through exploring the nature of the business research 'planning' layer and producing your research proposal, also in the 'planning' layer. Whether or not you decide to undertake observational research depends on the decisions you make in other steps in The Research Wheel, particularly the planning stage, when working on your research proposal.

WHAT IS OBSERVATIONAL RESEARCH?

In general terms, observation can be viewed as how we view the world. Angrosino (2007: 61) defines it as follows: 'Observation in the research context is a considerably more systematic and formal a process than the observation that characterizes everyday life'. Similarly, Wilson (2018: 98) defines it as 'A data-gathering approach where information is collected on the behaviour of people, objects and organizations without any questions being asked of the participants'. As with any definition, it is useful to consider the keywords or terms. Typically, when defining observational research, reference is made to 'systematic process', 'behaviour' and 'non-verbal communication'. This is because the fundamental nature of observation is collecting information on research subjects without asking questions. Furthermore, observation involves the detailed examination of participants within a naturalistic setting (Cowie, 2009). In relation to the latter point, an example here might be a researcher observing how sales employees interact with customers. The naturalistic setting in this instance is the retail environment.

Observational research can produce both qualitative and quantitative data. In quantitative observation, the researcher usually observes a large number of people, objects or organizations, collecting statistical information. Qualitative observation normally involves a smaller scale, and data are generated on the basis of semi-structured or unstructured observations. We examine these types of observations later in the chapter.

A key consideration when choosing observational research is that observation only measures behaviour; it does not provide answers as to 'why' the behaviour takes place or reveal individuals' attitudes towards their actions. Examples of behaviours that can be measured by researchers include: online shopping behaviour, physical actions within a retail environment, monitoring individuals on social media platforms, advertising viewing, and the physical products or brands that consumers have within the home.

Researchers can conduct different types of observational research. If you intend carrying out observational research, it is essential to think about your role as a researcher. Example questions include:

- Should I be an active participant when carrying out observations?
- Should I be a non-participant observer?
- Should I make my identity known or disguise my identity?
- Should I adopt a highly structured approach to my observation?

These are key questions you will need to consider if engaging in observational research as they relate to the nature of your research study.

Observation can be thought of as simply watching some action or activity and recording it in some way. However, Baker (2006) points out that observation is a complex research method. Certainly, when compared to other data collection methods, observation is complex as it often requires the researcher to play different roles and to use a number of techniques, including her/his five senses, to collect data.

Observation is unique in many respects when compared to other research methods. These include the training required, entering and leaving the study group, length of time in the field, sampling, and finally, data collection. Having said that, it is this uniqueness that makes it an interesting research method and one that warrants consideration by student researchers. What makes effective observation? According to Rowley (2004: 211), effective observation requires attention to the following:

- *What?* The development of the researcher's understanding of what is being observed.
- *Why?* The clear formulation of the question that is driving the observation.
- *How?* The choice of the type of observation including the choice between participant and non-participant observation, and covert and overt observation.
- *When?* Selection of the most appropriate times to conduct the observation. This may involve selection through the use of a rigorous sampling methodology, or may instead be based on a series of critical incidents (perhaps relating to service failures) specifically chosen to offer an insight into an issue.

DIFFERENT TYPES OF OBSERVATION

There are several different types of observation. Your choice is dependent on your research direction (including research questions and objectives of the research), access to sources and the resources available for conducting the research (Slack and Rowley, 2001). In essence, observation is typically categorized on the basis of participant and non-participant observation, and covert and overt observation (see Figure 13.2).

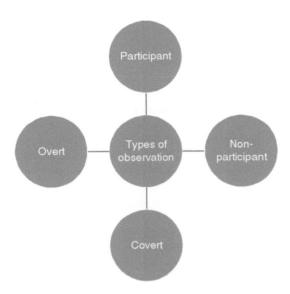

Figure 13.2   Types of observation

PARTICIPANT OBSERVATION

According to Timseena (2009: 76), 'Participant Observation is a process of data collection in which dialogue and interaction occurs between the researcher and people'. If you are a participant observer, then this involves engaging with the group being observed. A key outcome of participant observation should be insights concerning the behaviour, motivations, attitudes and perceptions of people within the culture in question (Jaimangal-Jones, 2014). By way of an example, if you are working and studying part-time, you may decide to observe your colleagues in the workplace. By doing this, you are also continuing to interact and perform your everyday tasks. An advantage of this type of observational research is that you have access to your research participants and you are also able to observe them in their natural setting. Moreover, as an observer able to see and interact with participants, you have a first-hand knowledge and understanding of the issues occurring in the work environment. A final advantage, and certainly relevant to the last point, is that data from participant observations can be a useful supplement to data gathered from other sources. For example, findings from participant observation might be compared with responses from an online survey.

However, there are limitations associated with participant observation. This type of observation may mean that how you interpret the observation is influenced by your own values, thus making it difficult to approach the research from an impartial viewpoint. For example, your perceptions about a person may influence how you interpret your observations. How do I decide whether to conduct participant observation? Consider the following questions:

- What is your research problem, the purpose of your research and research questions?
- To what extent do you have access to the research venue and the individuals you intend to observe?
- What is the cost of doing the research, not just in financial terms, but also resources?
- How much time do you have available to do the research?
- To what extent are you comfortable doing the role?

First, as noted earlier in the book, your research direction (including research problem, objectives and questions) should drive your data collection methods and analytical techniques. Most participant observation is exploratory in nature, typically recording the actions of individuals in a particular setting.

Second, you need to be clear on the level of access you have to the research environment, as well as the individuals. That is, make sure that you have the required ethics approval to engage in participant observation. Of particular concern is how you intend to disseminate your research findings as participant observation within your organization may generate sensitive information. If you have any doubts, consult with your research supervisor and the organization where the observation is taking place. Guest et al. (2013) make the point that the presence of the researcher or the researcher's data collection efforts may lead to a negative response from some of the people being observed. This negative response might simply be down to someone's dislike for being a part of your study. Another reason might be to do with fear of what will be done with the data.

Third, the cost of participant observation may not necessarily be expensive; however, it can be resource intensive. For example, if participant observation involves your own organization, it can take time to explain and share your research intentions with all of the research stakeholders. This may include senior management, your supervisor and employees within the business.

Fourth, the time it takes to undertake participant observation depends on your research objectives and the time frame set by your institution and possibly your employer (if you are doing a work-based project).

Finally, consider your role as a participant observer. Is it something you are likely to be comfortable with? How do you feel about observing colleagues or individuals within a natural setting? If observing colleagues, how will you address ethical issues, such as a potential conflict of interest?

NON-PARTICIPANT OBSERVATION

There are different levels of participant observation. For example, it can be distinguished on the basis of 'participant', 'non-participant', 'covert', 'overt', 'complete observer', 'complete participant', 'structured' and 'unstructured'. The complete participant and the complete observer are at opposite ends of the observation/participation spectrum. Unlike participant observation, if you take on the role of a complete observer (non-participant observer), then you do not interact with your research subjects. One way to think of non-participant observation is someone who is 'standing in the corner' and not interacting, but purely observing. By way of an example, if observing a board meeting, then you may sit in the corner of the room observing what takes place. This type of research may also involve the use of a camera or recording device to observe research participants. Again, the premise is the same – purely observation, with no interaction.

What are the advantages of being a non-participant researcher? A key advantage is that by not interacting with your participants, there is a strong likelihood that you will not affect their behaviour. Also, as a researcher, it gives you the opportunity to devote all of your attention to observing and recording the data. Conversely, by not participating, you may miss out on valuable verbal communication as you do not have the opportunity to engage and/or instigate a conversation.

Now that we have examined the different approaches to the 'participant' as an observer, it is also important to think about whether you make yourself known to your research participants. In this context, this is what we refer to as covert observation and overt observation. Let us look at these two approaches more closely.

COVERT OBSERVATION

Covert observation involves participating fully without informing members of the social group on which research is being done (Timseena, 2009). If you decide to be a covert researcher, then your research participants are unaware that they are being observed. By engaging in covert observation your participants are more likely to carry out their tasks in a typical way. Covert observation can be achieved by not making your identity known when visiting a store. An alternative approach is using sophisticated technology such as hidden cameras. Clearly, this approach does raise significant ethical concerns, such as informed consent and deception. There is also the question of what you intend doing with the recording. Is it simply for your own personal research purpose, or will it also be disseminated online?

Mystery shopping

An example of covert observation is mystery shopping. Here, the mystery shopper does not make their reasons for entering the shop and purchasing known. In some cases, it might be at a later date that a retailer receives notification that their customer service was observed and rated by a mystery shopper.

You may have worked as a mystery shopper, or possibly unknowingly served a mystery shopper. In retail, the mystery shopper's role is to conduct research on their shopping experience, while at the same time pretending to be an actual customer. The type of questions a mystery shopper might research include:

- What form of greeting or farewell was given by the sales assistant?
- How long did I have to wait to be served?
- How many people served me today?
- What was the sales assistant's product knowledge like?
- Did the store have the product(s) available?

What are the benefits of mystery shopping?

We can view the benefits of mystery shopping from both a customer perspective and the organization's perspective. First, customers benefit from mystery shopping as it is a tool designed to improve customer experience. If a mystery shopper has a bad overall experience, then the research findings will be reported back to the marketing research agency commissioned to do the research. Subsequently, this information is then reported to the organization who has commissioned the agency to carry out the research. Next, the organization should take steps to address any issues raised by the mystery shopper. Examples of possible issues might include poor customer service, lack of product availability or an unpleasant retail environment. Thus, the customer should ultimately benefit from any changes an organization implements in response to feedback from the mystery shopper.

How does an organization benefit from mystery shopping? Well, it can provide a useful insight into how employees work on a daily basis.

Disguised or covert observation is not only used by retailers. For example, in the past my research students have used mystery shopping when doing a group rebranding project on a leading sports brand. Students visited a number of stores and observed various aspects of the buying process.

Image 13.1 Mystery shopping is an example of covert/disguised observation

Source: iStock (photo ID: 171320567)

What are the disadvantages of mystery shopping?

Like all research methods, disguised observation has some disadvantages. First, the ethical nature of the research can be called into question as those employees being observed are not aware the observer is not a real customer. There is also the issue of what type of information and how it will be shared. From the researcher's perspective, a disadvantage of mystery shopping is that one visit is only a 'snapshot' of their shopping experience. In other words, a positive or particularly negative experience may not be a 'true' reflection of the typical service experience. One way to address this problem is to conduct multiple mystery shopping visits over a period of time. However, the downside to this is the additional costs involved and the employee(s) may react differently if they are aware that multiple visits are likely to take place.

Covert observation in action

An example of a study involving covert observation is that by Henriksen et al. (2020). The purpose of this research was to explore how the smartphone interacts with and impacts social interaction in the setting of the urban café.

The research methodology involved 108 observation situations and 52 unplanned in-depth interviews that focused on peoples' reflections on the social use of smartphones at the urban café. Research material was collected in the city centre of Trondheim, Norway. Covert observation focused on the actions of café guests, and unplanned in-depth interviews, i.e. short, open-ended interviews were conducted on the spot. The data were generated between the hours of 11am and 8pm on weekdays and weekends during November and December 2015. Observations took place across 13 different cafés. The researchers found groups of students reading for exams and preparing papers, adults taking time out from work or working with their laptops, friends meeting over a coffee, and mothers bringing their babies in strollers to socialize during maternity leave.

The researchers selected participants largely on the basis of age, the range being 20–40 years of age. Participants for the covert observations of 108 different social situations were selected on the basis of a simple inclusion criterion: they needed to be in groups of at least two people with at least one of them having a smartphone visible during their time at the café. Group size varied over time as people would join or leave while being observed. During their fieldwork, how they recorded their information evolved. For example, the researchers started taking notes regarding people sitting alone or arriving alone at the café with a smartphone visible. This is because it became apparent that many single visitors turned out to be waiting for someone as long as they did not start working on a laptop. The results of the research led to the researchers identifying three categories of smartphone use in social settings: interaction suspension, deliberately shielding interaction, and accessing shareables. The researchers selected 'social locations' in the form of cafés in which to conduct their research – a location where there is likely to be significant mobile phone usage and interaction between individuals and groups.

Covert observation does raise a number of ethical issues. These issues are addressed by Henriksen et al. (2020) in their article. For example, the researchers confirmed that interview participants were over 18 years of age and that no personal information would be recorded. Informed consent was collected during the invitation to be interviewed. Furthermore, the authors point out that 'covert observation is ethically accepted in public space – since anyone may observe anyone else, as long as reporting is strongly anonymized' (Henriksen, 2020: 5).

OVERT OBSERVATION

Unlike covert observation, engaging in overt observation means that research participants are aware that they are being observed. Another consideration when doing this type of observation is whether to observe in person or use a recording device such as a video camera. An example of overt observation is a regional manager of a telecommunications manufacturer conducting research on product performance. A work-based project, the regional manager shares with employees that they are carrying out the research. In this example, the regional manager is also involved in the day-to-day managerial tasks of the organization, so is also a participant observer.

There are limitations associated with overt observation. For example, in the case of the regional manager, employees might become suspicious of the manager's intentions. In other words, although the nature of the research might be communicated as purely part of an academic study, some employees may be 'suspicious' and consider there are other reasons for the study; quite possibly downsizing the workforce or restructuring.

Of course, one way to avoid suspicion from employees would be for the regional manager to conduct covert observation. There is another option – still carrying out overt observation, but acting as a non-participant. By way of an example, the regional manager may visit a factory in a different region and spend each day observing production, without actively participating in the day-to-day running of the factory.

One limitation of overt observation is the occurrence of 'observer bias'. This is where an observer may rate/comment on an individual (possibly a co-worker) more favourably out of a sense of allegiance. A researcher needs to be aware of the potential for observer bias and consider all of the ethical issues prior to conducting the research.

When considering observation roles and the relationship between participant/non-participant and overt/covert, see Figure 13.3. Each box contains an example of each respective observation.

	Participant observation	Non-participant observation
Overt observation	A researcher joins a voluntary organization and works as a part of the team on a project. She explains to the team that she is working on a research project about them and their organization.	The researcher is introduced by the trainer to employees taking part in the training session. The researcher then sits at the back of the room to conduct her observation.
Covert observation	A researcher pretends to be an employee to observe employee interactions within an organization's office environment.	Observing the interactions between customers and sales staff using a hidden camera.

Figure 13.3   Observation research roles

Another potential drawback of overt observation is that the act of being observed may change the behaviour of the participant (usually referred to as the 'Hawthorne effect'), thus impacting the value of the research findings. It is important to recognize that the researcher's presence will have some kind of influence on those being studied during observational research and this influence may be different for overt and covert observations (Strudwick, 2018).

METHODS OF OBSERVATION

As well as being distinguished on the basis of participant/non-participant and overt/covert, observation can also be viewed in relation to method (see Figure 13.4).

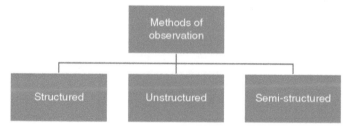

Figure 13.4   Methods of observation

STRUCTURED OBSERVATION

If doing structured observation, then you are observing and recording behaviour in a systematic way, typically using a coding schedule. In other words, the nature of your observation is deductive as you have a set of predetermined themes or codes that you intend observing. 'Structured observation requires less extensive data collection, since the observer only notes those incidents, or aspects of incidents that are of particular interest to the subject being observed; in turn, this facilitates data analysis' (Slack and Rowley, 2001: 39). For example, observers counting traffic can be viewed as a structured approach as this will normally involve observers using electronic or handheld counters and a record sheet. Similar to a structured questionnaire, structured observation makes use of a structured observation schedule (sometimes referred to as a checklist or form) for gathering data (see Figure 13.5). Using an observation schedule allows for increased reliability and makes the process consistent across observations. Moreover, if the same or similar structured observation schedule has been used in earlier studies, there is also the opportunity to compare research findings. Using a structured observation schedule may include a rating scale, and/or a tally, thus presenting an opportunity to conduct statistical analysis.

SAMPLE OBSERVATION SCHEDULE

Sales staff Research (Red Star Motors)

Date:

Start time:

Location:

Please tick in box to record occurrence

Actively approaches customers upon arrival								
Warm welcome								
Engages customers in conversation								
Shares latest product information								
Asks purpose of visit								
Soft-selling technique								

Figure 13.5   Structured observation schedule

UNSTRUCTURED OBSERVATION

If, on the other hand, you intend observing whatever you consider important, an approach 'shaped' by the observations, then your observations can be described as 'unstructured'. Here, you do not have a list of elements to observe. This type of observation tends to be undertaken at the start of a research project, where emphasis is on generating insights and an understanding. The next phase, or follow up after unstructured observation, might be structured observation.

SEMI-STRUCTURED OBSERVATION

Similar to semi-structured interviews, semi-structured observations will have an agenda of issues to observe, although there is also the flexibility in the observation process given the lesser degree of structure. This gives a researcher an opportunity to record unexpected or possibly unplanned for findings from their observations.

Image 13.2   Concept Cartoon 'Observational research'

Image 13.2 is a Concept Cartoon that shows characters expressing their views on observational research. Think about the different views, and if possible, use them to provoke a discussion with fellow students. What do you think? Do you share a viewpoint with one particular character?

ADVANTAGES AND CHALLENGES OF DOING OBSERVATIONAL RESEARCH

There are a number of advantages associated with observational research. First, observation allows the researcher to observe individuals in their natural setting. This is instead of using data to try to predict behaviour. Remember that observational research is typically about 'seeing' an individual's actions. These actions are not always the same as those shared in written or verbal form, such as answers to questions given in an online survey.

Second, observational research allows the researcher to observe behaviour individually and in a group setting. By way of an example, if you are an educator conducting research on student engagement in the classroom, participant observation allows you to take part in class discussions and also observe how students engage individually and when doing group tasks.

Third, observational behaviour is important for research where the emphasis is on non-verbal communication. For example, a researcher conducting research into the usage of public transport could administer a postal survey asking residents if they use the local bus service. However, the number of responses might be low; also how does the researcher know that participants give accurate answers when questioned how many times a week they use the local bus service? An alternative method would be to stand at the bus stop and physically count the number of people using the service.

Fourth, observation provides information about topics participants might be unwilling to talk about, unable to recall or unaware of. For example, researchers conducting research into TV viewing can use an electronic device to record the programmes and time spent watching television. However, using alternative data collection methods, such as interviews or online surveys may not capture accurate data as participants are unable to recall their television viewing habits.

Fifth, observation allows examination of activities or behaviour in real time. Again, when compared to other methods, the advantage of real-time observation means that it is relevant and up-to-date and not influenced by other factors.

Let us turn to the challenges. First, observational research can include a high level of observer bias. Subconscious opinions can affect the analysis. The way to address this is to consider your role as a researcher and to recognize and acknowledge potential biases before conducting your research.

Second, observations using qualitative research are based on interpretations and associated with the interpretivist philosophical stance. For example, how you interpret consumer actions within a store launching its January sales may not necessarily be the same interpretation of findings conducted by another researcher.

Third, observational research can be ethically challenging, time consuming and expensive to administer.

Fourth, as highlighted earlier in the chapter, there is always the potential for the Hawthorne effect – this is where participants may change their behaviour when they know they are being observed. One way to avoid this happening is to engage in covert observation.

Fifth, video/noted/audio recorded observations are influenced by what the observer chooses to record/analyze.

Finally, observation is only based on actions and does not give a 'complete picture' in terms of people's opinions and attitudes about a particular subject.

THE PROCESS OF DESIGNING OBSERVATIONAL RESEARCH

If you are considering conducting observational research, it is important to think about the steps involved. Remember that a starting point when choosing which research method(s) to use should not be methods, but the nature of your research topic, objectives, questions and methodological approach. In this section, we examine the observational research design, or in other words, the overall steps when conducting observational research.

RESEARCH AIMS AND CHOOSING THE RESEARCH SITE

Observation might be the only data collection method in your research. Alternatively, it could be one of several methods designed to address your research problem. At this stage in the process, emphasis is on thinking about the data required for your research. For example, observation is a field research method, so the researcher needs to consider the data required for the research.

Your choice of research site depends on your research questions. The location of enquiry should suggest the likelihood of observations of interest. For example, if you are undertaking research into how people engage with a fashion brand's outdoor advertising campaign, then your site (or 'field') of inquiry (the location of the billboard) needs to generate a large amount of footfall in order for the research to be worthwhile. Selecting two or three possible billboard sites will help to select the 'best' site in which to conduct the observations. The other consideration here is that the fashion brand's outdoor advert needs to be up long enough to permit the observations over a predetermined period of time.

GAINING ACCESS TO THE FIELD

Once the site is selected, the next step is to seek permission and gain access. Participant observers engaged in business research usually gain permission from management within organizations. These individuals are typically referred to as 'gatekeepers'. Knowing how to approach and negotiate access can be challenging for inexperienced researchers. However, Taylor et al. (2015) point out that students are likely to put gatekeepers at ease as most people expect students to have educational requirements to fulfil and keen students often attract help where required.

An essential part of observational research is clearly identifying and defining the 'field' for observation. The nature of the field depends on the research topic. In business research, this could be a physical place such as a shopping mall or an organization, such as an office environment. However, does the physical space also extend to the online space? For example, employees working within an organization have contacts with individuals outside of the workplace. In this respect, does the field extend to both the 'offline' and 'online' environment? The answer to this question depends on how you define 'field'. Clearly, when writing your methodology, define and justify your chosen field. It might be that the main interactions you intend to observe take place within the physical setting of an office environment.

Once you have defined your field, the next step for the researcher is to gain access to the site and individuals who are carrying out the action or activity. For students doing a work-based project, access is likely to be much more straightforward as research is typically based on their own organization. In contrast, where gaining access requires seeking permission, via perhaps sending an email or writing a letter, then this is certainly more challenging.

SAMPLING

Once you have received permission to enter the field, the next steps are to think about the actual process of 'what' to observe, addressing questions such as who, when, how, what and where you will carry out your observational research. Consider both 'time sampling' and 'event sampling'. The latter considers how often an event occurs, where the researcher records an event every time it takes place. For example, recording the number of times conflict occurs between employees. For time sampling, the researcher decides on a time and records what takes place at that time. Another key question for researchers is 'How many individuals or groups to observe?'. For example, if the focus of the research is on interaction in an open plan office environment, how many offices should be observed? Similarly, if the research topic is social media usage among teenagers, how many teenagers should be observed? An indicator of sample size is the research direction and methodological approach. For example, if conducting an interpretivist study, then the aim is unlikely to produce results that are intended for generalization to a population.

Typically, observers in the field use judgment sampling and draw on their knowledge of the literature and/or experience.

COLLECTING DATA

We examine collecting or recording of data later in the chapter. For now, it is worth noting that although the use of the pen and notebook are still used by researchers, there are now so many more options when it comes to recording data. Examples include the use of mobile phones, video and audio equipment. Where field notes are taken, separate notes are typically taken in the context of personal views and descriptive observations. As with all recording of data, it is better to record too much information as opposed to missing valuable data.

ANALYZING DATA

Analytical techniques feature later in the book. Remember that analysis can be either qualitative or quantitative. If the former, then this may involve arranging raw field data on the basis of categories. For example, if carrying out observations in the workplace, categories might include the headings 'conflict', 'relationships' and 'social'. Another type of analysis is content analysis – one approach here is to count specific words in the data. In essence, content analysis in this instance is turning qualitative into quantitative data.

EXITING (LEAVING THE FIELD)

The final step in observational research design is exiting or leaving the field of observation. To an extent, the approach taken here depends on the type of observation. Certainly, if undertaking participant observation in your workplace, then it is essential to make it clear to all participants when the research has come to an end. Again, there are ethical considerations here, not least thinking about debriefing and how to disseminate the research findings. In contrast, exiting with covert observation still requires ethical issues to be considered.

WHAT TO OBSERVE

The list of items you decide to observe during your research depends on your research objectives. These are likely to be hugely varied and there is certainly no one exhaustive list detailing everything to observe. However, Table 13.1 provides just some of the examples a researcher may consider observing.

Table 13.1   Examples of items to observe

Category	Includes	Researcher can record
Proxemics (space)	How close consumers stand next to one another	What are consumers' preferences concerning space? What do they suggest about their buyer habits?
Appearance	Age, gender, physical appearance	Does anything suggest membership of a particular reference group, e.g. football shirt/team?
Interactions	Interactions between customers and sales staff. How long does it take the employee to approach the customer, language, tone of voice, length of time?	Gender, age, position, ethnicity
Physical behaviour	What do people do? Who does what? Level of interaction?	How do individuals use their bodies and voices to communicate? How do they express their feelings?
Traffic	How many people/vehicles visit/pass every hour?	When people enter/exit, how long do they stay? What is their gender, ethnicity?

RECORDING YOUR OBSERVATIONS

Prior to conducting observational research, it is important to think about the process of actually observing and recording the data. As an inexperienced observer, it can be difficult knowing if you are seeing what you are looking for and recording what is needed (Conroy, 2017). Gorman and Clayton (2005) refer to the importance of systematic recording of observable phenomena or behaviour in a natural setting. For example, if using a video camera, what exactly is it that you are looking to record? How do you know what to record and what not to record? Field notes remain a common way of gathering data from participant observations. In some cases, researchers may use two notebooks – one that addresses the research questions or themes to be answered, while the other is intended for observations not necessarily relating to the research topic, but nonetheless of interest to the researcher. Key questions to consider when recording observations are as follows:

- What are you observing and what are the units of analysis?
- How will the data be observed?
- When will the observation(s) take place?
- How much time do you need to do the observations and record the data?
- How will the data be recorded?
- Where will the data be observed?

Let us examine each of these points more closely. First, make sure that you know what it is you intend to observe and the units of analysis. For example, when observing are you primarily interested in non-verbal communication, verbal communication or possibly both? In terms of the former, market researchers often examine what is referred to as kinesics and proxemics. The first of these relates to how body movements and gestures are used as a form of non-verbal communication, while proxemics is the branch of knowledge that deals with the amount of space that individuals deem necessary to set between themselves and others.

Other examples of what to observe when entering field settings are:

- Colour
- Sound
- Smell
- Objects
- Lighting
- Weather and temperature

An example of colour in observations might refer to the colour used for branding and brand identity. How does the retailer use colour in-store to influence consumer behaviour? Similarly, research into consumer behaviour within a retail environment may focus on other senses, such as How does the smell of freshly baked bread influence consumer behaviour?

Second, think about *how* the data will be observed. You may decide to use video recording equipment, observe in person or use other researchers. The latter can be problematic as not all institutions permit this type of research cooperation. Furthermore, it also means that you are relying on other individual(s) to interpret the research findings.

Third, when will the observations take place? Why might this be important? Well, by way of example, if you are observing consumer behaviour in a fashion retailer on a Saturday afternoon, then the number and type of customers might differ to those who shop during the week.

Fourth, consider the time you need to carry out and record the observations. Using a video camera means that you do not physically need to be present to conduct the observations. However, remember that this means you will need to still observe the videos and interpret the data.

Fifth, a number of options exist when it comes to recording the data. As we have examined, using a video camera is often used as it provides a permanent and accurate record of observations. However, it is important that you do not wholly rely on technology. Many researchers still take field notes as a back-up, or, in some cases, the only form of record. According to Thorpe and Holt (2008), 'field notes are contemporaneous notes of observations or conversation taken during the conduct of qualitative research'. Depending on the circumstances, the notes taken can be full or brief notations that can be elaborated on later. When taking field notes, the following points can be considered:

- *Note the primary observations* – these include keeping a chronological log, raw data, recording actions and non-verbal communication.
- *Reflection* – keeping field notes means ease of returning to and reflecting on actions.
- *Experiential data* – this includes data on the experience of conducting observations. Here, you might want to refer to your personal feelings, diary notes and emotional reaction to observational outcomes.
- *Pre-analysis data* – here, analysis takes place for possible themes and insights.
- *Forward planning* – keeping notes is always useful when planning to collect missing data by revisiting the field for follow up research.

Finally – where will the data be observed – is highlighted in Box 13.1.

BOX 13.1: RESEARCH SNAPSHOT

When deciding where observations will take place it is always useful to visit the site at different times of the day to develop an understanding of the environment, irrespective of the location, such as an office, shopping mall or community centre. Moreover, a physical map of the natural setting and a pilot study are important before you start your actual observations. This is because of the large number of factors that need to be considered when conducting observational research.

OBSERVATION AND ETHNOGRAPHY

The terms participant observation and ethnography are often used interchangeably in the context of qualitative research. Although both involve observation in a social setting, the role of an ethnographer goes beyond observation, as it can also involve different methods, as well as observation.

Typically, *ethnography* is carried out through participant (to a lesser extent non-participant) observation and interviews, with the researcher immersing him/herself in the regular, daily, activities of the people involved in the setting while recording observations (Green et al., 2015).

According to Draper (2015: 36) 'ethnography is concerned with describing people and how their behaviour, either as individuals or as part of a group, is influenced by the culture or subcultures in which they live and move'. Hammersley (2018: 4) points out that many of the definitions of ethnography contain different features, but if we put them together, we get a list along the following lines:

- relatively long-term data collection process
- taking place in naturally occurring settings

- relying on participant observation, or personal engagement more generally
- employing a range of types of data
- aimed at documenting what actually goes on
- emphasizes the significance of the meanings people give to objects, including themselves, in the course of their activities, in other words culture
- holistic in focus.

In simple terms, a fundamental aspect of ethnography can be viewed as gaining an insider's view through participating and observing in a group setting. By way of an example, an ethnographic study would be if you decided in order to learn more about a particular rural Chinese community, you would live and interact with the community on a daily basis. This might be over several weeks, months or even years. This type of research can provide deep and rich insights for the researcher. Ethnographic research can use a variety of methods to record data. This includes video, voice recorders and field diaries. Exploratory in nature, ethnographic research can lead to further qualitative and quantitative research.

OBSERVATION AND NETNOGRAPHY

Netnography is defined as 'a qualitative research methodology that adapts ethnographic research techniques to study the cultures and communities that are emerging through computer-mediated communications' (Kozinets, 2002: 62). In other words, netnography is the ethnographic study of communities on the web. It involves participation in an online community and examples include computer game players, car enthusiasts and mothers. Data collection is based on note taking and/or copying transcripts from the forum. Depending on the involvement of the researchers, netnographic studies range from non-participatory to participatory approaches, although many do take a passive stance (Costello et al., 2017).

Possible research questions associated with netnography are:

- How much do these posts influence customers and potential customers?
- What motivates people to post comments and other materials?
- Do people create an image or persona of themselves, to gain acceptance by others or to challenge others?
- Are their comments influenced by the opinions of those who have already posted?

NETNOGRAPHY IN ACTION

An example of netnography in action is a study conducted by Thanh and Kirova (2018). The main objective of their study was to thoroughly examine the wine tourism experience using a particular theory – the experience economy model.

To better understand the wine tourism experience and to answer the research question, the researchers adopted a qualitative research approach, as the nature of their research adopted an exploratory research design. Netnography was adopted and analysis based on the collection of consumers' reviews containing detailed information about their experiences published on the internet. The rationale for choosing netnography is that it is faster, simpler and less expensive than traditional ethnography and more naturalistic, objective and unobtrusive than focus groups or interviews.

The first step involved identifying the online communities most relevant to study the wine tourist experience. The researchers selected online reviews posted on TripAdvisor, and relative to the Cognac region in France as a wine tourism destination. Data were selected during a specific time period (August 2016). A cursory check on TripAdvisor showed that there were 5,552 reviews on the page for Cognac. The researchers then carefully selected only postings related to 'Visitations to vineyards, wineries, wine festivals and wine shows for which grape wine tasting and/or experiencing the attributes of a grape wine region are the primary motivating factors for visitors'.

The study considered a total of 825 original reviews posted on TripAdvisor by tourists who visited Cognac (France). To improve the reliability of the data collected, postings with no mention of the geographic origin and those in languages other than French or English were rejected. In terms of selecting reviews, the researchers excluded reviews less than 50 words long and noted that 10% of the sample reviews exceeded 400 words. To analyze the sample, the researchers developed a dictionary of themes based on the revised Experience Economy model. Finally, analysis included thematic analysis – this is something we examine later in the book.

WHAT MAKES AN EFFECTIVE OBSERVER?

In order to be an effective observer, you are likely to master a number of skills. These include:

- knowing the culture and the environment where the observations take place
- knowing your research subject(s)
- deciding how you will observe
- deciding how to record field notes.

There are several skills required to be an effective observer. Although by no means exhaustive, this section provides information on the key skills for you to consider if undertaking observational research.

First, an understanding is required of the culture and the environment where the observations will take place. Regarding the field or environment, there are several considerations that must be addressed. These include gaining permissions, choosing a location, selecting participants and familiarizing yourself with the culture. It is important to know the culture and the environment as this will make it easier to collect data and answer your research questions.

'Knowing the culture' is a broad term and may refer to local, national or corporate culture. For example, if conducting observational research within an advertising agency, the agency might use a hot-desking system. This is an office organization system where employees do not have assigned desks, but desks are used by different people at different times. Clearly, if you are undertaking participant observation and unaware of this system, then this will impact who you observe and the nature of the interactions between employees. Similarly, 'knowing the environment' in a business research context applies to a wide range of sites. By way of an example, conducting observational research in a shopping mall raises a number of issues. These include opening and closing times, security, where the greatest footfall takes place and, of course, research ethics such as seeking permission and how the environment may impact the recording of data.

Second, knowing your research subjects must be clear before carrying out observations. Examples here may refer to certain demographics, such as gender or age categories or possible membership groups. For example, in relation to the latter, if a researcher was observing fans' behaviour at a sporting event, then signifiers such as scarves and shirts clearly demonstrate the allegiance of a fan to a particular team. Of course, not all people may wear such signifiers. In this case, observation might be followed up with another data collection method, such as interviews.

Third, deciding how you will observe is something we looked at earlier in the chapter. Considerations here include participant observation, non-participant observation, covert observation and overt observation. Researchers also need to think about how the information will be recorded. For example, will this only involve the use of notebooks? Or, possibly, video recording equipment and the use a field notebook(s)? An effective researcher will be clear early in the research process and plan how they intend to carry out observations. Factors that may influence the decision associated with 'how' observation takes place include research aims, previous research, access and permission when entering the field.

In this section, we have examined the key skills required to be an effective observer. Other examples worth noting include the ability to concentrate for long periods of time, know how to accurately record data, the ability to recall information and effective communication skills. The latter point certainly applies in the context of asking permission to enter the field and engaging in participant observation.

HOW TO USE OBSERVATION IN YOUR RESEARCH

How do I know if observation is suitable for my research? This is a question I am sometimes asked by students considering using observational research. According to Jorgensen (1989), participant observation is most appropriate when certain minimal conditions are present:

- the research problem is concerned with human meanings and interactions viewed from the insiders' perspective
- the phenomenon of investigation is observable within an everyday life situation or setting
- the researcher is able to gain access to an appropriate setting
- the phenomenon is sufficiently limited in size and location to be studied as a case
- study questions are appropriate for case study
- the research problem can be addressed by qualitative data gathered by direct observation and other means pertinent to the field setting.

Unfortunately, observational research tends not to be a particularly popular method of research among student researchers. This is something I have indeed found among my own research students. The reasons for this are three-fold. First, observational research is not as familiar to students as other methods of data collection. Typically, interviews and surveys are often the first thought when it comes to data collection. Second, understanding the process associated with observational research is perceived as being more complex than other methods. Lastly, gaining access and ethics approval is likely to be more of a challenge than administering an online survey or simply conducting a small number of in-depth interviews.

COMBINING OBSERVATIONAL RESEARCH WITH OTHER METHODS

In this final section of the chapter, we will examine how observational research can be combined with other data collection methods. The examples featured here are from actual research studies.

EXAMPLE A

Skallerud and Grønhaug (2010) conducted research into Chinese food retailers' positioning strategies. The authors collected data in two stages, by means of observation and survey. The data from the two data collection methods were combined in the analyses. Observational research (i.e. expert assessments) were conducted in 152 retail outlets in order to assess their positioning strategies. Following this, the purchasing managers in the same retail outlets were personally interviewed by means of structured questionnaires.

In the first stage, multiple stores of all types were identified and recruited for the study. An experienced market research agency with branches in major Chinese cities and throughout Southeast Asia was employed for the data collection.

EXAMPLE B

The second example is a study by Elinwa (2020). Here, the researcher investigates the social experiences of Nigerian film audiences in viewing centres. To obtain detailed accounts of audiences' negotiating meaning during the process of film viewing, and to avoid culturally ingenuous generalizations, data were collected through active participant observation and unstructured interviews during the process of film viewing in a viewing centre. The researcher chose to collect the data using the ethnography research methodology. The recording of data involved using two A4 diaries. Journal records were read multiple times before summarization. In addition, data recorded from unstructured interviews were also transcribed and read multiple times before compression and then summarization. The analysis began by first reading the scripts. The researcher read each script at least six times before she was able to gain general insight into the data. After this, the researcher read the journal notes of the participant observation all over again.

In both examples A and B, you can see that the researchers started with observational research before conducting interviews. One advantage of using triangulation, in other words using multiple methods or data sources in qualitative research, is that studies using only one method are more vulnerable to errors linked to that particular method (Patton, 1999). For example, if you were conducting observational research by observing consumer behaviour in a supermarket setting, your observations may provide interesting findings on kinesics (the use of body language as a form of non-verbal communication) and proxemics (the amount of space the consumers in this case feel it is necessary to set between themselves and others). However, how do you know non-verbal communication accurately reflects consumers' thoughts? One way to address this question is by adopting triangulation (in the two cases here, using observational research and interviews).

Of course, observational research can be combined with other data collection methods. Once again, what is important is to think about your research questions, the relationship between research methods, and finally, the rationale behind triangulation.

This chapter concludes with a useful checklist from Slack and Rowley (2001: 41–42) of factors that need to be taken into account when using observation as a basis for data collection and analysis:

1. Gather and make use of as much contextual knowledge as possible about the situation under observation.
2. Be aware of the question or the problem to which a solution is being sought. Formulate objectives clearly and explicitly.
3. Seek ways of structuring observation.
4. Be alert to the potential for bias, and take all opportunities to cross check data.
5. Be alert to the potential for influencing behaviour and take any measures possible to minimize the effect of the observer.
6. Consider ethical issues, and clear these by asking appropriate permission wherever possible.

CHAPTER SUMMARY

- Observational research is a data-gathering approach where information is collected on the behaviour of people, objects and organizations without any questions being asked of the participants.

- If you are a participant observer, then this involves engaging with the group being observed.

- If you are a non-participant observer, then this does not involve engaging with the group being observed.

- If you decide to be a covert researcher, then your research participants are unaware that they are being observed.

- Engaging in overt observation means that research participants are aware that they are being observed.

- Observational research involves the systematic recording of observable phenomena or behaviour in a natural setting.

- Knowing the culture and the environment where the observations take place is a key skill of an effective observer.

- Ethnography can be viewed as gaining an insider's view through participating and observing.

- Participant observation is appropriate where the researcher is able to gain access to an appropriate setting.

QUESTIONS FOR REVIEW

1. What are the advantages and limitations associated with observational research?

2. Outline the different approaches to observational research.

3. Discuss the challenges associated with unstructured observation.

4. Outline the skills that make an effective observer.

5. Explain the reasons why participant observation might be an appropriate form of data collection.

6. What is meant by the term ethnographic research?

7. Give an example of covert observation used in consumer research.

8. Outline the ethical issues associated with observational research.

9. When taking field notes, outline the points a researcher engaging in observational research may wish to consider.

10. What is meant by the term 'netnography'?

STUDENT SCENARIO: TIM ENGAGES IN PARTICIPANT OBSERVATION

Tim is undertaking a work-based project at his local university. The project is the culmination of a two-year part-time degree into Small Business Management. As a part-time student, Tim's work-based project is based on the organizational performance of his family florist business. Tim decided to focus on participant observation as he is in the fortunate position of having access to employees and he also works part-time in the family business. By doing this, Tim is able to continue to interact and perform his everyday tasks. An advantage of this type of observational research is that he has access to his research participants and is also able to observe them in their natural setting.

Limitations associated with participant observation

Although Tim realized the advantages associated with participant observation, at the same time he was also aware of the potential drawbacks of conducting this type of observational research. Given the nature of the business – a small independently run family florist – Tim felt that he needed to share his research intentions with his parents, the owners of the business. In this respect, the nature of Tim's research would involve overt observation. Furthermore, Tim considered one of the benefits of his research approach was the ability to potentially implement his research findings.

Combining participant observation with other research methods

To address the limitations associated with participant observation, Tim's supervisor suggested that he engage in triangulation by combining different methods of data collection. As a result, Tim chose to conduct participant observation, observing both employees and customers and then to use the research findings to inform the second phase in his research – semi-structured interviews with customers. For his data collection, Tim produced a structured observation schedule and decided to conduct his observations over a 3-month period.

Covert and overt observation

As he would be observing both employees and customers, Tim thought carefully about whether or not to conceal his research when observing customers. Again, he decided that overt observation would be his preferred option for observing employees, as his family were aware of his study and supportive of his research. However, Tim chose covert observation, using hidden cameras within the shop, to observe customers. His rationale for selecting this approach was that cameras provided a less resource intensive way to observe customers and they also produced a permanent record of observations.

Questions

1. Give examples of alternative approaches to observational research Tim might like to consider. Give reasons for your answer.
2. Discuss some of the ethical issues Tim will need to consider given his approach to observational research.
3. Outline the benefits of combining data collection methods. In this case, participant observation and semi-structured interviews. Apply your answer to the student scenario.

Hint: Remember that there is no one 'best' approach to doing research. However, consider the research objectives when deciding your preferred method(s).

FURTHER READING

Alkhaldi, A.A. (2019) 'Language materials observation: Professional development training', *European Journal of Applied Linguistics Studies*, 2 (1).

This is an interesting educational study that focuses on classroom observation of language materials in the field of applied linguistics. The author develops a semi-structured observation schedule based on the related literature. Observations focus on teaching practice and materials in Jordanian classrooms.

Anesbury, Z., Nenycz-Thiel, M., Dawes, J. and Kennedy, R. (2016) 'How do shoppers behave online? An observational study of online grocery shopping', *Journal of Consumer Behaviour*, 15 (3): 261–270.

In this study, the researchers examine the way in which consumers shop online, such as the time taken to select categories and how quickly shoppers learn to navigate through a supermarket's site. The detailed behaviour of 40 shoppers was screen recorded while they each undertook an online shopping 'trip'. The observation procedure involved using video screen-capturing software to capture the shopper's choices, durations and site navigation.

Basil, M. (2011) 'Use of photography and video in observational research', *Qualitative Market Research*, 14, 246–257.

This article includes a number of insightful case studies that have used photography or video as part of observational research. The research highlights the potential uses of photography and video for researchers considering conducting observational research.

Clark, A., Holland, C., Katz, J. and Peace, S. (2009) 'Learning to see: Lessons from a participatory observation research project in public spaces', *International Journal of Social Research Methodology*, 12 (4): 345–360.

This article explores the use of public spaces by different social, ethnic and activity groups across the course of a 12-month period. The researchers draw on the experiences of and data collected by local non-academic researchers who were trained in a non-participatory semi-structured observation method.

Peters, K. (2010) 'Being together in urban parks: Connecting public space, leisure, and diversity', *Leisure Sciences*, 32 (5): 418–433.

This research explores the extent and nature of interethnic interactions by focusing on leisure activities in the public spaces of ethnically mixed neighbourhoods. Observations and semi-structured interviews are used to gather information about the interactions in and the meaning of urban public spaces.

REFERENCES

Angrosino, M. (2007) *Doing Ethnographic and Observational Research*. London: Sage.

Baker, L.M. (2006) 'Observation: A complex research method', *Library Trends*, 55 (1): 171–189.

Conroy, T. (2017) 'A beginner's guide to ethnographic observation in nursing research', *Nurse Researcher*, 24: 10–14.

Costello, L., McDermott, M-L. and Wallace, R. (2017) 'Netnography: Range of practices, misperceptions, and missed opportunities', *International Journal of Qualitative Methods*, 16 (1). doi: 10.1177/1609406917700647

Cowie, N. (2009) 'Observation', in J. Heigham and R.A. Croker (eds), *Qualitative Research in Applied Linguistics: A Practical Introduction* (pp. 165–181). New York: Palgrave Macmillan.

Draper, J. (2015) 'Ethnography: Principles, practice and potential', *Nursing Standard*, 29 (36): 36–41.

Elinwa, O.J. (2020) 'Audience readings and meaning negotiation in the film viewing space: An ethnographic study of Nollywood's viewing center audiences', *SAGE Open*. doi: 10.1177%2F2158244020939537

Gorman, G.E. and Clayton, P. (2005) *Qualitative Research for the Information Professional* (2nd edn). London: Facet.

Green, C.A., Duan, N., Gibbons, R.D., Hoagwood, K.E., Palinkas, L.A. and Wisdom, J.P. (2015) 'Approaches to mixed methods dissemination and implementation research: Methods, strengths, caveats, and opportunities', *Administration and Policy in Mental Health*, 42 (5): 508–523.

Guest, G., Namey, E.E. and Mitchell, M.L. (2013) *Collecting Qualitative Data: A Field Manual for Applied Research*. Los Angeles: Sage.

Hammersley, M. (2018) 'What is ethnography? Can it survive? Should it?', *Ethnography and Education*, 13 (1): 1–17.

Henriksen, I.M., Skaar, M. and Tjora, A. (2020) 'The constitutive practices of public smartphone use', *Societies*, 10 (4): 78.

Jaimangal-Jones, D. (2014) 'Utilising ethnography and participant observation in festival and event research', *International Journal of Event and Festival Management*, 5 (1): 39–55.

Jorgensen, D.L. (1989) *Participant Observation: A Methodology for Human Studies*. Newbury Park, CA: Sage. (Applied Social Research Methods, V.15).

Kozinets, R.V. (2002) 'The field behind the screen: Using Netnography for marketing in online communities', *Journal of Marketing Research*, 39 (1): 61–72.

Patton, M.Q. (1999) 'Enhancing the quality and credibility of qualitative analysis', *Health Services Research*, 34 (5 Pt 2): 1189.

Rowley, J. (2004) 'Researching people and organizations', *Library Management*, 25 (4/5): 208–214.

Skallerud, K. and Grønhaug, K. (2010) 'Chinese food retailers' positioning strategies and the influence on their buying behaviour', *Asia Pacific Journal of Marketing and Logistics*, 22 (2): 196–209.

Slack, F. and Rowley, J. (2001) 'Observation: Perspectives on research methodologies for leisure managers', *Management Research News*, 24 (1): 35–42.

Strudwick, R. (2018) 'Tensions in ethnographic observation: Overt or covert?', *Journal of Organizational Ethnography*. doi: 10.1108/JOE-11-2016-0022

Taylor, S.J., Bogdan, R. and DeVault, M. (2015) *Introduction to Qualitative Research Methods: A Guidebook and Resource*. London: John Wiley & Sons.

Thanh, T.V. and Kirova, V. (2018) 'Wine tourism experience: A netnography study', *Journal of Business Research*, 83: 30–37.

Thorpe, R. and Holt, R. (2008) *The SAGE Dictionary of Qualitative Management Research* (Vols. 1-0). London: Sage.

Timseena, B. (2009) 'Participant observation in field research: An overview', *Nepalese Journal of Qualitative Research Methods*, 3: 75–86.

Wilson, A. (2018) *Marketing Research: Delivering Customer Insights* (4th edn). London: Red Globe Press.

14

QUESTIONNAIRES

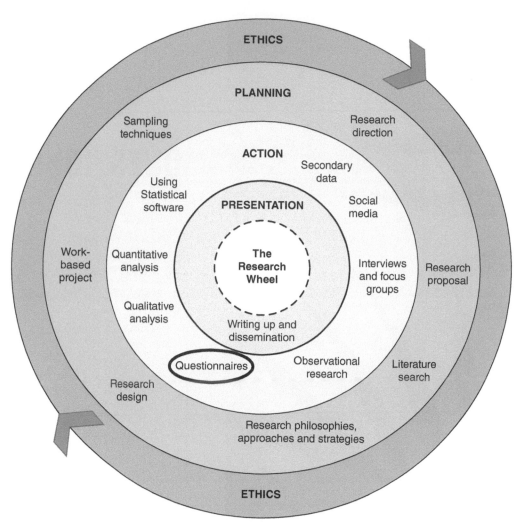

Figure 14.1 The Research Wheel

INTRODUCTION

The purpose of this chapter is to explore the use of questionnaires as a data collection tool. Questionnaires are often used in quantitative research, although they can also produce qualitative data by using open ended questions.

This chapter starts by examining how to define 'questionnaire', before moving on to look at the different types of questionnaires.

Next, we examine the advantages and disadvantages associated with using questionnaires as a data collection tool. In particular, the section compares the use of questionnaires with other data collection methods. Following this, the chapter devotes considerable attention to the questionnaire design process. In essence, this process takes the researcher through all of the essential steps when developing a questionnaire, from the starting point of considering the purpose, through to administering the questionnaire.

In the concluding part of the chapter, we examine three examples of actual research studies that have used a questionnaire. The purpose of these examples is so that you can see how a questionnaire is used in practice. Moreover, it may help you to develop your own ideas as to how a questionnaire might be incorporated into your research.

As you can see by Figure 14.1, 'Questionnaires' is in the 'Action' layer in The Research Wheel model (EPAP). This is because administering a questionnaire is part of actually carrying out your research. Once again, remember that the Action layer at this stage in the research process involves you conducting a number of activities, including collecting and analyzing data. You may have considered the ethical issues that come with using a questionnaire at an early stage in your research.

WHAT ARE QUESTIONNAIRES?

To ensure that you have a clear understanding of 'questionnaire' it is first important to make a distinction between 'questionnaire' and 'survey'. You will find in the research methods literature that the terms 'questionnaire' and 'survey' are sometimes used interchangeably. However, there is a difference. A survey is a data collection technique that seeks to determine the views of a sample using questionnaires or interviews. So, in this sense, a questionnaire can also be a survey, and is commonly referred to as a 'questionnaire survey'. Another view of questionnaire is that it is typically used to find answers to questions, such as the use of comment cards within a hotel. However, large scale studies involving questions and detailed analysis are commonly referred to as surveys.

Think of a questionnaire as containing a written set of questions, while a survey describes the overall process (Van Bennekom, 2002). This process includes the set of questions, together with the process of collecting and analyzing the response to these questions.

The questionnaire is a popular choice of data collection method among student researchers and is one of the most widely used data collection techniques within the survey strategy. Wilson (2019: 183) defines a questionnaire as 'the research instrument designed to generate the data necessary for accomplishing a project's research objectives'. Reference to the term 'instrument' implies that a questionnaire is similar to other instruments, such as interviews, similarly designed to generate data with a view to addressing a study's research objectives. Malhotra (2014: 334) provides a slightly more detailed definition of questionnaire: 'A structured technique for data collection consisting of a series of questions, written or verbal, that a respondent answers'. A distinction here is made between 'written' and 'verbal' as the latter relates to a questionnaire whereby the interviewer asks the questions to the respondent and then completes the questionnaire on the respondent's behalf. This process is typically referred to as an interviewer-administered questionnaire, where the interviewer reads the questions aloud and the respondent answer the questions. Hence, in simple terms, we can define *questionnaire* as 'a method of data collection that consists of a set of questions to generate data suitable for achieving the overall aims and objectives of a research project'.

Questionnaires are designed for many different purposes. For example, it is likely that you have completed a questionnaire(s) at some point during your study to evaluate a module. 'Evaluation' is a key reason for using questionnaires, whether it is evaluating students' opinion on a particular module, airline passenger views on their flight experience or a banking customer asked to evaluate their customer service experience.

Questionnaires tend to be used with descriptive or explanatory research. The former is all about seeking to describe aspects of the population, in particular, using 'what' questions. Explanatory research is quantitative in nature and seeks to understand the reasons, causes and effects that occur. In the context of a questionnaire, 'why' questions. A questionnaire can be used as a mono-method (one method) of data collection within a study; however, it can work especially well with other data collection methods. Again, the process of triangulation in the context of data collection can reduce the risk of chance associations and of systematic biases (Strauss, 1987).

Questionnaires are not particularly good for exploratory research. The main reasons for this are threefold. First, exploratory research uses open-ended questions. Although we examine these later in the chapter, for now, it is important to note that this type of question generates qualitative data, thus making it more time consuming to analyze given the lack of consistency in respondents' answers. Second, completing open-ended questions is time consuming for respondents. Consequently, the researcher is unable to ask a large number of questions as this will have a negative impact on overall response rate. Finally, other methods, such as narrative analysis are preferrable to a questionnaire, as the respondent has the opportunity to tell their 'story' in their own words. Having said that, questionnaires can work well as a data collection tool. According to Rowley (2014: 5), questionnaires are useful when:

- The research objectives centre on surveying and profiling a situation, to develop overall patterns.
- Sufficient information is already known about the situation under study that it is possible to formulate meaningful questions to include in the questionnaire.
- Willing respondents can be identified, who are in a position to provide meaningful data about a topic. Questionnaires should not only suit the research and the researcher, but also the respondents.

TYPES OF QUESTIONNAIRES

Before we explore the different types of questionnaires, whether or not you choose a questionnaire and the type of questionnaire are dependent on a number of factors. According to Saunders et al. (2015: 363), your choice of questionnaire will be influenced by a number of factors related to your research questions and objectives, as follows:

- characteristics of the respondents from whom you wish to collect data
- importance of reaching a particular person as a respondent
- importance of respondents' answers not being contaminated or distorted
- size of sample you require for your analysis, taking into account the likely response rate
- type of question you need to ask to collect your data
- number of questions you need to ask to collect your data.

In addition to the above points, your choice of questionnaire is also impacted by the resources you have available as well as the other steps in your research process. For example, if you have chosen to use a questionnaire as part of your research, then consider how this relates to the next step in your research – data analysis. In other words, the type of questions you use in your questionnaire will influence your choice of analytical techniques. By way of an example, if you ask a question 'What is your occupation?' and include a number of options, this type of question will generate data that can be analyzed using frequency counts. However, if you ask the question 'Please explain your occupation and your responsibilities', the answers here will generate qualitative data, therefore presenting alternative ways in which to analyze your data.

STRUCTURED QUESTIONNAIRE

From a broad perspective, we can think of 'questionnaire' as a dichotomy between 'structured' and 'unstructured'. The amount of structure in a questionnaire refers to whether questioning is structured or unstructured. According to Peterson (2000), completely *structured questioning* involves asking all research participants the same questions, the same way, in the same order. Furthermore, in a completely structured questionnaire, only closed-ended questions are used. By way of an example, a short-structured questionnaire with ten questions might be used by a library to determine users' views on their experience of using the library. Using the same ten questions, based on 'Yes' or 'No' questions, is a structured questionnaire as all of the answers are specific and designed to be completed in a short space of time. We look at closed-ended questions later in the chapter. A structured questionnaire is typically associated with quantitative research as the questions are designed to collect quantitative data.

UNSTRUCTURED QUESTIONNAIRE

Unstructured questionnaires are used to collect qualitative data and involve the use of open-ended questions. A completely unstructured questionnaire is usually associated with exploratory research. By way of an example, if a mobile phone manufacturer is testing a new product, they may use an unstructured questionnaire to collect insights from potential customers. The type of questions used by the manufacturer will be designed to generate a better understanding as to how the market may view the product, before moving on to the next stage in the product development process.

Finally, sometimes a researcher might want to generate a range of data, so therefore may prefer not to use either a structured or an unstructured questionnaire. In these circumstances, a semi-structured questionnaire is an option. This type of questionnaire uses a combination of closed-ended and open-ended questions.

THE ADVANTAGES AND DISADVANTAGES OF QUESTIONNAIRES

ADVANTAGES

There are a number of advantages and disadvantages associated with using a questionnaire as a data collection method. The main advantages of using a questionnaire can be summarized as follows (McClelland, 1994):

- they provide a cost-effective and reliable means of gathering feedback that can be qualitative as well as quantitative
- they allow you to obtain accurate information
- a survey questionnaire can provide accurate and relevant data through thoughtful design, testing and detailed administration.

First, a questionnaire can be a cost-effective means of data collection. This is one reason why it remains a popular choice of data collection among students. The typically low costs associated with administering a questionnaire also means it compares favourably to other data collection methods such as interviews and focus groups. For example, the latter often requires the cost of advertising for research participants, paying participants for their time and hiring a venue.

Second, a questionnaire takes less time when compared to other methods, especially in terms of the analytical process. This is because a questionnaire is usually associated with quantitative research. Hence, entering numerical data into a statistics software package and the subsequent analysis is less time consuming than qualitative analysis.

Third, a questionnaire can be used with a large sample size. The advantage of this is that you can survey the opinions of a greater number of people. However, in this instance, it can also be argued that sample size is only an advantage if the nature of your study is quantitative and aims to generate a representative sample.

Fourth, with a self-administered questionnaire there is a reduction in bias as the interviewer is not present.

DISADVANTAGES

Like all research methods, there are also certain disadvantages associated with using questionnaires.

First, a questionnaire is not suitable for all studies. For example, if the nature of your research is exploratory, then a questionnaire is unlikely to generate the data required in order to address your research questions. Remember that although a questionnaire can generate both quantitative and qualitative data, it remains a data collection tool usually associated with descriptive and explanatory research. In contrast, a questionnaire tends not to be a preferred option for generating a better insight and understanding about a particular topic. In this case, a researcher is more likely to use a method such as unstructured or semi-structured interviews.

Second, mailed or online questions might be filled in by someone else. By way of an example, if you are conducting research into employee views on sustainability, by targeting the senior management of leading food brands, you may decide to send a postal questionnaire to each senior manager. Yet, how do you know each questionnaire has been completed and returned by your intended audience? Similarly, an online self-completion questionnaire may not necessarily reach its intended audience.

Third, the nature of a questionnaire may not provide comprehensive information. Certainly, not to the same extent as other methods such as in-depth interviews. One way to overcome this issue is to consider using questionnaires with another type of data collection method(s). However, this decision is dependent on the nature of your research questions, together with other factors, such as the time you have in which to complete your research.

Fourth, respondents can give incomplete answers or lie on the questionnaire. Of course, there is also a chance that these issues occur with other methods, such as focus groups and interviews. However, often participants are likely to be more honest if a questionnaire is anonymous.

Fifth, if a questionnaire consists of a large number of closed-ended questions, such as those containing simple 'Yes' and 'No' or 'True' or 'False' questions, then this can result in 'tick box syndrome'. This means that if there is a clear pattern in the answers, the respondent 'ticks' each subsequent box without reading the question, as they presume the same pattern of answers will continue throughout the questionnaire. Examples are often found in medical or lifestyle questionnaires as typically the majority of respondents are not affected by any of the conditions listed on the questionnaire. One step a researcher can take to address this issue is to include a 'reverse question'. By including this type of question, there is a greater likelihood of avoiding 'tick box syndrome'. Figure 14.2 shows an extract from a hypothetical health and lifestyle questionnaire. The reverse question is question 5 (circled). However, the opposite can still happen, thereby leading to inaccurate data. Carrying out a pilot study can help to identify these types of issues with questioning techniques.

Question	Yes / No (please circle)
Have you been diagnosed with Parkinson's disease?	Yes / No
Have you suffered from kidney failure?	Yes / No
Have you suffered a heart attack, requiring hospital admission?	Yes / No
Have you ever contracted rabies?	Yes / No
Have you undertaken any form of exercise this year?	Yes / No
Have you taken early retirement on the grounds of ill health?	Yes / No

Figure 14.2   An example of a reverse question

Sixth, with a self-administered questionnaire, there is always a chance that a respondent may misinterpret a question as the interviewer is not there to provide guidance. If this happens, the response cannot be included in the final analysis. In many cases, this is not the fault of the respondent, but is the consequence of a poorly designed questionnaire or the researcher's inability to explain the question clearly.

Lastly, perhaps the main disadvantage of using a questionnaire is the challenges associated with questionnaire design. We fully examine the steps in questionnaire design in the next section.

QUESTIONNAIRE DESIGN

Designing a questionnaire can be a challenging task, even for experienced researchers. Some students tend to think of a questionnaire as developing the questions, then administering (sending out) the questionnaire to gather responses. However, in reality, there is a great deal more thought and steps required. Questionnaire design involves answering a number of questions and going through several steps in order to successfully carry out the process of collecting and analyzing data. The type of questions that need to be answered include:

- How can you ensure reliability and validity?
- How will the questions in the questionnaire address your original research objectives and research questions?
- What is the purpose of your questionnaire?
- What length should your questionnaire be?
- Will your questionnaire be combined with other data collection methods?
- How will you administer your questionnaire?

The questionnaire design process is essential in order to increase the likelihood of generating accurate information that will help the researcher to address their original research questions. Žmuk (2017: 50) points out that 'the process consists of certain steps out of which questionnaire formatting, question wording and response alternatives have the highest impact on questionnaire complexity'. Hence, it is advisable to follow the steps in the questionnaire design process, as illustrated in Figure 14.3.

In this section, we will examine each step in depth. Although the steps are illustrated as a linear process, as with many cases in research, in reality the steps are interrelated. For example, when conducting a pilot study, your findings may suggest that you need to revisit certain aspects of your questionnaire before administering the full survey. By way of an example, if a particular question is largely unanswered by participants, then to address this may involve rewording, or possibly removing the question from the questionnaire.

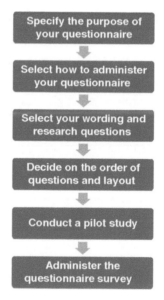

Figure 14.3   Steps in the questionnaire design process

STEP 1: SPECIFY THE PURPOSE OF YOUR QUESTIONNAIRE

Developing your question themes is driven by the nature of your research direction; this includes your research objectives and research questions. Remember that a questionnaire is an instrument, designed to allow you to address your research questions. Thus, the questions that feature in your questionnaire must be essential to your study. 'Interesting' questions, or in other words, those of secondary importance will of course add to the length of your questionnaire. Consequently, this may have a negative impact on response rate. I have sometimes seen students only realize certain questions should or should not have been included in their questionnaire at the analysis stage in their research. Clearly, this point is too late to make any changes. Hence, the importance of carrying out a pilot study.

At this stage in the questionnaire design process, the type of questions you are likely to ask include: Which themes need to be included in the questionnaire in order to address the research objectives? What demographic information is needed from the respondent? How will the results of the research be analyzed and presented? How will the questionnaire be structured?

STEP 2: SELECT HOW TO ADMINISTER YOUR QUESTIONNAIRE

Self-administered questionnaire

Broadly speaking, there are two ways in which to administer a questionnaire – self-administered or interviewer-administered. Let us examine each one in turn. First, a self-administered questionnaire is a structured form that requires the respondent to fill in the form themselves, without input from the interviewer. A self-administered questionnaire can be distributed using different methods, for example using post, email or online. The form tends to be structured and straightforward to complete as the interviewer is not present. The introduction of ambiguous questions and poor layout are likely to have a negative impact on response rate and affect the validity of the responses. The main advantage of the self-administered questionnaire is that it is straightforward to produce and does not require additional resources in terms of using an interviewer. Conversely, the key disadvantage of a self-administered questionnaire is that the interviewer is not involved so this increases the likelihood of a respondent making errors when answering the questions. Furthermore, self-administered questionnaires can generate low response rates.

Interviewer-administered questionnaire

An interviewer-administered questionnaire means that the interviewer is present when the respondent completes the questionnaire. For example, an interviewer working for a local authority may ask people in the street questions about their use of public transport. As the interviewer is asking the questions, there is the opportunity to ask more complex questions. If the respondent is uncertain about a particular question and requires clarification, the interviewer is present to answer their questions. However, one disadvantage of this method is that the respondent may feel pressurized to answer questions in a certain way. This sense of pressure would not be cause for concern if using a self-administered questionnaire. Which is the 'best' method for administering a questionnaire? There is no one 'best' method. So, if using a questionnaire for your own research, think about the nature of your research project. What is the purpose of your study? What type of questions do you want to ask respondents? Are they complex questions? Would a respondent be able to complete your questionnaire without assistance?

STEP 3: SELECT YOUR WORDING AND RESEARCH QUESTIONS

We briefly looked at questioning techniques in Chapter 12 when discussing interviews. The data collected via a questionnaire is dependent on the nature of the research questions. For example, the first question to ask yourself is, 'Is it essential for me to include this question in my questionnaire?'. If the answer is 'no', then there is no need to include the question, especially if it does not help you to address your original research questions.

According to Krosnick and Presser (2010: 264), when considering question design, the following points should be considered:

- Use simple, familiar words (avoid technical terms, jargon and slang).
- Use simple syntax.
- Avoid words with ambiguous meanings, i.e. aim for wording that all respondents will interpret in the same way.
- Strive for wording that is specific and concrete (as opposed to general and abstract).
- Make response options exhaustive and mutually exclusive.
- Avoid leading or loaded questions that push respondents toward an answer.
- Ask about one thing at a time (avoid double-barrelled questions).
- Avoid questions with single or double negations.

A key part of this stage in the questionnaire design process is deciding on your question structure, together with the type of questions you will use in your questionnaire (see Figure 14.3). In this section of the book, we focus on types of questions you may consider using in your own study. As shown in Figure 14.4, types of questions can be classified on the basis of structured and unstructured. Earlier in the chapter, we looked at structured and unstructured questionnaires. Each type of questionnaire is classified based on the type of questions.

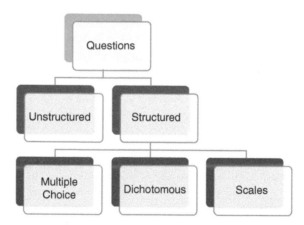

Figure 14.4   Types of questions

Unstructured questions

Unstructured or open-ended questions allow the respondent to provide a response in their own words. They generate qualitative data through open-ended questions. There are no options to choose from. Examples of open-ended questions are:

- What did you enjoy most about your holiday?
- Why do you prefer to commute to work by car?
- What are your views on the strategic partnership between organization A and organization B?
- Why did you decide to study at Viking University?

Open-ended questions are frequently used by researchers to gain more detailed information on a particular topic. They are associated with exploratory research as the nature of the questions are designed to allow the participant to provide an answer of their choosing. In other words, participants are not restricted by certain 'options.'

Structured questions

Structured questions require respondents to choose from available options. Closed-ended questions are an example of a structured question (see below). Other examples of structured questions we look at later in this section include: multiple-choice, dichotomous and scale questions.

Dichotomous questions

A dichotomous question is where there are only two possible answers. Closed-ended questions are dichotomous questions. Typically, a closed-ended question requires a 'yes' or a 'no' answer. A closed-ended question may also have multiple responses. See Figure 14.5 for examples of closed-ended questions.

Question	Yes/No (please circle)
Do you like Viking Cola?	Yes/No
Do you drink Viking Cola every day?	Yes/No
Do you find Viking Cola expensive?	Yes/No
Do you prefer Viking Cola to other brands?	Yes/No
Do you buy Viking Cola in a supermarket?	Yes/No

Figure 14.5   Examples of closed-ended questions

The advantage of closed-ended questions is that they allow for straightforward quantitative analysis, such as frequency counts. For example, we can determine the total number of respondents who buy Viking Cola. However, the downside is that they do not provide much in the way of detailed information. We can always include an open-ended question following a closed-ended question to find out more detail. Again, in the case of Viking Cola, if a participant answers 'Yes', then a follow up question might be 'Why do you buy Viking Cola?'

Questions should be designed in such a way so that:

- they are informed
- the respondent can remember so is therefore able to answer the question
- the respondent can articulate
- the questions take into account cultural issues.

Multiple-choice questions

Other closed-ended questions may require the respondent to select their answer from multiple response options. Multiple-choice questions should be written so that the selection of answers directly corresponds to the question being asked. Each of the responses needs to be mutually exclusive of the others so there is no uncertainty for the respondent. Figure 14.6 features an example of a multiple-choice question.

Question
1. Which of the following is a Chinese technology brand?
A. Amazon
B. Lenovo
C. Samsung
D. Hyundai

Figure 14.6   Example of a multiple-choice question

Scale-type questions

Scale-type questions take a number of different forms. In this section, we will examine some of the more commonly used examples.

Likert scale questions

Developed by the American psychologist Rensis Likert, a Likert scale question is an 'attitude question' that seeks to determine a respondent's attitude towards a particular topic. Typically, the respondent is required to 'tick' the response that best reflects their opinion. By way of an example, let us say that you have been emailed a customer satisfaction questionnaire by your supermarket. The questionnaire may include a question on product availability (see Figure 14.7). The table shows a five-point scale. A seven-point scale is sometimes used by researchers. However, this is often associated with a large sample size. Otherwise, a small sample size using a seven-point scale will end up with very small numbers on some of the points.

Statement	Strongly agree	Agree	Neither agree nor disagree	Disagree	Strongly disagree
Majestic supermarket has excellent product availability					

Figure 14.7   Example of a Likert scale question

Semantic differential scale question

A semantic differential scale question is intended to see how strongly the respondent holds an attitude. These scales include a progression from one extreme to another. Circling a number normally indicates the response. Figure 14.8 provides an illustration of a semantic differential scale question.

Rate the training material you receive within the organization (please circle the appropriate number)						
	1	2	3	4	5	
Interesting						Boring
Convenient						Inconvenient
Contemporary						Old fashioned

Figure 14.8 Example of a semantic differential question

A rank order scale question

A rank order scale question is a type of attitude-based question. 'Rank order' means that the respondent is required to rank an attitude statement in their order of preference. By way of example, let us say that you are conducting research into consumer preference for automobile brand ownership. Your questionnaire may include the following question: 'If you could own any of the following car brands, which would be your favourite?'. Figure 14.9 shows you how this question might look in a questionnaire. In this example, the respondent has indicated Mercedes as their first choice of car brand, followed by Audi and Volvo respectively.

If you could own any of the following car brands, which would be your favourite?

Brand	Rank order
BMW	
Audi	[2]
Toyota	
Mercedes	[1]
Ford	
Nissan	
Volvo	[3]

Figure 14.9 Example of a rank order scale question

The main advantage of a rank order question is that it allows a researcher to determine a respondent preference. This type of question is particularly suited where an organization is interested in comparing their product or brand to that of the competition. However, there are a number of disadvantages associated with rank order scale questions. These can be summarized as follows:

- Respondents may find it difficult to rank some items. This can certainly be the case if the question includes too many options.
- Respondents may not be familiar with this type of question. Hence, the importance attached to clearly explaining how to complete the question.
- The question may not be categorically exhaustive.
- The criteria used in the ranking may not be clear.
- Categories may differ across different cultures/markets.

Paired comparison scale

A paired comparison scale is similar to a closed-ended question as the respondent has to choose one of two options. For example, a question might be as follows: 'For each pair of breakfast cereals listed, put a tick next to the one you would most prefer if you had to choose between the two' (see Figure 14.10).

For each pair of breakfast cereals listed, put a tick next to the one you would most prefer if you had to choose between the two

____ Weetabix	____ Rice Krispies	____ Rice Krispies	____ Rice Krispies
____ Cornflakes	____ Weetabix	____ Cheerios	____ Cornflakes

Figure 14.10   Example of a paired comparison scale

Stapel scale

A stapel scale measures the attitude that consists of a single adjective presented vertically. The range of a stapel scale is between -5 to +5; there is no neutral point. Figure 14.11 shows an example of a stapel scale.

Please circle the number that best relates to your perception of Apple products:

Apple products are:

+5	+5	+5
+4	+4	+4
+3	+3	+3
+2	+2	+2
+1	+1	+1
Good quality	Expensive	Stylish
−1	−1	−1
−2	−2	−2
−3	−3	−3
−4	−4	−4
−5	−5	−5

Figure 14.11   Example of a stapel scale

Constant sum scale

A constant sum scale requires respondents to divide a fixed number of points among a number of attributes corresponding to the level of importance to the individual. Typically, the number of points is 100. Constant sum scales are not as commonly used in questionnaires as the likes of Likert scale questions. Although similar to rank order questions, the advantages of a constant sum scale are that the researcher is able to determine the scale of difference the respondents perceive between the different variables. Figure 14.12 shows an example of a constant sum scale. Here, you can see four examples of characteristics associated with a new set of headphones. The question relating to Figure 14.12 may read as 'Please allocate 100 points among the characteristics in such a way that represents your perceived level of importance. If you consider a characteristic to be totally unimportant, please allocate 0 points to it. Please check to make sure that the total points that you allocate add up to 100.'

Product characteristics associated with headphones	Number of points
Has an attractive design	
Is easy to use	
Is a quality product	
Is a leading brand	
	100 points

Figure 14.12   Example of a constant sum scale

Emoji (Emotion icons) rating scale

Emojis (emotion icons) can be used as a rating scale, for example using emoji and a scale, such as Very poor, Poor, Neither, Good, Excellent. Using emojis of smiley faces works particularly well when the researcher is seeking to gain feedback from people from different countries who speak different languages. For example, upon arriving at immigration at an international airport, you may have the option to rate your experience by using a touchscreen. Second, emojis are also useful if conducting research involving children. A study conducted by Gallo et al. (2017) used emojis when comparing children's liking and emotional responses to food images and actual foods. Emotion words and emojis relevant to children's experiences with food were identified through prior focus group testing with a group of 8 to 11-year-olds.

Image 14.1   Emojis can be used to measure customer satisfaction

STEP 4: DECIDE ON THE ORDER OF QUESTIONS AND LAYOUT

It is important to consider the sequence of questions in a questionnaire. Typically, a questionnaire starts with questions associated with personal characteristics or demographics, while more sensitive questions feature at the end.

The order of the questions and layout of the questionnaire relate to the physical characteristics. A clearly presented questionnaire is likely to generate effective and accurate data. However, what is equally important is that the questionnaire must be aimed at the intended target audience. A poorly selected sample can lead not only to a set of biased results, but also to a high non-response rate.

Question order

Your questions must be clearly presented and in a logical order. What do we mean by logical order? For example, one would expect to see questions relating to a specific topic in the same section of the questionnaire. By way of an example, questions relating to 'demographics' or 'personal characteristics' are usually grouped together. Examples here include age, gender, occupation and income. Similarly, let us say that you are doing research into extra-curricular activities undertaken by students while at university. These activities could be grouped into themes, such as 'Sports', 'Arts & crafts', 'Science' and 'Games' on the questionnaire and corresponding questions fall under each theme. Having a questionnaire with lots of random questions with no logical order means that respondents are less likely to complete the questionnaire.

According to Jones et al. (2013: 6), when ordering your questions in your questionnaire, consider the following:

> You should focus on what you need to know; start by placing easier, important questions at the beginning, group common themes in the middle and keep questions on demographics to near the end. The questions should be arrayed in a logical order, questions on the same topic close together and with sensible sections if long enough to warrant them. Introductory and summary questions to mark the start and end of the survey are also helpful.

Poor ordering of questions and complex layout are likely to have a negative impact on response rate. Bourke et al. (2016: 38) note that a researcher should:

- Include a cover letter or paragraph of text at the beginning of the questionnaire to describe the survey, who is sponsoring it, and its purpose. This must be highly motivating, if you want people to take the time to answer your questions! You may also tell the respondents here roughly how long it will take them to complete the survey and whether the survey is confidential and/or anonymous.
- Include clear instructions on how to complete the questionnaire and on how to navigate through the questionnaire. Avoid complex routing instructions however. Use of arrows is recommended.
- Include appropriate instructions on specific questions also – for example, 'tick as many as apply' or 'tick one box only'.

Generally, question order follows from first introducing broad topic-based questions, moving to narrow questions, followed by sensitive questions.

Layout

The layout of a questionnaire determines how easy it is for a respondent to read and to answer questions. There are a number of key considerations when designing your layout:

- Length
- Font size and formats
- How to deal with 'don't know' responses
- Single and multiple responses
- Routing
- Open-ended questions
- Thanking respondents for their cooperation
- Coding

Length

Deciding on the ideal length of your questionnaire is no easy task. On the one hand, you do not want to deter respondents by making your questionnaire too long. Conversely, it must be long enough so as to generate a sufficient amount of data. Unfortunately, there is little agreement about the optimal length of a questionnaire. In general, a shorter questionnaire elicits greater response and results in less abandonment than a longer one (Ritter and Sue, 2007). There are two steps you can take to determine the appropriate length of your questionnaire. First, look at questionnaires implemented by previous researchers in your chosen subject area. Second, conduct a pilot study to examine response rate.

Font size and formats

Font size and spacing should be clear and easy to read. Make sure to choose a font size that is big enough for respondents to read (minimum 12-point font) although this may have to be larger depending on the format. Your format may be paper-based, electronic, or possibly both. First, a paper-based questionnaire is likely to be more costly to produce; however, reducing printing costs should not be at the expense of producing a clearly presented questionnaire. Second, the advantage of electronic format is the flexibility and low cost to produce. Using a free online graphic design tool such as Canva (www.Canva.com) means you have the flexibility and templates to produce a professional-looking questionnaire. Finally, if you are producing both paper-based and electronic questionnaires, the emphasis here should be on creating the same questionnaire that works equally well across both formats.

How to deal with 'don't know' responses

In the context of your layout, having too many 'don't know' responses are encouraging the respondent to avoid answering the question. Conversely, by not including 'don't know', you are forcing respondents to answer the question, although if a respondent does really not want to answer a question, there is always the likelihood that they will leave the question blank. 'Don't know' answers can be used for certain questions. Examples here include the membership number for a professional organization. In short, use forced responses sparingly.

Single and multiple responses

Single and multiple response questions allow respondents to choose from a list of possible answers. In relation to the layout of your questionnaire, consider the number of potential responses for each question and how this may impact response rate and layout. For example, if asking a question, such as 'What is your preferred brand of coffee?', rather than listing every option, consider using 'other, please specify' to reduce space.

Routing

Question routing relates to respondents only asking questions relevant to them when completing the questionnaire. For example, including a question where the answer 'routes' the respondent to another question can be used if there is a likelihood that the respondent may answer 'No' to a question. See example below:

Q1   Are you a member of Viking Gyms?

Yes   (Go to question 2)   No   (Go to question 3)

The key point to remember when routing questions in this way is to make sure that the process is logical and clear to the respondent. Once again, a pilot study is essential here to make sure that question routing will be understood by respondents when carrying out the main study.

Open-ended questions

We examined open-ended questions earlier in the chapter. If you are using open-ended questions in your questionnaire, the most important consideration is to leave enough space for respondents to share their comments. There is nothing more frustrating for a respondent than having only a limited amount of space in which to share their answer. Moreover, this may mean an opportunity to gather valuable data is lost and could also impact negatively on response rate.

Thanking respondents for their cooperation

The final part of any questionnaire should always thank the respondent for taking time to answer the questions. If you are conducting follow up research, it is also useful to have a question asking respondents to express their interest in any future research.

Coding

Codes are symbols, usually numbers, which are used to identify particular responses, or types of response, in questionnaires and similar instruments (Robson, 1993: 256). Coding is used as part of your questionnaire in order to help process and analyze your data. Most of your data will involve quantitative analysis (something we look at in Chapter 16). For this reason, data will need to be entered into a computer software package that allows them to be analyzed. One of the most commonly used statistical software packages among student researchers is IBM SPSS Statistics (see Chapter 17). Gillham (2008: 40) points out that questions on a page should include:

- The questions (numbered in sequence).
- The answers, with their appropriate boxes.
- The coding column.

The last item is not essential, but will help you when you come to enter your data into the statistical software. See Figure 14.13 for an example of a question from a questionnaire and its coding.

Where is your salary range?			Research use only
	Less than £20,000	☐	8
	£20,000 – £29,999	☐	9
	£30,000 – £39,999	☐	10
	£40,000 – £49,999	☐	11
	£50,000 or over	☐	12

Figure 14.13   An example of a question from a questionnaire, including coding

STEP 5: CONDUCT A PILOT STUDY

Irrespective of the type of data collection method, it is always advisable to conduct a pilot study. According to Thomas (2004: 2), it is rarely possible to foresee all potential misunderstandings or biasing effects of questions and procedures, but conducting a pilot test will mitigate issues and enable you to do the following:

- Determine whether the cover letter or invitation is likely to work – that is, is the 'marketing' message Pilot Testing the Questionnaire clear and persuasive?
- Identify problems with question content, such as confusion with the overall meaning of a question and misinterpretation or misunderstanding of individual terms or concepts.
- Identify skip patterns that don't work as you intended.
- Determine whether formatting is 'user friendly'.
- Find out if everything 'works'.
- Gather evidence about the reliability of your questionnaire.
- Determine whether the coding for the analysis works as intended.
- Conduct a dress rehearsal to see that everything connects together as you planned.

Remember that a pilot study is effectively a 'trial run' to make sure that any problems or issues associated with the questionnaire can be addressed before administering the entire questionnaire. For example, I have conducted numerous studies in Asia and always carry out a pilot study. I have found that respondents do not always understand certain types of questioning techniques. A key consideration when conducting a pilot test is to make sure that the questionnaire is administered in exactly the same way as is intended in the full survey.

A questionnaire is reliable if it provides a consistent distribution of responses from the same survey universe every time. The validity of the questionnaire is whether or not it is measuring what we intend it to measure. Brace (2018) notes that piloting the questionnaire can be divided into three areas: reliability, validity and error testing. This leads us to consider the following points relating to these areas:

Reliability

- Do the respondents understand the questions?
- Does the questionnaire maintain the same level of engagement throughout?
- Do the interviewers understand the questions?
- Do responses vary based on the type of device being used?

Validity

- Can respondents answer the questions?
- Do the questions help to achieve the original research questions?

Error testing

- Does the technology work?
- Does the routing work?
- Have mistakes been made?
- How long will the fieldwork take?

STEP 6: ADMINISTER THE QUESTIONNAIRE SURVEY

As examined earlier in the chapter, there are two options when it comes to administering a questionnaire – self-administered and interviewer-administered. Questionnaires can be administered by an interviewer or answered by the respondents themselves. You also need to think about how you intend to send out your questionnaires. The main options are as follows.

Postal questionnaires

A postal questionnaire involves the researcher sending out questionnaires to the addresses of research respondents. These respondents within your sample may be 'cold' or have already agreed or expressed an interest in your research. If you are posting questionnaires to respondents 'cold', then you have had no previous contact with the respondents. This can lead to a low response rate as the recipient of your questionnaire has no knowledge of your research or your credibility as a researcher.

A telephone call to a potential respondent, followed by a postal questionnaire, can often help to increase response rate. By telephoning a potential respondent you are making them aware of your study. Furthermore, this also provides an opportunity for you to obtain verbal agreement that the person will take part in your research. From my experience, postal questionnaires are less popular than they used to be, certainly among student researchers. This is largely to do with the convenience and ability to reach a wide audience using an online questionnaire.

Web-based and email questionnaires

Email surveys are carried out by sending questionnaires via email to respondents. The researcher then hopes that the intended respondent returns the completed questionnaire via email. Ghorbani and Alavi (2014: 5) point out that email questionnaires are cost-effective and allow respondents to answer questions at their own convenience. Tse (1998) notes that email surveys are best suited to situations where:

- The population under study has universal or nearly universal email account ownership.
- There is no need to incorporate high-quality image or colour in the questionnaire.
- The inclusion of incentives will not greatly facilitate response rate and response quality.

Web-based questionnaires, sometimes referred to as Internet survey instruments, are a popular means of data collection among student researchers. The reason for this is that web-based questionnaires offer a number of advantages. These include lower cost than other methods, ease of data entry, an increasing number of recipients likely to accept the format, and reduced response time. In addition, the advantages can be summarized as follows:

- Data can be easily imported into data analysis software. The likes of Google Forms actually generate an Excel spreadsheet and allow the user to conduct statistical analysis.
- A web-based questionnaire has the potential to generate a large sample size.
- Compared to a paper-based questionnaire, a web-based questionnaire allows for easy correcting.
- A web-based questionnaire has the potential for wide coverage and generates a multiple response mechanism. For example, when creating a questionnaire survey in Google Forms, the link can be emailed and posted across numerous social media networks.

One of the most commonly used tools for creating a questionnaire is Google Forms. Another option is SurveyMonkey. For the majority of students, Google Forms is popular as it is free to use and allows the user to analyze their data. Many web-based survey applications offer free versions; these tend to be limited to number of responses, although might be suitable if you are conducting a pilot study. Table 14.1 provides an overview of some of the leading online survey tools.

Table 14.1 Comparing online survey tools

Name of online survey tool	Web address	Price	Responses per survey	Number of questions per survey
SurveyMonkey	www.surveymonkey.co.uk	FREE (basic plan)	View 40 responses per survey	10 questions per survey
Google Forms	www.docs.google.com	FREE	Unlimited	Unlimited
Typeform	www.Typeform.com	FREE (based on free plan)	10 responses per month	10 questions per Typeform
Zoho Survey	www.zoho.com	FREE (based on free plan)	100 responses per month	10 questions per survey

Source: www.surveymonkey.com, www.docs.google.com, www.Typeform.com, www.zoho.com (correct as of 19 March 2021)

The likes of Google Forms take away many of the time-consuming activities associated with more traditional data collection methods. The features of survey tools such as Google Forms allow the user to design different types of surveys, use different questioning techniques and also analyze data. The advantages of online survey tools are that many include rating scales, drop-down menus, multiple-choice questions and open-ended queries. The layout of the survey and questions is also controllable by the user (Maxymuk, 2009).

Covering letter

Irrespective of your chosen survey method, it is vital that you include a covering letter with your questionnaire. A covering letter should set out the nature of your research, what it hopes to achieve, address any ethical issues and, above all, state how it is likely to benefit the respondent. Effectively, a covering letter is your 'sales tool' – it is intended to encourage a potential participant to take part. A well-written covering letter can certainly increase your response rate. In contrast, those that are poorly written are likely to lead to a low number of replies. An example of a covering letter is as follows:

AN EXAMPLE OF A COVERING LETTER

Dear Mrs. Shaw,

My name is Richard Wang and I am a BSc Economics and Management student at Viking University. I am conducting research into the impact of the Covid-19 pandemic on the South East hospitality industry. There are several research studies on the impact of the pandemic on the hospitality industry at a national level, but as yet, little in the way of research focusing specifically on the South East region. I am inviting you to take part in this important piece of research and would be grateful if you could spare approximately 15 minutes of your time to complete the questions. These are based on:

- the background of your organization
- number of employees
- level of sales and market share
- future predictions concerning the hospitality industry in the South East region.

This is an important study. The advantages to participants who take part in this piece of research are as follows:

- It will contribute to research that carries regional and national significance.
- It will improve our understanding of the current and future hospitality sector in the South East region.
- All participants will receive a summary of the research findings.

I can assure you that all data collected in this study will be treated in the strictest confidence. I would therefore be grateful if you could please complete the questionnaire and return it in the enclosed self-addressed envelope. Alternatively, if you would like to complete an electronic version, please email me at the address below:

R.C.Wong@VikingUniv.ac.uk

Yours sincerely,
Richard Wong –
BSc Economics and Management student, Viking University.

BOX 14.1: RESEARCH SNAPSHOT

A covering letter when sending a questionnaire via email can either be attached to an email or embedded within an email. How you approach this task can make a difference in terms of response rate. For example, attaching a questionnaire in PDF format may exclude a number of potential participants who are unable to open PDF files. It is also important to think about what you type in the email's subject line. Simply referring to a title like 'Research' is too vague and may result in the person not even attempting to read your email. The title of the email should of course reflect the content, be concise and include the nature of the research topic. By way of an example: 'An important research study on Doing Business in China'.

Image 14.2   Concept Cartoon 'Administering a questionnaire'

Image 14.2 is a Concept Cartoon that shows characters expressing their views on how to administer a questionnaire. Think about the different views and use them to provoke a discussion with fellow students. What do you think? Do you share a viewpoint with one particular character?

If you are uncertain about how to administer your questionnaire, or perhaps having doubts about the type of questions to include in your questionnaire, there are a couple of steps you can take. First, ask your supervisor for their views on which method is the most appropriate. Second, look through past copies of student dissertations and journal articles that feature the use of a questionnaire as a data collection tool. This will help you to generate ideas as to what works best for your own research.

EXAMPLES OF STUDIES USING QUESTIONNAIRES

This section includes three examples of research studies that use a questionnaire as the main form of data collection method. The purpose of these examples is to illustrate how questionnaires are used in practice. Furthermore, they may also help you to generate ideas as to how you can use questionnaires as part of your own research.

Example A

In their study into entrepreneurial orientation and firm performance, Diaz and Sensini (2020) used a sample of organizations headquartered in Argentina in which to collect their data. A questionnaire was sent by email to the owner/manager of the companies. At the end of the survey, the researchers achieved

(Continued)

a 21.4% response rate. Stratified random sampling was carried out to ensure the representativeness of the extract sample. A pilot study was used to test a small sample of organizations to verify the structure of the questionnaire. Subsequently, the researchers improved the questionnaire to prevent the distortion of data and information. After the pilot study, the questionnaire was sent by email to all companies explaining the purpose of the research and other general information.

The questionnaire was divided into three sections. The first contained information about the company, owner and manager. The second section contained questions needed to measure the five dimensions of the entrepreneurial orientation and the firm's performance. The third section explored the perception of the reference context.

What is important to note about this particular study is that the researchers conducted a pilot study prior to actually launching their questionnaire. Moreover, the pilot study showed that there were issues with the content/structure that required changing before administering the final questionnaire. Again, conducting a pilot study is simply good practice and can certainly help to improve response rate. In the Diaz and Sensini (2020) example, the response rate was 21.4%. Is this a good response rate? The answer to this question is to compare the response rate with earlier, similar studies, and also the researchers' expectations as a result of the pilot test.

Example B

This second example uses a questionnaire as part of a two-phase study. A study by Dooris and Doherty (2010) used questionnaires to scope and explore 'Healthy University' activity taking place within English higher education institutions (HEIs).

The article reports the findings of a national-level qualitative study carried out during 2008 in order to investigate current 'Healthy University' activity taking place in England. The authors carried out a two-stage research process with HEIs. The first stage involved designing a brief, first stage web-based questionnaire using the online SurveyMonkey tool (www.surveymonkey.com), in order to audit current activity and identify a second stage, a purposive sample of universities interested and engaged in the 'Healthy University'.

A total of 117 HEIs received invitation emails and of these, 64 completed the survey, representing 55% of the sample. The data was summarized using the SurveyMonkey capabilities and thematic analysis undertaken.

In this study, what is interesting is that the researchers have used the responses from the first phase of a web-based questionnaire to identify potential participants for the second phase of the study.

Example C

In this third example by Khalid and Nawab (2018), the researchers conducted research into relationships between types of employee participation (delegative, consultative, worker director and worker union) on employee retention and the moderation of employee compensation in this relationship. The authors analyzed four types of employee participation, employee retention and compensation in two major sectors of Pakistan.

Data collection involved two mechanisms. First, a self-administered questionnaire was used to collect data from organizations in Islamabad, Rawalpindi, Lahore and Peshawar (response rate = 95%). Second, data were collected through emails (with two reminders after every three days' gap) from Karachi and Quetta (response rate = 62%). The total response rate from the manufacturing sector was 79.84%, while from the service sector, it was 82.30%.

In each sector organization, 650 questionnaires were distributed. The two samples were collected as convenience samples where the individual workers were personally approached in their workplaces.

After a brief introduction to this study, the voluntary participants were handed the surveys that were to be collected at the end of the day.

The research consisted of a group discussion, general interviews from two manufacturing organizations and two service organization managers, and doing pilot testing of the survey form. After completion of these three experiments, the survey form was modified in terms of simplifying the survey language and translating the survey form. Statistical analysis was later conducted on the research findings.

This study by Khalid and Nawab (2018) is a good example of how using different methods of collecting data can help to increase sample size and response rate. In this case, via post and email.

CHAPTER SUMMARY

- Questionnaires ask the same set of questions to research participants and are normally part of a survey strategy. Questionnaires are typically associated with quantitative research.

- Before designing your questionnaire, you need to know what data to collect in order to address your research questions.

- Your choice of type of questionnaire is dependent on your research objectives, research questions and resources available to you as a researcher.

- A questionnaire can be administered in a number of different ways, including self-administered and interviewer-administrated.

- When designing your questionnaire, consider the order and type of questions. The latter are distinguished on the basis of open-ended and closed-ended questions.

- The response rate you achieve when you administer your questionnaire is dependent on a number of factors, in particular whether or not a pilot study has been conducted.

- The validity and reliability of the questionnaire depends largely on how you frame your questions.

- The layout and structure of the questionnaire should be easy for participants to follow and read.

- All questionnaires should be pilot tested to test the validity and reliability of the questions.

QUESTIONS FOR REVIEW

1. How can a researcher aim to increase response rate through questionnaire design?

2. Why would a researcher choose to conduct a pilot study before administering their questionnaire?

3. Explain the steps in the questionnaire design process.

4. Why would a researcher choose to use a closed-ended question?

5. What are the differences between a self-administered and an interviewer-administered questionnaire?

6. What are the main considerations when designing the layout of a questionnaire?

7. Explain the advantages of using a questionnaire as a data collection method.

8. Explain the disadvantages of using a questionnaire as a data collection method.

9. What are the differences between a rank order question and a Likert scale question?

10. How can you increase the validity and reliability of your questionnaire?

STUDENT SCENARIO: SYLVIA'S QUESTIONNAIRE DESIGN

As part of her research project, Sylvia decided to carry out a questionnaire. Sylvia's research focused on sustainability strategies in the UK fashion industry. She was particularly interested in the views on sustainability among Generation Z (those born in the late 1990s). Sylvia chose to undertake a largely quantitative study, using a structured questionnaire to gather data on her research topic. The final questionnaire would be self-administered and shared online across a number of different social media platforms using Google Forms; for example, Sylvia intended sharing the link to the Google Form with her Twitter followers.

Questionnaire design

Sylvia was currently at the questionnaire design stage. She intended using a pilot study before carrying out the full study, so as to make sure to address any potential problems that might arise. Sylvia had never designed a questionnaire before, so used examples from journal articles and past student dissertations. She had a good understanding as to the content and layout of her questionnaire. The questions in the questionnaire needed to help address the research objectives and cover the key themes, such as how respondents define sustainability, the extent that respondents consider sustainability important in the UK fashion industry, whether or not respondents are prepared to pay a higher price for a product that is 'sustainable' and finally, the extent that sustainability is important compared to other buying factors.

Sylvia thought ahead to her analytical techniques and was interested in analyzing how demographics relate to questions concerning sustainability. Therefore, she intended including questions about age, gender, occupation and education. Furthermore, although a quantitative study, Sylvia decided to include a couple of open-ended questions towards the end of the survey, one of which would be 'Do you have any comments to make?'.

Questions

1. Sylvia intends using a structured questionnaire. Provide advice to Sylvia on what she will need to consider when designing her questionnaire.
2. Give examples of the types of questions Sylvia might use to gather data on respondents' views on sustainability in the UK fashion industry.
3. Outline the steps Sylvia can take to increase the response rate when administering her questionnaire.

Hint: Remember that all questions in a questionnaire must have a purpose – to help the researcher to achieve their research objectives and original research questions.

FURTHER READING

Burgess, T.F. (2001) *A General Introduction to the Design of Questionnaires for Survey Research*, Information System Services, University of Leeds.

A useful document for student and novice researchers that examines the steps in the questionnaire design process. In addition, there are also helpful examples of question types.

Codó, E. (2008) 'Interviews and questionnaires', in L. Wei and M.G. Moyer (eds), *The Blackwell Guide to Research Methods in Bilingualism and Multilingualism* (pp. 158–176). Oxford: Blackwell.

Contains insightful information on key aspects of the questionnaire design process. This includes planning, format and administering the questionnaire.

Dalati, S. and Gómez, J.M. (2018) 'Surveys and questionnaires', in J.M. Gómez and S. Mouselli (eds), *Modernizing the Academic Teaching and Research Environment* (pp. 175–186). Cham: Springer.

A detailed examination of self-administered survey questionnaires, including the advantages and disadvantages associated with this method. Moreover, the questionnaire design process is also discussed.

REFERENCES

Bourke, J., Kirby, A. and Doran, J. (2016) *Survey & Questionnaire Design: Collecting Primary Data to Answer Research Questions*. NuBooks.

Brace, I. (2018) *Questionnaire Design: How to Plan, Structure and Write Survey Material for Effective Market Research* (4th edn). London: Kogan Page.

Diaz, E. and Sensini, L. (2020) 'Entrepreneurial orientation and firm performance: Evidence from Argentina', *International Business Research*, 13 (8): 1–47.

Dooris, M. and Doherty, S. (2010) 'Healthy Universities: Current activity and future directions: Findings and reflections from a national-level qualitative research study', *Global Health Promotion*, 17 (3): 6–16.

Gallo, K.E., Swaney-Stueve, M. and Chambers, D.H. (2017) 'Comparing visual food images versus actual food when measuring emotional response of children', *Journal of Sensory Studies*, 32 (3): e12267.

Ghorbani, M.R. and Alavi, S.Z. (2014) 'Feasibility of adopting English-medium instruction at Iranian universities', *Current Issues in Education*, 17 (1): 1–16.

Gillham, B. (2008) *Developing a Questionnaire* (2nd edn). London: Continuum Books.

Jones, T.L., Baxter, M.A.J. and Khanduja, V. (2013) 'A quick guide to survey research', *The Annals of The Royal College of Surgeons of England*, 95 (1): 5–7.

Khalid, K. and Nawab, S. (2018) 'Employee participation and employee retention in view of compensation', *SAGE Open*, 8, 4: 1–17.

Krosnick, J.A. and Presser, S. (2010) 'Question and questionnaire design', in P.V. Marsden and J.D. Wright (eds), *Handbook of Survey Research* (pp. 263–314). Bingley, UK: Emerald Group.

Malhotra, N. (2014) *Basic Marketing Research* (4th edn). Harlow: Pearson.

Maxymuk, J. (2009) 'Online tools', *The Bottom Line: Managing Library Finances*, 22 (4): 135–138.

McClelland, S.B. (1994) 'Training needs assessment data-gathering methods: Part 1, survey questionnaires', *Journal of European Industrial Training*, 18 (1): 22–26.

Peterson, R.A. (2000) *Constructing Effective Questionnaires*. Thousand Oaks, CA: Sage.

Ritter, L.A. and Sue, V.M. (2007) 'The survey questionnaire', *New Directions for Evaluation*, 115: 37–45.

Robson, C. (1993) *Real World Research*. Oxford: Blackwell.

Rowley, J. (2014) 'Designing and using research questionnaires', *Management Research Review*, 37 (3): 308–330.

Saunders, M., Lewis, P. and Thornhill, A. (2015) *Research Methods for Business Students*. Harlow: Pearson Education.

Strauss, A. (1987) *Qualitative Analysis for Social Scientists*. Cambridge: Cambridge University Press.

Thomas, S.J. (2004) 'Pilot testing the questionnaire', in S.J. Thomas, *Using Web and Paper-based Questionnaires for Data-based Decision Making*. Thousand Oaks, CA: Sage.

Tse, A.C.B. (1998) 'Comparing response rate, response speed and response quality of two methods of sending questionnaires: Email vs mail', *Journal of the Marketing Research Society*, 40 (1): 353–361.

Van Bennekom, F.C. (2002) *Customer Surveying: A Guidebook for Service Managers*. Bolton, MA: Customer Service Press.

Wilson, A. (2019) *Marketing Research: Delivering Customer Insight* (4th edn). London: Macmillan International Higher Education.

Žmuk, B. (2017) 'Impact of questionnaire length and complexity on survey time: Comparison of two business web questionnaire versions', *Advances in Methodology & Statistics*, 14 (2).

15

ANALYZING AND MANAGING QUALITATIVE DATA

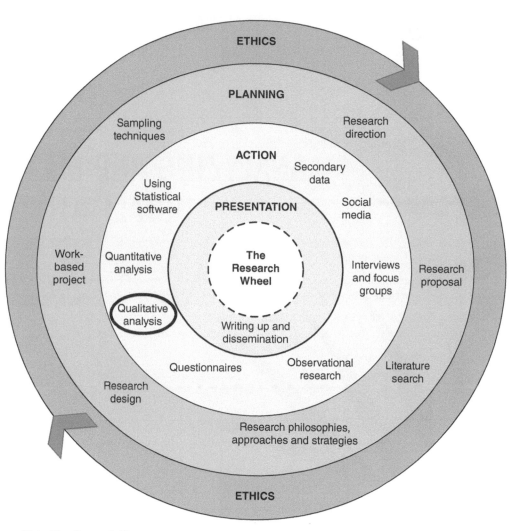

Figure 15.1   The Research Wheel

Learning objectives

By the end of this chapter, you should be able to:

- understand what is meant by qualitative analysis
- understand the differences between qualitative and quantitative data
- recognize how to prepare your data for qualitative analysis
- know the main types of qualitative data analysis
- understand the problems associated with qualitative analysis
- know how to manage qualitative data.

INTRODUCTION

This is the first of two chapters on how to analyze data. The focus of this chapter is on analyzing non-numerical data, or in other words, qualitative data. Some students think of qualitative data analysis as analyzing written text. Although qualitative analysis does include words, this is a very narrow view. Qualitative data analysis is much more than this as it includes other types of qualitative data, for example observations, visual data and verbal communication.

The chapter begins by examining what is meant by qualitative data analysis. Earlier in the book we looked at qualitative data collection methods. This includes observational research, interviews and focus groups. The next step in the research process is to consider how you intend to analyze your data. In reality, you should have chosen your qualitative analytical methods during the planning stage in your research. Certainly, this is something that should feature in your research proposal. Next, the chapter discusses the differences between qualitative and quantitative data analysis. There are a number of different approaches to analyzing qualitative data and distinguishing between 'qualitative' and 'quantitative' is not always a straightforward dichotomy.

The chapter then moves onto explore how to analyze qualitative data. Although there is no consensus among researchers on the steps involved when conducting qualitative analysis, many approaches proposed by various researchers feature 'common' steps. These start from transcribing your data, through to writing your report/project. Following this, we examine the main types of qualitative data analysis typically used by business and management students. These are: thematic analysis, narrative analysis, content analysis, Grounded Theory and discourse analysis. One of the challenges student researchers often face is deciding which analytical technique(s) to choose. To an extent, this is partly dependent on the choice of data collection method(s) and whether or not you decide to adopt a deductive or inductive approach to your research.

The chapter then features a brief discussion on using an appropriate software package. There are two leading packages on the market – NVivo and CAQDAS (Computer Assisted Qualitative Data Analysis Software). Finally, the chapter culminates with examples of research studies that have used qualitative data analysis. Again, the reasons for the inclusion of actual research studies are two-fold. First, to show you how each study has conducted qualitative analysis in practice. Second, they are chosen as they provide useful 'takeaways' for you if you are considering doing qualitative research as part of your own research project.

Figure 15.1 shows 'Qualitative analysis' in the 'Action' layer in The Research Wheel model (EPAP). Again, the Action layer means that you have put into practice everything planned for during the planning stage in The Research Wheel. This means your choice of analytical tools used to analyze qualitative data will have been decided early in the research process.

WHAT IS QUALITATIVE ANALYSIS?

In qualitative research, analysis of the collected data is a particularly important process that is hugely time consuming and requires patience (Shin et al., 2009). 'Time consuming' is often a characteristic associated with qualitative analysis as it involves timely processes, such as transcribing, data reduction and developing themes. According to Patton (1990: 22), qualitative data analysis is 'a detailed description of situations, events, observed behaviours, direct quotations from people about their experiences, attitudes, beliefs, and thoughts and excerpts or entire passages from documents, correspondence and records'. This definition nicely encapsulates the fundamental aspect of qualitative data analysis, that is, it takes a holistic view and 'goes beyond' referring to qualitative data analysis as simply analyzing text. Furthermore, references to words such as 'attitudes' and 'beliefs' signifies that it is interpretivist in nature.

Qualitative data analysis is exploratory and typically based on analyzing large amounts of data. Early in the analysis process it is essential to have a clear plan of the steps that need to be addressed in order to analyze your data. Often, one of the challenges students face is knowing which steps to take, particularly as there is no one definitive model to analyzing qualitative data.

The proposed steps in analysis vary between authors. For example, Miles and Huberman (1994: 10) make the point that qualitative analysis consists of essentially three activities – data reduction, data display and conclusion drawing/verification. As you will see later in the chapter, these activities are a fundamental part of doing qualitative data analysis, irrespective of the approach chosen to conduct your analysis.

When analyzing qualitative data, the likelihood is that your analysis will either be based on interview transcripts or field notes taken from observational research. Ideally, you will have audio or video recordings in which you can transcribe your data. This is typically the first step in the analytical process and requires a great deal of time and patience before moving onto the next step in your analysis.

Prior to conducting your analysis, you should have a clear idea as to your research approach. For example, will your approach be inductive or possibly deductive? This is important as it determines how you analyze your data. For example, a qualitative researcher who uses inductive analysis develops categories that emerge from field notes, documents and interviews. In other words, these are not imposed prior to data collection. Develop a system for how to conduct your analysis early in your research. Again, this should be set out within your research proposal.

THE DIFFERENCES BETWEEN QUALITATIVE AND QUANTITATIVE DATA

Earlier in the book, we examined qualitative and quantitative data collection. Remember that qualitative data collection is primarily associated with exploratory research, asking open-ended questions and is subjective in nature. These points are reflected in how to analyze qualitative data. In contrast, quantitative data is focused on objectivity, measurement and closed-ended questions. Schutt (2018) summarizes the following ways in which qualitative data analysis differs from quantitative data analysis:

- a focus on meanings rather than on quantifiable phenomena
- collection of many data on a few cases rather than few data on many cases
- study in depth and detail, without predetermined categories or directions, rather than emphasis on analyses and categories determined in advance
- conception of the researcher as an 'instrument', rather than as the designer of objective instruments to measure particular variables
- sensitivity to context rather than seeking universal generalizations

- attention to the impact of the researcher's and others' values on the course of the analysis rather than presuming the possibility of value-free inquiry
- a goal of rich descriptions of the world rather than measurement of specific variables.

Let us consider some of these points in more detail. The first point – qualitative data analysis focuses on meanings. This is certainly the case. A key part of qualitative analysis is looking for patterns and interpreting data. However, researchers undertaking qualitative analysis will sometimes convert qualitative data into quantitative data. This type of analysis is often referred to in the literature as 'quantitative content analysis' as it involves counting. We examine quantitative content analysis later in the chapter.

Second, 'collection of many data on a few cases' describes the nature of the exploratory aspect of qualitative analysis. For example, let us say that you are conducting qualitative analysis on answers to questions on mergers and acquisitions. These are from senior managers in financial organizations. The qualitative nature of data collection means that analysis will be based on results from these interviews. In essence, you will have a large amount of data from your interviews with managers, from a small number of cases (small number of managers).

Third, qualitative data analysis is certainly in-depth and requires familiarizing yourself with the data, making comparisons and the development of categories. However, it is also possible to conduct descriptive content analysis using predetermined categories. This does have its limits as it means that the researcher finds in the data only what they are looking for. In addition, the reliability of the research process depends on the skills of the researcher.

Fourth, as highlighted earlier in the chapter, the researcher is not using objective measures but is engaged in comparative analysis and interpretation of the data.

Fifth, sensitivity to context means focusing on analyzing the data from a small number of cases; the emphasis is not on making universal generalizations, as is often the case with quantitative research.

Sixth, qualitative analysis is largely not value-free as it represents the perspective of the researcher(s) and not the objective truth. So, this needs to be recognized by the researcher, together with its impact on the interpretation of the results.

Finally, emphasis is on describing data, but also understanding and interpreting data, as opposed to quantitative analysis where emphasis is on measurement of variables.

HOW TO ANALYZE QUALITATIVE DATA

It is important to note that there is no one definitive process for analyzing qualitative data. To a large extent, the steps are dependent on the type of qualitative analysis being undertaken and research questions. For example, if your research is concerned with analyzing and interpreting the advertising campaigns of leading health and beauty brands, then this will be very different to analyzing and interpreting data from unstructured interviews. One key difference here is that interpreting data from 'advertising campaigns' relates to visual data, while analyzing interview data involves transcribing your interviews and analyzing text. However, in both cases there is an element of interpretation. Hence, in qualitative data analysis, although there are differing views on the steps for preparing data for analysis, there are some common features such as 'transcribing' and 'interpretation'. In this section, we examine the key steps involved in the process of qualitative data analysis. The six analytical steps we are going to use can be summarized as follows:

1. Transcribing your data
2. Familiarize yourself with the data
3. Create coding frame (codebook) and code your data
4. Organize codes into categories and themes
5. Identify patterns and connections within and between categories
6. Interpretation and writing the report/project

STEP 1: TRANSCRIBING YOUR DATA

Once you have collected your video or audio data recording(s), you are then ready to engage in the process of converting audio and video data into a written document. This is called *transcription* (Wiggins, 2017). Irrespective of the type of qualitative data collection method – for example, perhaps you have chosen observational research, unstructured interviews, or focus groups – the first step in the qualitative data analysis process involves the transcribing of your data. For many student researchers, this will be data collected from interviews. In Figure 15.2, you can see a brief extract from an interview transcript that contains all of the key information from the interview – date of interview, name, organization and position. The initials 'AS' are the interviewee, while 'Q' represents 'question' from the researcher. The use of these references, together with the numbered lines, make it clearer and easier when it comes to later coding the data.

Transcribing data can be a hugely time-consuming process. Some researchers pay an organization that specializes in transcription services to carry out the work. The advantage of this is that you are employing someone specialized in transcribing data. In this respect, the process is likely to be much quicker than if you were to transcribe the data yourself. Another advantage of using a transcription service is that it allows you to devote more time to other aspects of your research, for example reviewing the literature or additional data collection.

Date of interview	Name	Organization	Position
10 January 2021	Ana Sanchez*	Viking International Supermarket*	General Manager

1. Q: Mrs Sanchez, please can you tell me your role with the joint venture.

2. AS: I was the manager of the joint venture.

3. Q: How did the joint venture come about?

4. AS: I understand it began with initial discussions between

5. senior management in both organizations. At the time, both

6. parties were keen to develop across international markets,

7. so there was a perception that a partnership could be a

8. 'win–win'.

9. Q: Are there restrictions on international supermarkets

10. forming a joint venture with local companies?

11. AS: Yes, there are a number of legal restrictions. At present,

12. it is still a challenging climate to develop international

13. partnerships. A key factor is having an understanding of

14. the cultural differences, together with key

15. macro-environmental issues.

Figure 15.2   Example of an extract from an interview transcript

However, there are disadvantages associated with using a transcription service or asking someone else to transcribe your data. First, the person transcribing your work is unlikely to be a subject specialist in your area of research. Ultimately, this means that it is unlikely they will be familiar with technical terms, abbreviations and any theories or models referred to by the research participant. If the transcriber then changes the wording, this may result in the original meaning of the answer being lost. Second, if you do your own transcribing, then you will have an invaluable opportunity to gain a deeper understanding of respondents' answers. It is also ideal preparation for later stages in the analytical process, such as reading and coding. If you do use a professional transcription service, my advice would be to check each transcript against your audio recordings. Although time consuming, it is important to check for the accuracy of your data.

Transcribing can also be combined with the process of creating analytic memos. Memoing during transcribing, and also reading and re-reading of the data, is a continuation of reflection. Memos are records of the researcher's emerging ideas about codes and their interconnections. They can be written anywhere, for example on a transcript, notebook or post-it note. There is no set format; they can be short or long. The purpose is to capture your thoughts when you make them. They are a documentation of the researcher's thinking processes rather than a description of a social context (Montgomery and Bailey, 2007).

If you have conducted observational research, then transcribing is likely to involve both audio and visual data. However, although the nature of your data are observations, rather than words, an important first phase of data analysis still entails transcribing your data in preparation for analysis. Once the data have been transcribed (most likely using a software package such as Microsoft Word or NVivo), the next step is to begin to familiarize yourself with the data.

STEP 2: FAMILIARIZE YOURSELF WITH THE DATA

The next step in the qualitative analysis process is all about familiarizing yourself with the data. This is an iterative process that requires reading through your data multiple times and writing down any ideas or interesting comments that emerge. Although time consuming, this process of familiarizing yourself with your data is an important step that takes place prior to coding your data. As well as reading through your transcripts, this step is also an opportunity to look over your notes you made during data collection and/or watching video recordings. In short, reading in this way is all about familiarization with the data.

STEP 3: CREATE CODING FRAME (CODEBOOK) AND CODE YOUR DATA

The next step in the analytical process is creating a coding frame and coding your data. Before we examine the process, it is essential to understand the key terms associated with coding. These include themes, codes, coding and categories. Sometimes these terms are used interchangeably, especially 'themes' and 'categories'; however, there is a difference. Only when you are familiar with the key terms can you begin to understand the nature of the coding process. See Table 15.1 for definitions of the key terms associated with coding.

Table 15.1   Definitions of the key terms associated with coding

Term	Definition
Coding	Identifying segments of meaning in your data and labelling them with a code as a means to categorizing the text in order to establish thematic ideas.
Code	A code is a label which shows the same theoretical or descriptive idea and is applied to data. This includes single words, sentences, phrases, paragraphs, parts of pictures and sections of an audio recording.
Theme	A way of linking together categories that convey similar meanings.
Category	A category is a group of codes that clearly have something in common.

An important part of the coding process involves something called a coding frame or code book (from now on referred to as coding frame). A coding frame allows the researcher to organize words and key phrases into themes. In simple terms, the coding frame should include definitions and examples of why you have coded something in a certain way.

O'Connor and Joffe (2020: 2) note that 'the coding frame is typically a list of codes, which may be organized according to higher order code categories, accompanied by code definitions and example data segments'. Once you develop your coding frame, it is then applied to the data.

Hannam and Knox (2005: 24) define a coding frame as 'a set of themes into which material can be allocated'. The authors go on to point out that the coding frame should be reliable. This can be achieved by two or more researchers analyzing the same material with the same objective and then uncovering the same results. See Table 15.2 for an example of a coding frame. In this example, the themes, such as 'Trust' and 'Commitment' are pre-determined. This means that we are establishing our coding frame before analyzing the data based on 'deductive themes'. These themes have emerged from the literature and/or our research questions. Developing a coding frame is essential if you have adopted a deductive approach to your qualitative analysis, as it sets out the coded concepts that you will need to look for when analyzing your data. An alternative approach to developing your coding frame is to use an inductive approach whereby the categories are derived from your data.

Your approach to developing your coding frame depends on the nature of your research questions, type of qualitative analysis and earlier studies. For example, if there are a number of existing studies that have used tried and tested coding, then you may wish to use the same approach, so as to compare your research findings. There is a 'third option' to developing a coding frame, that is to have a partially deductive and partially inductive approach where coding and re-coding takes place. By combining elements of deductive and inductive coding, the researcher is not restricted by one particular approach.

Table 15.2   An example of a coding frame for qualitative research

Themes	Coding example
Trust	We know our foreign partner will always deliver on time and is open regarding the sharing of technological information.
Commitment	We see this joint venture as being at least a ten-year venture.
Cooperation	We work closely together in aiming to achieve our strategic objectives.
Satisfaction	We are pleased with the venture in that there is regular exchanging of information.
Performance	We have achieved our set objectives over the short-term.
Dissolution	We are considering switching from a joint venture to a Wholly Owned Foreign Enterprise (WOFE) in the near future.

Source: Adapted from Wilson (2014)

Coding your data

Rather confusingly, 'coding' is a term that is used in the context of both qualitative and quantitative data. In quantitative data, coding is commonly referred to assigning numbers to survey question answers. The purpose here is to aid quantitative analysis when entering data into a statistics software package. In qualitative data analysis, coding is all about breaking down and defining what the data are all about. According to Linneberg and Korsgaard (2019: 260), 'Coding in its most basic form is the simple operation of identifying segments of meaning in your data and labelling them with a code'. Think of a 'code' as a keyword or phrase within your transcript or notes.

> A code in qualitative inquiry is most often a word or short phrase that symbolically assigns a summative, salient, essence-capturing, and/or evocative attribute for a portion of language-based or visual data. The data can consist of interview transcripts, participant observation field notes, journals, documents, drawings, artifacts, photographs, video, Internet sites, e-mail correspondence, literature, and so on. (Saldaña, 2015: 3)

This definition of 'code' highlights perfectly the eclectic mix of data associated with qualitative research – everything from drawings to internet sites.

The goal of coding is to 'fracture the data and rearrange it into categories that facilitate the comparison of data within and between these categories and that aid in the development of theoretical concepts' (Strauss, 1987: 29). However, why engage in coding? Reasons include:

1. *Retrieving data*, i.e. from the whole mass of data, particular words or statements can be searched for and retrieved to examine the 'fit' with other words or statements.
2. *Organizing the data*, i.e. words or statements can be reordered, put alongside each other and similarities and differences evaluated.
3. *Interpreting the data*, i.e. as words or statements are retrieved and organized in different ways, different interpretations of the similarities and differences can be made.

In short, coding is a process that helps to reduce data by considering its *retrieval, organization* and *interpretation*. Let us look at the above points.

First, retrieving data from the whole mass of data, such as words, statements can be used to see if they 'fit' with other words and statements. By way of an example, let us say that you have conducted 20 interviews with Human Resources managers on staff retention. If some of the respondents are referring to 'salary' as a reason why staff are leaving, while others may refer to 'promotion prospects', through retrieving and comparing the data you can examine the 'fit' and relationships between the answers given by the interviewees.

Second, organizing the data involves further comparative analysis by looking for differences and similarities. By way of example, let us say that you have conducted interviews with a sample of supermarket shoppers on customer satisfaction. Following the transcription and reading of your data, comments can be organized on the basis of 'positive', 'negative' and 'neither'.

Finally, interpreting the data is looking for reasons and an understanding of the answers given by respondents. With reference to the last point, this may include reasons why a participant has given a positive or negative answer.

As with developing your coding frame, there are two approaches to coding your data – *inductive* (or emerging) coding and *deductive* (or priori) coding. If you adopt the former, then you will develop codes from examining your data by using terms or phrases from the participants themselves. In contrast, with deductive coding, researchers use a pre-defined list of codes that are determined prior to analysis to code qualitative text. Furthermore, these codes are usually based on theoretical concepts or themes from the existing literature. By way of an example, let us say that you are interested in exploring consumer perceptions of luxury brand identities, by using an already established set of codes you would be following deductive coding. However, your argument against this approach might be that deductive coding hinders your ability to consider themes that emerge from your data that do not feature in the pre-defined list.

There is no one definitive approach to developing your codes. Figure 15.3 illustrates an example of initial coding of qualitative data. In this example, the researcher has included initial codes in the right-hand column, for example 'Negotiation process'. These codes are illustrated by words and will later be analyzed with a view to developing *categories* and *themes*. In this example, the study was based on inductive coding (codes emerged from the data). An alternative approach to using words for your codes is to use letters and numbers. Alternatively, colour coding for selected words and phrases.

Lastly, the purposes of coding procedures can be summarized as follows:

- build rather than test theory
- provide researchers with analytic tools for handling masses of raw data
- help analysts to consider alternative meanings of phenomena
- be systematic and creative simultaneously
- identify, develop and relate the concepts that are the building blocks of theory (Strauss and Corbin, 1990: 13).

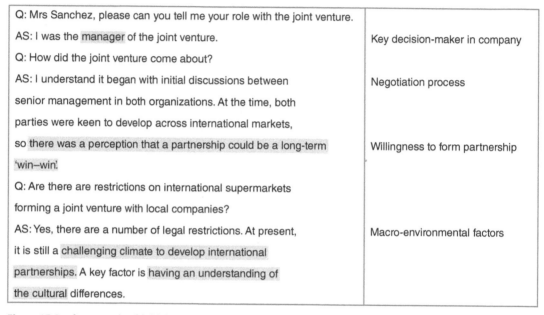

Q: Mrs Sanchez, please can you tell me your role with the joint venture.	
AS: I was the manager of the joint venture.	Key decision-maker in company
Q: How did the joint venture come about?	
AS: I understand it began with initial discussions between senior management in both organizations. At the time, both parties were keen to develop across international markets,	Negotiation process
so there was a perception that a partnership could be a long-term 'win–win'.	Willingness to form partnership
Q: Are there are restrictions on international supermarkets forming a joint venture with local companies?	
AS: Yes, there are a number of legal restrictions. At present, it is still a challenging climate to develop international partnerships. A key factor is having an understanding of the cultural differences.	Macro-environmental factors

Figure 15.3   An example of initial coding of qualitative data

STEP 4: ORGANIZE CODES INTO CATEGORIES AND THEMES

Once you have coded your data, the next step is your data needs to be retrieved so that you can carry out more in-depth exploratory analysis by combining your codes into patterns, themes and categories. A *category* is defined as a classification of concepts. This classification is discovered when concepts are compared one against another and appear to pertain to a similar phenomenon. Thus, the concepts are grouped together under a higher order, more abstract concept called a category.

For example, when grouping together the concepts of perception, satisfaction and cooperation, these could fall under the broad category of 'brand identity'. The process of creating categories is creative. 'Creating categories triggers the construction of a conceptual scheme that suits the data. This scheme helps the researcher to ask questions, to compare across data, to change or drop categories and to make a hierarchical order of them' (Basit, 2003: 144). Categories are formed by a group of codes, which later lead to the creation of themes. Think of themes as a way of linking together categories that express similar meaning. At this stage in the analytical process, emphasis is on developing a more meaningful understanding of the research findings.

STEP 5: IDENTIFY PATTERNS AND CONNECTIONS WITHIN AND BETWEEN CATEGORIES

A key aspect of interpreting data is looking for relationships between codes and developing categories and themes that you have identified within each transcript. The nature of the questions you might ask yourself concerning each category may include:

• Is there a relationship between categories?
• How important are these relationships?
• Is this consistent or does it contradict earlier research?

Although time consuming and challenging, attempting to answer these questions can be a rewarding exercise, especially as patterns and relationships in the data start to emerge. At this stage in the analytical process, you are moving beyond simply describing the data, to one of interpretation. As well as looking for relationships in the data, you are engaging in data reduction and moving from codes to categories to themes. Figure 15.4 shows an illustration of the outcomes of qualitative analysis. The 'codes' represent the keywords that have emerged from the data. These codes are then grouped together as they have something in common (categories). For example, 'recycling' and 'sustainability' are clearly associated with the category 'packaging'. Similarly, 'symbol' and 'sign' are associated with the category 'logo'. What links these categories together (the theme) is brand identity. A study may have generated one major theme, or possibly a number of themes may have emerged from the data.

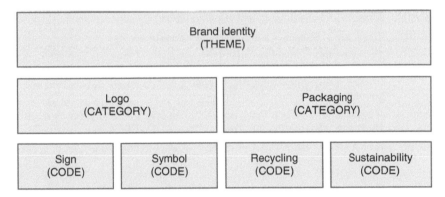

Figure 15.4   Moving from codes to theme

STEP 6: INTERPRETATION AND WRITING THE REPORT/PROJECT

The final analytical step is writing the report, such as a dissertation or journal article. Writing up is something we examine at length in Chapter 18. In terms of writing up qualitative findings, there are various methods used by researchers. Remember that qualitative data is not just written text. If your qualitative analysis is based on observational data, then there is also an opportunity to include visual data in your project. The use of visuals, such as word clouds, is a creative way of illustrating results. One notable way of presenting qualitative data is the use of verbatim quotes. If you have recorded and transcribed your data, then including verbatim quotations in your project gives the reader a view onto the world of the research participant. In short, their first-hand experience as opposed to purely numerical values or comments interpreted by the researcher.

Braun and Clarke (2012) make a clear distinction between writing a quantitative research report and a qualitative research report. In terms of the latter, writing and analysis are thoroughly interwoven – from informal writing of notes to the more formal processes of analysis and report writing. The purpose of your project is to provide a compelling story about your data based on your analysis. This is where structuring your results on the basis of clear themes can help to provide your story. The inclusion of verbatim quotations, structured on a thematic basis, helps to illustrate to your reader the kind of material you gathered through your inductive findings. In addition, Renner and Taylor-Powell (2003) also suggest creating a diagram with boxes and arrows as a useful way to show how the pieces of your research findings fit together.

TYPES OF QUALITATIVE DATA ANALYSIS

In the last section, we looked at the typical steps associated with qualitative data analysis. Although many aspects of these steps apply to various types of qualitative analysis, there are certain differences depending on your choice of analytical method. Table 15.3 shows a list of some of the more commonly used methods to analyzing qualitative data. By no means exhaustive, the purpose of the table is to provide a brief description of each method. Let us examine each one in turn.

Table 15.3   Approaches to qualitative data analysis

Approach	Description
Thematic analysis	A method for identifying, analyzing and reporting patterns (themes) within data.
Narrative analysis	The study of stories or a chronological series of events.
Content analysis	The systematic, objective, quantitative analysis of message characteristics. Quantitative content analysis involves the counting of data. Qualitative data analysis involves a qualitative approach to coding and its interpretations and does not use counting.
Grounded theory	A systematic approach that involves the discovery of theory that is shaped by the views of a large number of participants.
Discourse analysis	A broad term that relates to a number of ways to analyze written or spoken language.

THEMATIC ANALYSIS

According to Braun and Clarke (2006: 79), 'Thematic analysis is a method for identifying, analyzing and reporting patterns (themes) within data. It minimally organizes and describes your data set in (rich) detail'. As with any analytical method, the decision to use thematic analysis should be based on the overall research direction more than a desire to select an easy-to-follow method of analysis (Kiger and Varpio, 2020).

Earlier in the chapter, we defined a theme as 'a way of linking together categories that convey similar meanings'. Similarly, Joffe (2012) notes that a theme can be thought of as a 'specific pattern of meaning found in the data'. This can be directly observable, such as explicit reference to 'trust' across interview transcripts. Alternatively, it can contain more implicit reference to 'trust'. For example, if examining trust between organizational buyers and sellers, a buyer may imply that they trust their supplier to deliver products on time without mentioning the word 'trust'. Implication could be by reference to 'we have confidence that our supplier will deliver products on time'.

Researchers should be clear on the criteria that can and cannot be coded within such themes. As Joffe (2012) points out, in this sense, themes are patterns of explicit and implicit content.

Themes can be drawn from existing theory(s) on a particular research topic. Again, if you adopt this approach to your thematic analysis, it can be described as 'deductive'. In contrast, if you choose for themes to emerge from the raw data, then this can be described as an 'inductive approach'. Thus, theory is an outcome.

Thematic research is often associated with focus groups or interviews. A questionnaire using open-ended questions also produces qualitative data which makes it ideal for adopting thematic analysis. Table 15.4 shows a table from a study into themes associated with restaurant advertisements from a local newspaper. In the first column you can see themes, such as 'price' and 'location', while the column to the right shows the keywords associated with each theme.

Table 15.4 Common themes and keywords identified within restaurant advertisements

Common themes	Keywords
Price	Value for money; premium; competitive; payment methods.
Location	Address; size; amenities; parking; ease of access.
Promotion	Offers; special offers; discounts; loyalty; points.
Awards	Prizes; rating; reputation; ranking.
Service	Fast service; efficient; experienced staff; politeness.
Food	Menu; dishes; main course; starter.

Braun and Clarke (2012) recommend a six-phase approach to thematic analysis:

1. Familiarizing yourself with the data.
2. Generating initial codes.
3. Searching for themes.
4. Reviewing potential themes.
5. Under this point, Braun and Clarke (2012: 65) note key questions to ask:

   - Is this a theme (it could be just a code)?
   - If it is a theme, what is the quality of this theme (does it tell me something useful about the data set and my research question)?
   - What are the boundaries of this theme (what does it include and exclude)?
   - Are there enough (meaningful) data to support this theme (is the theme thin or thick)?
   - Are the data too diverse and wide ranging (does the theme lack coherence)?

6. Defining and naming themes.
7. Producing the report.

You will note that the process is similar to the six steps process to qualitative analysis we went through earlier in the chapter. However, the research aim here is to develop themes and a broad view meaning of data.

The type of data collected for thematic analysis is typically based on data collected using focus groups, interviews or narratives. In simple terms, the key steps in thematic analysis are – code, develop categories and then combine categories to form themes, as shown in Figure 15.4.

NARRATIVE ANALYSIS

Narrative analysis is the study of stories or a chronological series of events. Broadly speaking, there are two types of narrative: a personal narrative relating to someone's experience of a particular situation, and a 'life story' narrative that relates to someone's experience over a number of years.

An example of a personal narrative might be a consumer's account of the customer service they received when dealing with a particular company, while a 'life story' narrative might relate to someone's career progression since leaving school. Narrative analysis can be useful if you are conducting ethnographic research and are interested in the background of your respondents. Moreover, it can be useful for comparing the lives of individuals over time.

Key themes that can be explored when carrying out narrative analysis include asking the participant:

- to comment on a major event
- to discuss the most influential people in their lives
- to discuss significant life chapters
- to anticipate future career development
- to discuss personal ideologies or to reflect on decisions they have made.

You can illustrate your findings from narrative research using verbatim extracts from your interview transcripts. Below is an example of how to present a direct quote from a narrative study within the main body of a research project. This example is a personal narrative of a General Manager's working experience in their current role:

'In terms of establishing the pure-line programme, we are right on course. In terms of increasing market share, year-by-year we are doing that. And now we have another five-year objective, which we have just added on internally. And I think, based on the conversation I have had with my colleagues this morning, we are already ahead of the first year's target of that 5-year plan.'

(General Manager, UK Food Producer)

As mentioned earlier in the chapter, avoid simply listing verbatim comments in your research project. There needs to be evidence of critical analysis. For example, in terms of the quote from the General Manager of the UK food producer, how does his/her comment compare to other comments? Is this the 'norm' when compared to other responses? Is there anything particularly interesting about their comments?

CONTENT ANALYSIS

'Content analysis may be briefly defined as the systematic, objective, quantitative analysis of message characteristics' (Neuendorf, 2017: 2). There are numerous definitions of content analysis. In addition, the term is also viewed in the context of both qualitative and quantitative research. However, although content analysis can be used for qualitative research, the general consensus is that it is largely associated with quantitative research.

The advantage of content analysis is the ability to explore what is said (e.g. context) and not said (e.g. form) in successive stages of the interview.

Content analysis is often viewed as doing a word frequency count. Although this approach can be used when conducting content analysis, there are limitations with just relying on frequency counts. For example, a major potential limitation is that frequency counts may include words that are used out of context, or words that have multiple meanings (e.g. an institution can refer to a university, or a private or public sector organization). A respondent's level of English may also mean that certain words and phrases are used more frequently as a result of 'limited' English language capability.

'Content analysis is a way of systematically converting text to numerical variables for quantitative data analysis' (Collis and Hussey, 2003: 250). Content analysis usually involves the following steps:

1. Identify the unit of analysis – recording unit, sentence or paragraph.
2. Choose categories that are relevant to the issues being studied. They must be reliable, so that if someone else repeated the analysis they would find the same information (increased reliability).
3. Once you have chosen your categories, read through the material and apply these codes to units of text.
4. Tabulate the material. Present the categories and list the assertions under them.

First, the unit of analysis in content analysis is varied and can apply to words, sentences, grammatical structures or even themes (Prior, 2014).

Two alternative generic approaches to content analysis are typically taken: 'form orientated' (objective) analysis, which involves routine counting of words or concrete references; and 'meaning orientated' (subjective) analysis (Smith and Taffler, 2000: 627).

Content analysis is a method that is associated with the interpretation of both written and visual material. The latter is sometimes referred to by researchers as 'visual analysis' or more specifically 'visual content analysis'. Bell (2001: 14) defines *visual content analysis* as a systematic, observational method used for testing hypotheses about the ways in which the media represent people, events, situations, and so on. It allows the quantification of samples of observable content classified into distinct categories. An example of using visual content analysis is a study carried out by Kerkhoven et al. (2016). The aim of their research was to determine whether science education resources for primary school contained gender-biased visuals. The study involved analyzing visual content from science education resources on selected websites. Specifically, the total number of men and women depicted, and the profession and activity of each person in the visuals were noted.

Image 15.1   Content analysis includes verbal and visual analysis

Source: iStock (photo ID: 938423340)

Content analysis of visual material can involve analyzing images that may come from secondary or primary findings. Images may include television advertisements, photographs, outdoor advertising or pictures from magazine articles. For example, a study into celebrity endorsement in magazine advertising may involve searching the contents of a magazine publication for a six-month period.

Bell (2001: 14) notes examples of the typical research questions addressed using visual content analysis:

1. Questions of priority/salience of media content: how visible (how frequently, how large, in what order in a programme) are different kinds of images, stories, events represented? 'Agenda setting' studies of news broadcasts would be an example of this kind of question.
2. Questions of 'bias': comparative questions about the duration, frequency, priority or salience of representation of, say, political personalities, issues, policies, or of 'positive' versus 'negative' features of representation.
3. Historical changes in modes of representation of, for example gender, occupational, class, or ethically codified images in particular types of publications or television genres.

An example of visual analysis carried out by one of my former marketing students relates to 'the use of celebrity endorsement in TV advertising'. The analysis may involve asking questions such as:

- How many advertisements used celebrity endorsement?
- What is the message from each advertisement?
- What is the general content of each advertisement?

Ostensibly, it is less time consuming than discourse analysis or narrative analysis, but you may find that interpreting your data on the basis of visual images is more challenging than using written data. Remember that we can make a distinction between qualitative and quantitative content analysis. The latter involves coding, developing categories, and then counting and comparing the frequency of categories between groups. Data collection methods that are suited to content analysis, again, include interviews, focus groups and narrative research. Finally, Table 15.5 shows categories ranked by frequency of occurrence. In this example the categories are derived from interview transcripts. Interviewees were questioned on their working environment, including open-ended questions, such as 'How does your current role match your skills set?'. The most frequently occurring category is 'Communication', followed by 'Decision-making'.

Table 15.5   Categories ranked by frequency of occurrence

Rank	Category	Frequency
1	Communication	98
2	Decision-making	85
3	Negotiation	66
4	Creativity	42
5	Teamwork	36
6	Adaptability	28

GROUNDED THEORY

Grounded Theory is defined as a qualitative research design in which the inquirer generates a general explanation (a theory) of a process, action, or interaction shaped by the views of a large number of participants (Corbin and Strauss, 2008). In this case, theory is 'grounded' from the data, rather than being applied from the outset.

Grounded Theory was developed by two sociologists – Barney Glaser and Anselm Strauss. If you decide to use Grounded Theory, then you do not start with any preconceived ideas as to what theories might be developed from your data. The stages that researchers using Grounded Theory typically go through are as follows (Dillon and Taylor, 2015):

- Open coding
- Axial coding
- Selective coding
- Theoretical integration

Open coding

Open coding allows the researcher to see the direction in which to take their research so it can become selective and focused conceptually on a particular social problem (Glaser, 2016). It involves labelling and categorizing your data. In essence, the steps are largely the same for Grounded Theory as they are for other qualitative methods. Open coding aims to express the data in the form of concepts. For example, individual words and expressions are 'extracted' from the transcript and the meaning attached to them. Data can be coded line by line, sentence by sentence or paragraph by paragraph. The outcome of open coding is a list of codes. For example, see Table 15.6: the first column shows the concepts that have derived from the data, while the second column shows the open codes.

Table 15.6   Concepts that arose during open coding

Concepts	Open codes
Organization	Market share; number of employees; internal structure; culture; supplier networks; vision; mission; market coverage; market orientation; location of headquarters.
Communication	Electronic; internal; external; synchronous, asynchronous, time; channels; communication issues.
Customers	Loyalty; characteristics; buying process; target audience; size; location; satisfaction; dissatisfaction.
Brand	Logo; identity; loyalty; perceptions; image; colours; slogan; standardization; adaptation.
Trust	Personal; mistrust; corporate; organizational; long-term; commitment; contract.

Böhm (2004: 271) points out that in order to avoid simply paraphrasing, the following 'theory generating' questions are asked for the text.

- What? What is at issue here? What phenomenon is being addressed?
- Who? What persons or actors are involved? What roles do they play? How do they interact?
- How? What aspects of the phenomenon are addressed (or not addressed)?
- When? How long? Where? How much? How strongly?
- Why? What reasons are given or may be deduced?
- For what reason? With what intention, and for what purpose?
- By what means? What methods, tactics and strategies are used to achieve the goal? In coding researchers use their background.

Axial coding

Axial coding helps to refine and differentiate the categories that result from open coding. In this stage of the analysis, the researcher starts to select certain categories so as to put them in some kind of order. The researcher adopts a critical approach in an attempt to establish relationships between categories. Axial coding is based on relating categories with subcategories.

Selective coding

Selective coding is the last coding process in Grounded Theory. By this stage in the analysis, the researcher has identified all of the categories in the data. Selective coding is based on identifying a core category that represents the main theme of the research, i.e. the focal category to have been generated from the data. This is the category of data that accounts for most of the variation of the central phenomenon of concern and around which all the other categories are integrated.

Theoretical integration

It is important to stress that Grounded Theory is an iterative process of analysis and induction and not a linear step-by-step process. In general, Charmaz (2008: 27) refers to Grounded Theory methods as 'a logically consistent set of data collection and analytic procedures aimed to develop theory. Grounded Theory methods consist of a set of inductive strategies'. In short, the aim of Grounded Theory is to generate a theory/framework informed from data about a particular process or social phenomenon.

DISCOURSE ANALYSIS

Discourse analysis can be defined as 'the study of how people achieve things with language, or, in some versions, how language does things to people, sometimes despite their conscious intentions and interests' (Cocking and Drury, 2014: 88). In business research, discourse analysis might apply to transcripts of conversations, advertising campaign(s) and content from magazines. Given the qualitative nature of discourse analysis, sample size is not such an issue as the focus is on the way the language is used, as opposed to the number of participants and making generalizations to the wider population.

According to Hormuth (2009), one of the key advantages of discourse analysis in comparison to other qualitative methods is that authentic conversation is recorded and analyzed. This enables researchers to reconstruct and describe the actual communicative processes.

There are a number of approaches associated with discourse analysis. The main disadvantage is that it is extremely time consuming. A great deal of time is devoted to transcribing and interpreting data. Hence, it tends not to be a popular choice among business and management students.

USING COMPUTER-ASSISTED QUALITATIVE DATA ANALYSIS SOFTWARE

The approach to undertaking qualitative analysis can be done using a variety of software packages. Computer-Assisted Qualitative Data Analysis Software (CAQDAS) refers to specialized software packages that can be helpful when it comes to coding and counting the number of times a phrase or word feature in the data. However, many of the types of qualitative analysis discussed in this chapter can be undertaken manually or using Microsoft Word or Excel. For example, if using content analysis to count the number of times respondents refer to 'conflict' when discussing workplace culture, then Microsoft Word or Excel can be used to highlight and count the number of times respondents make explicit reference to 'conflict'. Linneberg and Korsgaard (2019: 260–261) point out that qualitative analysis does not necessarily require specialist software:

The basic coding operation can be done in various ways. In smaller projects with a limited amount of data, simple colour coding with markers may suffice, with one colour for each code. The copy-and-paste function in software such as Word or Excel will also allow you to copy portions of text or images from your data documents into new documents.

Having said that, many qualitative researchers now use specialist software such as NVivo. It is highly likely that your university or college will hold a copy(s) of these software packages. From my experience, NVivo tends not to be as widely used as quantitative software such as IBM SPSS Statistics. A full discussion on how to use NVivo is beyond the scope of this book (see Jackson and Bazeley (2019) in the further reading section of this chapter).

The likelihood is that you will use technology all the way through your qualitative research process. However, writing notes or memos is still a widely used practice by qualitative researchers. Weitzman (2000: 805–806) provides a useful checklist of some of the things computers can be used for to facilitate qualitative analysis:

1. making notes in the field
2. writing up or transcribing field notes
3. editing: correcting, extending or revising notes
4. coding: attaching key words or tags to segments of text, graphics, audio, or video to permit later retrieval
5. storage: keeping text in an organized database
6. search and retrieval: locating relevant segments of text and making them available for inspection
7. data 'linking': connecting relevant data segments to each other, forming categories, clusters or networks of information
8. memoing: writing reflective commentaries on some aspect of the data, theory or method as a basis for deeper analysis
9. content analysis: counting frequencies, sequences or locations of words and phrases
10. data display: placing selected or reduced data in a condensed, organized format, such as a matrix or network, for inspection
11. conclusion drawing and verification: aiding in the interpretation of displayed data and the testing or confirmation of findings
12. theory building: developing systematic, conceptually coherent explanations of findings; testing hypotheses
13. graphic mapping: creating diagrams that depict findings or theories
14. report writing: interim and final.

BOX 15.1: RESEARCH SNAPSHOT

An excellent way to show categories and their relationship with themes is to use a diagram. The two shaded themes in Figure 15.5 are 'Consumer preference' and 'Brand identity'. Remember that a category is a group of codes that clearly have something in common, whereas a theme is a way of linking together categories that convey similar meanings; for example 'logo', 'packaging', 'message' and 'colour' are categories that relate to the theme of 'brand identity'.

A process of using pen and paper to draw your ideas of possible categories, sub-categories and themes, illustrating their relationships, is all part of the iterative process of qualitative data analysis. Much of this chapter has discussed analysis in the context of textual data, but drawing your ideas in the form of a mind map is a useful exercise. Moreover, a diagram such as the one illustrated in Figure 15.5 can be used in your research project to show the reader the process you go through when analyzing your data.

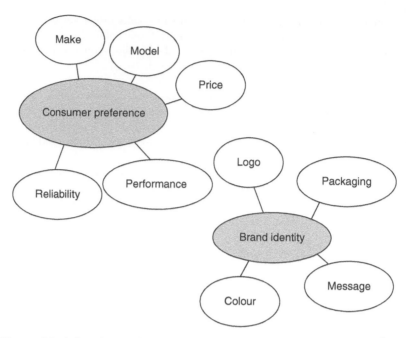

Figure 15.5   Themes (shaded) and categories

Image 15.2   Concept Cartoon 'Types of qualitative data analysis'

Image 15.2 is a Concept Cartoon that shows characters expressing their views on types of qualitative data analysis. Think about the different views and use them to provoke a discussion with fellow students. What do you think? Do you think narrative analysis is the best method for analyzing qualitative data?

EXAMPLE OF STUDIES USING QUALITATIVE ANALYSIS

In this part of the chapter, we examine two examples of studies that have used qualitative analysis. By now, you should be aware that there are many different approaches to both data collection and data analysis; the purpose of this section is to introduce you to just some of the ways researchers use qualitative analysis in practice. If you are considering conducting qualitative research, it is always useful to read journal articles that have used your intended approach as this can help to generate ideas and develop possible 'takeaways' for your own research. As with all data collection and analytical tools, once again, what drives your decision-making is the nature of your research objectives and research questions. Moreover, consider the existing body of literature on your chosen topic and also the views from your research stakeholders, such as your supervisor. Remember that qualitative data analysis is much more time consuming when compared to quantitative analysis, so do consider the time and resources required before conducting qualitative research.

Example A

In this first example, Hirudayaraj and Baker (2018) used content analysis to examine online Human Resource Development (HRD) job advertisements. The researchers used deductive analysis, whereby they analyzed the content of the job postings to cull out competencies (knowledge, skills and abilities) employers expected potential employees to possess or demonstrate. They then compared this 'content' consisting of expected HRD knowledge and skills against the competencies identified in the 2013 ASTD (the American Society for Training and Development) Competency Framework.

The researchers developed a coding sheet (coding frame) that represented ten areas of expertise and their accompanying sub-codes that reflected the task statements or activities. The coding framework included education qualifications, work experience, knowledge, skills, technical skills, industry and additional information and responsibilities. Next, the researchers went through manually individual job postings to locate each code, counted the number of times this code appeared in the data and kept a track of the counted codes to avoid duplicate counting. The job postings collected were predominantly from the following industries: health, education, manufacturing, technology, retail, government, banking, sports, insurance, non-governmental or not for profit, consulting, food, hotel, energy and entertainment.

Data calculations involved determining the counts of the areas of expertise then dividing by the total number of job ads evaluated (n = 459) to determine the percentage of each. The percentage of requirements by knowledge and responsibility elements were then displayed in a tabular format.

This is an example of quantitative content analysis as the facts are presented in the form of frequency expressed as a percentage or actual numbers of key categories (Berelson, 1952). The nature of the research is deductive as the researchers are using an existing framework – the 2013 ASTD Competency Framework. Conversely, if the researchers decided not to use a framework, then we can view the study as an inductive approach.

Example B

In this study by Conaway and Wardrope (2010), the authors used a Grounded Theory approach to thematically analyze the annual report letters written by the CEOs of 30 US-based companies and 24

(Continued)

Latin American-based companies listed on the New York Stock Exchange. The aim of the analysis was to ascertain common topics, stylistic (written) features and embedded cultural attributes.

The researchers adopted an inductive approach to analyzing the CEO letters and used open-coding as a means to discovering 'thematic patterns'.

Developing central themes

The authors encountered various central topics in a sentence or paragraph, so their process involved underlining the topic and noting it in the margin by writing a keyword. One of the participants – Fernando Cañas, Chairman of the Board of Banco de Chile – mentioned the topic of corporate governance when writing about an industry initiative, '... which is designed to modernize and make corporate governance rules more efficient ...'. Thus, the researchers noted the subject 'corporate governance' in the margin of the letter. Likewise, Chairman Cañas wrote later in the letter, 'Our Corporation also recognizes its role in the community and its efforts in this area are focused on producing a social benefit over time'. Here, the researchers noted 'social/community involvement' in the margin. Using these methods, the authors recorded these topics in the margins as they read through the letters.

Next, the researchers reviewed the keywords in the margins and looked for frequent repetition of words. Similar words were grouped together and placed in general categories or themes. CEO and Chairman Lorenzo Zambrano of Cemex Mexico, for instance, wrote about annual sales figures, compounded growth rates and operating cash flow in the first two paragraphs of his letter. Similarly, he discussed using free cash flow to reduce debt and the leverage ratio. Individual topics such as these were grouped under the general category of 'Financial Reporting'.

After developing the keyword list under various categories, the authors used content analysis software, NVivo 8, to process the extent to which reoccurring words and relationships appeared in the letters. Findings showed that the eight most common themes included: 'Financial reporting', 'Infrastructure and expansion', 'external environment', 'customer relations', 'corporate governance', 'leadership', 'social responsibility' and 'vision, mission, outlook'.

The researchers than used a table to show the results. The first column featured the list of themes ordered according to the total number of keyword references for that theme. When an NVivo search was conducted on each keyword, the total word count was calculated. Thus, the theme of financial reporting resulted in 1,096 words appearing in the data set related to financial reporting, which emerged as the predominant theme in both Latin and US letters.

This is an interesting article as the authors discuss explicitly the steps they went through when analyzing the data. The outcome of the research generated a total of eight themes. The generation of this number of themes is in keeping with many studies that use a Grounded Theory approach.

CHAPTER SUMMARY

- Qualitative data analysis is any kind of analysis that produces findings or concepts and hypotheses, as in Grounded Theory, which are not arrived at by statistical methods.

- In qualitative research, analysis of the collected data is a particularly important process that is hugely time consuming and requires patience.

- Visual data analysis involves analyzing images that may come from secondary or primary findings.

- Narrative analysis is the study of stories or a chronological series of events.

- Discourse analysis examines both spoken and written language.

- Grounded Theory is a method in which the theory is developed from the data, as opposed to applying theory from the outset.

- Quantitative content analysis is a way of systematically converting text to numerical variables for quantitative data analysis.

- Coding is identifying segments of meaning in your data and labelling them with a code as a means to categorizing the text in order to establish thematic ideas.

- A code is a label which shows the same theoretical or descriptive idea and is applied to data. This includes single words, sentences, phrases, paragraphs, parts of pictures, sections of an audio recording.

- The stages that the researchers using Grounded Theory typically go through are open coding, axial coding, selective coding and theoretical integration.

QUESTIONS FOR REVIEW

1. What are the advantages of qualitative data analysis?

2. Outline the steps you are likely to go through when analyzing qualitative data.

3. Discuss the challenges associated with qualitative data analysis.

4. Outline how you might illustrate verbatim comments within your research project.

5. Explain the reasons why participant observation might be an appropriate form of data collection.

6. What is meant by the term data coding?

7. Give an example of how content analysis might be applied in practice.

8. Outline the key difference between qualitative and quantitative data.

9. Give an example of how a researcher might use discourse analysis.

10. What is meant by the term 'discourse analysis?'

STUDENT SCENARIO: HEIDI'S CONTENT ANALYSIS OF ADVERTISING CAMPAIGNS

Heidi's research project aimed to investigate how UK supermarket Christmas magazine advertising campaigns had changed since the late 1970s. Heidi was particularly keen to examine the content, message and how communications and the brands had changed over time.

Using judgment sampling, Heidi took a sample of 50 Christmas advertising campaigns from leading glossy magazines from the period 1980 to 2020. These were based on several different supermarket brands. Heidi was keen to see how the advertising had come to rely more on a verbal and visual narrative (story) as opposed to a largely verbal, explanatory type of advertising.

(Continued)

Developing a coding frame

Heidi decided to develop a coding frame by using a combination of predetermined codes and codes that emerged from her analysis. The coding frame contained both code name, definition and an example. As part of her analysis, Heidi intended on using memoing to reflect on the analytical process and to also take notes. Heidi expected her coding frame to develop and change as she became more familiar with the data.

Using colour coding

Rather than using NVivo, Heidi decided to code her data using colour coding and Microsoft Word. First, she used each uploaded transcript in Microsoft Word to read through and familiarize herself with the data. Next, using the coding frame, Heidi assigned a colour to each code and highlighted the text or phrase that related to each code. For example, one of Heidi's explicit, predetermined codes referred to 'love'. In other words, each time the word 'love' was mentioned in the transcript, Heidi highlighted the word with the colour 'red'. However, coding also relied on implicit codes that implied the word 'love'. An example here is 'A father gave his daughter a Christmas gift under the Christmas tree'. In this example, 'love' was a predetermined code within Heidi's coding frame. Colours were also used for codes that emerged from the data.

Questions

1. Give an alternative approach to qualitative analysis Heidi might choose to adopt when analyzing her data.
2. Discuss why it is important for Heidi to code her data.
3. Outline the different ways Heidi can ensure reliability during the data analysis process.

Hint: Remember that there is no one definitive way to conduct qualitative data analysis. However, it is important to consider the relationship between the steps involved in the analytical process.

FURTHER READING

Flick. U. (2018) *Designing Qualitative Research* (2nd edn). London: Sage.

A concise introduction to qualitative research that includes an entire chapter on analyzing qualitative data.

Jackson, K. and Bazeley, P. (2019) *Qualitative Data Analysis with NVivo*. London: Sage.

A comprehensive guide on how to use NVivo software for qualitative data analysis.

Rodon, J. and Pastor, J.A. (2007) 'Applying grounded theory to study the implementation of an inter-organizational information system', *Electronic Journal of Business Research Methods*, 5 (2): 71–82.

This paper shows the application of Grounded Theory (GT) method in a research project. The authors provide a clear, systematic structure on their Grounded Theory building process, including coding.

Sbaraini, A., Carter, S.M., Evans, R.W. and Blinkhorn, A. (2011) 'How to do a grounded theory study: A worked example of a study of dental practices', *BMC Medical Research Methodology*, 11 (1): 1–10.

This is a useful article that gives a worked example of a Grounded Theory project. The authors aim to provide a model for practice. Although the paper is from the medical literature, it still offers a useful guide on how to do a Grounded Theory study.

Silverman, D. (2013) *Doing Qualitative Research: A Practical Handbook.* London: Sage.

A thorough book on qualitative research that includes a chapter on developing data analysis and using computers to analyze qualitative data.

Thorne, S. (2020) 'On the use and abuse of verbatim quotations in qualitative research reports', *Nurse Author & Editor*, *30* (3): 2.

A short article that discusses the importance and how to use verbatim quotations within qualitative research reports. These points are equally applicable to student researchers.

REFERENCES

Basit, T. (2003) 'Manual or electronic? The role of coding in qualitative data analysis', *Educational Research*, 45 (2): 143–154.

Bell, P. (2001) 'Content analysis of visual images', in T. Van Leeuwen and C. Jewitt (eds), *Handbook of Visual Analysis* (pp. 10–34). Thousand Oaks, CA: Sage.

Berelson, B. (1952) *Content Analysis in Communications Research.* New York: Free Press.

Böhm, A. (2004) 'Theoretical coding: Text analysis in Grounded Theory', in U. Flick, E. Von Kardorff and I. Steinke (eds), *What is Qualitative Research? An Introduction to the Field. A Companion to Qualitative Research* (pp. 270–275). London: Sage.

Braun, V. and Clarke, V. (2006) 'Using thematic analysis in psychology', *Qualitative Research in Psychology*, 3 (2): 77–101.

Braun, V. and Clarke, V. (2012) 'Thematic analysis', in H.E. Cooper, P.M. Camic, D.L. Long, A.T. Panter, D. Rindskopf and K.J. Sheranter (eds), *APA Handbook of Research Methods in Psychology* (pp. 57–71). Washington, DC: APA Books.

Charmaz, K. (2008) 'Grounded theory', in J.A. Smith (ed.), *Qualitative Psychology: A Practical Guide to Research Methods* (pp. 81–110). London: Sage.

Cocking, C. and Drury, J. (2014) 'Talking about Hillsborough: "Panic" as discourse in survivors' accounts of the 1989 football stadium disaster', *Journal of Community & Applied Social Psychology*, 24 (2): 86–99.

Collis, J. and Hussey, R. (2003) *Business Research: A Practical Guide for Undergraduate and Postgraduate Students* (2nd edn). Basingstoke: Palgrave Macmillan.

Conaway, R.N. and Wardrope, W.J. (2010) 'Do their words matter? Thematic analysis of US and Latin American CEO letters', *Journal of Business Communication*, 47 (2): 141–168.

Corbin, J. and Strauss, A. (2008) *Basics of Qualitative Research: Techniques and Procedures for Developing Grounded Theory* (3rd edn). London: Sage.

Dillon, S. and Taylor, H. (2015) 'Employing grounded theory to uncover behavioral competencies of information technology project managers', *Project Management Journal*, 46 (4): 90–104.

Glaser, B.G. (2016) 'Open coding descriptions', *Grounded Theory Review*, 15 (2): 108–110.

Hannam, K. and Knox, D. (2005) 'Discourse analysis in tourism research: A critical perspective', *Tourism Recreation Research*, 30 (2): 23–30.

Hirudayaraj, M. and Baker, R. (2018) 'HRD competencies: Analysis of employer expectations from online job postings', *European Journal of Training and Development*, 42 (9): 577–596.

Hormuth, J. (2009) 'The benefits of discourse analysis for human resource management', *German Journal of Human Resource Management*, 23 (2): 147–165.

Joffe, H. (2012) 'Thematic analysis', in D. Harper and A. Thompson (eds), *Qualitative Research Methods in Mental Health and Psychotherapy: A Guide for Students and Practitioners* (pp. 209–223). Chichester: Wiley-Blackwell.

Kerkhoven, A.H., Russo, P., Land-Zandstra, A.M., Saxena, A. and Rodenburg, F.J. (2016) 'Gender stereotypes in science education resources: A visual content analysis', *PloS One*, 11 (11): e0165037.

Kiger, M.E. and Varpio, L. (2020) 'Thematic analysis of qualitative data: AMEE Guide No. 131', *Medical Teacher*, 42 (8): 846–854.

Linneberg, M.S. and Korsgaard, S. (2019) 'Coding qualitative data: A synthesis guiding the novice', *Qualitative Research Journal*, 19 (3): 259–270.

Miles, M.B. and Huberman, A.B. (1994) *Qualitative Data Analysis: An Expanded Sourcebook* (2nd edn). Thousand Oaks, CA: Sage.

Montgomery, P. and Bailey, P.H. (2007) 'Field notes and theoretical memos in grounded theory', *Western Journal of Nursing Research*, 29 (1): 65–79.

Neuendorf, K. (2017) 'Defining content analysis', in K. Neuendorf, *The Content Analysis Guidebook* (pp. 1–35). Thousand Oaks, CA: Sage.

O'Connor, C. and Joffe, H. (2020) 'Intercoder reliability in qualitative research: Debates and practical guidelines', *International Journal of Qualitative Methods*, 19: 1–13.

Patton, M. (1990) *Qualitative Evaluation and Research Methods* (2nd edn). Newbury Park, CA: Sage.

Prior, L. (2014) *The Oxford Handbook of Qualitative Research*. Oxford: Oxford University Press.

Renner, M. and Taylor-Powell, E. (2003). *Analyzing Qualitative Data*. Programme Development & Evaluation, University of Wisconsin-Extension Cooperative Extension.

Saldaña, J. (2015) *The Coding Manual for Qualitative Researchers*. Thousand Oaks, CA: Sage.

Schutt, R.K. (2018) *Investigating the Social World: The Process and Practice of Research*. London: Sage.

Shin, K.R., Kim, M.Y. and Chung, S.E. (2009) 'Methods and strategies utilized in published qualitative research', *Qualitative Health Research*, 19 (6): 850–858.

Smith, M. and Taffler, R.J. (2000) 'The chairman's statement: A content analysis of discretionary narrative disclosures', *Accounting, Auditing & Accountability Journal*, 13 (5): 624–647.

Strauss, A. (1987) *Qualitative Analysis for Social Scientists*. Cambridge: Cambridge University Press.

Strauss, A. and Corbin, J. (1990) *Basics of Qualitative Research: Grounded Theory Procedures and Techniques*. Newbury Park, CA: Sage.

Weitzman, E.A. (2000) 'Software and qualitative research', in N.K. Denzin and Y.S. Lincoln (eds), *Handbook of Qualitative Research* (pp. 803–820). Thousand Oaks, CA: Sage.

Wiggins, S. (2017) *Discursive Psychology: Theory, Method and Applications*. London: Sage.

Wilson, J. (2014) *Essentials of Business Research: A Guide to Doing Your Research Project* (2nd edn). London: Sage.

16

ANALYZING AND MANAGING QUANTITATIVE DATA

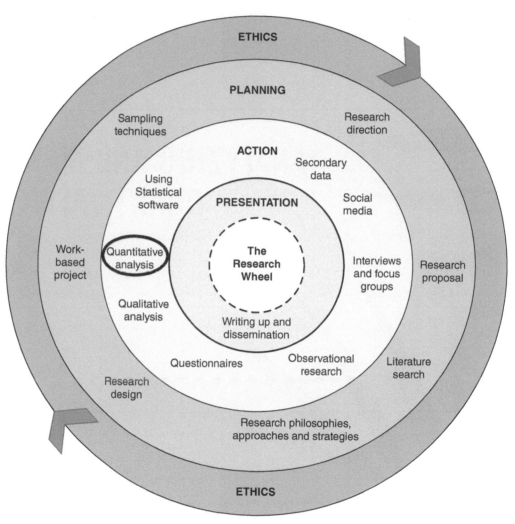

Figure 16.1   The Research Wheel

Learning objectives

By the end of this chapter, you should be able to:

- know what is meant by the term quantitative data analysis

- understand how to summarize data

- apply measures of central tendency

- apply measures of dispersion

- understand inferential statistics

- appreciate the role of the research supervisor in relation to quantitative data analysis.

INTRODUCTION

In the preceding chapter, we examined how to analyze qualitative data. In this chapter, we continue with our focus on data analysis, but our attention here turns to quantitative data analysis. The purpose of the chapter is to provide you with an introduction to the various methods you can use to analyze quantitative data.

A detailed discussion is beyond the scope of this book. However, it will cover the necessary steps required to conduct elementary quantitative analysis. Furthermore, in the next chapter, you will find a guide to putting what you have learned in this chapter into practice as we go through how to use IBM SPSS Statistics Version 27.

The chapter commences with a brief introduction to the nature of quantitative analysis and goes on to discuss the different methods you may consider when analyzing your data. The analytical methods you choose largely depend on the purpose of your research. When conducting quantitative analysis, it is important to know 'which' methods to use and 'why' you have chosen a particular method. Remember that the ability to justify your chosen analytical technique(s) is something your reader is likely to want to know. Moreover, certain conditions need to be met before choosing your methods of analysis. For example, the number and types of variable you are looking to analyze will ultimately influence your choice of quantitative methods.

Next, we look at how to organize your data for analysis, followed by how to summarize your data using descriptive statistics. This section also looks at presenting data.

Moving on, we examine inferential statistics. This includes inferential statistical techniques, such as correlation. The chapter then proceeds to discuss statistical software packages. The final section features examples of studies from academic journals that have used quantitative analysis. The rationale behind this section is to give you an insight into how quantitative analysis is used in practice.

As you can see by Figure 16.1, 'Quantitative analysis' is in the 'Action' layer in The Research Wheel model (EPAP). Remember that the Action layer is the stage in the research process involving a number of activities, not least collecting and analyzing data. If you are conducting a purely qualitative study, then quantitative analysis will not be something that you need to conduct during your research. However, it is still an important topic. This is especially the case if you have yet to decide on your research strategy – the extent you are going to use qualitative and/or quantitative data in your research.

WHAT IS QUANTITATIVE ANALYSIS?

Statistics is a branch of mathematics that is applied to quantitative data in order to draw conclusions and make predictions. In this sense, statistics is a discipline, but it can also be considered in the context of the data being collected. Statistics are used in all walks of life. For example, at the time of writing the 2021 census is being carried out in England, Wales and Northern Ireland. The census provides statistics from a national to a local level. Other examples include inflation figures, company sales figures, unemployment figures, interest rates and statistics on gross domestic product (GDP). In short, statistics are used in a variety of ways. Furthermore, they can be used to analyze past and current data, and forecast future projections. In simple terms, *quantitative data* is statistical and typically presented using charts, graphs and tables. Statistical techniques are used to describe and analyze variation in quantitative measures (Schutt and Chambliss, 2012).

If you have undertaken a positivist research philosophy, you will have gathered mainly, if not exclusively, quantitative data. In contrast, researchers who have adopted an interpretivist philosophy may also use quantitative data. For example, content analysis, which is a quantitative form of analysis, is typically associated with qualitative data. Quantitative analysis is usually associated with finding answers to 'What' and 'How much' questions. A range of quantitative analytical techniques can be used to analyze and interpret your data. We examine some of these techniques in this chapter. These include everything from simple tables to summarize your data, to multivariate tests to determine the strength of relationships between variables. Statistical data analysis is now typically done using computers. Statistical software packages such as IBM SPSS Statistics means that the time taken to prepare, conduct and interpret quantitative data has been markedly reduced. The likelihood is that your institution will have access to software, such as IBM SPSS Statistics, meaning that there is no need for you to be concerned about having to manually carry out calculations. Unfortunately, in some cases, students may recognize the value of statistics but fail to consider quantitative data analysis because they believe that the following concerns apply to them:

1.   I am no good at mathematics, and do not have the time to learn.
2.   I need a large sample for quantitative analysis.

With regards to the first point, certainly some statistical methods used to analyze quantitative data are difficult to learn, although methods used to describe data and make inferences to the wider population are relatively simple. Do not simply choose more complex methods to analyze your data because you think it is expected by your supervisor or may lead to a higher mark. Remember that the method(s) you choose should relate to your data collection, which in turn relates to your research direction. Again, think about the relationship between the steps in The Research Wheel model. Moreover, you can write an excellent project that does not go beyond the use of descriptive statistics. In essence, the quality of your data and the clarity of your analysis are more important than using complicated analytical tools. Moreover, it is essential that you understand 'why' you are using a certain technique and 'how' to interpret your results.

The second point tends to be more important if the intention of your research is to make inferences in relation to the wider population. In order to do this, you need a representative sample, although this does not necessarily need to be large in size (see Chapter 9). Research limitations mean it is not always necessary to have large quantities of data for analysis.

Albers (2017: 219) points out that 'many students regard quantitative data analysis as nothing more than taking the collected data, running a few statistical tests, and reporting the p value'. However, quantitative data analysis is much more than this. For example, we can make a distinction between *descriptive statistics* and *inferential statistics*. The former is used to summarize and describe data, while the latter is used to make inferences in relation to a wider population. Inferential statistics can also be subdivided on the basis of *non-parametric* and *parametric tests*.

Parametric tests are regarded as more powerful as they assume that the observed data follows a *normal distribution* (we examine this later in the chapter). Parametric methods are used when you are able to estimate the parameters of distribution in the population. Two of the main parameters are the *mean* and *standard deviation*. Non-parametric methods are used where a normal distribution cannot be ascertained. In other words, when you know nothing about the parameters and have a small sample size, then non-parametric tests must be used. Conducting quantitative data analysis can be viewed as a process (see Figure 16.2.). In this figure you can see that the process involves three basic steps. The diagram presumes that the researcher has collected his or her data.

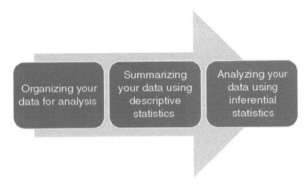

Figure 16.2   The quantitative data analysis process

We shall now explore each of the above steps in turn.

STEP 1: ORGANIZING YOUR DATA FOR ANALYSIS

Before you start carrying out quantitative analysis, your first step is to organize your data so that it is ready for analysis. This usually involves entering your data into a specialized software package such as IBM SPSS Statistics. When entering your data, you will start by creating a spreadsheet or matrix. Each column in your spreadsheet should represent a variable and each row represent a case (see Figure 16.3).

ID	Age	Service	Highest level of qualification	Fellowship status
001	28	5	2	1
002	33	12	3	2
003	58	20	1	2
004	42	14	2	3

Figure 16.3   Example of an extract from a data spreadsheet

Figure 16.3 is an extract of a spreadsheet from a large study looking in to the career information of employees working for a pharmaceutical organization. The first column indicates the 'case number'. As noted in Chapter 6, a single case might be a company, individual or possibly an event. We then have four variable types – 'age', 'service', 'highest level of qualification' and 'fellowship status'. This last variable refers to professional body membership. Each entry is a numerical value rather than text. This is because most statistical software packages do not recognize qualitative data. Hence, all data should be given a numerical value. For example, in the case of 'fellowship status' the coding used is as follows:

1 = Associate Fellow

2 = Senior Fellow

3 = Principal Fellow

You can see that from our brief extract in Figure 16.3, only ID 004 has achieved the highest fellowship status. Similarly, codes will be used for the other three variables. Coding in this way is usually planned before data collection. For example, allocating codes to respective questions within a questionnaire will make the task of preparing your data for analysis much easier. When assigning your codes, it is import-ant to consider the following points (Bryman, 2004: 146):

- the categories that are produced must not overlap
- the list of data must take into account all possibilities – this includes missing data and answers to open questions that might come under the heading 'other'
- there should be a clear set of rules governing how codes are applied – this is to ensure that coding is consistent over time.

VARIABLES

Before examining types of data used in research, it is important to understand some of the key termi-nology associated with quantitative analysis. First, we look at variables. So, what is a variable? In simple terms, a *variable* is something that can be measured or counted. Another term for variable is 'data item'. Examples of variables include age, gender, nationality, exam marks and salary.

Numerical variables can be described as 'continuous' or 'discrete'. A *continuous variable* is a numeric variable that can take any value, e.g. temperature, height and weight. The value given to an observation for a continuous variable can include values as small as the instrument of measure-ment allows. A discrete variable (also known as a categorical variable) is a numeric variable that is measured using specific values. A discrete variable cannot take the value of a fraction between one value and the next closest value. For example, the number of students in an exam hall is a discrete variable, we cannot say that the number of students is 45.5, 50.2, etc. Similarly, number of family members, number of mobile phones and number of chairs are discrete variables as they are mea-sured as whole units.

CATEGORIES OF DATA ANALYSIS

In the last section, we examined different type of variables. We can now go further and look at number of variables in the context of analysis. There are three categories of data analysis – univariate, bivariate and multivariate. Let us look at each one in turn.

First, *univariate analysis* is analyzing a single variable. For example, you may have conducted research into the ages of students on a postgraduate course. In this example, 'age' is the single variable. Univariate analysis is the simplest form of analysis as we are only concerned with one variable. Analysis here may involve using descriptive statistics, such as the mean, mode and range. Moreover, examples of how univariate data can be displayed include using pie charts, bar charts and frequency distribu-tion tables. This is something we examine later in the chapter. Univariate analysis does not examine two variables or the relationships between them. Another example would be 'nationality'. Here, your research is only concerned with the nationality of each of the research participants.

Second, *bivariate analysis* is used to find out if there is a relationship or correlation between two variables. For example, the strength of relationship between exams scores and hours revising. One way to visualize the extent of a relationship between variables is to create a scatter diagram (scatter plot). This 'visual snapshot' can give you an insight into the strength of the correlation between variables. Cross-tabulations can be used when conducting bivariate analysis. We examine this, together with how to use and interpret a scatter plot, later in the chapter.

Third, *multivariate analysis* is the analysis of simultaneous relationships among three or more variables. There are several ways to perform multivariate analysis. This depends on the nature of your research direction. Finally, the majority of methods associated with descriptive statistics are based on univariate data. Conversely, inferential statistics are typically associated with bivariate or multivariate data.

TYPES OF DATA

There are four scales of measurement – nominal, ordinal, interval and ratio. These scales are important when determining the type of statistics that may be legitimately employed (Doering and Hubbard, 1979). In order to select appropriate methods of analysis, it is essential that you understand these four types of data. Let us examine each one in turn.

Nominal

Nominal data are a discrete data type. They are data that cannot be measured numerically. In other words, it is named data and includes values that can be classified into categories. If, for example, you conduct a questionnaire survey into educational attainment, you may be interested in placing students into categories. Thus, 'fail' may be coded as 1, 'pass' 2, 'merit' 3 and 'distinction' 4. There are a limited number of methods that can be used to analyze nominal data. Typical methods include frequency counts and finding the mode (the value that appears the most often in a data set).

Ordinal

Like nominal, ordinal data are another type of discrete data. However, the main difference is that unlike nominal data, ordinal data can be rank-ordered. Let us say that you are interested in finding out the extent to which 'retail environment' is important to customer experience among a sample of customers. Using a 5-point Likert-scale question, perceived importance may be ranked from 1 to 5, where 1 = very important, 2 = important, 3 = neither important nor unimportant, 4 = unimportant, 5 = very unimportant. Examples of types of analysis suitable for ordinal data include frequency counts and percentages from a set of *ranked data*. Note that the distance across your set of categories might not be equal. Regarding the customer experience example, we cannot say that those customers who consider customer service as very important judge it to be 5 times more important than those who give a 1, although we can say what percentage of respondents tick each box on our 5-point Likert-scale question.

Interval

Interval data are continuous data types that have been achieved when the distance between the numbers is equal across the range, for example the difference between 4 and 5 is 1. This is equal to the difference between 5 and 6. The temperature scale of Fahrenheit and Celsius are typical examples of interval scales in that the zero in both scales is arbitrary. So, you cannot say that 40°C is twice as warm as 20°C. When dealing with interval data you need to be very careful not to make such claims. The *mean, mode* and *median* can be used to describe interval data.

Ratio

Ratio data are continuous data types and are very similar to interval data. The distinction between the two is that ratio data have a fixed zero point. Examples of ratio data include income, length, weight and height. Interval and ratio data allow for more precise levels of measurement than categorical data (nominal and ordinal). For example, an employee's salary might be given in exact figures (ratio), or listed in relation to other employees within the company (ranked). Interval and ratio data also offer a greater number of options when it comes to data analysis. We explore some of these options later in the chapter.

CODING

As we saw earlier in the chapter, all types of data should be coded numerically. For example, the *dichotomous variable* 'gender' is usually coded '1' and '2' when using statistical analysis software. The advantage of coding is that it will ultimately make your analysis easier and less confusing. Again, it is essential for most statistical software packages.

Coding during data collection

If you have adopted a deductive approach to your research and already have a set of predetermined categories, then you will most probably code your categories on your questionnaire survey. The advantage of coding at this stage is that it will save time later when carrying out your analysis. Furthermore, it can reduce the possibility of making errors when entering data as codes are predetermined and are consistent across all surveys.

Coding following data collection

If you are uncertain of the number and complexity of your responses, you may decide to implement your coding scheme after data collection, although for a collection tool such as a questionnaire survey, a predetermined set of codes for each question can make data entry and analysis less time consuming.

MISSING DATA

It is essential that you also code any missing data. Failure to do so is likely to impact on the interpretation of your results. A missing data code can be used to illustrate why data are missing. For example, a non-response might be indicated by a '99'. Coding missing data is required if you wish it to be excluded from your analysis.

Missing data may arise for a number of reasons. These include: a question is irrelevant to a respondent; a question is left blank as the respondent did not wish to complete it; and a question is not answered because the respondent did not understand it. The latter is sometimes a problem when conducting international or cross-cultural research. As highlighted earlier in the book, the number of non-responses or missing data can potentially be reduced by carrying out a pilot study.

STEP 2: SUMMARIZING YOUR DATA USING DESCRIPTIVE STATISTICS

Undertaking descriptive statistics not only allows you to describe your data, but also to present it in a number of different ways. Almost certainly you will be familiar with some of the techniques used to present descriptive statistics. These include frequency distribution tables, bar charts, pie charts and graphs.

When reading journal articles, you will often see that the author(s) who engage in statistical analysis use descriptive statistics as a starting point. The main advantage of summarizing the data in this way is that it provides the reader with a simple overview of your data prior to more complex analysis.

Table 16.1 presents the various methods that can be used when describing your data. Column two highlights the purpose of each method, while column three shows a brief example of how each method might be applied. The application of each of the methods depends on a number of factors. These include the number of variables, the type of data and the purpose. Let us examine the methods listed in Table 16.1.

Table 16.1 Examples of descriptive statistics

Method	Purpose	Examples of application
Frequency distribution tables	Summarizing data	Number and percentage of employees in each firm
Graphs and charts	Summarizing data	Advertising spend on different types of media
Mean, median, mode	Measuring central tendency	Analyzing exam scores from a finance exam
Standard deviation	Measuring dispersion	Analyzing the standard deviations from a finance exam
Range and interquartile range	Measuring dispersion	Analyzing the range from a finance exam
Index numbers	Describing change	Changes to retail prices
Cross-tabulations	Frequency distribution	A preference for a brand of cereal based on gender
Scatter diagrams	Frequency distribution	Exploring the link between car mileage and petrol consumption

SUMMARIZING DATA

Frequency distribution tables

A good starting point when analyzing your data is to look at the *frequency distribution* for each variable in your study. A *frequency* is a numerical value that illustrates the number of counts for an observed variable. For instance, in your research, you might be interested in the number of cars company directors have. When constructing a frequency distribution table, data is arranged in rows and columns. There are numerous ways to present a frequency distribution table. Indeed, you probably come across a variety of examples on an almost daily basis. Examples include everything from school to football league tables!

A table is also a good starting point for both presenting and summarizing your quantitative findings. Table 16.2 shows an example of a frequency distribution table based on 50 employees and the number of mobile devices they own. Remember that a response is not always guaranteed, so we may have a number of non-responses. In this case, all of the participants have responded to the question. If this were not the case, our table would also feature non-response frequencies.

Table 16.2 not only shows the frequency distribution for mobile devices, it also shows the percentage frequency distribution. This shows that 80% of employees own one mobile phone, 14% have two phones, and 6% have three phones. A percentage frequency distribution makes a useful addition to a frequency distribution table.

Table 16.2   Frequency distribution table: Number of mobile devices per person

Number of mobile devices	Frequency	Percentage
1	40	80%
2	7	14%
3	3	6%

Using a small sample size such as that for Table 16.2 is straightforward to incorporate into a frequency distribution table. However, adopting the same approach for large samples is simply not practical. To overcome this problem, you can group your observed values into classes. For example, if undertaking a large survey on employees' salaries, you can group the respondents into classes based on intervals of £5,000. For example, £10,000 or more, but less than £15,000; £15,000 or more, but less than £20,000, and so on. Using intervals of £5,000 is reasonable given the likely variation in salaries. However, where you are likely to have a wide range of observed values, you may wish to group them into slightly broader classes. In contrast, a narrower range would best suit a fewer number of classes.

The advantage of grouping your data is that it will make your table and results look more presentable. A potential problem is failing to recognize the types of data you are using when forming classes. For example, when using continuous data such as salary, it is sometimes easy to allocate data wrongly due to poorly defined intervals between classes. Let us look at an example of a frequency distribution table showing grouped data (see Table 16.3).

As well as showing grouped data, Table 16.3 also includes a cumulative frequency and cumulative percentage frequency distribution column. A cumulative figure is obtained by simply adding the observations from the previously stated (lower) classes. For example, when establishing the cumulative frequency for the third class in Table 16.3, we simply add the two lower classes, $3 + 11 + 7 = 21$. The same principles apply for cumulative percentage frequency distribution.

Table 16.3   Frequency distribution showing salaries among employees

Class	Frequency	Cumulative frequency	% frequency	Cumulative % frequency
<10,000	3	3	12	12
10,000<20,000	11	14	44	56
20,000<30,000	7	21	28	84
30,000<40,000	3	24	12	96
40,000<50,000	1	25	4	100

So far in this chapter, we have examined frequency distribution tables in relation to *univariate data*. Frequency distribution tables are also useful for examining *bivariate data*. A table that allows you to examine the relationship between two variables is called a *cross-tabulation*. We shall address this later in the chapter.

Graphs and charts

Wainer (2013: 11) noted, 'When looking at a good graph, your response should never be "what a great graph!" but "what interesting data!". A graph that calls attention to itself pictorially is almost surely a failure'.

A *graph* is a type of diagram used to present data. A graph can be used to analyze bivariate or multivariate data. Waters (1997: 107) offers the following advice when producing graphs:

- Always label the axes clearly and accurately.
- Show the scales on both axes.
- The maximum of the scale should be slightly above the maximum observation.
- Wherever possible, the scale on the axis should start at zero. If this cannot be done, the scale must be shown clearly, perhaps with a zigzag on the axis to indicate a break.
- Where appropriate, give the source of data.
- Where appropriate, give the graph a title.

Line graphs are ideal for analyzing trends over time (longitudinal data). For example, a line graph can be used to show the temperature changes over the period of a decade. Another example might be manufacturer sales trends over the period of one year. The data should be of at least interval, ordinal or ratio status. Figure 16.4 shows a line graph for three manufacturing companies – Bradshaw, Perez and TL. The graph illustrates the sales over the first six months of 2020. Clearly, Bradshaw has had the most successful start to the year.

A line to illustrate the trend over the entire time frame joins the data value for each respective time period, in this case six months (January to June 2020).

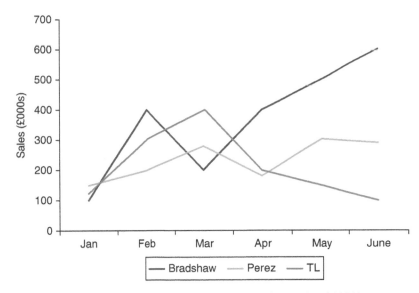

Figure 16.4   Sales for three manufacturing companies (for the first six months of 2020)

One advantage of graphs is that they can clearly illustrate the relationship between two variables. Moreover, DeShea and Toothaker (2015) note that exploring data with graphs can help to identify data entry errors. The authors provide an example of one of their undergraduate students where they saw an age typed as 91 instead of 19 years. A downside is that graphs tend not to be as visually appealing as charts.

Bar chart

A *bar chart* (or *graph*) compares a simple set of observations. Bars are used to represent the data. A bar chart is a straightforward way of summarizing either ordinal or nominal data. It involves bivariate analysis of the main characteristics of the distribution of the data.

Broadly speaking, there are two main types of bar chart: horizontal and vertical. Each bar is the same width, whereas the length represents the number of cases. A bar chart has a gap between each bar, while a histogram does not have any gaps because it represents continuous data. To illustrate, there are three consultancy organizations located in a business district. The number of major clients in each of their organizations is shown in Table 16.4

Next, let us put these data into a simple bar chart (see Figure 16.5).

Table 16.4   Number of major clients

	Consultancy organization		
	ZX Consulting	TPRM	Blackstone & Watkins
Retail	11	36	45
Construction	17	8	10
Travel	15	20	30
Financial Services	5	10	15

The main advantage of a bar chart is that it is a simplistic way of illustrating the relationship between two variables. On the other hand, a disadvantage is that a large number of cases representing small values can make the chart look cumbersome.

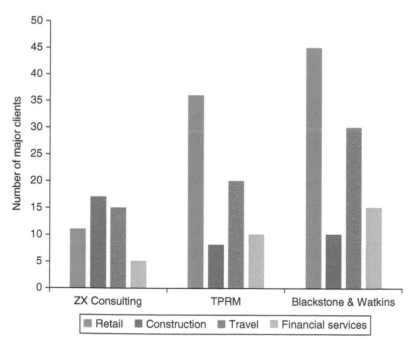

Figure 16.5   Number of major clients in consultancy organizations

Pie chart

A *pie chart* (or *graph*) is a common way for presenting simple statistics and used for summarizing categorical data. A pie chart is a circle divided into segments. Each segment represents a particular category. The size of each category is proportional to the number of cases it represents. Typically, the number of cases is represented by a percentage. Each segment has a different colour or pattern to clearly distinguish each category. Pie charts are straightforward diagrams that compare a limited amount of data. Figure 16.6 shows an example of a pie chart. In this example, a simple pie chart shows the mode of transport employees within a technology organization use to commute to work.

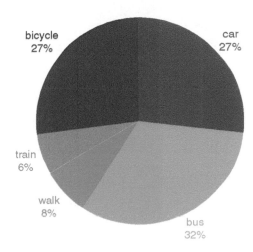

Figure 16.6   Mode of transport used for commuting to work

There are two main advantages associated with pie charts. First, they are a clear way of highlighting proportional differences. Second, the use of different colours makes it easy to distinguish between categories. Conversely, sometimes it can be difficult to divide categories into segments. This is especially true with fragmented data or when there are a large number of categories. A quick point on 3D pie charts – although a 3D pie chart looks more like a pie, they are not always clearly produced. This makes it difficult for the reader to interpret the pie chart. In short, simple charts often work best.

Tree maps

A *tree map* is similar to a pie chart. They are a useful visual for showing patterns of high and low values. They are sometimes used by the media to show how government spending is allocated. Tree maps use coloured rectangles of different sizes to show two measures for each dimension. The size of the rectangles distinguishes the proportion of the whole that is represented by each element. By way of an example, Figure 16.7 has a tree map showing the breakdown of total marketing spend by category. Our categories in this example are: outdoor advertising, radio advertising, print media, public relations and social media. The size of the rectangle in proportion to the whole represents the marketing spend, and the colour of the rectangle represents the category. More detailed tree maps can also break down further by defining sub-categories inside each category. In example Figure 16.7, this may involve breaking down social media into sub-categories of social media platforms, e.g. Facebook, Twitter and Snapchat.

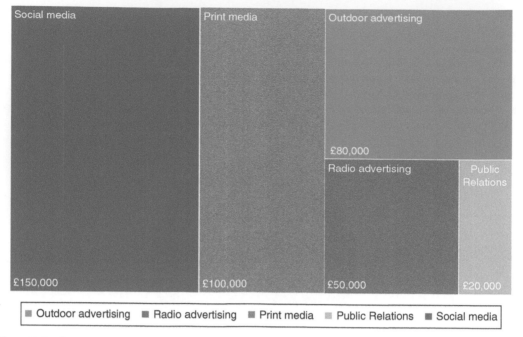

Figure 16.7   A tree map showing how Viking Anglia Ice Cream spends its marketing budget: Total £400,000

Histograms

A *histogram* is a type of bar chart that shows a frequency distribution of a set of data. It provides a clear indication of the nature of your distribution, in particular whether or not you have a *normal* or *skewed distribution*. It is a way of summarizing data that are measured on an interval scale (either discrete or continuous). The height of each bar represents each observed frequency.

Before compiling your histogram, you need to divide the range of values from your data set into groups. On the *x*-axis of your chart, each group is represented by a rectangle with a base length equal to the range of values within that particular group, and an area proportional to the total number of observations applicable to that group.

When compiling your histogram, it is important that you allocate a suitable number of groups. Too few or too many will negatively impact on the presentation of your frequency distribution. An advantage of a histogram is that it is easy to interpret the data. In addition, it is ideal where the class divisions are not the same. The main disadvantage is that it cannot provide precise individual values. By way of example, let us say that a delivery organization is keen to find out efficiency in terms of speed of delivery. The organization appoints a market research agency to conduct a pilot study on its busiest period – the week before the Christmas break. Following the agency's findings, the delivery organization intends to carry out further research in order to improve delivery times. Results from the research are summarized in a frequency distribution table (see Table 16.5), while the histogram of the same set of data is illustrated in Figure 16.8. The *y*-axis is the relative frequency, while the *x*-axis shows the delivery times.

Table 16.5   Frequency distribution table showing delivery times

Groups	Frequency
0–1 day	45
2–3 days	22
4–5 days	28
6–7 days	13

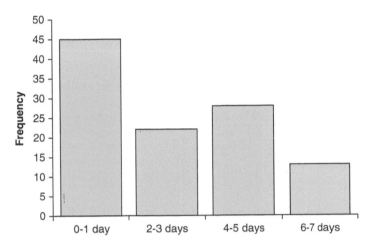

Figure 16.8   Histogram showing delivery times

MEASURING CENTRAL TENDENCY

Summarizing and presenting data is fine if we want a general overview of our obtained data. However, often we like to summarize data in a more concise way. A common way of doing this is to discuss the 'average'. Measures of *central tendency* are used to illustrate a typical outcome in a set of data. The main ways of measuring central tendency are the *mean*, *median* and *mode*. First, let us look at the mean.

Mean

The *mean* ($\bar{x}$) is the arithmetical average of a frequency distribution. The method of calculating the arithmetic mean is:

- add all observations together
- divide by the total number of observations.

We can distinguish between the population mean and the sample mean. Remember from Chapter 9 (sampling) that a sample is a sub-set of the population. First, the sample mean is denoted $\bar{x}$ and the formula for calculating the sample mean is as follows:

$$\text{Mean}\,(\bar{x}) = \frac{\sum x}{n}$$

where:

x = each observation

n = the total number of elements in the sample

Σ = the sum of

For example, if a researcher wanted to find the mean number of takeaway coffees bought by a sample of students over the course of a week, the process would be as follows:

Number of coffees bought over seven days: 25, 10, 11, 27, 25, 22, 20.

$$\bar{x} = \frac{\Sigma x}{n} = \frac{25 + 10 + 11 + 27 + 25 + 22 + 20}{7} = 20$$

The number of coffees bought over the course of the 7 days is 140. The mean number of coffees sold is 20.

The population mean is represented by the Greek letter *mu* (μ). It is given by the formula:

$$\mu = \frac{\Sigma x}{N}$$

where:

x = each observation

N = the total number of elements in the population

Σ = the sum of

If we are dealing with a set of grouped data, then we need to use a different formula for calculating the mean:
where:

x = each observation

f = the frequency

Σ = the sum of

For example, Table 16.6 shows the monthly salary among finance staff and is grouped into classes. Using the earlier cited formula, the mean monthly salary is:

$$\bar{x} = \frac{\Sigma fx}{\Sigma f} = \frac{£127,000}{50} = £2,540$$

The answer is that the mean monthly salary is £2,540.

One of the advantages of the mean is that it includes every score in a set of data. Also, if taking several samples from a population, the means are likely to be the same. The disadvantages are that the mean is sensitive to outliers (extreme values) and can only be used with interval or ratio data.

Table 16.6   Calculating the mean in a set of grouped data – monthly salary among finance staff

Monthly bonus (£)	Frequency (f)	Mid-values (x)	(fx)
<1000	6	500	3,000
1000–1999.99	10	1,500	15,000
2000–2999.99	18	2,500	45,000
3000–3999.99	8	3,500	28,000
4000–4999.99	8	4,500	36,000
	$\Sigma f = 50$	12,500	$\Sigma fx = 127,000$

Median

The *median* is also sometimes referred to as an average. It is the middle number in a set of numbers. The median can be found using the following formula:

$$M = \frac{n+1}{2}$$

where:

n = number of observations

For example, if you wanted to find the median in the following set of numbers: 32, 18, 58, 16, 10, the first step would be to put them in ascending order: 10, 16, 18, 32, 58. Next, apply the formula:

$$M = \frac{n+1}{2} = \frac{5+1}{2} = 3$$

So, the median is the third number in the sequence: 18.

If our list is made up of an even number, we can simply take the mid-value between the third and fourth values. For example:

$$8, 15, 19, 31, 39, 45$$

$$\frac{19+31}{2} = 25$$

Our median is halfway between the third and fourth values in our set of data (19 and 31). Therefore, the median is 25.

The median has two main advantages. First, it can be used with ordinal, interval and ratio data (it cannot be used with categorical data). Second, the median is unaffected by outliers. The disadvantages are that the median may not be a characteristic of the distribution if it does not follow a normal distribution, and it cannot be used for further statistical analysis.

Mode

The *mode* is the value that occurs the most often in your set of data. If, for example, we have the following set of data:

$$23, 19, 8, 19, 32, 49, 23, 19, 6, 31$$

the mode in the above example is 19, as it appears the most often: 3 times.

The advantage of the mode is that, unlike the mean and median, it can be used with nominal data. Moreover, it is very straightforward to determine and is unaffected by outliers. The disadvantage of the mode is that you can end up with more than one mode value. Moreover, it does not indicate the variation in a set of data and is sensitive to additional observations.

MEASURING DISPERSION

A key limitation of measuring central tendency is that it does not give us an indication of the shape of a frequency distribution. A measure that allows us to describe the spread of values in a distribution is referred to as a measure of *dispersion*. By combining measures of central tendency and dispersion you can gain a useful description of your set of data. Methods used to measure dispersion include the *standard deviation, range* and *interquartile range*.

Standard deviation

The *standard deviation* is represented by (S) for sample standard deviation and lower case sigma (σ) for population standard deviation. The standard deviation measures the spread of data around the mean value.

The steps in finding the standard deviation can be summarized as follows:

- Find the mean in your set of data (i.e. the difference between a particular value and the mean).
- Find the deviation from the mean for each value.
- Square the deviations from the mean to get rid of negative values (failure to do so will lead to an answer of zero).
- Find the sum of these values.
- Divide by the number of values in order to get an average (also known as the variance).
- Find the square root of the variance in order to find the standard deviation.

The standard deviation is expressed by the formula:

$$S = \sqrt{\frac{\sum (x - \bar{x})^2}{n - 1}}$$

where:

S = the sample standard deviation

x = an observation

$\bar{x}$ = the mean

n = the total number of observations

$\sqrt{}$ = the square root

Σ = the sum of

Please note, when calculating the standard deviation of a small sample, a better estimate is gained by dividing by $(n-1)$ rather than 'n'.

The formula for a set of grouped data is as follows:

$$S = \sqrt{\frac{\sum f(x - \bar{x})^2}{\sum f}}$$

where:

S = the sample standard deviation

x = the mid-point of each data class

f = the frequency of each class

$\sqrt{}$ = the square root

Σ = the sum of

By way of an example, let us say that you are researching the number of times (x) a packaging machine breaks down over the first quarter of the year (see Table 16.7).

Table 16.7   Finding the standard deviation

Month	x	$(x-\bar{x})$	$(x-\bar{x})^2$
January	6	-2	4
February	7	-1	1
March	9	1	1
April	10	2	4
Total	32		10

$$s = \sqrt{\frac{10}{3}} = 1.83$$

The standard deviation is 1.83.

An advantage of the standard deviation is that it uses every value in the population or group of sample data. However, because all items in a data set are used it can be influenced by extreme values.

Range

The *range* is found by subtracting the lowest value from the highest value in a set of data. If, for example, we have the following set of data:

3, 5, 6, 6, 8, 9, 14, 20, 24

The lowest value in our set of data is 3, while the highest is 24. By subtracting the lowest from the highest we get: 24 – 3 = 21. Therefore, our range is 21. The main advantage of the range is that it is easy to calculate and provides a clear indication as to the broadness or narrowness of a set of data. A key disadvantage is that a range based on a small sample size is likely to exclude extreme values. Conversely, the greater the sample size the greater the likelihood that extreme values will be included. Another disadvantage is that it does not tell us anything about the values within the range.

Interquartile range

As noted earlier, one criticism of the range is that it can be greatly affected by extreme values. The *interquartile range* helps to overcome this problem by measuring the spread between the upper and lower quartiles of a set of data (the middle 50%). As the interquartile range only focuses on the middle 50% of a range of data, it is not as sensitive as the range, although it is less susceptible to outliers.

Finding the interquartile range requires the following steps:

- List your data in order of size, beginning with the smallest first.
- Find the position of the median.
- Find the median in the data to the left of your median (lower quartile).
- Find the median in the data to the right of your median (upper quartile).
- Find the difference between the medians for the upper and lower quartile. This gives you the interquartile range.

The following example shows the interquartile range for a set of data.

An independent fashion retailer has recorded the number of returned products over a 12-month period (see Table 16.8).

Table 16.8   Number of returned products over 12 months

Jan	Feb	Mar	Apr	May	Jun	Jul	Aug	Sep	Oct	Nov	Dec
45	38	53	29	62	43	15	28	34	70	24	56

First, let us place the values in ascending order (Table 16.9).

Table 16.9   Number of returned products in ascending order

15	24	28	29	34	38	43	45	53	56	62	70

Next, find the median for the lower quartile (mid-value Q1) = 15, 24, 28, 29, 34, 38.

$$\text{Median} = 3\text{rd} + 4\text{th observations} \div 2$$

$$= \frac{28 + 29}{2} = 28.5$$

Now, find the median for the upper quartile (mid-value Q3) = 43, 45, 53, 56, 62, 70.

$$\text{Median} = 3\text{rd} + 4\text{th observations} \div 2$$

$$= \frac{53 + 56}{2} = 54.5$$

$$\text{Interquartile range (IR)} = Q3 - Q1$$

$$= 54.5 - 28.5 = 26$$

The interquartile range and median from our set of data can be shown as follows:

15, 24, 28, 29,	34, 38 43, 45,	53, 56, 62, 70
Lower quartile 28.5	Median 40.5	Upper quartile 54.5

Now, let us presume that the retailer only operated for 11 months of the year, thereby giving us an odd number of 11 observations (see Table 16.10).

Table 16.10   Number of returned products over 11 months

15	24	28	29	34	38	43	45	53	56	62

Find the lower quartile (mid-value Q1) = 15, 24, 28, 29, 34

Median = 3rd observation = 28

Median for the upper quartile (mid-value Q3) = 43, 45, 53, 56, 62

Median = 3rd observation = 53

Interquartile range (IR) = Q3 − Q1

= 53 − 28 = 25

If we wished to measure the spread of data based on the semi-interquartile range, our answer would be half of the interquartile range. Based on the first example, half of 26 is 13.

DESCRIBING CHANGE

Measuring dispersion allows us to examine the spread of data. However, this is based on a fixed point in time. How can we examine data that changes over time? For example, the percentage changes in fuel prices, house prices or interest rates? One method is to produce a simple index.

Index numbers

An *index number* shows how a quantity changes over time. Usually, the base period equals 100. Two of the most widely recognized indices are the FTSE 100, which is the list of the UK's top-performing 100 companies, and the Retail Price Index (RPI). The latter examines how people spend their income. It measures the fluctuation in the cost of a representative basket of goods and services. The RPI commenced in 1987. This therefore represents the base year. The base year can be represented by any given year, although it is typically a decade or more. This is for two reasons. First, historical data is often widely available. Second, when analyzing changes over time, we need a sufficient number of years to identify any possible trends.

Table 16.11   Average cost of a new home over time

Year	Average cost of a new home (£)
1950	1,891
1960	2,530
1970	4,057
1980	20,268
1990	58,153
2000	89,597
2010	170,365
2020	231,215

Source: Based on figures from SunLife (2020)

It is also worth noting that the base year does not have to be 100. For example, the FTSE 100 of leading shares has a base of 1,000.

The formula for calculating an index is as follows:

$$i = \frac{c/p}{b} \times 100$$

where:

c/p = cost/price

b = base value

Let us look at an example of an index. Table 16.11 shows how the average cost of a new home has changed over time. The base year (the first year when the data was collected) is 1950. Remember that 100 represents the base year.

The next step is to apply the formula so that we can clearly compare the extent that the data has changed over time (see Table 16.12).

Table 16.12   Average cost of a new home over time

Year	Average cost of new home	C/P × 100	Index number (I)
1950	1,891	$\frac{1,891 \times 100}{1,891}$	100.0
1960	2,530	$\frac{2,530 \times 100}{1,891}$	133.8
1970	4,057	$\frac{4,057 \times 100}{1,891}$	214.5
1980	20,268	$\frac{20,268 \times 100}{1,891}$	1,071.8
1990	58,153	$\frac{58,153 \times 100}{1,891}$	3,075.3
2000	89,597	$\frac{89,597 \times 100}{1,891}$	4,738.1
2010	170,365	$\frac{170,365 \times 100}{1,891}$	9,009.3
2020	231,215	$\frac{231,215 \times 100}{1,891}$	12,227.1

Weighted index numbers

A simple index such as car prices is fine if we are concerned about one observation over time. Yet, if we have a number of items, it is unlikely that we would place equal importance in respect of each item. In order to address this, we can allocate a weighting to each one.

Typically, a weighted price index is calculated at the end of each year, then comparisons are made over a given time period. A simple price index can be used to calculate the end year weighted price index. This is known as Paasche's Price Index and is represented by the formula:

$$\frac{\sum PnQn}{\sum P0Qn} \times 100$$

where:

$P0$ = base year prices

Pn = is the current year prices

Qn = current year quantity

Paasche's Index can only be calculated at the end of the current year as the weights are current year quantities in a price index. To illustrate, let us say that a model airplane manufacturer buys the following products from one of its suppliers during 2019 and 2020 (see Table 16.13).

Table 16.13   Model airplane manufacturer – supplier purchases (2019/20)

Parts	2019 Unit price (P0)	2019 Quantity (Q0)	2020 Unit price (Pn)	2020 Quantity (Qn)
Wings	40	50	44	60
Wheels	20	100	25	125
Glue	15	60	18	75
Batteries	28	125	32	150

Sum of $Pn \times Qn$ = (44 × 60) + (25 × 125) + (18 × 75) + (32 × 150) =

2,640 + 3,125 + 1,350 + 4,800 = 11,915.

Sum of $P0 \times Qn$ = (40 × 60) + (20 × 125) + (15 × 75) + (28 × 150) =

2,400 + 2,500 + 1,125 + 4,200 = 10,225

Thus, Paasche's Price Index = $\dfrac{11,915}{10,225} \times 100 = 116.53$

FREQUENCY DISTRIBUTION

Cross-tabulations

Earlier in the chapter, we looked at frequency distribution tables to gain an insight into frequency distribution of univariate data. A frequency distribution table can also be used to examine bivariate or multivariate data. This type of table is called a *cross-tabulation*.

A cross-tabulation is a table that shows the joint distribution of bivariate or multivariate data. In Table 16.14, the cross-tabulation shows the nationality by gender for business school students.

Table 16.14   Cross-tabulation showing the subject of study for business school students

Subject of study	Undergraduate students	Postgraduate students
Marketing	240	102
Human Resource Management	180	89
Business & Management	90	68
Accounting & Finance	170	80

The advantage of cross-tabulations is that they are simple to produce and allow for easy comparison between data. However, care should be taken with the number and types of variable. For example, too many variables will have a negative impact on the presentation of your table, and probably include several low values.

Scatter diagrams

A *scatter diagram* (sometimes referred to as a scatter plot) is essentially a graph used to assess the relationship between two variables. These are the independent variable using the *x*-axis, and the dependent variable the *y*-axis. The two variables are plotted on the graph to see whether or not a relationship exists.

Figure 16.9 shows the relationship between the years of service for employees of MPL Consulting. This can be described as a strong positive linear correlation. In other words, an increase in the value of one variable is associated with an increase in the value of the other.

A negative correlation happens when an increase in the value of one variable is associated with a decrease in the value of the other. For example, higher levels of unemployment might be associated with lower levels of property sales. If the points are scattered randomly throughout the graph, there is no correlation between the two variables. For example, see Figure 16.10, where there is clearly no correlation between age and driving test score. Another possibility is that the variables show a non-linear relationship. For example, this might be the case when examining the relationship between age and height.

A scatter plot is a helpful visual representation of data for understanding the relationship between two continuous variables and revealing potential outliers. An outlier is a value from a set of data that is inconsistent with other values. It can be much larger or much smaller than other values. You should not ignore an outlier, as it can impact on the results of descriptive statistics such as the mean. An outlier can be caused by one of two reasons – an error in measurement or radical behaviour from one of the participants. Either way, you need to establish reasons for the inconsistency before progressing with your research.

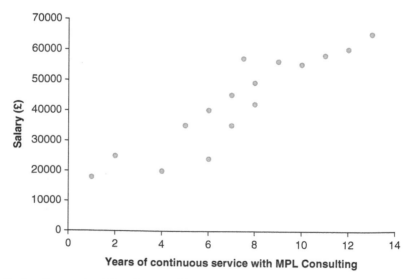

Figure 16.9   Scatter diagram showing a strong positive linear correlation

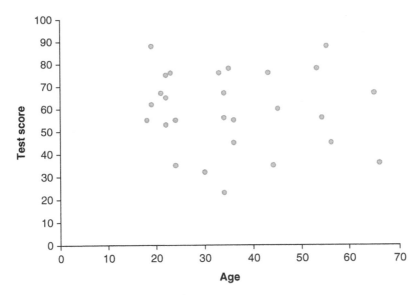

Figure 16.10   Scatter diagram showing no correlation

STEP 3: ANALYZING YOUR DATA USING INFERENTIAL STATISTICS

In the last section, we looked at descriptive statistics, the purpose of which is to summarize the data and to describe what occurred in the sample. If the nature of your research adopts a descriptive research design, then you may not undertake this last step in the quantitative analysis process. *Inferential statistics* are calculated so that they allow researchers to infer or generalize the findings from a sample to the entire population of interest. Inferential statistics can also be subdivided on the basis of *non-parametric* and *parametric tests*. A parametric test should only be applied if the following conditions are met: you have interval or ratio data, your sample is randomly drawn from the population, and your sample is from a population that is normally distributed. The *normal distribution* or *bell curve* is a graph that shows data scores that accumulate around the middle. The normal distribution proposes that the mean, mode and median are all equal. For example, the results of an exam would show the majority of exam scores would centre round the middle when the frequency curve is symmetrical. When the frequency curve is skewed, the mean, mode and median all have different values.

Determining whether or not your sample is from a population that is normally distributed is important as it will influence your choice of statistical tests. One can make this assumption using something called the *Central Limit Theorem*. The Central Limit Theorem is based on the notion that the average in a set of sample data drawn from a wider population is approximately distributed as a normal distribution if certain conditions are met. The main condition is that when a random, independent sample has at least 30 observations, the distribution of all sample means of the same-sized samples closely approaches a normal distribution of the population from which the sample is drawn. Hence, for sample sizes of above 30, you can assume that the sampling distribution of means will approximate to a normal distribution.

When a parametric test cannot be used, non-parametric tests should be applied. One advantage of these tests is that they make no assumptions about the distribution of the population.

Table 16.15   Examples of inferential statistics

Method	Purpose	Examples of application
Hypothesis testing (P/NP)	Estimation	H0 – There is no difference in the mean exam marks between male and female managers.
		H1 – There is a difference in the mean exam marks between male and female managers.
Pearson's product moment correlation coefficient (P)	Measuring association	Correlating gender with height.
Spearman's rank correlation coefficient (NP)	Measuring association	Comparing two managers' ranked assessment of ten employees.
Chi-squared test (NP)	Measuring difference	Do some manufacturers produce more faulty goods than others?
Student's t-test (P)	Measuring difference	Comparing the sample means of ages of female finance and marketing managers (independent t-test).
Simple regression (P)	Assessing the strength of relationship between variables	Strength of relationship between advertising spend and sales.
Multiple regression (P)	Assessing the strength of relationship between variables	Strength of relationship between advertising spend and training spend on sales.

Source: Adapted from Wilson (2014)

A number of parametric and non-parametric methods are associated with inferential statistics. Although by no means exhaustive, Table 16.15 summarizes the main methods that we will look at in this part of the chapter. It also includes the purpose of each method (a 'P' or 'NP' alongside each method indicates parametric or non-parametric respectively) and briefly illustrates how each method might be applied.

At this stage, do not be too concerned if you are unable to recognize the conditions required in relation to each of the examples in Table 16.15. By the end of this chapter, you should be in a position to develop your own examples for all of the methods listed here.

ESTIMATION

Estimation refers to estimating a population parameter from samples. It is unlikely that you will be in the fortunate position to have access to the entire population. If you have adopted a positivist approach to your research, the likelihood is that your intention is to estimate from your sample characteristics of the population. Two methods commonly used to estimate from samples are *hypothesis testing* and *confidence intervals*.

Hypothesis testing

Hypothesis testing is one of the main methods used in inferential statistics. It involves making a statement about some aspect of the population, then generating a sample to see if the hypothesis can or cannot be rejected. To test a hypothesis, you need to formulate a null hypothesis (H0) and an alternative hypothesis (H1). The former makes the assumption that there is no change in the value being tested. For example, 'no change' could relate to 'no difference' or 'no correlation'. For each null hypothesis there is an alternative hypothesis (H1). An alternative hypothesis tends to be vaguer than a null hypothesis, as will become apparent later on. The probability of rejecting the null hypothesis when it is true is referred to as the significance level. If the significance level is p≤0.05 (5% level), then you reject the null hypothesis. Conversely, if the significance level is p≥0.05, then you cannot reject the null hypothesis. Be careful with your wording. We cannot say 'accept'. The convention among researchers is to use 'cannot reject' the null hypothesis.

An example of a null hypothesis might be:

- H0: There is no difference between the driving test scores among male and female drivers
- H1: There is a difference between the driving tests scores among male and female drivers

The steps in hypothesis testing are as follows:

- State your null (H0) and alternative (H1) hypothesis.
- Choose a level of significance (typically the 0.05% or 5% level).
- Collect your data.
- Carry out statistical tests.

Make one of the following decisions:

1. Reject the null hypothesis (H0) and accept the alternative hypothesis (H1), or
2. Fail to reject the null hypothesis (H0) and subsequently note that there is not sufficient evidence to suggest the truth of the alternative hypothesis (H1).

Table 16.16   Possible outcomes of a hypothesis test

	H0 is true	H1 is true
Accept H0	No error	Type II error
Reject H0	Type I error	No error

Type I errors and Type II errors

Once you have carried out your hypothesis you should have reached a decision about whether to reject or not reject your null hypothesis, although, due to sampling variation, your conclusion will be subject to error. A *Type I error* is where the null hypothesis is true but rejected, while a *Type II error* is where the alternative hypothesis is true but rejected (see Table 16.16). If you set your level of significance too high (e.g. p>0.01), there is a greater likelihood of you making a Type II error.

Types of hypothesis test

Before carrying out a hypothesis test you need to decide which type of test to use. There are two types of test. The first of these is referred to as a 'two-tailed test', while the second is a 'one-tailed test'. Your choice is important as it will impact on how you word your alternative hypothesis. Let us look at each one in turn.

A two-tailed test is carried out to see if your hypothesis is above or below what you presume it to be. For example, you might believe that training (independent variable) has an effect on company performance (dependent variable); when using a two-tailed test, regardless of the direction of the relationship you hypothesize, you are testing for the possibility of the relationship in both directions. When the alternative hypothesis (H1) is written as not equal to ($\neq$), then you are indicating your intention to carry out a two-tailed test.

A one-tailed test is used when you are making a prediction that there will be an effect in a particular direction. For example, if students are given extra classes (independent variable), their exam marks will increase (dependent variable).

- If conducting a left-tailed test, H1 is written as follows:
- H1: μ < 200g
- If conducting a right-tailed test, H1 is written as follows:
- H1: μ > 200g

Confidence intervals

A *confidence interval* uses a range of values that is likely to comprise an unknown population parameter. A parameter is a population characteristic such as a proportion (p) or mean (m). Confidence intervals are generally more useful than straightforward hypothesis tests as they go beyond a simple 'reject the null hypothesis' or 'do not reject the null hypothesis' by providing a range of credible values for the population parameter.

First, it is important to make a distinction between confidence interval and confidence level. For example, if you collected data on job security from sales managers, 75% might say that they felt 'insecure' in their job. Hence, you might say that 75% of sales managers are insecure. You could support this by saying that you are 95% certain (confidence level) that this will represent the true population 95% of the time.

If, for example, we take a sample of 500 employees and find the mean age of 32, can we be sure that the mean age is representative of the population? Unfortunately, our mean (or point of estimate) is unlikely to be the same as the population, although it is likely to be close to the population mean but have some error. In order to address the problem of our point estimate, we can define a range (confidence interval) within which our population mean is likely to fall. The confidence interval is expressed with a level of confidence that the interval contains the true population parameter. Typically, most researchers use a 95% confidence level. This means that 95% of the probability falls between z values of –1.96 and +1.96. These represent the most commonly used critical values for calculating confidence limits. A *critical value* or z-score relates to the number of standard deviations that the sample mean departs from the population mean of a normal distribution. Other examples are shown in Table 16.17.

Table 16.17 Confidence level for each interval and respective critical value

Confidence interval (%)	Critical value
99	2.58
95	1.96
90	1.64

A confidence interval is used to estimate the true mean of an entire population. When the population standard deviation is known, the formula for a confidence interval (CI) for a population mean is represented by the formula:

$$\bar{x} \pm z^* \frac{\sigma}{\sqrt{n}}$$

where:

$\bar{x}$ = sample mean

± = margin of error

z = critical value

σ = population standard deviation

n = sample size

Let us say that you have conducted a study into the performance of chocolate production making equipment among a sample of 100 organizations. Your findings produce a mean length of operation before the equipment needs servicing of 150 hours, with a standard deviation of 25 hours. You now intend to determine the 95% confidence interval for the overall mean length of operation prior to servicing, among all organizations that use this type of equipment.

We have:

$$150 \pm 1.96 \times \frac{25}{\sqrt{100}}$$

Which gives us: 150 ± 4.9 (margin of error), i.e. from 145.1 to 154.9 operational hours before servicing.

In the above example, we assume that the standard deviation of the population is known. In reality, it is unlikely that we would know the standard deviation of a population but not its mean. In most cases, researchers need to use the sample standard deviation (S) and mean to estimate the population mean and standard deviation.

If you have a sample size (n>30), a confidence interval can also be used to estimate the proportion in a population.

This is represented by the formula:

$$p \pm z^* \sqrt{\frac{p(1-p)}{n}}$$

where:

z = critical value

p = sample proportion

n = sample size

$\sqrt{}$ = square root

Let us say that you have conducted a study into professional qualifications among independent accounting organizations. From your random sample of 100 organizations, you have established that 60 organizations have at least one employee who holds a professional qualification, thus x = 60 and n = 100.

$$P = x/n = 60/100 = 0.6$$

Now let us calculate the 95% confidence interval for the proportion of accounting organizations that have at least one employee who holds a professional qualification:

$$0.6 \pm 1.96 \sqrt{\frac{0.6(1-0.6)}{100}}$$

$$0.6 \pm 1.96(0.049)$$

$$0.6 \pm 0.096$$

$$(0.50, 0.70)$$

Thus, we are 95% confident that the true proportion of small firms who have an employee with a higher education qualification is between 50% and 70%.

Forecasting

Forecasting can be defined as the estimation of a set of values at a future point in time. Forecasting plays an important role in business. For example, many organizations engage in sales forecasting to allocate better control inventory levels, while governments forecast levels of inflation and unemployment, along with economic growth, to determine appropriate government policy. Forecasting financial data such as share prices is also important for both individual and organizational decision-making.

There are several different methods associated with forecasting. These include qualitative methods and economic models. In this section, I introduce you to one of the main categories associated with forecasting – *time series analysis*. This is an introduction to the subject. For a more detailed discussion on time series analysis, you will need to consult a book devoted to forecasting. See further reading.

Time series analysis

A *time series* is a series of data points that are typically measured over regular time intervals. Time series analysis involves using various methods to understand a time series in a 'historical' context, as well as to make forecasts or predictions. In relation to the latter, we shall now examine two of the commonly used methods of time series analysis – 'simple moving average' and 'weighted moving average'.

A *simple moving average (SMA)* is used to compare possible changes in a variable over time. It is found by calculating the mean for a given time period and represented by the formula:

$$SMA = \frac{A_1 + A_2 + \ldots + A_n}{n}$$

Where:

A = data point in given time period

n = number of periods to be averaged

The advantage of the simple moving average is that it is easy to calculate and provides a reasonably accurate estimate for forecasting. However, the main drawback is that it does not account for possible trends. For example, many seasonal products experience an increase in sales over the Christmas period. Ideally, this trend needs to be taken into account when forecasting. One way to do this is to weight your data.

A *weighted moving average* is where greater significance is placed on one part of your data set than the rest. For example, in a volatile economic climate the price of petrol may fluctuate to a large degree. Hence, you are more likely to give the most recent data in your set of fuel prices more significance than earlier data, as it gives better representation of the current state of the market.

MEASURING ASSOCIATION

If you have gathered bivariate data, then an interesting test would be to find out if your two variables are associated in some way. For instance, you might be interested in researching a possible association or *correlation* between age and salary among a group of employees. Remember that correlation does not mean causation. For example, if an umbrella manufacturer finds that there is a correlation between umbrella sales and annual rainfall, this does not necessarily mean that increased rainfall causes an increase in umbrella sales. Other variables are likely to impact on sales. These might include pricing, state of the economy, or possibly competition in the market.

A correlation coefficient is used for bivariate analysis. It measures the extent to which two variables are linearly related. Measurement is represented between – 1 and 1. A value of 1 represents a perfect positive correlation; a perfect negative linear relationship is represented by a value – 1, and a correlation coefficient of 0 means that there is no relationship between the two variables. In other words, both variables are perfectly independent.

In reality, it is unlikely that you will produce findings that are perfectly correlated or perfectly independent. Typically, values usually fall somewhere between +/– 1 and 0.

A straightforward way to find out if there is a correlation between two variables is to plot the data. As we have seen earlier in this chapter, a scatter plot is a simple way of doing this as it clearly illustrates the correlation between two variables. However, it does not measure the strength of the relationship between two variables. In essence, there are two types of correlation coefficient – Pearson's product moment correlation coefficient and Spearman's rank correlation coefficient. These are examined below.

Pearson's product moment correlation coefficient

Pearson's product moment correlation (r) is a parametric technique that measures the strength of association between two variables or bivariate data. For example, you may wish to examine a possible relationship between advertising spend and number of sales, or age and height among teenagers. The data used must be of an interval or ratio type and be normally distributed.

If your answer produces a strong relationship between your x and y variables, this does not mean that x causes y. We can go on to test this possibility by carrying out regression analysis.

Pearson's product moment correlation coefficient is represented by the formula:

$$r = \frac{\sum xy - \frac{\sum x \sum y}{n}}{\sqrt{\left(\sum x^2 - \frac{(\sum x)^2}{n}\right)\left(\sum y^2 - \frac{(\sum y)^2}{n}\right)}}$$

where:

n = the number of data pairs

y = the dependent variable

x = the independent variable

$\sqrt{}$ = square root

Σ = the sum of

By way of an example, a manufacturing plant wants to test the association between the number of breakdowns to its equipment over a period of 10 days and the consequent time taken to carry out the repairs. The data is set out in Table 16.18.

Using the data in Table 16.18, we can now enter this into the formula. Thus:

$$r = \frac{\sum xy - \frac{\sum x \sum y}{n}}{\sqrt{\left(\sum x^2 - \frac{(\sum x)^2}{n}\right)\left(\sum y^2 - \frac{(\sum y)^2}{n}\right)}}$$

$$r = \frac{285 - \frac{(49)\times(87)}{15}}{\sqrt{\left[191 - \frac{49^2}{15}\right]\left[585 - \frac{87^2}{15}\right]}}$$

$$r = \frac{285 - \frac{4,263}{15}}{\sqrt{\left[191 - \frac{2,401}{15}\right]\left[585 - \frac{7,569}{15}\right]}}$$

$$r = \frac{285 - 284.2}{\sqrt{[191 - 160.07][585 - 504.6]}}$$

$$r = \frac{0.8}{\sqrt{(30.93)(80.4)}} = \frac{0.8}{\sqrt{2,486.77}} = \frac{0.8}{49.87} = 0.016$$

Table 16.18   Production output data

Day	Number of breakdowns (x)	Time taken to repair (minutes) (y)	xy	x²	y²
1	4	5	20	16	25
2	5	4	20	25	16
3	5	5	25	25	25
4	2	10	20	4	100
5	2	4	8	4	16
6	1	8	8	1	64
7	2	5	10	4	25
8	3	4	12	9	16
9	6	5	30	36	25
10	2	4	8	4	16
11	4	6	24	16	36
12	5	12	60	25	144
13	2	5	10	4	25
14	3	6	18	9	36
15	3	4	12	9	16
Total	49	87	285	191	585

The next step is to interpret our result. This can be made by checking the values of the correlation coefficient (r):

- between 0.70 to 0.99 is a strong positive correlation
- between 0.40 to 0.69 is a medium positive correlation
- between 0 to 0.39 is a weak positive correlation
- between 0 to –0.39 is a weak negative correlation
- between –0.40 to –0.69 is a medium negative correlation
- between –0.70 to –0.99 is a strong negative correlation.

In our above example, the result is 0.016. This means that there is a weak positive correlation between the number of breakdowns and the time taken to repair each breakdown. We examine correlation when using IBM SPSS Statistics, in Chapter 17.

Spearman's rank correlation coefficient

Spearman's rank correlation coefficient (rs) is used to test the strength and direction of association between two ordinal variables. It is a test of association that is used for non-parametric data and can be used to aid either the proving or disproving of a hypothesis, e.g. the profit of an organization increases as size of the organization increases (see Table 16.19). The formula given to Spearman's rank correlation coefficient is as follows:

$$r_s = 1 - \frac{6\sum d^2}{n(n^2 - 1)}$$

where:

d = the difference between the two rankings of one item of data

n = the number of items of data

Σ = the sum of

Table 16.19   Ranked data based on organization size and profit

Company	Number of employees	Rank of employees	Profit (£)	Rank profit	Difference between ranks (d)	d^2
1	130	3	20,000	10	7	49
2	80	8	120,000	5	3	9
3	120	4	180,000	3	1	1
4	300	1	375,000	1	0	0
5	150	2	210,000	2	0	0
6	100	5	150,000	4	1	1
7	35	9	110,000	6	3	9
8	90	6	95,000	8	2	4
9	89	7	82,000	9	2	4
10	25	10	98,000	7	3	9

$$\Sigma \, d^2 = 49 + 9 + 1 + 0 + 0 + 1 + 9 + 4 + 4 + 9$$

$$rs = 1 - \frac{6(86)}{10(100 - 1)}$$

$$= 1 - \frac{516}{990}$$

$$rs = 0.48$$

As noted earlier, the closer the r value is to +1 or -1, the stronger the likely correlation. You should now be aware that our value for the above example of 0.48 for r means that there is a medium positive relationship.

Chi-square test for independence (of association)

The chi-square test for independence determines whether there is an association between two categorical variables. The formula is:

$$x^2 = \sum \frac{(O - E)^2}{E}$$

where:

O = observed frequencies

E = expected frequencies

The test only applies to categorical data that are counts or frequencies, not percentages. The simplest example of presenting the association between observations and categories is to use a 2 × 2 contingency table. For example, in the data set 'supermarket choice' customers are grouped into age categories – Generation X, Y (2 categories). Customers were asked whether price or quality was their preference when choosing a supermarket in which to shop (see Table 16.20). We can use the chi-square test to test the association between the row and column variables in a two-way table. Our hypotheses are as follows:

* H0: There is no relationship between generations and preference
* H1: There is a relationship between generations and preference
* The level of significance to be used in this case is 5%

Table 16.20   Generational groups and preference when choosing a supermarket

Preference	Gen X	Gen Y	Total
Price	50	60	110
Quality	20	35	55
Total	70	95	165

The steps in the chi-squared test are as follows:

1. Calculate the expected frequencies and the observed frequencies. To calculate the 'Expected value' for each cell, multiply each row total by each column total and divide by the overall total. First example below.

$$110 \times 70 \,/\, 165 = 46.67$$

Adopt the same process to establish other expected values. See Table 16.21.

Table 16.21   Expected frequency table

Factors	Gen X	Gen Y
Price	46.67	63.33
Quality	23.33	31.67

2. For each observed number in the table subtract the corresponding number $(O - E)$
3. Square the difference $(O - E)^2$
4. Divide the squares for each cell in the table by the expected number for that cell $(O - E)^2/E$
5. Sum all the values for $(O - E)^2/E$. This then gives you the chi square statistic.

To calculate point 5 in our example:

$$x^2 = (50 - 46.67)^2/46.67 + (60 - 63.33)^2/63.33 + (20 - 23.33)^2/23.33 + (35 - 31.67)^2/31.67$$

$$= 0.24 + 0.18 + 0.48 + 0.35$$

$$= 1.25$$

Next, we calculate the degrees of freedom (df). The degrees of freedom for a x^2 table are calculated with the formula:

(Number of rows – 1) x (Number of columns – 1). For our example $(2 - 1) \times (2 - 1) = 1$

Using a x^2 table, the tabular x^2 value at 0.05 level of significance and 1 df is 3.84. As the calculated x^2 of 1.25 is less than the tabular value, we fail to reject the null hypothesis and conclude that there is no significant association between generations in terms of preference.

MEASURING DIFFERENCE

Measuring the difference involves testing a hypothesis that there is a difference between an observed frequency and an expected frequency. In the last section, we looked at the strength of association between variables. The data we have used to carry out these tests has been ordinal, interval or ratio data. Earlier in the chapter, we looked at the chi-square test for association. The chi-square 'Goodness of Fit' test can be used when you have categorical data for one independent variable, and you want to examine whether the distribution of your data is similar or different to that expected. Another technique used to test the difference is the Student's t-test, which we examine below.

Student's t-test

The *Student's t-test* is a parametric technique used to test the difference between sample means. The samples must be gathered from two different populations. In short, the Student's t-test establishes the probability that two populations are the same in relation to the variable that is being tested. In order to carry out a t-test, your data must be normally distributed, of interval or ratio status and two data sets must have similar variances. In addition, for a paired t-test (see below) each data pair must be related.

T-tests infer the likelihood of three or more distinct groups being different. An independent t-test is used to test the difference between two independent groups, e.g. male and female. Let us say that you gathered data on IQ levels among female engineers and lawyers, and compared the sample means using the t-test. A probability of 0.4 means that there is a 40% chance that you cannot distinguish between your group of engineers and lawyers based on IQ alone.

A paired sample t-test is used to establish whether or not there exists a significant difference between the mean values of matched samples. It is often used to measure a case before and after some form of manipulation or changes have taken place. For example, you might use a paired t-test to establish the significance of a difference in exam performance prior to and after a professional training programme. A paired t-test can also be used to compare samples. For instance, our exam example may involve comparing the effectiveness of the training programme in improving exam scores by sampling employees from different companies and comparing the scores of those respondents who have taken part and those who have not taken part in the training.

BOX 16.1: RESEARCH SNAPSHOT

A key aspect of quantitative analysis is recognizing the type of data and the methods for presenting data. In your research project, pay attention to the 'how' you are presenting data, as well as 'what' the data means. Often, students are clear when presenting data, but not enough attention is given to analyzing and interpreting data. In addition, when analyzing data, do also consider how your results compare to earlier studies. For example, to what extent do they contradict or correspond to earlier studies?

ASSESSING THE STRENGTH OF RELATIONSHIP BETWEEN VARIABLES

The final section of statistical analysis often involves assessing the strength of relationship between variables.

Regression analysis

Although a detailed analysis and application of regression analysis is beyond the scope of this book, this part of the chapter provides a brief introduction into how it might be applied to your research. *Regression analysis* is a statistical technique for investigating the strength of a relationship between variables. Typically, the researcher aims to establish the causal effect of one variable on another. For example, the effect of an increase in price on consumer demand, or company size on performance. Essentially, there are two main types of regression analysis – *simple regression* and *multiple regression*.

Simple regression determines the strength of relationship between a dependent variable and one independent variable. It aims to find the extent that a dependent (y) and independent variable (x) are linearly related. A regression equation is often represented on a scatter plot by a regression line. A regression line is used to clearly illustrate the relationship between the variables under investigation. For example, in linear regression you might want to investigate the relationship between profit and advertising spend. First, let us look at the formula for linear regression, and then how this relates to our profit and advertising spend example. The formula is:

$$y = a + bx$$

where:

x = independent variable

y = dependent variable

a = point where the line intersects the y axis

b = gradient of the line

Profit = $a + bx$ advertising spend

Multiple *linear regression* aims to find a linear relationship between a dependent variable (y) and several independent variables (x). The multiple regression correlation coefficient (r^2) is a measure of the proportion of variability explained by, or due to, the linear relationship in a sample of paired data. It is represented by a number between 0 and 1. The formula for multiple regression is:

$$y = a + b_1 x_1 + b_2 x_2 + b_3 x_3 + b_4 x_4 + b_5 x_5 + b_6 x_6...$$

Let us say that our example of the relationship between profit and advertising spend was to take into account other factors. For instance, profit might also be affected by staff training expenditure, price, bonuses and competition. This would be represented in the following multiple regression formula:

$$\text{Profit} = a + (b1 \times \text{staff training expenditure}) + (b2 \times \text{price}) + (b3 \times \text{bonuses}) + (b4 \times \text{number of competitors}).$$

If the above equation was implemented, the regression coefficient indicates how good a predictor it is likely to be. Remember that the value produced is between –1 and +1. A figure of +1 indicates that your equation is a perfect predictor. Conversely, a value of 0 shows that the equation predicts none of the variation.

DECIDING WHICH STATISTICAL TESTS TO USE

Brown and Saunders (2008: 103–104) make the following suggestions before choosing a particular test:

- What is the research question I am trying to answer?
- What are the characteristics of the sample? For instance, are you using judgment sampling, snowball sampling, etc.?
- What types of data do I have?
- How many data variables are there?
- How many groups are there?
- Are the data distributed normally? If the data are not distributed normally, will this affect the statistic I want to use?
- Are the samples independent?
- Is the data representative of the population?
- Are the groups different?
- Is there a relationship between the variables?

STATISTICAL SOFTWARE PACKAGES

If your research involves quantitative data analysis, it is unlikely that you will do the work manually. Most computers have access to some kind of spreadsheet package, such as Microsoft Excel. These certainly allow you to carry out elementary statistical analysis. Yet, they do not have the range of options typically associated with statistical packages. Fortunately, there are now several excellent software packages on the market. Many of these are user-friendly and ideal for the student researcher. Two of the leading packages used in UK institutions are IBM SPSS Statistics and Minitab. This book is not intended to provide a comprehensive guide on how to use either of these packages. The important thing is that you recognize the advantages of using such a package as opposed to undertaking manual quantitative data analysis. The advantages of using a statistical software package are:

- it saves time
- you avoid the need to learn how to perform calculations
- it provides greater scope for your analysis
- data can be easily recorded, interpreted and presented.

Although there are clearly advantages associated with using a package such as IBM SPSS Statistics, there are still two important considerations. First, make sure you understand the purpose of statistical tests. Second, understand the circumstances in which they can be used.

Image 16.1   Concept Cartoon 'Quantitative data analysis'

In the Concept Cartoon in this chapter, characters are discussing the use of statistical methods. What do you think? Again, use the opportunity to discuss the scenario with your fellow students.

EXAMPLES OF STUDIES USING QUANTITATIVE ANALYSIS

In this section, we look at two examples of studies that have used quantitative data analysis. Again, the purpose of these examples is to show you how quantitative analysis is used in practice. Furthermore, you may find possible takeaways that you can use in your own research. Each study is from a different area of business and management.

Example A

The objective of this study by Asare-Nuamah (2017) was to assess the factors affecting international students' satisfaction at an Indian University. In terms of methodology, the researcher adopted a descriptive research design and quantitative research approach. The sample size comprised 29 international students. Data collection was based on a structured questionnaire. The entire population was taken as the sample size and a census survey was carried out. A simple probability sampling procedure was followed in selecting the respondents for the study.

Data collection involved using a structured questionnaire. The questionnaire had two sections. Section 'A' collected data on respondents' characteristics, while section 'B' collected data on students' satisfaction levels and made use of a five-point Likert scale that was comprised of 1 = strongly dissatisfied, 2 = dissatisfied, 3 = neutral, 4 = satisfied and 5 = strongly satisfied.

Descriptive data analysis was done using IBM Statistical Package for Social Sciences (SPSS) version 20. Statistical tools, such as mode and percentages, were used for the analysis of data. The researcher pointed out that the use of the mode gives a clearer picture in the case of Likert scale analysis as compared to mean.

To ensure content validity and to make sure the instrument was measuring what it was intended to measure, the researcher sought the views of experts in the design of the questionnaire. Initial views and feedback from students helped in designing the questionnaire to suit the need of the research and to enhance validity of the research and the instrument. The researcher also undertook in-depth discussion with experts to ensure that all variables needed to effectively collect data for the research were given importance and attention. The literature review also gave an idea of the variables that can and must be included in the questionnaire in order to fully understand and assess students' satisfaction.

The results indicated that students have high satisfaction for library, contact with teachers, class size, course content, reading materials and administrative services of the University.

Although clearly a small study, with a sample size of only 29 participants, this study gives you an insight into the relationship between data collection and data analysis. In this case, Likert scale questions were used and analysis focused on descriptive statistics.

The author refers to the mode – remember that the mode is the value that occurs most often within a data set. Researchers often use the median for Likert scale data, this is because those are ordinal (not interval) data.

Example B

In this second example, Mowbray and Hall (2020) examined the use of social media during job searching. Data supplied by young jobseekers in Scotland were analyzed to investigate the role of social media in job search. The research questions are as follows:

RQ1. What is the role of social media in job search?

RQ2. What factors influence social media use during job search?

RQ3. What impact does social media use have on job search outcomes?

The study was implemented sequentially in a two-stage iterative design. Qualitative data were gathered at the first stage to generate knowledge on social media use during job search at the level of the individual. When these data were analyzed, the researchers were then able to identify variables that could be used in the next stage of the research process. The qualitative data were used to generate questions for the survey due to the lack of previous studies specifically on social media and job search.

(Continued)

Interview, focus group and survey data supplied by young jobseekers in Scotland were analyzed to investigate the role of social media in job search. An extract from the survey focusing on 'General media use' is highlighted below, with the type of measure in brackets:

General social media:

1. Do you have a Facebook account (Nominal)?
2. How often do you use Facebook (Ordinal)?
3. How many Facebook friends do you have (Ordinal)?
4. Do you have a Twitter account (Nominal)?
5. How often do you use Twitter (Ordinal)?
6. How many Twitter accounts do you follow (Ordinal)?
7. Do you have a LinkedIn account (Nominal)?
8. How often do you use LinkedIn (Ordinal)?
9. How many LinkedIn connections do you have (Ordinal)?

For general social media use, a frequency distribution table was used to show the survey findings. Facebook was more popular than Twitter and LinkedIn. At the time of data collection, 96.6% (n = 539) of the respondents had a Facebook account. In comparison, 49.6% (n = 277) were on Twitter and 29.4% (n = 164) on LinkedIn.

An extract from the results showed that only social media variables are positively associated with the offer of telephone interviews. The highest coefficients are for using LinkedIn to look for jobs ($R^2 = 9.0\%$) and to contact someone about jobs ($R^2 = 10.9\%$). Therefore, out of all the measured variables in this analysis, LinkedIn use was the most closely associated with telephone interview invitations. The findings are statistically significant ($p < 0.01$).

This article is a good example of how to combine both qualitative and quantitative research. In terms of the latter, the authors used descriptive statistics, such as a frequency distribution table to analyze results. This is followed up with correlation analysis – an inferential statistical technique.

CHAPTER SUMMARY

- Quantitative analysis is usually associated with finding answers to 'What' and 'How much' questions.

- Statistics is a branch of mathematics that is applied to quantitative data in order to draw conclusions and make predictions.

- Parametric methods are used when you are able to estimate the parameters of distribution in the population.

- Non-parametric methods are used where a normal distribution cannot be ascertained.

- A variable is something that can be measured or counted. Another term for variable is 'data item'. Example of variables include age, gender, nationality, exam marks and salary.

- There are three categories of data analysis – univariate, bivariate and multivariate.

- There are four scales of measurement – nominal, ordinal, interval and ratio. These scales are important when determining the types of statistics that may be legitimately employed.

- The advantage of coding is that it will ultimately make your analysis easier and less confusing. Again, it is essential for most statistical software packages.

- A graph is a type of diagram used to present data. A graph can be used to analyze bivariate or multivariate data.

- There are two broad approaches to describing your data: measuring central tendency and measuring dispersion.

- Inferential statistics are calculated so that they allow researchers to infer or generalize the findings from a sample to the entire population of interest.

QUESTIONS FOR REVIEW

1. Give three examples of discrete variables. Justify your answer.

2. Explain the difference between descriptive and inferential statistics.

3. Give examples of univariate, bivariate and multivariate analysis.

4. What does 'measuring central tendency' mean and what are the main ways of measuring central tendency?

5. What does 'measuring dispersion' mean and what are the main ways of measuring dispersion?

6. Explain what a tree map is and give an example of how this might be applied by a researcher.

7. Explain what is meant by a Type I error and a Type II error.

8. What is regression analysis and what are the two main types of regression analysis?

9. What is a scatter diagram (scatter plot) and give an example of how this might be applied?

10. Explain what is meant by the term 'Spearman's rank correlation coefficient (rs)'.

STUDENT SCENARIO: SONITA PREPARES TO CONDUCT QUANTITATIVE DATA ANALYSIS

Sonita is studying on an MSc in Management degree and is at the analysis stage in the research process. The focus of her research is on the relationship between social media preference and brand preference. The latter looks at different types of brand categories in the supermarket industry – namely, 'value', 'standard' and 'premium'. Sonita was particularly interested to see if there was a relationship between demographics, such as age, gender and social class on social media and brand preference. She used an online questionnaire survey to gather her data. Chosen sampling methods used included a combination of convenience sampling and judgment sampling. Sonita used the latter based on the social media plat-forms she considered the most likely to generate the best response rate, together with the demographic

(Continued)

profile associated with each platform. She was pleased to achieve a 45% response rate (n = 125). Although Sonita had planned her data analysis process and techniques she intended to use when writing her research proposal, she was still keen to 'experiment' using different methods. Sonita had taken a course on how to use IBM SPSS Statistics and would be using the software package to analyze her data.

Univariate analysis

Sonita was familiar with data analysis, in particular, the fact that data analysis can be carried out using univariate analysis (the use of one variable in analysis), bivariate analysis (the use of two variables in analysis) and multivariate analysis (the use of three or more variables in analysis). Table 16.22 shows an extract to the question 'What is your social media platform preference?'

Table 16.22   Frequency distribution table – social media preferences

1.   What is your social media platform preference?

☐ 1 Facebook ☐ 2 Instagram ☐ 3 Snapchat ☐ 4 Twitter ☐ 5 WeChat ☐ 6 Other

	Frequency	Percent	Valid percent	Cumulative percent
1 Facebook	240	33.9	34	34
2 Instagram	124	17.5	17.8	51.8
3 Snapchat	66	9.3	9.6	60.4
4 Twitter	55	7.8	7.8	68.2
5 WeChat	138	19.5	19.7	87.9
6 Other	77	10.9	11.1	100.0
Total	700	98.9	100.0	
Missing	8	1.1		
Total	708	100.0		

Multivariate analysis

Table 16.23 is from Sonita's pilot study. In this table, we have three variables – age, gender and brand preference. When conducting her pilot study, Sonita was particularly keen to analyze her initial findings as the outcome would inform the final questionnaire survey. The focus of Sonita's study is very much on the relationship between variables. She intended presenting her final results using tables, charts, graphs, and bivariate analysis using cross-tabulations.

Table 16.23   Multivariate analysis – age, gender and brand preference

"What is your typical brand purchase?" (%)					
		under 35		35 and older	Age
		Male	Female	Male	Female	Gender
Brand preference	Value	15	18	25	30	
	Standard	35	38	40	36	
	Premium	50	44	35	34	
	Total	100	100	100	100	

Questions

1. Examine Table 16.22. How would you interpret the research findings?
2. Examine Table 16.23. How would you interpret the research findings?
3. Sonita has used a wide range of question techniques in her questionnaire survey. These include Likert scale, semantic differential scale, rank-order and open-ended questions. Outline other quantitative methods Sonita might use to analyze her data.

Hint: Remember that the type of quantitative methods you use is dependent on the type of data and research questions. Using analytical techniques is not just about the 'what' but also the 'why' you are using certain method(s).

FURTHER READING

Bergin, T. (2018) *An Introduction to Data Analysis: Quantitative, Qualitative and Mixed Methods*. London: Sage.

A concise book that focuses on a range of techniques for conducting quantitative, qualitative and mixed methods data analysis.

Kozak, M., Hartley, J., Wnuk, A. and Tartanus, M. (2015) 'Multiple pie charts: Unreadable, inefficient, and over-used', *Journal of Scholarly Publishing*, 46 (3): 282–289.

This paper examines the use of pie charts, in particular, the authors argue that the use of multiple pie charts are difficult to analyze and interpret.

Lutabingwa, J. and Auriacombe, C.J. (2007) 'Data analysis in quantitative research', *Journal of Public Administration*, 42 (6): 528–548.

An insightful article that discusses different steps in quantitative analysis, together with analytical methods.

REFERENCES

Albers, M.J. (2017) 'Quantitative data analysis: In the graduate curriculum', *Journal of Technical Writing and Communication*, 47 (2): 215–233.

Asare-Nuamah, P. (2017) 'International students' satisfaction: Assessing the determinants of satisfaction', *Higher Education for the Future*, 4 (1): 44–59.

Brown, R.B. and Saunders, M. (2008) *Dealing with Statistics: What You Need To Know*. Maidenhead: McGraw-Hill/Open University Press.

Bryman, A. (2004) *Social Research Methods* (2nd edn). Oxford: Oxford University Press.

DeShea, L. and Toothaker, L.E. (2015) *Introductory Statistics*. New York: Taylor & Francis.

Doering, T.R. and Hubbard, R. (1979) 'Measurement and statistics: The ordinal-interval controversy and geography', *Area*, 11 (3): 237–243.

Mowbray, J.A. and Hall, H. (2020) 'Using social media during job search: The case of 16–24-year-olds in Scotland', *Journal of Information Science*: 1–16.

Schutt, R.K. and Chambliss, D.F. (2012) *Making Sense of the Social World: Methods of Investigation*. Thousand Oaks, CA: Sage.

SunLife (2020) *History of House Prices in Britain*. Available at: www.sunlife.co.uk/articles-guides/your-money/the-price-of-a-home-in-britain-then-and-now/ (accessed 10 January 2021).

Wainer, H. (2013) *Visual Revelations: Graphical Tales of Fate and Deception from Napoleon Bonaparte to Ross Perot*. London: Psychology Press.

Waters, D. (1997) *Quantitative Methods for Business* (4th edn). Harlow: FT/Prentice Hall.

Wilson, J.S. (2014) *Essentials of Business Research: A Guide to Doing your Research Project*. London: Sage.

17

GETTING STARTED WITH IBM SPSS STATISTICS

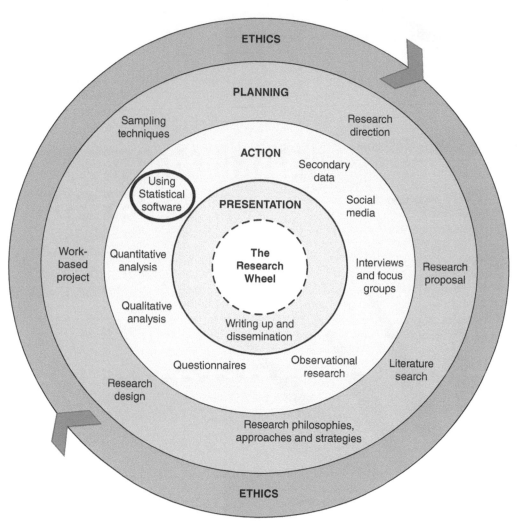

Figure 17.1   The Research Wheel

Learning objectives

By the end of this chapter, you should be able to:

- know how to prepare your data for analysis

- understand how to use the Data View and Variable View

- be able to create a data file

- know how to produce descriptive statistics using IBM SPSS Statistics

- know how to produce inferential statistics using IBM SPSS Statistics

- be able to analyze data using IBM SPSS Statistics.

INTRODUCTION

In the preceding chapter, we looked at quantitative data analysis, including brief reference to using statistical software packages. This chapter provides an introduction to how to use IBM SPSS Statistics version 27. It introduces *some of the more commonly used statistical methods* that you might use in your research project. Prior to carrying out your analysis, you will need to prepare your data. Hence, the chapter begins with a discussion on the preparation needed before analyzing data. This includes how to use the 'Variable View' and the 'Data View' in IBM SPSS Statistics.

Next, we examine how to produce descriptive statistics using IBM SPSS Statistics, including how to produce tables, graphs and charts. The remainder of the chapter includes examples of various statistical tests you can do. The emphasis in the chapter is not just on 'what' tests you can use, but also 'why' you are using them and how to interpret the results.

Finally, as with other chapters, there is a student scenario and questions for you to answer at the end of the chapter.

As you can see by Figure 17.1, 'Using Statistical software' is in the 'Action' layer in The Research Wheel model (EPAP). This is because like the two preceding chapters, the emphasis is on analysis. In particular, there are parallels with Chapter 16 as we are interested in quantitative analysis. Many of the analytical techniques discussed in the last chapter will be applied when using IBM SPSS Statistics.

WHAT IS IBM SPSS STATISTICS?

IBM SPSS Statistics is a software package designed for analyzing quantitative data. SPSS stands for 'Statistical Package for the Social Sciences'. It can be used to analyze data from a range of data collection methods, including online questionnaire surveys, observations and tests. The software is particularly suitable for student researchers doing survey research. It can provide a variety of functions, although its main usage is for analyzing and presenting data. IBM SPSS Statistics is widely used in colleges and universities, so there is a strong likelihood you will be able to use the software via your institution. The purpose of the remainder of this chapter is to introduce you to the software.

GETTING STARTED

The following steps refer to how to start IBM SPSS Statistics from the Start menu.
To Start IBM SPSS Statistics 27:

- Click the Start button on the taskbar, click IBM SPSS Statistics 27. If you are using the program for the first time the dialog box opens. Close the box.

THE DATA EDITOR WINDOW

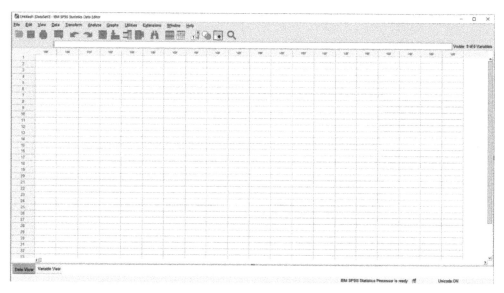

Figure 17.2   IBM SPSS Statistics Data Editor window

The Data Editor window opens with two view tabs (see Figure 17.2): Data View and Variable View. The former is used for entering data, while the latter for adding variables and defining variable properties. The Data Editor window contains several components.

First, the Title bar at the top of the screen displays the name of the file. Underneath the Title bar is the Menu bar. The menu contains the following:

1. File: Create new files and open existing files, save files and print.
2. Edit: Modify and copy text.
3. View: Change characteristics of windows.
4. Data: Used for defining variables, insert and sort cases and variables, select cases.
5. Transform: Rank and recode cases, and create new variables from existing data.
6. Analyze: Holds a selection of statistical procedures for analyzing data.
7. Graphs: Create a range of graphs and charts.
8. Utilities: Displays file and variable information.
9. Extensions: Additional tools and services provided by IBM SPSS Statistics.
10. Window: Arrange, select and control attributes of windows.
11. Help: Access to information on how to use the many features of IBM SPSS Statistics.

The additional features in the Data Editor window include the following:

- Underneath the Menu bar is the Data Editor toolbar.
- The columns with the headings Var are where to enter each variable.
- Each white rectangular box is a cell in which to enter data.
- Each numbered box to the left of the screen represents a case.
- In the bottom left-hand corner of the screen is the Data View tab and the Variable View tab.

Data View

The Data Editor opens in Data View. This is evident as the Data View tab is grey with a blue line underneath. Clicking on the Variable View tab switches from the Data View tab.

In Data View:

- Each row represents a case with each case listed numerically down the left-hand side. Your research participants can be cases. For example, if you have received 50 responses to your survey and intend entering the data into IBM SPSS Statistics, then you have 50 cases (or rows in which to enter the data).
- Each column represents a variable, e.g. gender, age, nationality and is presently headed Var until a variable is entered into the Variable View. Commonly defined variable types are string or numeric. Variable names must start with a letter. When defining a variable as numeric you need to specify number of decimal places. As you name your variables, make sure to make each one meaningful so that you remember what the variable represents.
- A cell is an intersection between cases and variables. Each response to a survey question is entered into a cell based on the variable type. For example, if in your survey you have a closed question, then you may enter 1 = Yes, 2 = No into the cell, depending on the respondent's answer.

Variable View

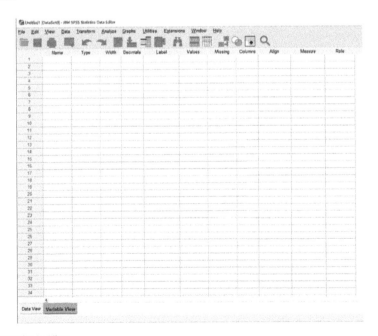

Figure 17.3   The Variable View

The **Variable View** is where to define variables by assigning variable names and specifying the attributes of each variable (see Figure 17.3). Click on **Variable View** in the bottom left-hand corner of the screen. We are now in the **Variable View** screen. The elements in the **Variable View** screen are as follows:

- Variable name is where you enter short and meaningful names to variables, for example, age, gender, Edu (level of education).
- Variable type determines how variables are to be entered. Clicking to the right of the cell brings up the **Variable Type** options.
- Variable labels allow users to describe what the variable name represents. To avoid confusion, variable labels must clearly define variable names.

CREATING YOUR FIRST DATA FILE

It is now time to create your first data file. First, you need to define the variables, and second, enter the data. Defining the variables should be planned in advance and certainly not left until just before entering your data. Once you have defined your variables, you are ready to start to enter the data.

Defining your variables

Assign your variables based on an extract from the data spreadsheet (see Table 17.1).

Table 17.1   Extract from a data spreadsheet

Subject	Age	Education	Monthly salary (£)	Online shopping monthly spend (£)
001	34	2	2,500	150
002	28	1	1,800	50
003	45	3	3,000	225
004	56	4	3,600	180
005	34	3	2,800	90
006	67	1	4,000	240
007	61	1	2,400	120
008	44	2	2,900	415
009	55	3	3,200	350
010	19	1	1,600	150
011	22	1	2,100	200
012	38	3	3,800	450

1. First, click the **Variable View tab** in the lower-left hand corner of the Data Editor window. The view should then turn grey with blue underline.
2. Type the name in the first cell under the **Name** column; type a word to identify the variable. The name must start with a letter and should not have any spaces. In some surveys each respondent is given a number in order to preserve anonymity, i.e., subject number. So, type **Subject** as the first variable and press enter. If you have made a mistake, to delete, click on the case number, followed by edit in Menu Bar and Clear.
3. The second variable related to the first question in our questionnaire is **Age**. We can refer to this as simply **Age**, so type this in the cell under **Subject**. You can call Education 'Edu', then 'Salary' (monthly salary of respondent) and 'Spend' (monthly online shopping spend).

Type

The two basic types of variable that you will use are numeric and string.

- *Numeric variables* can only have numbers allocated and are suitable for numerical calculations.
- *String variables* may contain letters, numbers or other characters.

When deciding whether a variable is string or numeric, nominal variables with many categories should be treated as string variables.

To change a variable type, left click on the small box on the right-hand side of the cell. This brings up the Variable Type dialog box (see Figure 17.4). If you select a numeric variable, you can then click in the Width box or the Decimal Places box to change the default values of eight and two characters respectively. For whole numbers, you can drop the decimals down to zero. If you select a string variable, you can indicate the number of characters to be allowed for data entry in this string variable. For example, if you had a variable type called Name, then this would be String.

1. In the case of the four variables in this example – Age, Education, Monthly Salary and Online Shopping Spend, there is no need to change the default Numeric setting.

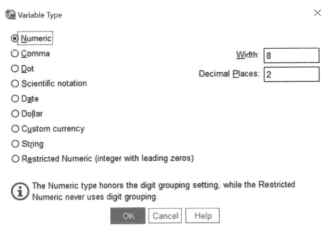

Figure 17.4   Variable Type dialog box

2. The next column is Label. This helps you to recognize the variable. For example, for Subject type the Label 'Respondent ID', for Age 'Age of Respondent', for Edu 'Level of education', Salary 'Salary of Respondent' and Spend 'Online Spending'. Your Variable View should now look like Figure 17.5.

3. The next column is Values. This is for entering the codes and what they represent. For example, out of our variables the question about highest level of education is a categorical variable. The categories are as follows: 1 = High School, 2 = A level or equivalent, 3 = Undergraduate degree, 4 = Postgraduate degree or higher. We are now going to enter these values into IBM SPSS Statistics. For the Edu variable, left click to the right of the cell under Values and a window will appear called Value labels. In the Value Box enter '1' and in the Label Box enter 'High School' and click Add. Next, enter '2' in the Value Box and 'A levels or equivalent' in the Label Box and click Add. Next, enter '3' in the Value Box and 'Undergraduate degree' in the Label Box and click Add. Finally, in the Value Box enter '4' and in the Label Box enter 'Postgraduate degree or PhD' then click the OK button. See Figure 17.6 showing value labels for the Edu variable.

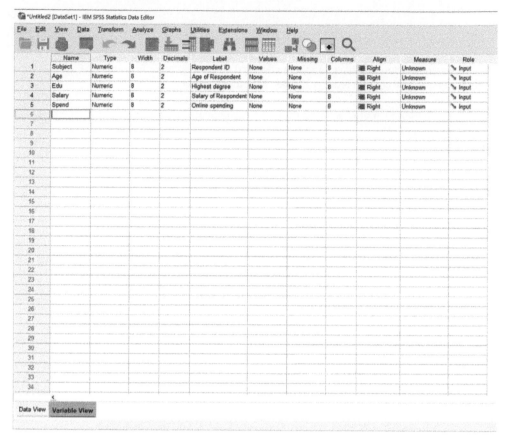

Figure 17.5   Variable View after entering Variable Labels

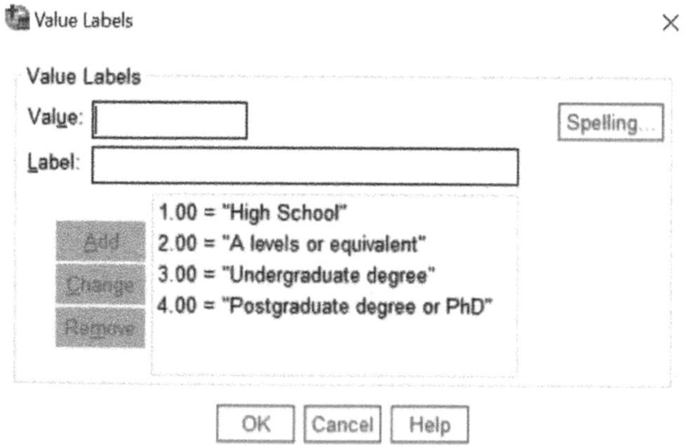

Figure 17.6   Value Labels for the Edu variable

4. The next column is **Missing** data. Sometimes respondents may miss out a question because they choose to do so or it is not applicable. If it is not applicable, then you should include this as an option in your questionnaire. Any non-responses must be coded. SPSS IBM Statistics provides a default measure for missing data or non-response. You can choose your own number, but make sure that the same number is used for all non-responses. Choose a number unlikely to be used and easily recognizable, e.g. 9999. In this example there are no missing data.

5. Columns refers to how many columns wide you would like the variable to be presented in the **Data View**. We will leave it at the default.

6. In the **Align** column, you can change the presentation so that scores for the variable are left justified, right justified or centred. We will leave it at the default.

7. In the **Measure** column, SPSS IBM Statistics gives you the following choice of measurement levels: nominal (categorical), ordinal (for example, rank order – high, medium, low), or scale. A scale variable is a numeric measurement such as height or weight. The current default measure is **Nominal** so we need to change **Respondent ID, Age of Respondent, Salary of Respondent** and **Online Spending** to **Scale** measure. First, in the Measure column for Subject, left click to the right of the cell. A drop-down arrow appears showing **Scale, Ordinal** and **Nominal**. Click on **Scale**. Repeat this process for all of the other variables except **Edu**. As **Edu** is a categorical variable, keep the measure as **Nominal**. Your **Variable View** should now look like Figure 17.7.

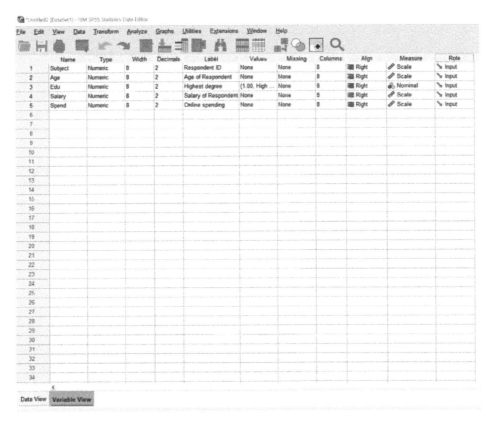

Figure 17.7 Variable View showing entered Measures

8. Role is a feature of newer versions of IBM SPSS Statistics. The column here is concerned with the role your variable is going to take in the analysis. For the procedures we are going to carry out it can be left as the default role of Input.

Once you have completed naming and defining the properties of the variables, save your work under the filename 'Shopping'. To save your work click on *File > Save As > Shopping>Save*
  SPSS IBM Statistics automatically adds the suffix '.sav'

Entering data

After defining your variables, you are now ready to start entering the data for each case from the data set as shown in Table 17.1. To do this:

1. Click the **Data View** tab in the lower left-hand corner of the Data Editor window. This should then turn grey with a blue underline.
2. Click in each cell to type your corresponding data. The entry is also displayed in the cell editor.

Once you have entered your data, your **Data View** screen should look like Figure 17.8

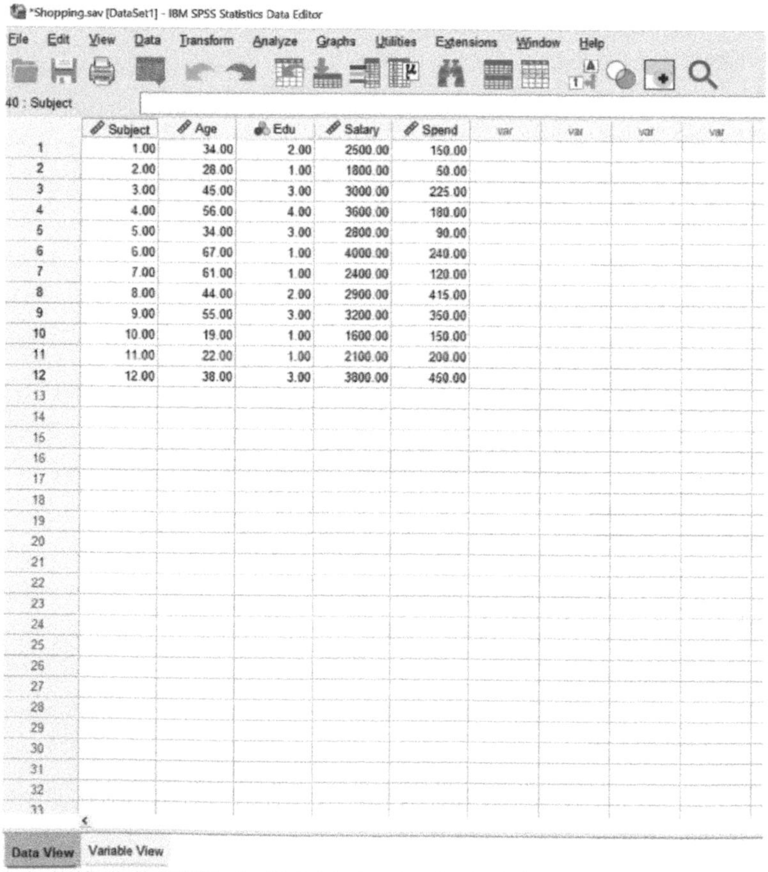

Figure 17.8   Completed data entry in Data View

When you have completed the data entry, again save your work by clicking on *File > Save*. Entering data can be time consuming and tedious. However, it is important to make sure that you enter the data accurately into the program, as incorrectly entered data will of course impact the results and analysis of your findings.

Recoding variables

In some cases, we may wish to recode a variable. This is done if we want to combine the values of a variable into fewer categories. For example, let us say that you have conducted a customer survey and one of the questions was on preferred delivery times. Instead of asking participants to enter the specific number of hours, one way is to group the data. This involves recoding. Let us look at an example. A researcher is doing research on the services provided by different delivery organizations. At this stage in the analysis, the researcher has decided to recode the 'Deliver time' variable. To do this, the researcher needs to decide how many categories will be used and which of the old values are going to be combined into the new categories.

Start by creating a data file by entering the data below (in Table 17.2). The location variable has the following values: 1 = North, 2 = South, 3 = East, 4 = West. The gender variable is coded as 1 for female and 2 for male.

Table 17.2   Data from delivery data set

Case no.	Gender	Delivery time (hours)	Location
1	1	12	1
2	2	26	3
3	2	40	2
4	1	19	4
5	2	42	4
6	1	35	1
7	1	27	2
8	2	47	2
9	2	13	3
10	2	15	1

For our 'Delivery' example, we are going to organize the data into two categories (see Table 17.3). This will allow us to compare customers of different groupings. For the purposes of this exercise the categories are as follows: 'non-standard delivery' and 'standard delivery'.

Table 17.3   Recoding delivery time variable to a new variable

The delivery time given by the respondent (from the Data View)	Speed (new variable)
12–37 hours	Non-standard
38–50 hours	Standard

Using IBM SPSS Statistics, we are now going to recode the Delivery variable.

1. Click on *Transform>Recode* into different variables.
2. Next, click on Delivery time in the list of variables and click on the transfer arrow to the left of the box. In the Output Variable Box give the variable a new name of 'Speed'.

3. Then, in the label box, give the new variable a label of 'Speed in 2 categories' and click on the Change button to tell IBM SPSS Statistics to make the changes.
4. The next step is to tell IBM SPSS Statistics how to create the new categories. Click on the Old and New Values button. We are now going to input the range of values for each category. Select Range, then type '12' underneath. Under 'through' type '37'. This is the fastest time from our 'non-standard' category.
5. Next, select Value in the New Value: Box and type 0 in the box. Then click Add. Now follow the same process for the other category, typing 1 in the New Value: Box.
6. Once you have entered details for each category, click Continue, followed by the OK button. IBM SPSS Statistics will then confirm that recoding has taken place.

We can now check to see our new category for 'Speed in 2 categories', using the following steps:

1. Click on *Analyze>Descriptive Statistics>Frequencies*. You should now see 'Speed in 2 categories [Speed]' in the variables list.
2. Click on [Speed in 2 categories] and click on the arrow to move to the Variables box.
3. Click the OK button.

If you now go to Variable View, you will see that there are no values for our speed category. Click on the values cell to enter value labels as follows: 0 = non-standard, 1 = standard. See the output in Table 17.4.

Table 17.4 Recoding a variable: Speed in 2 categories

Speed in 2 categories

		Frequency	Percent	Valid Percent	Cumulative Percent
Valid	non-standard	7	70.0	70.0	70.0
	standard	3	30.0	30.0	100.0
	Total	10	100.0	100.0	

DESCRIPTIVE STATISTICS

After you have entered your data into the Data Editor, the next step is to analyze your data using descriptive statistics. As we saw in the last chapter, summarizing and presenting your data typically takes place before inferential statistics. A good starting point when analyzing your data is to look at the *frequency distribution* or measures of central tendency.

Question 1: How many respondents hold a postgraduate degree or PhD?

FREQUENCY DISTRIBUTION ANALYSIS

We can use frequency distribution analysis to answer the above question. A descriptive statistical method, it involves counting how many respondents hold a postgraduate degree or PhD. Given the small sample size, we can simply count the number without using IBM SPSS Statistics. However, in your research, you may have entered data for several hundred participants. Thus, using statistical software is much less time consuming. When we run the frequencies test, IBM SPSS Statistics can also calculate the mean, median and mode to provide us further insight into the data. To answer Question 1 from the 'Shopping' data set we carry out the following steps:

1. Click *File > Open>Data>*Shopping.sav*>Open*
2. Click the Analyze menu, scroll down and point to Descriptive Statistics, and then click Frequencies.
3. In the Frequencies dialog box, select the variable that you want to analyze. In this example, click the 'Edu' variable in the box on the left, and then click the transfer arrow button. 'Edu' will then move to the Variable(s): box (see Figure 17.9).

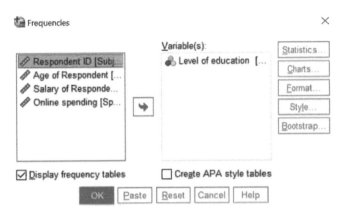

Figure 17.9   Frequencies dialog box

4. Ensure that the Display frequency tables box is ticked.
5. Click the OK button.

Table 17.5 shows the statistics and frequencies output for Level of education. The columns of the table display Frequency, Percent, Valid Percent and Cumulative Percent for each level of education.

Table 17.5   Frequency table for level of education

Statistics			
Level of education			
N	Valid		12
	Missing		0

Level of education		Frequency	Percent	Valid Percent	Cumulative Percent
Valid	High School	5	41.7	41.7	41.7
	A level or equivalent	2	16.7	16.7	58.3
	Undergraduate degree	4	33.3	33.3	91.7
	Postgraduate degree or PhD	1	8.3	8.3	100.0
	Total	12	100.0	100.0	

What can we interpret from the output? The most common level of education is High School, with 5, or nearly 42% out of the 12 respondents holding this level of education. Only one respondent holds a postgraduate degree or PhD. If this were a larger study, we could compare our findings to see to what extent the results compare or contradict with earlier research.

MEASURES OF CENTRAL TENDENCY

For the next task, we are going to use the measures of central tendency (mean, median and mode) when analyzing the Salary variable. The question for this task:

Question 2: What is the measure of central tendency for Salary?

If you have saved and closed the Shopping.sav file, open the file by carrying out the following steps:

1. Click File > Open>Data>Shopping.sav>Open
2. Click the Analyze menu, scroll down and point to Descriptive Statistics, and then click Frequencies.
3. In the Frequencies dialog box, select the variable that you want to analyze. In this example we are interested in the 'Salary of Respondents' variable in the box on the left, select and then click the transfer arrow button. 'Salary of Respondents' will then move to the Variable(s): box.
4. Ensure that the Display frequency tables box is ticked.
5. Click the Statistics button.
6. In the Frequencies: Statistics dialog box, select the Mean, Median and Mode in the Central Tendency section.
7. Click the Continue button.
8. Click the OK button.

Table 17.6 shows the statistics for salary of respondent. Here, we have measures of central tendency (Mean, Median and Mode). We also selected a frequency table so this is also included in the output. What do the results show? First, the Mean is just over £2,808 per month, Median is £2,850 per month and the Mode is £1,600 per month. However, in this data set multiple modes exist as every respondent has a different salary. This is evident from the frequency table.

Table 17.6   Measures of central tendency for salary

Statistics		
Salary of Respondent		
N	Valid	12
	Missing	0
Mean		2808.3333
Median		2850.0000
Mode		1600.00[a]

a. Multiple modes exist. The smallest value is shown

Salary of Respondent

		Frequency	Percent	Valid Percent	Cumulative Percent
Valid	1600.00	1	8.3	8.3	8.3
	1800.00	1	8.3	8.3	16.7
	2100.00	1	8.3	8.3	25.0
	2400.00	1	8.3	8.3	33.3
	2500.00	1	8.3	8.3	41.7
	2800.00	1	8.3	8.3	50.0
	2900.00	1	8.3	8.3	58.3
	3000.00	1	8.3	8.3	66.7
	3200.00	1	8.3	8.3	75.0
	3600.00	1	8.3	8.3	83.3
	3800.00	1	8.3	8.3	91.7
	4000.00	1	8.3	8.3	100.0
	Total	12	100.0	100.0	

MEASURES OF DISPERSION

A measure of dispersion (sometimes called a measure of spread) is used to describe the spread of values in a distribution. Examples include the range, interquartile range and standard deviation. Using our 'Shopping' data set, we are now going to find the standard deviation for online spending. The appropriate *measure of dispersion for interval*/ratio data is the standard deviation. For a recap on definitions relating to Measures of Dispersion, see Chapter 16.

Question 3: What is the range and standard deviation for online spending?

If you have saved and closed the Shopping.sav file, open the file by carrying out the following steps:

1. Click File > Open>Data>Shopping.sav>Open
2. Click the Analyze menu, scroll down and point to Descriptive Statistics, and then click Frequencies.
3. In the Frequencies dialog box, select the variable that you want to analyze. In this example, we are interested in the 'Online spending' variable in the box on the left, select and then click the transfer arrow button. 'Online spending' will then move to the Variable(s): box. We are also interested in Frequencies, so you can keep Display Frequency Tables selected.
4. Click the Statistics button.
5. In the Frequencies: Statistics dialog box, select Std. deviation and Range in the Dispersion section.
6. Click the Continue button.
7. Click the OK button.

Table 17.7 shows the statistics and frequencies output for Online spending. The output shows that the standard deviation is just over 126, while the range is 400. Remember that the range is the difference between the highest and the lowest values. Given this is a small data set, we can easily see from the frequency table that 400 is the correct answer.

Table 17.7   The range and standard deviation for Online spending

Statistics			
Online spending			
N	Valid		12
	Missing		0
Std. Deviation			126.42521
Range			400.00

Online spending		Frequency	Percent	Valid Percent	Cumulative Percent
Valid	50.00	1	8.3	8.3	8.3
	90.00	1	8.3	8.3	16.7
	120.00	1	8.3	8.3	25.0
	150.00	2	16.7	16.7	41.7
	180.00	1	8.3	8.3	50.0
	200.00	1	8.3	8.3	58.3
	225.00	1	8.3	8.3	66.7
	240.00	1	8.3	8.3	75.0
	350.00	1	8.3	8.3	83.3
	415.00	1	8.3	8.3	91.7
	450.00	1	8.3	8.3	100.0
	Total	12	100.0	100.0	

DESCRIBING YOUR DATA GRAPHICALLY

We can also use graphs, tables and charts to describe data. How you describe your data depends on the type of data you have. Table 17.8 shows the four basic types of data and how you can represent the data graphically. For a reminder on the different types of data, see Chapter 16.

Table 17.8   Representing different types of data graphically

Type of data	Bar chart	Pie chart	Histogram	Stem-and-leaf plot	Boxplot
Nominal	✓	✓			
Ordinal	✓				
Interval or Ratio (Scale in IBM SPSS Statistics)			✓	✓	✓

Before we start describing the data, we are going to add to our Shopping data set (see Figure 17.10). As you can see, we have three new variables – 'RetailerPref' (preferred online retailer) – this is based on a rank-order question. Second, 'Returns' (number of returned goods during 2020). Finally, 'ProductPref' (preferred product to buy online) – again this is based on a rank-order question from our survey.

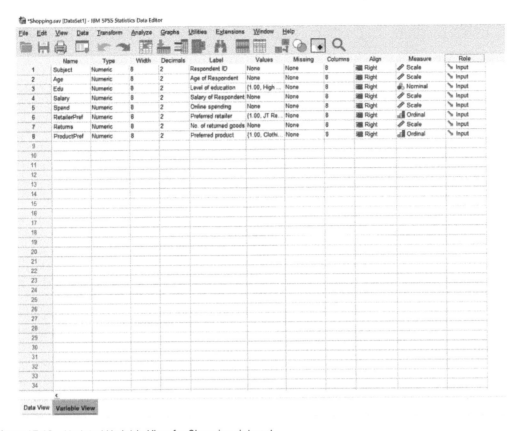

Figure 17.10 Updated Variable View for Shopping data set

To define our additional variables

Again, if you have saved and closed the Shopping.sav file, open the file by carrying out the following steps:

1. Click File > Open>Data>Shopping.sav>Open.
2. First, click the Variable View tab in the lower-left hand corner of the Data Editor window. The view should then turn grey with blue underline.
3. The first of our additional variables is Preferred Online retailer. We can refer to this as simply 'RetailerPref', so type this in the cell under Spend. We can now enter the Values as this is an Ordinal measure. The categories are as follows: 1 = JT Retail, 2 = Majestic Products, 3 = Shopilicious, 4 = Other. The last category is an option for those respondents who do not prefer to shop at any of the options from 1 to 3.

We are now going to enter these values into IBM SPSS Statistics. For the RetailerPref variable, left click to the right of the cell under Values and the Value labels will appear.

- In the Value Box enter '1' and in the Label Box enter 'JT Retail' and click Add.
- Enter '2' in the Value Box and 'Majestic Products' in the Label Box and click Add.
- Enter '3' in the Value Box and 'Shopilicious' in the Label Box and click Add.
- Finally, enter '4' in the Value Box and 'Other' in the Label Box, then click the OK button.

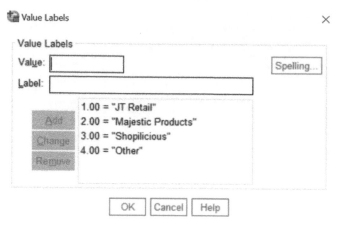

Figure 17.11   Value Labels for the RetailerPref variable

1. In the Measure column, change the Measure for **RetailerPref** to Ordinal.
2. Our second variable to add is '**Returns**' (number of returned goods during 2020). This is a Scale Measure so there are no Values to add. The Measure remains at default 'Scale'.
3. '**ProductPref**' (preferred product to buy online, again this is based on a rank-order question from our survey) is our final variable to add. Like **RetailerPref** this is also an ordinal variable. Following the same process you went through with the **RetailerPref** variable, add the following Values and Labels for '**ProductPref**':

    1 = Clothing and accessories
    2 = Electronics
    3 = Food
    4 = Other

After adding the three variables, you are now ready to start entering the data for all of the cases from the data set as shown in Figure 17.12. To do this:

1. Click the **Data View** tab in the lower left-hand corner of the **Data Editor** window. This should then turn grey with a blue underline.
2. Click in each cell to type your corresponding data (as shown in Figure 17.12).
3. Once you have entered the data in the **Data View** tab. Click on the **Save** button.

Missing values for a numeric variable

You will notice the spreadsheet contains a value of '9999'. This represents a missing value for Respondent 10 as they did not answer the product preference question. This could be for a number of reasons, such as:

- The respondent intentionally or unintentionally skipped the question.
- The respondent was not asked the question due to the routing of the questionnaire survey.
- The researcher made an error and failed to record the answer.
- The value is missing due to technology issues.

In this case, the missing value is represented by '9999' or in other words '9999' is a placeholder value. We could enter '0' as a placeholder value as the respondent has failed to answer. However, this is not as

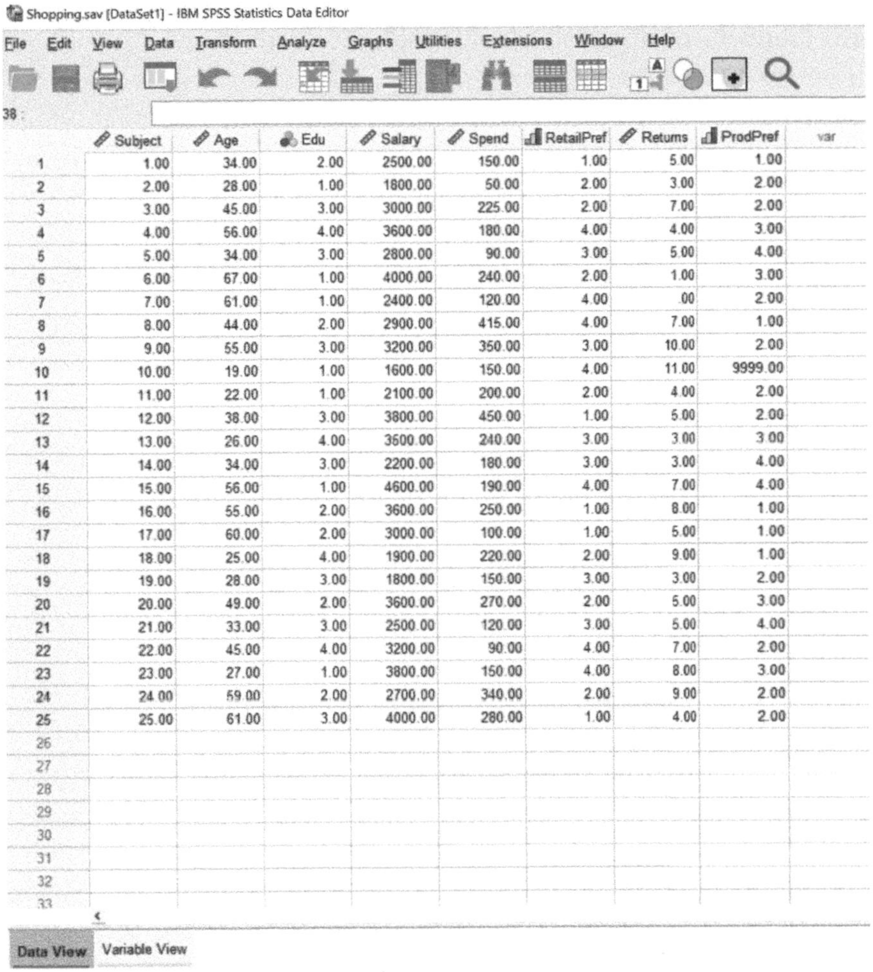

	Subject	Age	Edu	Salary	Spend	RetailPref	Returns	ProdPref	var
1	1.00	34.00	2.00	2500.00	150.00	1.00	5.00	1.00	
2	2.00	28.00	1.00	1800.00	50.00	2.00	3.00	2.00	
3	3.00	45.00	3.00	3000.00	225.00	2.00	7.00	2.00	
4	4.00	56.00	4.00	3600.00	180.00	4.00	4.00	3.00	
5	5.00	34.00	3.00	2800.00	90.00	3.00	5.00	4.00	
6	6.00	67.00	1.00	4000.00	240.00	2.00	1.00	3.00	
7	7.00	61.00	1.00	2400.00	120.00	4.00	.00	2.00	
8	8.00	44.00	2.00	2900.00	415.00	4.00	7.00	1.00	
9	9.00	55.00	3.00	3200.00	350.00	3.00	10.00	2.00	
10	10.00	19.00	1.00	1600.00	150.00	4.00	11.00	9999.00	
11	11.00	22.00	1.00	2100.00	200.00	2.00	4.00	2.00	
12	12.00	38.00	3.00	3800.00	450.00	1.00	5.00	2.00	
13	13.00	26.00	4.00	3600.00	240.00	3.00	3.00	3.00	
14	14.00	34.00	3.00	2200.00	180.00	3.00	3.00	4.00	
15	15.00	56.00	1.00	4600.00	190.00	4.00	7.00	4.00	
16	16.00	55.00	2.00	3600.00	250.00	1.00	8.00	1.00	
17	17.00	60.00	2.00	3000.00	100.00	1.00	5.00	1.00	
18	18.00	25.00	4.00	1900.00	220.00	2.00	9.00	1.00	
19	19.00	28.00	3.00	1800.00	150.00	3.00	3.00	2.00	
20	20.00	49.00	2.00	3600.00	270.00	2.00	5.00	3.00	
21	21.00	33.00	3.00	2500.00	120.00	3.00	5.00	4.00	
22	22.00	45.00	4.00	3200.00	90.00	4.00	7.00	2.00	
23	23.00	27.00	1.00	3800.00	150.00	4.00	8.00	3.00	
24	24.00	59.00	2.00	2700.00	340.00	2.00	9.00	2.00	
25	25.00	61.00	3.00	4000.00	280.00	1.00	4.00	2.00	
26									
27									
28									
29									
30									
31									
32									
33									

Figure 17.12 Final pilot study data spreadsheet

easy to distinguish when compared to unlikely values such as '9999'. We can set user missing values in the **Variable View**. In this example – the '9999' missing value for the 'ProductPref' variable – the steps taken to add this missing value are as follows:

1. For the **ProductPref** variable, click the right-hand corner of the **Missing** column cell to open the **Missing Values** dialog box.
2. Select Discrete missing values.
3. Enter **9999** in the **Discrete missing values** box and leave the other two boxes empty. See Figure 17.13. You can specify up to three distinct missing values, or you can specify a range of values plus one additional discrete value.
4. Click the **OK** button to save your changes then return to the **Variable View** screen.
5. The next step is to add a label to the value.
6. Click the right-hand corner of the Values cell in the **ProductPref** row.
7. Type **9999** in the **Value** field.

8. Type No Answer in the Label field. This represents a respondent has failed to answer the question.
9. Click Add to add this Label.
10. Click OK to save your changes.

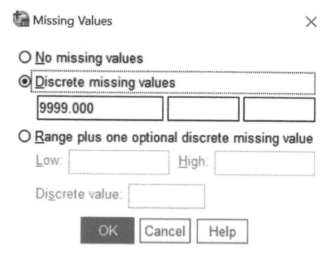

Figure 17.13   Missing Values dialog box

We can now check to see if the missing value is recognized by running a frequencies table:

1. Click the Analyze menu, scroll down and point to Descriptive Statistics, and then click Frequencies.
2. In the Frequencies dialog box, select the Preferred Product in the box on the left, and then click the transfer arrow button. 'Preferred Product' will then move to the Variable(s): box. Make sure that Display Frequency Tables is selected.
3. Click the OK button (see Table 17.9).

Table 17.9   Frequency distribution table showing missing value

Statistics			
Preferred product			
N	Valid		24
	Missing		1

Preferred product					
		Frequency	Percent	Valid Percent	Cumulative Percent
Valid	Clothing and accessories	5	20.0	20.8	20.8
	Electronics	10	40.0	41.7	62.5
	Food	5	20.0	20.8	83.3
	Other	4	16.0	16.7	100.0
	Total	24	96.0	100.0	
Missing	No Answer	1	4.0		
Total		25	100.0		

You can see from Table 17.9 that the Statistics box shows that one respondent out of the sample of 25 failed to answer the product preference question. If we than look at the frequency table, we can see that again one respondent did not answer the question. This represents 4% of the total sample.

Cross-tabulation (crosstabs)

To describe a single categorical variable, we use frequency tables. However, if we are interested in the relationship between two categorical variables, we can use crosstabs. We will now carry out a crosstabs analysis by analyzing two variables: Retail preference and Product preference. Again, if you have saved and closed the Shopping.sav file, open it by carrying out the following steps:

1. Click *File > Open>Data> Shopping.sav>Open*.
2. In **Data View**, click the **Analyze** menu, point to **Descriptive Statistics**, next click on **Crosstabs** (see Figure 17.14).

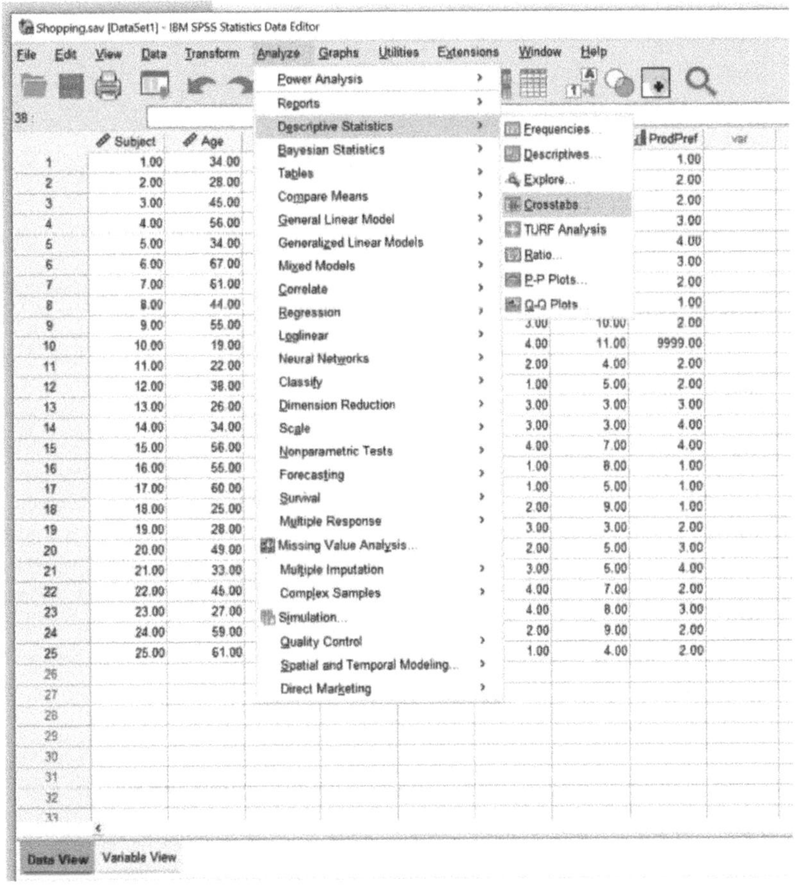

Figure 17.14   Crosstabs selected on the Analyze Menu

1. In the Crosstab dialog box, select the **Preferred retailer** variable in the left box, and then click the transfer window button to move it to the **Row(s)** box.
2. Next, select the **Preferred product** variable in the left box, and then click the transfer arrow button to move it to the **column(s)** box (see Figure 17.15).

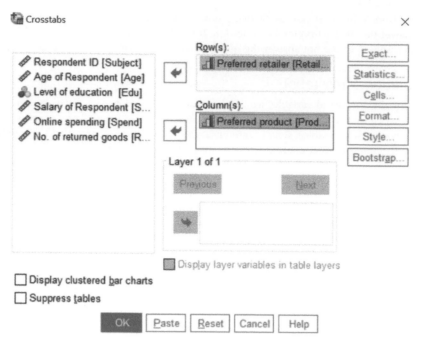

Figure 17.15　Crosstabs dialog box

3. The default is to count the observations. We can also include **percentages** by selecting **Cells** and under **Percentages** select **Column**.
4. Click **Continue**, followed by the **OK** button. The output viewer is shown in Table 17.10.

Table 17.10 shows two tables. The first table is **Case Processing Summary**, while the second is the **Crosstabulation matrix**. What do the results show? First, we can see in the Total column that the majority of respondents prefer Majestic Products (7), while JT Retail is the least preferred option (5). However, as this is a crosstabulation we are interested in the relationship between the two variables. The output shows that electronics is the most preferred product (10) and that 4 out of the 10 respondents prefer to buy electronics from Majestic products. The next step would be to find out 'why' the majority of respondents who prefer electronics, answered Majestic Products as their preferred retailer. Of course, this is a small sample and does not tell us much. However, if a large sample size produced similar results, then a possible next step would be for the researcher or Majestic Products to carry out research to establish 'why' their store is popular for the purchase of electronics.

Table 17.10　Crosstabs output

Case Processing Summary

	Cases					
	Valid		Missing		Total	
	N	Percent	N	Percent	N	Percent
Preferred retailer * Preferred product	24	96.0%	1	4.0%	25	100.0%

Preferred retailer			* Preferred product Crosstabulation					
			Preferred product				
			Clothing and accessories	Electronics	Food	Other	Total
Preferred retailer	JT Retail	Count	3	2	0	0	5
		% within Preferred product	60.0%	20.0%	0.0%	0.0%	20.8%
	Majestic Products	Count	1	4	2	0	7
		% within Preferred product	20.0%	40.0%	40.0%	0.0%	29.2%
	Shopilicious	Count	0	2	1	3	6
		% within Preferred product	0.0%	20.0%	20.0%	75.0%	25.0%
	Other	Count	1	2	2	1	6
		% within Preferred product	20.0%	20.0%	40.0%	25.0%	25.0%
Total		Count	5	10	5	4	24
		% within Preferred product	100.0%	100.0%	100.0%	100.0%	100.0%

Creating a bar chart

Using the same Shopping.sav file we are going to create a bar chart. Again, for further information on charts and graphs see Chapter 16. A bar chart is a straightforward way of summarizing either ordinal or nominal data. To produce a bar chart for variable 'ProductPref' (Product Preference) is as follows:

1. If you are not in the file, Click *File > Open>Data>* Shopping.sav>*Open*.
2. Click on Analyze > Descriptive Statistics > Frequencies. The Frequencies box will open.
3. In the Frequencies dialog box, select the variable that you want to analyze. In this example we are interested in the 'Preferred Product' variable in the box on the left. Click on Preferred Product and then click the transfer arrow button. 'Preferred product' will then move to the Variable(s): box.
4. Uncheck the Display frequency tables box.
5. Next, click on Charts. In the Frequencies: Charts box select Bar charts under Chart Type.
6. Select Frequencies in the Chart Values box. There is also the option to select Percentages, but for this example we are interested in frequencies.
7. Click the Continue button.
8. Click the OK button.

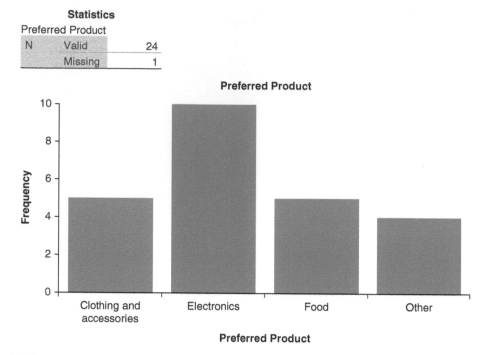

Figure 17.16   A bar chart for Preferred Product

Figure 17.16 shows from our sample of respondents, the preferred product to buy online is electronics. Note that the bars are not touching as the variable plotted on the x axis is not continuous.

Again, potential follow up research might be to ask the question 'why' there is a preference for electronics. Also, data here is from a small pilot study. For the main study, if we produced similar results, it would be interesting to see how findings compare to secondary data, for example research conducted by organizations such as Mintel and Statista. Adopting this typical analytical approach is important when considering the results in your research project.

Pie chart

A pie chart is ideal for illustrating the relative proportions (or percentages) for each category. Each category is displayed as a segment of a circular diagram. Think of a slice of pie, hence the name! We are going to produce a pie chart for the variable level of education. We have nominal data, so a pie chart is a suitable chart to use to analyze our data. To produce a pie chart for variable 'Edu' (Level of education) is as follows:

1. If you are not in the file, Click *File > Open>Data>* **Shopping.sav>***Open*.
2. Click on **Analyze > Descriptive Statistics > Frequencies**. The Frequencies box will open.
3. In the **Frequencies** dialog box, select the variable that you want to analyze. In this example we are interested in the 'Level of education' variable in the box on the left, click on **Level of education** and then click the transfer arrow button. 'Level of education' will then move to the **Variable(s): box**.
4. Uncheck the Display frequency tables box.
5. Next, click on Charts. In the **Frequencies: Charts** box select Pie charts under Chart Type.

6. This time select **Percentages** in the **Chart Values** box.
7. Click the **Continue** button.
8. Click the **OK** button.

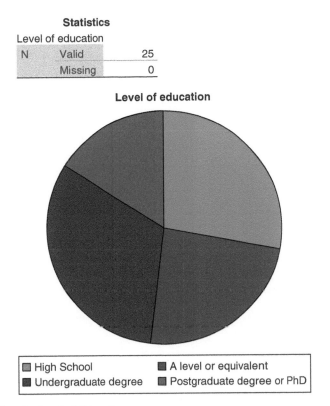

Statistics

Level of education

N	Valid	25
	Missing	0

Level of education

■ High School   ■ A level or equivalent
■ Undergraduate degree ■ Postgraduate degree or PhD

Figure 17.17   A pie chart for Level of Education

Figure 17.17 shows a Pie chart representing the percentage frequencies for each category in the highest level of education (Edu). The chart shows that the highest percentage of the respondents (32%) have an undergraduate degree. Running a frequency table will show the frequency counts.

Histogram

A histogram is a graph used to illustrate a distribution of continuous (interval or ratio) data. Hence, in a histogram the bars are not separated. In our example, we are going to plot **Online Spending**.

1. If you are not in the file, Click *File > Open>Data>* **Shopping.sav**>*Open*.
2. Click on **Analyze > Descriptive Statistics > Frequencies**. The Frequencies box will open.
3. In the **Frequencies** dialog box, select the variable that you want to analyze. In this example we are interested in the '**Online Spending**' variable in the box on the left, click on **Online Spending** and then click the transfer arrow button. '**Online Spending**' will then move to the **Variable(s): box**.
4. Uncheck the Display frequency tables box.

5. Next, click on Charts. In the **Frequencies: Charts** box select Histograms under Chart Type.
6. Click the **Continue** button.
7. Click the **OK** button.

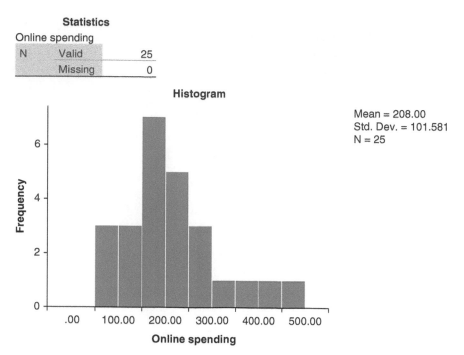

Statistics

Online spending

N	Valid	25
	Missing	0

Mean = 208.00
Std. Dev. = 101.581
N = 25

Figure 17.18   A histogram for Online Spending

For future reference, when plotting a histogram in IBM SPSS Statistics, you can also check the **Show normal curve on histogram box** (see Figures 17.19 and 17.20). This will show the distribution curve. A normal distribution is a bell-shaped curve, symmetrical and continuous. The mean, median and mode coincide at the centre. If the data has a normal distribution, then 68% of the observations will be within one standard deviation of the mean, 95% of observations will fall within 2 standard deviations of the mean and 99.7% of the observations will fall within 3 standard deviations of the mean.

Stem-and-leaf plot

A *stem-and-leaf plot* shows the frequency of values using a table which split each data value into two parts. The data are arranged in size order and each observation is divided into the first part or leading digit to represent the 'stem', and trailing digits represent the leaf of each value. Let us generate a stem-and-leaf plot in IBM SPSS Statistics for the **Salary variable**, as follows:

1. Click *File > Open>Data>*Shopping.sav*>Open.
2. Click the **Analyze** menu, scroll down and point to **Descriptive Statistics**, then click **Explore**.
3. Move **Salary** into the **Dependent List: Box** on the right.
4. Click on the **Plots** button.
5. Uncheck the Factor Levels together under Boxplots to None. Under Descriptive select Stem-and-leaf.
6. Click the **Continue** button.
7. Click the **OK** button for the results.

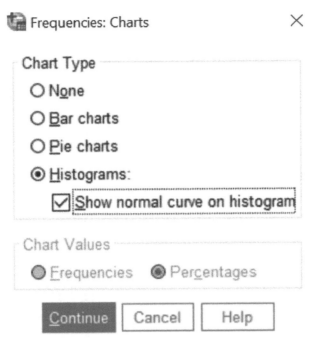

Figure 17.19   Frequencies: Charts with Show normal curve on histogram checked

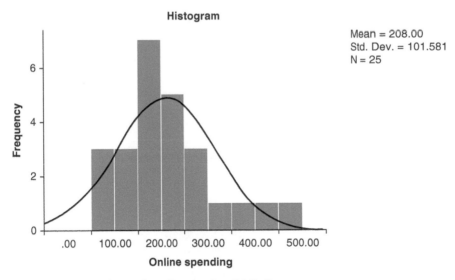

Figure 17.20   A histogram for Online Spending showing distribution curve

Boxplot (Box and whisker plot)

A boxplot is an ideal way of displaying the distribution of a continuous (e.g. interval) data variable. It shows the distribution information of a variable and displays the quartiles of the data. The whiskers of the box go from 0% quartile to the 100% quartile of the data. If you find that your sample includes any

Salary of Respondent Stem-and-Leaf Plot	
Frequency	Stem and Leaf
4.00	1. 6889
3.00	2. 124
5.00	2. 55789
4.00	3. 0022
6.00	3. 566688
2.00	4. 00
1.00	4. 6
Stem width:	1000.00
Each leaf:	1 case(s)

Figure 17.21   A stem-and-leaf plot for Salary of Respondent

outliers then they are displayed as data points outside the whiskers. The box spans from the 25% quartile to the 75% quartile and the median is displayed as a strong line inside the box (this is the 50% quartile). We are going to create a boxplot for Age.

1. Click *File > Open>Data>Shopping.sav>Open*.
2. Click the Graphs menu, followed by Chart Builder.
3. Click the OK button to define your chart.
4. In the Choose from box left click Boxplot.
5. Three Boxplot options will appear in the Choose from box (Gallery Tab) – Simple Boxplot, Clustered Boxplot and 1-D Boxplot. Hovering your cursor over each image will show the name of each Boxplot.
6. For this example, we are using a Simple Boxplot so left click Simple Boxplot and drag and drop into the 'Drag a Gallery chart here' window.
7. Left click Age of Respondent in the Variable Box and drag and drop to the y-axis.
8. Click the OK button (see the output in Figure 17.22).

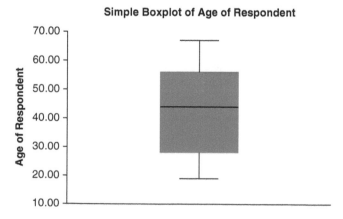

Figure 17.22   A simple boxplot of Age of Respondent

The box is drawn from Q_1 (lower quartile) to Q_3 (Upper quartile). The Interquartile range (IQR) is the distance between the upper and lower quartiles. In the box, the horizontal line in the middle is the median value (44 years of age) and the boxplot whiskers show the maximum and minimum vales, 67 and 19 years of age respectively.

Figure 17.23 'pulls together' what we have covered in this part of the chapter. The flowchart is based on 'describing a sample'. Column one asks whether you want to describe your sample statistically or graphically. For 'statistically', column two asks whether you want to calculate a measure of dispersion or central tendency. Column three is your type of data. Finally, the 'method' column shows the ways to describe your data. You will notice that for measuring central tendency using interval/ratio data that there is reference to 'skewed'. A skewed distribution means that the mean, median and mode have different values. A positive skewness means that the tail has a distribution to the right, while a negative distribution means that it has a tail to the left. For skewed data, use the median.

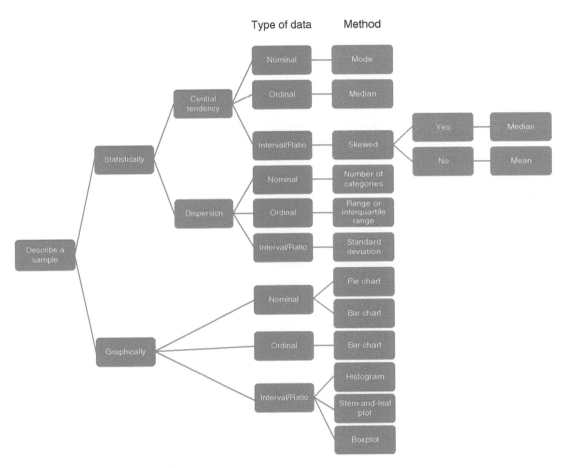

Figure 17.23   Describing a sample

BOX 17.1: RESEARCH SNAPSHOT

There are many different ways to describe data. Figure 17.23 provides a useful 'snapshot' of some of the ways you can describe data in your research. Remember that the techniques you choose are dependent on a number of factors. These include type of data, sample(s) and also the purpose of your research. Moreover, techniques used to describe data in earlier/similar studies may also influence your decision.

A note on the Chart Builder function

As when creating a boxplot, the **Chart Builder** function in IBM SPSS Statistics allows you to create and adapt a number of different charts. As a reminder, to access Chart Builder:

1. Click the *Graphs menu*>**Chart Builder**>**OK** button.

The main charts you can create using Chart Builder are highlighted in Figure 17.24. We have gone through the process of creating a boxplot using the Chart Builder function. Creating other charts is a similar process of 'drag and drop' in relation to your chosen chart and x and y axis.

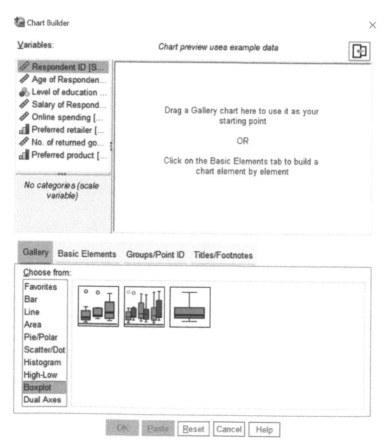

Figure 17.24   The Chart Builder function

ANALYZING DATA USING INFERENTIAL STATISTICS

In the last section, the focus of the chapter was on ways to describe data using IBM SPSS Statistics. In this part of the chapter, we look at inferential statistics. Inferential statistics are used to draw inferences about a population from a given sample.

PARAMETRIC OR NON-PARAMETRIC DATA

As a reminder, inferential statistics includes tests based on parametric or non-parametric data. The assumptions of parametric data are that the data is normally distributed, we are using interval or ratio data, and the data from different subjects are independent. Parametric tests are regarded as more powerful as they assume that the observed data follows a normal distribution. Parametric methods are used when you are able to estimate the parameters of distribution in the population. In contrast, when you know nothing about the parameters and have a small sample size, then non-parametric tests must be used. Moreover, non-parametric methods are used where a normal distribution cannot be ascertained.

As noted earlier in the chapter, a normal distribution is bell shaped and sometimes referred to as the Bell Curve. The right side will always mirror the left side. The mean, median and mode coincide and the range of the distribution is 6 standard deviation units (see Figure 17.25).

- 68% of the area approximately lies between +1 (SD) and -1 (SD) from the mean.
- 95% of the area approximately lies between +2 (SD) and -2 (SD) from the mean.
- 99.7% of the area approximately lies between +3 (SD) and -3 (SD) from the mean.

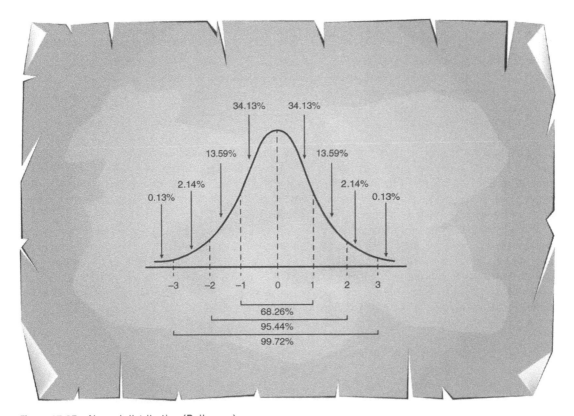

Figure 17.25   Normal distribution (Bell curve)

Source: iStock (photo ID: 669384668)

Many of the tests in this chapter are based on parametric tests. These include: mean, standard deviation, one sample t-test and Pearson's correlation test. An example of a non-parametric test is the chi-square test (see later in the chapter). The benefit of parametric tests is that we can draw more conclusions about population parameters such as the mean.

We can test to see if our data is normally distributed by running Kolmogorov-Smirnov and Shapiro-Wilk tests in IBM SPSS Statistics. These test the null hypothesis that the data is normally distributed. We can also use a Q-Q plot to show how the scores may deviate from the normal distribution. This is shown using a straight line (see later in the chapter).

For the methods used in this section, the data is from the final survey on online shopping, called Shopping2 (in digital resources). The data set is based on 100 responses with no missing responses.

One sample t-test

A one sample t-test is used to test the hypothesis that a sample mean is not significantly different from its presumed population mean. In order to carry out a one sample t-test there are a set of assumptions that should be met. First, you should have parametric data that should be continuous (interval or ratio scale). There should be just one score for each case and cases should be independent, or in other words, unable to influence each other. There should be no outliers (extreme observations). Also, the data should be drawn from a normally distributed population. We can test the assumption of normality using a variety of methods; however, a straightforward way is to inspect the data visually using a histogram or a Q-Q plot. We looked at how to produce a histogram earlier in the chapter. To run a Q-Q plot requires the following steps (based on shopping2 data set):

1. Click the Analyze menu, scroll down and point to Descriptive Statistics, then click Explore.
2. Click on the 'Online spending' variable in the box on the left, and then click the transfer arrow button to transfer 'Online spending' to the Dependent list: box.
3. Click on the Plots button
4. Click None in the Boxplots box.
5. In the Descriptive box, leave the Stem-and-leaf and Histogram boxes blank.
6. Select Normality plots with tests.
7. Click the Continue button.
8. Click the OK button.

From Figure 17.26, we can see that the residuals deviate from the 45-degree line; this may indicate that they are not normally distributed. If we consider the two statistical tests – Kolmogorov-Smirnov Normality Test and Shapiro-Wilk Normality Test – we can conclude that the sig. value for both the Kolmogorov-Smirnov test as well as the Shapiro-Wilk test is <0.05. This indicates that the data in this example significantly deviates from a normal distribution.

Let us look at an example of how to run a one sample t-test. According to a UK Government report, the average monthly salary is £1,950. We want to know if the mean monthly salary of people in our sample is equal to £1,950. This is our 'test value'. Our Shopping2 data set is a random sample of 100 respondents and we have recorded the monthly salaries in IBM SPSS Statistics. We will use the steps below to perform a one sample t-test to determine if the true mean monthly salary of those in our sample is equal to £1,950 based on the following null and alternative hypotheses:

- $H_0: \mu = \mu_0$ (the mean salary is equal to £1,950)
- $H_1: \mu \neq \mu_0$ (the mean salary is not equal to £1,950)

The significance level or p-value represents the probability that the null hypothesis is true. Often, researchers will use the value of 0.05 as a cut-off point (a critical value or alpha, α) that means that the null hypothesis has only a 5% chance of being true.

Tests of Normality

	Kolmogorov-Smirnov[a]			Shapiro-Wilk		
	Statistic	df	Sig.	Statistic	df	Sig.
Online spending	.144	100	.000	.941	100	.000

a. Lilliefors Significance Correction

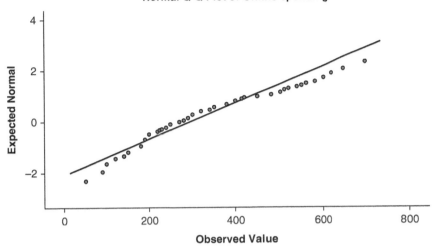

Normal Q-Q Plot of Online spending

Figure 17.26   Q-Q plot for Online Spending

Here are the steps followed to create a one sample t-Test in IBM SPSS Statistics:

1. Click the *Analyze menu> Compare Means>*One Sample T Test.
2. In the Test Variable box enter the variable Salary.
3. Move the variable Salary of respondent to the Test Variable(s) box.
4. In the Test value: box enter 1,950.
5. Click the OK button.

Table 17.11 shows the output for the one sample t-test. The statistical significance (p-value) Sig. (2-tailed) is $p < 0.001$ and therefore we reject the null hypothesis that the mean monthly salary of respondents is equal to the population mean of £1,950 and conclude that the mean salary is significantly different than £1,950.

Table 17.11   One sample t-test for monthly salary

One-Sample Statistics

	N	Mean	Std. Deviation	Std. Error Mean
Salary of Respondent	100	3156.0000	966.75235	96.67523

One-Sample Test

	Test Value = 1950					
					95% Confidence Interval of the Difference	
	t	df	Sig. (2-tailed)	Mean Difference	Lower	Upper
Salary of Respondent	12.475	99	.000	1206.00000	1014.1754	1397.8246

The one sample t-test can only compare a single sample mean to a specified constant. It cannot compare sample means between two or more groups. If in your research you want to compare the means of multiple groups to each other, you can run an independent samples *t-test* (to compare the means of two groups).

Independent samples t-test (Student's t-test)

Also known as the Student's t-test, this test compares the means of two independent groups in order to determine whether there is statistical evidence that the associated population means are significantly different. The assumptions for running an independent sample t-test include the dependent variable is a continuous variable (interval or ratio), the independent variable is categorical, a random sample of data from the population (random sampling method), independence of observations, a normal distribution (approximate), no outliers and homogeneity of variances. Homogeneity of variance (homoscedasticity) is the assumption in which the population variances (the spread around the mean) of two or more samples are considered equal.

In the shopping2 data set, respondents reported their usual monthly online spending, and whether or not they were in a managerial role. Let us say that we want to know if the average monthly spend online is different for managers versus non-managers. We can test whether the sample means for monthly online spending among managers and non-managers in our shopping2 sample are statistically different (and by extension, inferring whether the means for online monthly spend in the population are significantly different between these two groups).

We can express the hypotheses for this example as:

- H_0: μ non-manager – μ manager = 0 (the difference of the population mean is equal to zero)
- H_1: μ non-manager – μ manager ≠ 0 (the difference of the population mean is not equal to zero)

(μ manager and μ non-manager are the population means for manager and non-manager.)

Our sample data is based on two variables: 'Spend' (monthly on spending) and the variable 'Role' (0 = non-manager, 1 = manager). This is our independent variable, while the numeric variable Spend is our dependent variable. For this example, let us use α = 0.05.

Here are the steps followed to create an independent samples t-test in IBM SPSS Statistics:

1. Click the *Analyze menu> Compare Means>*Independent Samples T Test.
2. In the Grouping Variable box move the variable Role.
3. Move the variable Online spending (Spend) to the Test Variable(s) box.
4. Click on Role in the Grouping Variable box define groups, followed by Define Groups.
5. Type 0 (this represents our group of non-managers) in the Group 1 box and Type 1 in the Group 2 box (this represents our group of managers).
6. Click the Continue button.
7. Click the OK button.

Table 17.12   Independent samples t-test

Group Statistics

	Role	N	Mean	Std. Deviation	Std. Error Mean
Online spending	non-manager	55	293.9091	138.20171	18.63512
	manager	45	302.7778	147.56954	21.99837

Independent samples test		Levene's Test for Equality of Variances		t-test for Equality of Means						
									95% Confidence Interval of the difference	
		F	Sig.	t	df	Sig. (2-tailed)	Mean Difference	Std. Error Difference	Lower	Upper
Online spending	Equal variances assumed	.843	.361	–.310	98	.757	–8.86869	28.64034	–65.70450	47.96713
	Equal variances not assumed			–.308	91.440	.759	–8.86869	28.83046	–66.13315	48.39578

Analyzing the results from Table 17.12, since the p-value is greater than our significance level *of α = 0.05,* we fail to reject the null hypothesis. The p-value indicates how likely our sample result is if our population means are equal. In our example, p = .757 – a 75.7% probability.

The mean difference is calculated by subtracting the mean of the second group (manager) from the mean of the first group (non-manager), the mean difference being £8.87. We can conclude that the mean online spend for managers and non-managers is not significantly different.

Chi-square test of independence

The chi-square test of independence determines whether there is an association between two categorical variables (non-parametric data). The test uses a cross-tabulation. The categories for one variable appear in the rows, and the categories for the other variable appear in columns. If two variables each contain two categories, then cross-tabulation produces a 2 x 2 table containing 2 columns and 2 rows. To run a chi-square of independence, our data must be based on two categorical variables, there must be independence of observations, two or more categories (groups) for each variable and expected frequencies should be at least five for the majority of cells.

From the Shopping2 data set, respondents answered a question based on whether they are a car owner. The choices were car owner or non-car owner. Let us say we want to test the association between driver status (non-driver or driver) and role (non-manager or manager), using α = 0.05. Our null hypothesis (H0) is that there is no association between the two categories in each variable. To carry out the test, the procedure in IBM SPSS Statistics is as follows:

1. In *Data View*, click the **Analyze** menu, point to **Descriptive Statistics**, next click on **Crosstabs**.
2. Select **Driving** as the row variable and **Role** as the column variable.
3. Click the **Statistics** button.
4. Select **Chi-square** in the **Cross-tabs: Statistics** box and click the **Continue** button.
5. Click the **OK** button.

Table 17.13   Chi-square test of independence testing the association between Driver Status and Role

Case Processing Summary

	Cases					
	Valid		Missing		Total	
	N	Percent	N	Percent	N	Percent
Are you a driver? * Role	100	100.0%	0	0.0%	100	100.0%

Are you a driver? * Role Crosstabulation

Count

		Role		Total
		Non-manager	Manager	
Are you a driver?	Non-driver	29	19	48
	Driver	26	26	52
Total		55	45	100

Chi-Square Tests

	Value	df	Asymptotic Significance (2-sided)	Exact Sig. (2-sided)	Exact Sig. (1-sided)
Pearson Chi-Square	1.094[a]	1	.296		
Continuity Correction[b]	.714	1	.398		
Likelihood Ratio	1.097	1	.295		
Fisher's Exact Test				.321	.199
Linear-by-Linear Association	1.083	1	.298		
N of Valid Cases	100				

a. 0 cells (0.0%) have expected count less than 5. The minimum expected count is 21.60.

b. Computed only for a 2x2 table

Table 17.13 shows the case processing summary table. This includes the valid number of cases used for analysis (100). The cross-tabulation table shows the relationship between 'are you a driver?' and 'role' variables. Next, in the chi-square tests table we are concerned with the Pearson's chi-square. The value is 1.094. Since the p-value is greater than our significance level $(\alpha = 0.05)$ we do not reject the null hypothesis. There is not enough evidence to suggest an association between role and driving status.

CORRELATION

Correlations describe the relationship between two variables in statistical terms. Data collected using a variety of data collection methods can be analyzed to see if there is a relationship between two variables. For example, in business research, you might be interested to see if there is a relationship between training spend and number of sales made by an organization's salesforce.

Correlations can be plotted on graphs called a scatter plot (see below). This gives a visual representation of the strength of the relationship between two variables. The advantage of correlations is that it is an easy and quick way to see if there is a relationship between two variables. Furthermore, it is straightforward to conduct correlation analysis using IBM SPSS Statistics. Remember that when conducting correlation analysis, a value of 1 represents a perfect positive correlation; a perfect negative linear relationship is represented by a value –1, and a correlation coefficient of 0 means that there is no relationship between the two variables. In other words, both variables are perfectly independent.

SCATTER PLOT (OR SCATTER DIAGRAM)

A scatter plot is an ideal way of understanding the relationship between two continuous variables. The visual nature of a scatter plot can help to identify any potential outliers. Values of one variable are plotted on the x axis, while values of the other variable are plotted on the y axis. If there is no relationship between the two variables, then the scatter plot will show a random scatter of points. For example, you may expect the relationship between age and miles driven every month to show no relationship. However, bear in mind that certain factors could lead to a possible relationship, such as younger and older respondents using public transport more frequently due to possible savings. The way we can determine the strength of the relationship between age and miles driven is to run a scatter plot. In addition, a negative correlation describes a relationship in which one variable increases as the other decreases.

If higher values of the age variable occur with higher values of miles driven every month, then the scatter plot will show this positive relationship. Here are the steps followed to create a simple scatterplot in IBM SPSS Statistics:

1. Click the **Graphs menu**, followed by **Chart Builder**.
2. Click the **OK** button to define your chart.
3. In the **Choose from** box left click **Scatter/Dot**.
4. Click **Scatter Plot** – the top left-hand option – and drag-and-drop into the 'Drag a Gallery chart here' window.
5. You will be presented with **Scatter plot** showing 'Y-Axis?' and 'X-Axis?'. Ignore **Filter**.
6. Drag-and-drop the dependent variable **Online Spending** to the 'Y-Axis?' box and **Salary of Respondent** to the 'X-Axis' box.
7. In the **Linear Fit Lines** box (bottom right-hand corner), click **Total**.
8. Click the **OK** button.

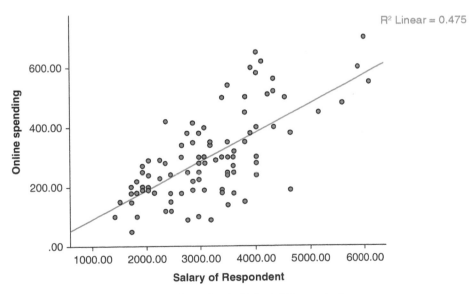

Figure 17.27   Simple scatter plot of Online Spending by Salary of Respondent

We can see from Figure 17.27 that there is a r^2 value (the *coefficient of determination*, square of the correlation) of 0.475. It measures the proportion of variation in the dependent variable (Online Spending) that can be attributed to the independent variable (Salary of Respondent), which means that 47.5% of the total variation in y can be explained by the linear relationship between x and y. If $r^2 = 0.475$, then $r = 0.689$. This is the *linear correlation coefficient*, which measures the strength and the direction of a linear relationship between two variables. Remember that the value of r is always between +1 and −1. So, based on our value of $r = 0.689$ we can state that there is a strong positive linear relationship between Online Spending and Salary of Respondent.

Pearson's correlation

Pearson's product-moment correlation coefficient (r) is used to measure the strength and direction of the linear association between variables. You must have parametric data for two continuous variables (interval or ratio). Other assumptions include cases should be independent and scores on both variables should be normally distributed. Again, this assumption can be assessed using a variety of methods, such as histograms and normal Q-Q plots.

Pearson's correlation assumes a linear relationship between the two variables. This means that when the value of one variable changes, the amount of change in the other variable is the same. We can assess this assumption by using a scatter plot. The final assumption relates to homoscedasticity. As highlighted earlier, this refers to the variance in one variable at each level of the other. Pearson's correlation assumes that this variance is constant. This can also be assessed using a simple scatter plot. If the scores on one variable show that they are spreading apart or getting closer together as the scores on the other variable increase, then the assumption of homoscedasticity has not been met. Here are the steps followed to carry out Pearson's Correlation in IBM SPSS Statistics:

1. In **Data View**, click the **Analyze** menu, point to **Correlate**, next click on **Bivariate**.
2. Click on '**Age of Respondent**' and then click the **transfer arrow** button to transfer '**Age of Respondent**' to the **Variables:** box.
3. Click on '**Salary of respondent**' and then click the **transfer arrow** button to transfer '**Salary of respondent**' to the **Variables:** box.
4. Under **Correlation Coefficients** accept the default which is Pearson.
5. Under **Test of Significance** select Two-tailed as this is a non-directional test.
6. Accept the default Flag significant correlations.
7. Click on **Options**. In the **Bivariate Correlations: Options** box, accept the default for Missing Values, which is Exclude cases Pairwise.
8. Click the **Continue** button.
9. Click the **OK** button.

Table 17.14   Pearson's correlation for Age of Respondent and Salary of Respondent

Correlations

		Age of Respondent	Salary of Respondent
Age of Respondent	Pearson Correlation	1	.414**
	Sig. (2-tailed)		.000
	N	100	100
Salary of Respondent	Pearson Correlation	.414**	1
	Sig. (2-tailed)	.000	
	N	100	100

**. Correlation is significant at the 0.01 level (2-tailed).

The results in Table 17.14 shows Pearson's correlation, its significance value and the number of cases (N = 100). We can see from the table that Pearson's correlation is .414 and that this is statistically significant at the 1% level ($p =\leq 0.01$). Thus, we can conclude that there is evidence to reject the null hypothesis of no correlation. Remember that correlation does not mean causation.

Spearman's rank-order correlation

Spearman's (*rho)* is a correlation coefficient used to measure the strength and direction of a relationship for two variables measured on a ratio, interval or ordinal scale. Both variables should be at least ordinal. Other assumptions that need to be met before using Spearman's correlation include there should be just one score on each variable for each case and cases should be independent. Spearman's correlation is suitable for correlating an ordinal variable with an interval or ratio variable as an alternative to using Pearson's *r* when its assumptions of normality and/or linearity cannot be met. Spearman's correlation is for use with non-parametric data.

This example of using Spearman's *rho* will measure the correlation between the **Retailer Preference** and **Product Preference** variables. Stated in the form of a null hypothesis:

HO = There is no relationship between Retailer Preference and Product Preference.

1. In **Data View**, click the **Analyze** menu, point to Correlate, next click on **Bivariate**.
2. Click on 'Preferred retailer' and then click the **transfer arrow** button to transfer 'Preferred retailer' to the **Variables: box**.
3. Click on 'Preferred product' and then click the **transfer arrow** button to transfer 'Preferred product' to the **Variables: box**.
4. Under **Correlation Coefficients** select Spearman.
5. Under **Test of Significance** select **Two-tailed** as in this is a non-directional test.
6. Accept the default Flag significant correlations.
7. Click on **Options**. In the **Bivariate Correlations: Options** box, accept the default for Missing Values, which is Exclude cases Pairwise.
8. Click the **Continue** button.
9. Click the **OK** button.

Table 17.15   Spearman's correlation for Preferred Retailer and Preferred Product

Correlations

			Preferred retailer	Preferred product
Spearman's rho	Preferred retailer	Correlation Coefficient	1.000	.090
		Sig. (2-tailed)	.	.375
		N	100	100
	Preferred product	Correlation Coefficient	.090	1.000
		Sig. (2-tailed)	.375	.
		N	100	100

The results in Table 17.15 shows Spearman's correlation, its significance value and the number of cases (N = 100). We can see from the table that Spearman's correlation coefficient is .090, a weak positive relationship and that this is not statistically significant (p = .375). Thus, we can conclude that there is no evidence to reject the null hypothesis.

LINEAR REGRESSION

Linear regression (simple linear regression) is used to find the relationship between two continuous variables (interval or ratio). Linear regression goes further than correlation by giving an indication of the ability of a predictor or independent variable to predict an outcome in a response or dependent variable. By way of an example, we could use linear regression to examine whether sales performance can be predicted based on sales training time. We looked at regression analysis in Chapter 16.

There are a number of assumptions to consider when using linear regression. The dependent variable is a continuous variable (measured on an interval or ratio scale). Raban and Rabin (2009) also point out:

- the relationship between the dependent variable and each independent variable is linear
- observations are independent of each other
- homoscedasticity (constant variance) of the errors of the dependent variable for each value of the independent variable
- normality (for any fixed value of X, Y is normally distributed).

In terms of whether the relationship between the dependent variable and each independent is linear, you can run a scatterplot to check this – something we did earlier in the chapter.

From the Shopping.2 data set we are going to use two variables: Monthly Salary of Respondent (independent variable) and Monthly Spend on Online Shopping (dependent variable). These are the steps for performing Linear regression in IBM SPSS Statistics:

1. In Data View, click the Analyze menu, point to Regression>Linear.
2. Move your dependent (outcome) variable into Dependent: box by clicking on the transfer arrow button. In this case Online Shopping.
3. Move your independent (predictor) variable(s) into Independent(s): box by clicking on the transfer arrow button. In this case the variable Salary of Respondent.
4. Click on the OK button.

Multiple linear regression can also be conducted using IBM SPSS Statistics. This measures how well multiple independent variables predict the value of a dependent variable (see further reading).

Table 17.16   Linear regression

Model Summary

Model	R	R Square	Adjusted R Square	Std. Error of the Estimate
1	.690[a]	.475	.470	103.24312

a. Predictors: (Constant), Salary of Respondent

ANOVA[a]

Model		Sum of Squares	df	Mean Square	F	Sig.
1	Regression	946913.176	1	946913.176	88.836	.000[b]
	Residual	1044595.824	98	10659.141		
	Total	1991509.000	99			

a. Dependent Variable: Online Spending

b. Predictors: (Constant) Salary of Respondent

Coefficients[a]

Model		Unstandardized Coefficients		Standardized Coefficients	t	Sig.
		B	Std. Error	Beta		
1	(Constant)	-21.371	35.412		-.603	.548
	Salary of Respondent	.101	.011	.690	9.425	.000

a. Dependent Variable: Online Spending

Table 17.16 first shows the 'Model Summary'. This gives us an R value (the simple correlation) of 0.690. This indicates a strong positive correlation. The R_2 value indicates how much of the total variation in the dependent variable (Online Spending) can be explained by the independent variable (Salary of Respondent). In our example, 47.5%. So, 47.5% of the variation in Online Spending can be explained by the model containing only Salary of Respondent.

The ANOVA table shows the statistical significance (Sig. column) – this indicates the statistical significance of the regression model. The p-value is less than 0.05, this then indicates the overall regression model significantly predicts the outcome variable.

The coefficients table shows the results from the regression analysis for the independent variable. 'Sig.' is the significance which indicates if our independent variable is a significant predictor of our dependent variable (Online Spending). We can see that Salary of Respondent is a significant predictor of Online Spending (p = .000).

Image 17.1   Concept Cartoon 'Using statistical software'

Image 17.1 is a Concept Cartoon that shows characters expressing their views on using statistical software. Again, think about the different views and use them to provoke a discussion with fellow students. What do you think? Do you share a viewpoint with one particular character?

INCLUDING IBM SPSS STATISTICS OUTPUT ON MICROSOFT WORD

When you have completed your statistical analysis, the next step is to copy the output to Microsoft Word. This includes graphs, tables and charts. You can create separate Word documents so as to organize your output. Using Copy and Paste you can copy from the **Output Viewer** window and paste into a Microsoft Word document. To export material to Microsoft Word:

1. In the **Output Viewer** window, right click a table, chart or graph. A box appears around the item you want to copy and a red arrow appears to the left of the table to show that it is selected.
2. Click **copy** on the shortcut menu.
3. Open your Microsoft Word document and right click in the Word document. Click **Paste** in the shortcut menu. The table is now copied into your Word document.

IBM SPSS Statistics is by no means the only statistical software available to students. Using Microsoft Excel is another option. Finally, the purpose of this chapter is to give you an introduction to using IBM SPSS Statistics. It is by no means exhaustive (see further reading at the end of this chapter for additional sources).

CHAPTER SUMMARY

- IBM SPSS Statistics is a software package designed for analyzing quantitative data. SPSS stands for Statistical Package for the Social Sciences.

- When creating your data file, you need first to define the variables, and second, enter the data.

- A numeric variable can only have numbers allocated and are suitable for numerical calculations.

- String variables may contain letters, numbers or other characters.

- It is important to consider your purpose, type of data and the nature of your sample(s) when considering how to analyze your data.

- When describing data, a distinction can be made between graphically and statistically.

- Statistical software is only a tool. You still need to be able to understand why you have chosen a certain method.

QUESTIONS FOR REVIEW

1. Which aspect of the distribution of a variable does the standard deviation measure?

2. Which measure of central tendency would you use to measure nominal data?

3. Which measure of central tendency would you use to measure ordinal data?

4. What is the difference between interval scale and ratio scale?

5. Which type of graph is used to show the relationship between two quantitative variables?

6. Which of the following describes continuous variables?

    a. Variables that are measured using an ordinal scale.

    b. Variables that are measured using an interval or ratio scale.

    c. Variables that are dichotomous.

    d. Variables that can be organized into categories.

7. What is meant by a Normal Distribution?

8. Which of the variables described below is ratio?

    a. The names of research participants.

    b. The distance travelled to work.

    c. The preference for different brands of breakfast cereal.

    d. The gender of research participants.

9. Which of the following is an example of a qualitative variable?

    a. Height

    b. Weight

    c. Religion

    d. Age

10. Give three examples of non-probability sampling methods.

STUDENT SCENARIO: LUCAS USES IBM SPSS STATISTICS TO ANALYZE HIS DATA

Lucas is doing a research project on the relationship between customer satisfaction and small business performance in the UK technology industry. A quantitative study, he is ready to analyze his data using IBM SPSS Statistics. The results from Lucas' questionnaire survey include the following data:

- the occupation of each respondent
- sales for each case (product)

(Coninued)

- number of customer complaints for each organization
- customer satisfaction in which goods are ranked in order of preference

Questions

1. Give examples of how Lucas can describe the data for occupation of respondent both statistically and graphically.
2. Give examples of how Lucas can describe the data for customer satisfaction in which goods are ranked in order of preference (both statistically and graphically).
3. Lucas is interested in the association between sales and number of customer complaints. Explain how Lucas can analyze the association between these two variables, together with the assumptions he will need to consider.

Hint: Consider the purpose and type of data when recommending how Lucas should analyze his data.

FURTHER READING

Field, A. (2018) *Discovering Statistics using IBM SPSS Statistics* (5th edn). London: Sage.

Now in its fifth edition, Andy Field's book is a comprehensive guide to using IBM SPSS Statistics. The book is supported with extensive online resources.

Pallant, J. (2020) *SPSS Survival Manual: A Step-by-step Guide to Data Analysis Using IBM SPSS* (7th edn). Maidenhead: Open University Press.

A useful guide for students. The book includes a wide range of statistical techniques.

Salkind, N.J. (2015) *Excel Statistics: A Quick Guide*. Thousand Oaks, CA: Sage.

Excel Statistics is a concise guide and an alternative to using IBM SPSS Statistics.

REFERENCE

Raban, D.R. and Rabin, E. (2009) 'Statistical inference from power law distributed web-based social interactions', *Internet Research*, 19 (3): 266–278.

18

WRITING UP AND DISSEMINATING YOUR WORK

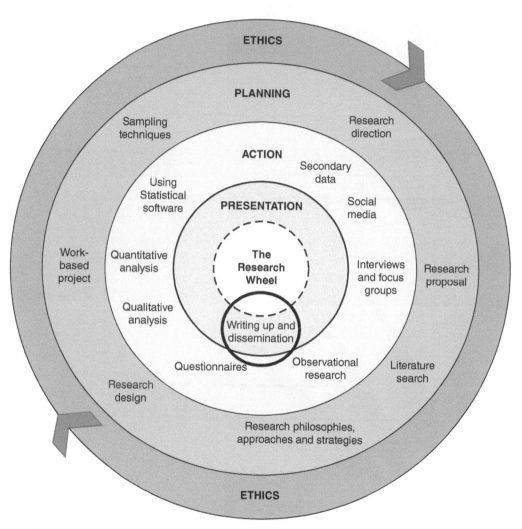

Figure 18.1   The Research Wheel

INTRODUCTION

In this final chapter, we look at how to write up, present and disseminate your research findings. The last of these three tasks does not always receive much attention from students. This is disappointing. Having worked hard on carrying out your research, there are now so many options when it comes to sharing or disseminating your work.

The chapter begins by discussing the steps associated with writing up a research project. For student researchers, there are essentially two options here. First, writing up as you go along. Second, writing up following the completion of your data analysis. Whatever you decide is really down to personal preference, although the choice you make should be made clear during the planning stage in your research, ideally, within your research proposal. Next, we examine the typical structure of a research project. Some of the steps here will be familiar to you as they are part of a research proposal. However, remember that a research proposal is only a plan or foundation. Your project is going to be written in much more depth. Following this, we look at the approaches for writing a research project.

Moving on, the chapter will then consider how to present and submit your work, before examining the viva voce and the marking of a research project. Next, we look at some of the ways to publish and disseminate your work, followed by the key success factors associated with writing a research project. Lastly, the chapter culminates with a group exercise. This is designed to 'pull together' everything you have learned throughout your research journey.

As you can see by Figure 18.1, 'Writing up' is in the final 'Presentation' layer in The Research Wheel model (EPAP). Prior to reaching the presentation layer you should have completed your data collection and analysis. For many students, writing up is the final stage in their research journey (as illustrated by The Research Wheel). However, do remember that research is an iterative process, so, although The Research Wheel shows 'Writing up' as the final step, remember that the nature of the wheel means that you may revisit some of the earlier steps. For example, you may start writing up, but need to later carry out further data collection as a respondent(s) has decided to withdraw from your study.

STARTING TO WRITE UP YOUR RESEARCH PROJECT

The way to start writing is to start writing. (Anon)

For many students, writing a dissertation or research project is likely to be the most challenging writing task during their degree. Typically, a research project is the culmination of a degree course and gives students an opportunity to write about a topic they are passionate about. However, a key question many students ask is, 'When do I start writing?'. In addition, another question sometimes asked is, 'Where do I start writing?'. Let us look at each of these questions in turn.

First, when you start writing is really a matter of personal choice. Personally, I prefer to write as I go along. The reason for this is that research is about reflection and revisiting steps (as illustrated by The Research Wheel). So, for example, it makes sense to start writing your literature review chapter early in the research process as you will read, write, reflect, read and so on throughout your research. However, some students prefer to write up at the end of the process. This works if you have a clear writing timetable.

Second, the answer to 'Where do I start writing?' might seem obvious. No, it is not always the beginning. For many researchers, adopting a methodological approach of starting to write the introduction, followed by literature review, then methodology, and so on, works best for them. However, you may find that your literature review is the best starting point. This is because writing a literature review is an ongoing process. Moreover, reviewing the literature can influence other chapters in a research project.

Prior to writing, it is essential that you have a clear writing timetable. This is something that should feature in every research proposal. However, it is likely that you will need to add more detail and adapt your timetable following the submission of your proposal.

PLANNING

Time management and thorough planning are essential when it comes to writing a research project. The former point is not only about managing your time, but also trying to find a writing routine that works for you. MacIntosh et al. (2015: 215) point out that:

> By the time you come to write a dissertation, you will have been writing since childhood and will have accumulated years of experience of what works best for you. We each typically have habits and contexts which enable us to write. It may be that the library, your home or a coffee shop is your venue of choice. Most people who write professionally, e.g. novelists, journalists, playwrights, have an established writing routine.

My advice would be to try to get in the routine of writing every day, no matter what. Even if you are only able to write for 30 minutes a day. What is important is that you are making progress. The other key point when planning your writing is to start early. You should be aware by now that a research project is a comprehensive piece of work and certainly not something that can be completed 'last minute'.

One way to allocate time is to do it on a chapter-by-chapter basis. Table 18.1 is a guide to how much time to allocate to writing up each chapter. I must stress that this is a guide. Clearly, people write at different speeds. It also depends on how many words you are expected to write.

A useful method for managing your time is the Pomodoro time management technique. The technique is named after the usage of a common kitchen timer in the shape of a tomato ('pomodoro' in Italian) and is based on 25 minutes of focused, uninterrupted work on one task, then 5 minutes of rest (Wang et al., 2010) (see Image 18.1).

Table 18.1 Time allocation to writing your research project

Chapter	Time allocation (weeks)
Introduction	2
Literature review	2
Methodology	1
Results and analysis	4
Conclusion and recommendations	1
Total	10

Source: Wilson (2014)

Image 18.1 Using a pomodoro timer can help to manage your time when writing

Source: iStock (photo ID: 509630263)

The Pomodoro technique can be helpful in motivating you to write as the timer is set at 25 minutes. Using the Pomodoro technique, first allocate 30 minutes in the day when you are least likely to have any distractions. Before writing, decide exactly what it is you want to write and prepare your writing environment – room, desk, chair, computer and surroundings. The focus here is solely on writing. Turn off any distractions, such as your mobile phone and emails. Do not browse the internet or answer the phone. In short, this is your writing time so 100% focus must be on the task at hand. Once you have written solidly for the full 25 minutes and the timer goes off, have a 5-minute break before deciding whether you are able to devote another 30 minutes. If you complete 4 or 5 consecutive pomodoros, take a longer break, such as 20 minutes.

The idea behind the Pomodoro technique is that it is designed to help you to work in a focused way for short blocks of time. This is ideal if you have other commitments, such as working part-time and other study tasks.

WRITING GROUPS

Although group projects are an increasingly used form of assessment, the likelihood is that you will be writing an individual piece of work. However, this does not mean that you have to write in isolation. There is no reason why you cannot form a group or join a writing community. Smith et al. (2009: 21) note several benefits associated with writing in groups:

- reducing isolation
- motivation to stick to project timelines
- critical friends with whom to discuss specific ideas, challenges and 'knotty problems'
- sounding issues out in advance of meeting a supervisor
- putting things in perspective if you are feeling stressed or under pressure
- sharing resources and search results.

From my own experience, I always actively encourage students to form writing groups. Informal meetings over a coffee can help to promote an exchange of ideas and lead to the benefits as outlined by Smith et al. (2009: 21). Additionally, there are generic issues faced by student researchers that can be discussed in a group setting. For example, knowing how to conduct a literature review or choosing a methodological approach.

Similarly, Duke (2018: 136) suggested some key points to help you to keep your writing on track:

- Know that writing is hard for everyone, you are not alone.
- Allow yourself to write badly. You can always edit later.
- Do not start writing with a pure blank page, put something – anything – on it.
- Learn to break down your writing task and use short periods of time productively to help move your writing forward even when life is too busy.
- Craft a clear statement encapsulating your main position and argument to give your writing structure and prevent you losing your focus.
- Develop a writing community to maintain motivation and make the writing process more enjoyable.
- Make writing a habit. This is the best way to prevent writer's block in the first place.

The second and third points here are particularly important. Write as often as you possibly can, even if you write badly. It is best to write and edit later, as opposed to editing as you write.

Time is a key factor when writing any research project. Cottrell (2014: 179) provides some helpful tips on helping you to get through writing up your research, as follows:

- Be kind to yourself during the writing process; give yourself plenty of rewards.
- Intersperse writing with other activities – do not make it an endurance test.
- Be prepared for some productive days, and others where the process may seem painfully slow.
- Organize your material from the perspective of your writing.
- Do not attempt to do it all at once – write as you go.

WRITING STYLE

Your writing style refers to how you put your words together. You will have probably developed your writing style through practice and feedback on your assessment. Moreover, writing a research proposal is an excellent way to develop your writing style, particularly when writing a preliminary literature review.

Essentially, there are two broad types of writing style – informal and formal. The former is more conversational, while the latter is more formal language that adopts a more serious, impersonal and detached tone. Let us look at two examples:

- Jack is dropping out of the course due to the really big pressure of study.
- Jack is withdrawing from his course of study due to the considerable challenges he is facing in his personal life.

Although both of these examples may convey the same meaning, the second example uses a more formal style of language and is a lengthier sentence. What level of formality should you apply when writing your research project? To answer this, consider the following questions:

- What level of formality is expected by my university or college?
- What level of formality is expected by my supervisor?
- Who is my target audience?

In many respects, these three questions can be considered collectively as guidelines for writing expectations are likely to be set out by your institution.

Avoid writing lengthy sentences. Make sure that your writing is clear, coherent and engaging for the reader. This last point is addressed by keeping 'on topic' and including material that is likely to prove of interest to the reader. A useful exercise is to read your work out loud, and ask yourself, is the writing clear and concise? Furthermore, it is also helpful to ask someone else to read through your research project prior to submission. Ideally, ask someone who is not a subject specialist to see if they are able to understand your writing. A research project should be written so a lay person can understand.

USING LONG SENTENCES

It is easy to write a long sentence. However, what is important is to be concise and clear in your writing. Consider sentence length when editing your work. Although there is no 'ideal' number of words, try to vary the length of your sentences so that your writing is more engaging. Too many long sentences make for dull writing. Consider the following examples:

1. Our current organizational performance is significantly impacted by the change in consumer buying habits because of a new product entering the European market.
2. There has been a significant impact on our current organizational performance. Clearly, consumers are turning away from the brand. This is due to a new product entering the market.

Notice the difference in the above examples. Obviously, the first of these is the longer and wordier sentence. By breaking up the two sentences, the second example reads better.

SIGNPOSTING

Signposting is an important part of academic writing. Think of signposting as a way of directing the reader through your work. In brief, the main points associated with the structure of your research project are set out below:

* Abstract – say what you will say (in brief)
* Introduction – say what you will say (in greater detail)
* Main body – say what you have to say in detail
* Conclusion – say what you have said

Signposting does not only apply to chapters or sections of your work, but also it is good practice to consider signposting throughout each chapter. For example, begin each chapter with an introduction and conclude each chapter with a summary to signpost your reader throughout your research project. The introduction should be brief and explain the purpose of the chapter. Similarly, your summary should be short and cover the salient points from the chapter.

Signposting in an introduction

Although by no means exhaustive, signposts in an introduction to a chapter include the following:

* The overall purpose of this chapter is to ... /the aim of this chapter is to ...
* The themes to be discussed in this chapter are: ...
* This chapter critically analyzes ...
* This chapter is divided into ... sections. First, section one will ... Second, section two will ...
* This chapter is organized in the following way ...

Signposting in a summary/conclusion

* In conclusion, ...
* To summarize, ...
* Clearly, this chapter has shown that the ...
* Several conclusions emerge from this chapter ...
* From the above, it is evident that ...

Retrospective signposting

A retrospective signpost is a useful way to highlight material already covered in your project. For example, a retrospective signpost might be used to remind the reader of a key point mentioned earlier within a chapter.

* Earlier in the chapter, the ...
* As highlighted earlier in the project, ...
* As noted in the last section ...

YOUR FIRST DRAFT

Your first draft is likely to include gaps in your work, inconsistencies and possibly repetition in places. Completing a first draft will clearly reveal to you the areas that require improvement. This is why it is always better to put words to paper and write, rather than spending time procrastinating on what content to include.

Writing your first draft is a major achievement. You now have a platform in place in which to build and refine your work. Prior to reworking your draft, arrange a meeting with your supervisor. The focus of the meeting should be on 'what you have achieved' and 'how you can improve your work'. In some institutions, a supervisor can read a complete draft or possibly one chapter before a student submits their final draft. If the latter, ask your supervisor to read the chapter you consider requires the greatest improvement.

Once you have received feedback from your supervisor, the next step is to start to improve on your first draft. At this stage, you do not need to start at the beginning, but can start on a particular chapter or section. Remember that there should be a 'common thread' running through your work, so chapter content will be interrelated. For example, the content of your literature review is dependent on the nature of your research objectives and research questions. Having a 'common thread' means that improving your draft is 'integrating' the chapters, sections and sub-sections. For example, your literature review must integrate with your introduction. You cannot review literature on a different research topic to what you have discussed in your introduction. If this is the case, then you may need to go back and change the focus of your literature review, or proposed research topic.

Reworking your draft also means tidying up the overall presentation. Check to make sure that pages are in order, you keep the same consistent font and size throughout, all tables and diagrams are labelled, your institution's choice of referencing system is fully and correctly applied throughout. You will find it useful to have a checklist of tasks to address when tidying up your draft. Some institutions create a checklist for students. If not, you can create your own.

It is important to make your research project 'reader-friendly' prior to submission. There are a number of ways you can do this. The following points are adapted from Levin (2005: 204, 102–103):

- Know your reader. Check expectations with your research supervisor as in many institutions the supervisor is the first marker. If there is flexibility in terms of structure, there may still be some academics who want to see a continuous piece of prose that is not divided up into chapters and sections. Check whether your project will be read by one of these.
- Give your reader clear 'signposts'. As highlighted earlier in the chapter, include a contents page, headings and sub-headings to help guide the reader through your work.
- There is no right length for chapters, but they usually turn out to have a 'natural' length. The introduction and conclusion are each usually around 10% of the overall word count, whereas the middle chapters – such as literature and methodology – can be anywhere between 15–25% of the overall word count.
- Using lists can provide clarity, but do not use them unnecessarily.
- Use illustrations, diagrams and tables where appropriate. For example, a relevant table can help to break up the text and summarize key points.
- Keep appendices to a minimum. Key charts and tables should feature in the main text. The appendix is not a 'dumping ground' for visuals.
- Do not introduce new material in your conclusion.
- If possible, after reworking your first draft, put it to one side for a couple of days. Then, print out and read your revised draft, noting any changes.

STRUCTURING YOUR RESEARCH PROJECT

There is no one definitive way to structure a research project. The structure depends on the type of project and your institution's submission requirements. However, there are some common features that one would expect to see in a research project. These include some kind of review of the literature and a research methodology. Though by no means exhaustive, the purpose of this section in the book is to discuss many of the typical features of a research project. The section also discusses what are referred to as 'preliminary features' and 'closing features'. These are features that come before and after the main chapters respectively. Before we look at these, let us consider the key chapters, starting with the introduction.

The traditional structure of a research project consists of five or six chapters: Introduction, Literature review, Methodology, Results and Analysis, and Conclusion.

CHAPTER 1: INTRODUCTION

Your introductory chapter should 'set the scene' and introduce the reader to the following:

- background to the study
- the research problem
- research direction (research objectives and research questions)
- layout of the study

Your introduction is the first chapter your reader is going to read so it is important to create a good impression early in your research project. The first few sentences of a research project need to engage the reader so that they want to keep reading. Think of these early sentences as a hook designed to capture the reader's attention – like bait on a fishing hook attracts a fish. There are various ways you can capture a reader's attention. First, you could use a short narrative to illustrate your point. Here is an example to a start of a research project that nicely illustrates 'the power of brand':

> Domino's Pizza in Russia was forced to end a promotion offering fans free pizza for life if they got the brand's logo tattooed 'in a prominent place' on their body after the campaign became too popular. (Deabler, 2018)

Second, you could use a quotation that is directly related to your chosen research topic. Later in your research project, you can then revert back to the quotation as to the extent you concur or refute the person's argument. Finally, consider using a striking visual or image to grab the reader's attention. Clearly, the visual must be related to your research topic, or more specifically, research problem.

An introduction should start with a clear background to the study. This is what I refer to 'as setting the scene'. For example, before a Shakespearean play takes place on stage, there is always a 'setting of the scene' before the play begins.

It is important to be explicit in your introduction as to the nature of your research topic. Remember the importance attached to answering the 'so what?' question. In other words, why are you doing the research? Although the introduction is the first chapter within a research project, it is likely it will be the last chapter you write. This is because certain aspects, such as research questions and background to the study are often refined during the research process. Again, we come back to the nature of research as being an iterative process, as illustrated by The Research Wheel model. In short, the purpose of the introduction is to provide the rationale for the study.

The final part of the introduction chapter is something that is associated with signposting. That is, it helps to guide the reader through your project. This is often referred to as 'layout of the study'. The way layout of the study is structured might read something like this:

In this chapter we have looked at the nature of the research topic and research direction. Chapter Two provides a critical review of the extant literature on the topic, Chapter Three explains the methodological approach, ...

Clearly, this is a shortened version of what you would find in a research project. However, you can see how to present the final part of your introduction.

CHAPTER 2: LITERATURE REVIEW

The first point to make about the literature review chapter is that it does not have to be called 'Literature review'. Second, you can write more than one literature review chapter. On the former point, you can name a literature review chapter on the basis of the content you are reviewing. The fact that you are writing a literature review chapter should be evident from your writing style.

The literature review is a critical review of what has been written on your research topic. As explained in Chapter 4, there are a number of different ways of structuring a literature review. For many business and management students, structure focuses on themes. In other words, a thematic approach. Again, signposting is essential to guide the reader through the review. A literature review should have a 'beginning', a 'middle' and an 'end'. The beginning includes an introduction that explains the purpose of the literature review and how it is to be structured. The main body will include headings and possibly sub-headings on the themes that relate to your research questions. Finally, a literature review should include a summary that 'pulls together' everything reviewed within the chapter and makes a clear 'link' between the literature and your study.

It is the final part of the literature review chapter that is not always fully addressed by students. The reader of your work will want to know how your work relates to the current body of literature on your subject.

CHAPTER 3: RESEARCH METHODOLOGY

Again, start your chapter with an introduction, explaining the purpose and structure of your chapter. Before starting to write your methodology chapter, it is useful to include a diagram of the elements of research methodology and how they apply to your study. An example here is *The Honeycomb of Research Methodology*. This is something many of my own research students use when writing their projects. The reasons for this are two-fold. First, a model or diagram such as this can be applied to your research. It provides the reader with a useful 'snapshot' of your chosen methodological approach. Moreover, a diagram is a helpful form of signposting as it is an indication of what you are going to cover within the chapter. Second, you can also use the model as a checklist when writing your methodology chapter.

Sometimes 'Research methodology' is referred to as 'Research design'. However, as we looked at earlier in the book, think of methodology as an umbrella term; research design falls under this. A research methodology typically includes the key elements as illustrated in Figure 18.2. Other features include sampling, reliability and validity. Your choice of methodological approach should also be supported. For example, if you have chosen to conduct an online survey using a convenience sampling method, then justify why you have made this choice.

A research methodology should not be a discussion on all the various types of research methodologies. Quite simply, this is not what is expected of you by the marker. The reader of your research project

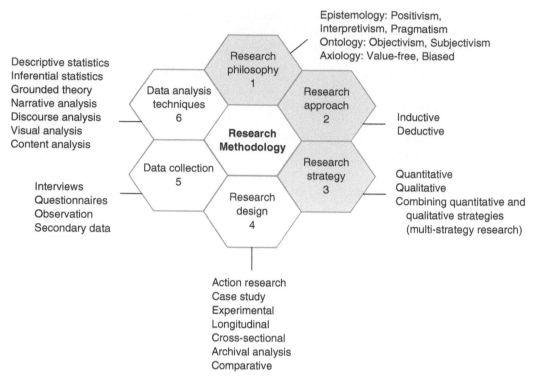

Figure 18.2   The Honeycomb of Research Methodology
Source: © Wilson (2014)

is expecting to see your choice of methodological approach and supporting evidence. For example, if you are using online focus groups to collect primary data, then explain why you have opted for online, as opposed to the more conventional type of focus group. A final important point – as you write your research methodology, try to avoid making it too general. A methodology that is too general often rambles and fails to engage the reader. By way of an example, rather than stating something quite generic such as, 'A focus group lasted for one-hour and consisted of a total of six participants', try to include details specific to your experience of conducting the focus group. Did it run smoothly? Did all participants arrive on time? What was the dynamic like during the focus group?

CHAPTER 4: RESULTS AND ANALYSIS

This chapter is sometimes referred to using a number of different headings, such as 'Findings', 'Research findings' or simply 'Results'. The title is often dependent on the nature of the research strategy. For example, if the researcher adopts a quantitative research strategy, then their analysis is based on statistical data. A key consideration here is how you present your research findings. To an extent, this depends on the nature of your study. For example, if you have undertaken a qualitative study, then the use of verbatim quotations is an excellent way to illustrate participant(s) views on a particular topic. In contrast, a quantitative study is more likely to use charts, graphs and tables to present numerical data. My suggestion here would be to try to use a variety of methods to present your data. Try to avoid adopting a 'death by pie charts' approach! Remember that using a variety of ways to present your data is going to make your research project all the more interesting to read.

CHAPTER 5: CONCLUSIONS AND RECOMMENDATIONS

In this final chapter, it is essential to be explicit as to how you have addressed your original research objectives. I even go as far as telling my students to re-state their objectives in the conclusion. This is an explicit way of showing the reader that each one has been fully addressed.

The chapter should also include a section on 'contributions'. A distinction can be made here between theory and practice. How has your research contributed to the current body of literature on your topic? For example, you may have used a theoretical framework from another discipline or possibly applied a theory in a different cultural context.

Other features of a conclusion chapter include 'limitations' and 'future or further research'. Examples of the former may comprise time constraints, difficulties accessing data and a general lack of resources. The purpose of having a section on future research is two-fold. First, it can be a reference to the 'next step' of what you would do differently if you were to conduct a follow up study. Although perhaps hypothetical, the second point is that your recommendations as to future research can be of benefit to other researchers interested in your research. In effect, you are 'passing on the baton' to another researcher(s). Thomas (2017) noted that a conclusion chapter should:

1. refer back to the introduction
2. chart the progress of any change
3. summarize briefly the main findings
4. acknowledge your project's limitations and weaknesses
5. outline any recommendations

BOX 18.1: RESEARCH SNAPSHOT

Two important points concerning your conclusion. First, do not introduce any new material. Second, a conclusion is typically 10–15% of the overall word count. Avoid writing a short discussion on your overall research. I find it particularly frustrating where a student has written an excellent research project, only to write a very brief conclusion. In some cases, this is because the student is approaching the word limit. Carefully break down the number of words to allocate to each chapter. Although only a guide, this can help to make sure that you devote enough to writing up your conclusion.

In this section, we have examined the main structure of a research project. There are also additional elements. These are commonly referred to as preliminary features and closed features.

PRELIMINARY FEATURES

Preliminary features come before the first chapter in your research project (the introduction) and include the following:

Title page

Your title should reflect the content of your research project. The likelihood is that you will change your title numerous times throughout your research. Avoid titles that are too generic, lengthy and lack clarity. In relation to qualitative research, Weaver-Hightower (2018) suggests mentioning the methodological approach in your title. The author argues that although not essential, this may help the reader to interpret your work. However, reference to methodology can also be included in the title of research based on quantitative research. Below are two examples of titles from academic journal articles. The first of these includes research design in the title, while the second refers to the type of quantitative analysis.

1. How women entrepreneurs build embeddedness: A case study approach. (Source: Aggestam and Wigren-Kristoferson, 2017.)
2. Descriptive analysis of graduate enrolment trends at Hispanic-serving institutions: 2005–2015. (Source: Garcia and Guzman-Alvarez, 2019.)

As well as reflecting the content of your research topic, you can include keywords or themes. Searching through titles of articles from academic journals can help you to develop your ideas on a possible title. As you can see from the two examples, using a colon can be useful for breaking up and improving the clarity of your title. In addition, what is interesting about the title of the paper from Garcia and Guzman-Alvarez (2019) is that the authors have also included the time frame from which the data is drawn (2005–2015). This is one way of narrowing the focus of your title. Remember that the title includes the first words of your research project. Thus, it is important to set a precedent by writing clearly. In particular, make sure to avoid making any spelling mistakes or grammatical errors in your title. This is not a good first impression! Depending on the institution, the title page usually contains the following information:

*   Full title of the research project, including any sub-titles
*   Student number and course name
*   Award for which the research project is submitted, for example, 'A research project/dissertation presented in partial fulfilment of the requirements for…. (name of course of study)'
*   Name of your institution
*   Name(s) of your research supervisor(s)
*   Month and year of submission

Figure 18.3 shows an example of a title page; this should be centred on the first page.

TITLE OF RESEARCH PROJECT

SUB-TITLE OF RESEARCH PROJECT

This Research Project is submitted as a partial fulfilment for the award of Bachelor of Honours in Business Studies by:

NAME OF STUDENT

STUDENT NUMBER

NAME OF SUPERVISOR

Viking University

© June 2021

Figure 18.3   Example of a research project title page

Acknowledgements

Typically, the Acknowledgements page comes after the title page in a research project. Although not essential, the acknowledgements page is an opportunity to thank all of those who supported you throughout your research. This is likely to be your research supervisor(s), friends, family and research participants.

The contents page

Your table of contents should include the number and title of each chapter in your research project. Chapter sub-headings should be clearly presented and numerically referenced. In addition, the contents page also includes a list of figures and tables that feature within your research project. Make sure to correctly format and number your pages. Numbering helps with signposting. For example, 'Figure 8.2 illustrates…', 'Table 5.3 shows that…'. Tables and figures should be numbered; this allows for explicit reference in the main text. See Figure 18.4 for an example of how to structure a contents page.

TABLE OF CONTENTS

University statement of originality

Acknowledgements

Table of contents

Abstract

List of tables

Chapter One: Introduction

1.1   Cultural capital, other social determinants and educational attainment

1.2   Statement of the research problem

1.3   Objectives of the study

1.4   Usefulness of the study

1.5   Layout of the study

Chapter Two: Cultural capital and educational attainment

2.1   Introduction

2.2   Defining and measuring cultural capital

2.3   The relationship between cultural capital, field and habitus

2.4   Cultural capital and educational attainment

2.5   Other forms of capital

Chapter Three: Other social determinants of educational attainment

3.1   Introduction

3.2   The influence of age on educational attainment

3.3   Gender issues and educational attainment

3.4   The complexity of ethnicity and educational attainment

3.5   Prior academic performance and the effect on educational attainment

3.6   Summary of key literature and how it relates to this study

Chapter Four: Research Methodology

4.1   Introduction

4.2   Theoretical perspective, research approach and research strategy

4.3   Sample and data collection procedure

4.4   Measures

4.5   Professional practice and ethical issues

4.6   Data analysis

4.7   Reliability and validity

(Continued)

Figure 18.4   (Continued)

Chapter Five: Results and discussion

5.1   Introduction

5.2   Descriptive statistics for the variables included in the study

5.3   Multiple regression analysis

5.4   Analysis of Model 1 – Control variables

5.5   Analysis of Model 2 – All variables

5.6   Analysis of Model 3 – Significant variables

5.7   Discussion on the hypotheses and research findings

Chapter Six: Conclusion and recommendations

6.1   Introduction

6.2   Contribution statements and educational implications

6.3   Limitations of the study

6.4   Future research

7.0   REFERENCES

8.0   APPENDICES

A – Questionnaire survey

B – Variables measurement

C – Summary of the hypotheses and findings

LIST OF TABLES

Table 4.1   Philosophical stance taken in this study

Table 5.1   Personal characteristics of student participants

Table 5.2   Parental background of student participants

Table 5.3   Grades for last semester, reading habits, cultural activities and extra-curricular activities

Table 5.4   Anticipated final degree mark

Table 5.5   Highbrow, middlebrow and lowbrow activities and measures

Table 5.6   Multiple regression

Table 5.7   Hypotheses and empirical findings

Figure 18.4   An example of how to structure a contents page

You will notice from Figure 18.4 that Chapters Two and Three do not include a chapter headed 'literature review'. Why? This is because in this particular example, the student has included two literature review chapters. Each review is associated with the chosen research topic. Hence, the respective chapter titles: 'Cultural capital and educational attainment' and 'Other social determinants of educational attainment'.

Abstract

The abstract provides a brief overview of your entire research project. This is usually the last part of the research project a researcher writes. Ideally, an abstract should be no more than 300 words and encapsulate the whole research project. This includes everything from the research context, objectives, methodology and key findings. Students often find writing an abstract challenging as it is difficult to give an overview of what is likely to be a 10,000 word+ project in no more than 300 words.

Something I recommend to all of my research students is to read through structured abstracts found in many peer-reviewed academic journals. The advantage of this is two-fold. First, it helps you to understand ways to reduce key parts of a research project into a small number of words. Second, the structured headings provide useful guidance. Although your institution may not require a structured abstract, creating headings can help you when breaking down your abstract into manageable 'chunks'. In the next part of the chapter, I have included an example of a structured abstract to illustrate how the authors have divided up each part.

An example of a structured abstract

- **Purpose** – This study aims to propose that a brand can be kept both prominent and fresh by using existing logos as well as logo varieties (i.e., slight modifications to the brand's existing logo).
- **Design/methodology/approach** – In two experimental studies, the authors exposed respondents to either the existing brand logo or to logo varieties, and examined their influence on brand prominence and freshness.
- **Findings** – The findings suggest that consumers subconsciously process logo varieties to which they are exposed in a similar way as they subconsciously process the existing logo of the brand, making both types of logo exposure effective for building brand prominence and freshness.
- **Research limitations/implications** – It would also be worthwhile to study the effect of logo varieties using other dependent measures than the ones employed in this study, such as purchase intent and behavioural measures (such as consumption behaviours).
- **Practical implications** – This research shows that logo varieties can be used alongside the existing brand logo to build prominence and freshness. These findings diverge from the findings typically reported in the branding literature that state that consumers resist changes to logos.
- **Originality/value** – This research not only demonstrates that exposure to logo varieties and existing logos evokes automatic effects (both types of logos outperform a control group in fostering brand-related outcomes) but also confirms that exposing consumers to the existing logo or logo varieties give less differential effects than one may think.

Source: Sääksjärvi et al. (2015)

Abbreviations, illustrations and list of tables

The first part of this feature is not essential, but it can be useful if your research project contains a large number of abbreviations. An example here would be an economics-related research project that may make reference to different multilateral organizations.

CLOSING FEATURES

Closing features come after the final chapter (the conclusion) in your research project. The closing features consist of references and appendices. Let us look at each one in turn.

References

Your list of references should correspond to all material cited in your research project. Some institutions may require both a bibliography and a list of references. In essence, a bibliography is a list of all those references cited in your research project, together with additional material you may have read but not cited. If in doubt as to what is required, do check with your research supervisor.

Many institutions use the Harvard referencing system. The Harvard system uses the author and date of publication in the main body of the text, for example, Henderson (2021). Material cited in the main text is included in a references list, which is listed in alphabetical order by author's family name. There are other referencing systems, such as the Vancouver system; however, no matter which system your institution requires you to use, what is important is that you are consistent in your referencing style.

Before submitting your work, ask yourself the question, 'Have I cited a sufficient number and range of sources?'. A list of references should contain strong evidence of research; this includes a wide range of sources.

Appendices

The appendix is where you can include additional information that readers might find interesting, but is not sufficiently relevant to be included in the main body of your research project. For example, perhaps a questionnaire template or interview transcripts. This last example may make your project extremely large, in which case it may not be an essential requirement of your institution. Morse (2006: 303) notes the type of material typically included in appendices is:

- Complete transcripts of interviews with key informants.
- Questionnaire design (including original form and English translation).
- Extended summaries of raw data (graphs or tables), but avoid including too much of this.
- Short explanations of exotic statistical tests if used in the report.

PRESENTING YOUR RESEARCH PROJECT

How you present your research project relates to overall presentation, as well as the presentation of data. Let us first look at the latter. If using tables to present your data, it is important to note the following:

- Make sure your data are suitable for a tabular format.
- Clearly label your table.
- Make sure that your table is legible.
- Make sure that the rows and columns are of equal proportions.
- If it is not your own work, make sure that you include your source.

Source: Wilson (2014: 317)

Tables can be used in a variety of ways. Students often use tables to illustrate results, especially when conducting quantitative research. However, tables can also be used in other parts of your research project. If including a table in your research project, make sure that it does not arrive unannounced. Every table should have a clear heading and include a discussion on the table content. As Cloutier and Ravasi (2021) point out, tables are not meant to be stand-alone entities; they need to be referenced, narrated and explained in the body of a research document. The purpose of a table can be to break up the text and to provide a snapshot on a particular area of your research. This includes everything from definitions of different terms in a literature review, to frequency counts showing characteristics of research participants. Table 18.2 shows an example of a frequency table from a study on celebrity endorsement.

Table 18.2　Frequency of respondents who agree with the statement: 'Celebrity has the power to change students' perceptions about the product'

	Frequency	Percentage
Strongly disagree	9	7.2
Disagree	28	22.4
Neither	28	22.4
Agree	36	28.8
Strongly agree	24	19.2
Total	125	100

Graphical techniques such as pie charts, graphs, pictures and word clouds (see Image 18.2) are alternative methods for presenting your data. Check with your institution's guidelines as to whether or not you can use pictures. Clearly, for some topics, pictures may add a significant contribution to a student's work. This is especially the case when doing qualitative research, where presentations are pictorial or textual. For example, research using visual content analysis may illustrate material from selected advertising campaigns and brand-related studies. The old *cliché, a picture speaks a thousand words*, is certainly the case with visual-related research topics. In the past, I have had students use visuals to good effect within their research, particularly in comparative studies. Showing pictures of how competing brands have evolved over time, or product development, are just two examples from many.

Image 18.2　An example of a word cloud

Source: iStock (photo ID: 458045187)

As with tables, any graphical techniques used should be clearly presented, labelled and referenced. Underneath all tables and graphical techniques, you should include the source. If the source is your own work, convention is to write: 'Source: Author's own work'. However, once again, do check with your institution's guidelines. Similarly, if using someone else's table or graphic, underneath cite: 'Source: author(s) surname(s) year of publication', for example 'Ricardo, 2020'. Finally, using the last example, if you have taken someone else's work but adapted it in some way, the convention is to write: 'Source: Adapted from Ricardo, 2020'.

Using graphical techniques can greatly enhance the presentation of your research. Moreover, it can also make your project more interesting and increase reader engagement.

The final approach to presenting data is using verbatim quotations. If you are undertaking qualitative analysis, including quotations is an ideal way of bringing a richness and depth to your research project (see Chapter 15 for more on qualitative analysis). It is best to indent long quotations (typically more than 40 words). All quotations should be put in quotation marks and written in italics and referenced in the main text in accordance with the referencing system you are using.

Once you have finished writing, editing and proofreading, you are finally ready to submit your research project. At this point in the research process, there are still a number of considerations. Most importantly, make sure that you understand your institution's submission requirements. This is something we examine in the next section.

Image 18.3　Concept Cartoon 'Structuring your research project'

The final Concept Cartoon in the book (Image 18.3) shows characters discussing the structure of a research project. Again, consider each character's opinion. What do you think? In groups, discuss your answers.

SUBMITTING YOUR RESEARCH PROJECT

How do you know you are ready to submit your research project? Once you have proofread your project, send it to your research supervisor to read. If this is not possible, then do make sure to proofread your work several times before submission. Understand the importance of deadlines and avoid submitting your work at the eleventh hour. I have known situations where students have left submitting their work to the final day, only to miss the deadline due to technology issues, such as problems with their laptop or an inability to access the electronic submission page. Similarly, if you need to submit a hard copy of your project, make sure not to leave printing to the last minute.

Your institution is likely to have regulations for submitting your project. Of course, these do vary from one institution to the next, although they are likely to include the following:

- Your research project must follow a set structure as per the 'Dissertation instructions'.
- It must contain key information on the title page, such as the project title and student number.
- It must be word-processed and/or submitted using a certain file type (such as PDF format).
- It must have 1.5 or double spacing (many institutions do not accept single spacing).
- A size 12 font must be used (typically Times New Roman, Arial, Calibri or Garamond).
- It must include a title page.
- A hard copy should be submitted using perfect or comb binding.
- A version must be submitted electronically (this tends to vary by institution).
- It must be submitted prior to the set deadline. A delay is likely to incur penalties such as a loss of marks.
- It should include a list of references.
- It should include a research project declaration form.
- It should include a student–supervisor meeting log (again, this can vary by institution).

Submitting your research project is likely to be the culmination of several years of study. Writing a project is a major undertaking for any students, so you should quite rightly be proud of your achievement.

THE VIVA VOCE

A viva voce is an oral examination and is a compulsory element of a PhD examination in the UK. However, it is also sometimes a feature of Master's and undergraduate assessment. To pass a viva, a student must not only possess a thorough understanding of their research topic, but must also be able to communicate this to the examiners (Cascarini and Lowe, 2004). Think of the examination as an oral defence of your work in response to the examiner(s) questions. Although a viva can be a stressful experience, it is made easier by having a clear understanding of the requirements and the name of your examiner(s). Higher level degrees usually have both an internal and an external examiner. However, for other undergraduate and Master's students there is often only one examiner from within the institution.

There are three key components of the viva (adapted from Tinkler and Jackson, 2002):

- *Skills*: As the viva is an oral examination, a key consideration here is the verbal skills of the student. Is the student able to explain and justify their work, interpretations and ideas during the viva? The ability to communicate clearly, perform well under pressure and 'think on one's feet' are all key skills for a successful viva performance.
- *Content*: Make sure you have an understanding of the purpose and content of the viva. Some institutions may not provide detailed guidelines, so it is always useful to discuss expectations with your

research supervisor. Where guidelines are provided, usually the assessment criteria specify that the student should be able to locate his/her research in the broader context and 'defend' the project.

- *Conduct*: The conduct of the viva is variable as different examiner(s) behave towards students in different ways. Often the viva is 'shaped' by the examiner in terms of the type of questions and topics covered.

The viva voce is a process that involves a number of steps. Broadly speaking, these steps are: preparation prior to the viva, during the viva and post-viva. Let us look at each one in turn. First, when preparing for your viva, it is essential that you are completely familiar with all aspects of your research. One step you can take to help with your preparation is to create a folder of your research project and use labels to organize the folder by topic or themed questions. Furthermore, you can also prepare a list of possible viva questions. A likely question will focus on research topic, for example: 'Please explain why you consider your choice of research topic important'. Another excellent way to prepare for the viva is to ask someone, ideally your supervisor, to do a mock viva with you. A mock viva will help you to articulate your research and reduce the pressure of having to present your work. Doing a mock viva with your supervisor will also give you to an opportunity to discuss and reflect on the process.

Second, during the viva, when asked a question, take your time before answering. It is better to take a moment before answering the question. If you do not understand the question, ask for clarification from the examiner. Moreover, if you do not agree with the views of your examiner, do not feel that you are obliged to agree with their view. However, if you do disagree, it is important to try to justify why.

Lastly, following your viva, the outcome of your viva examination depends on the nature of the qualification. However, for a PhD, the outcome is usually a pass with no amendments, a pass with minor amendments, a pass with major amendments or a straight fail. A viva can be stressful for students, but with plenty of preparation, a mock viva, working closely with your supervisor and an understanding of the guidelines, you are much more likely to enjoy the event. To help you to prepare for your viva, Table 18.3 includes examples of typical viva questions. Although by no means exhaustive, the questions cover all of the chapters in a research project.

Table 18.3   Examples of viva questions

Theme	Question
Questions relating to personal development	Who are the main stakeholders in this research?
	Why did you decide to do this degree/doctorate?
Question relating to the introduction	What was the motivation for your research?
	How did you decide on your final research topic?
	What was the original problem/research question?
	Specifically, which authors most influenced your thinking about your research questions?
Questions relating to the literature review	What do you consider to be the most important papers that relate to your research?
	How has your chosen subject developed?
	What has not been done before?
Questions relating to the research methodology	How would you describe your research methodology?
	What are the limitations of your research designs?
	What influenced you to choose this approach to your research?

Theme	Question
Results and analysis	How did you present your findings?
	How do you regard your work from the point of view of the reliability and validity of the findings?
	What are the major weaknesses of your research?
Conclusion and recommendations	To what extent did you achieve your research objectives?
	Where might this research go from here?

Source: Adapted from Wilson (2014); Remenyi et al. (2003)

THE MARKING OF A RESEARCH PROJECT

If you are an undergraduate or postgraduate student, then the likelihood is that you will not have to participate in a viva voce examination. Thus, you will be solely assessed on your written research project. Early in your research journey you should be well aware of the marking criteria, your supervisor's expectations and what constitutes as a 'good' and a 'bad' research project.

An excellent exercise to understand what makes a 'good' piece of work is to look through past copies of student research projects. This is something your supervisor and/or research methods tutor may share with you. If not, ask if you can see past copies of students' projects. Although your tutor is unlikely to tell you the mark awarded, they might be willing to share an indication as to the quality of work. The nature of the research topic is not important. What you are concerned with when looking through past projects is the structure, writing style and overall content.

In terms of marking criteria, this varies between institutions. However, the marking criteria weightings are likely to be based on chapters (see Figure 18.5).

Figure 18.5 shows four columns – 'Criteria', 'Marks available', 'Marks awarded' and 'Comments'. Although the marking criteria for your research project is likely to be different, you can use this as a guide when writing your research project.

PUBLISHING AND DISSEMINATING YOUR WORK

So far in this book, we have focused on the writing and submission of your research project. However, the research process does not have to end here. There are plenty of opportunities for you to publish and disseminate your work. Before discussing some of the options available, it is important to note the associated benefits of writing for publication. Rowley and Slack (2000: 20) pointed out the following benefits a new researcher can gain in writing for publication:

1. *Personal sense of achievement.* The sense of achievement associated with seeing your ideas in print and the recognition that others in your professional or academic circle have acknowledged that the work is worthy of wider circulation can be immense.
2. *Development of writing and communication skills.* These skills are valuable in all sorts of avenues, in work and academic study. In particular, it is invaluable to be able to write in different styles for different audiences.
3. *Curriculum vitae.* Publications always complement a CV, and add an external validation of your ideas. For anyone anticipating developing an academic or research career, publications are important evidence of your research output.
4. Visibility within appropriate professional and academic audiences.

Criteria	Marks available	Marks awarded	Comments
Abstract and Table of Contents. Does the abstract summarize: • What the report is about? • What the student did? • What the student found out? Is the Table of Contents clear and easy to follow?	5	3	The abstract provides a solid overview of the research project. However, the background is rather general in the sense that it discusses 'Made in China' and 'Chinese brand', yet the methodology suggests that the research is a single case study design based on the Chinese brand Haier. A lucid Table of Contents.
Introduction. Does the introduction: • Introduce the importance of the subject? • Set the content of the work in the world of branding? • Set out the research objectives?	5	3	The background to the study is rather lengthy. A discussion focuses on the development of Chinese brands and Haier's brand internationalization strategy. The latter is rather detailed and would have perhaps been better placed in the literature review chapter. Lacking a strong argument as to the importance of the research topic. For example, why is it important for brands to know how Chinese brands have evolved from 'Made in China' to established brands? Research Objectives and questions lack clarity in places.
Literature review. • Is there a good range of literature? • Is the literature relevant and up-to-date? • Does the student review critically the literature?	20	11	An introduction to the chapter would have made a useful addition. The start of your review on brand strategy features relevant key authors such as Aaker and Kotler. However, I would have liked to have seen a more critical approach adopted. For example, when defining 'brand strategy' – can we be critical of Aaker's definition? Some of your sources are now dated in the context of Chinese brand development. For example, the number of Chinese brands (Jia, 2013) and characterizing Chinese brands (Zhang, 2008) p.24. Certainly, Chinese brand international recognition is now unlikely to be described as 'low'. Your literature review lacks a summary setting out how the key points from the review 'link' to your research.

Figure 18.5 An example of an extract from a research project marking form

CONFERENCES

One way to disseminate your work is at national and international conferences, in the form of a poster or oral presentation (Quick and Hall, 2015). This usually involves submitting a short abstract of your work and then submitting the full paper at a later date. Depending on the conference, there are a variety of ways to present your research. One option is to create a research poster. As mentioned earlier in the book, the free graphic design platform 'Canva' (www.canva.com) includes a wide range of poster templates you can use to create your poster (see Image 18.4).

THE GLOBALISATION OF CHINESE BRANDS: A CASE STUDY APPROACH
Research Poster

INTRODUCTION

According to Fan (2006), Chinese companies are successful manufacturers, but have little knowledge of the merits of branding. Fan's (2006) article is now more than 15 years old. So, does China have a truly global brand? This is one of the main considerations in this study. There remains a dearth of literature on Chinese branding. The purpose of this study is to contribute to the extant literature on global branding, by applying John Quelch's seven features of a global brand to Chinese brands. Furthermore, the research focuses on key success factors of global branding.

RESEARCH DIRECTION

The aim of this research is to investigate the extent Chinese brands have achieved global brand status. Research objectives and corresponding research questions are as follows:
- To understand the extent Chinese brands have achieved global brand status
- To determine the factors that contribute to a successful global brand
- To analyse the perception of Chinese brands from an international perspective
- How have Chinese brands performed outside of their domestic market?
- What are the key success factors of a truly global brand?
- How do international consumers perceive Chinese brands?

KEY LITERATURE AND METHODOLOGY

This research draws on research conducted by leading authors on China, such as: Tim Ambler, John Quelch and Ying Fan. The latter's seminal (2006) article is particularly important as a means to analyse how Chinese brands have developed over the last 15 years.

In terms of methodology, this research adopts an interpretivist approach as the intention is to explore and look for understanding into a topic that has received limited attention.

A qualitative research strategy and case study research design examine international consumers' views of Chinese brands. Due to research limitations, convenience sampling is adopted, using a sample of 25 international students.

Data collection involves face-to-face interviews, while analysis will apply grounded theory (Glaser & Strauss, 1967). The rationale behind this approach is that the majority of existing research adopts a positivist stance. My intention is to complete the dissertation within a period of 3 months.

Image 18.4   An example of a research poster

Try to aim for conferences that include a theme closely related to your area of research. You are more likely to have your paper or poster accepted. Additionally, it is an ideal opportunity to network with academics and/or practitioners who specialize in your subject area. For example, in many subject areas of marketing, some of the main conferences taking place on an annual basis include The Industrial Marketing & Purchasing Group Conference, The Academy of Marketing Conference and the British Academy of Management Conference.

BLOGS

As noted in Chapter 11, a blog is a type of website, or at least part of a website. The word 'blog' is a shortened version of the term 'weblog'. Blogs contain a range of opinions and feature a variety of topics. You can create your own blog to disseminate your research and communicate your work to a wider audience. Creating a blog might just be the start of sharing your research. The advantage of having your own blog is the flexibility it provides in terms of content and layout. A blog works particularly well if your intention is to continue with your research, either formally or informally. However, if you consider publishing your work using a blog as a 'one off', then do check with your research supervisor if there is an opportunity to share your work via your School/Faculty blog.

PROFESSIONAL PUBLICATIONS

Professional or trade publications are written for a particular audience. For example, *Accountancy Age* (www.accountancyage.com/) is written for those in the field of accounting. Some trade magazines provide an outlet for students to submit elements of their research. An article in a trade magazine is very different to an academic piece of work found in a peer-reviewed journal (see later in this section). For one thing, an article in a trade magazine is likely to be much shorter in length. Second, your target audience is going to be largely made up of practitioners, so they are unlikely to have an interest in theory. If submitting an article to a trade magazine, as well as considering the target audience, you need to write something the publication's readership are going to find interesting. Hence, focus on one interesting outcome from your research that you believe has managerial implications.

Before writing an article, you can send your pitch to the editor via email. Alternatively, you can email your full article to the editor for consideration.

PEER-REVIEWED JOURNALS

Writing a journal article is an excellent way to share your work with an academic audience. If you are writing an undergraduate research project, there are potentially perhaps more suitable outlets to disseminate your work. Writing an article for an academic journal is different to writing a research project. The key differences are three-fold. First, your target audience is not your supervisor, second marker or an external examiner, but a larger audience, many of whom are likely to be experts in your chosen subject; hence, you need to make sure to accurately fulfil the journal's submission requirements. Martinsuo and Huemann (2020) compiled a useful list of basic issues that they encourage authors to consider when drafting their manuscripts for submission to the *International Journal of Project Management*. However, the authors also stress that these issues may well be relevant to other journals as well.

1. Write for your audience.
2. Justify and frame a novel contribution.
3. Tell a story with your paper.
4. Clearly delimit the scope.

5. Ensure validity.
6. Think and rethink the novel contribution.
7. Take care of the simple technicalities.

KEY SUCCESS FACTORS WHEN WRITING A RESEARCH PROJECT

The final section in this chapter focuses on the key success factors for you to consider when writing up your research project. This list is formed on the basis of over 20 years I have been supervising research projects. Though by no means exhaustive, it contains a useful 'checklist' for you to refer to when writing and prior to submitting your research project.

- Meet regularly with your research supervisor.
- Understand the nature of your research problem.
- Understand your institution's submission requirements.
- Have a clear research direction.
- Establish a writing routine.
- Develop a writing group/community.
- Create a well written and clearly structured literature review that adopts a critical approach.
- Demonstrate strong evidence of research – a wide range of sources.
- Make sure that all of the key elements of methodology are addressed.
- Make sure that your work is well presented with minimal typographical and grammatical errors.
- Adopt the same consistent referencing system, correctly applied throughout.
- Make sure that your conclusion fully addresses all of the research objectives.
- Make explicit reference to contribution to theory and practice.

This list is not ranked in any particular order. All of the above factors are important considerations when writing a research project. However, if I had to choose one factor above all others, it would be 'Meet regularly with your research supervisor'. Remember that the role of your supervisor is to guide and support you throughout the research process. Moreover, they are likely to be the first marker of your work. Quite simply, failure to meet with your supervisor is an opportunity missed. This is especially the case if she or he is a subject specialist in your chosen area of research.

GROUP TASK – 'BAKING THE RESEARCH CAKE'

This group exercise is called 'Baking the research cake'. It is designed to 'pull together' everything you have learned at each point in The Research Wheel model.

For the exercise, you will need a large sheet of plain paper and marker pens. Working in groups of four or five, discuss what you believe to be the main 'ingredients' of a research project. What exactly goes into the 'research cake?'. I suggest discussing the tasks between group members first before putting pen to paper. Produce a cake diagram showing all of the ingredients. Try to avoid simply naming chapters. If you were baking a research cake, what would the ingredients be? How are the ingredients related? Using the cake metaphor, do you see the cake as a series of layers?

This is a creative task designed to see if you can recall what goes into a research project. In addition, it determines your views on the relationship between the different 'ingredients'. The outcome of the task is a creative visual that can be used as a checklist when checking to see if you have covered all of the 'key ingredients' when putting together your own research project. See Figure 18.6 for an example, but do try to come up with your own creation!

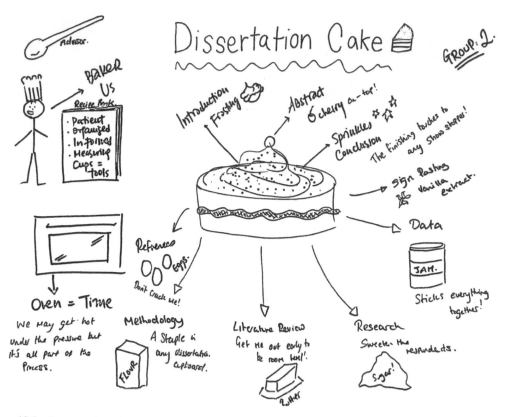

Figure 18.6 An example of 'Baking the research (dissertation) cake'

CHAPTER SUMMARY

- Time management and thorough planning are essential when it comes to writing a research project.

- The Pomodoro technique is named after the usage of a common kitchen timer in the shape of a tomato and is based on 25 minutes of focused, uninterrupted work on one task, then 5 minutes of rest.

- Make writing a habit. This is the best way to prevent writer's block in the first place.

- Your writing style refers to how you put your words together.

- Think of signposting as a way of directing the reader through your work.

- Your first draft is likely to include gaps in your work, inconsistencies and possibly repetition in places. Completing a first draft will clearly reveal to you the areas that require improvement.

- There is no one definitive way to structure a research project. The structure depends on the type of project and your institution's submission requirements.

- How you present your research project relates to overall presentation, as well as the presentation of data.

- Once you have proofread your project, send it to your research supervisor to read. If this is not possible, then do make sure to proofread your work several times before submission.

- To pass a viva, a student must not only possess a thorough understanding of their research topic, but must also be able to communicate this to the examiners.

- A key success factor when writing a research project is to meet regularly with your research supervisor.

QUESTIONS FOR REVIEW

1. What are the main chapter headings associated with a research project?

2. Outline the purpose of signposting.

3. Discuss the key features of a conclusion chapter.

4. Explain the purpose of an abstract and steps you can take to help to make writing one easier.

5. Outline the preliminary features associated with writing a research project.

6. Discuss the role of your research supervisor during the writing up of your research project.

7. Outline the closing features associated with writing up a research project.

8. Discuss the process of writing a first draft and reworking your draft.

9. Give examples of places where you can disseminate your work.

10. What is meant by the term 'writing style' and why is this important when writing your research project?

STUDENT SCENARIO: LUCY BEGINS WRITING UP HER RESEARCH

Lucy is in the final stages of writing her research project. The project is the culmination of a four-year part-time postgraduate degree in Management. As a part-time student, Lucy has had to plan her writing up timetable carefully, taking into account her work and other commitments. Early in the research process, Lucy chose to start writing early, as opposed to leaving the task until a few weeks before submission. She is in the process of writing her conclusion chapter and has arranged a meeting with her supervisor to talk through editing her work. Lucy has finally chosen a title for her research project: 'Personal and Organizational Networks and Conflict in Entrepreneurship: The Case of Small Business'.

Structuring the conclusion and recommendations chapter

Lucy's objectives focus on her research topic of networks in entrepreneurship. She has fully addressed each of her research objectives. In addition, there is a detailed section on recommendations. However,

(Continued)

Lucy is uncertain about what other features to include within her conclusion chapter. On the advice of her supervisor, Lucy is aware that her conclusion should take up approximately 10–15% of the overall word count.

Writing style

Lucy wanted to make sure that her research project was engaging to read. She was familiar with the importance of avoiding the use of long sentences and lengthy paragraphs.

One of the steps Lucy had taken to make her writing more engaging was to include the use of visuals, such as pictures associated with networks in entrepreneurship.

Questions

1. Give three examples of additional content Lucy should include in her conclusion chapter.
2. Critique the title of Lucy's research project.
3. Outline other ways Lucy can make her research project more engaging to read.

Hint: Remember that one way to make a research project more engaging to read is to provide direction to the reader. This includes a 'common thread' running through the research project.

FURTHER READING

Corden, A. and Sainsbury, R. (2006) *Using Verbatim Quotations in Reporting Qualitative Social Research: Researchers' Views*. University of York. Available at: www.york.ac.uk/inst/spru/pubs/pdf/verbquotresearch.pdf (retrieved 16 January 2021).

An interesting paper on the use of verbatim quotations. The authors investigate the inclusion of respondents' verbatim quotations within written reports of findings from applied social research.

Duke, T. (2018) 'How to do a postgraduate research project and write a minor thesis', *Archives of Disease in Childhood*, 103 (9): 820–827.

Although based on a non-business subject, this is an insightful article on how to do a postgraduate project. Many of the points are applicable across all subjects.

Hartley, J. and Cabanac, G. (2017) 'Thirteen ways to write an abstract', *Publications*, 5 (2): 11.

A useful guide highlighting the different ways to write an abstract.

O'Leary, Z. (2017) *The Essential Guide to Doing Your Research Project* (3rd edn). London: Sage.

A concise book on doing a research project. O'Leary devotes an entire chapter to the challenge of writing up, including the writing process.

REFERENCES

Aggestam, M. and Wigren-Kristoferson, C. (2017) 'How women entrepreneurs build embeddedness: A case study approach', *International Journal of Gender and Entrepreneurship*, 9 (3): 252–268.

Cascarini, L. and Lowe, D.G. (2004) 'Surviving a viva: A guide for candidates', *Journal of the Royal Society of Medicine*, 97 (10): 498–500.

Cloutier, C. and Ravasi, D. (2021) 'Using tables to enhance trustworthiness in qualitative research', *Strategic Organization*, 19 (1): 113–133.

Cottrell, S. (2014) *Dissertations and Project Reports: A Step by Step Guide*. New York: Palgrave Macmillan.

Deabler, A. (2018) 'Domino's realizes free pizza for life promotion was a bad idea', *Fox News*, 5 September. Available at: https://nypost.com/2018/09/05/dominos-realizes-free-pizza-for-life-promotion-was-a-bad-idea/.

Duke, D.C. (2018) 'When the words just won't come', in K. Townsend and M.N.K. Saunders (eds), *How to Keep Your Research Project on Track: Insights from When Things Go Wrong*. Cheltenham: Edward Elgar.

Garcia, G.A. and Guzman-Alvarez, A. (2019) 'Descriptive analysis of graduate enrollment trends at Hispanic-serving institutions: 2005–2015' *Journal of Hispanic Higher Education*. doi: 10.1177/1538192719835681

Levin, P. (2005) *Excellent Dissertations!* Maidenhead: Open University Press.

MacIntosh, R., Farrington, T. and Sanders, J. (2015) 'Writing up your research project', in K. O'Gorman and R. MacIntosh (eds), *Research Methods for Business & Management: A Guide to Writing Your Dissertation* (2nd edn). Oxford: Goodfellow Publishers Ltd.

Martinsuo, M. and Huemann, M. (2020) 'The basics of writing a paper for the International Journal of Project Management', *International Journal of Project Management*, 38 (6): 340–342.

Morse, S. (2006) 'Writing an effective research report or dissertation', in V. Desai and R.B. Potter (eds), *Doing Development Research*. London: Sage.

Quick, J. and Hall, S. (2015) 'The research dissertation: Planning, producing and writing a thesis', *Journal of Perioperative Practice*, 25 (11): 215–218.

Remenyi, D., Money, A., Price, D. and Bannister, F. (2003) 'The doctoral viva: A great educational experience or a gun fight at the OK Corral?', *Irish Journal of Management*, 24 (2): 105.

Rowley, J. and Slack, F. (2000) 'Writing for publication: The first steps', *Management Research News*, 23 (5/6): 20–27.

Sääksjärvi, M., van den Hende, E., Mugge, R. and van Peursem, N. (2015) 'How exposure to logos and logo varieties fosters brand prominence and freshness', *Journal of Product & Brand Management*, 24 (7): 736–744.

Smith, K., Todd, M. and Waldman, J. (2009) *Doing Your Undergraduate Social Science Dissertation*. New York: Routledge.

Thomas, G. (2017) *How to do your Research Project: A Guide for Students*. London: Sage.

Tinkler, P. and Jackson, C. (2002) 'In the dark? Preparing for the PhD viva', *Quality Assurance in Education*, 10 (2): 86–97.

Wang, X., Gobbo, F. and Lane, M. (2010) 'Turning time from enemy into an ally using the Pomodoro technique', in D. Šmite, N.B. Moe and P.J. Âgerfalk (eds), *Agility Across Time and Space* (pp. 149–166). Berlin, Heidelberg: Springer.

Weaver-Hightower, M.B. (2018) *How to Write Qualitative Research*. New York: Routledge.

Wilson, J.S. (2014) *Essentials of Business Research: A Guide to Doing Your Research Project* (2nd edn). London: Sage.

INDEX